UNDERSTANDING INDUSTRIAL AND CORPORATE CHANGE

Edited by
GIOVANNI DOSI, DAVID J. TEECE, AND JOSEF CHYTRY

OXFORD
UNIVERSITY PRESS

OXFORD

UNIVERSITY PRESS

Great Clarendon Street, Oxford OX2 6DP

Oxford University Press is a department of the University of Oxford.
It furthers the University's objective of excellence in research, scholarship,
and education by publishing worldwide in

Oxford New York

Auckland Bangkok Buenos Aires Cape Town Chennai
Dar es Salaam Delhi Hong Kong Istanbul Karachi Kolkata
Kuala Lumpur Madrid Melbourne Mexico City Mumbai Nairobi
São Paulo Shanghai Taipei Tokyo Toronto

Oxford is a registered trade mark of Oxford University Press
in the UK and in certain other countries

Published in the United States
by Oxford University Press Inc., New York

© Oxford University Press 2005

British Library Cataloguing in Publication Data

Data available

Library of Congress Cataloging in Publication Data

Data available

ISBN 0-19-926941-6 (hbk.)
ISBN 0-19-926942-4 (pbk.)

1 3 5 7 9 10 8 6 4 2

Typeset by Newgen Imaging Systems (P) Ltd., Chennai, India
Printed in Great Britain
on acid-free paper by
Biddles Ltd., King's Lynn, Norfolk

To the Memory of Keith Pavitt

CONTENTS

Contents

Understanding Industrial and Corporate Change: An Introduction

GIOVANNI DOSI[a], DAVID TEECE[b], and JOSEF CHYTRY[b]

([a] S. Anna School of Advanced Studies, Pisa, Italy and [b] University of California, Berkeley, CA, USA)

It has been just a little more than a decade (1992–) since *Industrial and Corporate Change* first appeared in print. We maintain that the papers published in our journal have made a difference to our understanding of technological innovation, institutional/organizational economics, and corporate strategy. In this volume we are publishing a selection of those papers to illustrate the powerful insights to industrial and corporate change which have been provided by some of our leading authors.

What is contained in this book, and more fully embellished through articles in the journal itself, is a rich tapestry of insights, models, and research results—much of it informed by the study of institutions and business history—which are helping scholars and policymakers understand the origins, sources, and nature of technological progress and productivity improvement in contemporary economic systems featuring private enterprises as major actors of both change and economic coordination. Using a variety of methodological approaches—including statistical and historical analyses, mathematical modeling and computer simulations, case studies, and appreciative theorizing, our authors offer novel contributions to the understanding of a variety of challenging issues, including:

(i)   the nature and sources of the purported 'bounds' of 'rationality' in decision-making;

(ii)   the links between individual and organizational behaviors in all circumstances when competences and incentives are far from being perfectly aligned;

(iii)   the role of organizational routines in economics, organizational theory, and artificial intelligence;

(iv)   the importance of rules and supervisory actions embedded in hierarchical constraints upon 'impulsive' individual behaviors in many organizational settings;

   (v)   the nature and evolution of exchange, power, and authority relationships in organizations;

  (vi)   the relationships between codified vs. tacit knowledge and their impact upon the patterns of technological change;

 (vii)   the emergence and evolution of different technological standards;

(viii)   the growth and development of financial markets;

  (ix)   the role of product- and technological diversity in the innovation process, and, more generally, the importance of decentralized efforts of exploration/experimentation in contemporary market economies;

   (x)   the counterintuitive tradeoffs between Intellectual Property Right (IPR) regimes and patterns of innovations;

  (xi)   the evolution of multidivisional organizational structures in large enterprises during the twentieth century.

Needless to say, it is extremely hard to map the foregoing topics into corresponding well-defined frontiers for state-of-the-art research, given the multiplicity of the theoretical and empirical challenges that they entail. However, at the cost of many oversights, let us try to flag some of them. In the *first* part of this volume the papers have to do with 'foundational' issues ultimately concerning, first, the nature of individual and organizational behaviors, and, second, the boundaries and inner structures of economic organizations and the relationships amongst them. On both grounds, we believe, these papers represent major contributions to the ongoing efforts to understand economic agency well beyond the confines of the rationality/maximization/equilibrium canons. Conversely, the papers included in the *second* part are more 'inductive' and historical, and deal with some crucial features of knowledge accumulation and of the co-evolution between technological knowledge and organizational forms.

1. *Rationality, Decisions, and Behaviors*

Some of the contributions included in this volume address the interpretation of individual and collective behaviors in all those—indeed *most frequent*—circumstances in which economic agents cannot be innocently assumed to display the canonic 'olympic' rationality. Roy Radner's article sharply sets the scene against the yardstick of L. J. Savage's classic axiomatization of 'rational' behavior under uncertainty (and his precocious awareness of its limits). What do economic agents—that is, what do most of us—do in all circumstances where the complexity decision tasks, in one way or another, go beyond what may be reasonably assumed to be an 'easy-to-optimize' problem? Clearly, it is an interpretative issue well rooted in Herbert Simon's path-breaking works on 'bounded' rationality. In Radner's words, 'as Herbert Simon emphasized in his work, the cognitive activities required by the Savage paradigm . . . are far beyond the capabilities of human decision-makers or even human/computer systems, except in the simplest decision problems' (p. 10).

But in turn, what does such 'boundedness' imply? One basic interpretation is simply that we tend to be *costly rational*, as Radner puts it, in the sense that we are bound to (i) economize on activities of observation (stemming from, for example, sample-size and 'multi-bandit' exploration costs), and (ii) experience constraints on information storage, communication, and information processing powers. However, a more radical view suggests that 'truly' bounded rationality has to do also with (i) inconsistency in decision *procedures*, (ii) ambiguity and vagueness in the cognitive frames by which agents (i.e. to repeat, all of us) attribute causal relations amongst observed variables, and (iii) related failures in the mappings between environmental *states, actions* and *consequences* in ever-expanding state-spaces and action-spaces.[1] Ultimately, Radner builds upon a rather *Simonesque* departure from olympian rationality and significantly expands upon it, hinting at frontiers of investigation ahead whereby agents (well in tune with a perspective pioneered by James G. March) may well be assumed to be also *procedurally inconsistent* (cf. March, 1994; Cohen, March, and Olsen, 1972; Dosi, Marengo, and Fagiolo, 2002, among others).

Another angle from which to tackle the 'bounds' of our 'rationality'—as conventionally defined in decision theory—focuses upon our frequent inter-temporal inconsistencies in expectations, commitments, and behaviors. This is the central theme of the article by Steven Postrel and Richard Rumelt, addressing our fragile and often inconsistent mechanisms of inter-temporal choice, which in turn seem to require some kind of *impulse-control procedures*. Certainly Radner's and Postrel and Rumelt's contributions depart from very different pieces of cognitive and behavioral evidence. However they converge in the conjecture that (in the case of both individuals and, much more so, of organizations) a variety of *routines* is likely to be put in place in order to (i) *imperfectly handle the division of cognitive and practical labor* amongst agents diversely constrained in their problem-solving capabilities, and, together, (ii) govern the motivational drives and the potentially conflicting interests of organizational members.

The paper by Michael D. Cohen *et al.* in this volume tries precisely to advance our understanding of the *nature and dynamics of such organizational routines* and other recurrent organizational action patterns. Building on a notion of routine as an 'executable capability for repeated performance in

---

[1] Much more on a germane critical review of parts of the state-of-the-art in the field is found in Dosi, Marengo, and Fagiolo (2002). See also the ambitious synthesis of research achievements and challenges ahead in experimental economies (regarding in particular coordination and learning) in Camerer (2003).

some context that has been learnt by an organization in response to selective pressures', the paper tries to distinguish routines in a strict sense from other patterns of organizational behaviors. Dimensions along which it is fruitful to distinguish among different types of organizational behaviors (e.g. rules of thumbs, routines, heuristics, and strategies) include the degrees of automaticity by which particular action patterns are elicited, the informational complexity of the decision rules, and the 'location' within the organization of the knowledge called for by any required action or ensemble of them.

2. Understanding the Boundaries, Inner Structures, and Behaviors of Economic Organizations

The ongoing research on the features of different organizational actions patterns links with an equally broad issue, namely the relationships between individual behaviors, on the one hand, and organizational structures and collective (organizational) behaviors, on the other. And the link is even more challenging whenever one abandons the strictest requirements of reciprocal behavioral consistency amongst 'rational' agents derivable from equilibrium interaction patterns. But, then, how do organizations hold together notwithstanding gross imperfections in incentive alignments? How do particular arrangements concerning intra-organizational flows of information, incentive schemes, learning procedures, and modes of income distribution happen to emerge and eventually prevail, at least in certain places and times? These questions are addressed in the chapters by Oliver Williamson, by Bruce Greenwald and Joseph Stiglitz, and by Masahiko Aoki—in different perspectives and with significantly different answers.

Williamson proposes a broad and detailed frame of interpretation of alternative modes of governance of economic interactions based on their comparative cost-economizing properties—*in primis*, concerning the costs of transaction governance. While well in tune with the rich flow of Williamson's contributions in this line of research, the article also offers a sharp (and possibly, to many readers, controversial) assessment of the links in organizations between cost-economizing considerations, hierarchical set-ups and power. One of the bottom lines of his argument is indeed that the importance of notions such as those of 'power' and 'trust' has been inflated in social sciences at large, and in organizational theory in particular. On the contrary, according to Williamson, one can go a long way in interpreting organizational forms 'predominantly from an efficiency perspective in which intended but limited rationality manifests itself as "incomplete contracting in its entirety". The efficiency perspective out of which transaction cost economics works further eschews Pareto optimality in favor of a remediableness standard—according to which an extant condition is held to be efficient unless a feasible alternative can be described and implemented with net gains' (pp. 132–3).

One of the reasons why such an interpretation of organizational forms is both challenging and controversial concerns precisely the abilities implicitly attributed to economic agents to work out the *best feasible* alternatives, and the abilities attributed to markets to select them. In both respects, Aoki's and Greenwald and Stiglitz's interpretations display significantly lower degrees of confidence in the general effectiveness of contemporary economic institutions in arbitraging away what is less than feasibly optimal.

Aoki argues on the ground of an original model—subsequently refined and explored also through insightful empirical application in Aoki (2002)—that distinct efficiency properties stem from specific *combinatorics* amongst different (i) organizational conventions, (ii) mechanism of transmission of information, and (iii) distributions of competences and scope of action across organizational members. A straightforward implication is that one should normally expect *coexistence of diverse organizational forms*, even when notionally facing identical environmental selective pressures. The two archetypes of the 'North American' and the 'Japanese' firms are good cases to the point: they have evolved, Aoki argues, as different modes of matching distinctly different intra-organizational information systems with equally different decision procedures, behavioral conventions and shared 'mental models'.

The distribution of information *across* organizations, and more specifically between financial institutions and business firms, is at the core of the paper by Greenwald and Stiglitz. Indeed it is part of the seminal contributions of the two authors to the understanding of financial institutions and their relationships with business firms. Financial institutions—Greenwald and Stiglitz argue—face five central problems, namely: (i) *selection* (i.e. sorting out 'good' and 'bad' projects and firms under conditions of imperfect and incomplete information); (ii) *enforcement* (i.e. how to verify the occurrence of the states-of-the-nature upon which payments often depend and make the receiver of funds comply with the terms of the contract); (iii) *incentives* (concerning the alignment of the interest of managers with those of fund suppliers); (iv) *management/ Public Good problems* (any effort to improve the quality of management is a 'public good' for all shareholders, but that also implies that the forces driving managers to serve shareholders interests may be particularly weak); and (v) *conflicting claims* (e.g. between shareholders and bondholders, etc.).

Financial institutions and contractual arrangements *imperfectly* handle those problems and change over times through evolutionary processes, 'in which the deficiencies in the market give rise to new contract forms, in which some of those in the market gradually learn how to exploit the new contract forms, and in which the market gradually learns the deficiencies in those forms, giving rise, in turn, to still new arrangements' (p. 190).

3. The Nature of Technological Knowledge and the Patterns of Technological Change

While there is a little doubt that the accumulation of technological know-ledge is a major driver of economic growth and change in all contemporary economies, systematic efforts to 'open up the technological blackbox', as Nathan Rosenberg put it, are relatively recent—in an expanding enterprise which is still far from over. Within such efforts, original—and, again, controversial—insights come from the papers by Robin Cowan, Paul David, and Dominique Foray; Keith Pavitt; Daniel Levinthal; and Paul David.

One issue with far-reaching implications concerns precisely the nature of technological knowledge itself. What are the (changing) boundaries between *tacit* and *articulated* knowledge? What are the relationships between articulation *and codification* of knowledge? And what are the drivers and constraints to codification efforts?

Cowan, David, and Foray address precisely these questions. They start from the fundamental distinction—shared by most students of innovation but still not fully acknowledged by the economic profession—between *information* and *knowledge*. In the Cowan, David, and Foray definition 'an item of information [is] a message containing structured data . . . Instead, it is the cognitive context afforded by the received that imparts meaning(s) to the information message: . . . the term 'knowledge' is simply the label affixed to the state of the agent's entire cognitive context' (p. 200). Given that much, the paper proposes a 'topography' for different knowledge activities (including the generation and use of both 'abstract' and 'practical') distinguished according to the articulation, codification, and presence/absence of 'codebooks' shared by the community of practitioners. The boundaries between different discrete types of knowledge and in particular the tacitness/codification boundary, the authors emphasize, are endogenous: they are influenced by organizational goals and by the prevailing costs and benefits from codification. By 'drawing the important distinction between knowledge that is codifiable . . . and that which is actually codified, and in focusing analytical attention upon the endogenous boundary between what is and what is not codified at a particular point in time, the paper also sets the scene for some related questions on the drivers of techno-logical learning and their conditioning influences' (p. 232).

How responsive are the 'codificability boundaries' to economic incentives—including, of course IPR regimes? And, more generally, how 'plastic' are the patterns of technological knowledge to economic inducements? Or, conversely, can one identify some intrinsic characteristics of specific bodies of knowledge relatively invariant vis-à-vis diverse economic conditions? Thus, for example, are there classes of technological problems which are intrinsically 'simpler' or 'harder' (Nelson, 2002)? Finally, can one identify some general features in the inner structure and in patterns of learning which hold across different bodies of knowledge? Addressing this set of questions, notions such as those of 'technological paradigms', 'technological systems' and the related one of 'technological trajectories', have been proposed to capture precisely the invariances associated with each body of knowledge and the ensuing incremental patterns of technological advance. In that case, how does one put together such 'gradualist' views of technological change with the relatively sudden occurrence of 'paradigm shifts' and Schumpeterian 'waves of creative destruction'?

This is the topic of the paper by Levinthal, imaginatively drawing upon the notions of 'punctuated equilibria' and 'speciation' as developed in contemporary biology. The work offers indeed a novel interpretation of the intertwinings between gradualism and 'revolutions' in the observed patterns of technological change, even when the latter are not the result of major discontinuities in the underlying technological paradigms (such as those associated with, for example, electrical vs. steam engine technologies, or vacuum-tubes vs. semiconductor-based computing technologies). 'As in the process of punctuation in the biological context', Levinthal argues, 'the critical factor is often a speciation event, the application of existing technological know-how to a new domain of application. The technological change associated with the shift in the domain is typically quite minor; indeed in some circumstances, there is no change at all. While the speciation event is in an immediate sense technologically conservative, it may have significant commercial impact which in turn may trigger a substantially new and divergent evolutionary trajectory.' Using the history of wireless communication technology for its testing ground, Levinthal suggests that 'the process of "creative destruction" occurs when the technology that emerges from the speciation event is successfully able to invade other niches, possibly including the original domain of application' (p. 238).

The contrast *gradualism vs. creative destruction* in technological change and the distinction between knowledge bases and artifacts are also at the center of the contribution of our mourned colleague and friend Keith Pavitt. A central point of departure of Pavitt's argument is that 'the firm's knowledge base both determines what it makes, and the directions in which it searches' (p. 275). It is a point which this contribution shares with an emerging evolutionary, capability-centered, perspective on the firm, seen as an ensemble of collective problem-solving procedures (i.e. routines and other persistent organizational traits: see, again Cohen *et al.*, in this volume) which store and reproduce a good deal of what the organization 'know'.[2] Given such a setting, Pavitt argues for a largely *incrementalist* view of knowledge accumulation, whereby 'competence-destroying' technological discontinuities are the exception rather than the rule: 'although they may have revolutionary effects, techno-logical discontinuities rarely encompass all—or even most of—the fields of knowledge that feed into a product. Typically they may affect the perform-ance of a key component (e.g. transistors vs. valves) or provide a major new technique (e.g. gene splicing). But they do not destroy the whole range of related and complementary technologies . . . that are necessary for a complete product' (p. 275).

Pavitt's point has fundamental ramifications. A *first* one is that in contem-porary economies, multitechnology and multidivisional firms 'with established R&D activities and a product range that has grown out of a common but evolv-ing technological competence has been and will continue to be "the largest sin-gle source of the new technological knowledge on which innovation depends"' (p. 270). A *second* consequence concerns the importance of the coordination and control of multiple specialized sources of knowledge within the organization. A *third* implication is that one should not overemphasize the importance of technological diversity across firms: rather, 'at the level of *product market* or *industry* there is similarity rather than diversity in the level and mix of tech-nological activities in competing firms; . . . the diversity exists downstream in . . . the product and process configurations that can be generated from the same or very similar base of technological knowledge' (pp. 273–4).

The first two points bear significant overlapping with Alfred Chandler's contribution, while the third links with Nathan Rosenberg's discussion, both in this volume. Let us start from the former.

Building on his previous accounts of the emergence of the modern American business enterprise, prompted by the railroad and telephone systems of the late nineteenth century, Chandler provides a fascinating interpretation of the many changes characterizing the typical large-scale American corporate organization since that period. 'The development of corporate strategies, structures and control systems in the US firms in modern capital-intensive industries rested on three sources—those developed in the management of railroads, those that come from the management of units of production (the factory or works) and finally those created by the corporate managers themselves' (p. 384).

---

[2] On the 'capability view' of organizations, also cf. Dosi, Nelson, and Winter (2000); on the relation-ship between organizational knowledge and organizational boundaries cf. Teece *et al.* (1994), and on the 'dynamic capabilities' shaping the direction of knowledge accumulation and strategic adjustment, cf. Teece, Pisano, and Schuen (1997).

The outcome has been the multidivisional 'M-form' corporation characterized by (i) a three-level organizational structure (the business unit, the division and the corporate headquarters); (ii) specific and novel accounting practices matching such an organizational structure; and (iii) a factory system that, whenever possible, incorporated tayloristic principles of division of labor and governance of production.[3] Such a multidivisional multitechnology structure—as Chandler has been arguing in many of his works—has fostered the exploitation of both economics of scale and scope (including, of course, the inter-technological complementarities discussed by Pavitt). The model, however, has been partly undermined since the late 1960s by several factors. First, the wave of mergers and acquisitions of the 1960s weakened the effectiveness of enlarged M-form organizations and increasingly disconnected the specific knowledge of top managers (if any) from the knowledge embodied in lower level operations. Second, especially since the 1980s, financial intermediaries became more aggressively involved in corporate restructuring, further strengthening a tendency in which 'top management decisions were becoming based on numbers, not knowledge' (p. 396). And third, 'control methods are also being redefined to take advantage of new, computer-based technologies and to meet the cost-cutting demands created by continuing powerful international and inter-industry competition' (p. 400). Today, the M-form still rules for most multiproduct multimarket firms, but Chandler's analysis points at the challenges that new technologies and new relationships between finance and industry are posing to the long-term governance of knowledge accumulation in contemporary corporations.

The role of *diversity*, as already mentioned, is one of the central topics also of Rosenberg's broad reflections on the role of 'economic experiments' in capitalist economies. The article, originally published just after the collapse of eastern European centrally planned economies, takes off from Karl Marx's path-breaking understanding of the innovation system of capitalist societies. A crucial feature of such a system is the possibility of undertaking multiple, possibly competing, technological and organizational *experiments*. In turn, such experiments are made possible by the existence of (i) a multiplicity of decision-makers, (ii) institutional measures meant to reduce risk and encourage experimentation itself (including the limited liability of investors), and (iii) some guarantee of appropriation of financial rewards to successful innovators. It is striking to remark the contrast between these basic ingredients of the 'unbound Prometheus' of capitalism and twentieth-century socialism, with its discouragement of experimentation through central planning,

---

[3] On this last point and its importance for the international dominance of the 'American model', cf. Kogut (1992).

the negligible freedom of action accorded to plant managers, the managerial risk-aversion of State bureaucracies, and the systematic neglect of consumers in production planning. At the same time, Rosenberg's ambitious article also sets the background for many challenging questions that have ultimately to do with the long-term properties of market economies and the comparative performances of different 'varieties of capitalism'—to use the expression of Hall and Soskice (2001).

One set of questions concerns the very effectiveness of market mechanisms in fostering and selecting amongst 'experiments'. To what extent do such mechanisms lead 'from the worse to some unequivocally best'? How do specific institutions shape the rates and directions of 'experimentation'? And, do they influence the types of technologies and organizational forms which are ultimately selected?

A crucial angle of investigation focuses upon the importance of the past in shaping the future of technological and economic outcomes. Clearly the more the past matters (e.g. in the form of inherited institutions, 'habits of thought', social conventions, organizational practices, shares skills, cultural values) the more one should also condition the outcomes of specific market interactions upon history-inherited conditions. Symmetrically, a complementary question regards the role of individual (micro) actions in shaping future (macro) streams of events.

The fascinating interpretation by David in this volume addresses the process of competition between direct and alternate current systems of electricity supply *c.*1887–92. It is a case which raises paradigmatic questions about the nature of 'technical progress', and more generally of 'economic progress', as 'uphill' processes. David's detailed reconstruction of the 'battle of the systems' is a revealing account of the subtle interrelations between individual behaviors and collective effects under conditions of dynamic increasing returns. A fundamental point is that 'by no means need the commercial victor in this kind of system rivalry be more efficient than the available alternatives. Nor need it be the one which adopters would have chosen if a different sequence of actions on the parts of others had preceded their own' (p. 319).

By the same token, 'for reasons having little to do with the ability of economic agents to foresee the future, or with anything more than an accidental and possibly quite transitory alignment of their private interests with the economic welfare of future generations, technological development may take a particular path which does prove eventually to have been superior to any available alternative' (p. 319). Indeed these turn out to be quite general properties of all dynamics in the domains of technologies, organizational forms and institutions characterized by some forms of dynamic increasing returns, network externalities, collective self-reinforcement effects or most other positive feedback processes. As David emphasizes, this is certainly 'a disquieting message for those who normally find comfort in the Panglossian presumption that the "invisible hand" of market competition—assisted sometimes by the visible hand of farsighted management—somehow has worked to shape ours into the most economically efficient of all possible worlds' (pp. 319–20).

Let us get back to some of the basic necessary conditions flagged in Rosenberg's article, mentioned above, for technological and organizational experimentations. Certainly, they include some form of *incentive compatibility* of experimentation efforts themselves. Granted that much, however, should such incentives necessarily take an economic form? A good part of the contemporary history of knowledge accumulation has involved a structure of incentives which happened to be very far from economic appropriation of the outcomes of search efforts. This certainly applies to 'pure' science, from Galileo to Einstein, but also to a significant part of seemingly 'applied' research endeavors (a good example is the discovery of the transistor with its far-reaching consequences into the development of microelectronics).

There are at least four major issues of stake here. *First*, what are the driving forces and the organizational arrangements nesting the search of a persistently expanding pool of scientific and technological opportunities? In this domain, *ICC* has a few long-lasting published contributions, especially concerning national and sectoral *systems of innovation*, including, among others, Nelson (1994) and (1996), Malerba and Orsenigo (1993) and (1997), Bell and Pavitt (1993). *Second*, what are the relationships between 'scientific search'—*stricto sensu* defined—and, technological developments? *Third*, how do *appropriability* conditions for the outcomes of successful technological innovations influence the rates of innovation themselves? For example, do higher expected rents stemming from tighter patenting regimes yield higher intensities of search and, ultimately, higher rates of innovation? And, *fourth*, what are the relationships between private rates of return to innovative search and the dynamics of collective welfare, however defined?

Sidney Winter's paper addresses the last two issues, showing—on the grounds of a simple model of industrial evolution—the possibility that strengthening appropriability regimes might yield (i) systematic falls in social welfare, and also (ii) decreasing rates of technological change. Given the current excitement about the unconditional virtues of ever-expanding property right regimes, Winter's work ought to be read as a precious, seminal insight into the subtle dilemma between incentive to innovate, to imitate, and to economically exploit what happens to be already commonly known.

This is an exciting set of issues, rarely explored by social scientists, despite their obvious importance to economic welfare and to society more generally.

In featuring these essays—almost exactly republished in their original form—we feature *ICC*, and its commitment to critical challenges. As editors of *ICC*, we encourage research that is original (with the chance to become pathbreaking) and directed toward big, tangled, knotty issues. We are happy to see our authors challenge the conventional wisdom, particularly when the conventional wisdom is unable to provide insights into important management and policy issues.

What is emerging from the pages of *ICC* is an interdisciplinary body of literature that is enriching our understanding of technological change, organizational processes, and organizational structures. We hope that the reader will be stimulated by the research essays of some of our leading authors, both here in this volume and in subsequent issues of *ICC* itself.

References

Aoki, M. (2002), *Toward Comparative Institutional Analysis.* MIT Press: Cambridge, MA.

Bell, M. and K. Pavitt (1993), 'Technological Accumulation and Industrial Growth: Contrasts between Developed and Developing Countries', *Industrial and Corporate Change*, 2:2, 157–210.

Camerer, C. F. (2003), *Behavioral Game Theory: Experiments in Strategic Interaction.* Princeton University Press: Princeton, NJ.

Cohen, M., J. G. March, and J. P. Olsen (1972), 'A Garbage can Model of Organizational Choice', *Administrative Science Quarterly*, 17, 1–25.

Dosi, G., L. Marengo, and G. Fagiolo (2002), *Learning in Evolutionary Enviroments.* Sant'Anna School of Advanced Studies, LEM Working Paper: Pisa.

Dosi, G., R. R. Nelson, and S. G. Winter (eds.) (2000), *The Nature and Dynamics of Organizational Capabilities.* Oxford University Press: New York and Oxford.

Hall, P. A. and D. Soskice (eds.) (2001), *Varieties of Capitalism: The Institutional Foundations of Comparative Advantage.* Oxford University Press: New York and Oxford.

Kogut, B. (1992), 'National Organizing Principles of Work and the Erstwhile Dominance of the American Multinational Corporation', *Industrial and Corporate Change*, 1:2, 285–325.

Malerba, F. and L. Orsenigo (1993), 'Technological Regimes and Firm Behavior', *Industrial and Corporate Change*, 2:1, 45–71.

Malerba, F. and L. Orsenigo (1997), 'Technological Regimes, Industrial Demography and the Evolution of Industrial Structures', *Industrial and Corporate Change*, 6:1, 83–117.

March, J. G. (1994), *A Primer on Decision Making: How Decisions Happen.* The Free Press: New York.

Nelson, R. R. (1994), 'The Co-Evolution of Technology, Industrial Structure, and Supporting Institutions', *Industrial and Corporate Change*, 3:1, 47–63.

Nelson, R. R. (1996), 'The Evolution of Comparative or Competitive Advantage: A Preliminary Report on a Study', *Industrial and Corporate Change*, 5:2, 597–617.

Nelson, R. R. (2003), 'On the Uneven Evolution of Human Know-How', *Research Policy*, 32, 909–22.

Teece, D., G. Pisano, and A. Schuen (1997), 'Dynamic Capabilities and Strategic Management', *Strategic Management Journal*, 18:7, 509–33.

Teece, D., R. Rumelt, G. Dosi, and S. Winter (1994), 'Understanding Corporate Coherence: Theory and Evidence', *Journal of Economic Behavior and Organization*, 23:1, 1–30.

Ziman, J. (ed.) (2000), *Technological Innovation as an Evolutionary Process.* Cambridge University Press: New York and Cambridge.

PART I

ECONOMIC BEHAVIORS AND ORGANIZATIONAL FORMS

Costly and Bounded Rationality in Individual and Team Decision-making

ROY RADNER

(Henry Kaufman Management Center, Department of Information Systems,
Leonard N. Stern School of Business, New York University, 44 West Fourth Street,
Suite 9-170, New York, NY 10012-1126, USA. Email: rradner@stern.nyu.edu)

The 'Savage paradigm' of rational decision-making under uncertainty has become the dominant model of human behavior in mainstream economics and game theory. However, under the rubric of 'bounded-rationality', this model has been criticized as inadequate from both normative and descriptive viewpoints. This paper sketches the historical roots and some current developments of this movement, distinguishing between attempts to extend the Savage paradigm ('costly rationality') and the need for more radical departures ('truly bounded rationality').

1. Introduction

Some kind of model of rational decision-making is at the base of most current economic analysis. This is certainly true of microeconomic theory and, in particular, recent theoretical research on the economics of organization. At the same time, there is a growing unease with the mainstream models of *Homo economicus*, and a small but growing body of economic theory in response to it. Such unease was already voiced at the beginning of the 20th century (if not before), but the work of Jacob Marschak and Herbert Simon provided the stimuli for a more intense level of activity. Interestingly enough, their work appeared almost at the same time that the publications of von Neumann and Morgenstern, L. J. Savage and John Nash established the foundations of the current rational-choice school of the theory of economic organization.

In this essay I shall sketch some of the roots of the current revolt against the mainstream, and also some of its branches. I shall confine myself to the roots and branches that relate most closely to what I call the 'Savage paradigm' of rational decision in the face of uncertainty. Thus I shall leave the game-theoretic aspects of organization theory aside.[1] I shall also confine myself to the economic theory literature, thus neglecting a large literature using a more sociological approach. Evidence of bounded rationality is not difficult to cite, at least the 'boundedness' part. Fortunately, I can refer the reader to the excellent review article by John Conlisk (1996).

My title, 'Costly and Bounded Rationality', reflects the two rather different approaches of Marschak and Simon. Marschak's work emphasized that the Savage paradigm could be extended to take account of costs and constraints associated with information acquisition and processing in organizations, without abandoning the notion of optimizing behavior. This approach found its most detailed expression in the theory of teams. Marschak was also interested in modeling the phenomenon of inconsistency in decision-makers' choices, and was one of the founders of the theory of 'stochastic choice'. However, even there he was interested in how, and to what degree, the real choices of decision-makers approximated, at least statistically, those of a fully rational person.

Simon was more concerned with behavior that could not so readily be interpreted, if at all, as 'optimizing'. As far as I know, he coined the term 'bounded rationality', and developed the concept in its relation to economics, psychology and artificial intelligence. However, in some of his publications he apparently considered bounded rationality to be a broader concept, subsuming costly rationality as a particular case. In order to avoid terminological disputes, I shall sometimes call the narrower concept 'truly bounded rationality'.

In this paper, I start with the theory of *unbounded* rationality of decision-making in the face of uncertainty, and with Savage's model as the archetype of such a theory. There is no doubt that Savage's purpose was *normative*. Near the beginning of *The Foundations of Statistics* he states:

> I am about to build up a highly idealized theory of the behavior of a 'rational' person with respect to decisions. In doing so I will, of course, have to ask you to agree with me that such and such maxims of behavior are 'rational'. In so far as 'rational' means logical, there is no live question; and if I ask your leave at all, it is only as a matter of form. But our person is going to have to make up his mind in situations in which criteria beyond the ordinary ones of logic will be necessary. So, when certain maxims are presented for your consideration, you must ask yourself whether you try to behave in accordance with them, or, to put it differently, how would you react if you noticed yourself violating them. (Savage, 1954, p. 7)

This quote describes a philosophical exercise. If there is any empiricism here, it is armchair empiricism about what 'reasonable and thoughtful' persons might think.

---

[1] See, however, some inflammatory remarks on the latter topic in Radner (1997).

My paper is written in the same spirit, as far as I can push it. But theorists of *costly and bounded* rationality face a dilemma. On the one hand, it is not rational to prescribe behavior that is hopelessly unrealistic. In particular, it is not realistic to expect even expert decision makers with computers to be fully logical (see Section 5.5). On the other hand, knowledge about cognitive costs and bounds is empirical. Nevertheless, my ultimate purpose here is normative. Given what we know about the cognitive costs and limits of decision-making in the face of uncertainty, what might it mean to make decisions rationally, if indeed there is any meaning at all?

One 'empirical' approach to rationality is to try to study how 'successful' decision-makers behave. I fear that this approach is fraught with difficulties, as Savage's own theory would explain. A discussion of this issue would fill a gap in the paper. For example, in an uncertain world, good decisions can often lead to bad consequences, and vice versa. Furthermore, in a world in which many uncertainties are never resolved, it is often impossible to tell *ex post* why the consequences of a decision were what they were. Recall that Savage's goal was to lay the foundations of inductive (i.e. statistical) inference, and in particular to rationalize many current statistical methods. At best, his model describes a set of 'rational' procedures for using information to make decisions. In this sense, his was a theory of *procedural rationality*.

I am, of course, aware that many economists use the Savage model, or something like it, as a *positive* theory to explain observed economic behavior and institutions. (This use of the model has even made inroads into other social sciences.) Mainstream positive economics holds on tenaciously to the Savage model, even though it is patently false if taken literally. However, this is not an issue that I address in this paper.

The term 'procedural rationality' brings with it connotations of dynamics and change. As explained in Section 3, in the Savage paradigm a decision-maker's preferences among actions and strategies are determined jointly by his or her 'tastes and beliefs'. The focus is on the dynamics of how a rational decision-maker revises his or her beliefs about the relative likelihoods of relevant events, in the light of new observations about the external world. However, *the decision-maker's underlying model of the world is fixed*, and the successive revisions of beliefs proceeds according to the calculus of conditional probability. (Technically, the underlying probability space remains unchanged.) In reality, decision-makers typically change their underlying models of the world from time to time, in response to stimuli other than observations consistent with the current underlying model. Whether there is a 'rational' way to do this in the spirit of the original Savage paradigm is an important and challenging question. I believe that there may be such a way, and in Section 5.4 I explore the idea in the context of a particular example.

The decision-maker's tastes are also subject to change. (In the jargon of economics, the decision-maker's tastes are represented by his or her *utility function*.) Some apparent changes in taste might be explained by the acquisition of new information about the consequences of action in a way that preserves the underlying model of the decision-maker, but there are often more deep-seated changes. For example, a recurrent theme in the management literature is the importance of the formation and maintenance of *values* in the firm (e.g. Mintzberg, 1989; Peters and Waterman, 1982). However, a serious examination of what has been written about the psychology and social psychology of human motivation is beyond the scope of this paper.

In Section 2, I sketch some of the roots of the ideas of costly and bounded rationality. In order to explain more clearly the branches that have subsequently developed, I found it desirable to sketch the elements of the Savage paradigm, which I do in Section 3. The topics of costly and truly bounded rationality follow in Sections 4 and 5 respectively. In particular, Section 5.4 sketches a proposed analysis of 'rational' model revision. Finally, in Section 6, I speculate on the senses (if at all) in which a 'boundedly rational' decision-maker can be said to be 'rational'. As I have already mentioned, my discussion is almost entirely confined to individual and team decision-making, as distinct from game-theoretic issues.

2. *Some Roots*

2.1 Uncertainty

Discussions of rational decision-making—unbounded and otherwise—have been closely tied to the consideration of uncertainty. The very beginnings of formal probability theory were in part stimulated by questions of how to act rationally in playing games of chance with cards and dice (Hald, 1990). Kenneth Arrow began his 1951 article, 'Alternative Approaches to the Theory of Choice in Risk-taking Situations', with the paragraph:

> There is no need to enlarge upon the importance of a realistic theory explaining how individuals choose among alternative courses of action when the consequences of their actions are incompletely known to them. It is no exaggeration to say that every choice made by human beings would meet this description if attention were paid to the ultimate implications. Risk and the human reactions to it have been called upon to explain everything from the purchase of chances in a 'numbers' game to the capitalist structure of our economy; according to Professor Frank Knight, even human consciousness itself would disappear in absence of uncertainty. (Arrow, 1951, p. 204)

During the first half of this century a number of alternative views were developed concerning the nature of uncertainty, the possibly different kinds of uncertainty and whether, or in what circumstances, it could be measured. I cannot review this development in any detail, but by the time Arrow wrote his article, a number of competing views had been formulated (see Arrow, 1951; Savage, 1954, ch. 4).

The first question was: what is one uncertain about? As the above quote suggests, economists tended to focus on uncertainty about the consequences of actions. One could also be uncertain about the laws of nature, or about the truth or falsity of mathematical propositions. Of course, to the extent that knowing the consequences of actions depended on knowing the laws of nature or the implications of mathematical axioms, uncertainty about the latter would be important for economic actions as well.

A second question was: can uncertainty be meaningfully measured (quantified)? I believe that there was general (but not universal) agreement that, if uncertainty could be quantified, then that quantification should obey the mathematical laws of probability. However, the 'frequentist' school reserved the legitimacy of probabilistic quantification to 'experiments' (planned or naturally occurring) that were repeated indefinitely under identical conditions. Thus, according to them, it would not be meaningful on 1 July 1998, to assign a probability to the event, 'President Clinton will not serve out his full term of office', or to the event that 'an economical method of producing energy by controlled fusion will be developed by 1 January 2001'. This view was espoused by Frank Knight (1921), who made the distinction between 'risk' and 'uncertainty', the former being measurable in an actuarial sense, and the latter not. Knight went on to apply this distinction to 'organizational economics' by asserting that, since 'uncertainty' (in his sense) could not be insured against, it was the peculiar role of economic entrepreneurs to bear this uncertainty in the hope of being rewarded with economic profits (i.e. profits beyond the returns due to the standard factors of production). He went on to say:

> When uncertainty is present, and the task of deciding what do takes the ascendancy over that of execution, the internal organization of the productive groups is no longer a matter of indifference or a mechanical detail. (Knight, 1921, p. 268)

The 'personalist school', which included a diverse set of methodologies, argued that the concept of probability was applicable to events outside of the frequentist realm. Some personalists went so far as to deny that the frequentist view could be applied meaningfully to any events at all, i.e. all probability judgements were 'personal'. (See Arrow's and Savage's accounts of the work of Ramsey, Keynes, Jeffries, Carnap and de Finetti. In some sense, the personalist view might also be ascribed to earlier authors, such as Bayes and Laplace.) The personalist view was given a solid foundation by Savage (1954), whose stated aim was to rationalize statistical practice. Ironically, his theory seems to have had only a modest effect on statistical practice. On the other hand, it was adopted by mainstream economists and game theorists as the dominant model of how decision-makers should (or even do) respond rationally to uncertainty and information. (See Section 3 for a summary of Savage's theory and its implications for economic decision-making.)

Central to the development of thinking about uncertainty was the simple idea that uncertainty about the consequences of an action could (or should) be traced to uncertainty about the 'state of the world' in which the action would be taken. An essential feature of the concept of the 'state of the world' is that it is beyond the control of the decision-maker in question. More precisely, its occurrence or non-occurrence is independent of the decision-maker's action. A further clarification was provided by the theory of games, put forward by von Neumann and Morgenstern (1947). In multiperson decision-making situations in which the participants have conflicting goals, the theory of games distinguishes between two aspects of the state of the world from the point of view of any single decision-maker, namely (i) the 'state of Nature', which is beyond the control of any of the persons involved, and (ii) the actions of the other persons. The latter has been called 'strategic uncertainty'. Economists (going back at least to Cournot, 1838), had struggled for a long time with how to incorporate strategic uncertainty into models of rational behavior in duopolistic and oligopolistic situations. Following the appearance of von Neumann and Morgenstern's book (1947), a number of different game-theoretic 'solution concepts' were put forward, and they generally predicted different outcomes, except in the special case of two-person zero-sum (or constant-sum) games. Nash's concept of 'non-cooperative equilibrium' (Nash, 1951), which was a generalization of Cournot's concept of oligopolistic market equilibrium, finally emerged as the 'solution' most popular with economists. However, in Nash's theory there was only strategic uncertainty, but no uncertainty about 'states of Nature'. Furthermore, his concept of non-cooperative equilibrium—or what is now usually called *Nash equilibrium*—did not entirely solve the problem of strategic uncertainty. The difficulty is that in a large number of game-theoretic models there are many Nash equilibria, and so the theory provides no good basis for predicting the actions of the other players.

Savage's book, *The Foundations of Statistics*, appeared in 1954, three years after Arrow's 1951 article. The synthesis of his approach with Nash's theory of games was initiated by Harsanyi (1967–68), and further developed by Selten (1975) and Kreps and Wilson (1982). The resulting theory of 'Nash–Harsanyi equilibrium' did not eliminate the difficulty of a multiplicity of equilibria.

Nevertheless, I think that it is fair to say that this synthesis now provides the dominant formulation of economic rationality, especially in the theoretical development of the economics of organizations.

In the remainder of this paper, I shall concentrate on a critique of this theory of rational behavior *as it is applied to single-person decision-making, or to multiperson situations in which the persons do not have conflicting goals*. A critique of the theory of strategic rationality is beyond the scope of the present paper, but for some remarks on this see Radner (1997).

2.2 The Savage Paradigm

A fuller sketch of the *Savage paradigm* of individual rational decision-making under uncertainty will be given in Section 3, but a few elements are needed here in order to introduce the notions of costly and bounded rationality. The essential building blocks of the theory are (i) a set of alternative *states of the world*, or simply *states*, which are beyond the decision-maker's control; (ii) a set of alternative actions available to the decision-maker, or as Savage calls them, *acts*; and (iii) a set of alternative *consequences*. An act determines which consequence will be realized in each state (of the world). Hence a parsimonious way to think about an act is that it is a function from states to consequences. The simplicity of this formulation hides a wealth of possible interpretations and potential complexity. I shall discuss these in more detail in subsequent sections, but here I shall allude only to a few of them. First, the decision-maker (DM) is assumed to have preferences among acts. These preferences reflect both the DM's *beliefs* about the relative likelihood of the different states, and the DM's *tastes* with regard to consequences. A few axioms about the independence of beliefs from consequences enable the DM to infer preferences among complicated acts from those among simpler ones. The DM is assumed (or advised) to choose an act that is most preferred among the available ones. I shall call this the assumption of *optimization*.

Second, if the decision problem has any dynamic aspects, then states can be quite complex. In fact, a full description of any particular state will typically require a full description of the *entire history* of those features of the DM's environment that are relevant to the decision problem at hand.

Third, the description of the set of available acts reveals—if only implicitly—the opportunities for the DM to acquire information about the state of the world and react to it. Together with the axioms about preferences among acts, this imposes a fairly stringent constraint on how the DM should learn from observation and experience. In fact, we shall see that this aspect of the model is what gives the Savage paradigm its real 'bite'. An act that describes how the DM acquires information and reacts to it dynamically is sometimes called a *strategy* (plan, policy). Savage described his point of view as follows:

> As has just been suggested, what in the ordinary way of thinking might be regarded as a chain of decisions, one leading to another in time, is in the formal description proposed here regarded as a single decision. To put it a little differently, it is proposed that the choice of a policy or plan be regarded as a single decision. This point of view, though not always in so explicit a form, has played a prominent role in the statistical advances of the present century. For example, the great majority of experimentalists, even today, suppose that the function of statistics and of statisticians is to decide what conclusions to draw from data gathered in an experiment or other observational program. But statisticians hold it to be lacking in foresight to gather data without a view to the method of analysis to be employed, that is, they hold that the design and analysis of an experiment should be decided upon as an articulated whole. (Savage, 1954, pp. 15, 16)

In a model of a sequential decision problem, the space of available strategies can, of course, be enormous and complex. This observation will be a dominant motif in what follows.

2.3 The Simon Critique

As Herbert Simon emphasized in his work, the cognitive activities required by the Savage paradigm (and its related precursors) are far beyond the capabilities of human decision-makers, or even modern human/computer systems, except in the simplest decision problems. This led him and his colleagues (especially at Carnegie–Mellon University) to investigate models of human decision-making that are more realistic from the point of view of cognitive demands, and yet do not entirely abandon the notion of rationality. As he put it,

> Theories that incorporate constraints on the information-processing capabilities of the actor may be called *theories of bounded rationality*. (Simon, 1972, p. 162)[2]

Simon was not the first to criticize the mainstream economic model of rational human behavior. The well-known economist J. M. Clark took time out during the First World War to study contemporary psychology, which effort resulted in 1918 in an article, 'Economics and Modern Psychology'. In a felicitous passage he wrote:

> If one wanted to be unfair to economists in general, he might select, for purposes of comparison with these psychological principles, a certain well known though fictitious character whose idiosyncrasies furnish alternate joy and irritation to

---

[2] Simon's interest in bounded rationality appears already in his early book, *Administrative Behavior* (1947). See also Simon (1955), and March and Simon (1958, esp. ch. 6).

modern readers of economics. He is a somewhat in-human individual who, inconsistently enough, carries the critical weighing of hedonistic values to the point of mania. So completely is he absorbed in his irrationally rational passion for impassionate calculation that he often remains a day laborer at pitifully low wages from sheer devotion to the fine art of making the most out of his scanty income and getting the highest returns from his employers for such mediocre skill as he chooses to devote to their service. Yet he cannot fail to be aware that the actuarial talent he lavishes outside of working hours would suffice to earn him a relatively princely salary in the office of any insurance company. So intricate are the calculations he delights in that even trained economists occasionally blunder into errors in recording them. (Clark, 1918, p. 24)

Savage himself was aware of the problem of bounded rationality. Early in his book he wrote, regarding the choice of a strategy (plan, policy):

> The point of view under discussion may be symbolized by the proverb, 'Look before you leap', and the one to which it is opposed by the proverb, 'You can cross that bridge when you come to it'. When two proverbs conflict in this way, it is proverbially true that there is some truth in both of them. . . . One must indeed look before he leaps, in so far as the looking is not unreasonably time-consuming and otherwise expensive; but there are innumerable bridges one cannot afford to cross, unless he happens to come to them.
>
> Carried to its logical extreme, the 'Look before you leap' principle demands that one envisage every conceivable policy for the government of his whole life (at least from now on) in its most minute details, in the light of the vast number of unknown states of the world, and decide here and now on one policy. This is utterly ridiculous, not—as some might think—because there might later be cause for regret, if things did not turn out as had been anticipated, but because the task implied in making such a decision is not even remotely resembled by human possibility. It is even utterly beyond our power to plan a picnic or to play a game of chess in accordance with the principle, even when the world of states and the set of available acts to be envisaged are artificially reduced to the narrowest reasonable limits. (Savage, 1954, p. 16)

Nevertheless, Savage felt that his model was a useful one for thinking about rational decision-making.

> Though the 'Look before you leap' principle is preposterous if carried to extremes, I would argue that it is the proper subject of our further discussion, because to cross one's bridges when one comes to them means to attack relatively simple problems of decision by artificially confining attention to so small a world that the 'Look before you leap' principle can be applied there. I am unable to formulate criteria for selecting these small worlds and indeed believe that their selection may be a matter of judgement and experience about which it is impossible to enunciate complete and sharply defined general principles. . . . On the other hand, it is an operation in which we all necessarily have much experience,

and one in which there is in practice considerable agreement. (Savage, 1954, pp. 16, 17)

Savage's approach remains the dominant method of 'mainstream' economists' theorizing about economic organization. In this methodology, the theorist sets up a rather simple model of the situation, and then applies the Savage paradigm, or some variation thereof, in its full force. Of course, the model has to be simple enough for the analyst to be capable of deducing interesting implications from the assumptions of 'full rationality'.

A different kind of approach, sometimes called 'behavioral', abandons the assumption of optimization in favor of some other model of decision-making, supposedly empirically based. Examples include 'satisficing', 'rules of thumb', 'routines', etc.[3] The development of these approaches has also had some interesting and close connections with the field of artificial intelligence, and Simon himself was an early contributor to both fields (e.g. Simon, 1981; Newell and Simon, 1972). Unfortunately, a serious treatment of this subject is beyond the scope of this paper.

2.4 Costly and 'Truly Bounded' Rationality

Simon's description of theories of bounded rationality as 'incorporat[ing] constraints on the information-processing capabilities of the actor' is broad enough to cover a number of different approaches. One approach deals with *costly rationality* without giving up the assumption of optimization. In this extension of the mainstream economic methodology, one explicitly models the constraints and/or costs relating to the cognitive capabilities of the DM, and assumes that the DM optimizes fully, subject to those constraints and taking account of the relevant costs. I shall call this the *extended Savage paradigm* (see Section 4). Early work in this spirit included the statistical research of Abraham Wald (1947, 1950), and the 'theory of teams', introduced by Jacob Marschak (Marschak, 1955; Radner, 1962; Marschak and Radner, 1972).

More radical approaches, which give up the assumption of optimization, are required to deal with the problems caused by *vagueness, ambiguity*, and *'unawareness'* in the decision-making situation. Even more troublesome is the *failure of logical omniscience*, which refers to the fact that the DM cannot know all of the logical consequences of what he knows. To avoid confusion with Simon's original terminology, I shall lump these diverse phenomena together under the heading *truly bounded rationality*, and discuss them in Section 5.

---

[3] For early work in this spirit, see Simon (1947, 1955, 1957) and March and Simon (1958). For a further formal analysis, see Radner (1975a).

3. *A Trunk: The Savage Paradigm*

The *Savage paradigm* of individual decision-making in the presence of uncertainty has already been briefly introduced in Section 2. In this section I shall give a fuller sketch of the theory, but this sketch will be far from complete or systematic. My limited goal here is to provide a background for the subsequent discussion of bounded rationality.[4]

As noted in Section 2.2, there are three essential building blocks of the theory:

1. a set *S* of alternative *states of the world*, or simply *states*, which are beyond the decision-maker's control;
2. a set *A* of alternative actions available to the decision-maker, or as Savage calls them, *acts*; and
3. a set *C* of alternative *consequences*.

An act determines which consequence will be realized in each state (of the world). Hence a parsimonious way to think about an act is that it is a function from the set of states to the set of consequences.

Savage illustrates the model with the following example:

> Your wife has just broken five good eggs into a bowl when you come in and volunteer to finish making the omelet. A sixth egg, which for some reason must either be used for the omelet or wasted altogether, lies unbroken beside the bowl. You must decide what to do with this unbroken egg. Perhaps it is not too great an oversimplification to say that you must decide among three acts only, namely, to break it into the bowl containing the other five, to break it into a saucer for inspection, or to throw it away without inspection. Depending on the state of the egg, each of these three acts will have some consequence of concern to you, say that indicated by Table 1. (Savage, 1954, p. 14)

TABLE 1. An Example Illustrating Acts, States and Consequences

Act	State of the sixth egg	
	Good	Rotten
Break into bowl	six-egg omelet	no omelet, five good eggs destroyed
Break into saucer	six-egg omelet, saucer to wash	five-egg omelet, saucer to wash
Throw away	five-egg omelet, one good egg destroyed	five-egg omelet

[4] The best systematic treatment is still Savage's book (1954, 1972), which includes extensive historical and critical remarks. A briefer, and somewhat more accessible, account is given in Part I of Marschak and Radner (1972).

Note that:

1. The set S has two alternative states (of the 'world'), namely 'the sixth egg is good' and 'the sixth egg is rotten'.
2. The set C has six different consequences, described in the six entries in the body of the table.
3. (i) The set A has 3 alternative acts:
    (i) break the sixth egg into the bowl;
    (ii) break the sixth egg into the saucer, then add it to the bowl if it is good, and throw it away if it is bad;
    (iii) throw the sixth egg away without breaking it.

The example can be used to illustrate two points. First, the DM's uncertainty about the consequences of action has been modeled as uncertainty about the state of the sixth egg, which is beyond the DM's control.

Second, acts (i) and (iii) can be thought of as corresponding to 'simple actions', taken without further information about the state of the sixth egg. On the other hand, act (ii) corresponds to a 'strategy' (plan, policy), according to which some information is first obtained (by breaking the sixth egg into the saucer), and then some appropriate further action is taken, depending on the information obtained (about the sixth egg). Note that the information is 'costly', since the saucer must be washed.

Typically, the set of states of the world for a decision problem will have many states, not just two. It corresponds to our everyday language to call a set of states an *event*. Thus, in the omelet example, there might be three states of the sixth egg: very fresh, moderately fresh and rotten. The first two states together would then comprise the event, 'the sixth egg is usable'.

Returning to the general model, Savage makes a number of assumptions about the DM's behavior in decision problems of this type. In this paper I can only highlight a few of those assumptions, and sketch their most important implications. First, it is assumed that the DM can rank all of the acts in order of preference. Implicit in this assumption is the interpretation that the DM will choose an act that is ranked highest in this preference order. (Some further mathematical assumption is needed to ensure that there will be at least one best act, e.g. this would be the case if the set of acts were finite.) At first sight, one might think that this is much too demanding a requirement. After all, in a complicated decision problem the DM will want some help, i.e. some method for finding the best act. However, additional assumptions about the structure of the DM's preferences make it possible (in principle) for him to infer his preferences among complicated acts (e.g. strategies) from his preferences among relatively simple ones. Taken together, these assumptions express the idea that the DM's tastes concerning consequences are independent of the states in which they occur, and his beliefs about the relative likelihood of different states (or events) are independent of the accompanying consequences. I shall call this requirement *the independence of tastes and beliefs*.

To some extent the postulate of independence of tastes and beliefs is a convention, in that its validity will depend on a careful description of states, acts and consequences. Savage gives the following example to illustrate this point. A person is about to go on a picnic with friends, but does not yet know where the picnic will be held. Furthermore, he will have no influence on that decision. Provisionally, we may regard the place of the picnic as the relevant state of the world. Before going on the picnic, the person

> . . . decides to buy a bathing suit or a tennis racket, not having at the moment enough money for both. If we call possession of the tennis racket and possession of the bathing suit consequences, then we must say the consequences of his decision will be independent of where the picnic is actually held. If the person prefers the [possession of the] bathing suit, this decision would presumably be reversed if he learned that the picnic were not going to held near water. . . . But under the interpretation of 'act' and 'consequence' that I am trying to formulate, this is not the correct analysis of the situation. The possession of the tennis racket and the possession of the bathing suit are to be regarded as acts, not consequences. (It would be equivalent and more in accordance with ordinary discourse to say the coming into possession, or the buying, of them are acts.) The consequences relevant to the decision are such as these: a refreshing swim with friends, sitting on a shadeless beach twiddling a brand-new tennis racket while one's friends swim, etc. (Savage, 1954, p. 25)

Savage's assumptions about the structure of the DM's preferences among acts imply the following proposition, sometimes called the *expected utility hypothesis* (EUH). Implicit in the DM's preferences are two scales. The first scale assigns *probabilities to events*, and obeys the usual mathematical laws of the calculus of probabilities. The second scale assigns *utilities to consequences*. (It is uniquely determined except for the choice of the origin and the unit of utility.) Using these two scales, one can calculate an *expected utility* for each act, in the usual way, since an act associates a consequence with each state. Thus for each state one calculates the product of its probability times the utility of the associated consequence, and then adds all of the products to obtain the expected utility of the act. Finally, the DM's preferences among acts is *represented by expected utility* in the following sense: *one act is as good as or better than another (from the point of view of the DM) if and only if the expected utility of the first act is greater than or equal to the expected utility of the second act.*

In one sense, the EUH is quite weak. No restrictions are imposed on the probability measure and the utility function implicit in the DM's preferences. To paraphrase an old saying, 'neither beliefs nor tastes are subject to dispute'. Furthermore, it can be shown that the specific form of the utility function represents not only the DM's preference ranking of consequences, but also his attitude towards risk. Thus the Savage axioms put no restrictions on the DM's attitude towards risk—he can be averse to risk, a risk-lover or some combination of the two. Thus two DMs can 'rationally' differ in their tastes, their beliefs and their attitudes towards risk.

On the other hand, the *EUH completely determines how a DM must update his beliefs, and hence his expected utility of acts, in response to new information*. In fact, his updating of beliefs must be governed by the mathematical laws of conditional probability, which in this case takes the form of the celebrated 'Bayes's Rule'. Hence the updating of beliefs by a DM who conforms to the Savage axioms is sometimes called *Bayesian learning*.

A simple example will illustrate the strength of the EUH in this context. Suppose that a 'black box' produces a potentially infinite sequence of zeroes and ones; denote the sequence by $\{X(t)\}$. Two DMs disagree about the probability law that governs this stochastic process, $\{X(t)\}$, but they agree on the following: any two sequences of the same finite length that differ only by a permutation of the zeroes and ones in them have the same probability. Suppose that the black box produces an infinite sequence $\{X(t)\}$ such that the relative frequency of ones is some number, say p, and suppose further that the DMs observe successively longer finite initial segments of the sequence, say

$$[X(1), X(2), \ldots, X(T)]$$

Then as T increases without bound, the DMs will asymptotically approach agreement that the black box produces a sequence of independent and identically distributed random variables, taking the values zero or one, and that the probability of a one is equal to p.[5]

The above example illustrates the *merging of opinions* of DMs who start with different beliefs about the state of the world, but who receive larger and larger 'chunks' of identical information. General conditions under which the merging of opinions occurs has been studied by a number of authors.[6] Space limitations do not allow me to review this material here, but I shall return briefly to the topic in Section 5.

[5] *Technical note*: The condition on which the DMs agree is called *symmetry* or *exchangeability*. In my loose statement of the proposition I have left out an important technical assumption, which is—roughly speaking—that the *a priori* beliefs of neither DM rule out as impossible any particular value of p (Savage, 1954, pp. 50–55).

[6] See Diaconis and Freedman (1986), for a review of the statistical literature up to that date; see also Sims (1971) and Jackson *et al.* (1999) for additional material.

4. *Branch I: Costly Rationality*

4.1 The Extended Savage Paradigm

As just sketched in the previous section, the Savage paradigm does not appear explicitly to take account of the costs of decision-making. However, nothing prevents the DM from incorporating into the description of the consequences of an act the costs—in terms of resources used—of implementing the corresponding actions. The costly activities involved in decision-making include:

1. Observation
2. Information processing, i.e. computation
3. Memory
4. Communication

The last category may be important when the decision-making process is assigned to a team of individuals.

If the resources used by these decision-making activities are limited, then those limits may impose binding constraints on the activities themselves, constraints that must be taken into account in the DM's optimization problem. If the constraints are on the *rate of resource use per unit time*, then more extensive decision-making activities may cause *delays* in the implementation of the eventual decisions. To the extent that a delay lowers the effectiveness of a decision (e.g. by making it more obsolete), we may think of delay as an 'indirect cost'.

We shall see that extending the Savage paradigm to incorporate the costs of decision-making may in some cases be natural, and in other cases problematic. The first class of cases I shall call *costly rationality*, which is the subject of the present section. My treatment will be more of an outline than a true discussion. Fortunately, there is a substantial literature on many of the subtopics, although the authors usually have not used the term 'costly rationality'.

4.2 Observation

The notion that observation is costly was implicit in the Neyman–Pearson theory of hypothesis testing, and was made explicit by Abraham Wald in his pioneering studies of sequential statistical procedures. (See Wald, 1950, for an influential codification of his general approach.) Examples of such sequential procedures include (i) the destructive testing of fuses and artillery shells, which falls under the more general rubric of *sequential analysis* (Wald, 1947); and (ii) clinical trials of new drugs, which is part of a more general topic with the curious name *bandit theory* (Basu *et al.*, 1990). The cost of observation also figures in more classical (non-sequential) statistical problems such as the design of sample surveys and agricultural experiment. Given some model of the costs of observation, the DM chooses the kind and amount of observation, optimally balancing the expected benefits of additional observations against their costs. Such decision problems fit naturally into the Savage paradigm, although taking account of these costs typically complicates the analysis. For example, in the case of clinical trials and other 'bandit' problems, the calculation of optimal policies quickly becomes computationally intractable for many problems of realistic size.

4.3 Information Processing and its Decentralization

Even after the information has been collected (e.g. by observation) it still must be further processed to produce the required decisions. This information-processing task may be quite demanding. Examples include (i) computing a weekly payroll, (ii) scheduling many jobs on many machines, (iii) managing multi-product inventories at many locations, and (iv) project selection and capital budgeting in a large firm. Such tasks are typically too complex to be handled by a single person, even with the aid of modern computers. In such circumstances the required processing of the information is *decentralized* among many persons in the organization.

The formal modeling of decentralized information processing is a relatively recent research topic. Computer science has provided a number of useful models of information processing by both computers and humans, and the decentralization of information processing in human organizations finds its counterpart in the theories of parallel and distributed processing in computer systems. Marschak and McGuire (1971) were probably the first to suggest the use of a particular model of a computer (the finite automation) to represent the limited information processing capabilities of humans in economic organizations. Reiter and Mount were early contributors to this line of research, and went further in analyzing economic organizations as networks of computers (see Mount and Reiter, 1998, and references cited there).[7]

One conclusion from this literature is what I have called *the iron law of delay* for networks of processors of bounded individual capacity. This 'law' can be paraphrased in the following way: *as the size of the information processing task increases, the minimum delay must also increase unboundedly, even for efficient networks and even if the number of available processors is unlimited.*[8]

---

[7] For more recent developments, see Radner (1993), Radner and Van Zandt (1992) and Van Zandt (1998a–c, 1999). See also papers presented at the recent conference organized by the CEPR on 'Information Processing Organizations', Free University of Brussels, 25–26 June 1999.

[8] Of course, a precise statement would require a precise description of the models in which it has been verified. See Radner (1997) and references cited therein for a fuller discussion.

4.4 Memory and Communication

Memory storage and communication among humans and computers are also resource-using activities, and cause further delays in decision-making. I shall not discuss these topics here, except to say that both the storage and transmission of information and the results of information processing seem to be relatively 'cheap' compared to observation and processing, at least if we consider computer-supported activities. The proliferation of large data banks, and the flood of junk mail, telephone calls and email, lend support to this impression. It appears that today it is much cheaper, in some sense, to send, receive and store memos and papers than it is to process them. Nonetheless, organization theorists should not, and have not, neglected the study of these activities. Game theorists have paid particular attention to models of players with limited memory (see Osborne and Rubinstein, 1994; Rubinstein, 1998, and references cited therein). For models of costly communication in organizations, and some implications for organizational structure, see, for example, Marschak and Reichelstein (1998) and Bolton and Dewatripont (1994).

4.5 Implications for Organizational Structure and Returns to Scale

The first implication of costly rationality for organizational structure is that in all but the very smallest economic organizations the process of decision making will be decentralized to some extent, i.e. distributed among several persons. Indeed, it is difficult to think of an economic organization with more than one member in which this is not the case. In itself, this says nothing about the 'decentralization of authority' in the every-day sense. In fact, the concept of 'authority' has proved elusive in the economic theory of organization, and I shall have nothing to say about it in this paper. (For some remarks on this topic, see Radner, 1997, pp. 336–338.)

The fact that decision-making is costly implies that a DM or organization will economize on the costly activities that are involved. In particular, since the incremental value of additional information typically declines after some point, a DM will not want to use all possible information for any one decision or group of related decisions. This in turn implies that, in an efficient organization, *different decisions or groups of related decisions will be based on different sets of information.* Hence, in a large organization both the information-processing and the decision-making will be distributed among many persons. In other words, in a large organization, *the decentralization of both information-processing and decision-making is inevitable.*

The implications for the architecture of this decentralization are less clear. The theory of teams was an early attempt to grapple with this question (Marschak,

1955; Marschak and Radner, 1972). One handicap of this attempt was that at the time there was no readily available model of the 'technology' of information-processing. Thus team theory compared the *benefits* of different organizational structures, but not their *costs*. Perhaps the time is ripe to return to some of those issues with the help of more recent models of information-processing.

Another complexity in the analysis of organizational structure is that the decentralization of information leads to a 'decentralization of power' (Radner, 1975b). I shall not even try to give a precise definition of this concept, but more recent studies of principal-agent relationships and other models of distributed (or 'asymmetric') information give some content to the idea. In other words, decentralization of information, together with diversity of goals among DMs in the organization, generates *strategic uncertainty*, with all its game-theoretic ramifications. As I have said above, I have put such considerations outside of the purview of the present paper (see, however, Dutta and Radner, 1995; Radner, 1992, 1997). Recall that in the theory of teams it is postulated that all the team members have the same goal, although they may have different information and make different decisions.

The renewed interest in the theoretical study of organizational structure, using both the tools of game theory and models of information-processing technology, has made progress, especially in the study of 'hierarchical' organizations. However, in my view we are still far from understanding why and under what circumstances firms are—or are not—organized hierarchically, and why economic activities are sometimes organized in firms and sometimes in markets (Radner, 1992).

A perennial topic in economic theory concerns the sources of increasing and decreasing returns to scale in firms, and in particular what are the organizational sources of scale effects. Economists have generally concluded that decreasing returns to scale should arise only when some input is held fixed.

Otherwise, at least constant returns to scale should be achievable by simply replicating a firm of a given size, and calling the collection of replicated firms a single 'firm'. On the other hand, one might hypothesize that

> there are organizational limits on returns to scale due to the problems of coordinating large numbers of activities within a single firm and operating in diverse environments. Such limits are theoretically possible because replication cannot be used to extend the scale of a firm at constant or decreasing cost. Replicating the activities of several small firms means that the subunits cannot communicate, coordinate their activities, or allocate resources, except as independent firms would do, such as through markets. There can be no headquarters that controls the subunits because such control would incur managerial costs and delays that the independent firms avoid. Such informationally disintegrated units could hardly [be regarded as] a single firm. (Van Zandt and Radner, 2000, p. 8)

As early as 1934, Nicholas Kaldor argued that the supply of coordinating ability must be limited in any single firm.

> You cannot increase the supply of coordinating ability available to an enterprise alongside an increase in the supply of other factors, as it is the essence of coordination that every single decision should be make on a comparison with all the other decisions made or likely to be made; it must therefore pass through a single brain. (Kaldor, 1934, p. 68)

However, the value of information and information processing, and the associated technologies, do not always follow the laws of the consumption and production of material goods. They also interact in surprising ways. To begin with, depending on how it is measured, the marginal value of information can be increasing at low levels of information, and decreasing at higher levels. Indeed, it can be shown that, under very general conditions, *the marginal value of information is increasing at sufficiently low levels* (Radner and Stiglitz, 1983). On the other hand, the law of large numbers (and similar theorems) imply that in standard sampling situations the incremental value of increasing the sample size is eventually decreasing. Applying team theory, Radner (1961) studied how the value of specific organizational devices varied with scale, but without regard to their costs.

On the technology side, Kenneth Arrow pointed out some time ago that the production and dissemination of information would typically show *increasing* returns to scale (Arrow, 1974). This would be so because the production of information usually requires a fixed expenditure of resources independent of the scale of the use or dissemination of the information (as in the case of research and development). The situation is even more striking today in the case of electronic communication, where the marginal cost of dissemination of information (including software) is often almost negligible compared to the initial development cost. The 'iron law of delay' (see Section 4.3 above) further complicates matters because the loss due to delay depends crucially on the intertemporal statistical properties of the relevant environment.

Even without multiplying such examples, it should not be surprising that returns to scale in decision-making activities show complex patterns. Van Zandt and Radner identify three informational scale effects:

> diversification of heterogeneous risks (positive), sharing of information and of costs (positive), and crowding out of recent information due to information processing delay (negative). [On the other hand, because] decision rules are endogenous, delay does not inexorably lead to decreasing returns to scale. However, returns are more likely to be decreasing when computation constraints, rather than sampling costs, limit the information upon which decisions are conditioned. [These] results

> illustrate the fact that informational integration causes a breakdown of the replication arguments that are used to [predict] nondecreasing technological returns to scale. (Van Zandt and Radner, 2000)

Finally, distributed information together with conflicting goals may lead to 'loss of control' or 'agency costs', which have their own peculiar scale effects. However, this takes us into game-theoretic models, which (I repeat) are beyond the scope of this paper.

5. *Branch II: Truly Bounded Rationality*

5.1 Introduction

Recall that in the Savage paradigm the DM has a model of the decision problem that is comprised of four building blocks:

1. a set S of alternative *states of the world*, or simply *states*, which are beyond the DM's control; subsets of S are the *events* about which the DM may be uncertain;
2. a set C of alternative *consequences*;
3. a set A of alternative *acts* available to the decision-maker; each act is a function from the set of states to the set of consequences;
4. a complete preference ordering on the set of acts.

In addition, several axioms are postulated concerning the preference ordering on the set of acts. Taken together, these axioms define a notion of *consistency* that is required of the DM by the paradigm. A preference ordering that is consistent in this sense can be represented by two numerical scales, a *personal probability scale* (defined on events) and a *utility scale* (defined on consequences). Of any two acts, one is preferred to the other if and only if it has a higher *expected utility*.

Among the difficulties a DM typically faces in trying to apply the Savage paradigm to a real decision problem are:

1. Inconsistency
2. Ambiguity
3. Vagueness
4. Unawareness
5. Failure of logical omniscience

As will be seen, these difficulties are somewhat related and overlapping. I mention 'ambiguity' because it is a term one often finds in the literature on decision-making. On the other hand, it appears difficult to distinguish in practice between 'ambiguity' and 'vagueness'. Hence, following Savage, I shall stick with the latter term.

In what follows, I give only a sketch of these difficulties and how they might be met. Savage (1954) devotes Chapter 4 and Section 5.6 to a more detailed discussion of inconsistency and vagueness. An account of more recent attempts to deal with some of these problems is given by Machina (1987, 1889).

5.2 Inconsistency

As is so often the case in this paper, I introduce the present topic with a quote from Savage.

> According to the personalistic view, the role of the mathematical theory of probability is to enable the person using it to detect inconsistencies in his own real or envisaged behavior. It is also understood that, having detected an inconsistency, he will remove it. An inconsistency is typically removable in many different ways, and the theory gives no guidance for choosing. (Savage, 1954, p. 57)

Some 'inconsistencies' have been observed so frequently, and have been so 'appealing', that they have been used to criticize the Savage axioms, and to form a basis for a somewhat different set of axioms. In particular, I have in mind the so-called 'Allais Paradox' and 'Ellsberg Paradox', which I shall not discuss here (see Machina, 1987).

In other cases, it has been argued that inconsistent preferences arise because the DM is forced to articulate preferences about which he is not 'sure'. (This explanation is related to 'vagueness'; see below.) To solve this problem, some authors have proposed the introduction of 'probabilities of a second order', according to which the DM thinks that some probability comparisons of events are more likely to be correct (for him) than others. Savage rejects this approach as 'leading to insurmountable difficulties . . . once second order probabilities are introduced, the introduction of an endless hierarchy seems inescapable. Such a hierarchy seems very difficult to interpret, and seems at best to make the theory less realistic, not more' (Savage, 1954, p. 58). The axioms of consistency can also be used to alleviate problems of 'unsureness' and the resulting inconsistencies. As de Finetti points out:

> The fact that a direct estimate of a probability is not always possible is just the reason that the logical rules of probability are useful. The practical object of these rules is simply to reduce an evaluation, scarcely accessible directly, to others by means of which the determination is rendered easier and more precise. (de Finetti, 1937, p. 60)

Another device to deal with 'unsureness' about preferences between acts is to relate this unsureness to uncertainty about some relevant state of the world. Going further, unsureness about preferences may also be due to uncertainty about what *are* the states of the world, i.e. about *what is the set of possible states*, a circumstance that can lead to a preference for 'flexibility' (see below).

It has been observed in experiments that inconsistencies in preferences are more frequent the closer the alternatives are in terms of preference. This observation led Marschak and others to the elaboration of models of 'stochastic choice'. Such models have become an important tool of the econometrics of demand (McFadden, 1999).

Finally, the DM's preferences can also be inconsistent (relative to the axioms) *because he makes mistakes in mathematics, or more generally, in logic*. This difficulty will be discussed below.

5.3 Vagueness and Unawareness

I have already alluded to the DM's possible vagueness about his preferences. However, he could also be vague about any aspect of his model of the decision problem, and is likely to be so if the problem is at all complex. Vagueness can be about the *interpretation* of a feature of the model, or about its *scope*, or both, as I shall explain in a moment.

A common source of vagueness is the need for the DM to limit artificially the scope of his model of the decision problem. One cannot expect the DM to plan his whole life as one grand decision problem. (See Savage's remarks about the 'Look before you leap' principle, quoted above in Section 2.3.) Instead, life is decomposed into a set of roughly independent or loosely linked decision problems, together with large parts that are more or less unplanned. As we shall see this creates problems of interpretation. Savage calls this the problem of 'small worlds', and provides some formal conditions under which a small-world decision problem can, without loss, be carved out of the grand decision problem (Savage, 1954, pp. 82–91). As one might expect, these conditions are quite restrictive, and will not provide much comfort in most realistic situations.

Typically, as the DM uses a particular model he will refine the interpretation and expand its scope. He may also become aware of states, consequences and acts of which he was not previously aware. Furthermore, *although he knows that these revisions will take place in the future, he cannot predict what they will be*. This dynamic process of model revision is a key feature of most applications of the Savage paradigm to real problems, but the theory implicit in the paradigm does not deal with this feature, at least not directly. *I see the development of a theory of rational model revision as a major challenge posed by the problem of bounded rationality* (see Section 5.4).

Consider first the problems of vagueness with respect to consequences. Recall that, in the Savage paradigm, all uncertainty about the consequences of action is reduced to uncertainty about the 'state of the world' in which the action takes place. Thus, given the true state of the world, there is no further uncertainty about the consequence of an action. However, in applications of the theory to real decision problems, the DM will typically be forced to simplify the model to such a degree that consequences are in fact uncertain, even given the state of the world (in the model). For example, in a simple model of a decision whether to buy a lottery ticket, the 'consequence' of owning the winning number might be thought to be receiving a prize of, say, $1 million (less the cost of the ticket). To put it slightly more accurately, the 'consequence' of winning is an increase in the DM's wealth of $1 million less the cost of the ticket. However, in order to correctly assess the utility of this consequence, the DM would have to know many things, such as his future income and health, the rate of inflation, etc., which will in turn depend on future actions and the further evolution of the state of the world (a history). In other words, the 'winning the lottery' is not a 'pure consequence' in the strict sense required by the theory.

In principle, given enough time and patience, the DM might be able to describe many of the various 'pure consequences' of winning the lottery, which would involve describing in detail all the possible future histories of all of the aspects if his life that concern him. Another difficulty is that there will be possible futures that he is not aware of and cannot even imagine. Although I cannot prove it, I feel that in practice this is less of a problem with respect to consequences. For example, as far as I know, the development of the atomic bomb was not even imagined in the 15th century. However, the consequences of dropping the bomb on Japan in the Second World War, if cast in terms of persons killed, property destroyed, etc., was probably imaginable, even though people living in the 15th century could not imagine the particular actions and states of the world that produced those consequences in 1945. Other, more cheerful, examples could easily be drawn from the history of technology, medicine, etc.

I turn now to the problems of vagueness about states of the world. The first problem is analogous to the first one concerning consequences. It is the practical difficulty of describing in full detail all of the relevant aspects of the past and future history of the DM's environment that, together with his actions, determine the consequences that directly concern him. If a decision model is not soon discarded as useless, it is likely to be refined by expanding the scope of the set of states. This will involve both describing states in more detail, and adding states. Some of the added states will have, or could have, been envisaged originally, but were omitted in the process of model simplification. Others will not even have been envisaged or imagined. In other words, as time goes on the DM will become aware of states of which he was previously unaware. Nevertheless, the thoughtful DM will anticipate that this will happen, and will try to take account of this in his decision-making process.

An important case of this arises in the DM's construction of the model itself. The concept of 'state of the world' is quite flexible, and can encompass what in everyday language are called 'laws of nature' and 'model parameters'. For example, if the DM believes that a certain stochastic process is a Markov chain, but does not know its parameter values, then the set of states can be expanded to include a description of the parameter values as well as the actual realization of the process. (This will be discussed more fully in the next section.) As the DM revises and expands the model, new parameters will be envisaged, and the set of states must be correspondingly revised. In the next section I shall illustrate how this might be done 'rationally'.

Finally, consider the problems of vagueness and unawareness about acts. Any vagueness and/or unawareness about consequences and states will, of course entail corresponding problems for acts. In addition, the DM may in the course of time discover or invent new acts. The history of technical change provides a rich store of such examples.

If the DM anticipates that he will become aware of new acts in the future, then, other things equal, he may prefer present actions that allow for 'flexibility'. The concept of flexibility has had many interpretations in the economics literature, and the subject has a long history, in part associated with the theory of money.[9]

I have the impression that the revision of a decision model to incorporate new acts is most often associated with the incorporation of new states into the model, although a substantiation of this hypothesis would require further study. I have already alluded to a corresponding impression with regard to consequences. This motivates the analysis in the next section.

5.4 A Bayesian Analysis of Model Revision

In the previous section I suggested that some process of model revision was an important component of most real dynamic decision problems. This leads to the question of what it might mean to engage in this process 'rationally'. In what follows I propose a Bayesian approach to this question, in the context of a special case of statistical model revision (Radner, 2000). I should emphasize that a general approach to the question that goes beyond this example has not yet been worked out, so what I shall present is more of a research program than a full-blown theory.

---

[9] For recent contributions, and further references, see Kreps (1992) and Jones and Ostroy (1984).

Suppose that the DM must make successive predictions, one period ahead, of each of a sequence of random variables, $X(0)$, $X(1)$, . . . , *ad infinitum*. It will be convenient to have a name for this sequence, so I shall call it the *X-process*. The prediction of each random variable $X(t)$ may be—but is not required to be—based on the past *history* of the X-process, defined by:

$$H(t - 1) = [X(0), . . . , X(t - 1)]$$

Let us say, provisionally, that the state of the world, s, for this problem is a particular realization, x, of the X-process, i.e.

$$s = x = [x(0), x(1), x(2), . . . , ad\ infinitum].$$

A *prediction strategy* for the DM is a complicated object. It determines

1. a prediction of the initial value, $X(0)$; and
2. for each subsequent period t and each history $H(t - 1)$, a prediction of $X(t)$ as a function of $H(t - 1)$.

Suppose that the DM is rewarded each period according to how accurate his prediction turns out to be. Then the relevant *consequence* is *the (infinite) sequence of eventual rewards*. Any particular policy determines a mapping from states (sequences of the random variables) to consequences (sequences of rewards); this mapping is an *act*.

In what follows it is not necessary to specify the DM's particular utility function on the set of consequences. Instead, we shall concentrate attention on DM's beliefs concerning the states, and how he updates his beliefs in the light of successively longer histories. To simplify the example further, suppose that the random variables $X(t)$ can take on only the values one or zero. According to the Savage paradigm, the DM's beliefs about the state can be scaled in terms of a probability law of the stochastic process of zeroes and ones.

For example, the DM might believe that the random variables $X(t)$ are independent and identically distributed (IID), with Prob$\{X(t) = 1\} = 1/6$, and Prob$\{X(t) = 0\} = 5/6$. [For example, as in tossing a 'fair die', with $X(t) = 1$ if the die comes up with one spot, and $X(t) = 0$ otherwise.] In this case, with a reasonable reward function, the DM will in each period ignore the previous history, and always predict a zero.

But what if the DM believes that the random variables are IID, but is uncertain about the probability that $X(t) = 1$? (For example, he thinks that the die might be biased.) In this case, the Bayesian approach would be to add a new state variable, call it p, and define the state as

$$s = (p,x)$$

[Recall that x denotes the infinite sequence, $\{x(t)\}$.] The DM's beliefs about the state would now have two components:

1. the marginal probability distribution of the 'parameter' p, called the *prior*; and
2. a family of conditional distributions of the X-process, given p, according to which, given p, the random variables $X(t)$ are IID, with $\text{Prob}\{X(t) = 1\} = p$.

Given any history, $H(t)$, the DM can calculate the conditional distribution of the parameter p given the history. This conditional distribution is called the *posterior distribution of p (given the history)*. (The formula for this calculation is called 'Bayes's Rule'.) The DM can then use this posterior distribution to calculate his prediction of the next random variable, $X(t + 1)$.

It is a striking theorem of Bayesian analysis that, if the DM's prior distribution of the parameter p is sufficiently 'open minded', then, if the true value of p is p^* (say), then the sequence of the DM's posterior distributions of p will become more and more concentrated in the neighborhood of p^*. In other words, the DM will asymptotically learn the true value of the parameter p. By 'open minded' I mean, roughly speaking, that the DM does not rule out as impossible any value of the parameter between zero and one.[10]

We are now in a position to consider the problem of model revision in the context of this example. Suppose that, in fact, the random variables in the X-process are not IID, but Markovian. This means that, in any period, the conditional distribution of the future random variables, given the history of the entire past, depends only on the value of the random variable in the preceding period. Will the DM ever discover this? To answer this question, I first observe that, under the hypothesis that the X-process is IID, in order to calculate the posterior distribution of the parameter after any history $H(t - 1)$, it is sufficient to know the number of ones in the history (in addition to the length, t, of the history). On the other hand, under the hypothesis that the X-process is Markovian, it is necessary (and sufficient) to know *three* numbers (in addition to t), namely, the initial value, $X(0)$, the number of ones that follow a zero, and the number of ones that follow a one. If the DM believes that the X-process is IID, then he will not make these more detailed counts, except out of idle curiosity, and hence will not discover that the process is Markovian.

To see more clearly what is going on, recall that if the X-process is Markovian, then it can be parameterized by a starting probability and a

---

[10] *Technical Note*: More precisely, 'open minded' means that the support of the prior is the entire unit interval. A more general statement of the theorem is that, if p^* is in the support of the prior, then conditional on $p = p^*$ the sequence of posterior probability distributions will converge weakly (i.e. in the weak* topology) to the point distribution with unit mass at p^*. A version of this theorem for more general sequences of IID random variables is due to Doob; see Diaconis and Freedman (1986).

transition matrix. To make things simpler, assume that the Markov process is *stationary and irreducible*, so we can dispense with the starting probability (it will be determined by the transition matrix). The transition matrix can be represented by a table:

		$X(t)$	
		1	0
$X(t-1)$	1	q	$1-q$
	0	r	$1-r$

The interpretation of the table is:

$$\text{Prob}\{X(t) = 1 \mid X(t-1) = 1\} = q$$
$$\text{Prob}\{X(t) = 0 \mid X(t-1) = 1\} = 1-q$$
$$\text{Prob}\{X(t) = 1 \mid X(t-1) = 0\} = r$$
$$\text{Prob}\{X(t) = 0 \mid X(t-1) = 0\} = 1-r$$

Here are some useful facts:

1. If $q = r$, then the Markov process is an IID process.
2. The Markov process is irreducible if q and r are strictly between 0 and 1.
3. If the Markov process is stationary, then for every period t:

$$\text{Prob}\{X(t) = 1\} = v = r/(1 - q + r)$$

It follows that *if the DM believes that the X-process is IID, but it is really Markovian with the above parameters (and with q distinct from r), then he will asymptotically come to believe the 'true parameter' of the IID process is p = v, and he will never learn the Markovian truth about the process.*

The only way out for this DM is for his not to be totally dogmatic about his belief that the X-process is IID, and experiment with the belief that it is Markovian. On the other hand, an extension of Doob's Theorem (see above) guarantees that *if the DM believes that the process is Markovian, and is open minded about the parameters, then if the process is in fact IID he will asymptotically learn that.*

We can, and should, consider further extensions of the process of model revision. It could be that the X-process is even outside the class of Markov processes, even though the DM does not envisage this at the start. For example, we might consider processes in which, for every period t, the conditional distribution of the future random variables, given the history of the entire past, depends only on the values of the random variable in the preceding k periods. This is sometimes called a *kth-order Markov process*. Clearly, for $h < k$, an hth-order Markov process is a special case of a kth-order Markov process. We can now imagine a never-ending process of model revision in which the

DM experiments with kth-order Markov process with larger and larger values of k.

We can now refine the question of how the DM might pursue such a process of model revision 'rationally'? I submit that ideally—if possible—*such a process should mimic the behavior of a Bayesian who is following the Savage paradigm from the beginning*, in other words whose prior beliefs do not rule out any of the models that the DM will eventually consider. This might seem to be an excessively demanding requirement, but the results that I have obtained so far suggest that it is attainable (Radner, 2000). Let $M(k)$ denote the model that the X-process is a kth-order Markov process, and recall that parameter space of the model $M(k)$ is essentially a subspace of that of the model $M(k + 1)$; in fact, I shall say that $M(k)$ *is* a subset of $M(k + 1)$. The basic idea is that every time the DM envisages a more general model, say from $M(k)$ to $M(k + 1)$, he extends his *prior distribution* to $M(k + 1)$ accordingly in a way that does not contradict the old prior within (i.e. conditional on) the subspace $M(k)$. He then continues to compute his posterior distributions as before, but with the new prior. However—and this is crucial for the interpretation of the process in terms of bounded rationality—he is not required to formulate a grand prior in advance, but only required to extend his prior incrementally, as he faces the prospect of using more and more general models.

Of course, in principle the DM can always eventually become aware of more general models than the one he is currently working with. For example, the class of all kth-order Markov processes does not exhaust the class of all stationary processes, and there are processes that are not even stationary. Here I must end the present discussion on a cautionary note. It can be shown that if the space of processes is 'too large' (i.e. if the parameter space is infinite-dimensional and 'very large' in some sense), it may not be possible to formulate a prior distribution on it that is 'open minded' in a useful way. Thus there will be limits to how well the process of model revision that I have roughly described above can guarantee that the DM will asymptotically learn the 'truth' about the process that he is observing.[11]

5.5 Failures of Logical Omniscience

Up to this point is has been assumed—if only implicitly—that the DM has no difficulty performing mathematical calculations or other logical operations.

---

[11] *Technical Note*: Although the set of all models $M(k)$, with k finite, does not exhaust the class of all stationary processes, one can approximate any stationary X-process by a stationary $M(k)$ process, provided the random variables take values in some finite set. However, it is an open question whether it is possible to put a prior distribution on the class of all such stationary processes in such a way that a Bayesian will asymptotically learn what the true process is.

In particular, having formulated a decision model, he will be able to infer what it implies for his optimal strategy. As has already been pointed out, this assumption is absurd, even for small-world models, except for 'Mickey Mouse' problems that are constructed for textbooks and academic articles. The crux of the matter is that, in any even semi-realistic decision problem, *the DM does not know all of the relevant logical implications of what he knows*. This phenomenon is sometimes called *the failure of logical omniscience*.

In the Savage paradigm, DM's are uncertain about events such as 'It will rain tomorrow in New York City', or 'If most countries do not take action to reduce the emissions of carbon dioxide into the atmosphere, then the average atmospheric temperature of the Earth will increase by 5°F in the next fifty years'. Examples of the failure of logical omniscience are:

1. A DM who knows the axioms of arithmetic is uncertain about whether they imply that 'The 123rd digit in the decimal expansion of pi is 3', unless he has a long time to do the calculation and/or has a powerful computer with the appropriate software.
2. Twenty years ago, a DM who knew the axioms of arithmetic was still uncertain about whether they imply Fermat's Last Theorem.

The following examples are closer to practical life, and possibly more intimidating:

3. Given all that a DM knows about the old and new drugs for treating a particular disease, what is the optimal policy for conducting clinical trials on the new ones?
4. Given all that is known, theoretically and empirically, about business organizations in general, and about telecommunications and AT&T in particular, should AT&T reorganize itself internally, and if so, how? (These examples are taken from Radner, 1997, p. 133.)

In commenting on this problem in 1954, Savage wrote:

> The assumption that a person's behavior is logical is, of course, far from vacuous. In particular, such a person cannot be uncertain about decidable mathematical propositions. This suggests, at least to me, that the tempting program sketched by Polya of establishing a theory of the probability of mathematical conjectures cannot be fully successful in that it cannot lead to a truly formal theory . . . (Savage, 1954, fn, p. 7)[12]

In spite of some interesting efforts (Lipman, 1999; Dekel *et al.*, 1998; Modica and Rustichini, 2000), I am not aware of significant progress on what it means to be rational in the face of failures of logical omniscience.

---

[12] For further discussion and references, see the 1972 edition of Savage's book.

6. *In What Sense(s) is a Boundedly Rational Decision-maker Rational?*

In the term 'bounded rationality', the first word reminds us that bounds on the cognitive abilities of human decision-makers, even when aided by modern computers, limit the extent to which their decision-making can conform to the Savage paradigm. On the other hand, the second word suggests that there is some sense in which such decision-making can be said to be rational. In this final section of the paper, I want to examine this presupposition.

As noted in Section 4, in some cases the Savage paradigm can be extended to incorporate the costs of, and constraints on, decision-making without abandoning the assumption of optimization. I called this 'costly rationality'. In fact, this is not really an extension of the paradigm, but merely a more sophisticated and detailed interpretation of the Savage model. In that sense, costly rationality retains the full meaning of 'rationality' in the Savage sense.

Nevertheless, this reinterpretation can be carried only so far in realistic situations. The DM must be content to work with highly simplified models, which in turn leads to a process of model revision—a potentially unending process. In Section 5.4 I sketched how, in some simple cases, the DM can devise a process of inference and model revision whose results eventually mimic those achieved by a Bayesian who is able to formulate a complete model from the beginning. In such cases, one may be justified in calling the *process of decision-making* 'rational'. I would like to think that, when applicable, this approach provides an instance of Simon's idea of 'rationality as process' (Simon, 1978).

Finally, I described the problems caused by 'failures of logical omniscience'. Here we come to the hard core of truly bounded rationality, which thus far presents the most difficult challenge to decision-theorists who strive to characterize the 'rationality' in 'bounded rationality'.

Acknowledgements

The present paper is a further development of part of Radner (1997), and as such it inevitably repeats many ideas in that paper. The reader will notice that I quote liberally from Savage's book, *The Foundations of Statistics*. It turns out that he anticipated most of the issues of costly and bounded rationality, and had something to say about them, even if he supplied few formal solutions. Thus in many instances I could not find a better way to express the relevant ideas than to use his own words. It would be too large a project to acknowledge my debts to all my friends and colleagues who have tried to help me think about this problem (some may judge unsuccessfully). At the very least, I must acknowledge the influences of Jacob Marschak, Herbert Simon and L. J. Savage, who introduced me to the topic. In addition, I thank Jim March and Sid Winter for stimulating discussions over the years, and specifically for comments on a previous draft of this paper.

References

The references cited in the body of the article have historical interest, provide an overview of a topic discussed and/or provide a key to other literature. The following references provide additional information on the application of notions of bounded rationality in economics and management: Arrow (1974), Majumdar (1998), McGuire and Radner (1986), Nelson and Winter (1982), Newell and Simon (1972), Radner (1992), Shapira (1997), Simon (1981), Williamson and Winter (1991) and Winter (1987).

Arrow, K. J. (1951), 'Alternative Approaches to the Theory of Choice in Risk-taking Situations,' *Econometrica*, 19, 404–437.

Arrow, K. J. (1974), *The Limits of Organization*. Norton: New York.

Basu, A., A. Bose and J. K. Gosh (1990), 'An Expository Review of Sequential Design and Allocation Rules,' Technical Report 90-08, Purdue University.

Bolton, P. and M. Dewatripont (1994), 'The Firm as a Communication Network,' *Quarterly Journal of Economics*, 109, 809–839.

Clark, J. M. (1918), 'Economics and Modern Psychology, I,' *Journal of Political Economy*, 26, 1–30.

Conlisk, J. (1996), 'Why Bounded Rationality,' *Journal of Economic Literature*, 34, 669–700.

Cournot, A. (1838), *Recherches sur les Principes Mathématiques de la Théorie des Richesses*. Hachette: Paris; trans. N. T. Bacon. R. D. Irwing: Homewood, IL.

de Finetti, B. (1937), 'La Prévision: Ses Lois Logiques, ses Sources Subjectives,' *Annales de l'Institut Henri Poincaré*, 7, 1–68.

Dekel, E., B. Lipman and A. Rustichini (1998), 'Recent Developments in Modeling Unforeseen Contingencies,' *European Economic Review*, 42, 523–542.

Diaconis, P. and D. Freedman (1986), 'On the Consistency of Bayes Estimates,' *Annals of Statistics*, 14, 1–26.

Dutta, P. K. and R. Radner (1995), 'Moral Hazard,' in R. Aumann and S. Hart (eds), *Handbook of Game Theory*, Vol. 2. North-Holland: Amsterdam, pp. 869–903.

Hald, A. (1990), *A History of Probability and Statistics and their Applications before 1750*. Wiley: New York.

Harsanyi, J. C. (1967–68), 'Games with Incomplete Information Played by Bayesian Players,' *Management Science*, 14, 159–182, 320–334, 486–502.

Jackson, M. O., E. Kalai and R. Smorodinsky (1999), 'Bayesian Representation of Stochastic Processes under Learning: de Finetti Revisited,' *Econometrica*, 67, 875–894.

Jones, R. A. and J. Ostroy (1984), 'Flexibility and Uncertainty,' *Review of Economic Studies*, 51, 13–22.

Kaldor, N. (1934), 'The Equilibrium of the Firm,' *Economic Journal*, 44, 70–71.

Knight, F. H. (1921), *Risk, Uncertainty, and Profits*. Houghton Mifflin: Cambridge, MA (reprinted 1957, Kelley and Millman: New York).

Kreps, D. (1979), 'A Representation Theory for "Preference for Flexibility",' *Econometrica*, 47, 565–577.

Kreps, D. (1992), 'Static Choice in the Presence of Unforeseen Contingencies,' in P. Dasgupta *et al.* (eds), *Economic Analysis of Markets and Games*. MIT Press: Cambridge, MA, pp. 258–281.

Kreps, D. and R. B. Wilson (1982), 'Sequential Equilibria,' *Econometrica*, 50, 863–894.

Lipman, B. L. (1999), 'Decision Theory without Logical Omniscience: Toward an Axiomatic Framework for Bounded Rationality,' *Review of Economic Studies*, 66, 339–361.

Machina, M. (1987), 'Choice Under Uncertainty: Problems Solved and Unsolved,' *Journal of Economic Perspectives*, 1, 121–154.

Machina, M. (1989), 'Dynamic Consistency and Non-expected Utility Models of Choice Under Uncertainty,' *Journal of Economic Literature*, 27, 1622–1668.

Majumdar, M. K. (ed.) (1998), *Organizations with Incomplete Information*. Cambridge University Press: Cambridge.

March, J. G. and H. A. Simon (1958), *Organizations*. Wiley: New York.

Marschak, J. (1955), 'Elements for a Theory of Teams,' *Management Science*, 1, 127–137.

Marschak, J. and R. Radner (1972), *Economic Theory of Teams*. Cowles Foundation and Yale University Press: New Haven, CT.

Marschak, T. A. and C. B. McGuire (1971), 'Lecture Notes on Economic Models for Organization Design,' Unpublished manuscript, University of California: Berkeley, CA.

Marschak, T. A. and S. Reichelstein (1998), 'Network Mechanisms, Informational Efficiency, and Hierarchies,' *Journal of Economic Theory*, 79, 106–141.

McFadden, Daniel (1999), 'Rationality for Economists?,' *Journal of Risk and Uncertainty*, 19, 73–105.

McGuire, C. B. and R. Radner (eds) (1986), *Decision and Organization*, 2nd edn. University of Minnesota Press: Minneapolis, MN.

Mintzberg, H. (1989), *Mintzberg on Management*. Free Press: New York.

Modica, S. and A. Rustichini (1999), 'Unawareness: A Formal Theory of Unforeseen Contingencies,' *Games and Economic Behavior*, 29, 15–37.

Mount, K. and S. Reiter (1998), 'A Modular Network Model of Bounded Rationality,' in M. K. Majumdar (ed.), *Organizations with Incomplete Information*. Cambridge University Press: Cambridge, pp. 306–340.

Nash, J. F. (1951), 'Non-cooperative Games,' *Annals of Mathematics*, 54, 286–296.

von Neumann, J. and O. Morgenstern (1944), *Theory of Games and Economic Behavior*. Princeton University Press: Princeton, NJ.

Nelson, R. R. and S. G. Winter (1982), *An Evolutionary Theory of Economic Change*. Harvard University Press: Cambridge, MA.

Newell, A. and H. A. Simon (1972), *Human Problem Solving*. Englewood Cliffs, NJ: Prentice Hall.

Osborne, M. and A. Rubinstein (1994), *A Course in Game Theory*. MIT Press: Cambridge, MA.

Peters, T. J. and R. H. Waterman (1982), *In Search of Excellence*. Harper & Row: New York.

Radner, R. (1961), 'The Evaluation of Information in Organizations,' in *Proceedings of the Fourth Berkeley Symposium on Probability and Statistics*. University of California Press: Berkeley, CA, Vol. 1, pp. 491–530.

Radner, R. (1962), 'Team Decision Problems,' *Annals of Mathematical Statistics*, 33, 857–881.

Radner, R. (1975a), 'Satisficing,' *Journal of Mathematical Economics*, 2, 253–262.

Radner, R. (1975b), 'Planning Under Uncertainty: Recent Theoretical Developments,' in M. Bornstein (ed.), *Economic Planning, East and West*. University of Michigan Press: Ann Arbor, MI.

Radner, R. (1992), 'Hierarchy: The Economics of Managing,' *Journal of Economic Literature*, 30, 1382–1415.

Radner, R. (1997), 'Bounded Rationality, Indeterminacy, and the Managerial Theory of the Firm,' in Z. Shapira (ed.), *Organizational Decision Making*. Cambridge University Press: Cambridge, pp. 324–352.

Radner, R. (2000), 'A "Bayesian" Analysis of Model Revision for a Class of Stationary Processes,' Stern School, New York University (unpublished).

Radner, R. and J. E. Stiglitz (1983), 'A Nonconcavity in the Value of Information,' in M. Boyer and R. E. Kihlstrom (eds), *Bayesian Models in Economic Theory*. North-Holland: Amsterdam, pp. 33–52.

Radner, R. and T. Van Zandt (1992), 'Information Processing in Firms and Returns to Scale,' *Annales d'Economie et de Statistique*, no. 25/26, 265–298.

Rubinstein, A. (1998), *Modeling Bounded Rationality*. MIT Press: Cambridge, MA.

Savage, L. J. (1954), *The Foundations of Statistics*. Wiley: New York (2nd edn, 1972, Dover: New York).

Selten, R. (1975), 'Reexamination of the Perfectness Concept for Equlibrium Points in Extensive Games,' *International Journal of Game Theory*, 4, 25–55.

Shapira, Z. (ed.) (1997), *Organizational Decision Making*, Cambridge University Press: Cambridge.

Simon, H. A. (1947), *Administrative Behavior*. Free Press: New York.

Simon, H. A. (1955), 'A Behavioral Model of Rational Choice,' *Quarterly Journal of Economics*, 69, 99–118.

Simon, H. A. (1957), *Models of Man*. Wiley: New York.

Simon, H. A. (1972), 'Theories of Bounded Rationality,' in C. B. McGuire and R. Radner (eds), *Decision and Organization*, 2nd edn (1986). University of Minnesota Press: Minneapolis, MN, pp. 161–176.

Simon, H. A. (1978), 'Rationality as Process and Product of Thought,' *American Economic Review*, 68, 1–16.

Simon, H. A. (1981), *The Sciences of the Artificial*, 2nd edn. MIT Press: Cambridge, MA.

Sims, C. (1971), 'Distributed Lag Estimation when the Parameter Space is Explicitly Infinite Dimensional,' *Annals of Mathematical Statistics*, 42, 1622–1636.

Van Zandt, T. (1998), 'Decentralized Information Processing in the Theory of Organizations,' in M. Sertel (ed.), *Economic Design and Behavior, Proc. XIth World Congress of the International Economics Association*, Vol. IV. Macmillan: London.

Van Zandt, T. (1998), 'Organizations with an Endogenous Number of Information Processing Agents,' in M. K. Majumdar (ed.), *Organizations with Incomplete Information*. Cambridge University Press: Cambridge.

Van Zandt, T. (1998), 'Real-time Hierarchical Resource Allocation,' Unpublished manuscript Northwestern University.

Van Zandt, T. (1999), 'Real-time Decentralized Information Processing as a Model of Organizations with Boundedly Rational Agents,' *Review of Economic Studies*, 66, 633–658.

Van Zandt, T. and R. Radner (2000), 'Real-time Decentralized Information Processing and Returns to Scale,' *Economic Theory* (forthcoming).

Wald, A. (1947), *Sequential Analysis*. Wiley: New York.

Wald, A. (1950), *Statistical Decision Functions*. Wiley: New York.

Williamson, O. E. and S. G. Winter (eds) (1991), *The Nature of the Firm*. Oxford University Press: New York.

Winter, S. G. (1987), 'Competition and Selection,' in J. Eatwell, J. Milgate and P. Newman (eds), *The New Palgrave*. Stockton Press: New York, pp. 545–548.

Incentives, Routines, and Self-Command*

STEVEN POSTREL and RICHARD P. RUMELT

(Anderson Graduate School of Management, University of California,
Los Angeles, CA 90024, USA)

Virtue, then, being of two kinds, intellectual and moral, intellectual virtue in the main owes both its birth and its growth to teaching . . . while moral virtue comes about as a result of habit, whence also its name (ἠθική) is one that is formed by a slight variation from the word ἔθωος (habit). . . .

Of all the things that come to us by nature we first acquire the potentiality and later exhibit the activity . . . but the virtues we get by first exercising them. . . . men become builders by building and lyre-players by playing the lyre; so too we become just by doing just acts, temperate by doing temperate acts, brave by doing brave acts.

This is confirmed by what happens in states; for legislators make the citizens good by forming habits in them, and this is the wish for every legislator, and those who do not effect it miss their mark, and it is in this that a good constitution differs from a bad one.

Aristotle, *Nicomachean Ethics*, 1103ª15–1103ᵇ5

1. Introduction

What is the source of the value added by organization? Two leading explanations are coordination of specialized efforts and control of opportunistic behavior. Both explanations assume that humans are boundedly rational—unable to process large amounts of information, to foresee all possible events, or to ferret out the facts known by others. In addition, control-of-opportunism theories (which have been dominant of late) assume that individuals are self-seeking and often dishonest. In models assuming opportunism, boundedness is invoked to establish the regime of action; within that regime, individuals behave coolly

* This paper was prepared for the Fourth International Week on the History of Enterprise, 'Organization and Strategy in the Evolution of the Enterprise,' organized by ASSI Foundation, Milan, Italy, October 3–5, 1991.

and strategically up to the limits of their ability, making no systematic errors. In these models, incentives, monitoring, and control procedures are seen as reducing the externality problems among individuals caused by cheating and shirking. In coordination models, organizational procedures are explained as necessary to reduce the probability that cooperating individuals will accidentally interfere with one another, leave vital tasks undone because they each expect someone else to perform them, or ignore information relevant to decisions. Both classes of explanation focus on the problems caused by the need for effective cooperation.

The primary contribution of these views is to explain the use of hierarchy, as opposed to arms-length market exchanges, as a method for governing transactions. However, there is a large range of organizational properties that remain unreached by these frameworks. In particular, little headway has been made in understanding the internal workings of organizations. Among the fundamental questions to which fully satisfying answers have yet to be given are the following.

1. Why is organizational change so difficult? In particular, why is it so difficult for firms to imitate best practice even after it has been recognized for a considerable time?
2. Why do organizations rely on such a preponderance of supervision and review mechanisms rather than on incentives?
3. Why do organizations create so many rules, policies, and routines rather than more general instructions to maximize objectives or achieve goals?

In this paper we argue that one promising path to progress in understanding internal organization is to reformulate the efficiency question in the light of a more complex model of man. A close look at the origins of capitalist institutions such as the factory and the white-collar business bureaucracy points to the centrality of a particular feature of human behavior not encompassed by current 'rational' models: impulsiveness and the consequent mechanisms of impulse control. Simply put, on a moment-by-moment basis, individuals have trouble taking those actions they believe are in their own long-term interest. They procrastinate, they let anger 'get the better of them,' they incur unsupportable debts, they daydream, they sleep late, they do not show up for work. A key feature of organization is that it provides external controls which help individuals reduce such deviations from their own best interests.

In addition to impulsiveness, the model we propose also assumes the existence of automatic thought and behavior. By automatic thought and behavior we mean that much of what people do and think, and especially what they do with greatest efficiency, is not under immediate conscious direction. Both of our assumptions flow from recent scholarship by cognitive and social psychologists, both are congruent with common experience, and both have profound import-ance for understanding the relationships among incentives, choice, and behavior. These assumptions break the tautological connection between incentives and behavior that characterizes economic man. As long as this connection is maintained, economic theorizing about the role of managers and the nature of organization is restricted to incentive design, monitoring, and the allocation of discretion. Our model of *impulsive man*, however, expands the role of man-agement to encompass the design and operation of a wide range of routines and practices designed to aid impulse control, provide cues and reminders about goals and priorities, embody best practice in repetitive procedures, help employees unlearn old dysfunctional habits and learn new more functional habits, and cultivate the moral sentiments necessary to support cooperation.

The arguments in this paper build on an extensive psychology literature about impulsiveness as well as on economists' studies of time-inconsistent choice. There is very little prior work, however, on linking these ideas to the structure of organizations. The notable exception is Akerlof's (1991) recent lecture on procrastination. Akerlof's model of procrastination is elegant and he offers a valuable treatment of the organizational implications of impulsiveness. He argues, as we do, that 'a major function of management is to set schedules and monitor accomplishment so as to prevent procrastination' (Akerlof, 1991, p. 7).

2. *Impulsiveness and Impulse Control*

In October of 1950, US forces had pushed the North Korean army out of the south and captured Pyongyang, the capital of North Korea, but on November 26, Chinese forces unexpectedly intervened. During the next 40 days, US forces retreated south, suffering terrible losses. During this period, many units of the US 8th Army were declared 'combat ineffective', having ceased to function with any cohesion. By contrast, the 1st Marine Division's epic retreat from the Chosin Reservoir was marked by continued cohesion and the maintenance of combat effectiveness despite heavy casualties inflicted both by China's 9th Army Group and by the bitterly cold winter.

According to military analysts, one of the main sources of this difference in performance between the 8th Army and the Marines was the differential enforcement of basic routines and field discipline. S. L. A. Marshall (1953, p. 19), the noted military historian, described Baker Company of the 8th Army's 2nd Infantry Division, just before it became the first unit to experience the surprise Chinese attack, in this way:

> For all its heaviness of spirit, Baker was remarkably light of foot on that particular
> morning. In fact, it was much too light. . . . All but twelve men had thrown away

their steel helmets. . . . The grenade load averaged less than one per man. . . . About one half of the company had dispensed with entrenching tools. . . . only a few men bothered to carry tinned rations on the march. Bedrolls and overcoats had been left behind.

These practices had serious consequences for Baker Company. With regard to the grenade loads, Marshall's history shows institutional accommodation to poor field discipline:

> From long experience, the 8th had ceased issuing grenades to its individuals except as an emergency arose. When pressure slackened, the men tended to discard grenades into the unit trucks. Movement shook the pins loose, and equipment had been lost because of this carelessness (Marshall, 1953, p. 251).

Analyzing the source of the 8th Army's breakdown, Cohen and Gooch (1990, p. 185) observe that the critical problems arose at the unit level:

> [The retreat] is the story of units who have no cleaning supplies for their weapons, who get into their sleeping bags for the night without digging in, who give up trying to establish communications with units on their left or right because they run out of field telephone wire.

By contrast, in the 1st Marine Division:

> discipline never broke. Battalion commanders checked that troops had dug foxholes before turning in, even though they had to chip away at half a foot of frozen dirt. Company commanders watched each man perform the painful but necessary ritual of changing his sweat-soaked socks every evening despite the howling cold, to prevent frostbite. . . . By enforcing such drudgery the marines retained their fighting effectiveness (Cohen and Gooch, 1990, p. 187).

It is a commonplace in the military that without 'discipline', soldiers may fail to perform the basic functions necessary to maintain their effectiveness.[1] Yet why should this be so? In the case just presented, whatever their interest in the strategic outcome of the war, individual soldiers surely had a keen interest in their unit's ability to resist attack, and certainly in their own protection against gunfire and cold. Why should it be necessary for the organization to enforce basic 'hygiene' rituals that are clearly in each soldier's best interest to perform?

---

[1] Military analysts place great weight on the maintenance of routine in assessing the potential effectiveness of troops. For example, writing during the first week of the Persian-Gulf War, Col. D. H. Hackworth's (1991, p. 32) negative appraisal of Iraqi capability was largely based on a Kuwaiti military officer's observations of Iraqi Republican Guard units in Kuwait: 'during the four months that he was with them he "never saw them perform maintenance on the vehicles or tanks" . . . Nor did they train or do battle drill. . . . Throughout the time this position was occupied, no one dug in, laid the guns, camouflaged, performed maintenance, or trained.'

'Rational man' never fails to act in his own self-interest and even 'bounded-ly rational man' should not make easily predictable errors in this regard. Yet the Battalion commanders of the 1st Marines foresaw that some men would need forcible reminders to avoid frostbite by changing wet socks for dry. They anticipated that although the soldiers 'knew' they should change socks and dig foxholes, they would also be tired and afraid, and experience powerful drives to rest and not move at all. The tension between these modes of thought is the familiar battle for self-control.

From the perspective of microeconomics, the impulse to neglect basic hygiene is irrational, even childish. But suppose that is our nature; suppose that people have two sources of 'value', one impulsive and short-term oriented and another more rational and capable of looking ahead to the longer-term consequences of action or inaction. This phenomenon is sometimes experienced as 'being of two minds'. Then, what must be judged for rationality is not just the urge, but the equilibrium between urges and controls, both internal and external. Soldiers may expect that their future impulses to neglect key tasks will be countered by watchful commanders (troops who can maintain discipline without commanders are termed 'elite forces'). In the 1st Marine Division, that expectation was fulfilled, the predictable impulses of the soldiers being countered by the maintenance of field discipline. However, in the 8th Army, the stress of battle and the inexperience of many commanders disrupted the equilibrium and cohesion was lost. *We argue that an important function of organization is to give aid and strength to people in their struggles for self-control.*

Theory of Impulsiveness

One general approach to the problem of impulsiveness is to treat it as impatience. In economic models, the value attached to the receipt of value V with delay t is usually assumed to be Ve^{-rt}, where r is the *discount rate*. If there are no constraints on borrowing or lending, standard theory predicts that each person should discount at the prevailing rate of interest (Fisher, 1930). Nevertheless, a number of studies have shown that most consumers frequently exhibit discount rates much larger than the rate of interest. For example, Hausman (1979) examined the purchase of a consumer durable with an average life of 9 years and measured an implicit discount rate of 25% with regard to price-efficiency trade-offs. Interestingly, the implied discount rate fell with income: consumers in the $10 000 annual income class exhibited a 39% discount rate, compared to 17% for those in the $25 000 income class. People have differing tastes for future versus current consumption just as they have different tastes for foods and activities, and some people place much greater weight on the present and near-term than on the future. Consequently, one person may save more or work harder than another because he places more weight on the future consequences of present (distasteful) actions. From this perspective, impulsive people are those with higher personal discount rates; they are not irrational, they simply are less concerned with the future.

The problem with this approach is that it does not explain the common inner sense of sometimes acting against one's own best interests, nor does it explain actions people may take to constrain and limit their future choices. There is, of course, a vast philosophical and psychological tradition exploring the inner conflict between appetite and reason, between 'lower' and 'higher' principles, or between the 'pleasure' and 'reality' principles. Recent scholarship has begun to identify these traditional tensions as flowing from the self-perception of having time-inconsistent preferences. In a pioneering paper, Strotz (1956) explored the conditions under which utility maximizing plans would actually be carried out (even when expectations about future events and desires have been verified). He showed that such consistency was guaranteed only for constant discount rates and argued that time-varying discount rates could explain '(1) spendthriftiness; (2) the deliberate regimenting of one's future economic behavior—even at a cost; and (3) thrift' (Strotz, 1956, p. 165). Thus, if people are 'hard-wired' with non-constant discount rates, then their plans about future choices will not be consistent with the choices actually made when the future arrives. If one knows that one's future desires will not be those one currently has about the future, which set of preferences will hold sway? It is possible that the psychology of the divided self is simply the self-awareness of one's own time-varying discount rates.

To make these issues explicit, consider the dieter. The dieter is unhappy with his weight and wishes to lose 30 pounds by restricting food intake over the next 4 months. The dieter announces his goal to friends and family, reads books on health and diet, and begins to keep a record of intake and weight. The dieter knows he must attend social functions frequently, but vows to avoid the rich foods and fancy desserts offered at these functions. However, at the first social occasion he is presented with an extremely rich dessert. The impulse to eat the dessert is strong and the dieter gives in, perhaps reasoning as follows: 'If I eat this dessert now, it will add an extra few days to my diet. Adding a few days to the end of my 4 month diet is a reasonable price to pay for this treat.' The next day the dieter realizes that his diet will fail if he keeps behaving in this way. Recognizing his weakness, he acts to strengthen his will. Among his options are actions such as (1) putting funds in 'escrow' with a friend that he wins back if he attains his weight loss goal, (2) calling hosts and hostesses in advance to request alternative desserts, and (3) sacrificing attendance at the social functions.

Note that the dieter is not just 'myopic'; if the dieter simply had a high discount rate, he would have never chosen to diet in the first place. He fully intended to abstain and nothing unexpected happened, yet he did not abstain when the crucial moment actually arose. Nor can a high discount rate begin to explain the third decision, to constrain or limit his own future actions. However, a rapidly declining discount rate reconciles these decisions.

To be concrete, let the utility at time T for payoff x received with delay t (i.e. at time $T + t$) be

$$U(x,t,T) = u(x) f(t). \tag{1}$$

That is, the utility function is separable and independent of the date T.[2] Here u is the static utility of the payoff and $f(t)$ is the discount due to deferral. By convention, $f(0) = 1$, and we assume that f is positive, differentiable, and decreasing in t. Consequently, there is a positive function $\rho(t) = -f'/f$ such that

$$f(t) = e^{-\int_0^t \rho(\tau)\, d\tau} \tag{2}$$

The function $\rho(t)$ is the 'instantaneous discount rate' at delay t. If $\rho(t) \equiv r$, then $f(t) = e^{-rt}$, the classic exponential case.

There are two rewards: L and S, with $u(L) > u(S)$, so that L is 'larger' than S when they are directly compared. However, receipt of L is delayed by d as compared with S. Finally, we assume that $u(S) > u(L)f(d)$, so that the decision-maker prefers getting the smaller reward immediately to waiting d for the larger payoff. When these conditions hold we say that S *proximity dominates* L: though smaller, it is preferred because it is received sooner.

The preference for S over L can be time-consistent or it can be *impulsive*, or in Ainslie's (1975) terms, *specious*. The test is whether or not the preference for S over L is reversed if both payoffs are additionally deferred. If the additional perspective gained by deferring both rewards causes a reversal of preference in favor of L, then the original preference for S was specious.

The conditions for *impulsive preference reversal* are that there be a t^* such that S is preferred for $t < t^*$ and L is preferred for $t > t^*$. In terms of the utility function (1) these conditions are

$$u(S)f(t) > u(L)f(t + d), \quad t < t^* \tag{3}$$

and

$$u(S)f(t) < u(L)f(t + d), \quad t > t^* \tag{4}$$

Clearly, t^* solves $f(t + d)/f(t) = u(S)/u(L)$. Furthermore, t^* will be unique, the above inequalities will hold, and the opposite sort of preference reversals will be ruled out if and only if $f(t + d)/f(t)$ is non-increasing and is decreasing at t^*. The corresponding conditions on $\rho(\tau)$ are that it is non-increasing and

---

[2] See Prelec and Loewenstein (1991) for a good summary of the assumptions lying behind separability as well as an extended discussion of time-inconsistency issues.

that $\rho\,(t^*) > \rho\,(t^* + d)$. These arguments and observations lead to the following propositions.

1. If $\rho(t)$ is constant ($f(t)$ is exponential), then preference for S over L is never specious.
2. If ρ is decreasing at some t, values of S, L, and d can always be selected which will exhibit impulsive preference reversal. Conversely, impulsive preference reversal implies that ρ is somewhere decreasing.
3. If ρ is always decreasing, the proximity domination is always specious.

Research on Impulsiveness

The idea that a declining instantaneous discount rate can induce impulsive behavior is elegant, parsimonious, and simpler than the reasoning lying behind the great body of psychoanalytic writings on unconscious urges.[3] More importantly, empirical work by psychologists has provided laboratory evidence bearing on all three of the key features of the theory: decreasing discount rates, impulsive preference reversal, and the use of commitments to strategically alter one's own behavior.

These studies have their root in Herrnstein's (1961) *matching law* which summarized the results of a number of animal studies. The matching law states that the relative time spent on a behavior is proportional to the amount and rate of reward, and inversely proportional to the delay of the reward. Taken literally, this law suggests that $f(t)$ is proportional to $1/t$, known in the psychology literature as the *hyperbolic discount function*. More recently, Loewenstein and Prelec (1992) have advanced a theory of intertemporal preference in which discount functions are generalized hyperbolas: $f(t) = (1 + \alpha t)^{-\beta/\alpha}$, where β measures impatience and $\alpha > 0$ determines the departure from a constant discount rate. The implied instantaneous discount rate is $\rho(t) = \beta/(1 + \alpha t)$, which becomes constant discounting when $\alpha = 0$. By Proposition 3 (above), with this discount function, if $\alpha > 0$ then proximity dominance is always specious.

Both Thaler (1981) and Benzion *et al.* (1989) aimed at estimating discount rates as a function of time delay. Both asked students questions about choice situations involving money and both found that discount rates fell dramatically with the amount of time delay. In the study by Benzion *et al.* the discount rates implied in choices involving future (positive) payments were (approximately)

---

[3] Thaler and Shefrin (1981) model impulsiveness by splitting the unitary decision maker into two conflicting selves. In their model an individual is an amalgam of a far-sighted 'planner' and a myopic 'doer'. Using an agency-theory approach, they are able to develop results on pension and savings behavior. Although their model preserves constant discount rates, it introduces complexities regarding which 'self' is in control on any given issue. It is also worth noting that the weighted average of two different constant-rate discount functions produces a decreasing discount-rate function.

29% per annum for a 6 month delay, 21% for a 1 year delay, 17% for a 2 year delay and 16% for a 3 year delay. These average results are consistent with $\rho = 0.29$ for the first 6 months of delay, and $\rho = 0.13$ thereafter. In addition, they found that gains were discounted more sharply than losses and small amounts more sharply than large amounts.

Most telling are the results on impulsive preference reversal in both animals and humans. The paradigm-setting experiments were carried out by Rachlin and Green (1972) and by Ainslie (1974) on pigeons. Rachlin and Green offered pigeons two keys (say A and B). Pecks on A induced a T second delay followed by the presentation of two keys, one providing food immediately (reward S), and the other providing twice as much food 4 seconds later (reward L). Pecks on B induced the same T second delay, followed by the presentation of a single key which provided only reward L. Faced with S and L, almost all birds chose S (proximity dominance). However, as T was increased (from less than 1 second to 16 seconds), three of the five birds began to choose the B key, blocking the availability of S. Reductions in T restored the former situation.

Working with undergraduate students, Solnick *et al.* (1980) asked subjects to solve math problems while being distracted by white noise, claiming the experiment was about noise pollution. Subjects could press either of two buttons, the first leading to an immediate, though short, cessation of the noise (reward S) and the other leading to a longer, though delayed, cessation (reward L). Most subjects chose the S button, but when an additional 15 second delay was added to both rewards, a majority altered their choice to the L button. This is a clear example of specious preference being reversed by the perspective provided by delay.

Ainslie and Haendel (1983) asked subjects to indicate their preferences for a variety of choices involving money and time. In one, subjects were asked whether they preferred $100 received immediately (S) or $200 to be received in 2 years (L). Most said they preferred the $100, exhibiting proximity dominance and an implied annual discount rate exceeding 41%. However, when shown a choice between $100 to be received in 4 years and $200 in 6 years, most preferred the latter, exhibiting impulsive preference reversal. Furthermore, most did not recognize the second situation as being the first with a 4 year delay, nor could they account for the reversal of preference.

Controlling Impulsive Behavior

Faced with knowledge of one's own temporally changing preference, how should one behave? The basic strategies are[4] (1) to arrange external restraints

---

[4] Ainslie (1986) describes the first four; the fifth might be considered to be a subclass of the third.

on future decisions, (2) to cultivate emotional responses that counter impulses, (3) to divert, restrict, or focus attention, (4) to develop principles or rules of behavior that help guide action, and (5) to develop habits or routines that guide behavior.

External restraints. In Rachlin and Green's (1972) experiment, some pigeons learned to use an external device to counter their own future impulsive behavior. Similarly, an academic who keeps putting off a project might agree to prepare a paper for a conference one year hence because the promise acts to sharply increase the costs of procrastination. Of course, people go further than simply accepting external constraints, they manufacture them to forestall future impulsive behavior. Dieters will pay health spas to enforce regimens; some even have their jaws wired shut. People create lifetrusts for their children in order to limit their own access to their money. The power of social sanctions to restrain future behavior is an element in announcements of commitments: announcing an engagement makes it more costly to act on an impulse to break off the relationship.

Moral sentiments. The emotions that counter impulse are what Adam Smith called moral sentiments. An unsocialized person who knows that stealing might lead to punishment may be at the mercy of a non-exponential time-preference. However, if the impulse to steal is also met with an immediate feeling of guilt and shame, then the internal battle is not between the salient now and the distant future, but rather between two concurrent values. Capacity to feel moral sentiments appears to be innate; the strength and content is dependent upon upbringing and other socializing experiences.

Distraction. The strength of an impulse may be reduced by simply distracting attention away from it. Waiting is easier if one thinks about something other than what is awaited; everyone knows that focusing on an appetite only serves to arouse it. Some distraction is achieved by avoiding stimuli: studying in the library forestalls the temptations of television and telephone. Psychologists have shown that people also have the ability to learn to ignore or 'tune out' certain stimuli, thus reducing the impulse to respond to them.

Rules. The most intriguing method of self-management is the creation of rules or principles to guide one's own behavior. For example, authors sometimes follow a rule of writing so many pages each day and an executive may have a rule that all incoming mail be answered that day. Many mountaineers follow a rule of pausing to rest only once each hour. Splitting the weekly pay into separate packets for food, clothing, rent, and savings is a time-honored self-imposed rule that foreshadows the routines of corporate budgeting. Schelling (1985) provides an insightful analysis of the various classes of such rules, pointing out that the best rules pose 'bright lines': for instance, exercising three times a week is a weaker rule than exercising every day.

Ainslie (1975) views rules as 'side-bets', with one's self-image as part of the stakes. He argues that one solution to the dieter's problem (described above) is for him to make a rule against deserts and to understand that he will only lose the weight if he has the willpower to keep the rule. Furthermore, 'it would not be necessary for anyone to hold the bet, since *the mere knowledge that this bet was necessary to avoid the specious rewards would make it binding*' (Ainslie, 1975, p. 479). The trick in this intrapsychic reputation game is to equate the impulse to eat the dessert with an immediate collapse in one's ability to follow the diet and, therefore, in the expected loss of all of the future rewards of the diet, not just its delay. If the immediate gain from the dessert exceeds the total discounted reward from weight loss, this trick will not work. However, the dieter can bundle this issue with another, 'betting' all the losses he might experience were his will-power to fail against each temptation.

Learned habit. The idea that one might learn to resist impulses by developing good 'habits' is as old as philosophy: Aristotle strongly emphasized the importance of repetition in forming the habit of countering impulses, equating character with good habits. The mechanism in question is *learning* and the proposition is that the self-reward of overcoming impulses can act as a reinforcer. The source of the self-reward is more difficult to pin down, although it is clearly associated with social norms or reduced cognitive dissonance with respect to internalized models of behavior.

The habits of moral philosophy are habits of cognition and guide conscious choice. However, the term habit also refers to routine or even unconscious behavior, and it too can be a source of impulse control. By virtually eliminating choice, habits render unpleasant action easier. For example, one of the authors increased his use of automobile seatbelts from occasional to always in order to set an example for his young daughter. After many years, the habit of fastening seatbelts was established, and he did not revert to his old ways. Acquiring the habit of buckling up dramatically reduced the cost of buckling up—he no longer had to allocate attention to consider the issue.[5]

---

[5] Note that the habits of moral philosophy, those *guiding* choice, are seen as primarily useful in helping to resist alluring temptations, and the habits of automatic behavior, those *eliminating* choice, are most useful in helping to take otherwise distasteful actions.

3. *Habitual Routines*

A 'habit' is a behavior that becomes easier or more rewarding with repetition.[6] A 'habitual routine' is a habit that consists of a sequence of actions and responses that, once initiated or triggered, proceeds with little or no conscious deliberation. This definition encompasses the possibility of branching—alternative subroutines that are triggered by particular stimuli in the course of executing a routine. In this section we examine the critical role played by habitual routines in organizational behavior, focusing on the connections between routines and impulse control. The argument advanced is that habitual routines aid in impulse control, but that impulsiveness also limits the degree to which people voluntarily invest in learning habitual routines.

Wedgwood

The central role of habitual routine is evident in Langton's (1984) treatment of Josiah Wedgwood's development of factory-based pottery production in England during the last half of the 18th century. Langton's primary concern is with reconciling the ecological view of organizations to the existence of aggressive forward-looking entrepreneurship. Langton's argument is that the real locus of natural selection in Wedgwood's firm was in the behavior of the potters. Wedgwood's strategy was to bring newly emerging factory practices to the pottery industry and thereby to produce a large volume of high-quality chinaware that could be sold to the growing middle-class. Wedgwood hired traditional country pottery workers and used operant conditioning, selectively rewarding and punishing various behaviors, to indoctrinate them in his new work methods. Langton relied on several careful histories of the region and industry, and it is worth quoting from him and his sources at length (Langton, 1984, pp. 343–45):

> Wedgwood began his firm with employees whose customs and attitudes were all, from a bureaucratic and capitalistic perspective, egregious vices. These workers were used to drinking on the job; they were used to working on a wide range of different tasks, more or less at their own discretion and without regard to overall coordination; and they were used to working flexible hours and taking time off for "St. Monday" and every wake and fair. When traditional potters did get down to business, "they worked by rule of thumb; their methods of production were careless and uneconomical; and their working arrangements arbitrary, slipshod

---

[6] The term 'habit' is also sometimes used to denote a ritual or an addiction. Rituals have no function other than their performance. The definition of addiction is difficult and controversial, but we take it to mean habits that are intrinsically rewarding (at least for a period) and which cannot be eschewed without considerable pain. Our interest is not with habits like these that are intrinsically rewarding, but with those that facilitate obtaining other rewards.

and unscientific: For they regarded dirt, the inefficiency and inevitable waste, which their methods involved, as the natural companions of pot making" (McKendrick, 1961, p. 38). . . .

Wedgwood resolved to change all this. . . . He obviously could not create the kind of work force he desired overnight, and he could not do it by the simple expedient of firing all those who failed to shape up immediately, since this would have left him with no help at all. To develop the kind of staff he desired, to give it a new culture, Wedgwood devised a remarkably sophisticated and astute program of behavior modification, based on an intricate mixture of rewards and punishments. . . .

To suppress the customary vices of the potters in his employ, Wedgewood published an incredibly detailed set of rules governing both production methods and conduct. He punished violations with stiff fines, deducted from wages. For example, "Any workman conveying ale or liquor into the manufactory in working hours" knew he would forfeit 2 shillings . . . Violations of certain rules, such as that against "strikeing or otherwise abuseing an overlooker," were punished by dismissal . . . Wedgwood also applied this ultimate bureaucratic sanction to those workers who simply would not shape up, who habitually violated his "Potters' Instructions. . . ."

The intricate blend of rewards and punishments that Wedgwood used to convert traditional potters into rational, industrial functionaries is clearly manifested in the job description he devised for the position of clerk of the manufactory who was

> to be at the works the first in the morning and settle the people to their business as they come in—to encourage those who come regularly to their time, letting them know their regularity is properly noticed, and distinguish them by repeated marks of approbation, from the less orderly part of the work people by presents or other marks suitable to their age, etc. Those who come later than the hour appointed should be noticed, and if after repeated marks of disapprobation, they do not come in due time, an account of the time they are deficient should be taken. . . . (McKendrick, 1961, p. 44)

Aided by the preaching of local evangelical pioneer John Wesley, Wedgwood's program 'certainly produced a team of workmen who were cleaner, soberer, healthier, more careful, more punctual, and more skillful and less wasteful than any other potter had produced before' (McKendrick, 1961, p. 46).

The example of Wedgwood's pottery factory at the beginning of industrialization clarifies some of the issues. Presumably, an individual potter who followed the practices Wedgwood insisted upon—sobriety, cleanliness, industry, frugality, precision—could have raised his income substantially, selling a larger quantity of goods at higher prices and lower costs. Yet few potters behaved this way before joining Wedgwood's factory. The hypothesis that the tradeoff of 'slack' for income was not desirable for potters is deflated by the fact that potters voluntarily took jobs in the factory and could have quit at any time. The hypothesis we wish to advance is that Wedgwood's factory provided a technology of behavior modification (in addition to possible gains from specialization that may have required coordination and monitoring). The potters joined the factory in order to attain the tradeoff of slack for income that they were unable to accomplish on their own.

Note that the original dysfunctional behavior of the traditional potters is not 'opportunism'. An opportunistic worker can be controlled by monitoring and by incentives tied to output; but workers who have bad habits or who are impulsive will not necessarily act functionally even when it is in their long-run best interest to do so. 'Bad' habits, dysfunctional culture, and impulsive behavior must be treated with training, incentives aimed at instilling new habits, 'moral' instruction (i.e. John Wesley), work routines that structure and cue desired behavior, and, to be sure, monitoring. Our thesis is that much of the fine structure of organizations, especially the structure of incentives and design of routines, is responsive to the problem of impulsive behavior and the existence of habits, both functional and dysfunctional.

Rosenberg and Birdzwell (1986) suggest that impulse control was also a factor in the development of factory production within the textile industry. The early textile industry was characterized by dispersed cottage production, which by the eighteenth century had largely evolved into a 'putting out' system wherein merchant-entrepreneurs contracted with individual artisans for work, took delivery of the final product, and then sold it for profit. According to Rosenberg and Birdzwell (1986, p. 159).

> The *irregular work habits of the cottage operators*, the problem of theft of materials, and the desire to gain greater control of the production process were recognized incentives for the adoption of the factory system even before the invention of factory machinery[7] [emphasis added].

Habits and Efficiency

The efficiency properties of habits have long been understood. William James (1899, pp. 114, 122) wrote that 'habit diminishes the conscious attention

---

[7] There is debate as to the relative importance of mechanization versus improved control in promoting the factory system. Rosenberg and Birdzwell (1986, p. 160) note that, 'there is still room for controversy over the relative importance of advantages of organization and advantages of technology in the introduction of the factory system in the textiles industry.' They conclude, however, that 'in the particular case of textile weaving, a general change to factory from cottage weaving would not have occurred had the only gains to the factory promoters been those attributable to savings in wages, longer hours, reduced theft, and other improvements in organization. Improvements in the productivity of the machines and in their ability to produce textiles of high quality were a necessary condition' (Rosenberg and Birdzwell, 1986, p. 179).

with which our acts are performed. . . . the more of the details of our daily life we can hand over to the effortless custody of automatism, the more our higher power of mind will be set free for their own proper work.' In the same vein, Whitehead said

> it is a profoundly erroneous truism, repeated by all copy-books and by eminent people making speeches, that we should cultivate the habit of thinking of what we are doing. The precise opposite is the case. Civilization advances by extending the number of operations which we can perform without thinking about them. Operations of thought are like cavalry charges in a battle—they are strictly limited in number, they require fresh horses, and must only be made at decisive moments.[8]

The power of routine is generated by several mechanisms: eliminating occasions for loss of self-control, reducing the psychic cost of action, focusing attention on important tasks, and facilitating skill development through repetitive practice. When engaged in a routine, deviations from programmed behavior are not even entertained, because of the high degree of automaticity involved in following the pattern. This suppression of considered choice prevents error.[9]

The idea that routines focus attention may seem odd. The point becomes clearer if perceptual and reflective resources are distinguished. For example, a trained firefighter approaching a closed door in a burning building has a subroutine 'feel door for heat before attempting to open' that is invoked when approaching a door. While 'thinking' about how much time is left before the roof collapses, perceptual attention will be fixed on the temperature of the door, thereby reducing the chance of a catastrophic accident.

There is considerable evidence that as learned habits become more automatic, mental resources are freed. Shiffrin and Schneider (1977), for example, studied search tasks and identified two modes: automatic processing ('parallel' search) and controlled processing ('sequential' search). As they varied the task difficulty, there was virtually no degradation in performance when automatic processing was being used. By contrast, performance fell off sharply with increases in task load when controlled processing was being used.

Even in activities where processing is not totally automatic, the role of routines in generating skill development through repetition is obvious, having been noted by everyone from Adam Smith to the Boston Consulting Group.

---

[8] Quoted without reference by Langer (1978, p. 40).

[9] Habitual routines help to reduce impulsive errors caused by fear, excitement, and stress. Much of the repetitive drill used in the military, police, and sporting arenas is designed to produce smooth performance even when emotionally-charged distractions bombard the individual. For example, basketball players are coached to develop ritualized routines whenever they shoot free throws—wipe your hands on your socks, bounce the ball three times, look at the front of the rim, etc. It is believed that these habits protect the players from the distraction of a roaring crowd and the pressure to make important shots.

Whether the task is cooking a duck, analyzing a real-estate project, doing algebra, or appraising a commercial loan application, learning habitual routines improves speed and accuracy and, perhaps most importantly, frees the individual to concentrate on refinements and strategic concerns. Just as there can be no strategy if tactical skills are not mastered, individuals and firms cannot undertake high-order tasks until the habitual routines that support them are well set. Another factor is that routine ways of doing things are much easier to improve than are unstructured approaches. By attacking a problem in the same way over and over again, a record of outcomes can be kept so that the work process becomes a controlled experiment. When behavior is unstructured, pinning down the causes of outcome variation is much more difficult.

Of course, habitual routines have traditionally been criticized by organizational scholars because they reduce flexibility and are essentially conservative in nature. Their dual nature arises in that they free resources for other tasks but also block change. In principle, this duality is no different from that attaching to the use of specialized resources. Just as in the case of specialized mechanical equipment, investment in specialized habitual routines improves efficiency but also exposes the investment to risk.

Our analysis puts this tradeoff in a different perspective. Routines 'compete' effectively with non-routine behaviors for implementation. This 'crowding out' effect of habitual routines is double-edged because non-routine actions are either impulsive deviations or functional adaptations to changed circumstances. Therefore, the degree to which there is a gain to routinization depends upon the degree to which it crowds out impulsiveness versus problem solving.

Investment in Habitual Routines

Habitual routines, once established, reduce impulsive behavior, but the establishment of a habitual routine is itself subject to impulsiveness. Consider a very simple habitual routine such as cleaning up a workplace at the end of the day. If workplaces are never cleaned up, tools will be lost or become inaccessible, worksurfaces will become unavailable and dirty, and key subroutines, such as tool maintenance, sharpening, and adjustment, will be undertaken only haphazardly. The routine of a daily clean-up uses the obvious trigger of day end to initiate the process, helping curb procrastination. Now imagine a technician who has not developed this habitual routine, but who agrees that it is a good practice. We shall make the even stronger assumptions that the technician knows and understands the future patterns of expected benefits and costs that follow from undertaking this practice. We assume that the benefits start immediately and are constant over time. Before the routine becomes a habit, it is aversive. However, as the activity is repeated, it becomes easier. Therefore, the 'cost' of the routine is high at the start, but diminishes with practice. The pattern of cost and benefit is that of an investment: net benefits are negative in the beginning, and positive in the future.

Because the formation of a functional habit has the character of an investment decision, impulsiveness may prevent the actions necessary to form the habit. Even though the clean-up routine is seen as worth developing (by assumption), the technician may fail to actually initiate the clean up on most days, perhaps being distracted by other tasks or interests. The technician does sometimes clean up; he just never develops a daily habitual routine of doing so. Notice that if the technician could get started on developing this habit, the 'cost' of the clean-up would begin to fall and soon the practice would become self-sustaining.

This explanation of the technician's failure to invest in forming a functional habit rests directly on the theory of impulsiveness. Although the technician knows that the clean-up habit is functional and that it will become less costly after some practice, if he has a sufficiently declining instantaneous discount rate he will nevertheless make the specious choice of deferral.[10]

The clean-up routine can become habitual because the required effort falls with repetition. The same logic applies to a habitual routine that is skill-enhancing. Consider, for example, the gain and effort patterns associated with learning to use a computer word processor. Here the level of perceived effort barely changes over time, but the level of performance increases dramatically with practice. Nevertheless, the net benefit pattern is negative at the beginning and only turns positive with practice. Thus, like the case of clean-up, some people will truly desire to learn word-processing but be unable to get started unless they join a training group or are forced to learn by an employer.[11]

Certain types of impulse control problems must be self-managed with the methods discussed in the previous section. In the case of habit development, it is common to employ external constraints and cues—this, after all, is what school is about. Think of a child struggling with his piano lessons. The need for constant repetition and practice before achieving the ability to play in

---

[10] Herrnstein and Prelec's (1991) intriguing theory of *melioration* provides a slightly different explanation for the choice of the poorer alternative. Based on a large body of empirical evidence, their theory is that in repeated choice situations, individuals allocate time or effort to equilibrate the *average* return per unit across alternatives. That is, average rather than marginal returns drive behavior. In the current context, this theory predicts that people do not correctly take into account the impact of their own actions on their future preferences. Were the technician a meliorator, his behavior would not reflect each repetition's value in diminishing the effort associated with all future repetitions.

[11] Much of the competition in microcomputer software in the past eight years has focused on adjusting the 'power curve': designing software that is powerful enough to warrant investment but which is not daunting to a beginner.

rewarding ways induces many to give up without attaining competence. Parents and teachers can help the learning process by reminding the flagging student of the need for practice, by setting aside certain times of the day for practice, by setting up attainable intermediate goals whose achievement will encourage the student, and by delivering rewards for serious practice efforts. These interim reinforcements and cues help to solve a problem of self-control. Without these aids the student may want to know how to play the piano, and may believe that the learning costs are more than made up for by the eventual rewards, but nevertheless find these intentions overwhelmed by the real-time unpleasantness of practice.

Investment in Changing Routines

We have noted that an individual who is learning a new routine experiences aversive feelings of discomfort and frustration. This aversion is magnified if the new routine replaces an old familiar habit, in part because the new routine leads to a temporary performance degradation, adding to the individual's frustration. Thus, organizational change, which involves unlearning old routines and learning new ones, can be more difficult and costly than creating a new organization.

Shiffrin and Schneider (1977) provide evidence on this issue. They studied the accuracy with which subjects performed a visual search-detection task as the number of repetitions increased. Accuracy rates rose from 56% in the first few trials to over 90% after 1500 repetitions. Subjects began the task using controlled (conscious) search, but gradually shifted to automatic processes. These subjects were then given a new search task in which the classes of target and background symbols were reversed; a control group worked on the tasks in the opposite order. Subjects found relearning the new task more difficult than learning the original task. On the relearning task, accuracy on the first few trials was only about 30% and rose to 90% only after about 2000 trials.

The implication is that there are potentially greater problems in impulse control with respect to changing routines than with learning new routines. *This hysteresis in the costs of learning may help explain why change is so difficult.* Even an entrepreneur like Wedgwood, starting with a fresh business concept, had to deal with conflicting habitual routines that were endemic among country potters, exclaiming 'it is very strange how long workmen are in quitting a habit they have been long accustom'd to' (McKendrick, 1961, p. 44).

The challenge of managing processes of learning and unlearning routines remains a key fact of organizational life. For example, F. Kenneth Iverson, chief executive officer at Nucor Corp., the leading steel minimill firm in the United States, told an interviewer that a major impediment to hiring senior executives from the steel industry was their 'bad habits':

> we've not had any success with older management [hired from old-line integ-
> rated steel companies]. Now we can hire a fellow who is 40 or under and that
> will work out OK, because over a period of time we can change him. But older
> than that we've found that we will never be able to change him. . . . Anyone who
> has worked a certain way . . . for years has very ingrained habits. It's very hard to
> break loose from that (Iverson, 1986, p. 42).

Nucor's difficulty in assimilating experienced steel company executives is the
complement of the problems the large integrated steel companies have in
changing their own organizations.

The more effective an organization is at inculcating efficient organizational
routines, the more difficult subsequent change becomes. Organizational
change requires that individuals unlearn habitual routines that have been
reinforced over a long period of time. One context in which this phenomenon
has become abundantly clear is in factories moving from traditional to 'pull',
or Kanban, systems of control. Under Kanban, the flow of work at each station is governed by the demand from the following station (a Kanban is a card
that functions as a work order). The key change, according to Oliver and
Wilkinson (1988, pp. 83–84), is that 'one does not just work for the sake of
it . . . but only when the containers, with Kanban attached, are there to be
filled.' They quote a team leader from a company that switched to the system:

> If a guy's been working the old system for 25 years you can't change it in
> 25 minutes. People want to work. It's difficult to say to a guy: 'Stop. Don't fill
> up any more. Stop. Stop.' Because he's used to working. . . . People get very
> jumpy when there's no work so they try to create work. . . . And it's very difficult.
> Sometimes you have to handcuff people (Oliver and Wilkinson, 1988, p. 84).

4. Organizations, Incentives, and Impulse Control

The impulse-control framework provides a parsimonious explanation for
many problematic features of organizations. In this section we discuss how
impulse-control theory can provide insights into the design of incentives,
monitoring, indoctrination, planning, and problem solving.

Incentives

The economic theory of organizations, and especially the agency-theory branch,
presumes that individual behavior is responsive to incentives. But incentives are
not preferences, and there may be distortions in the transformation of incentives

into preferences and, thence, into behavior. In agency theory, a principal can, with an appropriate contract, have his wishes implemented by a self-interested agent as long as he can observe some signal (e.g. output) that is correlated with the agent's actual behavior (e.g. effort).[12] Such a contract assigns to the agent payments that depend on the observed realizations of the signal, bribing the agent to take unpleasant actions that benefit the principal. However, if the agent is subject to impulsive behavior, this problematic link in the chain of causality renders contingent payoffs insufficient to guarantee optimal behavior.

Even though an agent might want to behave so as to gain the rewards specified in his compensation plan, the agent may need help from the organization. The most important form of this help is for measurement, feedback, and incentives to be applied frequently, so that the time lag between behavior and result is minimized. Another form of help is to make rewards and punishments vivid, certain, and manifestly connected to the specific behaviors desired. Incentive design, therefore, must have two aspects: *Rational preference alignment* is just the traditional economic theory of agency, the assignment of contingent payoffs across observable states of the world in order to make the agent's long-term, reflective choices consistent with the principal's goals. *Impulse control* involves positioning the payments in time and context to maximize their behavior-modifying effects.

We again turn to Nucor Corp. for an excellent example of an incentive design that is consciously driven by impulse control considerations. There, production teams receive weekly bonuses for turning out more billets of good steel per hour:

> If you work real hard and you get real good performance, you get the payment for that the next week so that you can very easily relate to the fact that you worked like a dog and there's the money—not at the end of the year, but now (Iverson, 1986, p. 47).[13]

This is reminiscent of Wedgwood's system of immediate fines for offenses against the rules of his factory, and in fact Nucor workers lose the day's bonus if they arrive to work five minutes late, and they forfeit the week's bonus if they are thirty minutes late. The salience of performance bonuses at Nucor is further enhanced by workers receiving the bonus payments in a physically separate check from their regular salary.

---

[12] One of the few general theorems of agency theory says that an optimal contract should condition payments on *all* information correlated with the agent's unobservable contribution to output (Holmstrom, 1979). Optimal contracts will therefore make payments contingent on any observable practices that affect output, although most of the models in the literature assume away the possibility of observing work practices.

[13] Nucor also pays a fraction of its profit-sharing retirement fund up front in cash, for similar reasons.

Agency theory ignores the significance of the timing and context of rewards and punishments (except for present value considerations) because it ignores the problem of impulse control. This omission is especially serious in the context of habit formation, where individuals need more help at first in order to break bad habits or to establish new ones.[14]

The idea that short-term rewards are part of a conditioning process is not novel. However, the treatment of this subject has generally presumed a behaviorist view of man that is at odds with the more rational reflective view necessary to understand managerial behavior. The impulse control framework, by contrast, allows an individual to choose or be willing to be conditioned in order to help deal with predictable problems of impulse control and to make certain behaviors more efficient by becoming more automatic.

The proposition that giving the 'correct' long-run incentives is not sufficient to induce the desired managerial behavior is a powerful adjustment to economic views of managerial work. The experience of ABC Supply Co., detailed in an interview with its founder, provides an especially clear example of the fine structure of incentive, review, and exhortation required to change managerial habits. ABC Supply is a rapidly growing wholesaler of roofing and building supplies with 1990 sales of $350 million. Kenneth Hendricks, the company's founder and chief executive officer, has generated its rapid and profitable expansion through a strategy of buying troubled roofing supplies distributors and correcting their managerial practices. Hendrick's basic theory is that these troubled firms suffer from two problems: lack of character and wasteful practices. His solution to the former issue is exhortation backed by termination:

> When managers don't work out, it's usually because of character problems. Of the ones that get fired, I'd say that 80% just plain don't care about anybody else. For example, they would not love their customers; they wanted to screw their customers. When employees see that, it destroys the character of the business (Hendricks, 1991, p. 36).

Just as Wedgwood found that he had to terminate workers who could not control their urges to steal, drink, and use violence, Hendricks is looking for managers with well-developed moral sentiments.

Hendrick's approach to the waste problem is to train his managers to use specific waste-reducing practices and to meet or surpass ABC Supply's numerical

---

[14] For evidence on the importance of reinforcement schedules for generating behavior, see Dews (1984) and Flak (1984). They go so far as to assert, mostly on the basis of animal experiments, that almost any reinforcer can be made to sustain any type of behavioral response with the appropriate schedule. The described effects of particular schedules on behavior are counterintuitive, but the general principle is that the interrelated pattern of behavior and reinforcement is a more powerful determinant of behavior than the size of the reward.

cost standards. The problem for these managers is to learn good habits and unlearn bad ones:

> They're in a failure culture, which we have to destroy and build a new one in its place. . . . [In our culture] we don't buy anything new. We buy used trucks, used buildings, used computers, and we make them work better than new. [Our] culture is. . . . getting rid of waste. These businesses are filled with waste, which is why they're failing. . . . That's true of most businesses. People don't see the waste because there are no standards (Hendricks, 1991, p. 36).

At ABC Supply, the process of unlearning bad habits and acquiring good ones is driven by four elements: standards, feedback, advice, and incentives. Standards are the first step in managerial behavior modification:

> the guy in this failing business hasn't ever had a standard . . . to go by. He might be working with three employees at $150,000 per employee, which means he has two too many. . . . We give them a standards sheet that runs down the company-wide P&L for the previous year. It shows the percentage of sales represented by each line on the P&L. You can compare those percentages with your own and get a pretty good idea of how you're doing.

Feedback is generated by delivering a monthly profit and loss statement for each store and showing it to all store employees. The P&L promptly and forcibly draws attention to problem areas and helps inculcate the routine of comparison of results to the standard. Advice consists of training in how to interpret the standards, information (and exhortation) on what practices have been shown to work, and cultivation of attention to detail. With a fast-growing company, many of ABC's managers are new and have difficulty in reading and understanding a P&L. The company trains them in this skill: it becomes a natural and automatic part of running their business. P&L consciousness in turn heightens the behavior-modifying effect of the monthly reports.

Incentives are the last part of ABC's behavior modification process. Employees at stores that beat the company standards receive annual bonuses, with 40% going to the manager and the rest distributed to the other store employees. These bonuses can amount to one-third or even one-half of an employee's base salary. The critical point is that these incentives, by themselves, are not sufficient to induce good practices. In fact, the incentives are clearly less than those obtained by the owner-managers before selling their business to Hendricks. The incentives seem to act as reinforcers to a learning process, a process that takes years. According to Hendricks (1991, pp. 38–39):

> I want them to catch on on their own. I want them to start doing things I didn't think of. It's important for them to feel the business is theirs, and not mine.

Sometimes that process takes two, three, even four years. But once they learn how to manage, they're there for life. . . . They see the bonus money, and their employees see the bonus money. Nobody really believes it, or gets it, until it happens. But once they ring the bell, everybody's on and things start falling into place.

The role of contingent payments at ABC Supply looms large, just as suggested by the economic theory of agency. What agency theory misses, however, is the overwhelming importance of reinforcement processes. Reinforcement enables an agent to leap the impulsive barrier that lies between a long-run preference for efficient behavior and current habitual routines.

Monitoring and Review

Supervision in organizations is normally much greater than can be explained by the need to control opportunism. In many work situations there are perfectly adequate measures of output, yet direct supervision is maintained. For example, office workers are frequently monitored continuously despite the fact that direct measures of productivity—forms processed—are available at the end of each day. Agency theory would try to explain this by supposing that some random, unobservable factor intervenes between worker effort and final output, so that output-contingent compensation is too risky for workers. In the context of office work this seems highly implausible. Impulse-control theory predicts that office workers know that there are objective measures of performance; nevertheless, they still might perform less well than they would like because of problems in self-discipline. Continuous supervision is a way of bringing into the present the reckoning at the end of the day.

Review is one of the means of monitoring middle-level and top-level managers in organizations. Managers who have cost or profit responsibility usually must prepare an annual budget with monthly components. As the year progresses performance with respect to the monthly budget targets is reviewed. This ritual is a common fact of organizational life. But what is the purpose of these monthly reviews? Should not the presence of an annual review at year end provide sufficient motivation during the year? It could be argued that the purpose of the reviews is to identify and solve problems, perhaps with the help of more experienced review officers. But the direction of communication in reviews is upward—it is the manager being reviewed who is supposed to identify problems and indicate solutions.

An explanation for ritualistic review that does fit the facts is the *control of attention* subject to impulsiveness. Attention is a limited resource. Simon (1985, p. 302) reminds us that deliberate thought is constrained by the 'bottleneck of attention—a serial, not parallel, process whose information capacity is exceedingly small. . . . People are, at best, rational in terms of what they are aware of, and they can be aware of only tiny, disjointed facets of reality.' The impulse to direct attention to the immediate, to pay attention to the 'squeaky wheel' rather than the journey's direction, is so commonly understood as to hardly deserve mention. It is precisely this impulse that generates the most frequently given management advice: 'make a list of what you need to do and start doing the tasks you have listed'. Indeed, a great deal of management consultation consists of nothing more than evoking from senior management their basic goals and then helping direct more organized energy towards their accomplishment.

Thus, the review of managerial activity serves to re-focus attention on important goals and activities. Annual review of performance may be sufficient to align *intended* behavior with the organization's goals, but annual lapses in attention would be unacceptably costly. Hence, monthly reviews of budgets and other objective review systems act to remind the reviewed about their own priorities.[15]

Indoctrination

Firms often devote substantial resources to exhortations, slogans, symbolic acts, morale-building exercises, etc. We claim that the purpose of these activities is not to convey information.

Consider sales meetings. These gatherings have been compared to pep rallies, with emotional speeches about the need to get out and sell, exhortations to beat the competition, praise of the company's products, and awards given to the most successful salespeople. The purpose of these events is straightforward. They are intended to 'psych up' and motivate the sales force. Although this makes little sense in a simple economic model, especially if salespeople receive commissions, the puzzle vanishes when we consider the problem of impulse control.

A salesperson on commission has a clear long-run incentive to work at selling until the marginal disutility of effort equals the expected commission. But selling is psychologically demanding; the salesperson faces constant rejection, has to initiate conversations with suspicious and sometimes hostile strangers, and sometimes must tout the virtues of a product that he or she knows is mediocre. In addition, if the salesperson is unsupervised in the field, the temptation to retreat from the battle may be overwhelming at times.

---

[15] Long exposure to such requirements may convert the organizational ritual into an individual habit for some managers, one that would be undertaken even if not required. It is common for managers from established firms who are used to these procedures to carry them along when they join new firms that have not yet adopted them.

The purpose of sales meetings, then, is to fortify the spirit of the salesperson with enthusiasm and confidence and to enable him to exert greater control over the impulse to shrink from the stresses of selling. The salesperson is to be inculcated with the moral sentiment that persistence and hustle are paramount virtues. Exposure to exemplary figures, whose sales successes can serve as a model, is combined with slogans and games. What is particularly interesting is that the participants in these meetings, especially the veterans, understand this manipulation. Nevertheless, the meetings appear to be effective. Thus, we have another case in which the organization helps individuals overcome problems of self-discipline.

Planning and Problem Solving

There has always been a tension in management thinking between the need for planning and the systems for carrying it out. Planning is essentially future oriented problem solving:[16] it necessarily involves consideration of non-routine actions (else it would be superfluous). Yet planning activities are themselves routine and necessarily occur in the present.

From an impulse-control perspective, the need for planning systems is obvious: habitual routines resist change throughout an organization and impulsive time-preferences induce procrastination with regard to the urgency for change. Thus, some overarching routine which cues the reviews of present routines is valuable. In simple terms planning systems aim to take potential future problems and transform them into current problems in order to garner attention.

Planning is usually cued by time. However, organizations face many problems that arise unpredictably, competing for attention with more routine tasks. To effectively focus rational reflection on *ad hoc* problems requires very careful attention to the structure of work routines. A good example of this kind of structure can be found in Kanban production methods. One of the crucial advantages of these systems is a pattern of continuous improvement in the production process. The basis for improvement lies in the notion that whereas large buffer inventories 'hide' problems, operating with small buffer stocks triggers an immediate problem-solving episode whenever anything goes wrong.[17] According to Oliver and Wilkinson (1988, p. 15),

---

[16] Planning also involves strong coordinative elements. Mintzberg (1979, p. 154) stresses this aspect, going so far as to define planning as 'the means by which the non-routine decisions and actions of an entire organization . . . can be designed as an integrated system'. We have chosen to concentrate on the forward looking and non-routine aspects of planning.

[17] The number of Kanban cards circulating in the production line acts as a control on the amount of work-in-process inventory.

if something is wrong the line will quickly be stopped and the problem corrected at source. Under this system the 'insurance policies' of buffer stocks, reserve staff and so on (which allow part of a process to go wrong without total disaster striking) are construed as obstacles to improvement. By permitting one to live with a problem, such spare resources remove the imperative to correct it.

Reid (1990, p. 151) describes the role of just-in-time methods in triggering problem-solving at Harley-Davidson:

Harley formerly used a complex, computerized Material Requirements Planning system that was based on maintaining safety stock. . . . But this just-in-case system covered up problems rather than solving them—it was a little like sweeping dirt under the rug. Suppliers continued to deliver substandard parts, machines continued to break down, systems continued to be inefficient. Instead of addressing these problems, the procedure was to put more and more safety stock in the stockroom. . . . with JIT, these are problems you can't live with any more, as you could when you had a security blanket of bulging stockrooms. As each problem is exposed, you are forced to identify its cause, fix it, and move on to the next problem that is revealed. It is a frustrating process, but it leads to a vastly improved manufacturing system.

A naive economic analysis might conclude that a firm could have its cake and eat it too by carrying out reviews when desirable and holding inventory levels that equate marginal stockout costs with marginal carrying costs. But the impulse-control framework warns us that the short-sighted desire for easy ways to keep the line moving may well dominate the rational long-run efficiencies of process improvement. Low inventory levels are an effective tool for committing to and cueing problem-solving.

5. *Conclusions*

We have argued that discipline is one of the sources of value provided by organization. In particular, we have proffered the idea that hierarchy acts to moderate and control impulsive behavior—a form of self-opportunism. As illustrated by our examples of Nucor and ABC Supply, long-term incentives may be insufficient to motivate individuals to behave in their own long-term best interest; short-term incentives, supervisor reminders, and inculcated habits are necessary, and individuals are usually cognizant of this fact.

It follows from this perspective that many elements of the fine structure of organizations are responsive to the problem of impulse control. Procedures for review and planning, as well as the timing and context of rewards and punishments, may not be intelligible absent consideration of the types of impulses to which agents are subject, their efficiency consequences, and the best ways of controlling them. The structure and pattern of monitoring and short-term incentives is most properly seen as a tool for reinforcing functional habits and routines which, in turn, are instrumental in obtaining long-term rewards.

The more general research program we encourage is that of enriching efficiency views of economic organization with more realistic models of human behavior. We do not advocate the abandonment of rational models, but we do suggest that individual and organizational rationality are 'engineered' outcomes, not natural endowments. The technologies of that engineering task are the proper subject of research in management.

Acknowledgement

Appreciation is extended to Steven A. Lippman for his many useful suggestions.

References

Akerlof, G. A. (1991), 'Procrastination and Obedience'. *American Economic Review*, 81, 1–19.

Ainslie, G. (1974), 'Impulse Control in Pigeons', *Journal of the Experimental Analysis of Behavior*, 21, 485–489.

Ainslie, G. (1975), 'Specious Reward: A Behavioral Theory of Impulsiveness and Impulse Control'. *Psychological Bulletin*, 82, 463–496.

Ainslie, G. (1986), 'Beyond Microeconomics: Conflict Among Interests in a Multiple Self as a Determinant of Value', in J. Elster (ed.), *The Multiple Self*, Cambridge University Press: Cambridge, pp. 133–176.

Ainslie, G. and V. Haendel (1983), 'The Motives of the Will', in A. T. Gottheil, A. T. McLellan and K. Druley (eds), *Etiology Aspects of Alcohol and Drugs Abuse*, Charles C. Thomas: Springfield.

Aristotle (1952), *The Works of Aristotle*. Trans. W. D. Ross, ed. Robert Maynard Hutchins. 2 vols. Encyclopaedia Britannica: Chicago.

Benzion, U., A. Rapoport and J. Yagil (1989), 'Discount Rates Inferred from Decisions: An Experimental Study'. *Management Science*, 35, 270–284.

Cohen, E. A. and J. Gooch (1990), *Military Misfortunes: The Anatomy of Failure in War*. The Free Press: New York.

Dews, P. B. (1984), 'Maintenance of Behavior by "Schedules": An Unfamiliar Contributor to the Maintenance of the Abuse of Substances and the Like', in P. K. Levison (ed.), *Substance Abuse, Habitual Behavior, and Self-Control*, AAAS Selected Symposium No. 59, Westview Press: Boulder, pp. 49–80.

Falk, J. L. (1984), 'Excessive Behavior and Drug-Taking: Environmental Generation and Self-Control', in P. K. Levison (ed.), *Substance Abuse, Habitual Behavior, and Self-Control*, AAAS Selected Symposium No. 59, Westview Press: Boulder, pp. 81–117.

Fisher, I. (1930), *The Theory of Interest*. Macmillan: New York.

Hackworth, Col. D. H. (1991), 'Mismatch in Kuwait.' *Newsweek*, January 28, 32–33.

Hausman, J. A. (1979), 'Individual Discount Rates and the Purchase and Utilization of Energy-Using Durable'. *Bell Journal of Economics*, 10, 33–54.

Hendricks, K. (1991), 'Waste Not, Want Not'. Interview by George Gendron and Bo Burlingham. *Inc*, March, 33–42.

Herrnstein, R. J. (1961), 'Relative and Absolute Strengths of Response as a Function of Frequency of Reinforcement'. *Journal of the Experimental Analysis of Animal Behavior*, 4, 267–272.

Herrnstein, R. J. and D. Prelec (1991), 'Melioration: A Theory of Distributed Choice'. *Journal of Economic Perspectives*, 5, 1–20.

Holmstrom, B. (1979), 'Moral Hazard and Observability'. *Bell Journal of Economics*, 10, 74–91.

Iverson, F. K. (1986), 'Steel Man Iverson'. Interview by George Gendron. *Inc*, April, 41–48.

James, W. (1899), *The Principles of Psychology*. Henry Holt and Company: New York.

Langer, E. J. (1978), 'Rethinking the Role of Thought in Social Interaction', in J. H. Harvey, W. Ickes and R. F. Kidd (eds), *New Directions in Attribution Research* (Volume 2). Lawrence Erlbaum Associates: Hillsdale, NJ, pp. 35–58.

Langton, J. (1984), 'The Ecological Theory of Bureaucracy: The Case of Josiah Wedgwood and the British Pottery Industry'. *Administrative Science Quarterly*, 29, 330–354.

Loewenstein, G. and D. Prelec (1992), 'Anomalies in Intertemporal Choice: Evidence and an Interpretation'. *Quarterly Journal of Economics*, 107, 573–598.

Marshall, S. L. A. (1953), *The River and the Gauntlet*. William Morrow & Co.: New York.

McKendrick, N. (1961), 'Josiah Wedgwood and Factory Discipline'. *The Historical Journal* 4, 30–55.

Mintzberg, H. (1979), *The Structuring of Organizations*. Prentice-Hall: Englewood Cliffs, NJ.

Oliver, N. and B. Wilkinson (1988), *The Japanization of British Industry*. Basic Books: New York.

Prelec, D. and G. Loewenstein (1991), 'Decision Making Over Time and Under Uncertainty: A Common Approach'. *Management Science*, 37, 770–786.

Rachlin, H. and L. Green (1972), 'Commitment, Choice, and Self-Control'. *Journal of the Experimental Analysis of Behavior*, 17, 15–22.

Reid, C. (1990), *Well Made in America: Lessons from Harley-Davidson on Being the Best*. McGraw-Hill: New York.

Rosenberg, N. and L. E. Birdzwell (1986), *How the West Grew Rich: The Economic Transformation of the Industrial World*. Basic Books: New York.

Schelling, T. C. (1985), 'Enforcing Rules on Oneself'. *Journal of Law, Economics, and Organization*, 1, 357–374.

Shiffrin, R. M. and W. Schneider (1977), 'Controlled and Automatic Human Information Processing: II Perceptual Learning, Automatic Attending, and a General Theory'. *Psychological Review*, 84, 127–190.

Simon, H. A. (1985), 'Human Nature in Politics: The Dialogue of Psychology with Political Science'. *The American Political Science Review*, 79, 293–304.

Solnick, J. A. (1980), 'An Experimental Analysis of Impulsivity and Impulse Control in Humans'. *Learning and Motivation*, 11, 61–77.

Strotz, R. H. (1955–56), 'Myopia and Inconsistency in Dynamic Utility Maximization'. *Review of Economic Studies*, 23, 165–180.

Thaler, R. H. (1981), 'Some Empirical Evidence on Dynamic Inconsistency'. *Economics Letters*, 8, 201–207.

Thaler, R. H. and H. M. Shefrin (1981), 'An Economic Theory of Self-Control'. *Journal of Political Economy*, 89, 392–406.

Routines and Other Recurring Action Patterns of Organizations: Contemporary Research Issues

Michael D. Cohen[1], Roger Burkhart[2],
Giovanni Dosi[3], Massimo Egidi[4], Luigi Marengo[4],
Massimo Warglien[5] and Sidney Winter[6]

([1]University of Michigan, Ann Arbor, MI 48109-1220, [2]Deere and Co., John Deere
Road, Moline, IL 61265, USA, [3]Department of Economics, University of Rome 'La
Sapienza', Via A. Cesalpino 12/14, 00161 Roma, [4]Laboratory of Experimental
Economics, [5]Department of Economics, University of Trento, Via Inama 1, Trento,
[5]Universita' degli Studi di Venezia, Ca' Bembo, S. Trovaso, Venezia 30123, Italy and
[6]The Wharton School, University of Pennsylvania, Philadelphia, PA 19104, USA)

*This paper reports and extends discussions carried out during a workshop held at the
Santa Fe Institute in August 1995 by the authors. It treats eight major topics: (i) the
importance of carefully examining research on routine, (ii) the concept of 'action patterns' in general and in terms of routine, (iii) the useful categorization of routines and
other recurring patterns, (iv) the research implications of recent cognitive results, (v) the
relation of evolution to action patterns, (vi) the contributions of simulation modeling
for theory in this area, (vii) examples of various approaches to empirical research that
reveal key problems, and (viii) a possible definition of 'routine'. An extended appendix
by Massimo Egidi provides a lexicon of synonyms and opposites covering use of the word
'routine' in such areas as economics, organization theory and artificial intelligence.*

1. Introduction

This paper reports the main lines of discussion that developed during a four-
day workshop held August 10–13, 1995, at the Santa Fe Institute, Santa Fe,
New Mexico. The workshop was devoted to exploring the difficulties and
promise of current research on organizational routines and related concepts.

We decided during the concluding day of our sessions that the productive
conversations we had held could be quite valuable to others if we could craft
an effective format for sharing them. Many of us were surprised, both by our

points of agreement and disagreement, and all of us felt that arguments made during the discussions contributed novel and valuable linkages to results and methods in related fields. It was our feeling that other researchers working on these issues could well benefit from an account of what was said.

This paper is therefore designed with the audience of fellow researchers— and especially graduate students—chiefly in mind. It reorganizes (and compresses) the chronological flow of our discussions in an effort to bring out major themes. In each of its sections it also contains commentary, pointers to literature and items of dispute, all added by the participants as they reviewed the working paper draft. Some comments of one participant evolved into a much larger argument that could not easily be sliced into separate chunks: this appears as Appendix A. Thus the document distils not only the four days of discussion, but some reflections on those discussions during the few weeks following the meeting while the draft was created and circulated for commentary.[1]

The seven gathered at the workshop were drawn from only a subspace of the many researchers working with the concept of routine. All shared a commitment to viewing actors through the lens of research in cognitive psychology on short-term memory limits, reasoning powers and differentiated forms of long-term memory and learning—an approach we will label 'cognitive realism'. All shared an approach to change processes in organizational systems as broadly evolutionary in their character ('an evolutionary approach to change'). All regarded as highly significant the 'political' and social forces within organizations, the many channels through which individual and local interests assert themselves at the expense of more global organizational concerns ('the diversity of "fitness" forces').

These common commitments probably contributed to the many points of agreement reached over the four days. Differences in emphasis between the three commitments probably account for many of the remaining points of contention.

What follows is a synthetic reconstruction of the conversations, indicating both significant agreements and issues that remained open (marked with an *). Each section closes with remarks contributed by workshop participants during revision of this paper, and attributed directly to them via their initials. Those participants (with their identifying initials) were: Roger Burkhart (R.B.), Michael Cohen (M.C.), Giovanni Dosi (G.D.), Massimo Egidi (M.E.), Luigi Marengo (L.M.), Massimo Warglien (M.W.) and Sidney Winter (S.W.). Some of Egidi's comments form a longer statement and are collected in the

---

[1] It might be thought of as a sort of 'flattened hypertext'. We are exploring the possibility of making it available for further commentary via the World Wide Web.

Appendix. (An eighth participant, Benjamin Coriat, was unable to attend due to an injury. Giovanni Dosi labored heroically to indicate at numerous points in the workshop positions he felt sure our colleague Coriat would have taken if he could have been with us. And Coriat has supplied some comments, generated during a review of our draft, and labeled B.C.)

The principal themes of the workshop, each of which is discussed in a section below, are as follows:

1. Why is it important to examine carefully research on routine?
2. What "action patterns" are under discussion?
3. How can routines and other recurring patterns be usefully categorized?
4. What are the research implications of recent cognitive results?
5. How can evolution be seen in relation to action patterns?
6. How can simulation contribute to better theory in this area?
7. What are examples of various approaches to empirical research that reveal key problems or results?
8. How might 'routine' be defined?[2]

2. *Why Is it Important to Examine Carefully Research on Routine?*

Our meeting grew out of an earlier session held during the winter of 1995 in Laxenburg, Austria, with the sponsorship of the International Institute of Applied Systems Analysis (IIASA). That meeting gathered numerous researchers working with evolutionary models of economic phenomena. During the course of the meeting it became clear that the concept label 'routine' was being used very widely, and—unfortunately—in widely varying senses. Routine is a fundamental concept in the Nelson and Winter (1982) approach to economic evolution, which was serving many of the researchers present as an intellectual point of departure. So it was especially of concern that many were using the concept with meanings that had drifted well away from the Nelson–Winter definition. And it soon became clear that, with the benefit of a dozen years of additional research by several hundred readers of their book, Nelson and Winter, who were present, also saw the definition of 'routine' as ripe for some reappraisal.

By the end of the meeting there was agreement on the potential of another, smaller gathering that would bring key participants together again for an

---

[2] We use single quotes when referring to the label for the concept indicated by the quoted term; double quotes are used in their normal way.

extended session focused strictly on routine: trying to clarify the concept in order to make empirical studies and theoretical models more coherent. The Santa Fe Institute and IIASA were eventually persuaded to jointly sponsor the meeting, since both have serious interests in research bearing on the concept.

Several of us attended other, more general, conferences on organization held in the intervening months and felt those meetings confirmed the timeliness of our decision. 'Routine' seems destined to be a keyword in a very large number of papers appearing in the mid-1990s. But an examination of the papers shows there has been little progress so far in reaching agreement on what routines are—and therefore on how or why social scientists should study them.

Commentary on 'Needed Examination'

L.M.   To some of us (to me at least!) routines (and, more generally, rule-guided behavior) appeal as a basic 'foundational' concept for an alternative theory of decision making to the neoclassical one. This endeavor goes far beyond the observation of organizational behavior, and requires a special effort in carefully defining the concept and formalizing it (maybe by boldly simplifying and losing a great part of the richness of different aspects which emerge from empirical observation). For this purpose the definition and formalization of routines given by computer scientists seems particularly appealing, but only partly overlapping with that emerging from the organization science/evolutionary economic tradition. (See the detailed comments along this line by M.E. in the Appendix.) Clarification on these definitional issues is, in my view, most needed.

M.W.   The concept of routine is probably paying the price for its success: as it diffuses, its meaning gets increasingly vague and subject to arbitrary extensions. This is to some extent the unavoidable side-effect of popularity (after all, the 'butterfly effect' has gone through much more cruel vicissitudes). However, some reasons for our discomfort are rooted in one of the original metaphors characterizing routines in the Nelson and Winter book. Much of the temptation of naming as 'routine' anything that is not new under the sun of organizational life may belong to their suggestion that routines are the 'organizational DNA': a metaphor that conveys the sense that routines are the organizational replicator, the fundamental structure undergoing reproduction. It thus becomes a natural temptation to claim that, whenever you observe some feature which is stable and reproducible over time or space, it has to be a routine. I think that the wise caveats that in Nelson and Winter's book came along with the introduction of the genetic metaphor have been largely overridden by this last in readers' minds. In contrast, cultural phenomena (to which economic evolution clearly belongs) present a wide variety of replicators, whose nature and level of aggregation is very diverse; some of the richness of cultural evolution resides in the way multiple replication processes interweave in quite complicated ecologies. So, I think that recognizing the diversity of replicators and replication processes in action within organizations and starting to define a more articulate language for speaking about them is a useful way to improve evolutionary thinking about firms, and is a good service to the notion of routine itself.

3. *What Action Patterns Are Under Discussion?*

Our clear principal focus is on action patterns that can be called 'routine'. However, 'other recurring action patterns' became part of the title of the workshop (and this paper) because we wanted to acknowledge that there are other recurring actions in firms that also merit close study, but may not exactly be routines. For example, there might be widely shared 'heuristics', rules of thumb used in common situations. They could give important regularity to firm actions and be important topics for research, but might lie outside a definition of 'routine'. Winter explored the topic of heuristics and other non-routine patterns in a short memo prepared for the group. A revised version of that memo is in the section on categorization below.

This meeting occurred because all the participants believe that useful theory about firms (and many non-profit and government agencies) must be solidly based in a realistic, empirically informed account of multi-person action. As Simon observed (1981), agents capable of perfectly tailoring their actions to their world would require no theory. Since they would optimize, one would need only a theory of that environment to which they flawlessly responded (and a statement of their goals). None of the participants believes that a good theory of firms (etc.) is likely to be found this way. All believe that firms are not frictionless reflections of their momentary environments, but rather highly inertial action repertoires, responding to—indeed perceiving—today's environment largely in terms of lessons learned from actions in days gone by.

In the consensus view, it is essential to understand how such action repertoires are assembled, maintained and modified. The perspective points a researcher's interest toward action patterns with these three properties:

1. Recurring (actions taken by the same actors at different times—or by different actors—that we want to call 'the same actions', e.g. approving a purchase order).

2. Selectable (actions—or patterns of action—that could be subject to forces that would make them more or less likely to recur, e.g. setting the R&D budget at 6% of total expenditure).
3. Set in an organizational context (the actions are not those of isolated individuals, e.g. trying alternative tools on an assembly line, not in one's basement).

*In addition, many felt the actions being discussed were typically not deliberative choices. They wished to preserve the prominence that tacitness and automaticity have generally had in distinguishing routine action from choice and problem solving. Some felt the 'other recurring action patterns' label in the workshop title was useful as it left a place for deliberative choices while keeping 'routines' for the non-choice cases, and yet another group (the 'imperialists') were happy to include deliberative choice under routines, leaving little in the other category. They note that even the standard of 'acting rationally' is evolving as decades roll by and fields like finance and operations research become more sophisticated. Thus young managers work hard to learn how to 'choose rationally' in school and their first jobs, and tend to stick to the patterns they have learned through the remainder of their careers, making rational actions a recurring pattern and potentially a species of routine.

*Finally, some embraced a distinction of 'action' and 'behavior' in order to resolve ambiguities that otherwise arise. When the same observable behavior occurs while very different intents are being accomplished (e.g. faxing an affected colleague the press release just before or after the public announcement), the cases might be coded as the same raw behaviors (fax the release), but interpreted by the actors as meaningfully different actions (pre-notified, or not). And different observable behaviors may occur in order to accomplish the same underlying intent (e.g. 'notify her before it's public', once by phone, another time by fax). Others felt it was acceptable to treat the two terms as interchangeable. Some felt that the distinction was meaningful but that behavior rather than action should be given priority in view of its greater observability. In the remainder of this account 'action' is generally used in a sense that includes intention. 'Behavior' is used to indicate directly observable events.

Commentary on 'Actions Under Discussion'

M.W. The problem whether to name as 'routine' all 'recurring action patterns' in organizations or just those that imply non-deliberate, automatic action may be a question of terminological taste. In any case, I think the substantive question is to start analyzing the structure of such action patterns and to make useful distinctions. Whether we want or not to call 'routine' the working of a kanban system in an assembly line, what strikes me is that we do not yet have a language for going too far in analyzing its working. To be sure, there is a lot of tacit knowledge and of non-deliberate behavior in the way workers can achieve coordination in a kanban system: there is more in it than workers or production engineers can say. But stability and replicability is assured to a large extent also by the following of explicitly stated rules and instructions (like 'stop working if you don't have any production kanbans authorizing it'), and by a carefully designed artifactual environment within which workers can learn coordinated behaviors. All these ingredients are 'recurring, selectable, and set in organizational context'—but they differ both in their cognitive nature and in the way they are reproduced. Moreover, if one wants to characterize a kanban system as a recurring action pattern, one has to look not only at those diverse ingredients, but also (and maybe chiefly) at the architecture of relations among those ingredients—how they fit reciprocally and with other processes such as set-up time reduction and working capital reduction. This relational architecture is itself recurring, selectable and set in an organizational context. Thus, whatever may be the terminological standard, the problem is finding a language for defining the ingredients of recurring action patterns and the architecture tying those ingredients together and giving them coherence.

L.M.   (i) I have some doubts on 'selectable' as a key ('definitional') property of routines. That all kinds of actions and action patterns are selectable (under a broad definition of 'selection') is rather obvious and I do not find it at all peculiar of routines. Certainly the role of selection pressure on the shaping and evolution of routines is a key issue, but I would not see selectability as a key discriminating characteristic of routines.

(ii) The discussion on automaticity versus choice (imperialists versus ?) is a basic one and should be perhaps more emphasized. To simplify the positions I see it in this way: those who stress the automaticity have in mind a very clear distinction between what is and what is not a routine. A standard psychological test (performing some other demanding activity while one is executing a routine) would perfectly discriminate. But this would probably narrow down (certainly too much for the economists, cf. my point under 'needed examination') the domain and the interest of the concept. On the other hand, the 'imperialists' (who basically have in mind the computer science view of routines) tend easily to an all-embracing definition (routine = executable procedure).

G.D.   In Dosi *et al.* (1995) we add two further characteristics of routines (which are there considered in terms of behavior patterns): (i) their context dependence and (ii) their invariance *vis-à-vis* fine informational change, once the context has been given. I think the former attribute is important in that it defines a set of behaviors which meets the logic of appropriateness (March, 1992). Hence, Mr Jones elicits specific behavioral repertoires which are appropriate to his being on an assembly line or having to answer a phone call, without having to select them by some backward inference from the ultimate consequences that they entail and often also without much intentionality. Regarding the second attribute, I have been quickly convinced by the Santa Fe meeting that it might induce some misunderstanding in that routines and other patterns of action might sometimes be extremely sensitive to signals from the environment (e.g. the behavioral pattern of a secretary might involve fine-tuning on the mood of the boss), although other action patterns display much higher invariance (e.g. spend 6% of sales on R&D; never hire a communist). However, I would maintain that in both cases the behavioral patterns themselves are rather inertial and relatively invariant to signals and feedbacks which could notionally call for their revision. Putting it another way, I am suggesting that the class of behavioral patterns we are discussing involves a major activity of information-framing and information-censoring which sustains their reproduction over time, often well beyond the circumstances which spurred their introduction.

4. How Can Routines and Other Recurring Patterns be Usefully Categorized?

Two approaches to this classification problem were developed for the workshop. One was based on the differing cognitive demands of various expressed action patterns. It appears immediately after this section as the first comment.

This first approach gave priority to cognitive processing loads as its forcing principle, and has the advantage of connecting to a rich and growing body of research on cognition. The second approach emphasized the demands of evolutionary change by focusing on classifying types of representations, each presumed to give rise to action patterns and thence to be subject to variation-yielding modification.

Thus if we are interested in an action pattern carried out by a group of actors in an organizational setting, we can ask how the representation of the action is maintained in the organization. Some answers, roughly clustered, might be:

1. In the memories of the individual actors for their respective roles in the overall pattern.

2. By means of locally shared language, with special significance given to terms used to trigger or carry out the actions. [Weick (1979) is especially informative on creation of shared meaning as a form of organizational memory.]

3. Via physical artifacts, such as tools, spatial arrangements,written codes of standard operating procedures or computer systems.

4. Via organizational practices such as archives, rotations of personnel, maintenance of working examples or by building key assumptions into organizational structure [e.g. 'architectural knowledge' of Henderson (1992)].

5. By means of globally shared language forms, such as formalized oral codes or pledges, or widely retold 'war stories'.

An interesting advantage of this type of classification arises from the importance in evolutionary analysis of sources of variation. By making explicit how an action pattern is stored between expressions, it suggests the processes that might be creating useful, or deleterious, variation. For example, forgetting is a far more active process for declarative memories of theories than for procedural memories of skills. This suggests greater stability over time for action patterns consisting largely of skilled actions by group members evoked in a performance context (e.g. an assembly sequence), and relatively greater variability for action patterns maintained via jointly held theories of how the environment works (a market projection for a new product). The formulation also helps make sense of frequent observations that changes in routines can be triggered by substitution of what were thought to be equivalent tools or raw materials, since these may have been serving a representational function. In turn, this observation provides a potential rationale for otherwise 'irrational' resistance to the turbulence of supply chains that flows from emphasizing price competition in purchasing.

Commentary on Categorization

S.W. ('routines resorted and glossed')   In their discussion of routines, Nelson and Winter apparently created an impression of themselves as 'lumpers' with respect to this conceptual category. Although a lot of different aspects and types of routines were discussed, there was also language in the book that created the impression in many readers that some unitary concept of 'a routine' was the key to our analysis. This note attempts to correct this misapprehension by pursuing a 'splitter' approach to routines (actually, to a category broader than 'routine' as I would now use that term). The distinctions involved in the 'splitting' here are at the cognitive level; they categorize different ways that a routine may relate to the cognitive functioning of the individuals involved in its performance.

This cognitive approach neglects, and hence risks obfuscating, the contextual aspects of routines. Context dependence is fundamental; the effectiveness of a routine is not measured by what is achieved in principle but by what is achieved in practice; this generally means that the routine might be declared effective in some specific contexts, but perhaps not in others. One important aspect of total context is the physical, which includes both the local/artifactual complements to the routine (e.g. the requisite plant and equipment) and the broader physical environment that was not produced for the benefit of the routine (e.g. climate, air pollution, radiation). A second major aspect of context is motivational/relational: what is the explanation for the fact that the human beings involved in the performance are willing to do what they do? The 'routine as truce' story is helpful here: once upon a time there was overt conflict, but in most cases it is largely over when the observer comes on the scene. What the observer sees is therefore the product of cognitive functioning constrained by sensitivity to the sources of conflict. However, the broader the temporal and geographical scale on which one seeks to address the motivational issues, the less of the problem is unlocked by the 'routine as truce' formulation.

The absence of these contextual factors from the following discussion implies that there are additional dimensions (perhaps several) on which some resorting and glossing of the routines concept might be called for. The case for making the distinctions noted below is not that they provide an exhaustive taxonomy, but that they provide a taxonomy that is useful, though partial.

The starting point here is the question 'what does an evolutionary theory really require about firm behavior if its basic evolutionary logic is to track?' The answer is the presence of some sort of quasi-genetic trait (QGT).

> QGT: Any trait that remains approximately constant in the organization over a period long enough for significant selective feedback to accumulate at a level where 'outcomes' are tested by an 'environment'. (An analytical distinction between an outcome that is 'tested' and an environment that does the testing is indispensable to an evolutionary view—but a change of unit/level of analysis may reclassify actual behaviors between these two categories.)

Some Types of QGTs, Distinguished by their Cognitive Aspects

I   **Routines** (in the broad sense, falling into two subcategories)

IA   *Routines (narrow sense):* complex, highly automatic (and at least in that sense 'unconscious') behaviors that 'function as a unit' and typically involve high levels of information processing that is largely repetitive over separate invocations of the routine.

IB *Rules of thumb:* quantitative, relatively simple decision rules that are consciously invoked and require low levels of information processing. Often, a rule of thumb yields a 'first approximation' answer to some quantitative question and shapes actual behavior only through this role as a target or norm.

I claim that the distinction is important, especially in understanding earlier literature; the idea that boundedly rational actors respond to a complex and uncertain or unknowable environment with simple rules captures what is going on with rules of thumb, but is far off the mark with routines (narrow sense) that are skill-like and may be awesomely complex and involve awesomely large amounts of unconscious information processing. Thus, the boundedly rational response has a big component of making the best of the situation by narrowing focus and suppressing deliberation, something quite different from the simplification response reflected in rules of thumb.

II **Heuristics and strategies** Concepts and dispositions that provide orientation and a common structure for a range of similar problem-solving efforts, but supply few, if any, of the details of individual solutions. (This is a very broad category; examples are identified by the combination of broad scope and prescriptive force: guidance toward a solution is provided over a substantial range of perceived problems. By contrast, a routine provides a detailed response to a narrow problem that may not even be perceived as a problem, since its 'solution' is at hand.)

III **Paradigms, cognitive frameworks** Mental models that are so fundamental to the cognitive activity of the actor that they affect perception as well as problem-solving and other cognitive functions; presumptions that underlie the actor's ability to see the world as meaningful and understandable. Although these models may have large articulable elements (as in scientific paradigms), they can also be inculcated as the result of long consistent experience, and in that case are often tacit. The specific influence on perception is generally tacit regardless of the amount of articulation possible in other respects: people cannot explain with any completeness why they perceive things as they do.

IV Examples

IVA *Routines (narrow sense):* The actions of a retail clerk in accepting payment, recording the sale, perhaps bagging the purchase, etc., or of a bank teller in executing the bank's side of a transaction. The sequence of steps executed in clearing a check. Accounting systems. Airline reservation systems. The actions of a team of workers at a particular station on an assembly line.

IVB   *Rules of thumb:* Rules for determining R&D expenditure or advertising expenditure in relation to sales. The markup number in a markup pricing formula. [By contrast, the cost number that is marked up is often the product of a cost accounting system that is an elaborate routine (narrow sense).]

IVC   *Heuristics and strategies:* In the realm of decision making: 'Do what we did the last time a similar problem came up.' In technology: 'Make process equipment larger (in physical volume) or faster (in cycle time).' 'Make the product smaller' (e.g. in semiconductor devices.) In business strategy: 'Always seek to be the number one or number two firm in every market you participate in—divest units that, over a period of time, fail to meet that standard.' 'Invest heavily in capacity to serve growing markets, so as to obtain learning curve advantages' (BCG doctrine). 'Stick to the knitting.' 'Quality is job no. 1.' In bargaining: 'Always ask for more than you would be willing to settle for.' 'Weigh the effect that a proposed settlement may have as precedent or signal.' In management: 'Centralize to achieve greater responsiveness to top management, and other advantages.' 'Decentralize to achieve greater responsiveness to customers, and other advantages.' As these examples suggest, a heuristic or strategy may permit concise articulation, but its consequences in behavior often depend on a much richer background of understanding that is not fully articulable.

IVD   *Paradigms and cognitive frameworks:* At a fundamental level, commitments to concepts like causality, with causes temporally preceding effects, or to two-valued logic, or to category systems (as in Lakoff, 1987), or to 'seeing is believing' (the naive version of the idea that there is a 'neutral language of observation').

At a not-quite-so-deep level, scientific paradigms in the Kuhnian sense (Newtonian physics, phlogistic chemistry, neoclassical economics), and their counterparts in technology (see especially Kuhn, 1962, Chapter 6, pp. 63–4). 'A scientific paradigm could be approximately defined as an "outlook" which states the relevant problems, a "model" [i.e. an "exemplar"?—S.W.] and a "pattern" of inquiry' (Dosi, 1984, p. 14). In broad analogy with the Kuhnian definition of a 'scientific paradigm', we can define a 'technological paradigm' as a 'model' and a 'pattern' of solution of selected technological problems based on selected principles derived from natural sciences and on selected material technologies.

Or, the uni-causal principle—the widely held intuitive belief that every identifiable and value-laden 'effect' must have a conceptually unique and commensurately value-laden 'cause'—a principle that provides grounds for conspiracy theories, often picks out 'pilot error' as the 'probable cause' of an airline disaster, attributes cancers and birth defects to handy environmental problems created by big money-grubbing corporations, etc.

At a more superficial level, the innumerable patterns of unconscious inference that derive from experience, typified by the tendency to perceive anomalous playing cards as normal—a black four of hearts is seen as a normal four of hearts or of spades (Bruner and Postman, 1949). Related mechanisms probably account for more consequential perceptual phenomena such as stereotyping on the basis of race, gender or ethnicity (note that the 'experience' base of the inference scheme need not be first-hand or statistically valid). In the worlds of management and policy, the powerful role of perception of a proposal as 'something that this organization is not likely to do' or 'something that will not attract majority support'.

Other QGTs

Although not having distinguishing cognitive features analogous to those of the types listed above, there are other types of QGTs that can provide the basic continuity needed for an evolutionary theory. In particular, there are *stable systemic traits:* traits that are not themselves 'structural' but that are stabilized over long periods by some combination of features of the organization. An operational definition of 'stable' is that the intraorganizational variation over time is small relative to the cross-sectional variation at a given time, or alternatively, that the intraorganizational variation over time for the trait in question is small compared to other traits of the same organization. In general, then, identification of a trait as 'stable' depends on the availability of some standard of comparison.

Examples of stable systemic traits: Budget allocations in a government bureaucracy or a multi-divisional corporation with a weak center (Williamsonian 'H-form' rather than 'M-form')—often describable by a simple formula involving historical allocation patterns and perhaps subunit contribution, even though no such formula is explicitly acknowledged in the decision process. Financial ratios reflecting, on average, the joint effect of a number of facets of business operations rather than any process focused on that ratio as such—sales/assets, working capital/assets, times interest earned, etc. (If these are explicitly attended to, perhaps because outsiders are believed to be attending to them, then they would be in the category of rules of thumb.)

Of course, mere constancy is not enough to identify something as a 'trait' of an organization or organism—just wait until that chameleon moves to a background of a different color and you will find what sort of 'trait' his color is. As the examples above suggest, it is something about the organization that is producing the observed stability and will tend to preserve it in the face of environmental change, even if the changes are ones that might suggest the need for some adaptation.

G.D.   (i) While I like the Winter taxonomy, I have some trouble on the current definition of the stable systemic traits (SSTs). The way I would interpret them is as relatively invariant ensembles of routines (narrow sense), rules of thumb and possibly heuristics. SSTs, in this definition, would then be the central level of observation in order to identify corporate capabilities as currently discussed in the business literature. That is, the proposition 'company X is good at doing Y' represents a statement on the collective properties of its routines, etc. Likewise it is at the level of SSTs that one might be able to discriminate among discrete types of organizational forms and model behaviors (e.g. Fordist or Toyotist).

(ii) It is true that rules of thumb are relatively simple, information-poor rules. However, behind the simple rule there are likely to be several routines (narrow sense) that make the rule operational.

5. *What Are the Research Implications of Recent Cognitive Results?*

One line of recent work in psychology has developed in a way that nicely reinforces traditional organization theory views of routine. Work on procedural memory in human individuals has shown that it has distinctive properties. It is centered on skills, or know-how, rather than on facts, theories or episodes (know-that) which seem to be more the province of an alternate, 'declarative', memory system. Procedural memory differs from declarative in its long decay times, and greater difficulty of transfer and of verbalization. This fits nicely with properties of routines observed in the field and in the laboratory (Cohen and Bacdayan, 1994; Egidi, 1994). And it appears to provide a firmer foundation in individual psychology for the characterization found in Nelson and Winter of routines as 'tacit' and highly stable analogs of individual skills.

While it is useful that procedural memory aligns with many characteristics of highly routinized action patterns, it seems likely that much effective organizational performance involves a mixture of such 'automatic' or 'tacit' elements together with a certain amount of 'decision-making' or 'problem-solving' that is much more deliberative and self-aware in its character.

The group engaged in detailed analysis of hypothetical examples in which choice points were embedded within relatively automatic sequences. The aim was to clarify questions about whether the choices were part of one routine or were better viewed at sutures joining together several smaller routines. This issue became known as the problem of 'grain size': whether a routine should generally be taken to be a rather large block of action, or a small block typically interleaved with other small routines and other forms of non-routine action.

The issues were additionally illustrated by observations from the Egidi–Cohen–Bacdayan experiments, where coherent chunks are small at early stages of play and become larger with experience. But even at late stages of experience, it is problematic whether players of the card game could be said to have one routine or rather a repertoire of several which are called upon as contexts vary. Different choices about the grain size or boundaries of routines lead to different predictions about how the system will maintain coherence as it encounters unexpected situations or problems.

Commentary on Cognition

The extended commentary by M.E., though relevant to most sections of the paper, is especially germane here. The reader who has not yet looked at the Appendix is encouraged to do so now.

G.D.   What generalizations can one draw from the existing literature in cognitive and social psychology with regard to 'learning modes'? It seems plausible to conjecture that the way people learn depends to some extent on the content of what is learned and the context in which it happens. Is it true? Is there some clear evidence?

M.W.   On the one hand, research in cognition has supported the idea that part of our knowledge is of the tacit (or, as is more commonly said, 'implicit') form. This provides a remarkable support to the routine hypothesis, although we need more empirical and experimental evidence, along the lines traced by the Cohen–Bacdayan–Egidi work, that characteristics of individual cognition can be mapped onto collective behavior. On the other hand, added conceptual dimensions have emerged that provide a richer picture and might help us in differentiating more sharply several distinct forms of organizational cognition. Four such dimensions look particularly useful to me.

Implicit/explicit   The notion of implicit knowledge matches quite closely with Polanyi's (1958) 'tacitness' issue. The cognitive literature has widely debated such issues in recent years, providing a precise characterization of implicitness and some empirical criteria for assessing it. I would like to report a concise but useful definition by Holyoak and Spellman (1993, p. 278): implicit knowledge is knowledge about covariations in the environment, learned by exposure to stimuli exhibiting the covariations, obtainable without attention or awareness, demonstrated by improved performance, but not fully verbalizable, and not fully manipulable, in the sense that it cannot be re-represented explicitly to serve as input to other procedures. (Holyoak and Spellman also review some assessment criteria derivable from such a definition.)

Distributed/local The local/distributed distinction has been closely related to the emergence of the debate on connectionism. A 'distributed' representation is one in which there is no single place where a concept or a pattern is stored and there is no explicit symbol for representing it, but instead representations arise from the joint activation of multiple elements (typically neurons). In a social context, the notion of distributed knowledge can be extended to the idea that a given routine has no place where it is represented (e.g. there is no explicit rule, stored in some record, fully describing it) and no one participant could entirely describe it, since the routine arises from the interactions among only partly overlapping, incomplete and inarticulate (possibly non-symbolic) individual knowledges (coordination in a team can easily have this character). Weick's discussion of the concept of 'mutual equivalence structures' suggests the distributed nature of knowledge embedded in most basic forms of stable organizational interaction (Weick, 1979, pp. 98–103).

Situated/context independent The idea that social knowledge can be not only distributed among individuals but also distributed among individuals and their environment brings us to the notion of situatedness: knowledge which is tightly coupled to a specific context, because such context acts as external memory and information processor. Research in cognitive anthropology has suggested that many 'routinized' competences can be of the situated kind (Suchman, 1987; Lave, 1988; Hutchins, 1995). This point was also made in Nelson and Winter (1983), where they argued that knowledge stored in human memories is effective only in some organizational context. It typically includes a variety of forms of external memory—files, message boards, manuals, computer memories, magnetic tapes—secondly, the context includes the physical state of equipment and of the work environment generally; finally, the context of information possessed by an individual member is established by the information possessed by all other members (Nelson and Winter, 1983, p. 105). However, I think the implications of such an assumption still have to be fully drawn in evolutionary theories of the firm (see the discussions of the role of artifacts in the following section).

Knowledge intensive/search intensive Any cognitive system experiences a trade-off between using search or stored knowledge as a basis for its actions (Newell, 1990). Newell also labels this as the preparation/deliberation trade-off. He points out that 'each situation leading to a response calls for some mix of deliberation and preparation' (Newell, 1990, p. 102), showing how a particular system can be located as points in the immediate knowledge (preparation)/search (deliberation) space. A long tradition in the bounded rationality literature discusses these issues in the organizational context (March and Simon, 1958, is still the basic reference). It still seems to me to provide useful distinctions. In particular, March and Simon suggest that search can also be routinized to a greater or lesser degree, implying that the preparation/deliberation distinction applies also within the boundary of routines rather than defining routines themselves.

Most of these dimensions are already present in the Nelson and Winter chapter on organizational routines; however, they seem to assume implicitly that such dimensions are highly correlated. But this appears to be a quite strong assumption: there is no reason to imagine that a routine lies on the left side of each axis. For example, there are routines that imply highly implicit forms of knowledge, but rely on shared rather than distributed knowledge. Search-intensive activities can rely on implicit rules of search while knowledge-intensive behaviors may rely on explicit standard operating procedures. Thus we can gain a richer description and useful distinctions by trying to plot our observations on those multiple axes.

Also the 'grain size' issue is strongly affected by how we plot actual patterns of action along those dimensions. For example, the definition of 'meta-routines' as routines that use routines as inputs to be processed would conflict with the assumption that implicitness (or tacitness) is a fundamental feature of routines; it is hard to imagine how implicit or distributed rules could be used as inputs of other rules—and in fact cognitive psychology suggests that only explicit, locally represented rules can be processed by higher-level rules (see the above cited definition by Holyoak and Spellman).

L.M.   Just a small point (strictly related to my earlier one) on the relation of routines to learning. One possible view is to consider routines as the 'fixed point' of a learning process. To make it a little extreme, this view would oppose non-routine behavior (the dynamic path) to routine behavior (the 'equilibrium'). Another view (more 'imperialist') would contend that at the beginning there were routines which get modified, selected, discarded in the learning process (itself driven by 'learning routines') and give rise to other routines. I certainly tend to be sympathetic with the latter view, as the former seems to have a lot in common with some neoclassical approaches to learning.

B.C. and G.D.   A crucial step when trying to bridge the evidence from cognitive psychology with organizational routines involves an explicit account of the double nature of routines, both as problem-solving action patterns and as mechanisms of governance and control. The issue is discussed in Coriat and Dosi (1994) with reference to the emergence of Tayloristic and Fordist routines in modern corporations. In brief, what we argue is that the painstaking establishment of a new set of routines (say those associated with Taylorism) involved both a different social distribution of knowledge but also a different distribution of power and control among individuals and social groups. And abundant witness of all that is the record of social conflict which accompanied the diffusion of such routines. There is a general issue here which pertains to the very nature and function of organizations. A good point of departure is March and Simon's (1993, p. 2) definition of organizations as 'systems of coordinated actions among individuals and groups whose preferences, informations, interests and knowledge differ. Organization theories describe the delicate conversion of conflict into cooperation.' In a similar fashion, Nelson and Winter (1982), after having defined routines also as truces among conflicting interests, proceed by emphasizing that: 'here we recognize the divergence of interests among organizations' and that 'for some purposes it is important, for some essential, to recognize the conflict of interest contained in and reflected by organizational behaviors'. The analysis of the purely cognitive aspect of organizational routines misses the point that they emerge and operate in a universe of (at least potential) conflict and diverging interests. Relatedly, one would like to see also experiments that are set in ways which account for both dimensions (e.g. a modified Cohen–Bacdayan–Egidi experiment involving distributional problems). Note also that the conflict-of-interest dimension is likely to be particularly important when analyzing the emergence of organizational routines (as opposed to their steady-state characteristics).

Moreover, it might not be totally irrelevant to revisit, in the new light of our discussion, older experiments which had a much stronger behavioristic flavor (see Milgram, 1974, on obedience to authority). And finally, see the interpretation of the nature of routines by Postrel and Rumelt (1991) who argue that they have a fundamental function of 'impulsiveness control'. One might not fully agree with such a quasi-Pavlovian view, but they certainly hint at the *lato sensu* political dimension of routines.

In this respect, one could analyze as a sort of extreme archetype the nature of routines in such organizations as armies (where one is likely to find a significantly different balance between their cognitive and their political contents as compared to, for instance, research teams). The general point here is that most organizational routines also involve the legitimation of an asymmetric distribution of power. Hence, together with the cognitive aspect of routines and their characteristics of truces, it is worth exploring their domination elements, whereby, paraphrasing Max Weber, the content of the command becomes a natural and automatic response of 'ruled' agents (Weber, 1968; Kemp, 1993; Dosi, 1995).

We are not experts in experimental design, but we think that a better understanding of how the political relations among actors shape cognitive and behavioral patterns should be high on the agenda.

G.D.   The issue of automaticity somewhat overlaps with the perspective from which we look at routines, i.e. do we consider them in their 'steady-state' form or from the point of view of origin? As to the former, I am convinced that varying degrees of automaticity are an intrinsic feature of routines (maybe one of their evolutionary values). Conversely, it might be more difficult to identify invariant patterns in the process of discovery/development of routines. In Dosi and Egidi (1991) we suggested that the problem-solving process is essentially an 'intelligent' search whose success yields the discovery of robust rules that can be quasi-idiotically applied thereafter. Note that if this holds, the same action might be a routine for someone and involve a highly deliberative activity for someone else. So a good deal of what we apparently see as 'expert knowledge' (cf. Lane *et al.*, 1995) might in fact be the outcome of highly routinized and automatic rules of evaluation and decision which we simply do not understand, not being experts ourselves.

6. How Can Evolution Be Seen in Relation to Action Patterns?

The meeting participants agreed that evolutionary accounts usually exploit a dualism of representation and expression. In the biological instance this occurs as the alternating roles of genotype and phenotype, in which a genome stores the pattern-guidance needed to reproduce its (evaluatable) phenotypic expression, and modifications of the genetic representation are the source of evolvable variation.

In the setting of human action patterns rather than organisms, the location and nature of the representations that guide enactment are not so sharp as the DNA on which so much current biology is focused. Nonetheless, it seems to make sense to distinguish representations (such as learned, skilled responses of machinists) from the action patterns (say, machine assembly steps) that occur when those representations are expressed.

*Some felt this distinction deserved considerable stress and saw representations as something to study in addition to the actions they might generate. (This was heartening for those interested in longitudinal field studies, where past expressions are not observable, but some historically preserved representations may be.) Others, while acknowledging the distinction, found it of lesser priority, preferring to focus on the observable form of the actions as expressed. (This is more consonant with 'ethnographic' field observation.)

There was agreement that selection forces in this setting are quite various, beginning with reduction of cognitive burdens on actors, but also including many other powerful organizational forces (e.g. issues of control, status, economic cost, shared mental models and general cultural context). Also selection operates at multiple levels, both within firms and in markets where individual firms are born, grow and die.

*There was contention over the relative research priority to be given to cognitive aspects of selection. Some see them as dominant factors, others as important along with many others or as varying in importance across situations.

Commentary on Evolution, Representation and Expression

R.B. For an evolutionary analogy to be applied to something called 'routines', a distinction must be preserved between units which are selected and behavior produced by these units which results in their selection. Mere action patterns are not enough, since their focus on description becomes only a restatement of the behavior by which an organization succeeds or fails. Evolution on a biological model assumes that the behavior of an organization, including any capacity to adapt, is constrained by elements that limit the range of actions and responses it can make. When behavior is controlled by such elements, change occurs either by change and reconfiguration of the elements themselves, or by selection (continuation, growth or collapse) of the organization that contains them.

The evolutionary analogy to organizations will always be relatively weak, since creation, diffusion and configuration of behavior-producing routines occurs on a continuous basis throughout an organization's lifetime rather than the fixed inheritance by which an organism lives or dies. Additionally, deliberate design and replication of structures to control and generate behavior is at least attempted by many organizations. Nevertheless, an evolutionary perspective would seem required to temper any presumed influence of rational and deliberate factors.

The challenge is to identify the various forms in which capacities of action (including decision-making) become embedded in organizations, to remain relatively inaccessible or impervious to change and thus a basis only for replication and selection. These forms may or may not resemble anything conventionally regarded as representations, but they may still be regarded as kinds of genetic units on which evolution proceeds. Cognitive learning is certainly one leading candidate for such lock-in of behavior, but patterns of learning and responsibility distributed across an organization, together with explicit policies and procedures, physical artifacts and arrangements, and social and political factors, can all be expected to play significant roles.

M.C.   The distinction between representations of routines and their realization strongly appealed to me. Among a number of nice features, an especially appealing one is that it offers an insight into the difference between routines and standard operating procedures (SOPs). These terms are often used interchangeably, but the distinction makes it natural to consider SOPs as one kind of representation, a formalized statement of what actions should occur. This separates SOPs from the actions occurring as routines are expressed in context. That is desirable since there is so much literature showing that real behavior diverges substantially from formalized SOPs. Indeed, 'working to rule' has proven an effective labor tactic for bringing an organization to a halt.

M.W.   The representation–expression dualism points to a key ambiguity in the DNA metaphor in Nelson and Winter's book: at which level do routines belong? If one takes the behavioral-level characterization of routines, which is implicit in Nelson and Winter, routines clearly belong to the expression-side. This has a profound implication: what is often reproduced is not the routine itself, but some kind of 'coded knowledge' which usually implies a mix of linguistic representation, rules and artifacts (although 'apprenticeship' processes may directly replicate the routine itself through forms of learning by examples—see, e.g., Lave and Wenger, 1991).

Consider two concrete examples:

'Best practice' diffusion has been a major focus of recent organizational management. In a way, it is built on the assumption that actual work experience generates successful routines to be reproduced and diffused—thus it seems to reinforce the 'routine' view. But if one looks at the actual reproduction process of such successful routines, one invariably finds a large effort to set up a 'technology of replication' that usually implies (i) learning a language within which to code successful routines; (ii) creating cognitive artifacts that can be diffused (through flowcharts and other replicable representations); (iii) translating the high-level description contained in the cognitive artifact in actual practice, generating a new routine adapted to the new context (see Hutchins and Hazelhurst, 1991, for a similar conceptualization of learning in the cultural evolution process). The awareness of this reproduction cycle is well expressed in the fact that managers mostly invest their attention in the 'techniques and tools for replication' rather than in actual routines to be replicated, although they know that what finally generates value is the routine (the expression) rather than the code (the representation).

*This is even more apparent in *'business process re-engineering'* (BPR), which in evolutionary terms might be thought of as a sort of organizational genetic engineering. In the BPR case, existing routines are used as materials to be manipulated mainly through deletion and recombination of their elementary components. Again, in order to make possible such manipulation, one has to code the routine in cognitive artifacts (e.g. work-flow graphs) amenable to engineering. Manipulation then happens at the representation level, and finally its outcomes are 'brought back to the field' generating new expressions (routines).

These examples point to the complexities of the process of reproducing patterns of actions, and to its inherent cultural nature, relying on our ability to code experience, to communicate it and to decode it in ways that may adapt it to new contexts.

G.D. In a paper that will appear in *Industrial and Corporate Change,* Benedicte Reynaud distinguishes between rules-to-be-interpreted and (interpreted) rules-to-be-executed. The distinction seems quite similar to the dichotomy between formally stated SOPs and actual behavioral patterns. Indeed, I totally agree that the relation between the two levels, however defined, is a promising area of investigation. However, I would not go as far as drawing an analogy with the genotypical–phenotypical distinction in biology. First, I am not convinced that representations are equivalent to some genotypical level. I would find it at least equally plausible to think of actual action/behavioral patterns as the genotypes, which reproduce via apprenticeship, and acculturation mechanisms within organizations, and imperfect imitation across organizations. Relatedly, it is not implausible to think of representations as sorts of imperfect and mostly *ex post* rationalizations of what has been done, should be done, one wished ought to be done.

Secondly, I would suggest a strong 'Lamarckian' interpretation of the coupled dynamics between behavioral patterns and their interpretation without any *a priori* hypothesis on the relative speed of change (how many times do new CEOs redefine SOPs just to find that people continue to do the same things renamed in different ways?).

G.D. and L.M. We note also that in the two examples suggested above by M.W.—the way we interpret them—it is quite clear that the objects of replication are routines themselves. However, the distinctive features of these examples of replication is that in the social domain there is no straightforward equivalence to sex, mitosis, etc. Therefore—unlike the biological models—we search for coding procedures which might indeed be more transient and conditional on particular contexts than so-called 'expressions' themselves.

7. *How Can Simulation Contribute to Better Theory in this Area?*

A significant recent development in computer science is the bifurcation of the artificial intelligence (AI) community into subschools, sometimes labeled 'symbolic' and 'behavioral'. Papers by Brooks (1991 a, b) and Maes (1993) give the flavor of the behavioral approach. It is strongly connected to robotics, to models of intelligence that can be instantiated in systems that take real actions in a messy real world. It assigns much of the responsibility for keeping track of details about the (changing) world to the world itself, rather than to an elaborate internal model of the world maintained by the software. Performance occurs as a modest number of simple rules interact with each other via their effects on the system's environment.

R.B. suggested that a number of the features of the 'behavioral' movement in AI were strongly consonant with some aspects of research on routine. For example, work on routine often sees artifacts and spatial arrangements as forming an essential part of the organizational memory from which the routine performance is drawn. It is argued that some organizational routines may have a distributed, implicit quality, so that it is not possible to find an account of the whole routine—or even an awareness that there is a routine—located in any one document or in any one person's head.

The discussion of simulation modeling echoed important dimensions of the discussion of cognitive aspects of routine. In simulation too there is a question of finding an appropriate blend or balance among tacit and deliberate elements. There was an extended discussion of efforts to model the learning of routine action patterns seen in the experiments conducted by Egidi (1994) and by Cohen and Bacdayan (1994). L.M. and M.C. both reported that it was possible to build simple systems of condition—action rules, such as Holland's (1995) classifier systems, that would reproduce a substantial portion of the actual moves made by subjects. However, they both agreed that it was very difficult to build a system that would learn such a set of rules with an amount of experience similar to the amount subjects have in the course of the experiment. (Reasonable competence is achieved after about ten hands of the card game task, of the order of 30 moves by each player.)

L.M. called the group's attention to work by Riolo (1990) on introducing foresight ('lookahead') into classifier systems. It is possible that such a capability would speed the learning process considerably. Bringing in lookahead gives a model elements of response to both experienced past and expected future. This seems similar to observations that show routines to contain both tacit and consciously deliberative elements.

Lookahead lends itself to a learning dynamic driven by 'surprise'—deviation of outcomes from expectations. This is increasingly an important factor in models of animal learning (Walker, 1987), and it is significant that Samuel's checker player, one of the greatest achievements of machine modeling of learning, is also driven by surprise. In the Samuel model, as in the experimental data, learning occurs on each action step, not just when a large-scale episode, such as a full game, ends in success or failure.

M.C. pointed out that the experimental task (a card game) was chosen because it drew on substantial knowledge that all subjects could be presumed to have. Times required for computer models to learn are often measured based on random initial knowledge. This is 'unfair' to the models. But once one begins to put knowledge into the models there are delicate problems of what to put in, and questions about how to assess the quality of the model's learning. The stable behavior at the end of learning by experimental subjects is relatively homogeneous and easy to model, but the important learning has occurred. However, the transient behavior of early stages of subject learning contains many 'mistakes' and false paths, and it would be very hard to get a model to reproduce such sequences accurately.

The discussion of simulation was broken off reluctantly with the shared observation that simulation of (systems of) routines could itself be the topic of a valuable conference. Beyond the issues mentioned above, several other themes were raised during the discussion:

1. Efforts to simulate routines of groups (as in the experimental card game task) suggest that the requirements of coordinating the actions taken by individuals place severe restrictions on how complex individual roles can be within a larger system. It is important to develop simulation tools that allow deeper explorations of such issues.

2. There is variation in what builders of models take as their fundamental objective: to model a routine in its 'steady state', for which a hand-crafted system of rules often suffices; or to model the learning process by which the steady state emerged, which clearly requires a commitment to some learning mechanisms of the individuals or an adaptive process acting on the relations among the individuals. The former approach is generally more manageable than the latter, and correspondingly less satisfying. (Steady-state systems of rules tend to be brittle in the face of variation, while the routine functioning they model tends to be fairly robust.)

3. Much of the interest in routines centers on what happens as systems of actors learn action patterns. However, there are a confusing variety of methods available for modeling individual learning. G.D. argued strongly for work on the classification of these alternatives into 'types',

with better understanding of the consequences for a modeling exercise of using one type or another.

4. Handling of time has been a serious deficiency of much previous simulation of organizational action. Many reported phenomena would be unlikely to remain if time were modeled in another, equally plausible way (Huberman and Glance, 1993). [For example, Conway's famous 'Game of Life' exhibits almost no interesting structure if updating of cell states is not perfectly synchronous (S. Page, unpublished).]

5. Theoretical development will be accelerated if it becomes easier to compare simulation models with each other (Axtell *et al.*, 1995), and if there are more opportunities for reuse of computer code—which will itself facilitate comparison.

Thus a computing architecture that would facilitate comparison and reuse could be of considerable value to the field. The SWARM system (Langton *et al.*, 1995) appears in demonstrations of early versions to offer many of these needed advantages. If SWARM does not prove sufficient, it might be valuable for a team of organizational researchers to devote themselves to creating another framework that would adequately facilitate the required comparison and sharing.

Commentary on Simulation

L.M.   I would mention here a very stimulating idea which is coming from simulation work: the approach which considers organizational routines as emergent properties of the interaction of distributed learning and adaptation processes. This also casts some light on the distributed nature of organizational routines (an aspect on which perhaps we didn't insist enough). (And see related comment on 'cognition' above.)

G.D.   We did not have much time to discuss in detail the relative values and limitations of modeling instruments and styles. Here are some relevant questions:

(i) Models of learning by artificial agents have been using a variety of techniques (neural nets, genetic algorithms, genetic programming, classifier systems, etc.). Is there any theoretical reason to choose one or the other? Under what circumstance do they yield similar results?

(ii) This leads to a more general question of the status of simulation models. I believe none of us is naive enough to think that our models represent how the mind or the organization actually works. But then one faces what we call in Dosi *et al.* (1995) 'weak isomorphism': under which conditions can we say that learning patterns in the model capture something isomorphic to learning individuals and organizations? Are we happy just with the fact that we are able to represent some mechanism of mutation and recombination among elementary cognitive and behavioral traits? And what about the way learning is driven in most models? More generally, thinking of our discussion on simulation models, I have a persistent feeling of an underlying epistemological ambiguity. Is the 'artificial reality' of our models understood as a sort of analog to experiments and empirical investigations? I really hope this is not so: simulation models (as well as economists' theorems) are ways of producing coherent and non-intuitive conjectures, but are a far cry from validating the conjectures themselves.

(iii) A direction of future enquiry that I consider promising is to build highly constructive models *à la* Fontana and Buss (1995) and thus begin to account for the endogenous emergence of higher-level entities.

B.C. and G.D.   It follows from our earlier comments on the 'double nature' of routines that we consider it urgent to model an explicit co-evolutionary origin of routines, i.e. to model evolutionary processes nested in multiple selection environments. For instance, think of action/behavioral patterns that evolve as driven by both their problem-solving coordination features and, at the same time, by the conflict among agents over who controls what. If we were able to do that, then we would also be able to compare the ensuing action patterns with those emerging in a 'pure problem-solving coordination mode' (such as in the current Cohen–Bacdayan–Egidi experiment) and, at the opposite end, those emerging in a 'pure adversarial no-problem solving mode' (in the spirit of prisoner's dilemma type adaptive learning; cf. Lindgren, 1992).

M.W.   A greater psychological accuracy of models of individual learning we employ for simulating organizational processes is of course highly desirable. However, in my view there are other directions in which substantial progress is at least as much needed.

Direct versus vicarious learning   Most models of machine learning of the kind exploited in organizational simulation are basically models of direct, experiential learning. However, a substantial part of the rate of progress in any social system is related to processes of diffusion of knowledge, which imply vicarious learning, or the ability to acquire knowledge from other people's experience (March *et al.*, 1991). Incorporating explicitly vicarious learning and diffusion mechanisms in our simulations might generate significant returns. In a pioneering paper, Hutchins and Hazlehurst (1991) have suggested some basic kinds of learning that a model of such a process needs to include: (i) direct learning of an environmental regularity; (ii) mediated learning about an environmental regularity from the structure of artifactual descriptions of it; and (iii) learning a language that will permit a mapping (in both directions) between the structure of the natural regularity and the structure of the artifactual description of it. I would add to that list that, in organizational contexts, some attention needs to be devoted to how structural features constrain or bias the way individual experience is diffused; organizational learning sometimes implies evolving those structural aspects, giving rise to a sort of 'architectural learning' [see Henderson (1992) on organizational structures, the 'architectural knowledge' they embody and organizational learning processes].

Learning at the organizational level   How well do machine learning models represent organizational versus individual level processes of learning? For example, one might argue that 'genetically inspired' models like genetic algorithms or genetic programming may leverage on processes which have little psychological plausibility at the individual level, but can be adapted to better match some organizational level dynamics [e.g. Cohen (1981) advances important remarks on organizational systems as 'parallel heuristics']. Furthermore, it would be desirable to model learning processes occurring simultaneously both at the individual and at the organizational level—a kind of multiple-level, nested dynamics for which the SWARM system seems to provide promising modeling tools.

Learning and evolution   Finally, understanding interactions between learning and evolution should be a primary concern for an evolutionary theory of the firm which claims that learning plays a fundamental role in shaping organizational life. There have been important advances in simulating, these processes in the field of artificial life (e.g. Ackley and Littinan, 1991; Parisi and Nolfi, 1995). These developments significantly parallel the rising interest within organization theory in complementarities between learning and selection (Levinthal, 1990), although much more structure should be put into the relationships among learning entities to provide significant insight in organizational matters. Again, the SWARM system may prove useful in supporting such efforts to simulate interactions between learning and evolution in organizational contexts, thanks to its ability to manage simultaneously dynamics occurring at different levels and with different timescales.

8. *What Are Examples of Various Approaches to Empirical Research that Reveal Key Problems or Results?*

We explored, more briefly than we had hoped, the fit between alternative empirical styles and the various substantive concerns. Among the observational methods reviewed were experiments, ethnographic field studies, longitudinal empirical studies and statistical/econometric approaches.

Discussion of experiments occupied considerable attention, probably for the simple reason that several experimentalists were present. To say the least, they were not a representative sample of all students of organizational routine. However, they were able to contribute especially detailed example material based on controlled multiple observations, and this rare asset was useful to the discussions.

There was general agreement that experiments can show gross evidence for routinization very clearly, and can provide data that support 'micro-genetic' analysis (Siegler and Crowley, 1991). This observation incorporates a distinction offered by Massimo Warglien, between the detailed content of an actual routine, which may be hard to measure, and the overall level of 'routineness' in the action, for which one may be able to construct workable indicators.

Explaining in detail the exact routines that emerge for a particular experimental work group can be very hard, however. This is so even when one has the advantages of extremely detailed data on actions and exact knowledge of the task environment. Still, it has been possible to define broad indicators of routinized action and measure their presence.

With respect to field studies, there is a possibility of exploiting this same distinction, looking for indicators of routineness, rather than—or along with—documenting actual contents of routines. Learning curve studies (Argote and Epple, 1990) provide a good example of evidence at the level of routinization without detailing the contents of the underlying routines. Others might include: implicit versus explicit representation of task requirements; methods of teaching skills to new members (formal schooling versus apprenticeship; Orr, 1990); and amounts of attention available for analysis of other, more novel tasks.

A further observation on field studies of the content of routine—not new, but very telling to those who have done it—was that data collection was very expensive, and progress requires 'an army of ethnographers'. The work generates richly suggestive results, and accumulation of such accounts, as in anthropology, provides essential grist for theory development. But the 'costs' of observations are also at the extraordinarily high levels typical of anthropology.

Thus while field observation will always be of major value, the high costs there suggest that some efforts should go into other approaches. An alternative is what were called longitudinal empirical studies: work on routine elements of action in an organization over years—or even decades—of existence. Here the research method is not direct observation, but rather reconstruction from the organization's written and oral histories, and perhaps from preserved artifacts such as products or machines. Thus in microelectronic firms, different devices may embody the same design competence, and they are usually classified in a same 'process family' despite being destined for very different usages. Therefore by tracking the rise and fall of such process families, one can learn a lot about the diffusion of specific design competences.

Finally, there is an approach that tries to extract evidence for routines, or other recurring patterns, via statistical analysis. Examples would include work on typical rates of mark-up or R&D investment, characterized by industries and eras (beginning with Cyert and March, 1963).

Commentary on Observation

M.C.   Video data from field sites presents many interesting possibilities for research on routine. At the moment, it is very time-consuming to analyze, but technical improvements relying on computers are beginning to emerge. (Suchman and Trigg, 1991; Carnegie-Mellon automatic segmentation project, http://www.informedia.cs.cmu.edu/), and the accumulation of video data sets will eventually offer possibilities for secondary and comparative analysis of field observations, which will be a major advance in our research options.

M.W.   Two remarks on 'routineness' and longitudinal studies:
On 'routineness': an advantage of measuring routineness rather than the actual routinized behaviors is that it puts less stringent constraints on our modeling strategies when trying to simulate learning processes. While machine-learning models can be poor in reproducing observed learned behaviors, many of them generate patterns of routinization that can decently match experimental or field observations (such as aggregate learning curves). In many cases, this can be enough for reasonable accuracy to be reached when the actual behavior is less relevant than its impact on organizational performance.

On 'longitudinal studies': a merit of longitudinal analysis carried over decades is not only that it sometimes avoids ethnographic costs (although it raises dramatically the costs of archival research), but also that it allows us to look at evolutionary dynamics (which are by their nature long-term ones) in ways that more accurate but shorter-term ethnographic studies would not allow. In particular, longitudinal studies may allow us to go through serious econometric (or econobiometric?) analysis and explore long-term patterns of innovation and diffusion of organizational replicators. If evolutionary theories of the firm want to take up the challenge of the population ecology of organizations, this seems to me an unavoidable step. Then the usefulness of the representation approach to categorizing suggested in the evolution section becomes apparent. Patterns of action and their diffusion are hardly trackable and measurable over long-term horizons, while at least some kind of representations are usually recorded in organizational archives. They may not tell us all the story about routines, but like fossil evidence, they supply important cues for understanding organizational evolution (especially if we can provide an understanding of the role of such elements in the cycle of the reproduction of patterns of action). This point is further reinforced if we embrace the point of view that representations (like artifacts), rather than expressions, are what actually get reproduced in organizational processes—in this case, representations might be not just a convenient substitute for closer observations of actual behaviors, but rather a more appropriate object of observation.

9. How Might 'Routine' Be Defined?

An agreed-upon definition was not seen as essential to progress in the meeting. However, considering a proposal did clarify many dimensions of variation in the group, and the result may be useful. The discussion produced some striking agreement along with the sharpest disagreements of the workshop.

The proposal discussed was R.B.'s. As amended from the floor, and after minor rearrangement in preparing this note, it was:

> A routine is an executable *capability* for repeated performance in some *context* that has been *learned* by an organization in response to *selective pressures.*

The terms emphasized are the key 'slots' of the definition. Any researcher using it would have to bring it into closer contact with a specific problem of observation or theory by giving more specialized accounts of the key terms. In its general form it runs a slight risk of including too many things, but it does have the virtue of showing how both a manufacturing competence and a computer program could be thought of together as routines. Each of the slots is discussed below, giving some expanded sense of its intended meaning and examples of how it could be specialized.

A *capability* was characterized as the capacity to generate action, to guide or direct an unfolding action sequence, that has been stored in some localized or distributed form (e.g. the ability of a group of factory workers to assemble an engine, of laboratory technicians to recognize cancerous cells, or of a computer package to return a Fourier analysis of a data stream).

Execution was conceived as possible only in some *context* within which action accomplishes some transformation. Context was seen as a powerful form of 'external memory' or representation of portions of the routine (e.g. the arrangement of tools and machines on a factory floor), and as a source of necessary inputs to actions. It provides the natural locus of attention for lines of research focused on the role of artifacts.

The characterization of routine as *learned* was noted to imply possibilities— but not certainty—of the tacitness and automaticity which have hallmarks of routine in many empirical studies. The term is used broadly to cover any of a wide variety of processes that could alter the probabilities of future enactments of the capability (e.g. individual actors in a team might be learning motor skills necessary for a particular team performance, learning might be occurring at the organizational level via changes in personnel or in training practices that change skill mix, improved computer programs might be generated by adaptive tuning methods). As with the other slots, the breadth of the term 'learning' means that a researcher must be guided by the trial definition to provide a more specific account.

Selective pressures is a broad term meant to indicate a wide variety of forces that could operate to make action sequences more or less likely (e.g. see above.) *This was one point of major divergence in the conversations, with some arguing that cognitive loads should receive clear priority as the forces most responsible for change and/or stability, while others argued for equal significance of many other factors such as personal incentives, status concerns or organizational culture.

Another difficulty noted for this term is the absence, in the organizational case, of a population of directly competing action sequences that might be expected by analogy to the biological case.

Some further notes on the definitional debate:

The proposed definition endorsed a view of learning and routine as very tightly coupled to each other, and hence excluded one-off performances from the category. This seemed to be generally accepted.

The proposal also acknowledged the duality of representation and expression, in an effort to situate routine in an evolutionary view of change. There was greater debate about this. *Attention to representations was seen by some as leading to research difficulties while others saw it as a welcome research opportunity. The closely related concern over distinguishing action from behavior was clearly evoked in discussing the proposal. Those advocating a 'behavioral' research focus again saw dangers in bringing intent into a central role and felt it increased ambiguity of observations, while proponents of the action-not-just-behavior line argued that an action viewpoint was needed to reduce ambiguity.

Winter contributed what he called his 'radical' view that achieving maximum tightness in key definitions may sometimes inhibit progress.

Commentary on Definition

M.C.   Looking at our discussion of ambiguity of observations and of action versus behavior, one might speculate that in research ambiguity of observation is conserved. What we debate is which rug to sweep it under.

Acknowledgements

This paper originally appeared as IIASA (International Institute for Applied Systems Analysis) Working Paper WPM-96-25 (March 1996) and SFI (Santa Fe Institute) Working Paper (November 1995). It presents the report of a working group meeting held under the joint sponsorship of IIASA and SFI in Santa Fe, New Mexico, on August 10–13, 1995.

Appendix. Accountants and Termites—A Longer Comment by Massimo Egidi

One of the issues raised during the SFI meeting was how to analyze the most relevant properties of routinized behaviors. While there is a largely dissonant use of the magic word 'routine' and other related keywords in different disciplines—economics, theory of organization, AI—and this creates confusion, I feel it useful to elaborate a small lexicon of synonyms and opposites. What follows is a reconsidered report of what I tried to say in Santa Fe, plus the lexicon.

Routine as a Set of Rules

Within the theory of computation, tradition considers 'routines' to be synonymous with 'programs', i.e. a list of instructions in a (artificial) language. Turing wrote his celebrated article on 'Computable Numbers', proposing his computing machine, in the same year (1936) in which Alonzo Church was completing his work on lambda calculus, and it soon became clear that the two systems were equivalent.

Since these two progenitors, Turing machines and lambda calculus, a large variety of mathematical representations of 'computing machines' have been proposed: URM machines, post systems, production systems, etc. All of them have been proved equivalent to a Turing machine.

Therefore a consolidated tradition exists which considers routines to be computable programs, which can be represented by a set of condition–action rules (i.e. production systems) or an equivalent computing device. It is obvious that in the social sciences strong resistance can arise against the notion of humans involved in a routinized activity as pure automata executing a set of condition–action rules: nobody likes being compared to a Pavlovian dog. However, before looking at the differences between the behavior of machines and men, I want to emphasize that this idea was implicit in Turing's scientific program, and imbued mathematical culture at the beginning of the

20th century, when the Hilbert program was dominant—and Hilbert's idea was, in fact, to mechanize all mathematical propositions via an axiomatic method in order to be able mechanically to decide the 'truth' or 'falsity' of any given proposition.

Turing's approach is implicitly based on a project to construct 'thinking machines' able to substitute for humans in their fundamental mental abilities. I propose to see to what extent this idea can be used to explain the features of human decisions and behaviors within organizations, my aim being to discover some of the desirable features of the notion of routine in organizational and economic contexts.

Let me start by reversing the Turing approach, i.e. by considering an experiment where men imitate the behavior of a Turing machine: many individuals execute mechanically a list of instructions, following the orders of some authority which coordinates their actions to realize a given task. Since the execution of the same list of instructions can be repeated many times, when the appropriate conditions arise, if individuals mechanically follow the instructions, the same sequence of behaviors will arise corresponding to the same set of conditions.

Therefore, an external observer would describe the team's behavior as 'routinized', because he observes that the same set of actions is performed in response to the same conditions.

One point to clarify is that when we observe a team of workers performing a task in a routinized way, we observe a set of coordinated actions repeatedly realized over time by the team, but do not directly observe motivations and rules. This distinction is crucial, even beyond our experiment of imitation. We follow the displacement of a set of rule-based behaviors as a dynamic process over time, at the immediate observational level: at this level, routinized behaviors can be interpreted in various ways, by referring to different models of human action. I will minimally assume that behaviors are the consequence of mental models and more stringently (but provisionally) that routinized behaviors are the outcome of the execution of a set of condition–action rules, stored in individuals' long-term memories. Is this purely a caricature of human behavior or does some family tie exist between the mathematical approach and real routinized human behaviors?

Observational Levels

Before answering this question, some preliminary problems relate to the observability and refutability of the mental models we assume. If we suppose individuals to be capable of forming an internal mental representation of the situation, based on symbols and their manipulation, we can find experiments to confirm or refute our approach not only at the behavioral level but also—and largely—at the level of mental models, with a sophisticated use of the methods of experimental psychology.

I emphasize that this level—interiorization of rules, memorization, etc.—is not unobservable. The problems in classical expected utility theory began when, with the experiments of Maurice Allais, and later of Kahneman and Tversky, it became possible directly to confirm or refute a large number of propositions claimed by the theory. The same holds for the empirical analysis of other mental activities involved in human behavior, like reasoning, problem solving, etc. Therefore, the more the methods of experimental psychology advance, the easier it is to verify on empirical grounds whether routinized behaviors in the real world are or are not rule-based, and more generally to what extent individuals act on the basis of an internal model of the world.

Cohen and Bacdayan's experimental model permits a large array of sophisticated stastistical methods to be used to conduct analysis either at the behavioral or at the mental level: it is in fact possible to examine the sequences of collective actions over time (behavioral level) or to operate at the level of subjective beliefs, models and expectations of the players.

Rules and Routinized Behaviors

If we assume as a starting point that routinized behaviors can be rule-based, we must carefully distinguish between the sequence of collective actions realized over time, and the set of rules which generate this sequence when applied by a team of individuals. It is quite a common habit to call the set of actions or behaviors 'routine', therefore confusing the two levels of analysis. Following the computational tradition we should consider 'routines' the algorithms (the set of rules) and 'routinized behaviors' the sequence of actions generated by the realization of the rules. But this is a purely nominal assumption, which I am ready to abandon provided that a different definition will preserve distinction between the two levels. Anyway, to avoid confusion in the following discussion I will not use the term 'routine' in the context of human behaviors and mental models, reserving for this term the usual meaning of theory of computation and referring only to routinized behaviors in order to indicate complex, collective, repetitive patterns of action. Let me clarify some further elements of the vocabulary used.

1. A 'rule'—here used with the limited meaning of condition—action rule—is a relationship which allows individuals to trigger an action when a condition is realized; the triggering can be automatic, like a stimulus–response mechanism, or deliberate and conscious.

2. In a dynamic process of coordination among many individuals, at any time the system configuration is composed by the events of the external environment plus the actors' behaviors. This configuration is the background from which 'conditions' emerge and are recognized by the actors. Once again the recognition of a condition may be automatic, like a stimulus–response mechanism, or deliberate and conscious.

3. Domain of applicability of condition–action rules—one important point is that in computation theory the set of rules is supposed to cover all contingencies, i.e. all the possible conditions with which individuals will have to cope.

4. A further point is that rules are defined a-temporally, i.e. they prescribe the action to be triggered in relation to a condition (or a set of conditions) which is defined independently of a specific date and of the system's configuration. This is a quite complex argument which relates to the 'compressibility' and 'representability' of knowledge and information, and I shall deal with the question only briefly: observe that a set of condition–action rules which compose a program must be completely specified if we want a machine to be able to execute it. This means that every configuration that the system can exhibit must match a 'condition' in the machine's list of rules. The same applies to fully routinized actors. In consequence, identifying an appropriate set of rules is a matter of high intelligence, because it requires one to 'reduce' all the complex features of the process to a few, essential traits which are described in the condition–action set. The possibility of reducing the system's features to few essential rules is not given in advance, but depends upon the nature of the problem involved. Chess is a good example, because it shows very modest compressibility: a winning strategy, which exists, cannot be represented with a reasonably limited number of rules. I suggest Chaitin's (1995) theory of complexity as a starting point for serious exploration of this issue.

The Problem of Identical Action

I have pointed out that at the most elementary level of observation, routinization is recognized by the observer when the 'same sequence of behaviors' corresponds to the 'same environmental conditions'; therefore the obvious problem is to define to what extent a sequence of behaviors can be defined as 'the same'. This question involves very subtle epistemological issues which I cannot raise here. I shall limit my discussion to pointing out that most of the problems involved are soluble if we accept the idea of rule-based actions: if we can prove that individuals use the same set of condition–action rules during their activity (by a protocol analysis, for example), then we can identify the routinized behaviors as 'the same', even though we observe behavioral variations over time. The same set of rules can in fact generate 'similar' blocks of actions if some of the conditions are 'similar' but not equal.

In Cohen and Bacdayan's game (1994) this aspect is quite clear: assume that each player adopts a stable set of rules, compatible with the rules adopted by the other, and applicable to every valid game configuration. In different runs, when players must find a card which is essential to achieve the solution, even if they apply the same set of rules, they can perform sequences of actions which may be quite different, depending upon the distribution of the covered cards. In this case I would not hesitate to consider the routinized behavior as the same, because all the reasonable elements of an 'identical action' are satisfied: the behaviors over time are partially different, but the generating mechanism is the same. As a counter-proof, examine what would happen if two Turing machines played the game: the sequence of actions would differ accordingly to the distribution of the covered cards, even though the machines were executing the same search algorithm.

What Happens in Real Organizations and with Men Instead of Machines?

I now turn to the original question, i.e. exploration of the differences between the behaviors of men and machines in the realization of a repetitive task.

1. When the actors are men, the rules that any individual adopts are quasi-exhaustive, i.e. they cover a large part of the possible contingencies but not necessarily all of them. Therefore a set of rules does not prescribe the action to be executed for every condition which may arise during the collective process.

    'Action' and 'condition' are terms which normally refer to a class of possible actions or conditions, e.g. the action 'Search for the two of hearts' can be realized in many different ways, i.e. refers to a class of possible actions. To realize the condition–action a machine must have a detailed search procedure, i.e. a fully exhaustive set of condition–actions to execute the program: therefore an executable machine program must recursively contain sub-procedures until all possible contingencies are covered.

    Quite different is the situation involving individuals, who normally do not memorize all the specific and detailed set of rules, because they are able to re-create parts of them in many different ways. Therefore we must accept that a micro-learning activity is normally at work, and consider situations in which an individual's activity is fully routinized, i.e. covers all possible contingencies with a memorized set of rules, as an extreme case. In these extreme situations behaviors are fully mechanized, and the learning process is inactive.

2. Call 'coordination rules' the rules which embody mutual relationships, i.e. prescribe actions which are compatible with the actions performed by the partners. Coordination rules are largely internalized by individuals, who do not need detailed and specific orders to realize the coordinated task. If an unexpected condition arises, there follows either a conflict among rules or the lack of rules, and coordination fails. A machine cannot work in these conditions, while the human reaction is typically to find a solution, i.e. start learning and exploring in the space of rules.

3. This suggests that a fully routinized activity is possible, or at least more likely to happen, when tasks are performed by isolated individuals. In coordination processes, in fact, purely routinized behaviors would require taking into account the reaction to the other's actions, including errors and conflicts, which require deliberation and learning: interactions are normally exponentially increasing with the number of participants. Therefore, to be covered by automatic rules, individuals would have to memorize an incredibly large number of rules—a situation very similar to chess. This aspect of the problem suggests that it is most likely that one will observe a purely automatized behavior—to which can correspond an automatized thinking (Weisberg, 1980)—at the level of isolated individual action, while this is quite rare and unstable in a widely coordinated action context.

4. Purely routinized collective behaviors are rather difficult to realize because, to cover any possible contingency, they require a huge set of rules governing the interactions among actors: this is the equivalent of complete markets with rational expectations in general equilibrium theory.

To activate a huge, possibly hierarchical set of rules, a large set of conditions must be recognized, and a great deal of information used and processed. Therefore, a complex activity of computation is required, which is difficult to reduce to an automatic execution of rules. I claim that there are limits to the complexity of the set of rules that can be activated by boundedly rational actors. Beyond this threshold, reasoning cannot be substituted for by purely automatic behavior. Chess seems exactly to configure situations where the threshold is surpassed and players cannot reduce their activities to the execution of a set of condition–action rules.

Routinized Behaviors

For the four reasons above I consider still unsurpassed the definition of routinized behaviors provided by March and Simon, i.e.

> We will regard a set of activities as routinized, [then,] to the degree that choice has been simplified by the development of a fixed response to defined stimuli. If search has been eliminated, but a choice remains in the form of clearly defined and systematic computing routine, we will say that the activities are routinized. (March and Simon, 1958, p. 142)

Here computing routine is used—I believe—in the meaning given to it by the theory of computation, as synonymous with the Turing machine or Turing algorithm. Following March and Simon, I shall use the term 'routinized behaviors' to mean behaviors which emerge as rule-based actions. As the psychological literature has emphasized, these behaviors are based on 'routinized thinking', which allows individuals to save on mental efforts; an experimental way to verify whether thinking is automatized is to check if subjects are able to perform some complex mental activity, like problem solving, while they are executing a different, repetitive task. The studies on the mechanization of thinking, the so called 'Einstellung effect', have a long tradition in psychology (Luchins, 1942; Luchins and Luchins, 1950; Weisberg, 1980).

If we take into account the observations on points 1–4, the above definition seems to fit accurately with most of the features assumed in Nelson and Winter's description of routines: automaticity, triggering of actions, complexity.

The features which seem not to be grasped by March and Simon's definition—with the previous remarks—are tacitness and awareness.

Awareness, Division of Knowledge, Repair of Patterns of Behaviors

Can behaviors be considered routinized independently of the degree of awareness of the individuals and irrespective of the level of tacitness of the knowledge involved? To frame the problem better, let us consider an extreme case of organizational shape, a top-down hierarchical organization whose members execute orders in a deliberate, conscious way. I assume a hierarchical, authority-guided, centrally designed activity such as were, historically, the accountants' offices in large business institutions and banks before the advent of the computer era. The everyday activity performed by large teams of accountants involved a huge computing and accounting activity, mostly deliberate. Moreover, the accounting process itself was the outcome of a deliberate design realized by a team of experts.

Can we avoid considering this process—where highly repetitive tasks were performed by the same team of employees in the same way everyday—as an example of routinized behavior? If we consider unawareness as a crucial feature of routinized behaviors, we should be tempted to say: no. The accounting process seems to be a perfectly deliberate, goal-oriented activity, realized by individuals clearly conscious of the goals they have to achieve and the means they use. The means are essentially the mathematical and financial algorithms created by 'experts' (from Pythagoras and Euclid to the most advanced financial mathematics of the time) which they carefully applied.

I subscribe to this opinion, and suggest that even this kind of activity cannot be reduced to a perfectly deliberate and conscious execution of instructions. The recursive character of knowledge suggests we be very prudent with the words 'awareness', and 'consciousness': in fact accountants—as all humans—are able to dominate mentally only a limited area of the knowledge, even of the specific knowledge required to perform their regular everyday task.

To be persuaded, think of some basic algorithms used by the accountants: counting, summing and multiplying. They use these algorithms to compute, but they have to know only the domain of applicability of the algorithm and the rules of application—which is a minimal and very bounded part of the involved knowledge. It is easy to show some elementary cases of these limitations. For example, everybody knows how to sum two numbers, but a very restricted number of persons know why the rules which compose the summing algorithm work, if there are different algorithms to sum, etc. In the event of a sudden global catastrophe, the surviving accountants presumably would not be able to reconstruct the theory underlying the mathematical algorithms they use in their everyday life (see various stories by Isaac Asimov). Individuals directly involved in a routinized activity may not be able to repair the pattern of cooperation to which they adapt if an eventual failure happens at a very deep level; a larger set of individuals, involved in the relevant knowledge, must intervene. This is the outcome of a characteristic feature of knowledge: its partial separability or 'orthogonality'. Part of knowledge can be used in a perfectly independent way from other parts which are indirectly involved, i.e. in terms of a problem-solving approach, there exist sub-spaces of problems which are orthogonal and independently solvable.

Therefore, even in the world of deliberate actions, where a symbolic representation is developed and a common language established, knowledge is never fully transparent to the limited minds of a single individual. In consequence, we have to admit the incomplete character of knowledge involved in the so-called 'deliberate' activities.

Perfect deliberativeness cannot exist and human behaviors are based on incomplete knowledge and partially opaque deliberations: this is also the reason for the cognitive delegation which characterizes the division of knowledge, and the origin of the conjectural and incomplete character of top-down hierarchical planning.

Now consider briefly the situation at the opposite extreme of the accountant example, i.e. assume that it is possible that a routinized pattern of behavior arises even if a common language does not exist, and individuals have an opaque internal representation of the problem. Here we move from accountants to forms of organizations where a 'conscious social mind', to cite Hayek, does not exist. Individuals act in a completely automatized way, as in a termite nest. But assume that Mister Brown, a worker who every day accomplishes his routinized work, this morning has a bad headache, does not respond 'normally' to some stimuli or does not recognize correctly the familiar patterns, and consequently does not trigger the correct action: a problem of mis-coordination arises, because Brown introduces a noise in the system. Does there exist a set of rules, memorized by all the workers, to solve this kind of problem? It is easy to understand that this can happen only to a limited extent, otherwise we ought to admit that there are no limits to human memory.

In general, the situation of conflicting goals, incompleteness in decisions, errors in responding to familiar conditions, etc., stimulates the onset of the learning process. Therefore, in the two extreme situations of purely deliberate and purely tacit systems of cooperation, learning is the fundamental force which stabilizes cooperation.

Limitations

Let me suggest the most important limitations in the above discussion.

1. Routinized behaviors can emerge in a huge set of different social contexts either at the individual or at the collective level. Even if we are mainly concerned with economic organizations, we cannot avoid recognizing that highly routinized behaviors in games, warfare, soccer, etc., are a widespread phenomenon. What seems to me common to all these situations is the existence of a challenging or conflicting environment in which coordination is required among a large number of individuals. I suggest that routinization can happen in many different ways, among which are the following: (i) an active search for a set of rules to coordinate a collective action; (ii) a passive adaptation to orders and rules issued by an external authority; (iii) a process of interiorization with a low level of comprehension, as happens in imitation and in the internalization of norms. For this reason it is reasonable to consider, as in the title of our meeting, 'other patterns of action' beyond behaviors which are cognitively routinized.

2. One of the most interesting features of routinized behaviors is their iner-
    tia, local stability and sub-optimality. The last property, emphasized by
    Nelson and Winter, allows us to go beyond the Chicago school approach
    (the optimality of an organization's behavior arises from selection), and
    to consider the possibility that economic institutions can remain in
    highly sub-optimal configurations for a long time without being able to
    establish new innovative internal rules. Innovation can therefore be
    better framed in its real difficulties and obstacles.

Local stability is a largely unexplored feature. To say that observed routinized behaviors are stable means that the rules governing behaviors do not
change: this is a symptom that a localized learning process does not lead to
the discovery of a new, more efficient set of rules. I have emphasized this cognitive explanation of the persistence of a set of rules within an organization.
But, recalling again March and Simon's book (1958, p. 215), let me suggest
that an equally relevant source of persistence (inertia) is that rules can be the
outcome of a locally solved conflict of interests. A set of rules governing an
organization can be stable because, as I have emphasized above, the team
involved does not discover new, more efficient rules. But also because of the
reallocative effects involved in the change of rules: any change would re-create
new internal conflicts that could not be easily solved. Consequently, even if
our discussion has been based on the cognitive aspect of rule-based behaviors,
I suggest that an important challenge for future research is to gain a better
understanding of the links between the cognitive and the conflictual forces
which give rise to the persistence of rules. From this viewpoint rules can be
to some extent considered social norms, and the internalization of norms
should be considered as one of most important sources of persistence.

Final Remarks

Turning to the problem of 'routine' definition, I consider fully satisfactory the
March and Simon definition of 'routinized behaviors' based upon mental
activity–inactivity. The exclusion of a psychological micro-foundation would
have the effect of excluding any chance to confirm experimentally our
assumptions on bounded rationality, tacitness and awareness: I would stress
that Polanyi's analysis of tacit knowledge (1958) and Hayek's theory of
knowledge incompleteness (1952) are deeply rooted in a theory of human
mind and of learning processes. Moreover, without experiments at the level
of mental models it would be impossible to decide which of the two explanation of behaviors—the rule-based approach and the opposite explanation
based on global optimality and rational expectations—can be confirmed.

The bounded rationality hypothesis and March and Simon's definition of routinized behaviors imply in my view the epistemological position that we must inevitably refer to experiments on human psychology in order to confirm our models and explain behaviors.

Everybody can agree that there are many possible models of mental activity. But whatever model we assume, routinized behaviors should, I believe, be based on the absence or the reduction of active thinking, i.e. on the emergence, in the mental activity involved, of automatization and tacitness: this is a question which involves not only economic but also political behavior. [See Hirschman's (1984) distinction between 'wanton' and 'non-wanton' choices.]

To conclude, we can decide to use the magic word 'routine' as a synonym for 'pattern of recurring routinized behaviors' as some of us suggested—and in this case the use of the word 'routine' as synonym for 'procedure' or 'program' should be excluded. Or, conversely, we can assume 'routine' to be synonymous with procedure, i.e. a set of rules which generates the repetitive behaviors: this is a purely nominal question.

My position rests on the idea that what matters is not how to use the magic word 'routine', but how to give a better framing and understanding of the process of routinization. As I suggested, even though we limit ourselves to the analysis of routinization as a cognitive process, many properties have to be explored to understand better the rise and modification of the rules governing economic organizations.

References

Ackley, D. and M. Littman (1991), 'Interactions between Learning and Evolution,' in C. Langton *et al.* (eds), *Artificial Life II.* Addison-Wesley: Reading, MA.

Allais, M. (1953), 'Le comportement de l' homme rationel devant le risque: Critique del postulats et axiomes de l'Ecole Americaine,' *Econometrica,* 21, 503–546.

Argote, L. and D. Epple (1990), 'Learning Curves in Manufacturing,' *Science,* 247, 920–924.

Axtell, R., R. Axelord, J. Epstein, and M. Cohen (1995), 'Aligning Simulation Models: A Case Study and Results,' Working Paper 95-07-065, Santa Fe Institute (*Journal of Computational and Mathematical Organization Theory,* in press).

Brooks, R. A. (1991a), 'New Approaches to Robotics,' *Science,* 253, 1227–1232.

Brooks, R. A. (1991b), 'Intelligence without Reason,' AI memo no. 1293. MIT Artificial Intelligence Laboratory: Cambridge, MA.

Bruner, J. S. and L. Postman (1949), 'On the Perception of Incongruity: A Paradigm,' *Journal of Personality,* XVIII, 206–223.

Chaitin, G. J. (1995), 'The Berry Paradox,' *Complexity,* 1(1), 23–30.

Church, A. (1936), 'An Unsolvable Problem of Elementary Number Theory,' *American Journal of Mathematics,* 58, 345–363.

Cohen, M. D. (1981), 'The Power of Parallel Thinking,' *Journal of Economic Behavior and Organization,* 2, 285–386.

Cohen, M. D. and P. Bacdayan (1994), 'Organizational Routines Are Stored as Procedural Memory: Evidence from a Laboratory Study,' *Organization Science,* 5(4), 554–568.

Coriat, B. and G. Dosi (1994), 'Learning How to Govern and Learning How to Solve Problems. On the Co-evolution of Competences, Conflicts and Organizational Routines,' IIASA working paper, Laxenburg, Austria.

Cyert, R. M. and J. G. March (1963, 1992), *A Behavioral Theory of the Firm,* 2nd edn. Blackwell: Cambridge, MA.

Dosi, G. (1984), *Technical Change and Industrial Transformation.* St Martin's Press: New York.

Dosi, G. (1995), 'Hierarchies, Markets and Power: Some Foundational Issues on the Nature of Contemporary Economic Organizations,' *Industrial and Corporate Change,* 4, 1–9.

Dosi, G. and M. Egidi (1991), 'Substantive and Procedural Rationality. An Exploration of Economic Behavior under Uncertainty,' *Journal of Evolutionary Economics.*

Dosi, G. L., Marengo, A. Bassanini and M. Valente (1995), 'Norms as Emergent Properties of Adaptive Learning,' IIASA working paper, Laxenburg, Austria.

Egidi, M. (1994), 'Routines, Hierarchies of Problems, Procedural Behavior: Some Evidence from Experiments,' IIASA working paper WP-94-58 July. In K. Arrow *et al.* (eds), *The Rational Foundations of Economic Behavior,* Macmillan (in press).

Fontana, W. and L. Buss (1994), 'The Arrival of the Fittest: Toward a Theory of Biological Organization,' *Bulletin of Mathematical Biology,* 1–64.

Hayek, F. A. (1952), *The Sensory Order. An Inquiry into the Foundations of Theoretical Psychology.* Routledge and Kegan Paul: London.

Henderson, R. M. (1992), 'Technological Change and the Management of Architectural Knowledge,' in T. A. Kochan, and M. Useem (eds), *Transforming Organizations,* pp. 118–131. Oxford University Press: Oxford.

Hirschman, A. O. (1984), 'Against Parsimony: Three Easy ways of Complicating Some Categories of Economic Discourse,' *Bulletin of the American Academy of Arts and Science.*

Holland, J. H. (1995), *Hidden Order: How Adaptation Builds Complexity.* Addison-Wesley: Reading, MA.

Holyoak, K. J. and B. A. Spellman (1993), 'Thinking,' *Annual Review of Psychology,* 44, 265–315.

Huberman, B. and N. Glance (1993), 'Evolutionary Games and Computer Simulations,' *Proceedings of the National Academy of Science USA,* 90, 7716–7718.

Hutchins, E. (1995), *Cognition in the Wild.* MIT Press: Cambridge, MA.

Hutchins, E. and B. Hazelhurst (1990), 'Learning in the Cultural Process,' in C. G. Langton *et al.* (eds), *Artificial Life II: Studies in the Sciences of Complexity.* Addison-Wesley: Reading MA.

Kahoeman, D. and A. Tversky (1986), 'Rational Choice and the Framing of Decisions,' in R. M. Hogart M. W. Reder (eds), *Rational Choice—The Contrast Between Economics and Psychology.* The University of Chicago Press: Chicago.

Kemp, D. A. (1993), 'Authority and Public Policy,' in R. Radner (ed.), *An Heretical Heir of the Enlightenment: Politics, Policy and Science in the Work of Charles E. Lindblom.* Westview Press: Boulder, CO.

Kuhn, T. (1962), *The Structure of Scientific Revolutions.* Chicago: Chicago University Press.

Lakoff, G. (1987), *Women, Fire and Dangerous Things: What Categories Reveal about the Mind.* Chicago University Press: Chicago.

Lane, A., F. Malerba, R. Maxfield and L. Orsinigo (1996), 'Choice and Action,' *Journal of Evolutionary Economics* (in press).

Langton, C., N. Minar and R. Burkhart (1995), 'The SWARM Simulation System: A Tool for Studying Complex Systems,' Draft working paper, Santa Fe Institute, http://www.santafe.edu/projects/swarm/swarmdoc/swarmdoc.html.

Langton, C. G. *et al.* (eds) (1992), *Artificial Life II.* Addison-Wesley: Reading, MA.

Lave, J. (1988), *Cognition in Practice.* Cambridge University Press: Cambridge.

Lave, J. and E. Wenger (1991), *Situated Learning.* Cambridge University Press: Cambridge.

Levinthal, D. (1990), 'Organizational Adaptation and Environmental Selection—Interrelated Processes of Change,' *Organization Science,* 2, 140–145.

Lindgren, R. (1992), 'Evolutionary Phenomena in Simple Dynamics of Prisoner Dilemma,' in C. G. Langton *et al.* (eds), *Artificial Life II.* Addison-Wesley: Reading, MA.

Luchins, A. S. (1942), 'Mechanization in Problem-Solving,' *Psychological Monograph,* 54, 1–95.

Luchins, A. S. and E. H. Luchins (1950), 'New EXPERIMENTAL Attempts in Preventing Mechanization in Problem-Solving,' *Journal of General Psychology,* 42, 279–291.

Maes, P. (1993), *Behavior-Based Artificial Intelligence: Proceedings of the 2nd Conference on Adaptive Behavior.* MIT Press: Cambridge, MA.

March, J. G. (1992), *A Primer on Decision-Making: How Decisions Happen.* The Free Press: New York.

March, J. G. and H. Simon (1958), *Organizations.* Wiley: New York; 2nd edn 1993, Blackwell: Oxford.

March, J. G., L. Sproull and M. Tanuz (1991), 'Learning from Samples of One or Fewer,' *Organization Science,* 2, 1–13.

Marengo, L. (1992), 'Coordination and Organizational Learning in the Firm,' *Journal of Evolutionary Economics,* 2, 313–326.

Milgram, S. (1974), *Obedience to Authority: An Experimental View.* Tavistock Institute: London.

Nelson, R. and S. Winter (1982), *An Evolutionary Theory of Economic Change.* Belknap Press: Cambridge, MA.

Newell, A. (1990), *Unified Theories of Cognition.* Harvard University Press: Cambridge, MA.

Orr, J. (1990), 'Sharing Knowledge, Celebrating Identity: War Stories and Community Memory in a Service Culture,' in D. S. Middleton and D. Edwards (eds), *Collective Remembering: Memory in Society.* Sage: Beverly Hills, CA.

Parisi, D. and S. Nolfi (1995), 'The Influence of Learning on Evolution,' in R. K. Belew and M. Mitchell (eds), *Adaptive Individuals in Evolving Populations: Models and Algorithms.* Addison-Wesley: Reading, MA.

Pentland, B. (1994), 'Reconceptualizing Routines: Grammatical Models of the Sequential Structure of Work Processes,' *Administrative Science Quarterly.*

Polanyi, M. (1958), *Personal Knowledge: Towards a Post-Critical Philosophy.* Routledge and Kegan Paul: London.

Postrel, S. and R. Rumelt (1991), 'Incentives, Routines and Self-command,' *Industrial and Corporate Change.*

Riolo, R. L. (1990), 'Lookahead Planning and Latent Learning in a Classifier System,' in J.-A. Meyer and S. Wilson (eds), *From Animals to Animals.* MIT Press: Cambridge, MA.

Samuel, A. L. (1959), 'Some Studies in Machine Learning Using the Game of Checkers,' *IBM Journal of Research and Development,* 3, 210–229.

Siegler, R. S. and K. Crowley (1991), 'The Microgenetic Method: A Direct Means for Studying Cognitive Development,' *American Psychologist,* 46, 606–620.

Simon, H. A. (1981), *The Sciences of the Artificial,* 2nd edn. MIT Press: Cambridge, MA.

Suchman, L. A. (1987), *Plans and Situated Action.* Cambridge University Press: Cambridge.

Suchman, L. A. and R. Trigg (1991), 'Understanding Practice: Video as a Medium for Reflection and Design,' in J. Greenbaum and M. Kyng (eds), *Design at Work: Cooperative Design of Computer Systems.* Erlbaum: Hillsdale, NJ.

Turing, A. M. (1936), 'On Computable Numbers, with an Application to the Entscheidungs-problem,' *Proceedings of the London Mathematical Society,* XLIII, 230–265.

Walker, S. (1987), *Animal Learning.* Routledge and Kegan Paul: New York.

Weber, M. (1968), *Economy and Society.* University of California Press: Berkeley.

Weick, K. (1979), *The Social Psychology of Organizing,* 2nd edn. Addison-Wesley: Reading, MA.

Weisberg, R. (1980), *Memory: Thought and Behavior.* Oxford University Press: New York.

Hierarchies, Markets and Power in the Economy: An Economic Perspective

OLIVER E. WILLIAMSON*

(University of California, Berkeley, California, USA)

This paper adopts the transaction cost economics perspective for purposes of examining hierarchies, markets, and power in the economy. Transaction cost economics works out of an economizing perspective in which markets and hierarchies are alternative modes of governance and the object is to ascertain which transactions go where and why. The role of power in this setup is strictly limited—partly because power tends to be myopic (transactions are not examined 'in their entirety') and partly because it is tautological. Power needs to be operationalized, whereupon the refutable implications that accrue to this perspective can be derived.

One of the leading purposes of the conference on 'Hierarchies, Markets and Power in the Economy' is to promote a broad interdisciplinary exchange. Because good interdisciplinary exchanges are hard to orchestrate, there ought to be a compelling reason. The reason here is simple: the role of hierarchies, markets and power in the economy cannot be understood adequately from the perspective of a single discipline. Given the participants, the papers, and the organization of the conference, I am confident that we will all have a better understanding of the issues when we leave.

Good interdisciplinary exchanges require that the participants talk with rather than by one another, which requires respect for several points of view. Focused perspectives—to include partisanship and even advocacy—nevertheless have a great deal to recommend them. For the purposes of this conference, I have been asked to provide a general introduction from an economic perspective (to include discussions of 'the nature and role of hierarchies in

* The author is Edgar F. Kaiser Professor of Business, Professor of Economics, and Professor of Law at the University of California, Berkeley. This article originally presented at the Conference on 'Hierarchies, Markets and Power', held at the Libero Instituto Universitario Cattaneo (LIUC), Castellanza, Italy, on 15–17 December 1994.

economic organization' and of 'the status and significance of 'power' and 'authority's and the way they relate to economic incentives').

Note that I have been asked to speak from an economic perspective rather than the economic perspective. That is felicitous, since there is not one single, unified economic perspective but many—neoclassical, behavioral, evolutionary, technological, agency theory, transaction cost economics and strategic/game theoretic perspectives being among them. Real differences notwithstanding, most of these adopt a 'rational spirit' and employ a 'systems approach' to the issues. That is where I begin the discussion, after which I shift to the more focused lens of transaction cost economics—which is, by construction, an interdisciplinary approach to economic organization in which law, economics and organization are joined.

The nature and role of hierarchies are briefly discussed in section 2. Power is the subject of section 3 and authority is treated in section 4. Concluding remarks follow.

1. *The Economic Perspective*

General

As described by Kenneth Arrow, 'An economist by training thinks of himself as the guardian of rationality, the ascriber of rationality to others, and the prescriber of rationality to the social world' (1974, p. 16). Taken in conjunction with the systems approach out of which economics works, this is a very powerful prescription.

To be sure, all of the social sciences have a stake in rationality analysis (Homans, 1958; Simon, 1978). What distinguishes economists is that they push the approach further and more persistently. As it turns out, that has been a productive exercise. Rationality is a deep and pervasive condition that manifests itself in many subtle ways (recall Adam Smith's reference to the 'invisible hand'). It has application to spontaneous and intentional governance alike, which is to say that it applies to organizations of all kinds—markets, hybrids, public and private bureaus. Yet rationality excesses—of which four kinds can be distinguished: oversimplification, maximization, natural selection and hyperrationality—are a chronic hazard.

It is elementary that what may be a fruitful simplification for some purposes can be an egregious oversimplification for others. Thus, although the theory of the firm-as-production function is a useful construction for examining a wide variety of price and output issues, it is not an all-purpose theory of the firm for purposes of ascertaining firm boundaries (the make-or-buy decision), the nature of the employment relation, the appropriate choice of financial instrument, corporate governance mechanisms, divisionalization and the like. To insist that the production function conception of the firm has universal application is to miss and/or misconstrue much of the relevant organizational action.

The general rational spirit approach is not, however, coterminous with orthodoxy. The response to those who would oversimplify is to insist that problems be addressed on whatever terms are most instructive. Theories of the firm (plural) rather than one, all-purpose theory of the firm (singular) is the appropriate way to proceed. The rational spirit approach does not preclude that there be several side-by-side alternatives out of which to work.

A second criticism of rationality analysis in economics is that many economists and fellow travellers assume that economic agents—consumers, investors, traders—are continuously engaged in maximization. Sometimes that is a poorly defined concept (Simon, 1978; Furubotn and Richter, 1991, pp. 26–28), in which event the exercise loses content; and sometimes maximization is justified not because it is realistic but because it is tractable.[1]

Relevant to this last is Herbert Simon's argument that 'Parsimony recommends that we prefer the postulate that men are reasonable to the postulate that they are supremely rational when either of the two assumptions will do our work of inference as well as the other' (Simon, 1978, p. 8). But while it is easy to agree that satisficing is a less demanding postulate than maximizing, the analytical toolbox out of which satisficing works is, as compared with maximizing apparatus, incomplete and very cumbersome. Thus if one reaches the same outcome through the satisficing postulate as through maximizing, and if the latter is much easier to implement, then economists can be thought of as analytical satisficers: they use a short-cut form of analysis that is simple to implement.[2] Albeit at the expense of realism in assumptions, and at the risk of overapplication, maximization often gets the job done.

The argument, moreover, that human agents lack the wits to maximize can sometimes be salvaged by invoking natural selection (Alchian, 1950; Friedman, 1953). That, however, is subject to the precaution that if selection 'is the basis for our belief in profit maximization, then we should postulate that basis itself and not the profit maximization which it implies in certain circumstances' (Koopmans, 1957, p. 141). Accordingly, we should 'expect profit maximization to be most clearly exhibited in industries where entry is easiest and where the struggle for survival is keenest' (Koopmans, 1957, p. 141).

---

[1] Milton Friedman describes the relevant trade-off as follows: 'The gains from greater accuracy . . . must . . . be balanced against the costs of achieving it' (1953, p. 17).

[2] Indeed, Simon has himself employed this approach (1976, p. 140).

The efficacy of selection remains controversial (Nelson and Winter, 1982; Barnett and Carroll, 1993) and early resolution does not appear to be in prospect. The following are nonetheless pertinent:

(i) selection pressures are manifold and subtle, especially within the economic domain, where selection operates at and through every contractual interface whatsoever—the most obvious being competition in final product markets and capital markers, but includes intermediate products markets and labor markets as well;

(ii) real differences between politics and economics notwithstanding, selection on efficiency operates within the political arena as well (Moe, 1990a, b; Stigler, 1992);

(iii) weak-form rather than strong-form selection often suffices, the distinction being that 'in a relative sense, the *fitter* survive, but there is no reason to suppose that they are *fittest* in any absolute sense' (Simon, 1983, p. 69; emphasis in original); and

(iv) selection reasoning is widespread throughout the social sciences (Simon, 1962; Hannan and Freeman, 1977, pp. 939–940;[3] Eccles and White, 1988, S24), which is to say that economics is not uniquely culpable.

The outer limits of hyperrationality reasoning are reached by the Arrow–Debreu model of comprehensive contracting, according to which contracts for all goods and services across all future contingencies are made between all agents at the outset. Although the Coase theorem, according to which the assignment of liability one way rather than another has no allocative efficiency consequences, is a partial rather than general equilibrium construction, it similarly assumes zero transaction costs (Coase, 1960). Analyses of both kinds make patently unrealistic assumptions about the cognitive ability of human actors to receive, store, retrieve and process information.

Counterfactuals are often illuminating, however, and there is no disputing that the fictions of comprehensive contracting/zero transaction costs have been productive. One instructive way to proceed is to use the counterfactual to display what an 'ideal' system would accomplish, thereafter to inquire into what factors are responsible for missing markers, in response to which non-market forms of organization often arise (Arrow, 1963), and where and why positive transaction costs arise, whereupon assignments of property rights one way rather than another do have efficiency consequences. Note, moreover, that the practice of looking ahead, discerning consequences, and factoring these back into the original organizational design does not require hyperrationality. 'Plausible farsightedness' (Williamson, 1993a, pp. 128–131) will often do—which invites economic organization.

[3] Hannan and Freeman take a weaker position in subsequent work (1989).

Systems Conception.   One of the advantages that Coase ascribes to economics, as compared with the other social sciences, is that economics works out of a systems conception of the issues (Coase, 1978, pp. 209–210):

> The success of economists in moving into the other social sciences is a sign that they possess certain advantages in handling the problems of those disciplines. One is, I believe, that they study the economic system as a unified interdependent system and, therefore, are more likely to uncover the basic interrelationships within a social system than is someone less accustomed to looking at the working of a system as a whole . . . [The] study of economics makes it difficult to ignore factors which are clearly important and which play a role in all social systems . . . An economist will not debate whether increased punishment will reduce crime; he will merely try to answer the question, by how much?

Thus even though such an approach may fail to relate to all of the pertinent issues and may even deflect attention from some, a systems conception of the issues often has a good deal to recommend it (Coase, 1978, p. 210).

Pertinent to this last is the question of what are the lessons for the other social sciences. One possibility is that, once the merits are displayed, other social scientists will undergo a conversion and adopt the farsighted contracting/systems approach out of which economics works. Were that to obtain, Coase projects that the advantage of economists in relation to practitioners of the 'contiguous disciplines' will accrue to those with deeper knowledge of the phenomena (Coase, 1978, p. 210; emphasis added):

> . . . if the main advantage which an economist brings to the other social sciences is *simply* a way of looking at the world, it is hard to believe, once the value of such economic wisdom is recognized, that it will not be acquired by some practitioners in other fields . . . [In that event] economists who try to work in the other social sciences will have lost their main advantage and will face competitors who know more about the subject matter than they do.

That, however, assumes that those social scientists who are persuaded of the merits of the systems conception out of which economics works will be able easily to internalize it.[4] Thomas Kuhn's remarks are pertinent (1970, p. 204):

> To translate a theory or world view into one's own language is not to make it one's own. For that one must go native, discover that one is thinking and working in, not simply translating out of, a language that was previously foreign . . . [Otherwise], like many who first encountered, say, relativity or quantum mechanics in their middle years, [a scholar] finds himself fully persuaded of the new view

---

[4] Although most noneconomists need to live with economics for a while before the approach becomes intuitive and congenital, a few undergo a mystical conversion. The latter are recognized as 'true believers'. They become missionaries and emphasize the endless powers of economics without regard or respect for its limitations.

... [yet is] unable to internalize it ... Intellectually such a [person] ... lacks the constellation of mental sets which future members of the community will acquire through education.

In the event that the systems approach out of which economics works is alien to many purveyors of the other social sciences, then economists and other social scientists will need to learn how to coexist with and complement one another.

Plainly, however, some noneconomists have accomplished the transition— March (1978), Coleman (1990), and the positive Political Theory movement being examples. Furthermore, some economists have invested heavily in the other social sciences—George Akerlof (1984), Jean Tirole (1986), and many of those associated with the New Institutional Economics movement being examples. Not everyone, moreover, needs to commit to research of a thoroughly interdisciplinary kind. Provided that specialists are respectful of what each side has to offer, fruitful exchange and collaboration are in prospect (Kreps, 1992).

Transaction Cost Economics

Transaction cost economics frequently invokes the fiction of zero transaction costs as a device by which to engage a systems view of a problem, thereby better to expose core issues. It immediately thereafter asks, however, wherein do positive transaction costs arise and why? Even more pertinent is to establish when and why differential transaction costs arise as between alternative modes of organization. The fiction of zero transaction costs is used thus as an entering wedge and is always and everywhere followed by an insistence on studying the world of positive transaction costs (Coase, 1984, 1992). The latter relieves excesses of hyperrationality and focuses attention on feasible organizational alternatives.

Note that whereas the fiction of zero transaction costs is thought mainly to apply to the study of property rights, the same fiction can be and has been used to examine organization. The result in both cases, moreover, is similar.

Within the property rights arena, the argument is this: the assignment of property rights has no allocative efficiency consequences because, in a world of zero transaction costs, the parties will bargain costlessly to an efficient solution whichever way property rights are assigned. The corresponding proposition in the organizations arena is that choice of governance structure is of no account—since any advantages that are ascribed to one form can be replicated costlessly by another (Williamson, 1979, p. 233; Hart, 1990, p. 156).

The 'real world', however, is beset by positive transaction costs—on which account the assignment of property rights and choice of governance structures do matter. Assuming that positive transaction costs are not so great as to block the assignment of property rights altogether (Demsetz, 1967; Arrow, 1969), then differential transaction costs will warrant the assignment of property rights one way rather than another. Similarly with respect to organization: except where positive transaction costs block the organization of some activities altogether, differential transaction costs will give rise to discriminating alignment—according to which some transactions will (for efficiency purposes) align with one set of governance structures and other transactions will align with others. Without more, however, this last is tautological. It needs to be operationalized, which describes the transaction cost economics project.

The general strategy out of which transaction cost economics works is set out elsewhere (Williamson, 1985, 1991a, 1993a). Crucial features include the following:

(i) the transaction is the basic unit of analysis;

(ii) the critical dimensions with respect to which transactions differ (for transaction cost purposes) are frequency, uncertainty and, especially, asset specificity (this last being a measure of asset redeployability);

(iii) each generic mode of governance (market, hybrid, private bureau, public bureau) is defined by a syndrome of attributes, whereupon each displays discrete structural differences of both cost and competence;

(iv) each generic mode of governance is supported by a distinctive form of contract law;

(v) predictive content turns on the argument that transactions, which differ in their attributes, are aligned with governance structures, which differ in their costs and competence, in a discriminating—mainly, transaction cost economizing—way;

(vi) additional predictive content obtains by treating the institutional environment (political and legal institutions, laws, customs, norms (North, 1991)) as the locus of shift parameters, changes in which induce changes in the costs (and, especially, in the comparative costs) of governance; and

(vii) transaction cost economics, always and everywhere, is an exercise in comparative institutional analysis—where the relevant comparisons are between feasible alternatives, whence hypothetical ideals are operationally irrelevant and the test for inefficiency is one of remediableness.

Transaction cost economics invites and has been the subject of considerable empirical testing (Joskow, 1988, 1991; Shelanski, 1991; Masten, 1993). Furthermore, it invites comparison with rival and complementary theories of organization in explanatory, predictive and empirical respects.

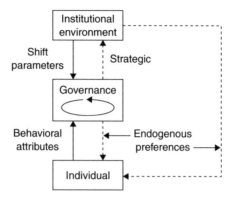

FIGURE 1. A layer schema.

The three-level schema out of which transaction cost economics works is set out in Figure 1. As shown, the institutions of governance (interfirm contracts, corporations, bureaus, nonprofits, etc.) are bracketed by the institutional environment from above and the individual from below. The main effects in this schema are shown by the solid arrows. Secondary effects are drawn as dashed arrows.

The institutional environment. The first of these main effects runs from the institutional environment of governance. Changes in the institutional environment (or, if making international comparisons, differences between institutional environments) are treated as shift parameters, changes (or differences) in which shift the comparative costs of markets, hybrids and hierarchies. Linking the institutional environment to the institutions of governance in this way is the source of numerous refutable implications (Williamson, 1991a). It furthermore permits transaction cost economics to relate more productively to recent research on comparative economic organization in which differences in the institutional environment are featured (Hamilton and Biggart, 1988).

Behavioral assumptions. The behavioral assumptions out of which transaction cost economics works are bounded rationality—behavior that is intendedly rational, but only limitedly so—and opportunism—which goes beyond simple self-interest seeking to make provision for self-interest seeking with guile. The import of this last is that the potentially adverse effects of simple self-interest seeking could be eliminated costlessly by asking the parties to make self-enforcing promises to behave 'responsibly' (in a joint profit maximizing way). That stratagem will not work if parties will renege on promises when it suits their purposes, in which event promises need to be buttressed with credible commitments.

Opportunism is a relatively unflattering behavioral assumption and many understandably prefer to describe self-interestedness in a more benign way—as, for example, 'frailties of motive and reason' (Simon, 1985, p. 303). Experience with the benign tradition in economics reveals, however, that such is fraught with hazard (Coase, 1964; Krueger, 1990; Williamson, 1991b). Robert Michels' concluding remarks about oligarchy are pertinent: 'nothing but a serene and frank examination of the oligarchical dangers of democracy will enable us to minimize these dangers' (1962, p. 370). If a serene and frank reference to opportunism alerts us to avoidable dangers which the more benign reference to frailties of motive and reason would not, then there are real hazards in adopting the more benevolent construction.

Ex post hazards of opportunism arise in a world of long-term, incomplete contracts implemented under uncertainty. Farsighted responses of several kinds can be distinguished. One would be to refuse to engage in such transactions (in favor of shorter and simpler transactions). A second would be to adjust the price of the complex transaction to reflect the added hazards. A third and deeper response would be to create *ex ante* safeguards (credible commitments), the effects of which are to mitigate opportunism. This last is to be contrasted with Machiavelli, who also subscribed to opportunism but viewed contracting myopically. Thus whereas Machiavelli advised his Prince to breach contracts with impunity—get them before they get us—transaction cost economics advises the Prince to devise (give and receive) credible commitments. Not only will the latter deter inefficient breach but it encourages investment in productive but otherwise risky assets and supports greater reliance on contract (as against no trade or vertical integration). Farsighted agents who give and receive credible commitments will thus outperform myopic agents who are grabby.

Organization has a life of its own. Organization theorists have long been alert to the existence of the subtle, unintended consequences that attend efforts to exercise control and have scolded economists and others who work out of a 'machine model' in which such effects are ignored (March and Simon, 1958, pp. 34–47). The arrow that turns back on itself in Figure 1 is intended to capture the proposition that organizations, like the law, have a life of their own. That is an important proposition and is ignored only at peril.

The existence of such effects demonstrates the need for deep knowledge about organizations, but it does not imply that the economic approach to organization (which easily misses such effects) is fatally flawed. To the contrary, the systems approach out of which economics works can and should make provision for all regularities whatsoever. Once apprised of predictable, recurring, unintended consequences, the informed economist will thereafter factor such effects into the *ex ante* design calculus. Unwanted costs will then be mitigated and unanticipated benefits will be enhanced—which approach tracks the earlier argument on dealing with opportunism exactly.

Because transaction cost economics is a more microanalytic contracting exercise and is more respectful of the discrete structural differences that define and distinguish alternative modes of organization than is economic ortho-doxy, transaction cost economics has helped to discern and explicate hitherto neglected contractual regularities. Among the more important of these are Fundamental Transformation and the impossibility of selective intervention.

The first of these explains when and why a large numbers bidding com-petition at the outset is transformed into a small numbers supply relation dur-ing contract execution and at contract renewal intervals. Such a transformation obtains for transactions that are supported by nontrivial durable investments in transaction-specific assets—which investments give rise to a condition of bilateral dependency (on which account identity matters and continuity of the exchange relation is the source of productive value). Classical market con-tracting—'sharp in by clear agreement; sharp out by clear performance' (Macneil, 1974, p. 738)—breaks down in these circumstances. The legal rules approach to contract thus gives way to the more elastic concept of contract as framework (Llewellyn, 1931; Macneil, 1978; Speidel, 1993).

The impossibility of selective intervention is the transaction cost economics answer to the query 'Why can't a large firm do everything that a collection of small firms can do and more?' Were it that a large firm could replicate small firm performance in all circumstances where small firms do well and intervene always but only where expected net gains from added coordination can be projected, then the large firm can always do as well as the collection of small firms (through replication) and will sometimes do better (through selective intervention). As it turns out, that is an impossible prescription because 'promises' to exercise dis-cretion only for good cause are not self-enforcing. That has several consequences, not the least of which is that incentives are unavoidably degraded when transac-tions are taken out of markets and organized internally. The upshot is that incentives and controls in firms and markets differ in discrete structural ways.

Other subtle (many of them intertemporal) consequences to which organ-ization theorists have been alerted and that can be subsumed within the sys-tems approach are:

(i) the Iron Law of Oligarchy;[5]
(ii) the successive build-up of identity/capability (codes, routines, culture/reputation);[6]

---

[5] See Michels (1962).
[6] See Polanyi (1962); Nelson and Winter (1982); Teece (1992); Kreps (1990).

(iii)   the benefits (such as information disclosure) that sometimes accrue to conflict;[7] and

(iv)   the intertemporal burdens of bureaucracy.[8]

The issues are discussed elsewhere (Williamson, 1993a, pp. 117–119). Suffice it to observe here that each of these effects takes on added significance when it is examined in a farsighted way—whereupon the ramifications of once unanticipated consequences are expressly introduced into the *ex ante* design calculus. Organization theory thus both informs and is informed by economics.

2. *The Nature and Role of Hierarchies*

The nature and role of hierarchies have been featured in transaction cost economics from the outset (Coase, 1937; Williamson, 1971, 1975; Alchian and Demsetz, 1972) and is an issue to which I return in section 4. My purpose here is to examine the alternative forms of hierarchy to which Masahiko Aoki (1990) recently has called to our attention.

Aoki distinguishes between the Western form of hierarchy (what he refers to as the *H*-form) and the Japanese form of hierarchy (the *J*-form). He also describes disturbances of three kinds: those that arise in stable, oligopolistic markets that produce standardized products; those that arise in markets where tastes change and/or demands shift rapidly; and those that involve novel technologies in which 'highly uncertain innovations involving new conceptualizations of market potential and highly specialized scientific approaches' are needed (Aoki, 1990, p. 9). Letting C_H and C_J be the cost of *H*-form and *J*-form respectively and letting $\Delta = C_J - C_H$, Aoki argues that Δ is positive for disturbances of types one and three, whereupon the *H*-form enjoys the advantage, but is negative for disturbances of type two, which is where the *J*-form excels (Aoki, 1990, pp. 3–9).

Aoki makes a plausible case for these assignments, but I would point out that (i) the comparisons refer strictly to equilibrium forms of organization; (ii) the comparison is strictly two-way (*J*-form versus *H*-form), which does not exhaust the possibilities; and (iii) type three disturbances are often associated with newly developing markets for which equilibrium concepts of organization are poorly suited. In consideration of all three, I suggest that a third form of organization, the *T*-form, where *T* denotes temporary or transitional, be considered.

---

[7] See Eccles and White (1988).
[8] See Williamson (1975, ch. 7; 1985, ch. 6).

T also denotes timeliness, which plays a huge role in the success and failure of firms that are operating in newly developing markets where technology and rivalry are undergoing rapid change. Change—being in the right place at the right time—is important in these circumstances, but it bears remark that firms that are flexibly positioned and quickly responsive have the edge. Large, mature and diffusely owned firms are at a disadvantage to smaller, younger and more entrepreneurial (concentrated ownership) firms in these circumstances (Williamson, 1975, pp. 196–207). Also, what may be thought of as 'disequilibrium' forms of organization can be important in real-time responsiveness respects.

Joint ventures and alliances should sometimes be thought of as *T*-forms of organization that permit the parties to remain players in a fast-moving environment. Each party being unable, by itself, to assemble and deploy the requisite resources in a timely way, the requisite resources are instead assembled by pooling. Thus construed, both successful and unsuccessful joint ventures will commonly be terminated when contracts expire. Successful joint ventures will be terminated because the combined effort has permitted each to remain viable and learn enough and/or buy time to go it alone. Unsuccessful joint ventures will be terminated because the opportunity to participate will have passed them by.

Our understanding of *T*-forms of organization is not good but is steadily improving (Nelson and Winter, 1982; Dosi, 1988; Teece, 1992; Barnett and Carroll, 1993; Teece *et al.*, 1993). Type three markets and *T*-form firms and associations require concerted study.

3. Power

Because *B* is bigger than *A, B* enjoys a power advantage in the exchange relation between them. Or because *A* is dependent on *B, B* has a power advantage over *A*. Or if *A* and *B* were initially on a parity, but a disturbance has occurred that works in *B*'s favor, then parity is upset and *B* now has more power.

Power is routinely invoked in these and other ways. Being a familiar condition, power is believed to be intuitively obvious and does not require explanation: 'Power may be tricky to define, but it is not that difficult to recognize' (Pfeffer, 1981, p. 3). I submit that there is less to power than meets the eye.

One of the problems with power is that it is a diffuse and vaguely defined concept. Within the commercial arena, the most ambitious effort to define power comes out of the 'barriers to entry' literature (Bain, 1956). That, however, is a deeply flawed exercise because differential efficiency and power are confused (Stigler, 1968). Recasting the issues in terms of strategic behavior discloses that power is a much narrower concept (Dixit, 1980; Williamson, 1983).

Most discussions of power never identify the critical dimensions on which power differentials work. Instead, it becomes an exercise in *ex post* rationalization: power is ascribed to that party which, after the fact, appears to enjoy the advantage. Related to this last is the propensity to examine power myopically. If *A* enjoys the advantage now and *B* enjoys the advantage then, and if *A* and *B* are in a continuing relation with each other, is it really useful to switch power assignments back and forth?

I argue that power has little to contribute to the study of contract and organization in circumstances where the parties to an exchange can and do contract in a relatively farsighted way. Since that varies with the circumstances, the argument is that power has relatively less to offer to the study of capital and intermediate product markets, has more bearing on labor and final product markets and is especially relevant to politics. Even with respect to this last, however, power plays a much more limited role than is widely believed.

The Problem of Tautology

Ronald Coase has defined a tautology as a concept that is 'clearly right' (1988, p. 19). In a world where confusion is the rule rather than the exception, important insights that help to unpack deep puzzles ought to be celebrated rather than disdained. There is nonetheless a grave problem with broad, elastic and plausible concepts—of which 'transaction cost' is one and 'power' is another—in that they lend themselves to *ex post* rationalization. Concepts that explain everything explain nothing.

The tautological status of transaction costs in the mid-1970s was described by Stanley Fischer as follows: 'Transaction costs have a well-deserved bad name as a theoretical device . . . [partly] because there is a suspicion that almost anything can be rationalized by invoking suitably specified transaction costs' (1977, p. 322, n. 5). There being too many degrees of freedom after the fact, the pressing need was to delimit the concept of transaction costs, thereby to give it operational (predictive) content before the fact.

John R. Commons (1934) took the first step by proposing that the transaction be made the basic unit of analysis. The question that then needed to be asked and answered was, 'What are the crucial dimensions with respect to which transactions differ?' Transaction cost economics began to overcome its tautological reputation only on asking and answering that question.

Power will not shed its tautological reputation[9] until a unit of analysis has been named and dimensionalized. Conceivably the transaction is the basic unit of analysis in the power arena as well. If so, that needs to be stated. Whatever the declared unit of analysis, the critical dimensions with respect to which that unit differs in power respects need to be identified. In addition, the analysis of power would benefit by adopting the farsighted systems view described above. Finally, power needs to develop the refutable implications that accrue to this perspective and demonstrate that the data line up.

Power and Efficiency

Efficiency plays a larger role in the degree to which parties are assumed to engage in contracting in a voluntary, relatively knowledgeable, and farsighted way. Voluntarism is widely disputed by sociologists (Baron and Hannan, 1994, p. 1116) and biases in decision processes—in dealing, for example, with low probability events (Kunreuther *et al.*, 1978), but to include probabilistic choice more generally (Tversky and Kahneman, 1984)—raise grave doubts about the competence of human actors to deal with complex events.

The opposites of voluntary, knowledgeable, farsighted contracting—namely, involuntary, uninformed and myopic contracting—are associated with power. Which description applies where and when? As developed below, power has less to contribute to the study of intermediate product markets and capital markets than it has to contribute to labor and final goods markets and to the study of politics.

Intermediate product markets. Resource dependency is one of the two dominant theories of organization (Friedland and Alford, 1991, p. 235), the other being population ecology. Resource dependency is very much a power perspective, the argument being that 'power' accrues to those social actors who provided critical resource for the organization and who cannot be readily replaced in that function' (Pfeffer, 1981, pp. 112–113).

Dependency, of course, is precisely the condition to which asset specificity refers. Given that all complex contracts are incomplete and that promises to behave continuously in a fully cooperative way are not self-enforcing, investments in transaction specific assets pose hazards. Resource dependency theory holds that the dependent party—which varies with the circumstances[10]—is

[9] James March concludes that 'Power has proven to be a disappointing concept. It tends to become a tautological label for the unexplained variance in a decision situation, or as a somewhat more political way of referring to differences in resources (endowments) in a system of bargaining and exchange' (1988, p. 6). This repeats an assessment that he had reached over 20 years earlier (March, 1988, pp. 148–149).

[10] Consider a buyer who purchases from a supplier who has made specific investments in support of the buyer's special needs. Suppose that demand falls significantly. The buyer says cut your prices or cancel the order. Given that the assets are nonredeployable, the dependent supplier slashes prices.

at the mercy of the other. Working, as it does, out of a myopic perspective, the theory holds that dependency is an unwanted and usually unanticipated condition. The recommended response to a condition of resource dependency is for unwitting victims to attempt, *ex post*, to reduce it.

Transaction cost economics regards dependency very differently because it works out of a farsighted rather than a myopic contracting perspective. Not only is dependency a foreseeable condition but, in the degree to which asset specificity is cost-effective, dependency is (i) deliberately incurred and (ii) supported with safeguards. Thus although less dependency is always better than more, *ceteris paribus*, deliberate recourse to asset specificity will be undertaken in the degree to which net benefits (due allowance having been made for safeguards) can be projected.

Pertinent to a net benefit assessment is whether the attendant hazards can be mitigated by crafting *ex ante* credible commitments (penalties, adaptive governance structures), the effect of which is to infuse confidence into trade. More generally, contract, under the transaction cost economics setup, is a triple in which price, asset specificity and contractual safeguards are all determined simultaneously. Safeguards, under this conception of contract, will progressively build up as asset specificity increases. In the limit, interfirm contracting will be supplanted by unified ownership (vertical integration). The evidence from the intermediate product markets is corroborative (Joskow, 1988; Shelanski, 1991).[11]

An interesting case in which the power versus efficiency perspectives collide is provided by contracting practices for gem-quality uncut diamonds. De Beers dominates this market (with an 80–85% market share) and is generally conceded to enjoy monopoly power. Such a condition would be expected to give rise to muscular contracting under a power perspective, and that appears to be borne out in practice. Thus Roy Kenney and Benjamin Klein describe contracting between the Central Selling Organization (CSO) of De Beers and 300 'invited' diamond traders and cutters as follows (1983, p. 502):

> Each of the CSO's customers periodically informs the CSO of the kinds and quantities of diamonds it wishes to purchase. The CSO then assembles a single box (or 'sight') of diamonds for the customer. Each box contains a number of folded,

But suppose instead that demand increases substantially. The buyer asks the supplier for more product. The supplier responds that this is very costly and that he will comply only if the buyer pays a large premium. The dependent buyer, who cannot obtain equivalent low cost product from unspecialized alternatives, pays. Dependency is evidently a variable (contingent) condition.

[11] Although resource dependency would also advise that safeguards should be created to get relief from dependency, that is strictly an *ex post* exercise. Because dependency is an unwanted condition, the main lesson is to avoid it in the future. Accordingly, parties will not renew dependent contracts when these expire and generic investments and spot contracts will be much more widespread under this perspective.

envelope-like packets called papers. The gems within each paper are similar and correspond to one of the CSO's classifications. The composition of any sight may differ slightly from that specified by the buyer because the supply of diamonds in each category is limited.

Once every five weeks, primarily at the CSO's offices in London, the diamond buyers are invited to inspect their sights. Each box is marked with the buyer's name and a price. A single box may carry a price of up to several million pounds. Each buyer examines his sight before deciding whether to buy. Each buyer may spend as long as he wishes examining his sight to see that each stone is graded correctly (that is, fits the description marked on each parcel). There is no nego-tiation over the price or composition of the sight. In rare cases where a buyer claims that a stone has been miscategorized by the CSO, and the sales staff agrees, the sight will be adjusted. If a buyer rejects the sight, he is offered no alternat-ive box. Rejection is extremely rare, however, because buyers who reject the dia-monds offered them are deleted from the list of invited customers.

Thus stones (a) are sorted by De Beers into imperfectly homogeneous cate-gories, (b) to be sold in preselected blocks, (c) to preselected buyers, (d) at non-negotiable prices, with (e) buyers' rejection of the sales offers leading to the withdrawal by De Beers of future invitations to purchase stones.

If this isn't muscle, what is?

Kenney and Klein, however, offer an efficiency interpretation. They observe (1983, p. 501) that gem-quality diamonds vary greatly in value, even after being sorted into more than 2000 categories (by shape, quality, color and weight). That being the case, there are private returns to searching through each diamond category to select the best stones. As this proceeds, the average value of the remaining stones will drop below the listed price. Picking-and-choosing thus has two costly consequences: oversearching and successive repricing. De Beers could respond by incurring added classification costs (e.g. sorting into 4000 categories), but it has responded instead by imposing a set of trading regularities. It assembles sights and offers these to invited buyers under all-or-none purchase rules and in-or-out trading terms.

The all-or-none purchase rule precludes buyers from picking-and-choosing individual diamonds. Being constrained to purchase the entire sight, it now makes sense to take a sample and ascertain whether the average value exceeds the asking price. The all-or-none purchase rule thus economizes on over-searching.

But what purposes are served by the in-or-out trading rule? Surely that smacks of muscle? Not necessarily. Although the all-or-none purchase rule reduces oversearching, picking-and-choosing has merely been moved from the level of individual stones to the level of sights. The purchase criterion becomes accept the sight if the estimated average value of the sample exceeds the per unit asking price, otherwise reject. De Beers is still, therefore, con-fronted with cherry picking.

What the in-or-out trading rule does is introduce an intertemporal dimension that further reduces search costs and brings reputation effects more effectively to bear. Given the in-or-out trading rule, a dealer who plans to be in business for a long time has an incentive to accept sights as presented, thereafter to ascertain in the marketplace whether he has received adequate value. The true valuation of a sight need not, therefore, be carefully determined through an *ex ante* assessment (oversearching) but is the automatic by-product of allowing the market to disclose value *ex post*. If sometimes De Beers is high and sometimes low, that will all work out.

If, however, a dealer is confronted with a series of sights in which the asking price exceeds realized value, then the presumption that De Beers is presenting fairly valued sights is placed in doubt. The next sight will therefore be carefully scrutinized and if it is refused sends a powerful signal that De Beers is not to be trusted. In a market where other dealers are knowledgeable and communication is good, that has powerful reputation effect ramifications (Kreps, 1990).

The combination of the all-or-none purchase rule with an in-or-out trading rule is thus to infuse greater credibility into a market that is otherwise fraught with high transaction costs. It is in the interests of the system that these costs be reduced.

Note that this efficiency interpretation takes initial conditions—namely, the De Beers monopoly—as given. Conceivably that is too passive, in that, as a matter of good public policy, the De Beers monopoly should be broken up. That, however, is another story (and may or may not be feasible). The confusion to be avoided is to assume that nonstandard practices at the contracting stage invariably magnify power disparities at the initial stage. That needs to be shown rather than assumed.[12] The details are where the action resides. These need to be explained in a coherent way.

Capital markets.   Samuel Bowles and Herbert Gintis contend that 'capital markets tend to penalize non-hierarchical enterprise structures' (1993, p. 93) and aver that 'Capital markets concentrate power because rational lenders prefer to transact with organizations with undemocratic political structures quite independently of their administrative structure' (1993, p. 94). By contrast, I argue that the only preference to which capital reliably relates is that of seeking high (risk adjusted) returns. According to the latter view, undemocratic political structures are relevant only as these have a bearing on contractual hazards. Holding the investment project constant, capital will be priced on

---

[12] Yet another example in which power and efficiency explanations collide is over the interpretation of franchising restraints—where size asymmetries between franchisor and franchisees are commonly great. For a discussion, see Klein (1980) and Williamson (1985, pp. 181–182).

better terms for those political structures to which lower hazards are projected, *ceteris paribus*.

The Bowles and Gintis argument is akin to one advanced earlier by John Bonin and Louis Putterman, who define a worker-managed enterprise by the single proviso that 'ultimate decision-making rights are vested in the workers, and only in the workers' (1987, p. 2). Because Bonin and Putterman contend that this proviso is innocuous, they declare that there is no objective reason why capital should ask for a risk premium in dealing with such enterprises.

I submit that different forms of finance need to be distinguished and that equity capital incurs added risk when it is excluded from decision making, which is what the worker-management proviso demands.[13] My argument is an application of the proposition that debt and equity are not merely financial instruments but are also governance instruments. Contrary to the Modigliani and Miller (1958) theorem, transaction cost economics maintains that debt and equity need to be matched to the attributes of a project for which finance is needed.

The argument, in brief, is this (Williamson, 1988):

(i)   easily redeployable assets are appropriately financed by debt;
(ii)   highly nonredeployable assets are ones for which equity finance is more well suited;
(iii)   the governance structure associated with debt is more legalistic and works out of rules while that associated with equity is more hierarchical and allows greater discretion;
(iv)   the board of directors is a discretionary control instrument that is efficiently awarded to residual claimants—namely, to equity in firms in which investments in durable, nonredeployable physical assets are significant;
(v)   refusal to award control over the board of directors in such firms to equity finance poses an investment hazard, the effect of which is to raise the effective price of finance; and
(vi)   some firms—mainly professional firms (law firms, accounting firms, investment banking, consulting)—involve negligible investment in firm-specific physical assets and are appropriately organized as worker-controlled partnerships.

According to the 'power' view of capital in which 'political preferences' are featured, the scarcity of worker-managed enterprises is explained by the hostility of capital to democratic decision making. The efficiency view, by

---

[13] Bonin and Putterman, joined by Jones, now evidently agree (Bonin *et al.*, 1993, p. 1309).

contrast, is that equity capital must have access to (is virtually defined as) discretionary control, whence democratic decision making is poorly suited to organize firms for which significant investments in specific capital are required. The efficiency view is borne out by the data (Hansmann, 1988).

Labor and final product markets. It is more plausible to assume that parties to a transaction are knowledgeable for transactions between two firms than it is for transactions between firms and workers or, especially, between firms and consumers. That is because of information asymmetries in which firms often enjoy an information advantage in relation to both workers and consumers.

Thus, many final consumer and some labor market transactions are characterized by (comparatively) shallow knowledge, confusion, inability to craft a specialized governance structure, weak reputation effects and costly legal processes. Although groups of consumers could and sometimes do create their own specialized agents to contract on their behalf, there are serious collective action problems in forming such groups and in excluding free-riders (Arrow, 1969). Unlike firms, moreover, consumers are rarely able to integrate backward—thereby to relieve the troublesome transaction by placing it under unified ownership. (Backward integration into day care by parents who organize nonprofit day care facilities is an exception (Ben-Ner and Van Hoomissen, 1991).)

To be sure, the producers and distributors of hard-to-measure goods and services sometimes can and do create added safeguards through branding, warranties, authorized service and the like. Whether best private efforts of buyers and suppliers to concentrate the costs and benefits can be further improved on with net gains (remediableness) is then the question. Public ordering may be warranted if best private efforts are severely wanting. Consumer protection regulation—information disclosure, standards, legal aid—often has these origins.

Similar arguments apply to labor, although here the possibility of private collective action is often more feasible. Transaction cost economics observes in this connection that the efficiency benefits of collective action, including associated governance structure supports, will vary with the degree of human asset specificity. Accordingly, labor unions ought to arise earlier and governance ought to be more fully elaborated in firms where human asset specificity is great (Williamson *et al.*, 1975; Williamson, 1985, ch. 10).

Differences between the 'industrial pluralists'—Harry Schulman, Archibald Cox, Arthur Goldberg, Justice Douglas—and Katherine Stone over the interpretation of the Wagner Act are pertinent. The former adopted what, in effect, was an efficiency view: the purpose of the Act was to harmonize labor relations, promote cooperation and please the parties. By contrast, Stone (1981) advanced an adversarial interpretation, according to which the purpose of the Act was to equalize power. Thus, whereas the pluralists viewed arbitration as a means by which to resolve disputes in favor of the idiosyncratic needs of the parties, Stone recommended a legalistic approach in which the National Labor Relations Board is directed to 'interpret the language of the written agreement, *not please the parties*' (Stone, 1981, p. 1552, n. 238, emphasis in original).

Although a legalistic approach to contract is understandably recommended by those who prefer confrontation, that can be a costly way to organize society. For better or worse (depending on one's preferences), the efficiency view has prevailed. Interestingly, Japanese economic organization can be interpreted as an effort to move to a higher degree of contracting perfection (Aoki, 1990; Williamson, 1991c).

Politics. The idea that politics is the product of knowledgeable and farsighted contracting is surely preposterous. 'Everyone knows' that voting is irrational and that to expend efforts to vote knowledgeably is especially irrational. Robert Ellickson (1993) responds that politics is a consumption good, whence participation has a rational basis. Still, political choices are often complex and ignorance is widespread.

Terry Moe   (1990a, b) has reframed the issues in terms of interest groups. He maintains that while voters in general are poorly informed, interest groups not only have extensive knowledge of the issues but also understand a great deal about the consequences of structural choice. Thus, whereas bureau design is a matter with which voters express concerns only after the fact, when they can observe how a bureau operates, interest groups are actively involved in the *ex ante* design of bureaus and know what they want. As Moe and Caldwell bluntly put it, 'on issues of structure, virtually all pressures come from the groups . . . structural politics is interest group politics' (1994, p. 173)— which is to say that politics is an exercise in power.

There are more and less efficacious ways to exercise power, however, and the economic approach advises that bureaus will be designed with farsighted purposes in mind. In the degree to which the current majority perceives that its hold on political office is insecure, forward looking politicians will recognize that those very same bureaus through which favors are awarded to a target population could become instruments for reversing earlier actions (perhaps even to reward the opposition) by successor administrations. Therefore, agencies will be designed with reference to both immediate benefits (which favors responsive mechanisms) and possible future losses (which often favors crafting inertia into the system). The creation of a bureau will be attended therefore by some degree of (apparent) design inefficiency—that being the forward thinking way to protect weak political property rights (Moe, 1990a, b). What is furthermore noteworthy is that such inefficiencies may be irremediable—given the rules of the game.[14]

The issue of remediableness also arises in George Stigler's recent examination of political choice. He queries whether an 'apparently inefficient' political program should be regarded as inefficient if the program in question has passed 'the test of time'. Consider the US sugar program, which Stigler describes as follows (1992, p. 459):

> The United States wastes (in ordinary language) perhaps \$3 billion per year producing sugar and sugar substitutes at a price two to three times the cost of importing the sugar. Yet that is the tested way in which the domestic sugar-beet, cane, and high-fructose-corn producers can increase their incomes by perhaps a quarter of the \$3 billion—the other three quarter being deadweight loss. The deadweight loss is the margin by which the domestic costs of sugar production exceed import prices.

How is such a program to be assessed? A common interpretation is that the deadweight loss represents inefficiency: 'The Posnerian theory would say that the sugar program is grotesquely inefficient because it fails to maximize national income' (Stigler, 1992, p. 459). The fact that the sugar program has statute-based, rather than common law-based, origins is, purportedly, a contributing factor.

Stigler takes exception with efficiency of law scholarship both in general (the statute-based versus common law-based distinction) and in his interpretation of the sugar program. The problem with the argument that the common law is efficient while statute law is problematic (Landes and Posner, 1987) is that it rests on an underdeveloped logic (Stigler, 1992, pp. 459–461). More pertinent for my purpose is Stigler's argument that 'Maximum national income . . . is not the only goal of our nation as judged by policies adopted by our government—and government's goals as revealed by actual practice are more authoritative than those pronounced by professors of law or economics' (Stigler, 1992, p. 459).

Rather than appeal to deadweight losses in relation to a hypothetical ideal, Stigler proposes that the appropriate criterion is the test of time, according to which criterion he declares that the 'sugar program is efficient. This program is more than fifty years old—it has met the test of time' (Stigler, 1992, p. 459).

---

[14] As it turns out, recourse to inefficiency by design is employed—as rent and/or property rights protective measures—in the private sector as well (Teece, 1986; Heide and John, 1988; Helper and Levine, 1992). The apparent disjunction between politics and commerce is therefore not as great as Moe suggests. What we observe in both are variations on a weak property rights theme.

In effect, the test of time is a rough-and-ready way to assess remediableness—the assumption being that if there were a cheaper, feasible and implementable alternative then it would be implemented. That test makes no provision for organizational breakdowns, however, and it assumes that the democratic process has been and is working acceptably. I address these issues elsewhere. On making allowance for egregious intertemporal breakdowns of organization and/or politics, the Stiglerian test of time criterion is reformulated as a rebuttable presumption (Williamson, 1993b).

The upshot is that efficiency plays a significant role even in the power arena (politics), especially if the relevant test for inefficiency is that of remediableness.

4. Authority[15]

As discussed in section 1 under the heading 'transaction cost economics', transaction cost economics maintains that each generic mode of organization is supported by a distinctive form of contract law. That contradicts the view that the firm is no different from the market in contractual respects, as argued by Alchian and Demsetz (1972, p. 777):[16]

> The single consumer can assign his grocer to the task of obtaining whatever the customer can induce the grocer to provide at a price acceptable to both parties. That is precisely all that an employer can do to an employee. To speak of managing, directing, or assigning workers to various tasks is a deceptive way of noting that the employer continually is involved in renegotiation of contracts on terms that must be acceptable to both parties . . . Long-term contracts between employer and employee are not the essence of the organization we call a firm.

That it has been instructive to view the firm as a nexus of contracts is evident from the numerous insights that this literature has generated. But to regard the corporation only as a nexus of contracts misses much of what is truly distinctive about this mode of governance. As developed below, bilateral adaptation effected through fiat is a distinguishing feature of internal organization. But wherein do the fiat differences between market and hierarchy arise?

One explanation is that fiat has its origins in the employment contract (Barnard, 1938; Simon, 1951; Coase, 1952; Masten, 1988). Although there is a good deal to be said for that explanation, I propose a separate and complementary explanation: the implicit contract law of internal organization is that of forbearance. Thus, whereas courts routinely grant standing to interfirm

---

[15] This section is based on my treatment in Williamson (1991a, pp. 274–276).
[16] Both have modified their positions since. See Alchian (1984) and Demsetz (1988).

disputes over prices, the damages to be ascribed to delays, failures of quality, and the like, courts will refuse to hear intrafirm disputes—between one internal division and another—over identical technical issues. Access to the courts being denied, the parties must resolve their differences internally. Accordingly, hierarchy is its own court of ultimate appeal.[17]

The underlying rationale for forbearance law is twofold:

(i) parties to an internal dispute have deep knowledge—both about the circumstances surrounding a dispute as well as the efficiency properties of alternative solutions—that can be communicated to the court only at great cost; and

(ii) permitting internal disputes to be appealed to the court would undermine the efficacy and integrity of hierarchy.

If fiat were merely advisory, in that internal disputes over net receipts could be pursued in the courts, the firm would be little more than an 'inside contracting' system (Williamson, 1985, pp. 218–222). The application of forebearance doctrine to internal organization means that parties to an internal exchange can work out their differences themselves or appeal unresolved disputes to the hierarchy for a decision. But this exhausts their alternatives. When push comes to shove, 'legalistic' arguments fail. Greater reliance on instrumental reasoning and mutual accommodation result. The argument that the firm 'has no power of fiat, no authority, no disciplinary action any different in the slightest degree from ordinary market contracting' (Alchian and Demsetz, 1972, p. 777) is exactly wrong: firms can and do exercise fiat that markets cannot.

Viewing fiat and the zone of acceptance through the lens of efficiency leads to different predictions that obtain when these same features are interpreted in terms of power. According to the efficiency perspective, the zone of acceptance will be broad or narrow depending on the nature of the transaction. The idea here is that (holding the nature of the task constant), workers will ask for greater compensation if the zone across which they are expected to be compliant includes a larger set of disfavored jobs, *ceteris paribus*. Accordingly, a zone will be widened to include more potentially adverse assignments only in the degree to which that is perceived to be cost-effective.[18]

Arguments that power manifests itself in the design of jobs go back to Adam Smith and Karl Marx and have been surveyed recently by James

---

[17] To be sure, not all disputes within firms are technical. For a discussion of personnel disputes, see Williamson (1991a, p. 275).

[18] This does not imply that all tasks will be made as narrow and repetitive as possible. If job variety is valued by workers, greater variety will be introduced in the degree to which this is cost-effective. Given, however, any specification of the task, workers will ask for more compensation if the zone of acceptance is expanded to include more disfavored outcomes.

Rebitzer (1993, pp. 1401–1409). It being beyond the scope of this paper to assess these issues here, I merely make four points:

(i) persistent inefficiency in the design of jobs in a competitively organized industry reflects either a condition of market failure (private gains with systems losses) or a condition of disequilibrium contracting;

(ii) inefficiency by design is more apt to be incurred where value or rent dissipation is the concern (and in any event may not be remediable);

(iii) power-serving purposes that have inefficiency consequences are continuously threatened by credible contracting structures to which the parties attach confidence; and

(iv) the relevant efficiency criterion for job design is not a hypothetical (but unattainable) ideal but is that of remediableness.

5. *Conclusions*

As described above, the economic approach to the study of organization works out of a rational spirit perspective in which parties approach contracting in a farsighted way. Transaction cost economics adopts this perspective and moves it to a more microanalytic level of analysis than is customary in economics and develops the microanalytics in a more operational way than has been customary in organization theory or than was attempted by the older type of institutional economics. Kenneth Arrow's remarks are pertinent (1987, p. 734):

> Why . . . has the work of Herbert Simon, which has meant so much to all of us, nevertheless had so little direct consequence? Why did the older institutional school fail so miserably, though it contained such able analysts as Thorstein Veblen, J. R. Commons, and W. C. Mitchell? I now think that there are two answers; one is that in fact there are important specific analyses, particularly in the work . . . of the New Institutional Economics movement. But it does not consist primarily of giving answers to the traditional questions of economics—resource allocation and the degree of utilization. Rather, it consists of answering new questions, why economic institutions have emerged the way they did and not otherwise; it merges with economic history, but brings sharper nanoeconomic . . . reasoning to bear than has been customary.

Thus, whereas transaction cost economics deals with many of the microanalytic phenomena with which organization theory has long been concerned, it examines these predominantly from an efficiency perspective in which intended but limited rationality manifests itself as 'incomplete contracting in its entirety'. The efficiency perspective out of which transaction cost economics works further eschews Pareto optimality in favor of a remediableness standard—according to which an extant condition is held to be efficient unless a feasible alternative can be described and implemented with net gains.

A huge number of puzzling phenomena are reinterpreted in this way and a large number of predictions (which, as it turns out, are variations on a small number of transaction cost economizing themes) are realized. Such regularities by no means exhaust all of the interesting variety that is out there. The economizing lens is nevertheless a useful place to start.

References

Akerlof, G. (1984), *An Economic Theorist's Book of Tales*. Cambridge University Press: New York.

Alchian, A. (1950), 'Uncertainty, Evolution and Economic Theory', *Journal of Political Economy*, 58 (June), 211–221.

Alchian, A. (1984), 'Specificity, Specialization and Coalitions', *Journal of Institutions and Theoretical Economics*, 140 (March), 34–49.

Alchian, A. and H. Demsetz (1972), 'Production, Information Costs, and Economic Organization', *American Economic Review*, 62 (December), 777–795.

Aoki, M. (1990), 'Toward an Economic Model of the Japanese Firm', *Journal of Economic Literature*, 28 (March), 1–27.

Arrow, K. J. (1963), 'Uncertainty and the Welfare Economics of Medical Care', *American Economic Review*, 53 (December), 941–973.

Arrow, K. J. (1969), 'The Organization of Economic Activity: Issues Pertinent to the Choice of Market Versus Nonmarket Allocation', in *The Analysis and Evaluation of Public Expenditure: The PPB System*. Vol. 1, US Joint Economic Committee, 91st Congress, 1st Session, US Government Printing Office: Washington DC, 59–73.

Arrow, K. J. (1974), *The Limits of Organization*. First edition, W. W. Norton: New York.

Arrow, K. J. (1987), 'Reflections on the Essays', in G. Feiwel (ed.), *Arrow and the Foundations of the Theory of Economic Policy*. NYU Press: New York, 727–734.

Bain, J. (1956), *Barriers to New Competition*. Harvard University Press: Cambridge, MA.

Barnard, C. (1938), *The Functions of the Executive*. Harvard University Press: Cambridge, MA (fifteenth printing, 1962).

Barnett, W. and G. Carroll (1993), 'How Institutional Constraints Affected the Organization of the Early American Telephone Industry', *Journal of Law, Economics, and Organization*, 9 (April), 98–126.

Baron, J. and M. Hannan (1994), 'The Impact of Economics on Contemporary Sociology', *Journal of Economic Literature*, 32 (September), 1111–1146.

Ben-Ner, A. and T. Van Hoomissen (1991), 'Nonprofit Organizations in the Mixed Economy', *Annals of Public and Cooperative Economics*, 62 (4), 519–550.

Bonin, J. and L. Putterman (1987), *Economics of Cooperation and Labor Managed Economics*. Cambridge University Press: New York.

Bonin, J., D. Jones and L. Putterman (1993), 'Theoretical and Empirical Studies of Producer Cooperatives', *Journal of Economic Literature*, 31 (September), 1290–1320.

Bowles, S. and H. Gintis (1993), 'The Revenge of Homo Economicus: Contested Exchange and the Revival of Political Economy', *Journal of Economic Perspectives*, 7 (Winter), 83–114.

Coase, R. H. (1952), 'The Nature of the Firm', *Economica N. S.*, 4 (1937), 386–405. Reprinted in G. J. Stigler and K. E. Boulding (eds), *Readings in Price Theory*. Richard D. Irwin: Homewood, IL.

Coase, R. H. (1960), 'The Problem of Social Cost', *Journal of Law and Economics*, 3 (October), 1–44.

Coase, R. H. (1964), 'The Regulated Industries: Discussion', *American Economic Review*, 54 (May), 194–197.

Coase, R. H. (1978), 'Economics and Contiguous Disciplines', *Journal of Legal Studies*, 7, 201–211.

Coase, R. H. (1984), 'The New Institutional Economics', *Journal of Institutional and Theoretical Economics*, 140 (March), 229–231.

Coase, R. H. (1988), 'The Nature of the Firm: Influence', *Journal of Law, Economics, and Organization*, 4 (Spring), 33–47.

Coase, R. H. (1992), 'The Institutional Structure of Production', *American Economic Review*, 82 (September), 713–719.

Coleman, J. (1990), *The Foundations of Social Theory*. Harvard University Press: Cambridge, MA.

Commons, J. R. (1934), *Institutional Economics*. University of Wisconsin Press: Madison, WI.

Demsetz, H. (1967), 'Toward a Theory of Property Rights', *American Economic Review*, 57 (May), 347–359.

Demsetz, H. (1988), 'The Theory of the Firm Revisited', *Journal of Law, Economics, and Organization*, 4, 141–162.

Dixit, A. (1980), 'The Role of Investment in Entry Deterrence', *Economic Journal*, 90 (March), 95–106.

Dosi, G. (1988), 'Sources, Procedures, and Microeconomics Effects of Innovation', *Journal of Economic Literature*, 26 (September), 1120–1171.

Eccles, R. and H. White (1988), 'Price and Authority in Inter-Profit Center Transactions', *American Journal of Sociology*, 94 (Supplement), S17–S51.

Ellickson, R. (1993), 'Property in Land', *Yale Law Journal*, 102 (April), 1315–1400.

Fischer, S. (1977), 'Long-Term Contracting, Sticky Prices, and Monetary Policy: Comment', *Journal of Monetary Economics*, 3, 317–324.

Friedland, R. and R. Alford (1991), 'Bring Society Back In', in Walter Powell and Paul DiMaggio (eds), *The New Institutionalism in Organizational Analysis*. University of Chicago Press: Chicago, IL, 232–266.

Friedman, M. (1953), *Essays in Positive Economics*. University of Chicago Press: Chicago, IL.

Furubotn, E. and R. Richter (1991), 'The New Institutional Economics: An Assessment,' in E. Furubotn and R. Richter (eds), *The New Institutional Economics*. Texas A & M Press: College Station, TX, 1–32.

Hamilton, G. and N. Biggart (1988), 'Market, Culture, and Authority', *American Journal of Sociology*, 94 (Supplement), S52–S94.

Hannan, M. T. (1989), *Organizational Ecology*. Harvard University Press: Cambridge, MA.

Hannan, M. T. and J. Freeman (1977), 'The Population Ecology of Organizations', *American Journal of Sociology*, 82 (March), 929–964.

Hansmann, H. (1988), 'The Ownership of the Firm', *Journal of Law, Economics, and Organization*, 4 (Fall), 267–303.

Hart, O. (1990), 'An Economist's Perspective on the Theory of the Firm', in O. Williamson (ed.), *Organization Theory*. Oxford University Press: New York, 154–171.

Heide, J. and G. John (1988), 'The Role of Dependence Balancing in Safeguarding Transaction-Specific Assets in Conventional Channels', *Journal of Marketing*, 52 (January), 20–35.

Helper, S. and D. Levine (1992), 'Long-Term Supplier Relations and Product-Market Structure', *Journal of Law, Economics and Organization*, 8 (October), 561–581.

Homans, G. (1958), 'Social Behavior as Exchange', *American Journal of Sociology*, 62, 597–606.

Joskow, P. L. (1988), 'Asset Specificity and the Structure of Vertical Relationships: Empirical Evidence', *Journal of Law, Economics, and Organization*, 4 (Spring), 95–117.

Joskow, P. L. (1991), 'The Role of Transaction Cost Economics in Antitrust and Public Utility Regulatory Policies', *Journal of Law, Economics, and Organization*, 7 (Special Issue), 53–83.

Kenney, R. and B. Klein (1983), 'The Economics of Block Booking', *Journal of Law and Economics*, 26 (October), 497–540.

Klein, B. (1980), 'Transaction Cost Determinants of "Unfair" Contractual Arrangements', *American Economic Review*, 70 (May), 356–362.

Koopmans, T. (1957), *Three Essays on the State of Economic Science*. McGraw-Hill Book Company: New York.

Kreps, D. (1990), 'Corporate Culture and Economic Theory', in J. Alt and K. Shepsle (eds), *Perspectives on Positive Political Economy*. Cambridge University Press: New York, 90–143.

Kreps, D. (1992), '(How) Can Game Theory Contribute to a Unified Theory of Organizations', unpublished manuscript.

Krueger, A. (1990), 'The Political Economy of Controls: American Sugar', in M. Scott and D. Lal (eds), *Public Policy and Economic Development*. Clarendon Press: Oxford, 170–216.

Kuhn, T. S. (1970), *The Structure of Scientific Revolutions*. University of Chicago Press: Chicago, IL.

Kunreuther, H., *et al.* (1978), *Protecting Against High-Risk Hazards: Public Policy Lessons*. John Wiley & Sons: New York.

Landes, W. and R. Posner (1987), *The Economic Structure of Tort Law*. Harvard University Press: Cambridge, MA.

Llewellyn, K. N. (1931), 'What Price Contract? An Essay in Perspective', *Yale Law Journal*, 40 (May), 704–751.

Macneil, I. R. (1974), 'The Many Futures of Contracts', *Southern California Law Review*, 47 (May), 691–816.

Macneil, I. R. (1978), 'Contracts: Adjustments of Long-term Economic Relations under Classical, Neoclassical, and Relational Contract Law', *Northwestern University Law Review*, 72, 854–906.

March, J. G. (1978), 'Bounded Rationality, Ambiguity, and the Engineering of Choice', *Bell Journal of Economics*, 9 (Autumn), 587–608.

March, J. G. (1988), *Decisions and Organizations*. Basil Blackwell: Oxford.

March, J. G. and H. Simon (1958), *Organizations*. John Wiley & Sons: New York.

Masten, S. (1988), 'A Legal Basis for the Firm', *Journal of Law, Economics, and Organization*, 4 (Spring), 181–198.

Masten, S. (1993), 'Transaction Costs, Mistakes, and Performance: Assessing the Importance of Governance', *Managerial and Decision Economics*, 14, 119–129.

Michels, R. (1962), *Political Parties*. Free Press: Glencoe, IL.

Modigliani, F. and M. H. Miller (1958), 'The Cost of Capital, Corporation Finance, and the Theory of Investment', *American Economic Review*, 48 (June), 261–297.

Moe, T. (1990a), 'The Politics of Structural Choice: Toward a Theory of Public Bureaucracy', in O. Williamson (ed.), *Organization Theory*. Oxford University Press: New York, 116–153.

Moe, T. (1990b), 'Political Institutions: The Neglected Side of the Story', *Journal of Law, Economics, and Organization*, 6 (Special Issue), 213–254.

Moe, T. and M. Cladwell (1994), 'The Institutional Foundations of Democratic Governance: A comparison of Presidential and Parliamentary Systems', *Journal of Institutional and Theoretical Economics*, 150 (March), 171–195.

Nelson, R. R. and S. G. Winter (1982), *An Evolutionary Theory of Economic Change*. Harvard University Press: Cambridge, MA.

North, D. (1991), 'Institutions', *Journal of Economic Perspectives*, 5, (Winter), 97–112.

Pfeffer, J. (1981), *Power in Organizations*. Pitman Publishing: Marshfield, MA.

Polanyi, M. (1962), *Personal Knowledge: Towards a Post-Critical Philosophy*. Harper & Row: New York.

Rebitzer, J. (1993), 'Radical Political Economy and the Economics of Labor Markets', *Journal of Economic Literature*, 31 (September), 1394–1434.

Shelanski, H. (1991), 'A Survey of Empirical Research in Transaction Cost Economics', unpublished manuscript, University of California: Berkeley, CA.

Simon, H. (1951), 'A Formal Theory of the Employment Relation', *Econometrica*, 19 (July), 293–305.

Simon, H. (1962), 'The Architecture of Complexity', *Proceedings of the American Philosophical Society*, 106 (December), 467–482.

Simon, H. (1976), 'From Substantive to Procedural Rationality', in S. J. Latsis (ed.), *Method and Appraisal in Economics*. Cambridge University Press: Cambridge, 129–148.

Simon, H. (1978), 'Rationality as Process and as Product of Thought', *American Economic Review*, 68 (May), 1–16.

Simon, H. (1983), *Reason in Human Affairs*. Stanford University Press: Stanford, CT.

Simon, H. (1985), 'Human Nature in Politics: The Dialogue of Psychology with Political Science', *American Political Science Review*, 70, 293–304.

Speidel, R. (1993), 'Article 2 and Relational Sales Contracts', *Loyola of Los Angeles Law Review*, 26 (April), 789–810.

Stigler, G. J. (1968), *The Organization of Industry*. Richard D. Irwin: Homewood, IL.

Stigler, G. L. (1992), 'Law or Economics?' *Journal of Law and Economics*, 35 (October), 455–468.

Stone, K. (1981), 'The Postwar Paradigm in American Labor Law', *Yale Law Journal*, 90 (June), 1509–1580.

Teece, D. J. (1986), 'Profiting from Technological Innovation', *Research Policy*, 15 (December), 285–305.

Teece, D. J. (1992), 'Competition, Cooperation, and Innovation: Organizational Arrangements for Regimes of Rapid Technological Progress', *Journal of Economic Behavior and Organizations*, 18 (June), 1–25.

Teece, D. J., R. Rumelt, G. Dosi and S. Winter (1993), 'Understanding Corporate Coherence: Theory and Evidence', *Journal of Economic Behavior and Organization*, 22 (January), 1–30.

Tirole, J. (1986), 'Hierarchies and Bureaucracy: On the Role of collusion in Organizations', *Journal of Law, Economics and Organization*, 2 (Fall), 181–214.

Tversky, A. and D. Kahneman (1974), 'Judgment under Uncertainty: Heuristics and Biases', *Science*, 185, 1124–1131.

Williamson, O. E. (1971), 'The Vertical Integration of Production: Market Failure Considerations', *American Economic Review*, 61 (May), 112–123.

Williamson, O. E. (1975), *Markets and Hierarchies: Analysis and Antitrust Implications*. Free Press: New York.

Williamson, O. E. (1979), 'Transaction-cost Economics: The Governance of Contractual Relations', *Journal of Law and Economics*, 22 (October), 233–261.

Williamson, O. E. (1983), 'Credible Commitments: Using Hostages to Support Exchange', *American Economic Review*, 73 (September), 519–540.

Williamson, O. E. (1985), *The Economic Institutions of Capitalism*. Free Press: New York.

Williamson, O. E. (1988), 'Corporate Finance and Corporate Governance', *Journal of Finance*, 43 (July), 567–591.

Williamson, O. E. (1991a), 'Comparative Economic Organization: The Analysis of Discrete Structural Alternatives', *Administrative Science Quarterly*, 36 (June), 269–296.

Williamson, O. E. (1991b), 'Economic Institutions: Spontaneous and Intentional Governance', *Journal of Law, Economics, and Organization*, 7 (Special Issue), 159–187.

Williamson, O. E. (1991c), 'Strategizing, Economizing, and Economic Organization', *Strategic Management Journal*, 12, 75–94.

Williamson, O. E. (1993a), 'Transaction Cost Economics and Organization Theory', *Industrial and Corporate Change*, 2 (2), 107–156.

Williamson, O. E. (1993b), 'Redistribution and Inefficiency: The Remediableness Standard', unpublished manuscript.

Williamson, O. E., M. L. Wachter and J. E. Harris (1975), 'Understanding the Employment Relation: The Analysis of Idiosyncratic Exchange', *Bell Journal of Economics*, 6 (Spring), 250–280.

The Evolution of Organizational Conventions and Gains from Diversity

MASAHIKO AOKI

(Department of Economics, Stanford University, Stanford, CA 94305, USA.
Email: aoki@leland.stanford.edu)

This paper investigates, by using a highly abstract evolutionary game model, the mechanism of evolution of different organizational conventions, as well as roles of free trade, integration, experiments, emulation and entrepreneurial foresight for exploring gains from organizational diversity. It focuses on an aspect of organization as a voluntary association of economic agents trying to overcome the bounds of their rationality, scope of action and competence, rather than as an 'instrument' for entrepreneurial maximizing behavior, and identifies two generic forms of organization as an information system. The paper concludes by discussing the relevance of the evolutionary game model for understanding actual organizational evolutionary processes in North America and Japan.

1. Introduction

A 'design' approach is adopted by two otherwise distinct theories of the firm (organization): the contract theory and the team theory. The contract theory analyzes an aspect of the firm's organization in terms of incentive instruments that are optimally designed under incentive compatibility and participation constraints. The second-best instruments are responsive to values of exogenous parameters. Relevant parameters include, besides the usual technological parameters, those specifying agents' outside options and the initial distribution of information among them. The team theory *à la* Marschak – Radner takes the coordination mode of organization as the object of design (who is to process what information and communicate with whom) while suppressing the problem of incentives. It is shown that there can be a variety of organizational coordination modes other than classical hierarchy, but that their relative efficiency also depends on various exogenous parameters specifying technological interdependencies among tasks, the level of communications technology, types and levels of agents' information processing skills, etc. (Aoki, 1986, 1995; Cremer, 1990; Radner, 1993; Bolton and Dewatripont, 1994; Maskin *et al.*, 1997).

The results of the design approach may be taken to imply that the organizational form (as a combination of incentive instruments and coordination mode) will tend to converge among firms in the same industry facing similar technological parameters (provided that their participation constraints are the same). However, we often observe a variety of organizational forms in the same industry across regions and economies in spite of similar technological parameters. For example, there are remarkable differences in the organizational form among the high technology firms clustering in Silicon Valley, Route 128 and Ohta Ward in Tokyo (e.g. Okimoto and Nishi, 1994; Saxenian, 1994). Continental Europeans and the Japanese have introduced tax incentives and other policy measures to stimulate the development of venture capital financing, but the clustering of high-tech entrepreneurial firms in a critical mass *à la* Silicon Valley has not so far emerged as intended. On the other hand, organizational forms tend to be conventionalized in each economy or region, although there are variations, experiments and mutants. Entrepreneurs try to experiment with a new organizational form or emulate an organizational form that evolved elsewhere and has proved to be competitive in a particular industry. However, usually the outcome of such experiments and emulations, even if they occur within a critical mass, is neither a dramatic switch from one convention to another nor a 'chaotic' cohabitation of widely divergent organizational forms. Rather, they are likely to result in a 'modification' of a conventional organizational form that may significantly alter some characteristics of the existing conventions while retaining their other basic characteristics. Alternatively they may lead to the emergence of a new clustering of entrepreneurial firms, as in Silicon Valley. Thus references are often made to national or regional forms of organization, e.g. Silicon Valley firms, the 'American system of manufacture' (Rosenberg, 1969), German firms, Japanese firms. Some argue that interregional/national differences in organizational forms and implied organizational competence may explain the patterns of regional/national advantage in industry and trade (e.g. Dosi *et al.*, 1990).

However, unlike the naturally endowed resources that constitute the source of Ricardian comparative advantage, the organizational form is a human contrivance. As such, should it not be transplantable (mobile) across national economies? Why can each economy not easily adopt the most suitable organizational form for each industry? Why do we tend to observe a similar organizational form (organizational convention) in one locality/economy? Or is such an observation superficial and misled by transitory phenomena, and will competitive selection eventually weed out inefficient organizational forms which do not fit the emergent technological imperatives of each industry, as Alchian (1950) and Friedman (1953) argued some time ago?

This paper tries to understand at a highly abstract level the essential nature of the diversity of organizational forms as well as that of the mechanism of evolution of different organizational conventions. I focus on an aspect of organization as a voluntary association of economic agents trying to overcome the bounds of their rationality, scope of action and competence, rather than as an 'instrument' for entrepreneurial maximizing behavior. However, note that by this I do not mean to disregard the intention of each agent to maximize his own pay-off in the following discussion. On the contrary, although an agent's capacity to fully realize such an intention may be limited, it constitutes an essential ingredient of the model to be constructed.

The discussion in this article is divided into three parts. The first, preliminary part (Section 2) introduces a framework for dealing with an aspect of an organizational form—the information systematic aspect—as a choice variable rather than as technological data. It identifies two generic forms of organizations when economic agents are bounded in their information processing capacity but try to overcome the limits through cooperation in the organization. This framework originates in previous works by Aoki (1986) and Cremer (1990), who tried to understand the comparative informational efficiency of different organizational forms within the team theoretic approach. Section 2 provides a basic, bounded-rationalistic justification for identifying two generic forms of intra-organizational information systems as a basic building block of evolutionary game-theoretic analysis. Although they appear to be very abstract, as demonstrated elsewhere (Aoki, 1995) and further discussed in the third part of the present article, many empirically observed organizational forms of historical importance may be seen to be related to either of the two. An important point which can be derived from previous works is that either of the two forms may not have an absolute advantage, independent of parameters describing industrial technology and market conditions, and of the level of information processing capacity of agents, as well as the level of information and communications technology. Therefore, it is important to understand the nature of the evolution mechanism, as well as the competitive selection, of organizational forms under the constraints of the bounded-rationality of agents. Using a simple evolutionary game model as an illustrative tool, the second part (Section 3 and 4) of the article is engaged in this and other related inquiries such as: 'Is a particular form of organization likely to grow and establish itself as a convention across industries in each economy?' or 'Is an efficient arrangement of organizational forms able to emerge in each economy entailing a diversity of organizational forms across industries?'. If the first is the case, how can a barrier to transition from an inefficient organizational convention to an efficient cross-industrial arrangement be reduced? Even if the barrier is high, can potential gains from diversity be realized through regional specialization and free trade?

Can the rational foresight of entrepreneurs help the economy to escape from the trap of historical determinism and self-organize the efficient combinations of diverse organizational forms across industries?

The concluding part discusses the implications and limits of the model for interpreting evolutionary organizational dynamics across economies. It argues that, although the formal model presented in this article is at an extremely simple and abstract level, actual evolutionary processes in North America and Japan may be seen as processes of complex ramifications of one of the two generic organizational forms. It also explains that actual innovation often occurs as a modification of indigenous practices (strategies) through learning from perceived foreign practices. In that sense, organizational diversity is a source of organizational innovation and there are thus dynamic gains from the diversity.

2. *Two Generic Forms of Organizations and Corresponding Skills*

This section provides a simple framework for treating an aspect of a firm's organizational form—the information system—as an economic choice variable rather than technological data. Suppose that one unit of an output can be produced and marketed within a period by an organization of two agents performing different tasks. The objective of the organization is to reduce the cost of unit output as much as possible under environmental uncertainty (output price is determined by the market in a manner specified in the next section). The cost reduction may be achieved by adjusting the operation level of each task in response to changing input market conditions, technological environments, etc. There are two interactive effects of simultaneous adjustment of operational levels of the tasks on the cost reduction outcome. First, the tasks may be competing for the use of limited organizational assets (physical or human). Second, adjustment in the intensity levels of the two tasks may need to be aligned to enhance their effectiveness (e.g. a result of R&D cannot be implemented without effort at the manufacturing site). If the first effect is relatively stronger, the marginal cost reduction from an increase in the intensity level of one task will decline while that of the other task simultaneously increases. If the second effect is relatively stronger, the opposite will be true. In the first case the two tasks are referred to as being substitutes, while in the latter they are complementary.

Further, the cost reduction effect of adjustment of the operational level of each task is uncertain, contingent on the state of environmental variables. With a common prior knowledge about the environment variables, the agents may agree on a certain level of operation for each task *ex ante* and proceed to implement it. However, if the agents can jointly or separately process the information regarding emergent environmental conditions to improve on the priors and choose operation levels of the tasks accordingly, the efficiency of the organization may be enhanced in spite of any extra costs that might be incurred (in terms of time and effort for sampling environmental variables, the use of organizational assets, etc.). The question is, how should this information processing activity be organized between the two agents? Assume that the environments of both tasks can be correlated to a certain degree, but not perfectly (otherwise the two tasks do not need to be distinguished). There are two generic systems of information processing in our simple setting: differentiated and assimilative (Cremer, 1990; Aoki, 1995). The *differentiated* information system is the one in which each agent is specialized in the processing of information regarding the environment, forms his own posterior beliefs and makes a decision regarding the intensity level of his own task accordingly. However, to achieve the organizational objective of cost reduction, both agents must agree *ex ante* on respective decision rules to be employed *ex post*. In the *assimilated* information system, both agents jointly process information about that part of the environment common to both tasks, and use the shared information (together with private environmental information relevant only to the respective tasks) as a basis for choosing the intensity levels of the respective tasks.

The difference between the two generic systems is reflected in the between type of 'mental model' (Denzau and North, 1994), or information processing skill, that each system requires the agents to embody. In our setting, the mental models of the agents are simply composed of two rules: an inference rule that transforms observations (of samples) regarding environment variables into posterior beliefs; and a decision rule that transforms posterior beliefs into a choice of the intensity level for the respective task. The assimilated information system anticipates both agents to share the type of mental models where common posterior beliefs (with some noise) are inferred from pooled samples and decisions are made accordingly. The differentiated information system anticipates each agent to acquire a mental model to form his/her own posterior belief from his/her own samples, but the decision rules need to be consistent with the organizational objective. The principal-agent theory of organization focuses on decision rules that are incentive compatible for agents to follow. In contrast, my focus in this article is on the inference rule portion of mental models, i.e. the rules the agents apply in observing and deriving inference about the environment relevant to cost reduction. Below, the capacity for making an inference according to the type of mental model fitting the differentiated information system is referred to as an *individualized* (information processing) skill. On the other hand, the information processing capacity tailored to the assimilated information system is referred to as a *contextual* (information processing) skill, since the corresponding mental models may be constructed and shared by the agents within the context of a particular organization.

Agents' information processing capacities represented by different mental models may be made comparable by evaluating the precision (in the Bayesian sense) of an observation of the environmental variable in each model relative to its prior precision.[1] From previous studies (Cremer, 1990; Aoki, 1995) it is known that, for the same level of information processing capacity of the agents, the relative performance in cost reduction of the two generic systems depends on the technological interrelationship of the two tasks: if the two tasks are complementary, the assimilated information system performs better, while under the condition of substitutability the differentiated information system performs better.[2] If the two tasks are complementary, it is desirable to simultaneously adjust the intensity levels of two tasks in the same direction. Decisions based on assimilated information can meet such an imperative better than those based on differentiated information. If the two tasks are substitutes, such an adjustment falls more easily into conflict with the availability constraint of organizational assets. Thus, there are good logical grounds for positing that there is no single organizational form and corresponding type of mental model of agents that is superior regardless of technology. Depending on the technology, either of the two generic information systems may fare better. But the question to be asked in this article is whether or not this technological factor alone determines the choice of an organizational form (information system) of industry in the economy.

Let us summarize the discussion above in order to introduce a building block of the evolutionary model for examining this issue. A firm is organized by the matching of two agents. In the following evolutionary game model, I assume that the agents invest in one skill type for their lifetime. Agents may invest in the individualized skill type only prior to entry into a market in which they are matched to organize firms. They are mobile in the market. However, as contextual skills can be formed only posterior to entry into a particular organization, what agents invest in prior to entering the market are preparatory skills that are malleable according to the specific needs of an organization afterwards. It may be appropriate to refer to such preparatory skills as proto-contextual skills. But for the sake of briefness, we will also refer to such preparatory skills simply as contextual in spite of slight abuse of the word. If two agents who have invested in an individualized skill type are

---

[1] This definition can be extended to the case of multiple environmental variables. See Aoki (1995).

[2] This proposition can be extended to the case where there are more than two tasks. See Prat (1996).

matched to form a firm, its information system will be a differentiated one, whereas if two agents who have invested in the proto-contextual type are matched, it will be an assimilated system. Suppose further that there are two types of industries, B and D. The differentiated information system has an efficiency advantage in industry B (because of substitutability of tasks), whereas the assimilated information system has an efficiency advantage in industry D. If a mismatching of two different skill types occurs, that organization will be the least efficient in both industries.

This assumption can be represented by two matrices, one for each industry, showing the costs of unit-production contingent on the matching of skill types. Denote the skill types by I (=individualized) and C (=contextual), and the unit output cost of the industry B (alternatively D) by b_{jk} (alternatively d_{jk}), when the matching of skill types j and k (=I or C) occur. We have

$$
B = \begin{bmatrix} b_{II} & b_{IC} \\ b_{CI} & b_{CC} \end{bmatrix} \quad \text{and} \quad \Delta = \begin{bmatrix} d_{II} & d_{IC} \\ d_{CI} & d_{CC} \end{bmatrix}
$$

where $b_{II} < b_{CC} < b_{IC} = b_{CI}$ and $d_{CC} < d_{II} < d_{CI} = d_{IC}$. Additionally, it is assumed that $b_{CI} - b_{CC} < d_{CI} - d_{CC}$ and $d_{IC} - d_{II} < b_{IC} - b_{II}$, implying that the cost reduction gain from a particular skill-matching is greater in the industry in which that matching has a comparative advantage. These matrices will be used as technological data for the model of organizational evolution in the following sections.

3. *The Evolution of Organizational Conventions*

In the previous section I focused on the internal structure of the firm. I will leave this now to form an overview of the economy-wide strategic interplays of economic agents. Suppose that the population of an economy consists of a continuum of economic agents with a unit measure. Time runs continuously. Each agent invests in one skill type, $\varsigma = C$ or I, for his lifetime (he dies or quits work at a certain rate) and works in one of the two industries, $i = B$ or D. Let us denote the distribution of the population over skill types and industries at a particular moment in times as $m = (m_{CB}, m_{CD}, m_{IB}, m_{ID})$, where $m_{CB} + m_{CD} + m_{IB} + m_{ID} = 1$ and $m_{\varsigma i}$ represents the proportion of the population who choose industry i with skill type ς [when needed, the symbol (t) may be attached to variables to make it explicit that they are evaluated at time t]. I assume that a firm is formed by the matching of two agents in a manner specified momentarily, and that it can produce two units of output at any moment with the unit cost as specified in matrices B *and* Δ.[3]

Regarding matching technology, I assume the following. Agents equipped with individualized skills are mobile between the two industries at any moment in time. On the other hand, contextual skills are geared toward a particular industrial-organizational context. Therefore, agents equipped with contextual skills are not as easily mobile across industries (organizations) as agents who have invested in individualized skills. Because of their relative immobility, agents with contextual skills select matching partners more carefully. I assume that the probability of agents with contextual skills being matched with their same type in industry i is given by:

$$\Pi_{Ci} = \left[\frac{m_{Ci}}{m_{Ci} + m_{Ii}} \right]^{\gamma}, \quad i = B, D$$

where $0 < \gamma \leq 1$. If $\gamma = 1$, matching is random; if it is <1, matching is positively assortative. (I will state shortly how perfect mobility of an individualized type can be formulated.) The revenue of the firm, net of production cost, is equally shared between the two agents forming the firm.

All the agents in the economy have identical consumption tastes and spend their incomes on the products of the B and D industries in the proportions of β and δ, where $\beta + \delta = 1$. Recalling that each firm produces two units of the product, the total outputs of industries B and D are $(m_{CB} + m_{IB})$, $(m_{CD} + m_{ID})$ respectively. Unit prices of products B and D are given by the unit-elasticity inverse demand functions $p_B = \beta/(m_{CB} + m_{IB})$, $p_D = \delta/(m_{CD} + m_{ID})$ respectively. To ensure the existence of an equilibrium with positive profits, we assume that the cost coefficients (bs and ds) are all <1.

The average pay-offs of agents possessing contextual skills and working in industries B and D are given by:

$$u_{CB} = \frac{\beta}{m_{CB} + m_{IB}} - \Pi_{CB}b_{CC} - \left(1 - \Pi_{CB}\right)b_{CI}$$

$$u_{CD} = \frac{\delta}{m_{CD} + m_{ID}} - \Pi_{CD}d_{CC} - \left(1 - \Pi_{CD}\right)d_{CI}$$

For example, an agent who enters the B-industry has the probability Π_{CB} of being matched with an agent of the same type, and consequently bearing the cost b_{CC}, while having the probability $1 - \Pi_{CB}$ of being mismatched with an

---

[3] An alternative modeling strategy could be to consider a matching game defined on two populations instead of one: a population of entrepreneurs whose strategy set is composed of organizational forms and industry choices, and a population of workers whose strategy set is composed of skill types and industry choices. More realistic though this alternative modeling may appear, doing it will add little substance to the results obtained in this paper.

agent of a different skill type and consequently bearing the larger cost, b_{CI}. He receives an equal share of the net revenue with his partner, whoever she may be.

Likewise, the average pay-offs of agents with individualized skills working in industries B and D are:

$$u_{IB} = \frac{\beta}{m_{CB} + m_{IB}} - \Pi_{IB}b_{II} - \left(1 - \Pi_{IB}\right)b_{IC}$$

$$u_{ID} = \frac{\delta}{m_{CD} + m_{ID}} - \Pi_{ID}d_{II} - \left(1 - \Pi_{ID}\right)d_{IC}$$

where Π_{Ii} ($i = B, D$) is the probability of agents with individualized skills being matched with others of the same skill type in industry i. These probabilities can be determined by the labor market clearing conditions:

$$\left(1 - \Pi_{Ci}\right)m_{Ci} = \left(1 - \Pi_{Ii}\right)m_{Ii}, \quad i = B, D$$

That is, even if agents miss a correct matching, they are matched with an agent of the different type and there is no unemployment.

The agents with individualized skills do not select the same skill type with a higher probability, but are more flexible in choosing the industry. I assume that they can instantaneously choose the industry in which they can expect to earn a higher income, so that the following arbitrage condition holds at any moment of time:

$$(m_{IB}, m_{ID}) = \text{argmax}_{m_{IB} + m_{ID} = 1 - m_{CB} - m_{CD}}[m_{IB}u_{IB} + m_{ID}u_{ID}]$$

That is, the agents with the individualized skill type are allocated between the two industries in such a way as to equalize their expected incomes.

With this, I have completed the specification of the state of the economy at any moment in time characterized by the distribution of population $m = (m_{CB}, m_{CD}, m_{IB} + m_{ID})$ The next task is to describe a dynamic process of the economy over time, along which the distribution of the population evolves, and inquire into the nature of the equilibria of such a process. Though I do not explicitly model the dynamics, a brief description of a process which might underlie such a model may be stated as follows.

Agents invest in a specific skill type for a lifetime and cannot change it until they exit the economy, although they are mobile across industries (organizations) as specified so far. At each moment in time a small fraction of the population is replaced by a new generation of individuals, most of whom mimic the strategies of their parents. A small fraction of them choose their strategies to mimic the existing strategy with the highest average pay-off. I will introduce later the possibility that an even smaller fraction experiments with random choice. As a result, only the most successful type will increase its relative share in the population. Letting u = max[u_{CB}, u_{CD}, u_{IB}, u_{ID}] I define the *best response evolutionary dynamics* as a path characterized by the following conditions:

$$\frac{dm_{\varsigma i}}{dt} < \varepsilon\,(u_{\varsigma i} - u)$$

for some $\varepsilon > 0$, if and only if $u_{\varsigma i} < u$ and $m_{\varsigma i} > 0$;

$$\frac{dm_{\varsigma i}}{dt} = 0$$

if $u_{\varsigma i} < u$ and $m_{\varsigma i} = 0$, where $\varsigma = <C,I>$ and $i = <B,D>$; and

$$\sum_{\varsigma i_\varepsilon < C,I > \times < B,C >} \frac{dm_{\varsigma i}}{dt} = 0$$

An *equilibrium* of these evolutionary dynamics is any population distribution $m^* = (m^*_{CB}, m^*_{CD}, m^*_{IB}, m^*_{ID})$ for which $(dm_{\varsigma i}/dt) = 0$ for all ς and i. Such a distribution can be realized when there exists ς_1 and ς_2 for which

$$u^*_{\varsigma 1 B} = u^*_{\varsigma 2 D}$$

$$u^*_{\varsigma 1 B} \geq u^*_{\varsigma B} \text{ for } \varsigma \neq \varsigma_1; \text{ if } > u^*_{\varsigma B} \text{ then } m_{\varsigma B} = 0$$

$$u^*_{\varsigma 2 B} \geq u^*_{\varsigma D} \text{ for } \varsigma \neq \varsigma_1; \text{ if } > u^*_{\varsigma D} \text{ then } m_{\varsigma D} = 0$$

$$\text{If } u^*_{Ii1} > u^*_{Ii2} \text{ then } m^*_{Ii2} = 0$$

The last condition reflects the utility maximizing behavior of the mobile agents with individualized skills. They do not participate in an industry unless they are assured of at least the same pay-offs as can be expected in the other industry. An equilibrium is said to be an *evolutionary equilibrium* if it is locally asymptotically stable (Freedman, 1991). All states near an evolutionary equilibrium will eventually evolve toward it.[4] We can prove:

PROPOSITION 1.   *There are nine equilibria for the best-response evolutionary dynamics, all of which are Nash equilibria. Among them four are evolutionary equilibria and only one is Pareto efficient, characterized by a diversity of organizational forms.*

Equilibria of evolutionary dynamics are listed in Table 1. (The proof is routine, so is omitted. The stability properties may be intuitively grasped by consulting Figure 1.)

   Of the nine equilibria, the *P-equilibrium* is the unique Pareto optimal equilibrium in which an optimal diversity of organizational forms (the most efficient matching) is realized in both industries (*L-equilibrium* is a pathological

———

[4] In the setting of the current model, any evolutionary equilibrium of the current dynamics is also an evolutionarily stable strategy in Maynard Smith's sense.

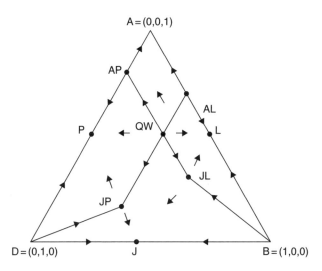

FIGURE 1. Simplex (m_{CB}, m_{CD}, $m_{IB} + m_{ID}$) representation of best response evolutionary dynamics and multiple equilibria.

TABLE 1. Equilibria of Evolutionary Dynamics

Equilibrium	Condition	Stability
P	$u_{CD} = u_{IB} = u^P > u_{CB}, u_{ID}$	stable
A	$u_{IB} = u_{ID} = u^A > u_{CB}, u_{CD}$	stable
J	$u_{CB} = u_{CD} = u^J > u_{IB}, u_{ID}$	stable
L	$u_{CB} = u_{ID} = u^L > u_{CD}, u_{IB}$	stable
AP	$u_{CD} = u_{IB} = u_{ID} = u^{AP} > u_{CB}$	saddle
JP	$u_{CB} = u_{CD} = u_{IB} = u^{JP} > u_{ID}$	saddle
AL	$u_{CB} = u_{IB} = u_{ID} = u^{AL} > u_{CD}$	saddle
JL	$u_{CB} = u_{CD} = u_{ID} = u^{JL} > u_{IB}$	saddle
QW	$u_{CB} = u_{CD} = u_{IB} = u_{ID} = u^{QW}$	source

equilibrium in which less efficient matching is sustained in both industries). In the *A-equilibrium* and *J-equilibrium* all the agents adopt a single skill choice strategy, either individualized or contextual, regardless of industry. Once these two equilibria are established historically, it would be difficult to upset them in spite of their suboptimality, because the deviation of a small group of agents from the corresponding equilibrium strategy would be heavily penalized by the larger risk of mismatching. The adoption of the prevailing homogeneous skill choice would then become a *convention*. Hereafter we refer to the *A-equilibrium* (*J-equilibrium*) and the *A-convention* (*J-convention*) interchangeably. Since neither of these organizational conventions has an absolute advantage but only a relative one, different economies internalizing different organizational conventions may enjoy absolute advantages in different industries. The following proposition provides information regarding their Pareto ranking.

TABLE 2. Equilibrium Population Distributions and Pay-offs: a Numerical Example

Eq	m^*_{CB}	m^*_{CD}	m^*_{IB}	m^*_{ID}	u
P	0.000	0.500	0.500	0.000	0.700
A	0.000	0.000	0.525	0.475	0.652
J	0.475	0.525	0.000	0.000	0.652
L	0.500	0.000	0.000	0.500	0.600
AP	0.000	0.156	0.533	0.311	0.638
JP	0.311	0.533	0.156	0.000	0.638
AL	0.328	0.000	0.164	0.508	0.583
JL	0.508	0.164	0.000	0.328	0.583
QW	0.333	0.167	0.167	0.333	0.566

PROPOSITION 2. *If $\beta = \delta$, $b_{II} = d_{CC}$ and if $b_{CC} = d_{II}$, $u^A = u^J$. Difference $u^A - u^J$ is increasing β, $d_{CC} - b_{II}$ and $b_{CC} - d_{II}$.*

Proof. See the appendix.

Table 2 illustrates the equilibrium distribution of strategies and the associated values of pay-off levels for the numerical examples of $\beta = \delta = 0.5$, $\gamma = 1$ and cost matrices:

$$B = \begin{bmatrix} 0.3 & 0.5 \\ 0.5 & 0.4 \end{bmatrix} \quad \text{and} \quad \Delta = \begin{bmatrix} 0.4 & 0.5 \\ 0.5 & 0.3 \end{bmatrix}$$

Figure 1 depicts the distribution of the equilibria in the three-dimensional simplex representing (m_{CB}, m_{CD}, $m_{IB} + m_{ID}$) for the same numerical values. The areas containing the evolutionary equilibria P, A, J and L are the basins of attraction for the respective equilibria, which are the sets of all initial points that eventually converge to the corresponding equilibria via the best response evolutionary dynamics. The topology (qualitative nature) of the phase diagram will remain the same as the parameter values of the technologies, consumer tastes and assortative matching technology change. Some of the quantitative responses of the basins of attractions to parameter value changes are analyzed in Section 5.

4. *Mechanisms of Exploiting Gains from Diversity*

The model of the previous section indicates that the Pareto efficient industrial structure involves a diversity of organizational forms, contingent on the technological and market parameters of each industry, whereas the economy in which some type of organizational convention prevails cannot achieve the same level of efficiency. The efficiency gains from the diversity of organizational forms are referred to below as the *gains from organizational diversity*. The model so far has not predicted which evolutionary equilibria will be likely to emerge, except that it solely depends on the initial condition. As discussed heuristically by Aoki (1995), however, any economy (national or local) is more or less characterized by the relative uniformity of organizational form, although it may be preceded by a period of cohabitation of diverse organizational experimentation.

Imagine that at the initial stage of the economy a more primitive organizational mode, say 'classical hierarchy' (CH), prevailed, in which constituent tasks served by simpler skills produced an output (say, with cost 0.5) according to commands specified *ex ante* by a proprietor-entrepreneur. Imagine further that multiple organizational experiments subsequently emerged which relied on the information processing capacity at the task level. They can be 'functional hierarchy' (FH), based on a differentiated information system, or team-oriented 'horizontal hierarchy' (HH), based on an assimilated information system [for a precise conceptualization of FH and HH see Aoki (1995)]. Like the numerical examples in Table 2, each of them may be able to produce one unit of a product at the cost of 0.3 in its relatively advantageous industry and at the cost of 0.4 in its relatively disadvantageous industry, provided that appropriate information processing skills are supplied and matched. It may be considered the role of entrepreneurs to mediate assortative matching of such still-scarce skills, although they were not explicitly introduced in the model presented in the previous section.

In the beginning, there might be competition among new organizational forms, but once one form gained momentum, even if another form were potentially more efficient in some industry, evolutionary pressure might make the sustainability of that other form harder, at least at the economy-wide level. This is so because, with the fear of the greater risk of mismatching, it becomes ever less advantageous for the new generation to invest in the type of skills tailored to a less dominant organizational form (this is an instance of strategic complementarity). Alternatively, more intensive assortative matching might be sought among the holders of relatively scarce types of skills, which might result in a local congregation of a unique organizational form which constitutes a niche in the economy. Thus the presence of evolutionary pressure suggests that organizational diversity, in the sense of cohabitation of diverse organizational forms across industries in one economy/locality, may not be taken for granted. However, the possibility of multiple equilibria also suggests that the evolution of different organizational conventions across economies and localities may occur. Given such a possibility of organizational diversity, let us now consider several possible avenues for exploiting the gains from diversity: free trade, economic integration, mutation based on emulation or invasion (foreign direct investment) and design based on rational expectations.

Free Trade

First, let us consider if the gains from organizational diversity could be exploited by free trade among economies/localities. This subsection deals with gains from trade between two economies that have historically developed two different organizational conventions, A-equilibrium and J-equilibrium.

Let the population size of the two economies, A and J, be n^A and n^J. Let n^A_{Ii} be the size of the population of A-economy engaged in i-industry ($i = B, D$), and n^J_{Ci} be that of the J-economy. Assume that the tastes of the populations of the two economies are identical, as specified in the previous section. Then perfectly integrated markets determine the price level of the B-product at

$$p^B = \frac{\beta(n^A + n^J)}{n^A_{IB} + n^J_{CD}}$$

and that of D-product at

$$p^D = \frac{\delta(n^A + n^J)}{n^A_{ID} + n^J_{CD}}$$

Assuming that the organizational convention of each economy persists after market integration, because of a barrier to free mobility of agents across the borders of two economies so that

$$u^A_{IB} = p^B - b_{II}, \quad u^A_{ID} = p^D - d_{II}, \quad u^J_{CB} = p^B - b_{CC},$$
$$u^J_{CD} = p^D - d_{CC}$$

there are three possible classes of trade equilibrium, depending upon the relative size of the two economies.

(i) If

$$\Psi^{-1}(b_{II} - d_{II}) \le \frac{n^A}{n^A + n^J} \le 1$$

for Ψ defined in the proof of Proposition 2, then it holds that

$$u^A_{IB} = u^A_{ID}, \quad u^J_{CB} = 0$$

This is the case in which the J-economy, being smaller and enjoying the efficiency advantage in industry D, becomes specialized in that industry. However, the supply capacity of the J-economy is so small that part of the population of the relatively larger A-economy is also engaged in that industry as well to meet demands. From the equilibrium condition

$$u^A_{IB} = u^A_{ID}$$

it holds that

$$\Psi\left(\frac{n^A{}_{IB}}{n^A + n^J}\right) = b_{II} - d_{II}$$

and the price level remains the same as in the closed A-economy. Therefore there are no gains from trade for the larger A-economy, but for the J-economy there are aggregate gains—quasi-rent from the organizational advantage in its specialized industry.

(ii) If

$$0 \leq \frac{n^A}{n^A + n^J} \leq \Psi^{-1}(b_{CC} - d_{CC})$$

then

$$u^A{}_{ID} = 0, \quad u^J{}_{CB} = u^J{}_{CD}$$

This is a case symmetric to (i) in which the smaller A-economy is specialized in industry B for which it has an efficiency advantage.

(iii) If

$$\Psi^{-1}(b_{CC} - d_{CC}) \leq \frac{n^A}{n^A + n^J} \leq \Psi^{-1}(b_{II} - d_{II})$$

then

$$u^A{}_{ID} = u^J{}_B = 0$$

This is the case where two economies, which are relatively equal in size but heterogeneous in organizational convention, are engaged in mutually benefi-cial free trade. Both economies are specialized in the industries for which they have efficiency advantages.[5]

If the conventions of both economies are taken as exogenously fixed, all the equilibria described above correspond to what will emerge in the neo-Ricardian model when the skill distribution is exogenously given (Krugman and Obstfeld, 1994, chapter 2). In the present model the skill distribution and, accordingly, the distribution of the organizational form are endogenous variables. Therefore, when the organizational forms are fixed at subefficient

---

[5] The neo-Ricardian feature of our model is responsible for this unrealistic implication that both economies are completely specialized in one industry. In the real world a substantial flow of intraindustry trade is observed. One way of reconciling our model with this phenomenon without invoking the Krugman—Helpman type sophistication is to regard the B- and D-industries as groupings of products based on organizational advantage (e.g. logic chips may be regarded as a B-product most efficiently pro-duced by individualized skills, whereas memory chips may be regarded as a D-product most efficiently produced by contextual skills).

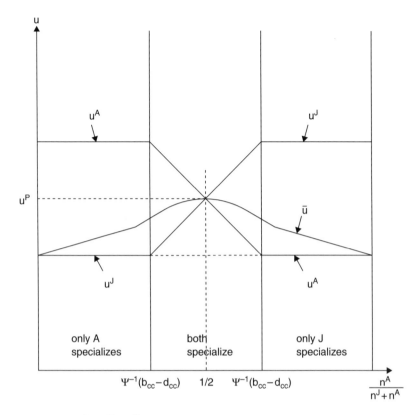

FIGURE 2. Free trade welfare effect.

conventions, the aggregate gains from free trade do not match those available from optimal organizational diversity (*P*-equilibrium), except for the unlikely case in which the relative size of the two economies n^A/n^J happens to be equal to the ratio of demand parameters β/δ.

Figure 2 depicts the welfare gains from free trade for a symmetric case. The line $\bar{u}$ represents the average pay-offs of the agents weighted by the size of the populations. The distance between u^J (alternatively u^A) and $\bar{u}$ measures the per capita quasi-rent from the organizational innovation accruable to individual agents of the smaller *J*-economy (the *A*-economy). Thus, we have:

PROPOSITION 3.   *The gains from free trade are greater for a smaller economy which has developed an organizational advantage in some industry. However, the quasi-rent from the organizational advantage will decline as the relative size of the economy becomes larger. The global gains from free trade will not reach the optimal level except by chance.*

Geographical Economic Integration

Present-day international economic interactions are not limited to trade. Another possibility of realizing the gains from organizational diversity is the integration of two economies which have developed different organizational conventions, each having superior efficiency in a different industry (for example, one may interpret European integration as having a modicum of this feature). In the following proposition, 'economic integration' is interpreted as the merger of two separate evolutionary games.

PROPOSITION 4. *For any technological and demand conditions, the integration of two economies which have developed the A- and J-conventions will lead to Pareto efficient organizational diversity, provided that neither of them is too large nor too small vis-à-vis another economy. Precisely, with the total population size being normalized as* $n^A + n^J = n_{CS} + n_{CD} + n_{IB} + n_{ID} = 1$, *the post-integration best response evolutionary dynamics will converge to the P-equilibrium if the pre-integration size of the A-economy,* n^A, *is in the neighborhood of* $m^{QW}_{IB} + m^{QW}_{ID}$ *(the population share of the individualized skill type at the post-merger QW equilibrium).*

Proof. Omitted.

I interpret this proposition as indicating a kind of path-dependent property of evolutionary dynamics: once an organizational convention has been formed in a closed economy and has acquired a certain scale, it will continue to exist, even if the initial condition which facilitated its emergence disappears. On the other hand, even a potentially efficient organizational innovation may become extinct by 'premature' integration with a larger economy if that innovation has arisen in a relatively small economy.

Organizational Experiments

As we have seen, the gains from diversity through free trade are incomplete in our model. In any case, the possibility of trade in the real world may be limited by various technological and politico-economic reasons (e.g. transportation costs, intrinsic immobility of certain goods and services, trade barriers). However, the source of possible gains from diversity in our model is organizational form, which is a human contrivance. Therefore, we need to examine the possibility of internal exploitation of the gains from diversity. Even though it is not situationally rational for agents not to conform to an established convention, they may experiment in unconventional skill formation, e.g. by investing in individualized skills within the context of *J*-convention or, alternatively, the contextual skills within the context of *A*-convention. These random experiments are analogous to mutations in biological evolution, independent of the natural selection of the fittest. Social mutations may occur when a small proportion of the population is replaced by a new generation which is not bound by a traditional convention—for example, a number of agents who are exposed, educated and trained in a foreign convention return to the home country, or a foreign firm makes direct investment and consciously selects workers fitting the convention in its host economy (positive assortative matching). What would be the long-term outcome of evolutionary selection when such mutations occur? Is it still difficult to upset old social conventions?

To explore this issue theoretically in the context of a closed economy, let me introduce the notion of the cost of transition from one evolutionary equilibrium to another. Let us imagine that possible 'states' of the economy are composed only of the nine equilibria of evolutionary dynamics described in the last section. Among them, refer to the four evolutionary stable equilibria, P, A, J and L, as *quasi-permanent* states and the five unstable equilibria, AP, AL, JP, JL and QW, as *transitory* states. We define the *cost of transition*, C_{HK}, from a quasi-permanent state H to another quasi-permanent state K by the least upper-bound of the proportion of the current population at H, who must mutate in order to cross the intermediate transitory state, HK, to reach K (e.g. for the case of transition from L to P, the intermediate state is QW; see Figure 1). Remembering that the individualized type can be mobile between two industries, the cost is defined as

$$C_{HK} = \|m^b - m^{bk}\| = 1/2 \left[\left| m^b{}_{CB} - m^{bk}{}_{CB} \right| + \left| m^b{}_{CD} - m^{bk}{}_{CD} \right| \right.$$
$$\left. + \left| m^b{}_{IB} - m^b{}_{ID} - m^{bk}{}_{IB} - m^{bk}{}_{ID} \right| \right]$$

The cost of transition, C_{kh}, from K to H may be defined symmetrically. Figure 3 displays the costs of transitions between the quasi-permanent states based on the numerical example given in Table 2. It shows that it is more costly for the unique Pareto efficient state, P, to transit to another state than for the opposite to occur. This property generally holds. The property roughly indicates that it would be relatively more difficult to upset the Pareto efficient state once it is achieved.[6]

---

[6] Theoretical refinement is not the purpose of this paper. However, it may be of some interest to point out the following theoretical property of the present model. Take the set of four quasi-stable equilibria and consider all possible 'trees' among them. [The tree is a half-order relation on the set of states such that: (i) each element except one has only one immediate successor; and (ii) there is only one element which is a (immediate or indirect) successor to all the other elements in the set. The last element, which is also excepted in (i), is called the root of the tree.] For each tree, calculate the aggregate costs of transition and identify the minimum aggregate cost tree from all the trees having H as the root. Refer to the minimum aggregate cost as the 'cost of transition to H'. Finally, compare the costs of transition to all four quasi-permanent states. The root of the minimum cost tree among the four is P in our model. According to Kandori *et al.* (1993) and Young (1993), the root of the minimum cost tree is indeed the unique long-term equilibrium of stochastic evolutionary dynamics in which agents from a finite population experiment with a very small probability at a discrete time interval. However, our model comprises the continuum of the agents' revising strategy on a continuous time scale. In continuous models the dynamic property of a stochastic evolutionary game may depend on various parametric specifications of the model (Fudenberg and Harris, 1992).

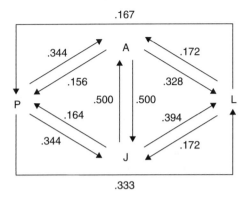

FIGURE 3. Costs of transition.

It is also interesting to note that for this example the cost of transition from *A* to *P* is smaller than that from *J* to *P*. This property arises because of the flexible mobility of the individualized skill type across industries, and holds in general for cases in which technologies and demands are 'symmetric' in that

$$b_{II} - b_{IC} = d_{CC} - d_{CI}, \quad b_{II} - b_{CC} = d_{CC} - d_{II}, \quad \beta = 1/2, \quad \gamma = 1$$

This is intuitive and proof is omitted.

PROPOSITION 5. *For cases of symmetric technological and demand parameters with random matching, the cost of transition to the efficient diversity is smaller than the A-convention than for the J-convention.*

It is interesting to examine how this disadvantage of the *J*-convention can be overcome by introducing the possibility of assortative matching, as well as asymmetry in demand and technological parameters. This question is answered by the following proposition.

PROPOSITION 6. *The cost of transition from the J-convention to the efficient diversity, P, is reduced as* β, $(b_{IC} - b_{CC})/(b_{CI} - b_{II})$, $d_{CC} - b_{CC}$ *and* γ *become smaller.*

Proof. See the appendix.

This proposition may be interpreted as follows. Suppose that the *J*-convention prevails in the economy so that the *D*-industry is run efficiently but not the *B*-industry. In this situation, if the product demands for *B*-product are not so large and/or if the relative efficiency of the conventional organizational form is very low in the *B*-industry, the convention may be upset more easily in that industry by the external shock of mutation. The productivity differential between the two industries under the convention will have the same effect. These results are consistent with often observed stylized facts that organizational conventions are rather robust in a relatively efficient economy but that organizational learning sometimes proceeds at a faster rate and generates a new organizational form when a large productivity gap with a foreign economy is perceived (Aoki, 1995). Also, if the degree of positive assortative matching is greater so that the contextual skill type tends to congregate more, less evolutionary pressure will be exercised on individualistic mutants because of the reduced risk of mismatching. Then the mutant organizational form becomes more viable and there will be an increasing chance of transit to efficient organizational diversity. This is analytically clear, but a conventional argument does not seem to necessarily run in this vein.

Skill Formation (Organizational Design) Based on Rational Foresight

Evolutionary dynamics are characterized by two elements of bounded rationality: (i) myopic choice of skill type and industry by the agents without any foresight but rather on the basis of observed behavior of the current population; and (ii) inertia, which makes a complete, instantaneous, optimal adjustment impossible. These two bounded-rationality factors were responsible for the path-dependent selection of a non-optimal equilibrium (the emergence of an organizational convention). The previous subsection indicates that mutations may play a role in helping the economy to overcome historical determinism. However, the barrier to realizing the gains from organizational diversity by means of mutations may remain formidable (in our numerical example close to 8% of the population needs to mutate at one time!). One may thus wonder whether adding some element of 'rationality' and a gradual accumulation of organizational innovation may help the economy to realize the efficient choice of an organizational arrangement. We therefore ask the following question: if a small number of agents are successively able to form foresight regarding the potential future value of an unconventional organizational form, choose a strategy accordingly and adhere to it over time, will the economy gradually self-organize the efficient organizational diversity?

It is difficult to present a convincing formulation of expectations which carry a certain bounded rationality feature. Therefore, I make the following compromise: a certain proportion of the population, called a group of entrepreneurs, randomly selected at each moment in time, form perfect foresight and base their strategic choices on that expectation, while others are attached to current strategies with inertia. I assume that the relative size of the entrepreneur at each moment in time is proportional to the conceived magnitude of disequilibrium, i.e. the greater the discrepancy of the potential asset values between the two skill types, the more agents will base their choices on future expectations. I will show that, far from the evolutionary equilibria, the entrepreneurial expectation plays a significant role in wiping out the historical constraint. However, it does not necessarily imply that the economy will definitely converge to the efficient state of organizational diversity. Far from evolutionary equilibria a bifurcation of the dynamic equilibrium path occurs, with one path converging to the efficient organizational diversity and the other to an inefficient evolutionary equilibrium (convention).

In order to make the analysis tractable, I introduce two restrictions into the model, although I conjecture that the essential argument is expected to be carried out for a more general case. First, I assume in this section that the matching of agents with contextual skills is also random (i.e. $\gamma = 1$). Second, I assume that the agents choosing the C-strategy are always engaged in the technologically advantageous D-industry. Thus the strategy set of the agents is reduced to the binary strategy choice of I versus C. The agents choosing the I-strategy can be mobile between the B and D industries at any moment in time, as before. Diagrammatically, this assumption reduces the domain of the agent's strategic choice to the one-dimensional border line (simplex) connecting the apices $D = (0,1,0)$ and $A = (0,0,1)$ of the two-dimensional simplex depicted in Figure 1.

On the one-dimensional simplex $[DA]$, define $\Delta u_C = u_{CD} - u_{IB}$ and let Q_C represent the implicit net asset value of acquiring the contextual skill relative to the individualized skill. Given the rate of interest on riskless assets, ρ, the arbitrage condition requires:

$$\frac{dQ_C}{dt} + \Delta u_C(t) \leq \rho Q_C(t)$$

with equality if $m_{CD} > 0$. In other words, the implicit net asset value is determined at the level at which the sum of expected net capital gains and the current net income from possessing the asset are equal to the interest income available from investing the same value of wealth in safe assets.

Suppose that at each moment in time a group of agents randomly selected from the population can perceive the implicit net asset value Q_C correctly and base their investment decisions on that expectation. Specifically we assume:

$$\frac{dm_{CD}}{dt} = \lambda Q_C(t)$$

where λ represents the level of the entrepreneurial spirit in the economy. The formula implies that the higher the net asset value of the contextual skill Q_C is, the greater the relative size of the entrepreneur group. The above two differential equations define the Krugman-Matsuyama type equilibrium dynamic paths. Then the following proposition holds.

PROPOSITION 7. *If $d_{IC} + d_{CI} - d_{CC} - d_{II} > \rho^2/4\lambda$, the dynamic path bifurcates when it is far from the evolutionary equilibrium.*

Proof. See the appendix.

This proposition suggests that if there is a higher cost of mismatching in the *D*-industry and a higher level of entrepreneurial spirit, and, if entrepreneurs discount the future less, then it is less likely that history alone will determine the outcome of the evolutionary dynamic path. The entrepreneurs' foresight matters, but the direction of their activity is not clear. It does not necessarily lead to efficient organizational diversity, but may lead to the formation of a subefficient homogeneous convention. Which way the economy evolves may depend on some historically unique factors that the economic model of this paper is unable to capture. We need to accumulate more comparative and historical information regarding the evolution of organizational forms before being able to construct a more insightful model of organizational evolution.

5. *The Limits and Relevance of the Evolutionary Game Model*

One of major objectives of this paper has been to show how different organizational conventions could arise in different economies/localities and become a source of relative industrial advantage/disadvantage, even if potential technologies and tastes were the same everywhere. The reason for the evolution of multiple suboptimal organizational conventions is neither convexity nor externalities, as focused on recently in economics, but complementarity among the strategic choices of agents. If a large proportion of the population adopts a certain strategy, it becomes the best response for agents to adopt the same strategy. The apparent difference from the contract theory of the organization which prescribes/predicts a (second) best response of the principal to exogenous parameters arises from the fact that the contract theory treats the outside options open to the principal and agents as exogenously given, while in evolutionary models, alternatives open to each agent are determined endogenously as a result of the strategic interplay of agents.

The model presented here is extremely simple: there are only two skill types and two organizational forms. Technological and market conditions are parametrically fixed. Although the setting of the model thus remains at an extremely abstract level, I hope that it captures some fundamental factors which underlie the observed diversity of organizational forms across economies. More specifically, I submit that if one compares two (possibly polar) cases of organizational evolution in North America and Japan, one cannot fail to notice the striking relevance of the distinction made in this paper between individualized and contextual skill types.

Think of some of the notable examples of innovation in the area of work organization which were initiated and institutionalized in North America, such as the so-called 'American manufacturing system' developed in the last century in New England that surprised contemporary Europe with its competitive threat (Rosenberg, 1969; Pine, 1993); the Taylorist scientific management movement [whose innovative nature has often been misunderstood; see Wrege and Greenwood (1991)]; and the subsequent development of functional hierarchies, bureaucratization of the employment system (Jacoby, 1985; Baron *et al.*, 1986) and job controlled unionism in the 1930s. All these examples have a common characteristic in having either introduced or institutionalized a new method of combining individualized skills at progressive degrees of maturity— skills that became embodied in individual workers, engineers and managers through professional and vocational training, even though some elements of organizational contextuality cannot be entirely ignored. The organizational innovation which has recently taken place in Silicon Valley seems to have evolved somewhat along the same line, although it is legitimately regarded as a radical departure from traditional functional hierarchies in which bureaucratic control of highly segmented jobs was the norm.[7]

If we turn to historically known examples of organizational practices and innovations which affected the evolutionary path of organizational practices in Japan, a striking contrast to the American path is immediately discernible: for example, the dormitory system of the female workers when the privately run industrial factory system emerged late in the last century; the design of the seniority and bonus payment system by advanced factories at the beginning of the twentieth century as a means of restraining excessive resignations of skilled workers; reliance on collective, ad-hoc problem-solving by the workers on the shop floor in response to various production problems arising from the scarcity of tools and materials during the Second World War; the transformation of the American-born, engineer-led quality-control system into shop-floor-level work-group practices; and the evolution of the 'kanban' system which partially emulated an inventory restocking method used by American supermarket firms in the 1950s (Aoki, 1988, 1997; Fujimoto, 1997; Okazaki and Okuno-Fujiwara, 1997).

In contrast to the American case, reliance on workers' 'mental models' horizontally sharing information channels within the context of a particular organization is a distinct attribute, even though more recent innovations seem

---

[7] See Aoki (1999, chapter 12) for a model of Silicon Valley which purports to explain how it differs from, as well as conforms with, the traditional functional hierarchies and why it evolved in a peripheral region of North America.

to increasingly accommodate elements of the workers' individualized information processing skills. For example, the now famous 'kanban' system cannot be implemented without the ability of individual workers to cope with emergent events on the spot, such as breakdown of machines or spotting defective parts. But even these abilities are backed up by the workers' information networking channels (e.g. mutual help in teams, the sharing of engineering and production knowledge through job rotation and cross-functional meetings, company-specific training programs). It is worth noting that, when the idea of the 'kanban' system was brought back to America in the 1980s as a lesson from the so-called 'Japanese management', it was transformed into something different, yet consistent with the American path—the 'lean production method' which would reduce inventories and hierarchical layers of production control by flexible matching (outsourcing) with specialized suppliers.

The brief observations in the last two paragraphs also indicate the limits of applying the results of a 'stationary' evolutionary model for interpreting real phenomena, however. By 'stationary' I refer specifically to the assumption that the strategic choice set of each agent is exogenously given and fixed. Therefore, in our theoretical model, 'innovation' in one economy can occur only in the form of a shift from one equilibrium to the one characterized by diversity. Competition among economies often induces an attempt to emulate an organizational convention prevailing in a foreign economy which may be perceived to be superior. However, as just mentioned above regarding the evolution of the 'kanban' system and its recycling into North America, learning from a foreign practice may result not in a simple transplant, but rather in the formation of a hybrid with indigenous organizational practice. Also, entrepreneurial experiments that eventually lead to the rise of a new organizational form may actually be enriched ramifications of existing strategies, as in the case of Silicon Valley firms.

Thus actual organizational evolutionary processes involving innovation may not then be characterized as a mere shift from one convention (such as the J- or A- equilibrium) based on one type of 'mental model' to a diversity merely mixing the two (such as the P-equilibrium). Rather, it can be characterized as a process that expands the space of strategies which the agents actively devise and choose. One conjecture is that such a process may be characterized by successive equilibria, at each of which one type of mental model is sequentially enriched from autonomous design and learning—something similar to what Denzau and North (1994) identified as the process of 'punctuated equilibrium'. In that attempted emulation may often lead to an (unintended) efficient hybrid, a diversity of conventions across economies may become a source of innovations, and there may be dynamic gains from organizational diversity. However, in order to understand such a process, we need to go beyond the scope of conventional 'stationary' evolutionary modeling as presented in this paper.

Acknowledgements

An earlier version of this paper has been circulated since 1993. I am grateful to numerous people who have made critical comments and valuable suggestions for substantially improving on it. I particularly thank Robert Boyer, Joshua Gans, Hideshi Itoh, Michihiro Kandori, Anne O. Krueger, Andreas Mas-Colell, Preston McAfee, Aki Matsui, Kiminori Matsuyama, John Rohmer and participants of workshops at the Bank of Italy, Universitat Autonoma at Barcelona, UC Berkeley and San Diego, and Universities of Keio, Stanford, Waseda, Tokyo and Kobe. This version was also presented at the Seventh World Congress of the Econometric Society (Tokyo) in 1995. Robert Hauswald, Serdar Dinc and Ichiro Shinkai provided helpful research assistance. The usual caveats apply.

References

Alchian, A. (1950), 'Uncertainty, Evolution and Economic Theory', *Journal of Political Economy*, 58, 211–221.

Aoki, M. (1986), 'Horizontal and Vertical Information Structure of the Firm', *American Economic Review*, 76, 971–983.

Aoki, M. (1988), *Information, Incentives, and Bargaining in the Japanese Economy*. Cambridge University Press: Cambridge.

Aoki, M. (1995), 'An Evolving Diversity of Organizational Mode and its Implications for Transitional Economies', *Journal of the Japanese and International Economies*, 9, 330–353.

Aoki, M. (1997), 'The Role of Community Norms and States in East Asian Rural-inclusive Economic Development and Institution-building', in Y. Hayami and M. Aoki (eds), *Institutional Foundation of East Asian Economic Development*, Macmillan: Houndmills, pp. 529–551.

Aoki, M. (1999), *Toward a Comparative Institutional Analysis*. MIT Press: Cambridge, MA, in press.

Baron, J. N., F. N. Dobbin and P. Devereaux (1986), 'War and Peace: the Evolution of Modern Personnel Administration in U.S. Industry', *American Journal of Sociology*, 9, 350–383.

Bolton, P. and M. Dewatripont (1994), 'Firms as Networks of Communications', *Quarterly Journal of Economics*, 109, 809–839.

Cremer, J. (1990), 'Common Knowledge and the Co-ordination of Economic Activities', in M. Aoki, B. Gustafsson and O. E. Williamson (eds), *The Firm as a Nexus of Treaties*. Sage Publications: London, pp. 53–76.

Denzau, A. T. and D. North (1994), 'Shared Mental Models: Ideologies and Institutions', *Kyklos*, 47, 3–31.

Dosi, G., K. Pavitt and L. Soete (1990), *The Economics of Technical Change and International Trade*. Harvester Wheatsheaf: New York.

Freedman, D. (1991), 'Evolutionary Games in Economics', *Econometrica*, 59, 637–666.

Friedman, M. (1953), *Essays in Positive Economics*. University of Chicago Press: Chicago, IL.

Fudenberg, D. and C. Harris (1992), 'Evolutionary Dynamics with Aggregate Shocks', *Journal of Economic Theory*, 57, 420–441.

Fujimoto, T. (1997), *The Evolutionary Theory of Production System: Organizational Capability and Emergent Process in Toyota* (in Japanese). Yuhikaku: Tokyo.

Jacoby, S. (1985), *Employing Bureaucracy. Manager, Unions, and the Transformation of Work in the American Industry, 1900–1945*. Columbia University Press: New York.

Kandori, M., G. Mailath and R. Rob (1993), 'Learning and Mutation, and Long-run Equilibrium in Games', *Econometrica*, 61, 29–56.

Krugman, P. (1991), 'History versus Expectations', *Quarterly Journal of Economics*, 56, 651–67.

Krugman, P. and M. Obstfeld (1994), *International Economics: Theory and Policy*, 3rd edn. HarperCollins College Publishers: New York.

Maskin, E., Y. Qian and C. Xu (1997), 'Incentives, Scale Economies, and Organizational Forms', mimeo, Harvard University.

Matsuyama, K. (1991), 'Increasing Returns, Industrialization, and Indeterminacy of Equilibrium', *Quarterly Journal of Economics*, 56, 617–650.

Okazaki, T. and M. Okuno-Fujiwara (1997), 'Evolution of Economic System: The Case of Japan', in Y. Hayami and M. Aoki (eds), *Institutional Foundation of East Asian Economic Development*. Macmillan: Houndmills, pp. 482–521.

Okimoto, D. I. and Y. Nishi (1994), 'R&D Organization in Japanese and American Semiconductor Firms', in M. Aoki and R. Dore (eds), *The Japanese Firm: Sources of Competitive Strength*. Oxford University Press: Oxford.

Pine, B. J. (1993), *Mass Customization: The New Frontier of Business Competition*. Harvard Business School Press: Boston, MA.

Prat, A. (1996), 'Shared Knowledge versus Diversified Knowledge in Teams', *Journal of the Japanese and International Economies*, 11, 181–195.

Radner, R. (1993), 'The Organization of Decentralized Information Processing', *Econometrica*, 61, 1109–1146.

Rosenberg, N. (ed.) (1969), *The American System of Manufactures: the Report of the Committee on the Machinery of the United States 1855 and the Special Reports of George Wallis and Joseph Whitworth 1854*. Edinburgh University Press: Edinburgh.

Saxenian, S. (1994), *Regional Advantage*. Harvard University Press: Cambridge, MA.

Wrege, C. D. and R. G. Greenwood (1991), *Frederick W. Taylor, the Father of Scientific Management: Myth and Reality*. Irwin: Barridge, IL.

Young, H. P. (1993), 'The Evolution of Conventions', *Econometrica*, 61, 57–84.

Appendix

Proof of Proposition 2

Let us introduce an auxiliary function:

$$\Psi(x;\beta) = \frac{\beta}{x} - \frac{1-\beta}{1-x}$$

which is decreasing in variable x and increasing in parameter β (this function plays very important roles in various proofs in the following sections). In terms of this function, A-equilibrium is characterized by $\Psi(m^A_{IB}) = b_{II} - d_{II}$ and $m^A_{ID} = 1 - m^A_{IB}$ while J-equilibrium is characterized by $\Psi(m^J_{CB}) = b_{CC} - d_{CC}$ and $m^J_{CD} = 1 - m^J_{CB}$. If $\beta = \delta$, $\Psi(m) = -\Psi(1-m)$. Therefore, with the rest of the conditions of the proposition, it holds that $m^A_{ID} = m^J_{CD}$ and $u^A = u^J$. The second part of the proposition easily follows from the monotonicity of Ψ.

Proof of Proposition 6.

First, consider the case $\gamma = 1$. From the *JP*-equilibrium condition:

$$u^{JP}_{CB} = u^{JP}_{CD} = u^{JP}_{IB}$$

$$\Psi\left(m^{JP}_{CB} + m^{JP}_{JB}\right) = \frac{1}{m^{JP}_{CB} + m^{JP}_{IB}}\left[m^{JP}_{CB^b_{CC}} + m^{JP}_{IB^b_{CI}}\right] - d_{CC}$$

$$= \frac{1}{m^{JP}_{CB} + m^{JP}_{IB}}\left[m^{JP}CB^{b}_{IC} + m^{JP}IB^{b}_{II}\right] - d_{CC}$$

From this it is derived that

$$\frac{m^{JP}_{IB}}{m^{JP}_{CB}} = \frac{b_{IC} - b_{CC}}{b_{CI} - b_{II}} =_{\text{def}} \kappa$$

and

$$\Psi(m^{JP}_{CB} + m^{JP}_{IB}) = \frac{b_{CC} + b_{CI}\kappa}{1 + \kappa} - d_{CC}$$

Therefore as κ gets smaller, the line going through $D = (0,1,0)$ and m^{JP} gets less steep (see Figure 4). On the other hand, by the definition of *J*-equilibrium, $\Psi(m^{J}_{CB}) = b_{CC} - d_{CC}$. As the function Ψ is monotone decreasing in the variable and $b_{CC} < b_{CI}$, it holds that $m^{JP}_{CD} + m^{JP}_{IB} < m^{J}_{CB}$. As the function Ψ is monotone increasing in parameter β, the smaller $d_{CC} - b_{CC}$ and β, the closer m^{J} and m^{JP} are located to D. All these geometrical effects of parameter value changes make the distance $\|m^{J} - m^{JP}\|$ shorter. Proof for the case of $\gamma \neq 1$ is

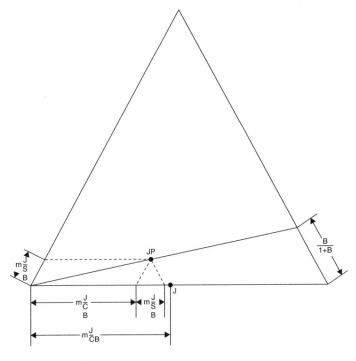

FIGURE 4. Illustration of Proposition 6.

straightforward. From the *JP*-equilibrium condition $u^{JP}{}_{CB} = u^{JP}{}_{CD} = u^{JP}{}_{IB}$, we can derive

$$\left(1 - \left(\frac{1}{1+x}\right)^{\gamma}\right)[(b_{CI} - b_{CC})x - (b_{IC} - b_{II})] = -(b_{CC} - b_{II})x$$

where $x = (m^{JP}{}_{IB})/(m^{JP}{}_{CB})$. By differentiating this with respect to γ we get $dx/d\gamma > 0$, which implies that the line going through D and m^{JP} gets less steep as γ declines.

Proof of Proposition 7

An equilibrium dynamic path described by the two equations in the text is depicted in Figure 5. Size m_{CD} is measured on the line $[D,A]$ left from the right endpoint, A, and size $m_{IB} + m_{ID}$ is measured right from the left endpoint, D. The point K^* is a switching point. On the segment K^+ left to point K^* agents adopting *I*-strategy are specialized in *B*-industry, while on segment K^- to the right of it they are distributed between *D*- and *B*-industries (they are enjoying the same expected pay-offs). On K^+ we have

$$\Delta u_C = -\Psi(1 - m_{CD}) + (b_{II} - d_{CC})$$

and its value declines with respect to m_{CD}. By linearizing the dynamic equations around the equilibrium point, P, we find that the characteristic roots of the differential equations are given by $\frac{1}{2}[\rho \pm \sqrt{(\rho^2 - 4\Delta u'_C\lambda)}]$ where

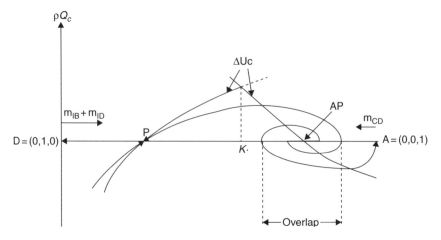

FIGURE 5. Bifurcation of equilibrium path on $(0, m_{CD}, m_{IB} + m_{ID})$.

$\Delta u'_C = d\Delta u_C/dm_{CD}$ is evaluated at P. Therefore, one root is positive and another negative at equilibrium P, making it a stable node.

The dynamic path in region K^- is more complicated. In this region, imposing $u_{IB} = u_{ID}$, we derive

$$\Delta u_C = -\frac{d_{IC} + d_{CI} - d_{CC} - d_{II}}{d_{IC} - d_{II}} \Psi(m_{IB}) + \text{constant}$$

with m_{IB} determined by

$$\Psi(m_{IB}) = b_{II} - d_{II} - \frac{m_{CD}}{1 - m_{IB}}(d_{IC} - d_{II})$$

Differentiating the second equation with respect to m_{CD} and rearranging, we derive

$$m'_{IB} = \frac{dm_{IB}}{dm_{CD}} = \frac{(d_{IC} - d_{II})m^2_{IB}}{\alpha - (d_{II} - b_{II})m^2_{IB}} > 0$$

so that Δu_C increases with respect to m_{CD} in this region, provided the demand parameter for B-product, β, is not too small. If $\Delta u'_C$ is smaller than $\rho^2/4\lambda$ at AP-equilibrium, both characteristic roots are real and positive so that the linearized system steadily diverges from the AP-equilibrium. Depending on whether the initial point is to the left or to the right of AP, the equilibrium path converges to the P- or A-equilibrium uniformly (in the latter case after switching to the equilibrium path defined by the differential equation system on K^+). History (the initial position) uniquely determines the equilibrium path in this case.

However, if $\Delta u'_C > \rho^2/4\lambda$ at AP, then there are two complex characteristic roots, and the linearized system diverges from the AP-equilibrium in expanding oscillations. If the initial point, m_{CD}, lies inside a certain range around the AP-equilibrium, i.e. in what Krugman calls the 'overlap', the self-fulfilling expectation equilibrium path bifurcates, culminating in the P- or the A-equilibrium as shown in Figure 5. At the A-equilibrium, the value of Q_C becomes zero and remains so thereafter. Although it is complicated to derive a general condition for the existence of the overlap in terms of parameter values, the condition in Proposition 7 provides a sufficient condition, a proof of which can be given as follows. Let

$$\xi = d_{IC} + d_{CI} - d_{CC} - d_{II}$$

From the AP-equilibrium condition, $u_{IB} = u_{ID} = u_{CD}$,

$$\Psi(m^{AP}_{IB}) = b_{II} - \frac{1}{\xi}(d_{IC}d_{CI} - d_{II}d_{CC}) \overset{\text{def}}{=} \zeta$$

Then at the *AP*-equilibrium,

$$\Delta u_C' = \frac{\xi}{d_{IC} - d_{II}} \Psi'(m^{AP}{}_{IB}) m^{AP'}{}_{IB}$$

$$= \xi \left[\beta + \left(\frac{(\Psi^{-1}(\zeta))}{1 - (\Psi^{-1}(\zeta))} \right)^2 (1 - \beta) \right] \left[\frac{1}{\beta - (d_{II} - b_{II})(\Psi^{-1}(\zeta))^2} \right]$$

$$> \xi \left(1 + \frac{(d_{II} - b_{II})(\Psi^{-1}(\zeta))^2}{\beta - (d_{II} - b_{II})(\Psi^{-1}(\zeta))^2} \right) > \xi$$

Therefore, if the condition of the proposition holds, $\Delta u'_C > \rho^2/4\lambda$.

Information, Finance, and Markets

The Architecture of Allocative Mechanisms[1]

B. GREENWALD[a] and J. E. STIGLITZ[b]

([a]Columbia University and [b]Department of Economics, Encima Hall,
Room 401, Stanford University, Stanford, CA 94305, USA)

Bankers and businessmen have long recognized the importance of finance, financial constraints, and financial institutions for the vitality and growth, both of their enterprises and of the economy. Yet, while these financial factors may have played a central role in economic theories of the nineteenth and early twentieth centures [see for example Hawtrey (1919)], for almost a half century they have been subordinated to a secondary role by economic theorists. In seeking to explain business cycles, the most recent fashion among American academic economists—real business cycles—attributes no role at all to financial institutions; while in the earlier new classical theories (and even much of Keynesian theory[2]) all financial analysis is subsumed under the control of the money supply.

[1] October 1990 revision of paper presented at International Conference on the History of Enterprise: Finance and the Enterprise in a Historical Perspective, Terni, Italy, September 18, 1989. Financial support from the National Science Foundation, the Olin Foundation, and the Hoover Institution is gratefully acknowledged. This paper was written while B. Greenwald was at Bell Communications Research.

[2] Keynes must be given part of the blame for these developments: his aggregation of long term bonds and equities ignored the fundamental differences between these two forms of capital, differences which play a central role in explaining business fluctuations.

If Keynes set the economics profession on the wrong road, Modigliani and Miller—appearing a quarter century after the publication of Keynes' *General Theory*—provided the intellectual underpinnings for what was by then standard practice among macro-economists. They provided a set of assumptions under which financial structure truly made no difference. While for almost 15 years following Modigliani and Miller, the profession sought to show that their result was more general than even they had realized (see for example Hirshleifer, 1966; and Stiglitz, 1969, 1972a), it has only been in the past 15 years that we have gradually come to understand why the theorem is of little relevance (see for example Stiglitz, 1988a, and the references cited there).

The econometric work examining firm behavior, particularly with respect to investment behavior, provides an important cautionary tale: while the earlier work of Kuh and Meyer (1959) had provided strong suggestions that, at least for many firms, financial factors were important in determining their investment behavior, the later work of Jorgenson and his co-authors (see Hall and Jorgenson, 1967) employing the so-called neoclassical theory of investment excluded these variables, simply because they (wrongly) believed that 'economic theory' argued that they should have been excluded. While 'measurement without theory'

In looking at macro-economic theories of long term growth, this narrowing of theoretical vision has been, if anything, even more extreme. Neoclassical growth theory ignored the role of financing institutions altogether (e.g. Solow, 1956) and the few attempts to look at the role of financial markets (e.g. Foley and Sidrauski, 1970) focused narrowly on the effects of money supply decisions. In our view, while the former perspective is simply wrong, the latter approach not only represents a vast oversimplification, but it is a misleading one: the prescriptions which emerge, both with respect to micro- and macro-policy, are, at best partial, at worst, suspect. Thus, it is significant that in empirical economic analyses (e.g. in development economics and economic history) there is extensive debate on the role of financial institutions in stimulating growth which is almost invisible in the theoretical arena.

This paper is divided into three sections. The first defines the economic problems with which the financial institutions are concerned. It argues that the central function of financial institutions is to overcome, or at least deal with, the information problems which, in their absence, would impede the agglomeration of capital and its transfer from those who have resources to those who can most effectively use it. The second shows the variety of ways with which modern economies address these problems, identifying the strengths and weaknesses of the alternative mechanisms, discusses briefly how these institutions have evolved, and identifies the legal and technological changes that were required for the development of these financial institutions. The third section explores the relationship between the financial constraints which arise out of the informational imperfections and the evolution of the firm. It serves to illustrate the impact of financial institutions on real resource allocations, and to suggest why neoclassical models, which systematically ignored financial institutions and constraints, may be seriously misleading.

1. *The Role of Financial Institutions*

There are two reasons for the development of financial institutions[3]: some enterprises require more capital than any single individual has at his disposal (the agglomeration function); and those who are in the best position to invest

---

may not be the best approach to understanding economic systems, and while it may be true that 'data can never speak for themselves', we should at least listen to the strong whispers of the data, and not be over confident in our theories, particularly when they contradict common sense.

[3] There are other reasons, with which we shall be less concerned in this paper; principal among these is risk diversification.

(to innovate, to monitor, etc.) are not necessarily those who have resources (the transfer function[4]).[5]

To accomplish these functions, financial institutions must select among alternative uses of those funds (the selection function), and they seek to encourage prudent behavior on the part of those to whom they have provided funds, to ensure that the funds are used in a way which will reap the providers of the fund the expected return, both by designing contractual (implicit and explicit) arrangements and by direct monitoring (the control function).[6]

It is important to realize, at this juncture, the basic differences between financial (capital) markets and other markets, in which goods are traded contemporaneously. In capital markets, money today is exchanged for a *promise* of returns in the future. The promise is always, in effect, a contingent promise: in the case of a bond, the promise takes the form, 'I will pay a certain amount, provided that I can; and if I can't, certain other consequences follow. . . .' In the case of equity, the promise takes the form, 'I will pay a fraction of my profits. I will decide the fraction, and I will decide how profits are defined. Trust me! If I don't pay you a dividend, I will reinvest the money in the firm, and you will receive a return in the form of a capital gain.'

It is precisely this difference which explains why financial markets are not, and cannot be, run as auction markets: why lenders, for instance, do not simply lend to those who are willing to offer to pay the highest interest rates. Those who promise to pay the highest interest rates may not, in fact, be those for whom the expected return is highest.[7]

Banks and other financial institutions are in the business of directly allocating resources, of making judgments about the best uses of capital, or at least, about which users are most likely to pay the promised returns. Prices (interest rates) play a role in the allocative mechanism—they define, for instance, the opportunity cost of the funds; but the allocative mechanism is fundamentally a *screening* mechanism, in which prices play a secondary role. Thus, in contrast to markets for homogeneous commodities, in which the role of institutions (firms and market makers) can reasonably be approximated by the interaction of supply and demand, in studying financial markets and the allocation of funds the role of institutions is central.

---

[4] Indeed, in the natural life cycle of a firm, in the early stages the firm needs more capital than it generates, while in later stages it may generate more profits than it can profitably invest.

[5] The adduced reasons for financial institutions are really reasons either for the existence of a capital market or for financial institutions. Below, we explain why credit markets are not like auction markets, that is, why financial institutions are required.

[6] Both the selection (or screening) function and the control function can be thought of as information problems: imperfect information is an impediment to the functioning of financial markets, and it is a principal objective of financial institutions to overcome these informational impediments.

[7] This point has been emphasized by Stiglitz and Weiss (1981) and Stiglitz (1988b).

A Simple Formal Model

Consider a simple situation in which an agent (entrepreneur or manager) offers participation in a project to investors. The amount to be raised is V. Without these funds no project may be undertaken. Assume that the project is completed after a fixed period and there is a return, π, which is available for distribution to both investors and the agent. This return depends on the amount of funds actually committed to the project, k, which may be either greater or less than V depending on whether the agent himself makes a positive or negative investment; on the underlying attractiveness of the project, θ, and on the actions taken by the agent, e, which include not only active management of the project and effort expended, but also the steps that the agent takes to appropriate the benefits of the project for himself.[8] Formally,

(I.1) $\pi = h(k,e,\theta), \quad h_k > 0,\ h_e > 0,\ h_\theta > 0$

The return to investors, R, depends upon the way in which the total return, π, is divided. For simplicity we will assume that a fraction, α, is paid out to investors. Thus,

(I.2) $R = \alpha\pi = \alpha h(k,e,\theta)$

In practice, π is neither observable nor known with certainty at the time funds are raised. Moreover, it may be only imperfectly observable by the time the project terminates. The level of investment, k, may also not be observed *ex ante* and may be observable only imperfectly and at high cost *ex post*. The same applies to the actions of the agent, e, and the attractiveness of the project. They will be difficult to observe both before and after the fact. Finally, while α may be specified *ex ante*, in many contracts (e.g. payment of corporate dividends) it is not.[9]

The central problems of financial management, in this context, are (1) how to determine an appropriate level of V (and the form in which V is raised) given the imperfect nature of information concerning all the determinants of R (these decisions affect both the beliefs of investors concerning what they might expect and the incentives of the agents), and (2) how to monitor and/or control (directly or indirectly, completely, or more likely, partially) the variables θ, k and e so that appropriate decisions in the interests of the investors are made.

---

[8] From this perspective, greater efforts expended to divert funds from the firm to the manager represent smaller values of e.

[9] Moreover, α may itself be a function of other variables. The relationship between R and π will, of course, differ for different financial instruments.

Impediments to the Development of Financial Markets

Given the importance ascribed to financial markets and institutions in modern economies, it is perhaps remarkable that they have developed so late. Though antecedents of modern capital markets have, of course, existed for a long time, the scale of modern institutions and the range of financial instruments which they offer are truly unprecedented.

Yet, upon further reflection, the natural impediments to the development of financial markets are stupendous, and we should, perhaps, be impressed that they work as well as they do.

Recent research has identified five central problems facing financial markets, which are related to the functions of financial intermediaries about which we spoke earlier. These problems arise, in varying forms and in varying degrees, with essentially all financial instruments used to raise capital. In some cases, they may arise with such force as to make it virtually impossible to raise capital in the open market, or to use certain instruments (such as equity).

(a) **The selection problem.** The fundamental problem facing capital markets can be put starkly: there is an infinite supply of charlatans in the market, those who are willing to take others' money for their own uses. Moreover, like the students in our courses, all of whom believe that they are in the upper half of the class, even honest entrepreneurs are likely to have an inflated view of the returns to their projects. And there is little reason to believe that the correlation between individuals' beliefs in their returns and the actual returns are sufficiently high (even if we could solicit honest views concerning what those expected returns are) to warrant allocating scarce funds on the basis of those expectations.

In terms of the model outlined above, the existence of an almost infinitely elastic supply of charlatans means that at $V > 0$ there is a very large supply of projects at which $R \leq 0$ either (a) because $k = 0$ and/or (b) levels of e are chosen which make π either zero or, if access to credit is available in some form, less than zero[10] or (c) there was no real project opportunity so that $\pi = 0$, given θ, for all k and e, or (d) because, after the fact, the unobservable true level of π, while positive, is reported to be zero by the agent. In any of these cases, there are a number of projects, N, which are indistinguishable from 'valid' projects, for which the return is $R^N \leq 0$. If we denote the returns of similar seeming legitimate projects as R^L and there are a fixed number of L of these, the average return to projects offered investors is

(I.3)
$$\bar{R} = \left(\frac{N}{N+L}\right)R^N + \left(\frac{L}{N+L}\right)R^L$$

[10] In this interpretation, π is profits after paying off debtors.

Investors will in the long run only make continuing investments if

(I.4) $$V(1 + \rho) < \overline{R}$$

where ρ is an appropriate required expected rate of return encompassing both the time value of funds and returns for risk. Since L and R^L are fixed, determined by the available technologies and resources, for any $V > 0$, there is an N large enough and a R^N small enough so that $\overline{R} < (1 + \rho)V$. Thus, no financial markets consistently capable of raising positive funds will exist unless there are some limitations on N and R^N.

We have perhaps put the matter too strongly in ascribing the selection problem to the infinite supply of charlatans and dreamers. The problem is actually more generic: it arises whenever there are asymmetries of information between providers of capital and those seeking capital concerning the returns to projects. For instance, insiders (the firm managers and controlling shareholders) almost inevitably have more information concerning the firm's prospects than outsiders. They are most keen to sell the shares of their enterprise when the market has overvalued them. When the market has undervalued them, they are obviously reluctant to sell their shares. The market recognizes this, and there is considerable evidence that, in the absence of other information to the contrary, the market interprets a firm's willingness to issue shares as a negative signal concerning its quality; that is, the price of shares falls dramatically upon (the announcement of) a share issue. Of course, firms are aware of this, and this explains, in part, the relatively little reliance on new share issues. Indeed, in the absence of risk aversion, it can be shown that there would be no market for equities.[11] (But of course, in the absence of risk aversion, the adverse risk bearing effects which are associated with the use of debt rather than equity finance would not be present.)[12]

Finally, we should emphasize that the selection problem arises even when there is no asymmetry of information, and where borrowers are not intentionally cheating lenders. If there is a large supply of individuals who are overconfident of their abilities, investors have a problem of screening the unproductive investments from the truly productive investments. They cannot simply rely on the price system as a selection device.

While the selection problem arises in both credit and equity markets, the scope that equity contracts provide for charlatans makes these contracts extremely attractive to them, and makes the selection problem central there.

---

[11] These issues have been discussed at greater length by Greenwald *et al.* (1984) and Myers and Majluf (1984).

[12] There remain adverse incentive and selection effects. See for example Stiglitz and Weiss (1981).

(b) The enforcement problem. The equity contract is supposed to pay equity holders a fraction of the firm's profits. But typically, the contract leaves the fraction of the profits to be paid, as well as the definition of profits, to the discretion of the firm's managers (board of directors). The scope for diversion of funds to the use of managers or controlling shareholders appears to be great.

Indeed, even in the case of income bonds (where firms promise to pay a certain amount to bondholders out of the firm's income, provided that there is sufficient income), firms have manipulated the definition of income in a way to evade paying amounts due, so much so that currently income bonds are seldom used, in spite of their risk sharing advantages to corporations.[13]

Formally, we have

(I.5) $$R = \alpha \hat{\pi}$$

where $\hat{\pi}$ is the declared profit level. $\hat{\pi}$ may be substantially less than π.[14]

In this subsection, we have actually identified two separate enforcement problems: (i) the difficulty of verifying the state of nature, or the variables upon which the payments to the supplier of funds are supposed to depend; and (ii) the difficulty of making the receiver of the funds comply with the terms of the contract. The latter problem is the one that the literature on sovereign debt has focused, but the fact that there are large legal costs in enforcing a contract make it apparent that this problem may be more pervasive. Indeed, the fact that in bankruptcy owners of equity typically walk away with something, even though debt claimants do not have their claims fully satisfied is evidence to the importance of these enforcement problems.

(c) The incentive problem. Since firms' managers reap only a fraction of the returns to their managerial efforts, their incentives are attenuated (Ross, 1973; Stiglitz, 1974a; Jensen and Mechling, 1976). More generally, the interests of the managers do not coincide with the interests of the shareholders. This has

---

[13] Gale and Hellwig (1985) and the recent literature on sovereign debt (Eaton and Gersovitz, 1981; Eaton, *et al.*, 1986) has emphasized the enforcement problem.

A recent literature (under the rubric of 'costly state verification') (Townsend, 1979) has developed, arguing that enforcement costs (or more precisely, the costs of the required verification) are less with debt than equity contracts. Providers of capital only have to verify the state of nature if the borrower fails to make the promised payment. As an explanation of the use of debt rather than equity, the theory has been criticized both on the grounds that the costs of verification do not appear to be that significant (the other explanations accordingly seem more persuasive); more importantly, *given* that there are outstanding equities, for which, in the simple models at least, state verification is required, there are no *marginal* verification costs associated with issuing additional equities.

As we noted above, the cost of verifying income (profits) was an impediment to the early development of equity markets, and remains an impediment to the use of income bonds.

[14] This corresponds to point (d) made in the discussion preceding equation (I.3).

been made dramatically clear in recent takeover controversies.[15] These discrepancies affect a whole range of decisions.

(d) The Management/Public Good Problem. Since, in principle, all shareholders receive the same amount per share any efforts by a shareholder (or group of shareholders) to improve the quality of management (the return to their shares) redounds to the benefit of all shareholders. (The same is true for any other class of claimants.) Therefore, Management and efforts to improve Management are Public Goods.[16] Thus, in corporations with widely held shares, the forces driving managers to serve shareholder interests may be particularly weak.

(e) The Conflicting Claims Problem. While the interests of all claimants within a class (shareholders, bondholders) coincide[17], the interests of different classes of claimants frequently conflict. This too was seen most dramatically in several of the recent LBO's (Leverage Buyouts) within the US, where the value of debtors' claims decreased dramatically as the value of equity claims increased.[18] While debt contracts show a cognizance of this possibility, with provisions which restrict the actions which the firm can undertake, the debt contract can seldom anticipate all the actions which the firm might undertake which would decrease the value of their claims. While future debt contracts are likely to provide some insurance against losses arising from LBOs, firms will, undoubtedly, devise new methods of transferring wealth from other claimants on the firm to themselves.

Difficulties Facing Equity Issues: An Application of General Principles

In terms of the model developed above, when equity issues are undertaken as part of the continuing financing efforts of a long-lived firm whose common stock is publicly traded, the population of investors/shareholders changes continuously over time. Thus, there is no longer a well-identified investor population associated with a particular investment project whose interests the

---

[15] Hannaway (1989) has emphasized the range of activities over which discrepancies in interests may arise. Information which may be of limited value to the firm may be of considerable value to the individual, in, for instance, signalling to others his competency and command of the situation.

Shleifer and Vishny (1988) have, similarly, stressed managers' incentives for making themselves indispensable to the firm, thus increasing the amount that they can extract from the firm (managerial entrenchment).

[16] This point has been emphasized by Alchian and Demsetz (1972), Grossman and Hart (1980), and Stiglitz (1982, 1985).

[17] Except, of course, to the extent that controlling shareholders can divert some of the firms' assets to their own interests.

[18] The potential for this has long been recognized in the theoretical literature, see, for instance, Stiglitz (1972a).

project's managers can be required, at least in theory, to serve. This, in turn, calls into question the definition of appropriate behavior of a project's managers, since decisions which benefit shareholders at time, t, may adversely affect the interests of shareholders at a later time, $t + 1$.[19,20] The common answer to these difficulties both in law and economic theory is to assume that in making decisions at time t, managers serve the interest of current shareholders (i.e. those who hold stock at time t).[21] For simplicity we will assume that there are only two periods of interest. In the first, the managers of the firm make a set of financing decisions, the market price of the firm's equity is determined on an open market in response to those decisions (a reaction anticipated by the firm's managers), funds are raised and operating plans are undertaken. In the second period, the results of the initial operating and investment decisions are revealed and returns to investors are determined accordingly. In addition, we will assume that a fraction β of the initial shares are sold by shareholders after financing decisions are announced in period one (and, therefore, a fraction $1 - \beta$ are retained through period two).[22] Formally, therefore, the proper objective function for such a firm's managers is to maximize

(I.6) $$\beta V_0 + (1 - \beta)\Gamma\alpha\hat{\pi} - c(k)\text{Prob}(\pi \leq R^*)$$

where V_0 is the initial post-financing-decision market value of the firm, Γ is the fraction of the firm held by its initial shareholders (this is one if no new equity is sold), R^* now represents the promised level of repayment on the firm's debts, $\hat{\pi}$ is declared profit, c is now the penalty associated with bankruptcy, and we now assume that bankruptcy penalties involving the reorganization of the firm now increase with the size of the firm. If an amount of new equity, E, is raised in the financing period, then

(I.7) $$\Gamma = \frac{V_0}{V_0 + E}$$

Assume further that a firm's managers have their own agenda to which they respond at least partially, reflected in their utility function, which we represent as a function of θ, the nature of the project, k, and the resources devoted

---

[19] And in the absence of perfect information, later shareholders may not be able to protect themselves by reducing their willingness to invest.

[20] Only in special cases, such as where there is a complete set of state-contingent securities, will there be no ambiguity about what the firm should do, see Stiglitz (1972a,b, 1974b) or Grossman and Stiglitz (1977, 1980).

[21] It should be apparent, however, that only under severe restrictions will this policy, of maximizing the current market value, or expected utility of current owners, be (constrained) Pareto efficient; see for instance Stiglitz (1972b).

[22] The standard theoretical justification for such an assumption is that of an overlapping generations model in which most wealth is held by older investors who sell it off for consumption goods over time.

to the project effort. For clarity, we distinguish between 'e', the effort devoted to increasing π, and $\hat{e}$, the effort devoted to underreporting, which we model as simply a function of the discrepancy between π and $\hat{\pi}$, for any project. Thus, we represent the managers' utility function by $\hat{u}[e, \theta, k, \hat{e}(\pi - \hat{\pi}, \theta, k)]$, where $\hat{u}$ embeds within it the managerial compensation schemes which define the financial rewards received by the managers. It will be convenient in the following discussion if we simply represent the managers' utility in terms of the variables e, θ, k, and $\hat{\pi}$:

(I.8) $$u(e, \theta, k, \hat{\pi}) \equiv \hat{u}[e, \theta, k, \hat{e}(\pi - \hat{\pi}, \theta, k)].$$

Then what actually is maximized reflects to some extent the managers' own utility:

(I.9) $$\beta V_0 + (1 - \beta)\Gamma\alpha\hat{\pi} - c(k)\,\mathrm{Prob}\,(\pi \le R^*) + \psi u$$

and this is maximized, as before, subject to the constraint that

(I.10) $$\hat{\pi} \le \pi(e, k, \theta)$$

ψ represents the weight the manager places on his own agenda (utility). (The conventional principal agent literature assumes that ψ is infinite, that is, the manager simply maximizes his own expected utility, given the incentive schemes he faces.[23])

This model can be used to illustrate several of the impediments to equity markets to which we referred earlier:

(a)   The conflicting claims are reflected in difference in judgments concerning the weights to be associated with current market value versus future profitability, the parameter β above.[24]

(b)   As holding periods of shareholders become extremely short, β tends towards one, and only the initial value, V_0, matters to managers. This, in turn, means that signals become overwhelmingly important relative to actual performance and, like financial markets without fraud sanctions (see the discussion below), equity markets will tend to collapse completely.[25]

---

[23] We suspect that that formulation exaggerates the extent to which employees in general follow self-interested policies. There appear to be many instances where individuals 'do their job'—and do it well—not simply because their financial rewards increase the better they perform. (This holds even if we take into account the increased likelihood of promotion for good behavior, and the increased likelihood of dismissal for poor performance.) This is particularly true in managerial jobs where it may be little more difficult to do a good job than a poor job, and individuals receive considerable satisfaction from doing a good job. The fact that their company is number one, or that they have done better than their rivals, is satisfaction enough.

[24] This only reflects conflicting claims among shareholders, not the conflicts between shareholders and bondholders.

[25] The proof of this claim follows from a straightforward comparative statics analysis of the Greenwald–Stiglitz–Weiss (1984) model.

(c)   The managerial incentive problem—the conflict between managers' incentives and that of the 'firm' (whatever β is employed)—is reflected in the term

$$u[e, \theta, k, \hat{e}\,(\pi - \hat{\pi}, \theta, k)]$$

which, we noted, is assumed to have imbedded in it the managerial incentive compensation scheme. It is generally not possible to find managerial compensation schemes (with risk averse managers) so that when they maximize their 'utility', shareholder welfare (for any β) is maximized.

2. Coming to Terms with Capital Markets Impediments: the Architecture of Allocative Mechanisms

In spite of these seeming impediments to the transfer and agglomeration of capital, capital is transferred and agglomerated. This is one of the hallmarks of modern capitalism. We thus need to ask, how do modern economies overcome these impediments? What were the changes in the legal, economic, and social structure which facilitated the development of modern equities markets, and which enabled these markets to overcome the significant barriers to the effective functioning of these markets?

Trust

Historically, in the absence of a well functioning legal system, there are two mechanisms which have worked to ensure the fulfillment of contracts: trust and reputation.

Trust played an important role in the early development of capital markets, in which financial transactions were often concentrated among members of a well defined ethnic group or community. In such a context, social sanctions were a more effective instrument for the enforcement of contracts than economic sanctions.[26] (The fact that transactions occurred within a relatively small group also mitigated the information problem: the participants in the transactions likely had considerable information about each other.) It is, perhaps, ironic that the development of capitalist financial institutions depended, to a large extent, on non-capitalist ethics and control mechanisms, a point to which we shall return later.[27] But as economic development proceeded, the increasing scale of enterprise made it impossible to limit raising

---

[26] The recent literature on sovereign debt has made clear the limited effectiveness of economic sanctions. See, for instance, Eaton *et al.* (1986).

[27] Albert Hirschman has stressed a similar point in some of his recent writings.

and transferring funds within the members of a close knit community. Moreover, in some cases, social bonds within the community weakened, reducing the force of social sanctions as a discipline device.

Reputation

For reputation to be effective, there must be a continuing flow of profits: otherwise there would be no incentive to maintain one's reputation. Reputations provide an effective barrier to entry, which may allow the profits to be sustained. Again, we note an irony: the viability of capitalist financial institutions depends on limitations on the degree of competition.[28] The flow of profits associated with banks, which surely rank among the most important of the financial intermediaries, arose, in most countries, from governmentally imposed restrictions on entry combined with the rights to print money (fractional reserve banking). The profits generated by these government-granted monopolies depended, in part, on the assets which were available in which reserves could be held. The fact that in England government debt provided a relatively safe investment opportunity yielding a positive return gave British banks the flow of profits, which not only provided depositors with some direct insurance of the safety of their funds, but also provided banks with an incentive to maintain their reputation, an incentive which reduced the likelihood that the funds would be invested in an excessively risky manner. In this view then the stability of the British government's national debt was closely linked with the successful development of some of its financial institutions.

However, for reputation to be an effective incentive for those who raise equity to pay a return to their investors, the firm must have plans to have recourse once again to the equity market. But such future recourse to the equity market may have disadvantages as well: for it may imply dilution of the original owners' equity claims. Furthermore, each return to the equity market is a negative signal, with adverse affects on the firms' market value (see Gale and Stiglitz, 1989). If it is not the desire for future access to the equity market which provides the firm with an incentive to pay a return to equity owners, what does? It is the legal strictures, which require that all shareholders (controlling and non-controlling) be treated the same, and the limitations imposed by the legal system in the ability of controlling shareholders to divert funds to their own interests.[29]

---

[28] The limitations on competition are endogenous, rather than exogenous, and in equilibrium, though existing firms earn positive profits, there are zero profits associated with entry. See for example Stiglitz (1987).

[29] Two other mechanisms are often suggested as imposing discipline on managers: (a) shareholder voting and (b) take-overs. There are good theoretical reasons for suspecting that these mechanisms are of only limited efficacy (see Stiglitz, 1982, 1985; Grossman and Hart, 1980) and observation of firm behavior seems consistent with this view.

Changes in Legal Structure

Trust and reputation, while they may have sufficed for simpler capital markets, by themselves were not sufficient for the development of effective, widespread financial markets. For this, two innovations in the legal structure were required.

First, the principle of limited liability had to be recognized. Without limited liability, the costs that charlatans could impose on investors would be unlimited and investors would be unwilling to turn over funds to others about whom they had very limited information, even if those others contained only a relatively small fraction of charlatans.

Once limited liability constraints are imposed so that $R^N \geq 0$, then the average return to investors is bounded below by

$$\bar{R} \geq \left(\frac{L \cdot R^L}{N + L} \right),$$

which may be small if N is very large relative to L, but which nevertheless provides the possibility of $V \geq 0$. Historically, of course, limited liability has always been characteristic of debt contracts. The lender is not held responsible for the uses to which his money has been put. At worst, he loses his money. Hence, the early existence of borrowing and lending. However, in order to provide for the risk-spreading opportunities inherent in equity markets, explicit limited liability laws for equity investors are essential. Unfortunately, limited liability by itself would still, given an extensive supply of charlatans, create only limited opportunities for raising financial resources, since investors would pay only small levels of V for projects.[30]

Secondly, a legal system which could effectively prosecute securities fraud[31] was required. Without such a system, the ability of firm managers to divert resources is essentially unfettered, and again, the costs of not knowing the honesty of the managers (or of not monitoring borrowers' activities) would effectively deter most investment. As it is, even with fraud statutes, the scope for managerial diversion of funds for their own benefits (as recent episodes of managerial behavior in the face of take-over bids testifies) is not insignificant.

---

[30] A further complication associated with unlimited liability concerns the impact of the wealth of other investors on the returns to any particular investor. Since 'poor' investors provide little additional protection to other investors in the event of loss, investor pools made up of such investors will be undesirable. Individual investors must, therefore, investigate not only the quality of the investment project in question, but the wealth of their co-investors as well, considerably complicating the investment process. At the same time, 'rich' investors possibly provide positive protection to co-investors at considerable cost to themselves and doing so provides them with a disincentive to invest. As a result, investment pools will be adversely selected to consist only of poorer investors with fewer funds who, accordingly, are likely to have greater than average risk aversion.

[31] As will be apparent from our discussion below, we are using the term, fraud, in a very broad sense.

Again, this condition can be expressed in terms of our simple model. The actual levels of θ, e, k and, where π is unobservable, the declared level of π, are determined by the objective function of a project's agent. Thus, in the polar case where he maximizes his own utility, his behavior is defined by the problem[32]

$$\max_{\{e,\, k\}} u\,(e, k, \hat{\pi}, \theta)$$

where $\hat{\pi}$ is the declared level of profit and θ enters the agent's decision whether or not to bring a particular project to market. We have hitherto assumed essentially that u_e, u_k, and $u_{\hat{\pi}}$ are all less than zero (hence the tendency to strip the project's owners of any possible return). However, once mechanisms for prosecuting fraud are in place, the agent's objective function may now be specified in an entirely different way. A contract may be written between investors and their agent which merely specifies a promised return, R^*, on any given project. If 'fraud' is interpreted as the payment of a penalty in the event of failure to deliver on such a promise, then the objective function of the agent becomes

$$\max_{\{e,\, k\}} u\,(e, k, \hat{\pi}, \theta) - \hat{c}\,\text{Prob}(\alpha\hat{\pi} \leq R^*)$$

where $\hat{c}$ is the cost of 'fraud', $\text{Prob}\,(\alpha\hat{\pi} \leq R^*)$ is the probability of being (found) guilty of fraud and, of course, this problem must now be solved subject to the constraint that

$$\alpha\hat{\pi} = \hat{R} \leq \pi(e, k, \theta)$$

since declared 'dividends' must actually be paid. As $\hat{c}$, the penalty for fraud, becomes very large, agents will (1) always declare a value of 'profits' sufficient to provide the promised rate of return, where this is feasible; (2) take actions, e, and make investments, k, which ensure that promised returns, R^*, can feasibly be paid and (3) avoid undertaking projects where θ is such that condition (2) cannot be fulfilled with high probability.

Fraud penalties thus not only deal directly with the 'enforcement' problem; they also have incentive effects. Furthermore, they may enhance the ability of good firms to signal that fact; when there is a fraud penalty, promises ('R^*') convey information; better firms will, in general, promise more.[33] Moreover, fraud penalties deter charlatans from entering the market. Thus, fraud penalties also enhance the economy's ability to solve the selection problem.

[32] Identical results obtain if he maximizes the more general objective function (I.8).
[33] Certain technical conditions have to be satisfied for this to be the case.

If effective fraud enforcement is interpreted to mean a level of c sufficiently high to ensure that promises are normally fulfilled, it will imply that

$$\overline{R} \approx R^*$$

for the project universe as a whole and, with diversification, that

$$V = \overline{R}/(1 + \rho)$$

is substantially positive. Historically institutions, like debtors prisons, have developed to serve precisely these fraud policing functions.

However, while such fraud control mechanisms may be essential to the functioning of financial markets they create a new set of financing problems in solving old ones. Typically, the returns to investment projects are uncertain even to the agents who undertake and manage them. Thus, as the cost of fraud, c, increases it not only deters fraudulent investors, but also deters legitimate projects. The chance of incurring fraud costs accidentally may either (a) limit the scope of projects, or (b) lead to serious underestimates of promised returns (and, hence, underfinancing) or (c) deter the undertakings altogether. This is especially likely if agents are risk averse. As a result, the vigorous fraud control approach described above must be tempered either (1) by limiting penalties and/or (2) by developing approaches for excusing fraudulent performance under circumstances beyond the agent's control and/or (3) by providing financing without explicit return promises (i.e. equity finance). Yet these tempered measures, which might be thought of as constituting an imperfect legal control system, reintroduce the original problems posed by the agent's private knowledge of e, π and k.

The Modern Corporation

The development of the large, modern corporation was, to a large extent, made possible by the improvements in financial markets, and at the same time represented an intrinsic part of those improvements. We want to call attention to four aspects of these developments.

First, while the development of accounting practices and auditing procedures made the *internal* control of the firm feasible, it also enabled investors to monitor more effectively what was going on within the firm. These accounting standards made it possible to define fraud more precisely and to detect it more easily. In the context of the model, audit and punishment systems could be applied to reduce deviations between $\hat{\pi}$ and π and deviations of e, k and θ from desirable levels.

Secondly, the large scale firm could make use of systems of peer monitoring to reduce the likelihood of fraud. In a small firm, the owner/manager could doctor the books, with little scrutiny from anyone else. In a large scale firm, with multiple checks, fraud (diversion of funds meant for the common interests of shareholders in general to the interests of a few) required the complicity of a large number of individuals, making such diversion less likely.

At the same time, the modern corporation created an 'internal capital market'. Funds could be transferred around the country, allocated to regions and used where returns were highest. The firms created a community to replace the ethnic communities, in which members knew each other well, and while social sanctions may be limited, economic sanctions (being fired, denied promotion within the hierarchy) could be quite effective.[34] (Indeed, in recent years, it has been very much the fashion to speak of the culture of a corporation.) In most cases within the United States, the corporation developed a specialized knowledge associated with certain markets (products). As a result, while capital was efficiently allocated within certain spheres, large discrepancies might arise between returns in different markets. But the informational and other problems discussed above provided an important barrier to the flow of funds. (Chandler has rightly emphasized the importance of the lowering of transportation costs to the development of national markets. The national markets in the US were sufficiently large that dis-economies of scope set in when firms attempted to cross into new markets. The emergence of conglomerates provides a possible exception—yet the failure of so many of the conglomerates suggests that these diseconomies were considerable, outweighing the obvious gains from arbitraging across markets.)

Finally, corporations facilitate the functioning of the reputation mechanism. Firms create an asset called good will, based on the firm's reputation, and it pays current owners to maintain that asset.[35] This, in turn, implies that investors may be more willing to provide long-established corporations with funds. In effect, the firm's incentive to maintain its reputation reduces the investors' monitoring costs.[36,37]

Venture Capital

Modern corporations as mechanisms for allocating capital face two problems. The first, which we have just discussed, is their specialization within an industry. The second is specialization in certain competencies relevant to the

---

[34] The circumstances under which these are effective incentive devices are explored in Stiglitz and Weiss (1983).

[35] See Eaton (1986).

[36] Stiglitz and Weiss (1983) show that the intertemporal interlinking of loans (making the availability of funds at one date dependent on the firm's performance at an earlier date) increases banks' expected returns.

[37] At the same time, it needs to be recognized that the information costs which give the modern corporation a role in allocating capital also give rise to considerable managerial discretion. While capital may be more efficiently allocated, some of the efficiency gains are appropriated by the managers, with the

operation of large well-defined continuing enterprises with extensive but fragmented authority delegated to individuals or groups of individuals. Both of these specializations may render corporations particularly unsuited to operate in nascent markets where success depends on familiarity with new technologies and demand behaviors on the one hand and specific characteristics (e.g. imagination, risk preference) on the other hand which are not prevalent in large modern corporations. Accordingly, a disproportionate amount of innovation arises in new and small enterprises. The problems we discussed earlier concerning the functioning of capital markets arise forcefully, and cannot be resolved through the institution of the modern corporation. To fill this gap, special institutions have grown up in the United States which constitute the venture capital industry.[38]

The industry itself has many of the aspects of early financial market developments. Venture firms typically operate in a tightly-knit community, sharing projects among members of that community and engaging, by design, in a continuing stream of projects. As a result, reputation is critical to the effectiveness of the venture capital firms themselves and strong cultural ties bind these firms together with investors. At the same time, the entrepreneurs who are funded by the venture capital firms are closely tied to and highly dependent upon the venture capital firms. Consequently, venture capital firms tend to have detailed information on the operations of the projects they fund, and potentially strong sanctions in the event of misfeasance. The venture capital firms usually also have detailed specialized knowledge of the industries in which their entrepreneurs operate so that they are adept at evaluating relative entrepreneurial performance. The similarities to early capitalist communities appear to be striking.[39]

Further Impediments to Efficient Capital Markets

We began this paper with a list of problems which all financial markets face, and proceeded to show how certain changes in the economic and legal environment had facilitated the development of financial markets. We now want to raise some questions about how some more recent developments may, in the near future, serve to impede the functioning of capital markets.

---

providers of capital reaping only a part of the returns. While the mechanisms described in this paper may limit the fraction of the returns which can be so appropriated, the total amount which managers can obtain in a large corporation may be enormous.

[38] The relatively small scale of most European markets in the period of the initial growth of most large corporations may account for the fact that European corporations have tended to be less highly specialized than US corporations and, hence, have themselves substituted to a greater extent for the venture capital industry in the United States.

[39] See Sahlman (1989) for a detailed description of the venture capital industry in the United States.

First, we spoke earlier about the ability of corporations' managers to divert resources to their own purposes, and the role of the legal system in preventing fraud. Belatedly, managers have discovered that there is a wide range of *legal* ways by which funds can be diverted to their purposes. In one recent take-over, the old managers walked off with $100 million. To make matters worse, in several states, the legal system has reinforced the rights of managers, and have made take-overs more difficult. Take-overs are one of the mechanisms by which shareholders can ensure (or make it more likely) that their assets are well managed, and that the market reflects accurately the true value of those assets.

Secondly, the improvements in the secondary market for equities have led to an increase in short term trading of securities. Moreover, an increasingly large fraction of funds on the market originate in pension funds, managed by fiduciary agents, many of whom are judged by the short run performance of their portfolio. In short, the problems of which Keynes wrote more than a half-century ago, where investors focus on short term returns rather than the long term, are far more important today than they were when he was writing.

The consequences of this focus on the short term have been discussed extensively elsewhere. Here, we note one additional effect: the focus on the short term increases the signaling costs associated with issuing equities, and hence results in fewer firms issuing equity.[40,41]

3. *Finance and the Evolution of the Firm*

The neoclassical theory of the economy pictures capital as a liquid: it flows smoothly throughout the economy, until the rates of return in all sectors are the same. The picture we have drawn is markedly different: the problems (largely informational in character) which we have described above create large barriers to the free flow of capital. Capital inside the firm is different from capital outside the firm. As a result, there may be large differences in the observed rates of return across firms or sectors of the economy.

Why are the normal forces of arbitrage not effective in overcoming the differences? Our analysis has provided at least a partial answer to this question: what we observe are *average* rates of return, say within a sector. Those outside the sector may be less able to select good projects within the sector, so their expected marginal returns may be much lower; and outside suppliers of funds may fear that (for any of the reasons delineated earlier) they may not be able to obtain the same rates of return on, say, new issues of equity.

---

[40] Greenwald *et al.* (1984) characterize the equilibrium size of the new equities market for any given β. This result is obtained by examining how the equilibrium changes as β changes.

[41] Summers and Summers (1989) and Stiglitz (1989) argue that an appropriately designed turnover tax may be used to encourage longer term holdings of equities.

But why do existing firms not borrow additional funds? First, firms may not be willing to borrow more, given the limited issue of equity, for to do so would expose them to additional risk, which they cannot divest. This is the fundamental difference between debt and equity: while debt entails a fixed obligation, equity does not; hence with debt, there is always a chance of bankruptcy (see Greenwald and Stiglitz, 1988; 1990).

Secondly, lenders may not be willing to lend: with asymmetric information, moral hazard, and enforcement problems, credit markets will, in general, be characterized by credit rationing (see Stiglitz and Weiss, 1981, 1983, 1986, 1987). Lenders are not concerned with the marginal return to investment, only with the fraction of the total returns which they can appropriate. The total return in one sector may be higher than in another, but the (expected) fraction which they can appropriate may be lower. Credit markets will not serve to equate (expected) returns to investments.

Of course, industries with high returns will have an incentive to reinvest a large fraction of their high profits back into the enterprise, and this reinvestment will eventually drive down the rate of return. Thus, there is a tendency for returns to capital to be equated *in the long run*, but the mechanism by which this occurs is quite different from that envisaged by the traditional neoclassical model. Moreover—and more importantly—new industries are constantly being created. Returns in these new industries may, accordingly, be significantly higher than in older, established industries, so that observed inequalities in rates of return may be persistent (though which industries are enjoying above normal rates of return may be always changing).

Kalecki (1939), Kaldor (1956) and Robinson (1956) (and perhaps Marx and Rosa Luxembourg) postulated models in which investment by firms was tied to their profits. In these models, the main source of investment funds was firms' retained earnings.[42] For several decades, these models have been criticized for being 'ad hoc'—whether they are realistic is quite another matter. The advances in the theory of financial markets described in this paper have provided micro-foundations for the kinds of constraints on financial markets which underlay these models. The assumptions concerning information and contract enforcement are undoubtedly more reasonable than the assumptions of costless and perfect contract enforcement and perfect (or at least symmetric) information underlying the neoclassical model.

We now show how these ideas can be used to develop simple models of the evolution of firms. To begin with, we assume that there is equity and credit rationing: firms must rely on retained earnings to finance their investment. For simplicity, we assume that the output-capital ratio is fixed at b, and the

---

[42] In this view, then, Kaldor's formulation of the aggregate savings function may provide a better description of the economy than Passinetti's formulation (1962).

labor-capital ratio is fixed at l. K_i denotes the capital of the ith firm, and w the wage rate. Assume that the firm retains and invests a fraction s of its profits. Then

(III.1) $$dK_i/dt = sbK_i - swlK_i$$

or

(III.2) $$d\ln K_i/dt = m(w) \equiv s(b - wl)$$

We thus obtain Gibrat's law: firms grow proportionately.

Assume the labor force grows at a fixed rate n, and that the rate of change of real wages is a function of the unemployment rate (a real Phillips curve). Let aggregate capital be denoted by K:

(III.3) $$K = \Sigma K_i$$

Aggregate employment is then

(III.4) $$L = lK.$$

The employment rate is then

(III.5) $$lK/N = e$$

where N is the aggregate labor supply. The real Phillips curve postulates that

(III.6) $$d\ln w/dt = g(e) = g(lk), g' > 0$$

where $k = K/N$.
In steady state,

(III.7) $$g(e^*) = 0$$

or

(III.8) $$K^* = Ne^*/l$$

Summing the firm capital accumulation equations over all firms,

(III.9) $$dK/dt = d\Sigma K_i/dt = \Sigma K_i m(w) = m(w)\Sigma K_i = m(w)K$$

or

(III.10) $$d\ln k/dt = m(w) - n$$

In long run equilibrium, this implies that

(III.11) $$d\ln K/dt = m(w) = n$$

or

(III.12) $$w^* = m^{-1}(n) = (sb - n)ls$$

Thus, in the long run wages adjust so that employment and capital grow exactly at the same rate as the labor supply. It is easy to verify that the dynamics described by the differential equations III.6 and III.10 give rise to limit cycles.[43]

The model we have just described is completely non-stochastic. If we postulate that there are some diseconomies of scale (if we think of the number of firms in the economy as fixed at N, firms that are much larger than average are slightly less productive than smaller firms) and that there is some randomness in the accumulation process, then

(III.13) $\qquad \mathrm{d}\ln K_i/\mathrm{d}t = M(w, K_i/K)\varepsilon_i, \quad \text{with } E\varepsilon = 1$

Define $v_i = K_i/K$, so, in long run equilibrium with $\mathrm{d}\ln K/\mathrm{d}t = n$,[44]

(III.14) $\qquad \mathrm{d}\ln v_i/\mathrm{d}t = \hat{M}(w, v_i)\varepsilon_i - n$

The discrete time analogue to III. 14 is a stochastic process which, it can easily be verified, satisfies all of the Champernowne conditions. There exists a steady state distribution of (relative) firm sizes, in which the tail of the distribution satisfies (approximately) Pareto's law.[45]

Extension to Firms which are Equity but not Credit Constrained

The analysis can be extended in a straightforward manner to firms which are equity but not credit constrained. For simplicity, we use the Greenwald–Stiglitz (1988) model in which costs of bankruptcy give rise to risk averse behavior on the part of firms; and these costs of bankruptcy are proportional to the scale of the firm. In that model, while firms can borrow as much as they wish at the actuarially fair interest rate (which takes into account in an appropriate manner the probability of default), because increased borrowing gives rise to an increased probability of default, firms choose to limit their borrowing. They show that firms will have an equilibrium debt equity ratio, d^*. Thus, if their working capital or equity is denoted by E, their debt is d^*E, and their total capital is $(1 + d^*)E$. The change in the expected equity of the firm is then given by

(III.15) $\quad \mathrm{d}E_i/\mathrm{d}t = b(1 + d^*)E - \rho d^*E - w\,l(1 + d^*)E_i \equiv \mu(\rho, w)E_i$

---

[43] The aggregate equations are of the form of the Volterra – Lotka equations, see Akerlof and Stiglitz (1969). In the case where b is a function of the capital employment ratio (and hence of w), there is convergence to the steady state, but the path of convergence may entail oscillations.

[44] In effect, we are assuming that there are enough different firms that the law of large numbers allows us to ignore, at the aggregate level, the variations in ε, and that the diseconomies of scale are sufficiently weak that the slight fluctuations in the distribution of K_i/K can also be ignored [i.e. we assume that $\Sigma\, M(w, K_i/K)K_i\varepsilon_i \approx m(w)K$].

[45] See Champernowne (1953) or Stiglitz (1969).

where ρ is the safe rate of interest. It is clear that III. 15 is exactly of the same form as III.2: our new model also gives rise to Gibrat's law. It should also be clear that other specifications of firm risk aversion (bankruptcy costs) and/or technologies can give rise to equations describing the evolution of the firm of the form.

(III.16) $$\mathrm{dln}\ E_i/dt = \hat{\mu}(\rho, w, E_i)$$

To complete the model, we need to determine ρ. If we postulate that households have a savings function of the form

(III.17) $$S = s(\rho, w)Y$$

where Y *is household income*, $wlK + \rho\ d^*E$; where E is aggregate equity,

$$E = \Sigma E_i$$

and K is the aggregate capital stock,

$$K = [1 + d^*(\rho, w)]E$$

then in equilibrium, household savings must be equal to the increase in firm debt:

(III.18) $$d^*(\rho, w)dE/dt = d^*(\rho, w)E\mu(\rho, w) = s(\rho, w)Y$$

The steady state is determined by the pair of equations

(III.19) $$d^*(\rho, w)\mu(w, \rho) = s[wl(1 + d^*) + \rho\ d^*]$$

and

(III.20) $$\mu(\rho, w) = n$$

Substituting III.20 into III.19, we obtain

(III.21) $$d^*(n - s\rho - swl) = swl$$

Normally, we would expect $\mu_1 < 0$ (increasing the rate of interest reduces the rate of equity accumulation) and $\mu_2 < 0$ (increasing the wage rate reduces the rate of equity accumulation). Similarly $d_1 < 0$ (increasing the rate of interest that has to be paid on debt reduces the optimal debt equity ratio) and $d_2 < 0$ (increasing the wage rate, which reduces the profitability of output, makes production less attractive, and hence reduces the desired amount of borrowing). Accordingly, so long as the savings rate does not *decrease* too rapidly as π increases (it seems unlikely) and so long as the savings *rate* does not decrease too rapidly as wages increase (which also seems unlikely), both III.20 and III.21 are negatively sloped curves. It appears that there can be multiple steady states: a low wage, high interest rate equilibrium in which firms have a high debt equity ratio; and a high wage, low interest rate equilibrium in which firms have a low debt equity ratio. In both equilibria, the steady state employment rate and per capita output are the same. The distribution of income and the economy's financial structures differ across equilibria. In a more general version of this model, in which the capital output ratio may differ, the different equilibria will then be associated with different levels of per capita income.

It is easy to extend this model to incorporate stochastic elements, as well as exogenously or endogenously determined changes in the rates of productivity growth, whether arising from learning by doing or investment in R&D (see Greenwald and Stiglitz, 1990). In the latter case, differences in financial structure will be associated with different patterns of investment (differences in willingness to take risks): economic equilibria in which there is a low debt equity ratio will be associated with higher rates of investment in R&D, and accordingly higher rates of technological progress. The formal development of these models will, however, take us beyond the scope of this paper.

The main points of this exploration would, moreover, be largely unaltered by these final extensions. These main points are that modern theories of financial market imperfections (chiefly related to informational problems) (a) provide effective theoretical support for much of the existing less theoretical literature on the role and importance of financial institutions and (b) serve to rehabilitate many of the early growth models and the conclusions concerning economic development that arose out of the earlier literature.

4. *Conclusions*

There are a few simple messages underlying the analysis of this paper:

1. Capital markets are different from other markets. They entail exchanges of money today for a *promise* of a return in the future. Ensuring that those promises can and will be fulfilled is a major concern of financial markets.

2. Difficulties in ensuring contract fulfillment presented a barrier to the development of modern financial markets. (In the text, we noted five major impediments to the development of financial markets.) Legal changes—the development of limited liability and enforceable fraud standards—combined with technological/economic advances (e.g. in accountancy and auditing) facilitated, and in some cases, were necessary for the development of modern capital markets.

3. Still, there remains a tension: the observed financial contracts may differ markedly from those that would arise in a world in which the problems we alluded to earlier did not arise. For instance, the functions of risk sharing

would be well served by equity contracts; yet equity contracts suffer greatly from information asymmetry problems, as well as enforcement difficulties, so that relatively little reliance is placed on equity as a source of new finance.

4. These limitations on financial markets mean that financial markets function markedly differently from the way envisaged in traditional neoclassical theory. Rates of return across sectors may differ. The firm takes on a role as an important financial institution.

5. At the same time these limitations, and the associated disparities in rates of return, give rise to two concomitant pressures: There is, first, the pressure for financial innovations. Leveraged buy-outs and junk bonds represent two recent examples of these financial innovations in the United States. At the same time, there will always be those who will seek to take advantage of existing and new contract forms for their own advantage, to define the boundaries of the fraud statutes, and to exploit common perceptions of contract interpretations, and the limitations of trust and reputation as contract enforcement mechanisms. Golden parachutes and a variety of other forms of managerial entrenchment in the United States are but two recent examples.[46]

The process is best described as an evolutionary one, in which the deficiencies in the market give rise to new contract forms, in which some of those in the market gradually learn how to exploit the new contract forms, and in which the market gradually learns the deficiencies in those forms, giving rise, in turn, to still new arrangements. We suspect, for instance, that the true risks associated with the junk bond, a financial form lying between the standard bond and an equity, will only be fully recognized as the economy enters its next recession.[47,48] Since the behavior and function of firms is so closely linked with finance, with the contractual arrangements by which it raises funds, this evolution of financial instruments will be intertwined with the evolution of the firm. And since the behavior and evolution of the economy as a whole depends on the behavior and evolution of the firms which comprise it, understanding the growth and development of modern industrial societies must

---

[46] The evolutionary nature of the market—and the fact that learning in this environment appears, in one sense, quite rapid, and in other sense, quite limited—is illustrated by the S & L debacle in the United States. The S & Ls were quick to respond to the new economic situation that they found themselves in in the 1980s, but they seemed not to have learned from history the risks associated with having too large a fraction of one's portfolio in correlated assets, nor did they grasp the possibility that prices of real estate may fall dramatically. The S & L crisis has also made it clear that the line between fraud and 'moral hazard' may be a fine one. The crisis has forced changes in financial regulations, which in turn will give rise to adaptations of the financial institutions.

Whether mortgage insurance and the development of national mortgage markets represent permanent changes in financial structure, or the temporary (mal-)adaptation of markets to a situation in which, for several decades, real estate markets have had relative stability—the problems of the Great Depression receding into ancient history—only time will tell.

[47] Though the junk bond itself may be partially a response to legal changes which reduced the economic costs of bankruptcy.

[48] See, for instance, Asquith and Mullins (1991).

begin by a study of the history and evolution of financial markets. This is the task before us in this conference. We hope our paper has provided a helpful conceptual framework with which to undertake this task.

References

Alchian, A. and H. Demsetz (1972), 'Production, Information Costs and Economic Organization', *American Economic Review*, 62, 777–795.

Akerlof, G. and J. Stiglitz (1969), 'Capital, Wages and Structural Unemployment', *Economic Journal*, LXXIX, 269–281.

Asquith, P. and D. Mullins (1991), 'Returns and Default Rates on High Yield Bonds', *Journal of Finance*, in press.

Champernowne, D. G. (1953), 'A Model of Income Distributions', *Economic Journal*, LXIII, 318–351.

Eaton, J. (1986), 'Lending with Costly Enforcement of Repayment and Potential Fraud', *Journal of Banking and Finance*, 10, 281–293.

Eaton, J. and M. Gersovitz (1981), 'Debt with Potential Repudiation: Theoretical and Empirical Analysis', *Review of Economic Studies*, 48, 289–309.

Eaton, J., M. Gersovitz, and J. Stiglitz (1986), 'Pure Theory of Country Risk', *European Economic Review*, 30, 481–513.

Foley, D. and M. Sidrauski (1970), 'Portfolio Choice, Investment and Growth', *American Economic Review*, 60, 44–63.

Gale, D. and M. Hellwig (1985), 'Incentive-Compatible Debt Contracts I: The One-Period Problem', *Review of Economic Studies*, 52, 647–664.

Gale, I. and J. E. Stiglitz (1989), 'The Informational Content of Initial Public Offerings', with Ian Gale, *Journal of Finance*, XLIV, 469–478.

Greenwald, B. and J. E. Stiglitz (1988), 'Money, Imperfect Information and Economic Fluctuations', in Meir Kohn and S. C. Tsiang (eds), *Finance Constraints, Expectations and Macroeconomics*, Oxford University Press, pp. 141–165.

Greenwald, B. and J. E. Stiglitz (1991), 'Financial market Imperfections and Productivity Growth', *Journal of Economic Behavior and Organization*, 13, 321–345.

Greenwald, B., J. Stiglitz, and A. Weiss, A. (1984), 'Informational Imperfections in the Capital Markets and Macro-economic Fluctuations', *American Economic Review*, 74, 194–199 (paper presented to the American Economic Association, December 1983).

Grossman, S. and O. Hart, (1980), 'Takeover Bids, the Free Ride Problem and the Theory of the Corporation', *Bell Journal of Economics*, 11, 42–64.

Grossman, S. and J. Stiglitz (1977), 'On Value Maximization and Alternative Objectives of the Firm', with S. Grossman, *Journal of Finance*, XXXII, 389–402.

Grossman, S. and J. Stiglitz (1980), 'Stockholder Unanimity in the Making of Production and Financial Decisions', *Quarterly Journal of Economics*, 94, 543–566.

Hannaway, J. (1989), *Managers Managing: The Workings of an Administrative System*. Oxford University Press, Oxford.

Hall, R. and Jorgenson (1967), 'Tax Policy and Investment Behavior', *American Economic Review*, 57, 391–414.

Hawtrey, R. (1919), *Currency and Credit*. Longmans, Green and Co., New York.

Hirshleifer, J. (1966), 'Investment Decisions under Uncertainty: Applications of the State-Preference Approach', *Quarterly Journal of Economics*, 80, 252–277.

Jensen, M. and Mechling (1976), 'Theory of the Firm: Managerial Behavior, Agency Costs and Ownership Structure', *Journal of Financial Economics*, 3, 305–360.

Kaldor, N. (1956), 'Alternative Theories of Distribution', *Review of Economic Studies*, 23, 83–100.

Kalecki, M. (1939), *Essays in the Theory of Economic Fluctuations*, Allen and Unwin, London.

Keynes, J. M. (1936), *The General Theory of Employment, Interest and Money*. Macmillan, London.

Kuh, E. and J. R. Meyer (1959), *The Investment Decision*. Harvard University Press, Cambridge.

Myers, S. and N. Majluf (1984), 'Corporate Financing and Investment Decisions When Firms Have Information that Investors Do Not', *Journal of Financial Economics*, 11, 187–221.

Modigliani, F. and Miller (1988), 'The Cost of Capital, Corporation Finance and the Theory of Investment', *American Economic Review*, 48, 261–267.

Passinetti, L. (1962), 'Rate of Profit and Income Distribution in Relation to the Rate of Economic Growth', *Review of Economic Studies*, 29, 267–279.

Robinson, J. (1956), *The Accumulation of Capital*. Macmillan, London.

Ross, S. (1973), 'The Economic Theory of Agency: The Principal's Problem', *American Economic Review*, pp. 134–139.

Sahlman, W. (1989), 'Venture Capital Industry in the United States', Harvard Business School Working Paper.

Shleifer, A. and R. Vishny (1988), 'Managerial Entrenchment', paper presented to conference at Princeton University.

Solow, R. (1956), 'A Contribution to the Theory of Economic Growth', *Quarterly Journal of Economics*, LXX, 65–94.

Stiglitz, J. (1969), 'A Re-Examination of the Modigliani-Miller Theorem', *American Economic Review*, 59, pp. 784–793.

Stiglitz, J. (1972a), 'Some Aspects of the Pure Theory of Corporate Finance: Bankruptcies and Take-Overs', *Bell Journal of Economics*, 3, 458–482.

Stiglitz, J. (1972b), 'On the Optimality of the Stock Market Allocation of Investment', *Quarterly Journal of Economics*, 86, 25–60.

Stiglitz, J. (1974a), 'Incentives and Risk Sharing in Sharecropping', *Review of Economic Studies*, 41, 219–255.

Stiglitz, J. (1974b), 'On the Irrelevance of Corporate Financial Policy', *American Economic Review*, 64, 851–866 (presented at a conference in Hakone, Japan, 1970).

Stiglitz, J. (1982), 'Ownership, Control and Efficient Markets', in W. F. Sharpe and C. Cootner (eds), *Financial Economics: Essays in honor of Paul Cootner*, Prentice Hall, Englewood Cliffs, 118–158.

Stiglitz, J. (1985), 'Credit Markets and the Control of Capital', *Journal of Money, Credit and Banking*, 17, 133–152.

Stiglitz, J. E. (1987), 'Imperfect Information in the Product Market', in *Handbook of Industrial Organization*, Vol. 1, Elsevier Science Publishers, pp. 769–847.

Stiglitz, J. (1988a), 'Why Financial Structure Matters', *Journal of Economic Perspectives*, 2, 121–126.

Stiglitz, J. (1988b), 'Money, Credit and Business Fluctuations', *The Economic Record*, 307–322.

Stiglitz, J. (1989), 'Using Tax Policy to Curb Speculative Short-Term Trading', *Journal of Financial Services Research*, 3, 101–115.

Stiglitz, J. and A. Weiss (1981), 'Credit Rationing in Markets with Imperfect Information', *American Economic Review*, 71, 393–410.

Stiglitz, J. and A. Weiss (1982), 'Incentive Effects of Termination: Applications to the Credit and Labor Markets', *American Economic Review*, 72, 912–927.

Stiglitz, J. and A. Weiss (1986), 'Credit Rationing and Collateral', in J. Edwards, J. Franks, C. Mayer and S. Schaefer (eds), *Recent Developments in Corporate Finance*, Cambridge University Press, New York, 101–135.

Stiglitz, J. and A. Weiss (1987), 'Credit Rationing with Many Borrowers', *American Economic Review*, 228–231.

Summers, L. and V. Summers (1989), 'When Financial Markets Work Too Well: A Cautious Case for a Securities Transaction Tax', paper presented to the Annenberg Conference on Technology and Financial Markets, Washington, DC, February, 1989.

Townsend, R. (1979), 'Optimal Contracts and Competitive Markets with Costly State Verification', *Journal of Economic Theory*, 21, 265–293.

PART II

KNOWLEDGE, ORGANIZATIONS, AND TECHNOLOGICAL EVOLUTION

The Explicit Economics of Knowledge Codification and Tacitness

ROBIN COWAN[a], PAUL A. DAVID[b] and DOMINIQUE FORAY[c]

([a]University of Maastricht, MERIT, Maastricht, The Netherlands, [a]Stanford University and All Souls College, Oxford, UK and [c]University of Paris—Dauphine & IMRI (CNRS), France. Emails: paul.david@economics.ox.ac.uk/pad@leland.stanford.edu, r.cowan@merit.unimaas.nl and dominique.foray@dauphine.fr)

This paper attempts a greater precision and clarity of understanding concerning the nature and economic significance of knowledge and its variegated forms by presenting 'the skeptical economist's guide to "tacit knowledge"'. It critically reconsiders the ways in which the concepts of tacitness and codification have come to be employed by economists and develops a more coherent re-conceptualization of these aspects of knowledge production and distribution activities. It seeks also to show that a proposed alternative framework for the study of knowledge codification activities offers a more useful guide for further research directed to informing public policies for science, technological innovation and long-run economic growth.

1. Introduction: What's All this Fuss over Tacit Knowledge About?

With increasing frequency these days references appear in the economics literature to 'tacit knowledge'. More often than not the meaning of this term itself is something that remains literally tacit—which is to say, those who employ it are *silent* as to its definition. Something is suggested nevertheless by the common practice of juxtaposing mention of tacit knowledge and references to 'codified knowledge'. What is all this about? Why has this distinction been made and what significance does it have for economists?

Polanyi (1958, 1967) introduced the term into modern circulation by pointing to the existence of 'the tacit dimension of knowledge', a form or component of human knowledge distinct from, but complementary to, the knowledge explicit in *conscious* cognitive processes. Polanyi illustrated this conceptualization by reference to a fact of common perception: we all are often aware of certain objects without being focused on them. This, he maintained, did not make them the less important, as they form the context that renders focused perception possible, understandable and fruitful. Reference to the findings of Gestalt psychology in regard to other perceptual phenomena formed another important aspect of Polanyi's conceptualization of tacit knowledge: people appear to be perceptually (and/or intellectually) aware of some objects and things about the world only as *entities*—as illustrated by the identification of a particular human face or voice.[1] Knowledge of this kind consists of *holistic* understandings, and thus is not completely amenable to purely reductionist analyses.

Subsequently, the term 'tacit knowledge' has come to be more widely applied to forms of personal knowledge that remain 'UN-codified' and do not belong in the category of 'information', which itself is thought of as an ideal-type good having peculiar economic features that differentiate it from other, conventional economic commodities.[2] One may observe the growing practice among economists of juxtaposing 'tacit' and 'codified' knowledge, which casually applies the former term as a label for the entire (residual) category of knowledge that cannot be seen to be conveyed by means of codified, symbolic representations, i.e. transmitted as 'information'. In this process of inflating the usage of the term, the emphasis upon context and contextual under-standing that was present in psychological references to the 'tacit dimension' of human knowledge has been largely discarded. Tacit knowledge thus has come to signify an absolute type, namely: 'not codified knowledge'. Among economists it is used more and more in this way, without explicit definition, and therefore without further explication of the conditions that might under-lie 'tacitness' or the resort to codification of knowledge.

But, more than having become merely another overly vague bit of fash-ionable economic jargon, 'tacit knowledge' now is an increasingly 'loaded' buzzword, freighted with both methodological implications for micro-economic theory in general, and policy significance for the economics of science and technology, innovation, and economic growth. Indeed, references to 'tacitness' have become a platform used by some economists to launch fresh attacks upon national policies of public subsidization for R&D activities, and equally by other economists to construct novel rationales for governmental funding of science and engineering research and training programs.

---

[1] Polyani (1967, pp. 4–6): 'I shall reconsider human knowledge by starting from the fact that we can know more than we can tell . . . Gestalt psychology has demonstrated that we may know a physiognomy by intergrating our awareness of its particulars without being able to identify these particulars . . .'

[2] Most significant, from the economist's viewpoint, is the absence of super-additivity and the neglig-ible marginal costs of transmitting information. These properties and their implications are discussed more fully in the following text, but the canonical references are Nelson (1959) and Arrow (1962).

The first-order result of all this would seem to have been the creation of a considerable amount of semantic and taxonomic confusion. In and of itself, this might be both expected and tolerable as a transient phase in any novel conceptual development. Unfortunately, one cannot afford to be so sanguine, because those very same confusions are being exploited to advance economic policy conclusions that claim to be grounded upon propositions that are well established (if only recently recognized in economics) about the existence of different kinds of knowledge pertinent to scientific, technological and organizational innovation. In our view, however, such claims in many instances are neither analytically nor empirically warranted.

This essay responds to a felt need for greater precision and clarity of understanding concerning the nature and economic significance of knowledge and its variegated forms, by presenting what might be described as 'the skeptical economist's guide to "tacit knowledge"'. Our skepticism, however, does not extend to questioning the seriousness of the array of issues that economists and others have been discussing under the general rubric of tacit knowledge, which truly are important and deserving of careful consideration. Furthermore, we acknowledge that some of the now-classic contributions to the economics of scientific and technological innovation, when regarded from an epistemological perspective, appear unwarrantedly simplistic in their handling of some subtle questions concerning 'knowledge' and 'information', and the relationship between the two.

Our immediate purposes in this paper are to critically reconsider the ways in which the concepts of tacitness and codification have come to be employed by economists, and to develop a more coherent re-conceptualization of these aspects of knowledge production and distribution activities. We seek to show, further, that a proposed alternative framework for the study of knowledge codification activities—perhaps because it rests upon explicit microeconomic foundations—offers a more useful guide for further research directed to informing public policies for science, technological innovation and long-run economic growth.

The following section elaborates on our contention that the terminology and meaning of 'tacitness' in the economics literature, having drifted far from its original epistemological and psychological moorings, has become unproductively amorphous; indeed, that it now obscures more than it clarifies. Among the matters that thereby have been hidden are some serious analytical and empirical flaws in the newly emerging critique of the old economics of R&D. By the same token, we also can identify equally serious flaws in the novel rationale that has recently been developed for continuing public support of R&D activities, based upon the alleged inherent tacitness of technological knowledge.

An explicit re-examination of some fundamental conceptual underpinnings in this area is therefore in order. Although this requires that we re-open questions which readers coming to the topic from economics may feel are settled well enough for their purposes, a persuasive case can be made for doing so; and setting it forth in section 3, we seek to show that a new taxonomic framework would prove helpful in clearing away a number of the conceptual confusions that presently are impeding the progress of research in this area. Such a framework is proposed in section 4, providing a topography of 'knowledge transaction activities', the salient features of which are discussed in section 5. A number of advantages afforded by the novel conceptual structure (those that are discernible *a priori*) are indicated in section 6. But, as the proof of any pudding of this kind is to be found only in the eating, we proceed to put it to practical use in section 7, where we consider the economic costs and benefits of codification activities in different knowledge environments, thereby exposing the main endogenous determinants of the dynamic path of the boundary between what is and is not codified in the existing state of knowledge. Section 8 concludes with some brief comments indicating the implied directions for theoretical and empirical work needed to further explore this promising vein in the economics of knowledge.

2. How the Tacit Dimension Found a Wonderful New Career, in Economics

To motivate this undertaking we begin with a closer look at the intellectual background of the increasing frequency with which the notion of tacit knowledge currently is entering economic policy discussions. It is fair to say that economists have not had much preparation to deal with the recent debates that are emerging in their midst over the nature of knowledge and the significance of its tacit dimension. This is understandable, because the popular social science career of this concept began elsewhere . . . long ago, and in a far distant discipline.

Must economists now prepare themselves to become ever more deeply involved in discussions of the nature of knowledge, and begin to care about the various categories into which other disciplines claim knowledge should be sorted? Is this not something better left for epistemologists and others of similar philosophical inclination? Although one might be tempted to answer the latter in the affirmative, it is now too late to ignore the very meaning of something that a large and growing number economists and other social scientists seem bent upon discussing. It seems helpful, therefore, to approach the subject with some background awareness of the historical path by which 'tacitness' made its way from the philosophical writings of Polanyi (1958, 1967) into widespread currency in the economic journals.

2.1 The Roots in the Sociology of Scientific Knowledge, and Cognitive Science

The pioneering role was taken by those who called themselves 'sociologists of scientific knowledge' (SSK), thereby distinguishing their purpose and approach from that of the then mainstream Mertonian school in the sociology of science. Proponents of the SSK program were more interested in the role of social forces (under which both economic and political interests were subsumed) in shaping the cognitive aspects of scientific work. The traditional approach in the sociology of knowledge had, by contrast, tended to focus attention upon the role of macro-institutional settings, reward structures and the like, in mobilizing resources for the pursuit of scientific knowledge and organizing the conduct of research. By and large, it had thereby eschewed direct engagement with the epistemological issues that occupied philosophers of science, and so it appeared to accept if not endorse the latter's formal accounts of 'the scientific method' as the 'disinterested confrontation of logically derived propositions (theory) with empirical evidence (fact)'.

That picture, however, did not appear to square with the one found by some SSK-inspired students of contemporary scientific practice. They observed that some kinds of knowledge deployed in scientific inquiry—most notably that relating to the assembly and operation of experimental apparatus and instrumentation, and the interpretation of the data which these generated—were not communicated as hypotheses or codified propositions, or by any means resembling the formalized modes of discourse with which philosophy of science traditionally had been preoccupied. Rather, working scientists appeared to be more occupied with 'craft knowledge', and much of what seemed crucial to their research efforts was not being transmitted among them in the form of any explicit, fully codified statements.

Collins's (1974) notably influential study in this vein examined the early construction of the TEA laser in a number of laboratories, and reported that none of the research teams which succeeded in building a working laser had done so without the participation of someone from another laboratory where a device of this type already had been put into operation. For Collins, '[t]he major point is that the transmission of skills is not done through the medium of written words'. Subsequent contributors to the sociology of scientific and technological knowledge have read this and other, kindred observations as showing that 'the diffusion of knowledge could not be reduced to the mere transmission of information' (Callon, 1995).

A contrast thus was posed between the 'algorithmic model' of knowledge production, which is concerned exclusively with the generation of consistent propositions and the transmission of explicit declarative statements, on the one hand, and the so-called 'enculturation model' of scientific activities on the other. This distinction was invoked primarily by philosophers and sociologists who sought to challenge the idea that science, and specifically the modern scientific method, was a source of 'privileged' statements. The putative privilege in question derived from the implication that scientific statements could be stripped from the social contexts in which they had been formed and in which they had acquired meaning, and consequently could be promulgated as part of an authoritatively universal, 'codified' body of knowledge about the physical world. Challengers of that view leaned heavily on the seeming importance of tacit knowledge in the actual conduct of scientific activities.

At this juncture in the narrative a few remarks should be entered about the distinction observed here between 'information' and 'knowledge', terms that we shall continue to avoid using interchangeably. We find it useful to operationally define an item of information as a message containing structured data, the receipt of which causes some action by the recipient agent—without implying that the nature of that action is determined solely and uniquely by the message itself. Instead, it is the cognitive context afforded by the receiver that imparts meaning(s) to the information-message, and from the meaning(s) follow the specific nature of the induced action(s). The term 'knowledge' is simply the label affixed to the state of the agent's entire cognitive context.[3]

The algorithmic model to which reference has been made above, strictly interpreted, implies the absence of any meaningful distinction between information and knowledge. Under this approach all the cognitive and behavioral capabilities of whatever human or non-human agent is being described must have been reduced to 'code', that is, to structured data and the necessary instructions for its processing. Only in that way could a purely algorithmic actor generate further data and/or instructions for future actions— whether those were physical actions, or simply the processing, classification, storage, retrieval and transmission of information. It is possible, therefore, to say that what an (algorithmic) economic agent 'knows' is nothing more nor less than 'information'.

---

[3] From the foregoing it should be evident that we do not find it helpful to conflate 'what humans learn in order to assimilate, digest and use information' with the concept of 'tacit knowledge', and thereby to arrive at the glib but empty formalization: 'information = codified knowledge' and 'knowledge' = 'tacit knowledge' + 'information'. The definitions offered in the text make explicit the distinctive usage of the terms *data, information* and *knowledge* in Dasgupta and David (1994), David and Foray (1995) and Cowan and Foray (1997). As we point out below, when knowledge is defined in this way, i.e. as an attribute of individual agents, some delicate conceptual issues arise when one tries to be precise in extending the notion by speaking of 'social knowledge' as the attribute of some collectivity of agents.

To stop there, of course, would be to ignore, *inter alia*, the manifest differences between intelligent human agents and computers. Humans create new categories for the classification of information, and learn to assign meanings to (sensory) data inputs without the assistance of programmed instructions of which they are consciously aware. Not surprisingly, then, the term 'knowledge' is applied in ordinary language when referring to human capacities that appear to be accessed without the intermediation of any formal code. In other words, humans (and other living creatures) 'know things' that they have not acquired as 'information' and which, not having been reduced to symbolic representations (code), are held in forms that are not readily available for communication to others—at least not explicitly as 'information-bearing' messages. At the same time, however, it is no less important to notice that the capacities of humans to 'decode', interpret, assimilate and find novel applications for particular items of information entail the use of still other items of information. These latter equally are part (and may well form the critical part) of the 'cognitive context' within which the recipient of a given message assigns to it 'meaning(s)'. Moreover, there is nothing in this observation that would imply a lack of awareness on the part of the individual concerned about the pertinent 'information context', or any inability to transmit it to others.

2.2 From Evolutionary Economics to Management Strategy and Technology Policy

For some considerable time, economists took little if any interest in the question of separating the notion of knowledge from their idea of information, and scarcely noticed the sequel distinction that other disciplines had drawn between the algorithmic and enculturation models of learning and associated behaviors. But things have moved on from that stage, and in several directions. A parallel and related course of development also has been evident in the management studies literature, from the early formulations such as that provided by Winter (1987), to the recent wave of books on 'knowledge management', as exemplified by Leonard-Barton (1995), Nonaka and Keuchi (1995) and Davenport and Prusak (1998).

Thus, the importance of tacit knowledge as a strategy asset is acknowledged today by students of rational management practices on the one hand,[4] and at the same time is cited as being crucial by critics of the 'algorithmic'

---

[4] The definition of 'knowledge' given in the text (above) is broadly consonant with, albeit rather more spare than, the way the term is being used in this literature, as may be seen by the following 'working definition' offered by Davenport and Prusak (1998, p. 5): 'Knowledge is a fluid mix of framed experience, values, contextual information, and expert insight that provides a framework for evaluating and incorporating new experience and information. It originates and is applied in the minds of knowers.'

approach of modern economic analysis of all aspects of human behavior. In its latter manifestations, the concept of the inextricable tacitness of human knowledge forms the basis of arguments brought not only against the residue of behaviorist psychology which remains embedded in the neo-classical formulation of microeconomic analysis, but against virtually every construction of rational decision processes as the foundation for modeling and explaining the actions of individual human agents.

Whether the emergence of these disparate intellectual developments can be said to constitute scientific 'advance', however, remains another matter. Quite clearly, the challenge being brought against algorithmic representations of knowledge generation and acquisition goes much deeper than arguments for 'bounded' rationality following the work of Newell and Simon (1972); and it has been argued in far more sweepingly general terms by critics of the whole artificial intelligence (AI) program such as Hofstader (1979) and, more recently, Penrose (1989, 1997). In those quarters, tacit knowledge has come to stand for the aspects of human intelligence that cannot be mimicked by *any* (computer) algorithm.

It may be remarked that were the latter rather nihilistic arguments against the quest for AI to be read as statements conditional on the presently available and *foreseeable* states of technology, rather than as absolute assertions of impossibility, this would leave room for the boundary between tacit knowledge and knowledge of other kinds to be other than inextricably fixed. Instead, what was tacit, and correspondingly what was not, would be subject to some future readjustments by improvements in the performance of computer hardware and software—because increasing processing speeds, reduced access times, expanded storage and more efficient algorithm designs permitted the faithful reproduction of an increasing range of human capabilities.[5] The resolution of debates over the mutability of this boundary would carry many implications for economics, but, as will be seen, the way in which the idea of tacitness has come to be used opens the possibility that still other, non-technological conditions also are influential in determining what knowledge is codified and what is not.

One may locate the seedbed of the modern flowering of economic discussions of tacit knowledge in the early attention that was directed to Polanyi's writings by Nelson and Winter's (1982) widely noticed critique of neoclassical analysis and initiation of a program of research in evolutionary

---

[5] Balconi (1998) explores the effects of changes in the modern technology of steel product manufacturing upon the boundary between the codified and the tacit elements of the knowledge deemed relevant for production operations and worker training. The relevance here is simply that this boundary is mutable under the influence of technological changes other than those in the domain information technology narrowly construed.

economics.[6] Their discussion of the parallels between individual human skills and organizational capacities (Nelson and Winter, 1982, ch. 4) gave particular prominence to the concept of tacit knowledge, and expanded upon its significance for economists concerned with the internal workings of the firm.[7] Those passages remain as perceptive and stimulating, and as fresh and balanced today as when they first appeared, almost two decades ago, and it is a pity that a larger proportion of the economists who now talk about tacit knowledge and its implications do not appear to have acquainted themselves with this 'local source'.[8]

What Nelson and Winter (1982) say about the nature and significance of tacitness in knowledge conveys not just one sharply defined concept, but a nexus of meanings, each carrying somewhat distinctive implications. Their first reference to the term (1982, p. 73), for example, offers only a parenthetical clarification: 'The knowledge that underlies skillful performance is in large measure tacit knowledge, *in the sense that* the performer is not fully aware of the details of the performance and finds it difficult or impossible to articulate a full account of those details' (emphasis added).

Yet, as is made clear shortly following this statement, Nelson and Winter accept Polanyi's (1967) account of such situations as being contextual, rather than absolute: 'the aim of a skillful performance' may 'be achieved by the observance of a set of rules which are not known as such to the person following them'. Reference then is made to Polanyi's earlier philosophical work, *Personal Knowledge* (1958, p. 49), where an example is presented of a swimmer keeping himself buoyant by regulating respiration, yet remaining unconscious of doing so. In this case the operant rule ('never empty your lungs fully') plainly is one that is articulable, could be known to another person, and so might be transmitted verbally by a swimming instructor—were the latter aware of the principle of buoyancy. In other words, Nelson and Winter

---

[6] For the subsequent elaboration of a more thorough-going rejection of microeconomic optimization in the evolutionary models of Schumpeterian competition, see e.g. Dosi (1988), Dosi *et al.* (1988) and Dosi and Egidi (1991). Evolutionary modeling in economics now spans a wide range of practice in regard to how 'bounded' the bounded rationality of agents is assumed to be. Anderson (1994) discusses this and other issues in the algorithmic representation of the general class of 'Nelson–Winter type' models.

[7] Skinner (1994, p. 11) points out that the use made of Polanyi's concept by Nelson and Winter (1982) emphasized what cognitive scientists refer to as the 'granularity' of the efficient mode of mental storage for learned skills and procedures ('routines'), rather than for the storage of declarative statements. Skinner suggests that, in developing the former theme, Nelson and Winter were influenced strongly by the previous work in cognitive science and AI, e.g. by Newell and Simon's (1972) formulation of a production system model of information processing for 'learning,' and the idea of learned routines being holistically stored for recall (as 'scripts')—a concept due to Shank (1988), who was a leading figure in cognitive science and AI fields on the faculty of Yale University during the 1970s and 1980s (as were Nelson and Winter).

[8] Had things been otherwise, it seems only reasonable to suppose that we would have been spared at least the more serious confusions and unwarranted generalizations that have become commonplace in the literature.

(1982, p. 77) do not insist, any more than did Polanyi, that tacitness implied 'inarticulability', even though the inarticulability of some (personal) knowledge logically implied that the latter would remain tacit.

On the question of 'awareness', Nelson and Winter (1982, p. 78) recognize that the skillful performer may have 'subsidiary awareness' of the rules that are being followed, while being 'focally aware' of some other—most probably novel—facet of the task in which she is engaged. This reinforces an appreciation of the contextual boundaries within which knowledge will be tacit, rather than explicitly recognized and articulated. Yet, if one can describe behavior in terms of 'rule conformity', then it is clear that the underlying knowledge is *codifiable*—and indeed may have previously been codified.

Most significant still, for what we shall say about the more recent strain of the literature on tacitness, is Nelson and Winter's (1982, p. 78) acknowledgement that this quality *is not inherent in the knowledge*. They write: 'The same knowledge, apparently, is more tacit for some people than for others. Incentives, too, clearly matter: when circumstances place a great premium on effective articulation, remarkable things can sometimes be accomplished'. In amplification of this point, they offer the example of an expert pilot giving successful verbal instruction via radio to a complete novice as to how to land an airplane—even though the 'expert' had never had occasion previously to make explicit what was entailed in his successful performance of a landing. Indeed, their section on 'Skills and Tacit Knowledge' concludes by emphasizing that

> . . . costs matter. Whether a particular bit of knowledge is in *principle* articulable or necessarily tacit is not the relevant question in most behavioral situations. Rather, the question is whether the costs . . . are sufficiently high so that the knowledge *in fact* remains tacit (p. 80).

This important set of observations deserved much more attention and elaboration than it has been accorded by the subsequent literature, and we have sought (in section 7, below) to begin the work of rectifying this oversight.

It is unfortunate that these more complicated aspects of the concept had been all but forgotten, were they ever widely grasped when 'tacitness' made its debut on the economic policy stage. Among the most notable of the uses to which the idea of tacit knowledge is being put on the more mundane levels at which most economists operate, and certainly the uses that have the greatest impact in economic policy circles, has been the qualification—and in some instances the outright rejection—of the practical policy conclusions drawn from the classic information-theoretic analysis of the economics of R&D activities.

Following the seminal work of Arrow (1955, 1962) and Nelson (1959), an entire generation of economists treated scientific and technological knowledge as 'information'. To that degree, they reasoned, the knowledge generated by research activities possessed certain generic properties of public goods. Much of the case for government subsidization of science and engineering research, and for innovative activity more generally, came to be grounded on the proposition that *qua* information, such knowledge could not be optimally produced or distributed through the workings of competitive markets.

Nowadays we are more and more frequently instructed otherwise. In the newer understanding of science and technology as being pursuits inextricably involved with tacit knowledge, it is claimed that the old public policy rationales are exploded; the essential understandings are said to be the portion of knowledge that remains uncodified, and so deprived of the public goods properties that would result in informational spillovers and market failure. Thus, as this argument concludes, the traditional economic case for subsidizing science and research in general collapses, as there is little or no basis for a presumption of market failure. Similar arguments are advanced in the context of policy debates over the role of intellectual property rights in providing incentive for innovation: the claim is that the information presented (in codified form) in a patent is insufficient to allow others to actually make use of the patented invention, and it is the correlative 'tacit knowledge' that resides with the innovator that provides the real source of private, rent-appropriating (monopoly) power.[9]

But, at the same time, tacit knowledge is invoked by defenders of government subsidization of science as part of a strategic innovation policy. A standard argument against public subsidy to science is that foreigners engaging in applied, commercially oriented R&D would free-ride (since information is a public good and travels freely) by exploiting the basic knowledge discoveries that *our* researchers vie to codify for disclosure in the scientific journals and similar archival publications. To this, the proponents of a strategic role for tacit knowledge reply, nations and regions, like individual enterprises undertaking R&D investments, can count on the benefits of 'sticky data'—to use von Hippel's (1993) arresting term. Knowledge does not travel freely, a condition that rests largely on the importance of tacit knowledge residing only in the heads of the scientists and engineers engaged in its production. Codified knowledge may have low marginal costs of transmission and is thus slippery and hard to contain, but that is largely irrelevant if what one needs is its 'sticky', tacit counterpart.[10]

---

[9] For further discussion see Arundel and Kabla (1999). The force of such claims would seem restricted largely to the case of process patents rather than product patents. Arundel (1996, 1997) reports that the CIS survey of EU firms found that 18–20% of respondent companies in the size range above 199 employees regarded process patents as a 'very important or crucial' source of competitive advantage, whereas in the case of product patents the corresponding figure was in the 30–40% range.

[10] In subsequent work, von Hippel (1994) generalizes the idea of stickiness so that it covers all situations in which there is an appreciable cost of transferring information, relevant for innovative activities. In principle, at least, von Hippel's use of the notion of 'stickiness' makes no distinction between transfer costs consisting of pure rents imposed by the owners of intellectual property rights, on the one hand, and real

The inherent 'stickiness' of certain kinds of knowledge, consequently, enables business (or other) entities to protect their ability to appropriate the benefits derivable from their research investments fully, by controlling access to the repositories of uncodified knowledge. For this, minimal recourse is required to the protection of intellectual property in the form of patents and copyrights; a mixture of trade secrecy law and labor law (master–servant relations) governing the behavior of current and former employees may be enough. Thus, curious though it may seem, the tacit dimension of scientific and technological knowledge has found a new career for itself in science and technology policy debates: it is beginning to supplant its now dubious companion, 'codified knowledge', as the core of a new rationale for government research funding intended to build national and regional 'competitiveness' through innovation.

According to this application of the argument, even though the essential tacit knowledge concerning how to exploit what has been invented might be less than perfectly 'sticky', what this implies is that its economic benefits are only available to be captured locally. In other, more formal, terms, it is asserted that the marginal costs of knowledge transmission rise very rapidly with 'distance' from the context in which such knowledge was generated. Research by-products in the form of technological knowledge—being concerned with how best to get instrumentation involving chemical, mechanical, electrical and optical processes to work—are seen as inherently more strongly tacit in nature. That is held to be particularly beneficial for would-be commercial developers who are able to situate closer to the locus of such discoveries (see e.g. Pavitt, 1987; Nelson, 1992; Patel and Pavitt, 1995).

A broad policy implication following from this is that for an economy to have a strong, innovative manufacturing sector, it is necessary also to have correspondingly strong applied and basic research activities situated in close proximity to the production operations themselves. The new innovation strategy perspective that has now formed around the concept of tacitness in the business management literature is illustrated by the following passage (Kay, 1999, p. 13):

> Since 'knowledge that'—the characteristic discoveries of natural science—is easily transmitted, one solution [to the problem of creating 'knowledge-based competitive advantages'] is to continually innovate and stay one step ahead. And that kind of innovative capacity depends on knowledge that isn't 'knowledge that', but 'knowledge how'—i.e. Tacit knowledge. Tacit knowledge can take many forms, but it cannot be written down. It is unique to an organization—and therefore cannot be copied . . . The benefits of such tacit knowledge arise only through a culture of trust and knowledge-sharing within an organization . . .

---

social resource costs such as those entailed in physically transporting an expert for the purpose of demonstrating the proper use of a novel product or process in a distant location.

Such considerations apply not only to scientific and engineering know-how, but also, and perhaps more strongly, to marketing, and internal management knowledge pertaining to business organizations, all of which have strongly contextual elements that make them 'natural' contributors to what von Hippel (1994) refers to as 'sticky information'.

Thus, a notion that took its origins in the psychology of visual perception and human motor skills has been wonderfully transmuted, first from an efficient mode of mental storage of knowledge into a putative epistemological category (having to do with the nature of the knowledge itself), from there into a phenomenon of inarticulable inter-organizational relationships and finally to one of the keys to corporate, and perhaps also national, competitive advantage!

A corollary of arguments in the latter vein is that the case for granting public subsidies and tax concessions to private companies that invest in R&D would seem to be much weakened, were it not for the difficulties caused these firms by the circulation of their research personnel.[11] Scientific and engineering staff are able to carry critical tacit knowledge off to potential rival firms that offer them better terms of employment, including equity ownership in 'start ups' of their own. In the logic of this approach, recognition of the criticality of tacit knowledge argues for further strengthening of trade secrecy protections, to block those 'leakages' and altogether eliminate the market failure rationale for governmental support of the performance of R&D by the private sector.[12] That leaves the way open for those who wish to mount an essentially 'techno-mercantilist' argument for R&D subsidies, grounded on the idea that the country can benefit from job-creation, etc., if its firms win the race to be first to launch new products in international markets. It is, in effect, a new strategic trade policy argument, grounded on the claim that tacit knowledge permits national appropriation of the direct and indirect benefits of monopolizing international product niches by being 'first to invest'.

We see a need to put the economics of tacit and codified knowledge on analytically firmer and terminologically more precise foundations than those upon which most of the recent literature presently rests. The foregoing account of the wonderful career that has thrust 'the tacit dimension' into the science and technology policy limelight serves, at least, to identify a number

[11] We can observe that the more things change the more they stay the same. We have moved from the view that the problem to be solved arises from the fact that a firm's *knowledge* is easily appropriated by other firms. Acknowledging the importance of tacit knowledge, and thus that the initial problem may not be so severe, we face a 'new problem' stemming from the fact that a firm's *knowledge workers* are easily appropriated by other firms. In both cases the general issue remains, however—fluidity of knowledge or information (whether transmitted through codified knowledge or labor mobility) is good for the economy but may be bad for the individual firm that bears the costs of enlightening its competitors.

[12] See, for example, Kealey (1996) on industrial secrecy as the suitable 'remedy' for the problem of informational spillovers from research, and the critique of that position in David (1997).

of issues that are of sufficient importance to warrant much more careful consideration. The notion that the economic case for public support of science and engineering should now be based upon the inherently tacit and 'craft' nature of research activities certainly is rather paradoxical. Taken at face value, it would suggest that intellectual property protection is unjustified, since, in the 'natural' state of things, there are no 'externalities' of new knowledge. By implication, the patent system's exchange of monopoly of use for 'disclosure' allows the patentee to retain the tacit knowledge without which the information contained in the patent really is useless.

But, before rushing to discard everything we know about the economics of R&D, scientific skepticism instructs us to pause and ask whether the epistemological foundations of these new propositions really are all that solid. We should therefore question whether the economic functioning and attributes of tacit and codified knowledge are well understood by those who would invoke those matters in the context of current innovation policy debates.

3. *Codification and Tacitness Reconsidered*

It will be easiest for us to start not with the concept of tacit knowledge but at the opposite and seemingly less problematic end of the field, so to speak, by asking what is to be understood by the term 'codified knowledge'. Its obvious reference is to *codes*, or to standards—whether of notation or of rules, either of which may be promulgated by authority or may acquire 'authority' through frequency of usage and common consent, i.e. by *de facto* acceptance.

Knowledge that is recorded in some codebook serves *inter alia* as a storage depository, as a reference point and possibly as an authority. But information written in a code can only perform those functions when people are able to interpret the code; and, in the case of the latter two functions, to give it more or less mutually consistent interpretations. Successfully reading the code in this last sense may involve prior acquisition of considerable specialized knowledge (quite possibly including knowledge not written down anywhere). As a rule, there is no reason to presuppose that all people in the world possess the knowledge needed to interpret the codes properly. This means that what is codified for one person or group may be tacit for another and an utterly impenetrable mystery for a third. Thus *context*—temporal, spatial, cultural and social—becomes an important consideration in any discussion of codified knowledge.

In what follows, we make extensive use of the notion of a codebook. We use 'codebook' both to refer to what might be considered a dictionary that agents use to understand written documents and to apply it also to cover the documents themselves. This implies several things regarding codification and codebooks. First, codifying a piece of knowledge adds content to the codebook. Second, codifying a piece of knowledge draws upon the pre-existing contents of the codebook. This creates a self-referential situation, which can be particularly severe when the knowledge activity takes place in a new sphere or discipline. Initially, there is no codebook, either in the sense of a book of documents or in the sense of a dictionary. Thus initial codification activity involves creating the specialized dictionary. Models must be developed, as must the vocabulary with which to express those models. When models and a language have been developed, documents can be written. Clearly, early in the life of a discipline or technology, standardization of the language (and of the models) will be an important part of the collective activity of codification. When this 'dictionary' aspect of the codebook becomes large enough to stabilize the 'language', the 'document' aspect can grow rapidly [for a further discussion of this issue see Cowan and Foray (1997)]. But new documents will inevitably introduce new concepts, notation and terminology, so that 'stabilization' must not be interpreted to imply a complete cessation of dictionary-building.

The meaning of 'codification' intersects with the recent literature on economic growth. Much of modern endogenous growth theory rests on the notion that there exists a 'world stock of knowledge' and, perhaps, also a 'national knowledge-base' that has stock-like characteristics. This is true particularly of those models in which R&D is seen as both drawing upon and adding to 'a knowledge stock' which enters as an input into production processes for other goods. How ought we to characterize this, or indeed any related conceptualization of a world stock of knowledge? Implicit in this literature is that this stock is codified, since part or all of it is assumed to be freely accessible by all economic agents in the system under analysis. Unpacking this idea only partially suffices to reveal some serious logical difficulties with any attempt to objectify 'a social stock of knowledge', let alone with the way that the new growth theory has sought to employ the concept of an aggregate knowledge stock.[13]

The 'new growth theory' literature falls squarely within the tradition emphasizing the public-goods nature of knowledge. So, one may surmise that

[13] See Machlup (1980, pp. 167–169) for a discussion of 'the phenomenological theory of knowledge' developed by Schutz and Luckmann (1973, chs 3–4). The latter arrive at a concept described by Machlup as: 'the fully objectivated [sic] knowledge of society, a social stock of knowledge which in some sense is the result of a socialization of knowledge [through individual interactions involving private stocks of subjective but inter-subjectively valid knowledge] and contains at the same time more *and* less than the sum of the private stocks of subjective knowledge. . . . This most ingenious phenomenological theory of the stock of knowledge in society is not equipped to deal with . . . the problem of assessing the size of the stock and its growth.'

the world stock of knowledge surely has to be the union of private stocks of codified knowledge: anything codified for someone is thereby part of the world knowledge stock. Such reasoning, however, may involve a fallacy of composition or of aggregation. One might reasonably have thought that the phrase 'world knowledge stock' refers to the stock available to the entire world. But if the contextual aspect of knowledge and codification (on which, see *supra*) is to be taken seriously, the world stock of codified knowledge might better be defined as the *intersection* of individuals' sets of codified knowledge—that being the portion that is 'shared' in the sense of being both known and commonly accessible. It then follows that the world stock of knowledge, being the intersection of private stocks, whether codified or tacit, is going to be very small.[14]

The foregoing suggests that there is a problem in principle with those models in the 'new growth theory' which have been constructed around (the formalized representation of) a universal stock of technological knowledge to which all agents might contribute and from which all agents can draw costlessly. That, however, is hardly the end of the difficulties arising from the primacy accorded to the accumulation of 'a knowledge stock' in the recent literature on endogenous economic growth. The peculiarities of knowledge as an economic commodity, namely, the heterogeneous nature of ideas and their infinite expansibility, have been cast in the paradigm 'new economic growth' models as the fundamental non-convexity, responsible for increasing returns to investment in this intangible form of capital. Heterogeneity implies the need for a metric in which the constituent parts can be rendered commensurable, but given the especially problematic nature of competitive market valuations of knowledge, the economic aggregation problem is particularly vexatious in this case.

Furthermore, the extent to which the infinite expansibility of knowledge actually is exploited therefore becomes a critical matter in defining the relevant stock—even though in most formulations of new growth theory this matter has been glossed over. Critics of these models' relevance have quite properly pointed out that much technologically relevant knowledge is not codified, and therefore has substantial marginal costs of reproduction and re-application; they maintain that inasmuch as this so-called 'tacit knowledge' possesses the properties of normal commodities, its role in the process of growth approaches that of conventional tangible capital.[15] If it is strictly

---

[14] It is clear that the availability of two operators—union and intersection—when combined with two types of knowledge—tacit and codified—leads to a situation in which 'the world stock of knowledge' is going to take some further defining.

[15] This view could be challenged on the grounds that knowledge held secretly by individuals is not distinguishable from labor (tangible human capital) as a productivity input, but, unlike tangible physical capital, the existence of undisclosed knowledge assets cannot be ascertained. Machlup (1980, p. 175), in the sole passage devoted to the significance of tacit knowledge, adopts the latter position and argues that: 'Generation of socially new knowledge is another non-operational concept as long as generation is

complementary with the codified part of the knowledge stock, then the structure of the models implies that either R&D activity or some concomitant process must cause the two parts of the aggregate stock to grow *pari passu*. Alternatively, the growth of the effective size of the codified knowledge stock would be constrained by whatever governs the expansion of its tacit component. Pursuing these points further is not within the scope of this paper, however; we wish merely to stress once again, and from a different perspective, that the nature of knowledge, its codification or tacitness, lurks only just beneath the surface of important ideas about modern economic growth.

Leaving to one side, then, the problematic issue of defining and quantifying the world stocks of either codified knowledge or tacit knowledge, we can now turn to a fundamental empirical question regarding tacit knowledge. Below, we address explicitly whether some situations, described as rife with tacit knowledge, really are so, but for the moment we can make an important point without entering into that issue.

Some activities seem to involve knowledge that is unvoiced—activities which clearly involve knowledge but which refer only seldomly to texts; or, put another way, which clearly involve considerable knowledge beyond the texts that are referred to in the normal course of the activity.[16] Thus we can ask: why is some knowledge silent, or unvoiced? There are two possible explanations: the knowledge is unarticulable or, being capable of articulation, it remains unvoiced for some other reason.

Why would some knowledge remain unarticulable? The standard economist's answer is simply that this is equivalent to asking why there are 'shortages', to which one must reply 'there are no shortages' when there are markets. So, the economist says, knowledge is not articulated because, relative to the state of demand, the cost and supply price is too high. Articulation, being social communication, presupposes some degree of codification, but if it costs too much actually to codify, this piece of knowledge may remain partly or wholly uncodified. Without making any disparaging remarks about this view, we can simply point out that there is some knowledge for which we do not even know to begin the process of codification, which means that the price calculation could hardly be undertaken in the first place. Recognition of this state of affairs generates consensus on the uncodifiable nature of the

---

not complemented by dissemination. . . . Only if [an individual] shares his knowledge with others can one recognize that new knowledge has been created. Generation of knowledge without dissemination is socially worthless as well as unascertainable. Although "tacit knowledge" cannot be counted in any sort of inventory, its creation may still be a part of the production of knowledge if the activities that generate it have a measurable cost.'

[16] We note that activities involving 'unvoiced knowledge' are often assumed to involve thereby tacit knowledge. We argue below that this is too hasty.

knowledge in question. We raise this to emphasize the important point in what follows that the category of the unarticulable (which may be coextensive with the uncodifiable) can safely be put to one side. That, of course, supposes there is still a lot left to discuss.

It is worth taking note of the two distinctions we have just drawn, and the degree to which they define coextensive sets of knowledge. Knowledge that is unarticulable is also uncodifiable, and vice versa: if it is (not) possible to articulate a thought so that it may be expressed in terms that another can understand, then it is (not) possible to codify it. This is the source of the statement above that articulation presupposes codifiability. It is not the case, though, that codifiability necessitates codification; a paper may be thought out fully, yet need not actually be written out. Operationally, the codifiability of knowledge (like the articulable nature of a thought) cannot be ascertained independently from the actions of codification and articulation. But, when we consider the question of the status of knowledge with reference to multiple contexts, the preceding strictly logical relations (implied by a single, universal context) are not exhaustive categories. Thus we see the possible emergence of an additional category: codified (sometime, somewhere) but not articulated (now, here).[17] This observation implies that care needs to be taken in jumping from the *observed* absence of codified knowledge in a specified context to the conclusion that only some non-codifiable (i.e. tacit) knowledge is available or employed.

It is within the realm of the codifiable or articulable-yet-uncodified that conventional price and cost considerations come into play in an interesting way, for within that region there is room for agents to reach decisions about the activity of codification based upon its costs and benefits. We shall discuss the factors entering into the determination of that knowledge-status more fully below.

4. A Proposed Topography for Knowledge Activities

We now proceed to examine a new knowledge topography, from which it will soon be evident that the realm of 'the tacit' can be greatly constricted, to good effect. The new topography we propose is meant to be consulted in thinking about where various knowledge transactions or activities take place, rather than where knowledge of different sorts may be said to reside. We should emphasize that as economists, and not epistemologists, we are substantively more interested in the former than in the latter.

[17] In understanding these distinctions it is important to remember that we are discussing knowledge activities, and the kinds of knowledge used in them. Thus we can observe activities in which the knowledge has been codified at some point in history but is not articulated in current endeavors.

By knowledge activities we refer to two kinds of activities: the generation and use of 'intellectual (abstract) knowledge'; and the generation and use of 'practical knowledge', which is mainly knowledge about technologies, artifacts (how to use this tool or this car, or how to improve their performances) and organizations.

Given that definition, we need to clarify the distinction between knowledge embodied in an artifact and codified knowledge about an artifact. The distinction between embodied and disembodied knowledge is a nice way for economists to capture features of intersectoral flows (of technologies), particularly in an input–output framework. Therefore, the fact that knowledge is embodied in a machine tool is not to be conflated with the codification problem. Knowledge about the production and the use of artifacts, however, falls within our set of issues about codification: does the use of this new tool require the permanent reference to a set of codified instructions or not? We can put this point in a slightly different way. From the perspective of a producer, any artifact, from a hammer to a computer, embodies considerable knowledge. The artifact often is an exemplar of that knowledge, and can sometimes be thought of as a 'container' or 'storage vessel' for it, as well as the means through which the knowledge may be marketed. From the point of view of the user, however, this is not necessarily the case. While any user will admit that the producer needed a variety of kinds of knowledge to produce the artifact, this is of little practical interest. The knowledge of interest to the purchaser of a hammer or a PC, whether codified or not—and indeed that often is the issue—is how to use the artifact, rather than the knowledge that was called upon for its design and fabrication. Of course, the latter may bear upon the former.

Part of the reason for this interpretation of what is to be located in our topography is simply that discussions about 'where knowledge resides' are difficult to conduct without falling into, or attempting to avoid, statements about the relative sizes of the stocks of tacit and codified knowledge, and their growth rates. By and large, pseudo-quantitative discussions of that sort rarely turn out to be very useful; indeed, possibly worse than unhelpful, they can be quite misleading. Although there is no scarcity of casual assertions made regarding the tendency toward increasing (relative) codification, the issue of the relative sizes of the constituent elements of the world stocks of scientific and technological knowledge resists formal quantitative treatment. That is to say, we really cannot hope to derive either theoretical propositions or empirical measures regarding whether or not the relative size of the codified portion must be secularly increasing or decreasing, or alternatively, whether there is a tendency to a steady state. The fundamental obstacle is the vagueness regarding the units in which 'knowledge' is to be measured.

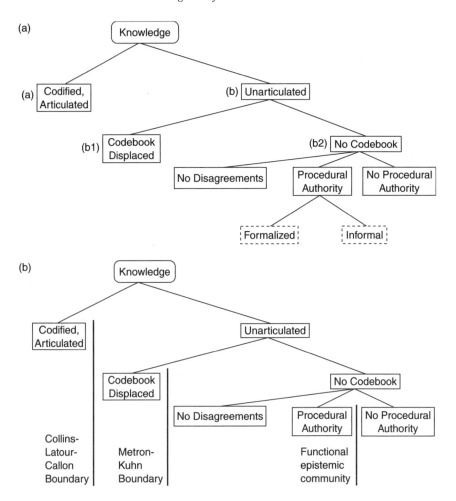

FIGURE 1. (a) A tree structure for codified and uncodified knowledge. (b) Boundaries in the knowledge space.

To begin, we shall consider a topological tree structure in which distinctions are drawn at four main levels. A tripartite branching on the uppermost level breaks the knowledge transaction terrain into three zones: articulated (and therefore codified), unarticulated and unarticulable. Setting the third category aside as not very interesting for the *social* sciences, we are left with the major dichotomy shown in Figure 1:

(a) *Articulated (and thus codified)*. Here knowledge is recorded and referred to by 'the group', which is to say, 'in a socio-temporal context'. Hence we can surmise that a codebook exists, and is referred to in the usual or standard course of knowledge-making and-using activities.

(b)   *Unarticulated*. Here we refer to knowledge that is not invoked explicitly in the typical course of knowledge activities. Again, the concept of a context or group is important.

In case (a) a codebook clearly exists, since this is implicit in knowledge being or having been codified. In case (b) two possible sub-cases can be considered. In one, knowledge is tacit in the normal sense—it has not been recorded either in word or artifact, so no codebook exists. In the other, knowledge may have been recorded, so a codebook exists, but this book may not be referred to by members of the group—or, if it is, references are so rare as to be indiscernible to an outside observer. Thus, at the next level, 'unarticulated' splits into two branches: (b.1) in the situation indicated to the left, a source or reference manual does exist but it is out of sight, so we say the situation is that of a *displaced codebook*; and (b.2) to the right lie those circumstances in which there truly is no codebook, but in which it would be technically possible to produce one.

(b.1)   When a codebook exists, we still may refer to the situation in which knowledge is unarticulated because within the group context the codebook is *not manifest*; it is not explicitly consulted, nor in evidence, and an outside observer therefore would have no direct indication of its existence. The contents of the codebook in such situations have been so thoroughly internalized, or absorbed by the members of the group, that it functions as an implicit source of authority. To the outside observer, this group *appears* to be using a large amount of tacit knowledge in its normal operations.[18]

A 'displaced codebook' implies that a codified body of common knowledge is present, but not manifestly so. Technical terms figure in descriptive discussion but go undefined because their meaning is evident to all concerned; fundamental relationships among variables are also not reiterated in conversations and messages exchanged among members of the group or epistemic community.[19] In short, we have just described a typical state of affairs in what Kuhn (1962) referred to as 'normal science'; it is one where the knowledge base from which the researchers are working is highly codified but, paradoxically, its existence and contents are matters left tacit among the group unless some dispute or memory problem arises. We may analogously describe 'normal technology' as the state in which knowledge about artifacts is highly codified but the codebook is not manifest.

---

[18]   Here we may remark that the ability to function effectively, possibly more effectively with the codebook out of sight (e.g. to pass closed-book exams), often is one criterion for entry, or part of the initiation into the group. Not being truly an initiated 'insider' is generally found to be a considerable impediment to fully understanding the transactions taking place among the members of any social group, let alone for would-be ethnographers of 'laboratory life'.

[19]   This often infuriates outsiders, who complain vociferously about excessive jargon in the writings and speeches of physicists, sociologists, economists, psychologists and . . .

Identification of the zone in which knowledge is codified but the existence of codification is not manifest is an extremely important result. But it poses a very difficult empirical problem (or perhaps a problem of observation). This point is crucial in understanding the economic problem raised by the management of knowledge in various situations: when the codebook is displaced and knowledge is highly codified, new needs for knowledge transfer or storage (or knowledge transactions generally) can be fulfilled at a rather low cost (the cost of making the existing codebook manifest), whereas when there is no codebook at all, the cost will be very high (the cost of producing a codebook, which includes costs of developing the languages and the necessary models).

This suggests that it would be useful to reconsider closely the many recent empirical studies that arrive at the conclusion that the key explanation for the observed phenomenon is the importance of tacit knowledge. That perhaps is true, but it is quite difficult to document convincingly; most of such studies fail to prove that what is observed is the effect of 'true tacitness', rather than highly codified knowledge without explicit reference to the codebook. By definition, a codebook that is not manifest will be equally not observed in that context, so it is likely that simple proxies for 'tacitness' (such as whether communication of knowledge takes place verbally in face-to-face transactions rather than by exchanges of texts) will be misleading in many instances. Differentiating among the various possible situations certainly requires deep and careful case studies.

(b.2)   When there is no codebook, we again have a basic two-way division, turning on the existence or non-existence of disputes. There may be no disagreements. Here there is stabilized uncodified knowledge, collective memory, convention and so on. This is a very common situation with regard to procedures and structures within organizations. The IMF, for example, has nowhere written that there in only one prescription for all the monetary and financial ills of the world's developing and transition economies; but, its advisers, in dispensing 'identikit' loan conditions, evidently behaved as if such a 'code' had been promulgated. Such uncodified-but-stable bodies of knowledge and practice, in which the particular epistemic community's members silently concur, will often find use as a test for admission to the group or a signal of group membership to outside agents.

Where there are disagreements and no codebook is available to resolve them within the group, it is possible that there exist some rules or principles for dispute resolution. Elsewhere, such 'procedural authority' may be missing. This is the chosen terrain of individual 'seers', such as business management gurus like Tom Peters, and others who supply a form of 'personal knowledge about organizational performance'. Equivalently, in terms of the outward characteristics of the situation, this also might describe the world of 'new age' religions—in contradistinction to structured ecclesiastical organizations that refer to sacred texts.

There is, however, another possibility, which creates a three-fold branch from node b.2: it may be the case that when disagreements arise there is some procedural authority to arbitrate among the contending parties. Recall that the situation here, by construction, is one in which the relevant knowledge is not codified, and different members of the organization/group have distinct bodies of tacit knowledge. When these sources of differences among their respective cognitive contexts lead to conflict about how to advance the group's enterprise or endeavor, the group cannot function without some way of deciding how to proceed—whether or not this has been explicitly described and recorded. Clearly, once such a procedure is formalized (codified), we have a recurrence of a distinction paralleling the one drawn at the top of the tree in Figure 1, between codified and 'unarticulated'. But this new bifurcation occurs at a meta-level of *procedures* for generating and distributing knowledge, rather than over the contents of knowledge itself. We can, in principle, distinguish among different types of groups by using the latter meta-level codified–tacit boundary. So the whole taxonomic apparatus may be unpacked once again in discussing varieties of 'constitutional' rules for knowledge-building activities. But that would carry us too far from our present purposes.

5. *Boundaries in the Re-mapped Knowledge Space and Their Significance*

Across the space described by the foregoing taxonomic structure it is possible to define (at least) three interesting boundaries. The 'Collins–Latour–Callon' boundary would separate articulated codified knowledge from all the rest— assigning observational situations in which there was a displaced codebook to the same realm as that in which learning and transmission of scientific knowledge, and *praxis*, were proceeding in the absence of codification. The line labeled 'the Merton–Kuhn boundary' puts codified and codebook-displaced situations together on its left side, and would focus primary attention there— as it constituted the distinctive regions occupied by modern science. That would leave all the rest to general psychological and sociological inquiries about 'enculturation processes' involved in human knowledge acquisition.

Our branching structure recognizes that it is possible, nonetheless, for *epistemic communities* to exist and function in the zone to the right of the Merton–Kuhn boundary. Such communities, which may be small working groups, comprise knowledge-creating agents who are engaged on a mutually recognized subset of questions, and who (at the very least) accept some commonly understood procedural authority as essential to the success of their collective activities. The line labeled the 'functional epistemic community boundary' separates them from the region immediately to their right in the topography. Beyond that border lies the zone populated by personal (and organizational) gurus of one shape or another, including the 'new age' cult leaders in whom procedural and personal authority over the conduct of group affairs are fused.

As is clear from the foregoing discussion, there are two quite distinct aspects of knowledge that are pertinent in the codified–tacit discussions, although they are often left unidentified. On the one hand, knowledge might or might not be presented or stored in a text. This is the notion associated with codification. On the other hand, there is the degree to which knowledge appears explicitly in standard activities. Here, we can think of knowledge as being *manifest* or not. Figure 2 elaborates these two properties in a tableau. For this purpose we have used a 3×3 matrix, in which one axis represents the extent of codification: codified, partially codified, and uncodified; the other axis represents the extent to which the knowledge is manifest, or commonly referred to in knowledge endeavors: manifest, alluded to, and latent.

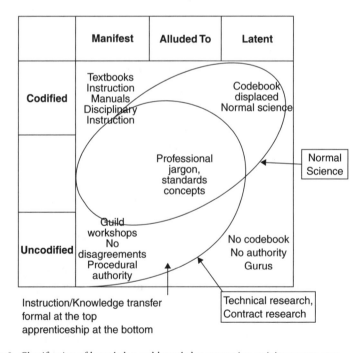

FIGURE 2. Classification of knowledge and knowledge generation activity on two axes.

These divisions that are indicated along the vertical and horizontal axes are patently arbitrary, for mixtures in the ordinary human knowledge activities form a continuum, rather than a set of discrete boxes.

To make clearer the meaning of Figure 2, it may be useful to look specifically at the four extreme cases: the corners north-west, south-west, north-east and south-east. Both the codified–manifest case (the north-west corner) and the uncodified–latent case (the south-east corner) describe situations which are easily comprehensible because the criteria fit together naturally. The codified–latent case (the north-east) was described as a situation in which the codebook is displaced while knowledge is not tacit. Finally the uncodified–manifest case (south-west) describes situations in which agents start to make their discoveries, inventions and new ideas manifest (in order to diffuse them) but still cannot use a full and stabilized codebook to do so; and even 'writing' a book with which to make this new knowledge manifest does not necessarily imply codification. It is possible that the vocabulary or symbolic representation employed is highly idiosyncratic, that there are many ambiguities, and so on. This implies that while certain aspects of codification may be present (in knowledge storage and recall, for example), other important aspects (such as an agreed vocabulary of expression) can be missing.

The overly sharp coordinates nevertheless give us a tableau which can be used heuristically in distinguishing major regions of the states-space within which knowledge-groups can be working at a given moment in their history. Instruction or deliberate knowledge transfer is thus roughly situated in the tableau's 'manifest' column, spilling over somewhat into the 'alluded to' column. Formal instruction comes near the top ('codified'), whereas apprenticeship lies near the bottom ('uncodified') of the array. The world of normal science inquiries extends across the ellipse-shaped region that is oriented along the minor diagonal (southwest–northeast axis) of the array, leaving out the north-west and south-west corners. In the former of the two excluded regions codified knowledge is most plainly manifested for purposes of didactic instruction, in which reference is made to textbooks, grammars and dictionaries, manuals, reference standards, and the like. In contrast, most craft apprenticeship training, and even some computer-based tutorial programs, occupy the lower portion of the 'soft-trapezoidal' region covering the left side of the array in Figure 2: a mixture of both codified and uncodified procedural routines are made manifest, through the use of manuals as well as practical demonstrations, whereas other bodies of codified knowledge may simply be alluded to in the course of instruction.[20]

---

[20] A number of interesting examples are presented in Balconi's (1998) study of worker training programs in the modern steel-making industry, showing that what formerly could justifiably be described as 'rules of the art' have been transformed into codified knowledge of a generic sort, as well as explicit

The boundaries of the world of engineering and applied R&D also extend upwards from the south-west corner in which closed, proprietary research groups function on the basis of the uncodified skills (experience-based expertise) of the team members, and their shared and manifest references to procedures that previously were found to be successful. But, if we are to accept the descriptions provided for us by articulate academic engineers, those boundaries are more tightly drawn than the ones within which science-groups operate; in particular they do not reach as far upwards into the area where there is a large body of latent but nevertheless highly codified knowledge undergirding research and discovery (see, e.g., Vincenti, 1990; Ferguson, 1992).

6. *On the Value of This Re-mapping*

What value can be claimed for the topography of knowledge activities that we have just presented? Evidently it serves to increase the precision and to allow greater nuance in the distinctions made among types of knowledge-getting and transferring pursuits. But, in addition, and of greater usefulness for purposes of economic analysis, it will be seen to permit a more fruitful examination of the influence of external, economic conditions upon the codification and manifestation of knowledge as information. A number of the specific benefits derived from looking at the world in this way warrant closer examination, and to these we now turn.

6.1 On the Topography Itself

Figures 1 and 2 clean up a confusion concerning the putative tacitness of the working knowledge of scientists in situations that we have here been able to characterize by applying the 'displaced codebook' rubric. A number of studies, including some widely cited in the literature, seem to have placed undue reliance upon an overly casual observational test, identifying situations where no codebook was manifestly present as instances showing the crucial role of 'tacit knowledge', pure and simple (see e.g. Collins, 1974; Latour and Woolgar, 1979; Latour, 1987; Traweek, 1988). It now should be seen that this fails to allow for the possibility that explicit references to codified sources of

---

operating procedures for the plant in question. According to Balconi (pp. 73–74), an overly sharp distinction has been drawn by Bell and Pavitt (1993) when they contrast the nature of the 'learning within firms' that is necessary to augment the content of the formal education and training conducted by institutions outside industry. In the cases she discusses, 'the aim of training [provided within the industry] is to transmit know-how by teaching know-why (the explanations of the causes of the physical transformations carried out [in the plant]), and know-what (codified operation practices)'.

'authority' may be supplanted by the formation of 'common knowledge' regarding the subscription of the epistemic community to that displaced but nonetheless 'authoritative' body of information.

The location of the Collins–Latour–Callon boundary in Figure 1, and its relationship to the regeneration of knowledge in tacit form, signifies that this latter process—involving the mental 'repackaging' of formal algorithms and other codified materials for more efficient retrieval and frequent applications, including those involved in the recombinant creation of new knowledge—rests upon the pre-existing establishment of a well-articulated body of codified, disciplinary tools.[21]

Economists' recent concerns with the economics of knowledge tend to lie in the 'no disagreements' (uncodified, manifest) box in Figure 2. We are talking here about the literature that views reliance upon 'sticky data' or 'local jargons' as methods of appropriating returns from knowledge. This is the region of the map in which knowledge-building gives rise to the 'quasi' aspect of the description of knowledge assets as quasi-public goods. The immediate implication is that to determine the degree to which some particular pieces of knowledge are indeed only quasi-public goods calls for a contextual examination of both the completeness of the codification and the extent of manifestation.

The argument has recently been advanced, by Gibbons *et al.* (1996), that an emergent late twentieth century trend was the rise of a new regime of knowledge production, so-called Mode 2. This has been contrasted with the antecedent dominant organizational features of scientific inquiry, associated with Mode 1: in particular, the new regime is described as being more reliant upon tacit knowledge, and transdisciplinary—as opposed to the importance accorded by Mode 1 to the publication of codified material in areas of disciplinary specialization as the legitimate basis of collegiate reputational status, selection decisions in personnel recruitment, and the structuring of criteria for evaluating and rewarding professional performance. Doubts have been raised about the alleged novelty and self-sufficiency of Mode 2 as a successor that will displace the antecedent, highly institutionalized system of research and innovation (see e.g. David *et al.*, 1999, and references therein). But the main point to be noted in the present context is that such coherence and functionality as groups working in Mode 2 have been able to obtain would appear to rest upon their development of procedural authority to which the fluid membership subscribes.

---

[21] Further, in much the same vein, it is quite possible that practiced experimental researchers, having developed and codified procedures involving a sequence of discrete steps, may be observed discussing and executing the routine in a holistic manner—even to the point of finding it difficult to immediately articulate every discrete constituent step of the process. The latter is a situation found quite commonly when experienced computer programmers are asked to explain and document the strings of code that they have just typed. The phenomenon would seem to have more to do with the efficient 'granularity' for mental *storage and recall* of knowledge, than with the nature of the knowledge itself, or the manner in which it was initially acquired.

6.2 On Interactions with External Phenomena

How do changes in information and communications technologies impinge upon the distribution of knowledge production and distribution activities within the re-mapped space described by our topography? The first and most obvious thing to notice is the endogeneity of the boundaries (which we discuss more fully in the next section). In the new taxonomy there are two interesting distinctions: knowledge activities may use and produce codified or uncodified knowledge, or they may use and produce knowledge that is either manifest or latent. We should re-state here that 'boundary' is not being used in reference to the distribution of the world knowledge stock, but instead to the prevailing locus of the activities of knowledge agents in a specific cognitive, temporal and social milieu. Nevertheless, it is most likely to be true that the situation of a group's knowledge stock will be intimately related to, and possibly even coterminous with, the location of its knowledge production activities.

Organizational goals affect the manifest–latent boundary. Activities that couple teaching with research, for example, will be pushed towards the more fully 'manifest' region of the state space. This consideration will be important in studies of the economics of science, and of the institutional organization of academic research activities more generally.[22]

The positioning of the endogenously determined boundary separating the codified from the uncodified states of knowledge activities will be governed by the following three sets of forces, which we examine at greater length below. For the present it is sufficient simply to note that these include: (i) costs and benefits of the activity of codification; (ii) the costs and benefits of the use of the codified knowledge (data compression, transmission, storage, retrieval, management, etc.); and (iii) feedbacks that arise because of the way codified knowledge is used to generate further codified knowledge.

A given discipline's age (or the stage of development reached in the life cycle of a particular area of specialization) affects both of the boundaries. The evolution of a discipline, a technological domain (or of a research group or a community of practitioners) may now be described as a movement in the two-dimensional plane of the tableau in Figure 2. Let us illustrate this by taking a lead from Kuhn (1962) and begin, early in the life cycle of a research program, with activities centered in the south-east corner of the array: a disparate collection of individual researchers and small teams, working without any commonly accepted procedural authority, generating knowledge that remains

---

[22] A recent exemplification of the application of the approach formalized here is available in Geuna's (1999) studies of the economics of university funding for research in science and engineering, and how different funding structures affect the types of activity within the modern European university system.

highly idiosyncratic and uncodified, and having only a very restricted scope for transmission of its findings beyond the confines of the immediate work-group(s). Subsequently, if and when these investigations have begun bearing fruit, work in the field coalesces around a more compact set of questions and the locus of its knowledge activities shifts westward, as agents make their discoveries and inventions manifest either in physical artifacts, conference presentations and published papers. This is where the codification process begins. But even though scholarly texts may be produced, because the concepts involved and language in which these reports are couched have not yet been thoroughly standardized, codification must still be considered very incomplete. Thenceforward, the emerging discipline's course follows a northerly track, spreading towards the north-east as disputes arise from inconsistencies in description and interpretation, and conflicts emerge over the specifics of the way the language is to be standardized. As these debates are resolved and closure on a widening range of issues is achieved, the characteristic activities migrate eastward in the space of Figure 2, landing up in the region where most of the actual research activity is carried on within the 'latent–codified' and 'manifest–partially codified' domains that typify normal science.

7. *The Economic Determinants of Codification*

The preceding exposition focused first upon the conceptual distinctions separating types of knowledge activities and then upon the locations of knowledge activities in the space thus delineated. In any topographic discussion there is a temptation to treat boundaries between regions as having been imposed from outside the system that is under examination. In a sense this is proper, in that structures are often in principle distinct from the activities that make them. But inasmuch as we are dealing here with knowledge, and the latter is seen today to be so central to the process of economic growth, a treatment of the subject would be more useful were it to deal with the genesis of our structural boundaries and the forces that determine their positions in different areas of knowledge formation. This becomes all the more relevant inasmuch as the main concern here is not primarily taxonomic; we are less interested in delineating the nature and varieties of human knowledge than in being able to explain and predict the changes taking place in the character of economically significant knowledge activities.

Another way of highlighting this issue is to return briefly to the previous discussion of the critique of the implicit assumptions of new growth theory in regard to the composition of the knowledge stock. Both sides in this incipient debate over the economic role of the tacit dimension have tended to accept a view of the 'composition of knowledge by type' (i.e. the codified–tacit mix) as being determined exogenously, outside the sphere of economics—and, therefore, as a matter that may be left to the epistemologists, cognitive scientists and students of human psychologists. But, in focusing upon those extra-economic conditions bearing upon the supply side of knowledge production and distribution activities, that implicit approach ignores the influence of the range of considerations that impinge upon the *demand* for codified versus uncodified knowledge. Some of these factors involve institutional arrangements affecting the structure of relative rewards for codification activities, whereas others have to do with the state of available technologies affecting the costs of rendering knowledge in codified form and the storage, retrieval and transmission of information. In the remainder of this section, therefore, we make a start towards a more systematic economic analysis of the matter.

7.1 The Endogeneity of the Tacitness–Codification Boundary

Any individual or group of agents makes decisions about what kind of knowledge activity to pursue and how it will be carried on. Should the output be codified or remain uncodified? Are the inputs to be made manifest or latent in the production process? For an economist, there is a simple one-line answer: the choices will depend on the perceived costs and benefits. The implication is that where knowledge activities are located (the extent to which agents codify their knowledge for example) will depend on economic considerations, and that the boundaries may move in response to changes that are external to the knowledge system *per se*. The significance of this requires some further discussion, if only because it represents a novel (if obvious) departure from the usual way in which the problem of tacitness has been framed.

In analyzing the economics of this choice, we need—even more so than above—to consider only knowledge which is codifiable. Several different situations can arise: knowledge can be in a state of true tacitness but codifiable; the codebook can exist or not; and it can be displaced or not. Each situation generates its own cost–benefit structures, which we will address through the concept of the knowledge activity environment.

The endogeneity of the tacit–codified boundary (or the Merton–Kuhn boundary in Figure 1a) refers to the fact that the agents pursuing a knowledge activity have a choice regarding whether or not to codify the knowledge they use and produce. In practice, the extent to which both 'new' and 'old' knowledge becomes codified in a particular environment is determined by the structure of the prevailing costs and benefits of doing so. Many factors—such as the high cost of codifying a certain type of knowledge, to take the simplest example—can decrease the incentives to go further, by lowering the private marginal rate of return on codification investments. A low rate of return may in turn result in the existence of a large community of people possessing tacit knowledge. In other words, there will be a market for the workers whose functions include the storage and transfers of the knowledge from firm to firm. Of course, the presence of a thick labor market as a medium through which knowledge can be accessed further reduces incentives to codify, provided that the heterogeneity, perishability and autonomy of these organic knowledge repositories does not give rise to offsetting costs. (See the discussion of policy issues in section 2, above.)

A self-reinforcing, positive feedback process of that kind can generate multiple equilibria. If, for example, there are high returns to codification, more knowledge will be codified. This will decrease the value of alternative (thick labor market) means of maintaining and distributing (tacit) knowledge. As the market for labor to perform that function shrinks, the relative value of codification would tend to increase further. Thus there are two possible equilibria: one with significant resources devoted to codification and a resulting high incentive to codify; and one with few resources so devoted, a thick, active market for skilled labor as the mechanism for storing and disseminating knowledge, and thus low incentives to codify. This conclusion rests on there being substitutability in the production process between the types of knowledge transferred by these two mechanisms.

This focus on endogenous limitations indicates that costs and benefits and the resulting incentive structures are pivotal in shaping the dynamics of codification. Emphasizing the role of the incentive structures by no means implies that the codification of new forms of knowledge is an instantaneous process: moving the boundaries between codified and tacit parts of the stock of knowledge is a matter of long-term technological and institutional evolution, involving changes in incentive structures, and in costs and benefits.

7.2 Costs, Benefits and the Knowledge Environment

In order to understand the sources and magnitudes of costs and benefits, it is necessary to put them in the context of the knowledge environment. A first and straightforward point is that the incentives will depend to a very great extent on the possibility of proceeding to codification on the basis of pre-existing codebooks [languages, models and techniques, in the terminology of Cowan and Foray (1997)].

When the language and the model already exist, the fixed costs, those born to generate the now standard models and languages, have already been sunk: languages and models have been developed by past work, and are known by codifiers and users. Such a situation describes both cases in which codebooks are manifest and those in which codebooks are displaced. The idea here is that some existing body of well-developed, stable, codified knowledge, often one that is displaced, contains the necessary concepts and relations with which to codify the knowledge in question. The only cost then is the variable one. On the other hand, if codebooks do not exist, or are incomplete or ambiguous, costs of codification entail more than simply the variable costs. Further, before a language has been standardized and is stable, linguistic ambiguity implies that codes which appear to represent codified knowledge can change their meanings as the language is developed and refined, and as vocabulary expands and changes. It is thus useful to differentiate between contexts of stability and contexts of change.

7.3 Costs and Benefits in a Stable Context

In a stable context—when there is a community of agents who have made the necessary initial investments to develop a language and to maintain efficient procedures of language acquisition for new entrants—the transfer of messages can be assimilated to transfer of knowledge, and storing messages means recording knowledge.

On the benefits side, the efficiency gains from codification will be greater in very large systems that must coordinate the complementary activities of many agents. We identify five classes among such situations: (i) systems involving many agents and many locations; (ii) systems strongly based on recombination and reuse, and which take advantage of the cumulativeness of existing knowledge (rather than on independent innovation); (iii) systems that require recourse to detailed memory; (iv) systems which need particular kinds of description of what (and how) the agents do; and (v) systems characterized by an intensive usage of information technologies. We take these up for further discussion *ad seriatim*.

First, codification will provide high benefits in stable systems characterized by specific requirements of knowledge transfer and communication. Such needs may arise from a tendency towards delocalization and externalization, or from the development of cooperative research, entailing a spatial distribution with activity at many places. This first effect can be appreciated without any ambiguity, for example, in science. It operates, however, within a given 'clique' or network—that is, a community which shares common codes and codebooks (whether or not the latter are manifestly present to hand) and such tacit knowledge as is used in interpreting messages exchanged among the members.

Second, in (stable) systems of innovation where advances and novelties mainly proceed from recombination, reuse and cumulativeness, benefits of codification are important. Gibbs (1994, 1997) claims that the very limited progress in the productivity of software engineering is due to an excessive dependence on craft-like skills (in contrast, for example, with chemical engineering). The schema that Gibbs has in mind is that once an algorithm is written as a piece of code, it can be used in many applications—at least in principle. The practical difficulty in doing so arises in part because of a lack of standardization both in the way code is written and the way algorithms are employed. This lack of technological rationalization impedes the full realization of the opportunities provided by the reuse and recombination model.

Third, codification holds out great benefits for systems that require extensive memory and retrieval capacities (e.g. firms and organizations that have extended product or process development cycles or high rates of personnel turnover, and institutions confronted by a major technological bifurcation). In those settings, under-investment in codification increases the day-to-day costs of locating frequently applied knowledge; and, where there are critical bodies of knowledge that are not kept in more-or-less continuous use, inadequate codification and archiving heightens the risks of 'accidental uninvention'. For example, according to Mackenzie and Spinardi (1995), in the nuclear weapons design process specific local and uncodified knowledge was so important that there was a constant appreciable risk that critical elements of the knowledge base would be lost simply through the turn-over of scientists and engineers—a risk of technological retrogression, or at best of costly reconstruction of the organization's previous capabilities (competencies).

The same argument is readily extended to apply in situations where knowledge has been thoroughly codified in the form of algorithms, or operating instructions, but the text of the 'source code' for these—or an understanding of the language in which it was recorded—has ceased to be readily decipherable, or has simply been misplaced or destroyed. The result is a paradoxical one: the technology in which the knowledge has been embedded may continue to work, as is the case when the computer implements the machine-language version of its instructions. But, as has been found to be the case with some major pieces of 'legacy software', the human agents, being no longer able to read or write the source code, are unable to emend or elaborate those machine-language encoded instructions. Nor can they locate and correct defects in the original source code, defects whose existence has become painfully evident. It is possible that even beyond the range of such algorithmic technologies, cultural inventions and culturally transmitted skills important for activities upon which social welfare depends—such as those involved in dispute resolution—may become lost because 'the market' for agents possessing tacit knowledge of that kind is undermined by the competition of more fully codified (legal) procedures.

Fourth, systems that require accurate descriptions of what agents are doing (either to meet quality standards constraints, to patent innovations or to enter into contractual relations with a partner) would greatly benefit from codification. Here we can also include systems confronted with inefficient market transactions, where the traditional mechanisms of legal warranty, insurance, reputation and test are not efficient means to mitigate the effects of information asymmetry in regard to product and service quality (Gunby, 1996). If, however, it is feasible to record production practices, some of the asymmetry can be removed, as the buyer given this information is in a better position to judge the prospective quality of the output. The widely diffused procedural certification standards belonging to the ISO 9000 series were based upon what was, in essence, a linguistic innovation aimed at facilitating codification of quality assurance practices.

Fifth, and last but not least, a sort of cross-situation deals with the lack of productivity gains from the use of information technology (IT), due to incomplete codification. Fully taking advantage of the potential productivity gains of IT typically demands not only the adoption of the technology but also organizational change (see e.g. David, 1991, 1994, 2000; Cowan, 1995, and references therein). But a firm undergoing organizational change does not want to lose functionality in the process. The firm must develop jointly the new technology and organizational structures that will reproduce old functions and create new ones (see David 1991, 1994). It is obvious that if too much of the old functionality resides in tacit knowledge, or depends heavily on it, this task will be extremely difficult. When the presence of tacit knowledge operates as a bottleneck, impeding the full realization of productivity potential, the firm can expect great benefits from codification (Baumol *et al.*, 1989). This, indeed, may be a critical role played by management consultants, to whom earlier reference was made.

In all these cases, where important operations of transfer, recombination, description, memorization and adaptation of existing knowledge (to IT) are required, it would be very costly and inefficient to keep this knowledge tacit. Thus, there can be under-investment in codification, coexisting with 'excess of tacitness'. Given the nature, degree and pace of recent technical change, it is likely that the current equilibrium involves an allocation of resources devoted to knowledge generation and transmission under conditions of incomplete codification and deliberate under-documentation.

Nonetheless, private resources continue to be poured into the production of differentiated 'information' that is idiosyncratically coded, whether deliberately or inadvertently, because such practices support the producers' intentions to capture private 'information rents'. Such practices also occur within business corporations (and other bureaucracies) where the internal reward mechanisms have failed to align the interests of individuals (possessing specialized knowledge) with those of the larger organizational entity. There, as in the cases where there are social inefficiencies due to the persistence in an uncodified state of knowledge that could be made more widely available in codified form for use by competing business entities, the design of incentive mechanisms is likely to prove more effective than the provision of less costly codification technologies, or the imposition and enforcement of formal disclosure requirements, in eliciting a collectively beneficial change in strategic behaviors.

Many other, rather more subtle issues are involved in considering the means through which firms and other entities can manage a process of codification where a large portion of the critical knowledge base required for functioning of the organization (its so-called 'core competencies') has not been articulated. Quite often one hears of businesses which (in times of stress) apply for help from some external management consultant, who will try to identify what things the troubled firm really 'knows how' to do well. A large body of modern management literature has been spun around that conceptualization of the consultant's role, so it may be reassuring to notice this implication of our topographic structure: collective procedural knowledge may remain unarticulated even though, at some cost, it is perfectly (or at least workably) 'codifiable'.

A more interesting issue for the skeptical economist to ponder in that connection is simply why is it that the organization—having somehow acquired and successfully deployed its 'core capabilities' without needing to make them explicit—should suddenly require, or find it profitable to employ, the costly services of outside management consultants to break the spell of 'tacitness'. In most of the specific cases discussed in the literature of professional business management that question is not posed explicitly. But, there is a suggestion that the organization, perhaps through the attrition of key personnel, may have 'forgotten' what it once understood tacitly and was therefore able to act upon collectively. Another possibility is that the operating environment of the firm might have been radically altered, without prompting a timely revision of the collective awareness of the mismatch created between the opportunities now facing the enterprise and its capabilities for exploiting them. The presumption, therefore, is that it will take too long, or be too risky, to go through a tacit, trial-and-error learning process. Bringing explicit analysis to bear—and so codifying the organization's understanding of itself and its new situation—then is deemed to prove either more expedient or less costly, or both, than continuing to operate in tacit mode (see Cobenhagen, 1998).

7.4 Costs and Benefits in the Context of Change

While many knowledge activities take place in a relatively stable context, some particular domains or sectors are characterized by knowledge environments exhibiting ongoing rapid transformations.

Models and languages are fluid, and the community of agents conversant with the models and languages is itself changing. The fluidity of the language implies that there is uncertainty about what the messages actually mean, because there is uncertainty, and perhaps change, with regard to the vocabulary in which they are written. Even when scientific papers express new discoveries, or re-examine old results in some 'natural' language, much jargon specific to the subject matter remains; 'terms of art' are employed whose meanings are lost on outsiders; and, in formal modeling, definitions of variables specific to the model may remain in flux as the model itself is modified and reconciled with observational data. In an important sense, the progress of research involves—and requires—the stabilization of meanings, which is part of the social process through which the stabilization of beliefs about the reliability of knowledge comes about.

To the extent that codification is taking place under those conditions, the benefits deriving from it have substantial 'spillover' elements, as they contribute largely to the modeling and language development parts of the exercise. There may be competition among different basic models, and so among the basic tenets and vocabulary of the language. Until this competition is resolved, the community of potential knowledge generators and users will have difficulty communicating, and the value of knowledge codification that arises from dissemination will be reduced. Thus the codification process in this environment generates some immediate value, which derives both from worth of the content of the messages that agents can transmit and interpret with less effort and expense, and from the value to the agent of storage and retrieval of his own knowledge. However, it has greater value as an investment good: a contribution to the resolution of the competition among variant languages and models.

It is in the context of change that we expect to find situations of 'excess codification'. That is to say, the accumulation of successive generation of codes can prevent the development of radically new knowledge, simply because explicating and understanding it would require entirely new codes. As argued by Arrow (1974, p. 56), codification entails organizational rigidity and uniformity while increasing communication and transaction efficiency:

> the need for codes mutually understandable within an organization imposes a uniformity requirement on the behavior of participants. They are specialized in the information capable of being transmitted by the codes, so that they learn more in the direction of their activity and become less efficient in acquiring and transmitting information not easily fitted into the code.

It is clear, therefore, that codification can have unfortunate consequences for creativity and radical changes. Like a larger category of coordination mechanisms to which technical interoperability standards belong, codified knowledge can be a potent 'carrier of history'—encapsulating influences of essentially transient and possibly extraneous natures that were present in the circumstances prevailing when particular codes took shape. Having that power, it can become a source of 'lock in' to obsolete conceptual schemes, and to technological and organizational systems that are built around those.[23]

The second problem we have thus identified deals with 'excess inertia'. There are high fixed costs to be borne in the process of codification, especially when the cognitive environment is changing. Roughly put, costs of learning and developing languages in which new codes are being written will be incurred during the period when the knowledge environment is in flux, whereas benefits will accrue (from some of those investments) during a subsequent period of stabilization and widespread dissemination of the information. During a period of change, infrastructure is developed, languages and models are built, learned and standardized, and a community of agents with shared tacit knowledge grows. All of these investments contribute to a reduction in the fluidity of the knowledge environment, and conduce to hastening the enjoyment of the increasing returns from more widespread application that are permitted by the stabilization of organizational and technological knowledge. As a network of users of the knowledge expands, learning costs continue to decline and coordination externalities are likely to grow more significant as a source of social benefits.

If developing new languages and models allocates the fixed cost to one generation while many future generations benefit from the new infrastructure to codify knowledge, there is an intergenerational externality problem which can result in a lack of adequate private (or social) incentives for allocating resources to the development of more powerful codes and systematizing those that already exist. Solutions that would help mitigate this kind of time inconsistency problem entail the development of relevant markets (which may significantly increase the benefits even for the first generation of developers), or the creation of infinitely lived institutions that do not discount the future so strongly. Alternatively, society may rely upon the cultivation of altruistic preferences for the welfare of coming generations, to whom a greater stock of useable knowledge can be bequeathed (see Konrad and Thum, 1993).

8. *Conclusions and the Direction of Further Work*

This paper has looked intensively and critically at one of the several dimensions David and Foray (1995) identified in their schematic description of the

---

[23] The argument follows that developed by David (1994) regarding the sources of path-dependence in the evolution of organizations and institutions, without reiterating the important respects in which those social entities differ from technological constructs.

space in which 'knowledge-products' were distributed.[24] Our focus has been maintained on the most problematic and, for many economists, the most esoteric of the three axes defining that space: the dimension along which codification appeared at one extremum and tacitness occupied the other. This has permitted some further unpacking of the economic determinants of codification decisions, and the resources committed thereto, and has revealed that the term tacit is being used so loosely in the current economics of science and technology literature that important distinctions, such as the one separating that which is uncodified in a particular context and that which will not (likely) be codified at all, are blurred or entirely lost.

Also lost from view in too many treatments now appearing in the economics literature dealing with tacit knowledge and experience-based learning (learning 'by doing' and 'by using') is the important difference between procedural knowledge (know-how) and declarative propositions (know-what and know-why) about things in the world. Although the subject of tacit procedural knowledge, and its regeneration in the process of working with previously codified routines, has been highlighted by Cowan and Foray (1997) and touched upon at several places here, the nature of the technological constraints and the role of economic factors affecting the scope for codification in 'cycles of learning and knowledge transformation' are topics that deserve and are likely to repay more thorough exploration.

In drawing out the important distinction between knowledge that is codifiable (in the sense of articulable) and that which actually is codified, and in focusing analytical attention upon the endogenous boundary between what is and what is not codified at a particular point in time, it has not been possible to adequately discuss some quite important 'conditioning' influences. Most notably, this essay has had to leave for future treatment the ways in which the nature of the intellectual property rights regime and the disclosure conventions of various epistemic communities affects private strategies concerning the degree of completeness with which new knowledge becomes codified.

Those interactions, as much as the effects of changes in information technology, will have to be studied much more thoroughly before economists can justly claim to have created a suitable knowledge base upon which to anchor specific policy guidelines for future public (and private) investments in the codification of scientific and technological knowledge.

---

[24] The other two dimensions of that space are the continuum between secrecy and full disclosure, and the spectrum of asset ownership status ranging from legally enforced private property rights to pure public goods. See David and Foray (1995, 1996) for further explication.

Acknowledgements

This article originated in a report prepared under the EC TSER Programme's TIPIK Project (Technology and Infrastructure Policy in the Knowledge-Based Economy—The Impact of the Tendency Towards Codification of Knowledge). That draft was presented for discussion by the 3rd TIPIK Workshop, held at BETA, University of Louis Pasteur, in Strasbourg, April 2–4, 1999, where it elicited many helpful comments and suggestions from our colleagues. We acknowledge the contributions of the TIPIK teams lead by Patrick Cohendet, Franco Malerba and Frieder Meyer-Kramer to improving both the substance and the exposition of our arguments, even though it has not been possible for us to do justice to all of their good ideas in the present paper. We are grateful also to Keith Pavitt for his probing critique of an earlier draft, and to W. Edward Steinmueller and an anonymous referee for their editorial questions and recommendations.

References

Anderson, E. S. (1994), *Evolutionary Economics: Post-Schumpeterian Contributions*. Pinter: London.

Arrow, K. J. (1955), 'Economic Aspects of Military Research and Development,' RAND Corporation Memorandum D-3142, August 30.

Arrow, K. J. (1962), 'Economic Welfare and the Allocation of Resources to Inventive Activity,' in R. Nelson (ed.), *The Rate and Direction of Technical Change*. National Bureau of Economic Research: New York.

Arrow, K. J. (1974), *The Limits of Organization*. Norton: New York.

Arundel, A. (1996), 'Enterprise Strategies and Barriers to Innovation: Preliminary Descriptive Results for the CIS Subjective Questions,' paper prepared for EIMS, DGXIII, Luxembourg, May.

Arundel, A. (1997), 'Enterprise Strategies and Barriers to Innovation,' in A. Arundel and R. Garrelfs (eds), *Innovation Measurement and Policies*, pp. 101–108. European Commission, EIMS publication 50.

Arundel, A. and I. Kabla (1998), 'What Percentage of Innovations are Patented? Empirical Estimates for European Firms,' *Research Policy*, 27, 127–141.

Balconi, M. (1998), 'Technology, Codification of Knowledge and Firm Competences,' *Revue Internationale de Systémique*, 12, 63–82.

Baumol, W., S. Batley Blackman and E. Wolff (1989), *Productivity and American Leadership: The Long View*. MIT Press: Cambridge.

Bell, M. and K. Pavitt (1993), 'Technological Accumulation and Industrial Growth: Contrasts between Developed and Developing Countries,' *Industrial and Corporate Change*, 2, 157–201.

Callon, M. (1995), 'Four Models of the Dynamics of Science,' in S. Jasanoff (ed.), *Handbook of Science and Technology Studies*, pp. 29–63. Sage: Thousand Oaks, CA.

Cobenhagen, J. (1999), 'Managing Innovation at the Company Level: A Study on Non-sector-specific Success Factors,' PhD dissertation (to be defended), Maastricht University.

Collins, H. M. (1974), 'The TEA Set: Tacit Knowledge in Scientific Networks,' *Science Studies*, 4, 165–186.

Cowan, R. and D. Foray (1997), 'The Economics of Codification and the Diffusion of Knowledge,' *Industrial and Corporate Change*, 6, 595–622.

Cowan, R. (1995), 'The Informatization of Government as an Economic Opportunity,' *STI Review*, 16.

Dasgupta, P. and P. A. David (1994), 'Towards a New Economics of Science,' *Research Policy*, 23, 487–521.

Davenport, T. H. and L. Prusak (1998), *Working Knowledge: How Organizations Manage What they Know*. Harvard Business School Press: Boston, MA.

David, P. A. (1991), 'General Purpose Engines, Investment and Productivity,' in E. Deiaco, E. Hornell and G. Vickery (eds), *Technology and Investment*, pp. 141–154. London: Pinter Publishing.

David, P. A. (1994), 'Why are Institutions the "Carriers of History"?: Path Dependence and the Evolution of Conventions, Organizations and Institutions,' *Economic Dynamics and Structural Change*, 5, 205–220.

David, P. A. (1997), 'From Market Magic to Calypso Science Policy: A Review of T. Kealey's *Economic Laws of Scientific Research*,' *Research Policy*, 26, 229–255.

David, P. A. (2000), 'Understanding Digital Technology's Evolution and the Path of Measured Productivity Growth: Present and Future in the Mirror of the Past,' in E. Brynolfsson and B. Kahin (eds), *Understanding the Digital Economy*. MIT Press: Cambridge, MA (forthcoming).

David, P. A. and D. Foray (1995), 'Accessing and Expanding the Science and Technology Knowledge Base,' *STI*, 16, 13–68.

David, P. A. and D. Foray (1996), 'Information Distribution and the Growth of Economically Valuable Knowledge: a Rationale for Technological Infrastructure Policies,' in M. Teubal *et al.* (eds), *Technological Infrastructure Policy: an International Perspective*, pp. 87–116. Kluwer Academic Publishers: Dordrecht.

David, P. A., D. Foray and W. E. Steinmueller (1999), 'The Research Network and the New Economics of Science: from Metaphors to Organizational Behavior,' in A. Gambardella and F. Malerba (eds), *The Organization of Inventive Activity in Europe*, pp. 303–342. Cambridge: Cambridge University Press.

Dosi, G. (1988), 'Sources, Procedures and Microeconomic Effects of Innovation,' *Journal of Economic Literature*, 26, 1120–1171.

Dosi, G. and M. Egidi (1991), 'Substantive and Procedural Uncertainty,' *Journal of Evolutionary Economics*, 1, 145–168.

Dosi, G., C. Freeman, R. Nelson, G. Silverberg and L. Soete (eds) (1988), *Technical Change and Economic Theory*. Pinter: London.

Ferguson, E. S. (1992), *Engineering and the Mind's Eye*. MIT Press: Cambridge, MA.

Geuna, A. (1999), *Resource Allocation and Knowledge Production: Studies in the Economics of University Research*. E. Elgar: Cheltenham.

Gibbons, M., C. Limoges, H. Nowotny, S. Schwartzman, P. Scott and M. Trow (1996), *The New Production of Knowledge*. Sage: London.

Gibbs, W. W. (1994), 'The Crisis in Software,' *Scientific American*, 241, 261–267.

Gibbs, W. W. (1997), 'Taking Computers to Task,' *Scientific American*, 277, 282–289.

Gunby, P. (1996), 'Explaining Adoption Patterns of Process Standards,' PhD Dissertation, Department of Economics, The University of Western Ontario.

Hofstader, D. (1979), *Gödel, Escher, Bach: An Eternal Golden Braid*. Basic Books: New York.

Kay, J. (1999), 'Money from Knowledge,' *Science and Public Affairs*, April, 12–13.

Kealey, T. (1996), *Economic Laws of Scientific Research*. Macmillan: London.

Konrad, K. and M. Thum (1993), 'Fundamental Standards and Time Consistency,' *Kyklos*, 46, 607–632.

Kuhn, T. (1962), *The Structure of Scientific Revolutions*. University of Chicago Press: Chicago, IL.

Latour, B. (1987), *Science in Action: How to Follow Scientists and Engineers Through Society*. Harvard University Press: Cambridge, MA.

Latour, B. and S. Woolgar (1979), *Laboratory Life: The Construction of Scientific Facts*. Princeton University Press: Princeton, NJ.

Leonard-Barton, D. (1995), *Well-springs of Knowledge*. Harvard Business School Press: Boston, MA.

Machlup, Fritz (1980), *Knowledge: Its Creation, Distribution and Economic Significance. Vol. I. Knowledge and Knowledge Production*. Princeton University Press: Princeton, NJ.

Mackenzie, D. and G. Spinardi (1995), 'Tacit Knowledge, Weapons Design and the Uninvention of Nuclear Weapons,' *American Journal of Sociology*, 101.

Nelson, R. R. (1959), 'The Simple Economics of Basic Scientific Research,' *Journal of Political Economy*, 67, 323–348.

Nelson, R. R. (1992), 'What Is "Commercial" and What is "Public" about Technology and What Should Be?,' in N. Rosenberg, R. Landau and D. Mowery (eds), *Technology and the Wealth of Nations*, ch. 3, pp. 57–72. Stanford University Press: Stanford, CA.

Nelson, R. R. and S. Winter (1982), *An Evolutionary Theory of Economic Change*. Harvard University Press: Cambridge, MA.

Newell, A. and H. A. Simon (1972), *Human Problem Solving*. Prentice-Hall: Englewood Cliffs, NJ.

Nonaka, I. and H. Keuchi (1995), *The Knowledge Creating Company*. Oxford University Press: New York.

Patel, P. and K. Pavitt (1995), 'Patterns of Technological Activities: Their Measurement and Interpretations,' in P. Stoneman (ed.), *Handbook of the Economics of Innovation and Technical Change*, pp. 14–51. Blackwell: Oxford.

Pavitt, K. (1987), 'The Objectives of Technology Policy,' *Science and Public Policy*, 14, 182–188.

Penrose, R. (ed.) (1997), *The Large, the Small and the Human Mind*. Cambridge University Press: Cambridge.

Penrose, R. and M. Gardner (1989), *The Emperor's New Mind: Concerning Computers, Minds, and the Laws of Physics*. Oxford University Press: Oxford.

Polanyi, M. (1967), *The Tacit Dimension*. Doubleday: New York.

Polanyi, M. (1958), *Personal Knowledge: Towards a Post-critical Philosophy*. Routledge & Kegan Paul: London.

Schutz, A. and T. Luckmann (1973), *The Structures of the Life-world* [translated by R. M. Zaner and A. T. Engelhardt Jr]. Northwestern University Press: Evanston, IL.

Shank, R. (1998), 'What is AI, Anyway?,' in D. Partridge and Y. Wilks (eds), *The Foundations of Artificial Intelligence: A Sourcebook*. Cambridge University Press: New York, pp. 3–13.

Skinner, R. E. (1994), 'Making Tacit Knowledge Explicit,' Working Paper, Stanford Knowledge Systems Laboratory, Stanford University.

Traweek, S. (1988), *Beam Times and Life Times: The World of High Energy Physicists*. Harvard University Press: Cambridge, MA.

Vincenti, W. G. (1990), *What Engineers Know and When They Know It: Analytical Studies in Aeronautical History*. The Johns Hopkins University Press: Baltimore, MD.

von Hippel, E. (1993), 'Trading in Trade Secrets', *Harvard Business Review*, February/March, 59–64.

von Hippel, Eric (1994), ' "Sticky Information" and the Locus of Problem Solving: Implications for Innovation,' *Management Science*, 40, 429–439.

Winter, S. G. (1987), 'Knowledge and Competence as Strategic Assets,' in D. J. Teece (ed.), *The Competitive Challenge*, ch. 8, pp. 159–184. Ballinger: Cambridge, MA.

The Slow Pace of Rapid Technological Change: Gradualism and Punctuation in Technological Change

DANIEL A. LEVINTHAL

(The Wharton School, University of Pennsylvania, Philadelphia, PA 19104
and Graduate School of Business Administration, Harvard University,
Boston, MA 02163, USA)

Discussions of technological change have offered sharply contrasting perspectives of technological change as gradual or incremental and the image of technological change as being rapid, even discontinuous. These alternative perspectives are bridged using the punctuated equilibrium framework of evolutionary biology. Using this framework, it is argued that the critical event is not a transformation of the technology, but speciation— the application of existing technology to a new domain of application. As a result of the distinct selection criteria and the degree of resource abundance in the new domain, a new technological form may emerge. The new technological form may be able to penetrate other niches and, in particular, may precipitate a process of 'creative destruction' and out-compete prior technologies. This framework is applied to an historical study of wireless communication from the early experimental efforts of Hertz to the modern development of wireless telephony.

1. Introduction

Discussions of technological change have offered sharply contrasting perspectives. On the one hand, we have arguments regarding the gradual, incremental nature of technological change (Dosi, 1983; Rosenbloom and Cusumano, 1987; Basalla, 1988). In contrast, others have offered the image of technological change as being rapid, even discontinuous (Tushman and Anderson, 1986; D'Aveni, 1994). Indeed, the *locus classicus* of evolutionary perspectives of technological change (Schumpeter, 1934) offers the dramatic imagery of 'waves of creative destruction'.

How might these alternative perspectives be reconciled? As suggested by Tushman and Romanelli (1985), the punctuated equilibrium framework of evolutionary biology (Gould and Eldridge, 1977) offers a powerful lens with which to view processes of both gradualism and discontinuous change. Management theorists, however, have tended to apply the punctuated equilibrium framework to a given level of analysis, whether it be a management team (Gersick, 1991), organization (Tushman and Romanelli, 1985) or technology (Tushman and Anderson, 1986). These arguments correspond to an early view within the biological literature of what Simpson (1949) termed quantum evolution. The most prominent proponent of this perspective was Goldschmidt (1940), who argued for the importance of occasional mutation events with substantial developmental effects. Within evolutionary biology, this quantum view of change has been generally abandoned (Strickberger, 1996).

The modern perspective, introduced by Gould and Eldridge (1977), hinges not on a single mutational event but on speciation—the separation of reproductive activity. The initial speciation event is minor in the sense that the form does not differ substantially from its predecessor. However, as a result of a separate reproductive process driven by genetic drift and a possibly distinct selection environment, the speciation event may trigger a divergent evolutionary path.

These ideas are applied here to provide insight into the pace and nature of technological change. Discontinuities are generally not the product of singular events in the development of a technology. As in the process of punctuation in the biological context, the critical factor is often a speciation event, the application of existing technological know-how to a new domain of application. The technological change associated with the shift in domain is typically quite minor; indeed, in some instances, there is no change in technology. While the speciation event is, in an immediate sense, technologically conservative, it may have significant commercial impact which, in turn, may trigger a substantially new and divergent evolutionary trajectory.

The lineage development of a technology within a new domain of application differs as the result of two basic forces. First, the new domain of application may have a distinct basis of selection; the critical attributes of functionality and degree of price sensitivity are likely to differ substantially across domains. Second, domains may differ substantially in the resources associated with them. A modest niche may only sustain a moderate rate of technological progress. In contrast, a more mainstream market may permit a much faster pace of development.

The process of 'creative destruction' occurs when the technology that emerges from the speciation event is successfully able to invade other niches, possibly including the original domain of application. This is the situation Christensen and Rosenbloom (1995) identify in the disk drive industry, where the drives developed for the initial niche market of portable computers ultimately become viable in the mainstream desktop market. However, such 'invasion' of the original, or predecessor, application domain need not occur. The domains may differ sufficiently in their selection criteria that the two forms can coexist.

These ideas are developed in the context of the history of wireless communication. The history of wireless communication is traced from the early experiments of Hertz on the existence of electromagnetic waves to the advent of cellular phone systems. In examining this broad history, three sets of considerations are highlighted. First, the degree of technological change required for wireless communication to enter a new domain of application is examined. Second, the distinct selection, or performance criteria, in each domain of application are identified. The identification of the selection criteria, in turn, provides a basis to consider the lineage development of wireless technology within a domain of application. Although the technological shifts associated with the speciation events were quite modest, the commercial impact of these speciation events was often dramatic. The commercial import of these speciation events fostered rapid lineage development of new techno-logical forms, which in turn provided the basis for subsequent speciation events. In this manner, an incremental view of radical technological change is set forth.

Wireless communications encompasses an enormous range of devices, technologies and domains of applications. The discussion here focuses on the principal developments within this broad arena. The analysis begins with the initial experimental transmission of electromagnetic waves by Hertz. The initial speciation event examined is the development of wireless telegraphy. The subsequent speciation events addressed are the shift to the wireless transmission of voice communication in the form of wireless telephony and broadcast radio. Clearly there are a number of other 'branches' that could be considered, including paging devices, microwave transmission and broadcast television. For the purposes of an article-length treatment of these issues, it is necessary to bound the domains considered. Indeed, even within these bounds, it is a challenge to provide a rich, yet succinct account of the technological changes.

Niches and Speciation

The core of any viable speciation theory is a mechanism for the disruption of the within-species pattern of ancestry and descent (Eldredge and Cracraft, 1980). This separation may occur by a variety of means. The mode most emphasized in the biological literature (Mayr, 1963) is geographic separation.

This may be a wholly new niche (allopatric speciation) or, as Bush (1975) suggests what may be more common, the exploitation of the periphery of an existing niche.

How might we characterize niches with respect to human ecology (Hawley, 1950)? While this has been a long-standing challenge, with regard to the more narrow problem of the evolution of technological artifacts, the task is a bit less daunting. In the fields of marketing, strategic management and economics, populations of (potential) consumers are distinguished by the functionality they desire and their willingness to pay for these various attributes of functionality (Lancaster, 1966; Kotler, 1991).

A key element of innovative activity is the identification of promising domains of application for existing technologies. This argument provides a somewhat different perspective on the Schumpeterian notion of entrepreneurship as a creative recombination of existing ideas (Schumpeter, 1934). Creative recombination has generally been interpreted as the melding of two functionally distinct technologies; the emphasis here is on the recombination of technology from one application domain to another. The identification of promising domains of application is often quite uncertain. Basalla (1988, p. 141) notes that

> When an invention is selected for development, we cannot assume that the initial choice is a unique and obvious one dictated by the nature of the artifact. Each invention offers a spectrum of opportunities, only a few of which will ever be developed during its lifetime. The first uses are not always the ones for which the invention will become best known. The earliest steam engines pumped water from mines, the first commercial use of radio was for the sending of coded wireless messages between ships at sea and from ships to shore, and the first electronic digital computer was designed to calculate firing tables for the guns of the United States Army.

This creative linkage of technology to application domain is a quintessential entrepreneurial activity.

Lineage Development: Selection Criteria and Resource Abundance

Given the speciation event, why might we observe a radically divergent technology emerge and why might this lead to a rapid pace of technological change? The nature and pace of technological change are driven by two elements of the selection process. The first is a process of adaptation: the technology becomes adapted to the particular needs of the new niche that it is exploiting. The second element corresponds to the resource abundance of the niche. As a result, the mode of development is influenced by the particular features of the niche, while the pace of development is driven by the resources that this niche is able to provide.

A technology naturally adapts to the niche to which it is being applied (Basalla, 1988). This adaptation reflects the distinctive needs of the niche regarding functionality. The new application domain may value particular elements of functionality that were largely irrelevant to the prior domain to which the technology was applied. In the case of Christensen and Rosenbloom's (1995) work on the disk drive industry, we see that the attributes of size, weight and power requirements become relevant in the new niche of portable computers. These same attributes had had little relevance for manufacturers of desktop machines.

These needs should be viewed both in terms of the relative importance of various attributes, such as different price/performance tradeoffs among potential consumers, but also the minimal threshold of functionality for a technology to be viable in a given application domain (Adner and Levinthal, 1997). A horseless carriage that is likely to break down after a quarter of a mile is a novelty, not a substitute for a horse.

The other class of factors are the resources available to sustain the innovative activity. While a new application domain may have a distinct set of selection criteria, if the resources in this niche are quite limited, then we should not expect to observe the rapid development of new technological forms. It is the combination of a distinct selection criteria and the availability of substantial resources to support innovative efforts associated with the new application domain that results in a speciation event with dramatic consequences for technological development. The pace of development becomes much more rapid if the technology is able to satisfy the needs of not only the possibly peripheral niche to which it may have first entered but, as the technology develops in functionality or cost is reduced, the technology may subsequently penetrate larger, more mainstream niches.

Punctuation and Speciation

Ideas of punctuated equilibrium have been associated with Schumpeter's notion of creative destruction (Tushman and Anderson, 1986). Creative destruction occurs, however, not as a direct result of a speciation event. The phenomenon of creative destruction is associated with the 'invasion' of the technological form that has evolved in the new domain of application into other domains, including the domain of application of the antecedent technology.

Radial tires were initially developed in the distinct niche of high-performance sports cars (Foster, 1986). This niche valued the high performance of these tires. The resources made available from the success of radials in this niche led to increased efficiency in the production process. That reduction in cost, in conjunction with a different attribute of radials—their greater longevity relative to bias-ply tires—allowed radial tires to penetrate the mainstream niches of replacement tires and ultimately the original equipment market of automobile manufacturers.

This successful 'invasion' of the mainstream niche is the dramatic event on which commentators tend to focus. However, that dramatic invasion is the outcome of a substantial period of development in a relatively isolated niche. Indeed, a development process that could only occur because this alternative application domain has distinct selection criteria that allows a new technological lineage to emerge. Prior to any lineage development, there is little possibility that the new technological form can out-compete the refined variant of an established technology in its primary domain of application. As Rosenberg (1976) argues in his analysis of the development of the machine tool industry, even those technologies which ultimately became widely diffused, general-purpose technologies initially focused on the needs of a particular application domain.

What permits the new technology to have some basis of viability is the existence of niches, or peripheral elements of existing niches, that exhibit a somewhat different set of selection criteria. The initial substantiation of the new technology is very unlikely to dominate the existing technology 'on its own terms'. The distinct niche provides the resources with which the new technology may develop. The path of lineage development may allow the new technology to successfully invade other niches and, in Rosenberg's term, become a general-purpose technology.

In many cases, this invasion of other niches may not occur. As a function of the resources available to support technological development and the distinct selection criteria in the new application domain, even in its developed form the new technology may not be viable in other niches. For instance, the teletype endured even with the full development of telephone technology, because it had the attribute of providing a written record that was valuable in business transactions, as well as allowing for asynchronous communication. Its demise waited for the development of an alternative form of written networked communication—improved facsimile technology and the development of large-scale computer networks. A final component in the persistence of a technology in a given domain of application are various forms of switching costs. These may be costs incurred by individual actors, or more tellingly, costs associated with network externalities (David, 1985; Arthur, 1989).

Figure 1 summarizes the argument. A technology undergoes a process of lineage evolutionary development within a given domain of application. At

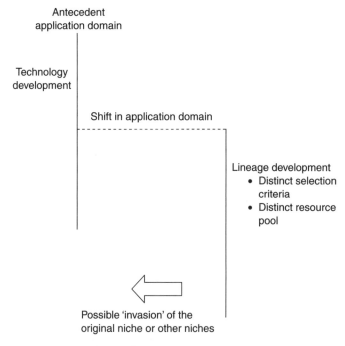

FIGURE 1. Speciation in technological development.

some juncture, that technology, or possibly set of technologies, is applied to a new domain of application. The technological shift necessitated by this event is argued to be modest. The lineage development that ensues within the new domain of application, however, may result in a technology quite distinct from the antecedent technologies with which this lineage was initiated. There are two basic factors that may differentiate the evolutionary path of this new lineage: the distinct set of selection criteria in the new application domain and the set of resources available in this domain. The technology may remain specific to this niche or, as it develops, it may be able to penetrate other application domains. In particular, the developed form of the new technological lineage may result in the 'creative destruction' of the technology associated with the antecedent application domain.

Melding of Technological Lineages—Convergence and Fusion

The argument developed here has focused on the development of a new technological lineage as a result of applying existing technology to new domains of application. New lineages may also emerge as the result of

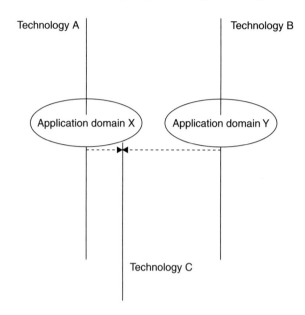

FIGURE 2. Technological convergence.

melding or hybridizing two formerly distinct technologies in a common application domain (Kodama, 1992; Yoffie, 1996). This common domain may be an application domain to which one of the two antecedent technologies is already associated, as characterized in Figure 2, and can be viewed as a process of technological convergence. Consider the development of the CAT scanner (Teece, 1987). In terms of the figure, medical imaging can be viewed as application domain X, to which X-ray technology (technology A in the figure) is already associated. Computer technology (technology B in the figure) is previously associated with data processing (application domain Y) and is creatively combined with X-ray technology in the context of medical imaging to form the new technology of CAT scanning (technology C).

Alternatively, one may observe the melding, or fusion (Kodama, 1992), of two technologies not formerely linked with one another in an application that is novel with regard to both of the antecedent technologies. Such a process is characterized in Figure 3. Kodama (1992) suggests that the melding of optics and electronics in the context of fiber-optic communications technology is an example of such fusion. Technology fusion 'blends incremental technical improvements from several previously separate fields of technology to create products that revolutionize markets' (Kodama, 1992, p. 70).

Biological evolutionary processes are not capable of such convergence or fusion. By definition, species are not capable of interbreeding with other species

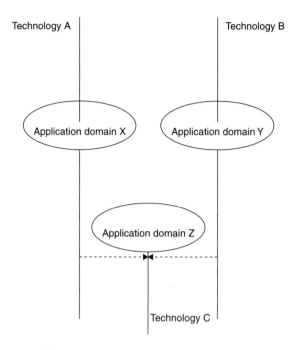

FIGURE 3. Technological fusion.

and producing fertile offspring (Strickberger, 1996). The evolution of technologies, however, is not restricted to processes of natural reproduction. Agents of technological change are continually generating the 'creative recombinations' of which Schumpeter spoke. Many of these creative recombinations produce new forms that prove unviable in the market place. Witness the many variants of pen-based computing and personal digit assistants (PDAs) that have been commercial failures (McGahan *et al.*, 1997).

In the history of wireless communication, there are clear examples of both technological convergence and fusion. In particular, at several junctures the lineage development of wireless technology was greatly facilitated by the 'borrowing' of technical knowledge formerly associated with other application domains. Thus, there are important examples of the pattern depicted in Figure 2, including the application of technology from the electric power industry to the development of more powerful transmitters for wireless telegraphy and the application of key findings from Edison's efforts at developing an incandescent light to the development of improved receiver technology for wireless telegraphy—a development effort that ultimately led to the discovery of the vacuum tube.

2. *Development of Wireless Communication Technology*

The development of wireless communication technology has, at many junctures, been heralded as revolutionary, including the introduction of wireless telegraphy, radio broadcasting and wireless telephony. However, these seemingly radical changes provide a striking illustration of the characterization offered here of gradual technological evolution within a lineage with dramatic changes initiated by the application of existing technology to new domains of application. As indicated in Figure 4, the development of wireless communication technology can be construed as consisting of four distinct epochs, with each epoch corresponding to a different application domain, and associated with each application domain a distinct selection environment regarding functionality and resource availability.

The initial developments by Hertz occurred as a result of his interest in testing Maxwell's theoretical work regarding electromagnetic waves. The critical functionality in this application was the reliable measurement of electromagnetic waves. For the second application domain of wireless telegraphy, a new functionality of distance was required. This selection criteria focused efforts at enhancing the power of transmitters and increasing the sensitivity of receivers. The effort to develop superior receivers for wireless telegraphy (and an effective repeater for wired telephony) ultimately led to the development

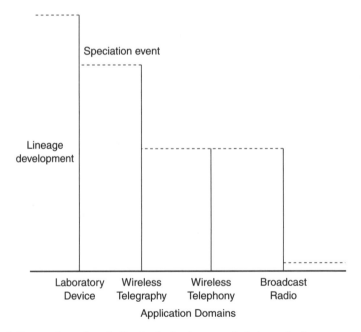

FIGURE 4. Punctuation and gradualism in the development of wireless technology.

of the vacuum tube (Aitken, 1985). The vacuum tube provided the basis for a continuous wave transmitter, a technology which was readily applied in the new application domains of radiotelephony and broadcasting.

These shifts in domain of application are significant breakpoints in the technology's development. The initial prototype of the technology, however, that entered a given new domain, whether it was Hertz's laboratory equipment, Marconi's early wireless or initial efforts at broadcast radio, was readily derived from the existing state of knowledge. The shifts were nevertheless important in that they signaled a shift in selection criteria, or, put differently, the critical functionality of the technology. The entry to a new application domain not only changed the selection criteria, but it also radically changed the resources available to support the development of the technology. Contrast Hertz's assembly of components laying about the laboratory he took over in Karlsruhe, Germany with Marconi's ability to generate financial backing for a corporation to pursue the commercial application of electromagnetic waves as an alternative to wired telegraphy (Garratt, 1994) and the commitment of resources by the already established corporate entities of Westinghouse, RCA,[1] and General Electric to its refinement.

Each of the four application domains is briefly outlined. The analysis of each application domain is organized around two sets of issues. One is the technological requirements of introducing wireless technology into the new application domain. Was the innovative use of wireless technology in a new application domain preceded by major technological developments initiated with that purpose in mind, or was the technology able to enter the new domain of application as a result of the lineage development in the context of an existing application domain? The other issue addressed is the nature of the selection criteria across application domains that causes wireless technology to diverge and take on distinct forms.

Experimental Demonstration of Radio Waves

Distinct selection environment of new application domain. While there were a number of amateur and professional scientists experimenting with electromagnetic waves in the mid-1800s, Hertz had a quite focused goal of validating experimentally Maxwell's hypothesis that electromagnetic waves traveled at the speed of light—indeed, that light was simply the range of the electromagnetic spectrum that could be seen by the human eye. Hertz had

---

[1] The name Radio Corporation of America (RCA) is potentially confusing in this context. RCA was founded by General Electric, AT&T and United Fruit (joined later by Westinghouse) in order to pool their patents in the pursuit of wireless telegraphy (Aitken, 1985). RCA was not founded in anticipation of broadcast radio and indeed the emergence of broadcast radio shortly after the founding of RCA caused considerable conflicts among the parent companies.

a minimal threshold of functionality that electromagnetic waves be measurable. This required a predictable source of electric charge, a detector tuned for waves of the length and frequency that were emitted, and a method of measuring the ensuing wavelength (Garratt, 1994).[2] This was not a trivial accomplishment in Hertz's time. This same degree of functionality constituted a maximum for his purposes as well. He had no need or interest in sending a signal beyond the confines of his laboratory and the signal need not convey anything other than its existence for his purposes.

Technological requirements of shift. Hertz was neither the first to consciously emit electromagnetic waves, nor the first to detect such transmissions. By 1842, Joseph Henry had detected spark transmissions from a distance of over 30 feet (Susskind, 1964). Not only was there past and ongoing experimental work, but the theoretical foundation for the properties of electromagnetic waves had been well developed by Maxwell and subsequent researchers. Maxwell's work not only indicated the existence of such waves, but also the effect of conductors, the phenomenon of interference or stationary waves, and the knowledge of how to produce waves of a given length (Lodge, 1902).

In addition, existing experimental practice in optics included an ability to measure wavelengths (Garratt, 1994). By directing waves on a reflector, the emitted and reflecting waves would interfere with one another and produce a series of 'standing' waves that could be measured. Aitken (1975) suggests that this application of ideas from optics to the longer waves of radio frequencies was Hertz's most original contribution. While certainly creative, it is also consistent with the theoretical argument developed here in that it represents an application of an existing 'technology' from optics to a new domain of application of electromagnetic waves.

Hertz also made substantial refinements in the methods by which electrical discharges could be generated and controlled. Starting from the well-established practice of using a Lyden jar to store and discharge electricity, 'it was through these small, incremental, one-step-at-a-time changes that Hertz's transmitter came into existence' (Aitken, 1975, p. 54). The antenna that Hertz developed could radiate waves more effectively than the Lyden jar and the frequency of the oscillations could be controlled by manipulating the inductance and capacitance of the antenna according to the established principles developed by Maxwell.

---

[2] A more subtle requirement for Hertz was that he could only effectively measure short electromagnetic waves. A critical element of the experiment (see the subsequent section) was the use of interference to generate stationary waves. Hertz's laboratory was a lecture hall 15 m in length. In order to measure a stationary wave, there had to be at least two peaks in the electromagnetic wave between the radiating antenna and the reflecting device. With a long electromagnetic wave, Hertz would not be able to generate two peaks within the physical confines of his laboratory.

Wireless Telegraphy

Technological requirements of shift.   The required insights to initiate wireless telegraphy were more commercial than technological. One of the first articulations of that vision was an article in 1892 in a popular publication called the *Fortnightly Review* by Cookes, a prominent scientist and lecturer. In this publication, he suggested the possibility of 'telegraphy without wires, posts, cables, or any of our present costly appliances'. Cookes went on to address what was preventing this vision from becoming a practical reality. He noted that Hertz had already shown how electromagnetic waves could be focused and radiated in a desired direction and received at a distance. All that was necessary was to improve devices that already existed: simpler and more certain ways of generating waves of desired length, more delicate receptors and better means of directing the waves.

The only modification of Hertz's equipment necessary to provide at least a limited wireless telegraph was the addition of a Morse coder at the transmitter and the already existing filing-tube receiver as a detector. Indeed, Lodge, in his lectures on Hertz's experiments to the British public, generated a wireless Morse code message. Lodge, however, framed his public lectures and demonstrations as contributions to the electrical theory of vision and titled his lectures to the British Association 'On Experiments Illustrating Clerk Maxwell's Theory of Light' and 'On an Electrical Theory of Vision' (Garratt, 1994). For Lodge, the generation of a coded message was simply a by-product of demonstrating the existence of Hertzian waves. In terms of technological artifacts, there was nothing new in the equipment that Marconi used to demonstrate the possibilities of wireless telegraphy to the British postal service, consisting of essentially the same type of transmitter and receiver that Lodge had used in his public lectures two years earlier.

Distinct selection criteria.   Lodge himself, quoted below, expressed the sense that it was the result of a fundamentally different focus and set of objectives, rather than technological barriers, that caused him and other researchers not to pursue aggressively the commercial development of wireless technology (Lodge, 1902, pp. 45, 84).

> Numbers of people have worked at the detection of Hertz waves with filing tube receivers, and every one of them must have known that the transmission of telegraphic messages in this way over moderate distances was but a matter of demand and supply. . . . There remained no doubt a number of points of detail, and considerable improvements in construction, if the method was ever to become practically useful. . . . The idea of replacing a galvanometer . . . by a relay working an ordinary sounder or Morse was an obvious one, but so far as the

present author was concerned he did not realize that there would be any particular advantage in thus with difficulty telegraphing across space instead of with ease by the highly developed and simple telegraphic and telephonic methods rendered possible by the use of a connecting wire. In this non-perception of the practical uses of wireless telegraphy he undoubtedly erred. But others were not so blind.

In contrast to Hertz and Lodge, Marconi, with little formal education, was focused exclusively on the commercial possibilities that electromagnetic waves offered. Marconi founded the Wireless Telegraph and Signal Company in 1897 to pursue the commercial development of this technology. The choice of the particular commercial markets with which to apply the technology illustrates the importance of peripheral niches. Preece, the director of the British postal service, in commenting upon Marconi's system after the initial demonstrations, stated that wireless telegraphy was appropriate for 'small islands, lighthouses, and above all moving ships' (Aitken, 1976, p. 216). Wireless communication was to be used in special circumstances in which the existing technology was not feasible. In particular, there was no consideration to wireless as a substitute for the existing technology of wired telegraphy. The first customers of the firm were the British Army and Navy (Basalla, 1988). The initial non-military market was the maritime industry which used the technology for ship-to-shore communication.

The Marconi Company subsequently engaged in one market, transatlantic communication, that at first blush looks as if it was in competition with an existing technology, that of undersea cables. However, this capability to engage in transatlantic transmissions was not initially developed to compete with the existing wired telegraphy system, but to provide maritime coverage for the east coast of North America and the approaches to Europe (Maclaurin, 1949). Consistent with this aim, the US-based transmitting station was located at Cape Cod—appropriate for maritime communications but not an obvious location for connecting to or competing with the existing system of transatlantic telegraphy used by the newspapers and financial organizations. Subsequent development efforts at transatlantic wireless telegraphy were prompted by a concern with the vulnerability of undersea cables during wartime and the monopolistic pricing of the cable operators.

The focus of Marconi and others interested in the commercial development of wireless technology was on very long wavelengths in the belief that these lower frequencies would generate a signal that covered greater distance (Maclaurin, 1949). This shift in the area of the electromagnetic spectrum provides a narrow, technical illustration of the idea of shifting selection criteria. Hertz, constrained by the physical limits of his laboratory, could only succeed in his experiments if he were able to generate much higher frequency waves than had previously been used. The pioneers of the commercial development of the technology completely abandoned this range of the spectrum in pursuit of their goal of long-distance communication.

Lineage development: development of continuous wave.   To achieve greater distance than that realized with the existing systems of radio transmission, Marconi experimented with alternative antenna designs, a process of experimentation that ultimately resulted in what is now termed a ground-plane antenna (Garratt, 1994). In principal, it was no different from the standard dipole antenna in use at that time; the key refinements were that it was vertically polarized and that the earth served as one of the dipole arms. These changes substantially increased the range of transmission and formed the basis for Marconi's subsequent efforts, including the initial transatlantic transmissions. The basic virtue of the new antenna design was that it permitted the use of longer wavelengths, which were not restricted to line-of-sight usage.

As Marconi focused his attention on the very long range transmission of transatlantic coverage, he and the Marconi Company supplemented the use of large antennas with increased voltage of the transmission itself. Indeed, Marconi ultimately brought in engineers from the electric power industry to help develop the desired high-voltage systems (Aitken, 1976)—an example of convergence of formerly distinct technological lineages.

The most profound lineage development, at least with respect to the opening up of new potential domains of application, consisted in changes in the electrical charge itself. The spark transmitter developed by Hertz and built upon by Marconi and others generated a series of damped sine waves. When Hertz measured the length of standing waves, he was actually measuring the strongest signal present, not the only signal. A spark transmitter was inherently a 'dirty radiator', polluting the spectrum with radiation that was unnecessary and interfering with the signals of other users (Maclaurin, 1949).

A continuous-wave transmitter awaited the development of the vacuum tube. While the vacuum tube was critical in paving the way for wireless communication of the human voice, and in turn wireless telephony and radio broadcasting, the development of the vacuum tube occurred in the context of efforts to enhance the sensitivity of receivers for wireless telegraphy and the transmission of long-distance, wired telephone transmissions. Fleming, the developer of the diode, was a university professor who was retained by the Marconi Company to improve its transmitting and receiving apparatus (Inglis, 1990). He developed a more sensitive detector for radio signals—a device called a rectifier which converts the alternating current of electromagnetic waves to direct current. The utility of the diode was limited by its inability to amplify electrical signals. This limitation was overcome by de Forest's innovation of the triode,[3] an invention that grew out of the need to enhance the sensitivity of wireless receivers (Inglis, 1990). An unintended consequence of de Forest's refinement of the triode for Federal Telegraph was the discovery that it oscillated, which implied that the device could generate a continuous wave and not merely act as a detector of radio waves.[4]

The further development of the triode was stalled both by technical challenges and by the conflicting patent claims of Fleming and de Forest (Aitken, 1985). By 1912, however, de Forest was able to construct a crude amplifier for voice circuits that he demonstrated to AT&T's engineers (Inglis, 1990). At the time, AT&T was eagerly searching for an amplifier, or repeater, that would make transcontinental wired telephone service possible (Inglis, 1990). With their understanding of amplification, AT&T engineers were able to considerably refine de Forest's device and by 1915 achieved a transcontinental telephone circuit using electron tube amplifiers, or repeaters (Inglis, 1990). As a by-product of that effort, 'they also developed much of the electron tube apparatus required for wireless telephony and broadcasting transmitters' (Inglis, 1990, p. 32). The legal dispute over intellectual property rights was ultimately settled by the pooling of patents, controlled at that time by General Electric, American Telephone & Telegraph, and Westinghouse, and the founding of RCA in 1920 (Aitken, 1985), with RCA having the mission to commercially apply vacuum tube technology for wireless telegraphy and AT&T having the right to use the technology for its phone system.

It is important to note that two of the important actors in the development of wireless telegraphy, Fessenden and Elwell, did consider the possible implications of their innovative efforts for wireless transmission of voice communication and, indeed, they both made attempts to apply their technology to that end.[5] Their failure in wireless telephony and broadcast radio was both a result of the limitations of the current technology (they both lacked a continuous wave transmitter) and, equally important, an inability to identify and pursue a market that would support their efforts.

Fessenden pushed spark technology to its limit with the alternating spark transmitter, which emitted a rapid series of sparks and in that manner approximated a continuous wave. Elwell developed the oscillating arc transmitter. Both developments in transmission technology were applied to

---

[3] The triode was simply a diode with an electrical control grid added. The virtue of the control grid was that by application of a low-power input signal to the grid, an output signal of much greater power could be produced (Inglis, 1990).

[4] Indeed, there is strong evidence to suggest that de Forest was actually unaware of this property of his invention until it was pointed out by others (Aitken, 1985).

[5] De Forest, subsequent to his development of the audion to enhance the reception of wireless telegraphy, applied the audion to both the reception of wireless telegraphy and wireless telephony, although without much commercial success (Aitken, 1985). However, in his efforts at wireless telephony, he used an oscillating arc for a transmitter and not a vacuum tube.

wireless telegraphy, with Elwell's efforts at Federal Telegraphy having much greater commercial impact than Fessenden's efforts at National Electric Signaling Company (NESCO). However, neither of their efforts in transmitter development were ultimately applied to the context of wireless communication of voices.

The one important lasting contribution of this research program was not a technological artifact, but Fessenden's identification of the heterodyne principle. This discovery stemmed from Fessenden's search for a more sensitive receiver. The heterodyne principle itself, the mixing of two waves of different frequency to produce a new wave with a frequency determined by the difference of the two input waves, was already well known in the context of audio frequencies. Fessenden's contribution was to apply this concept at radio frequencies and note the potential it held for transforming an inaudible radio wave to an audible frequency.[6]

Broadcasting

Technological requirements of shift. The term 'broadcast', in the context of wireless communication, originated with the Navy, where it referred to the transmission of a radio message, initially wireless telegraphy and then wireless telephony, to multiple receiving stations without the need to acknowledge receipt of the message (Archer, 1938). Both Fessenden and de Forest engaged in experimental radio broadcasts. On Christmas Day of 1906, Fessenden broadcast music to radio operators on Navy vessels and ships of the United Fruit Company out in the Atlantic, who had been previously alerted by telegraph (Aitken, 1985). De Forest broadcast from the Metropolitan Opera House in 1910 (Douglas, 1987). However, both Fessenden and de Forest engaged in these broadcasts to generate publicity for their companies and were not contemplating the possibility of commercial radio broadcasts.[7] Furthermore, the sound quality of these broadcasts was rather poor. Neither Fessenden or de Forest were using continuous wave transmissions—a necessary precondition for high-quality wireless transmission of voices. The broadcasts were striking to their listeners because of the novelty of communication of voices, but were not sufficiently clear to be used for general listening (Douglas, 1987).

---

[6] For instance, if a radio wave with a frequency of 100 kHz is mixed with a wave of 98 kHz, it will produce a new wave, in the audible range of 2 kHz (as well as a high-frequency wave determined by the sum of the two input waves of 198 kHz).

[7] Wireless entrepreneurs in many instances funded their initiatives by direct (and largely unregulated) sales of stock to an often naive public. Indeed, in the case of the companies founded by de Forest, the 'profits' he and his business partners pocketed derived from stock sales, not from revenue from operations (Douglas, 1987).

What is conventionally viewed as the first radio broadcast in the modern sense of that term occurred in 1920 and is attributed to Frank Conrad, a Westinghouse engineer and amateur radio operator who participated in Westinghouse's efforts in the development of vacuum tubes for radio-telephones.[8] Westinghouse had received a special license from the US Government to build and operate two experimental stations for telegraphic and telephonic communication, one of which was located at the company's East Pittsburgh plant and the other at the home of Conrad (Dunlop, 1970). Conrad began playing records on his amateur station on a regular basis and by September of that year a Pittsburgh department store began advertising and selling simple receivers with which Conrad's broadcasts could be heard (Dunlop, 1970). Westinghouse, recognizing the publicity Conrad was receiving and noting the possible profits from the sale of receivers to a new class of consumers, decided to develop its own station, KDKA, in October 1920.

What is striking about this episode is that the innovation of broadcasting was largely a conceptual, rather than a technical breakthrough:

> KDKA, with its six 50 watt tubes, was indeed using 'state of the art' technology, but nothing that had not been familiar to radio engineers for several years. It was no technical breakthrough that created the broadcasting industry almost overnight. What made the KDKA experiment significant . . . was its disclosure that a market existed and that it could be reached with a relatively small invest-ment. That market was, initially, the community of radio amateurs, individuals who knew how to string up a wire antenna and tune a crystal set and were delighted to share those skills with their friends, families, and neighbors. But beyond those amateurs was a vast potential audience with an apparently insatiable appetite for news and music whose existence had previously been almost totally unsuspected. (Aitken, 1985, pp. 471–472)

The critical technical stumbling block for radio broadcasting lay with the transmission of voice communication over the airways. This was a challenge that was overcome in the pursuit of more sensitive receivers for wireless tele-graphy and a repeater for wired telephony. The reception of a continuous wave modulated by an audio frequency was not problematic—any simple rectify-ing detector would serve to demodulate the signal and reproduce the sound in earphones or, after amplification, in a loudspeaker. It was for this reason that simple crystal sets were so effective in the early days of broadcasting.

The modest technical demands of early receivers for a broader consumer market are illustrated by RCA's development efforts in this area. Sarnoff, the

---

[8] Furthermore, for the current argument, identifying the first broadcast is not critical. What is import-ant is that the initial experiments in broadcast were not preceded by self-conscious scientific efforts to make these broadcasts possible and, indeed, that such efforts were not required.

one corporate actor who seemed to anticipate the possibilities of commercial broadcasting, pushed the RCA technical committee early in 1920 to fund a project for a 'radio music box'. Engineers at GE had estimated that it would cost ~$2000 to build a prototype and that it could be done in 4–6 weeks (Aitken, 1985). RCA's technical staff, while skeptical about the effort, agreed to go ahead. The experimental broadcasts of Conrad, and Westinghouse's subsequent development of its own radio station obviously changed the saliency for RCA of the mass consumer market for radio receivers, as well as for other latent participants. Nonetheless, the modest engineering commitment necessary to develop a 'radio music box' indicates the incremental nature of that effort.

Lineage development.   Early radio broadcasting technology was primitive, but with its dramatic commercial success the technology developed rapidly. The early transmitters had <5 kW of power and were of low efficiency. They used the techniques of low-level grid modulation that AT&T had developed for wireless telephony (Inglis, 1990).

Radio receivers themselves went through substantial changes during the early years of radio broadcasting. Many early receivers used a 'cat's whisker' crystal detector, rather than an electron tube, and earphones were often used in place of loudspeakers (Inglis, 1990). Often these receivers were sold as kits that were assembled by users. Tuning was a particular problem in early receivers. To change stations, each stage in a series of amplifiers had to be turned individually and precisely with an array of knobs on the front panel (Inglis, 1990). Batteries were used as a power source for early sets. By the mid-1920s, these sets began to be supplemented by receivers using Armstrong's superheterodyne circuit that could run on alternating current (Inglis, 1990). The superheterodyne had perhaps a more important virtue of enhancing tuning.

The major development in radio technology subsequent to the superheterodyne was the development of frequency modulated (FM) broadcasting. Ironically, though FM transmission was developed to enhance the quality of radio broadcasting, it had little impact in its intended domain of application for many decades. The early important commercial uses of FM transmission were in wireless telephony for mobile communication.

Armstrong developed prototypes of FM transmission in the early 1930s and publicly demonstrated a working wide-band FM system in 1935 (Erickson, 1973). FM's slow commercial development in broadcasting stemmed from a number of sources. First, ownership of amplitude modulated (AM) broadcasting rights were a valuable asset that the established broadcasters did not want to see diluted by the opening up of the spectrum that FM, which was targeted at higher frequencies, represented. In addition, Sarnoff and RCA had committed to the development of television broadcasting which would compete for the same high-frequency region of the spectrum as FM broadcasts. Thus, for both sets of reasons, the established radio broadcast systems resisted Armstrong's innovation (Erickson, 1973). Finally, one could argue that the greater audio quality of FM did not offer an appreciable advantage for the bulk of radio broadcasting—news, radio shows and the popular music of the time. Only for classical music was there a clear benefit to the FM system. It was only with the growth in popularity of rock music in the late 1960s that there was a mass need for the higher fidelity of FM broadcasting. Furthermore, the relatively low price of FM broadcasting rights was a further reason that the new stations dedicated to rock music were attracted to FM transmissions. It was FM's broadcasting other virtue, the much greater freedom from interference, that caused it to have an early important role in wireless telephony (Calhoun, 1988).

Wireless Telephony and Mobile Communication

Distinct selection criteria. The slow development of wireless telephony, in contrast to the rapid development of broadcast radio, illustrates the importance of the viability of the speciated technology in its new domain of application. Elwell, using his arc transmitter, was able to demonstrate the wireless transmission of voices between Stockton and Sacramento, California in 1910. However, in the context of a California already heavily wired for phone communication, it was not a commercially viable substitute (Aitken, 1985).[9] There was the further problem that AT&T would not allow a wireless competitor to interconnect with its wired system—a problem that was to plague the more contemporary efforts at wireless telephone service of MCI (Cantelon, 1995).

Wireless telephony proved viable not in the mainstream application domain of phone service to fixed locations, but in settings in which mobile communications were important. Initially, this was in the context of maritime applications (ship-to-shore and ship-to-ship communications). Realizing the importance of wireless communication technology for coordinating the fleet and perhaps anticipating involvement in World War I, the US Navy began a program to develop ship-to-ship and ship-to-ship voice communication in 1915. By 1929, commercial radiotelephone services began to be offered on luxury cruisers. Not only did maritime applications place a high value on the functionality provided by wireless communication, but the large size and power requirements of wireless telephony at that time did not hinder their

---

[9] It is interesting to note in this regard that in contemporary times, wireless telephony may be a viable substitute to wired phone systems in the context of transitional economies which have a poor infrastructure of wired phone service (Lavin, 1996).

use on-board ship. These considerations of size and power requirements were, however, an important limitation in applying wireless telephony to mobile land-based communication.

In addition to the value of wireless telephony to offshore islands and ships, it held great promise for transoceanic communication. Indeed, submarine cables capable of transoceanic voice transmission did not come into existence until 1955 (Coates and Finn, 1979). In contrast, AT&T established the first transoceanic telephone link between New York and London, in conjunction with the British Post Office, in 1927 (Colpitts, 1971). Thus, the diffusion of radiotelephony across application domains paralleled that of wireless telegraphy, first with maritime applications and subsequently transoceanic applications. Land-based mobile communication, an application domain distinctive to wireless telephony, had to await further lineage development of the technology.

Lineage development.   Public service agencies, particularly police departments, took the lead in the development of land-based mobile communications (Kargman, 1978). Civilian use of land-based mobile communications started as early as 1921 with experiments by the Detroit police force with radio dispatch (Noble, 1962). The Police Commissioner was concerned that the 'modern' automobile had given the criminal an advantage in speed that could not be overcome by the use of police cars controlled by telephone call-boxes (Noble, 1962). The early car radios proved unreliable in that they could not withstand the buffeting of mobile use. Subsequent work on receiver technology, particularly the work of Bates refining the superheterodyne design, led to the first operational system in 1928 (Calhoun, 1988). These initial systems only allowed for one-way communication from the base to the patrol cars. With the reduction in the size of transmitters, two-way transmission capabilities were developed in 1931, and by 1934 radio dispatch technology was widely diffused among municipalities.

Although widely diffused, mobile communications still had important limits. In particular, there were a variety of problems associated with propagation disturbances. Radio signals were broadcast using amplitude modulation, where the strength of the signal varied to convey sound. Armstrong's system of communicating by modulating the frequency of the radio wave (i.e. FM) proved an enormous benefit in that it overcame the problem of static—or random amplitude noise from natural and man-made sources (Calhoun, 1988). This was a particular problem for mobile communications, since the receiver was constantly changing its position and problems of static and 'flutter' could not be overcome by manual tuning as in the case of a fixed location receiver. Another important virtue of FM for mobile communication is that FM requires far less power, allowing for smaller receivers and transmitters.

These two advantages resulted in FM quickly becoming the dominant mode of transmission for mobile communication. In contrast, as noted earlier, the feature of greatly enhanced dynamic range and hence fidelity did not provide a basis for successful early penetration in radio broadcasting. By 1939, the Connecticut State Police established the first FM communication system (Noble, 1962). Calhoun (1988, p. 28) suggests that 'the advent of FM technology was the first great watershed in mobile radio. . . . Although there have been major advances in network-level architecture, improvements in components and in the network interface, *no fundamental breakthroughs in the technology of the basic mobile radio link have reached the market since the late 1930s'* (emphasis in the original). Again, it is important to keep in mind that Armstrong developed the FM system to enhance the quality of radio broadcasts. Its application in mobile communication was not intended and did not provide the motivation for his efforts.

World War II provided a tremendous stimulus to refine FM-based mobile communications. Several hundred thousand mobile radios were manufactured for the war effort, resulting in improvements in packaging, reliability and cost (Calhoun, 1988). The technical history of mobile communications equipment design since 1940 is in many important respects a history of developments to improve the efficiency of spectrum utilization (Noble, 1962). During the 1940s, requests for spectrum for two-way mobile radio increased dramatically for uses ranging from police, fire departments, electric, gas and water utilities, railroads, buses, streetcars, trucks and taxis (Calhoun, 1988). There have been two foci of this effort to more efficiently utilize the limited spectrum for mobile communication: the reduction of transmission bandwidths, referred to as channel splitting, and the development of automatic trunking of radio communications.

A mobile telephone service that allowed users to interconnect with the land-line system was initiated in St Louis in 1946 by AT&T (Calhoun, 1988). These systems were an immediate success. Within a year, a mobile telephone service was offered in over 25 US cities at rates of $15.00 a month and 15¢ a minute (Calhoun, 1988). The systems used FM transmission with a single powerful transmitter that provided coverage of >50 miles, a range more than adequate for most metropolitan areas.

The penetration of mobile telephone services was constrained by the limited channels available for use. Ratios of subscribers to channels of 50–100 were common (Calhoun, 1988). As a result, the service was quite poor with the probability of a phone call being 'blocked', because all available channels were in use, becoming as high as 65% (Calhoun, 1988). As recently as 1976, the New York metropolitan area of 20 million people had only 12 channels available for mobile phone use.

The major development that overcame this constraint of limited spectrum was the development of cellular systems. The notion of cellular system architecture was initially put forth by Bell System engineers in the 1940s. The cellular idea departed from the convention adopted from broadcasting of a single transmission source. Rather, there would be many low-powered transmitters providing coverage for a portion of a broader region. The enormous advantage of this system is that a given channel or frequency could be 'reused' across cells. Conceptually, as cells are made smaller, it is possible to increase the system capacity indefinitely. Practical development of such a system posed significant system engineering challenges to gracefully 'hand-off' a call as a user passed from one cell into another.

Furthermore, a viable cellular system still required a certain critical mass of channels or spectrum. Therefore, while Bell engineers laid out the system requirements for a cellular system as early as 1947, the Federal Communications Commission (FCC) did not allocate sufficient spectrum to mobile telephone use to make the development of such a system viable (Calhoun, 1988). Television, which the FCC tended to view as more of a mass medium of communication, and thereby more worthy of spectrum allocation, received the bulk of the high-frequency spectrum. In 1949, when deciding how to allocate the ultra high-frequency (UHF) band of the spectrum, the FCC declined the Bell System's proposals, refusing to allocate any of the UHF spectrum to mobile telephony and instead created 70 additional television channels.

In the face of the tremendous underutilization of the UHF frequencies by broadcasters and the overwhelming need for spectrum allocation for mobile communications, the FCC finally began to reconsider its position (Calhoun, 1988). However, it was not until 1982 that the FCC ruled that two 20 MHz licenses would be issued for each metropolitan area (Calhoun, 1988). The first US cellular system, operated by AT&T, began in Chicago in October 1983 (Calhoun, 1988).[10] Digital systems hold the further promise of allowing each frequency, even within a cell, to sustain multiple conversations and, as a result, can greatly expand the carrying capacity of a given frequency allocation at a much lower cost than cell-splitting.

3. *Technical Forms and Niches*

The speciation events in wireless communication consisted largely in creating new opportunities, though in some cases they ultimately led to the replacement of existing technologies. Wireless telegraphy was developed to

---

[10] AT&T, however, was to be a cellular operator for a total of 79 days as the Bell System was broken up and the regional Bell Companies took over cellular operations.

serve remote locations such as lighthouses and ships. The subsequent niche it entered was that of long-distance transoceanic service. In this application domain, wireless faced competition from the established technology of transoceanic cables. Though cable and wireless telegraphy have coexisted, it is a competition that wireless has largely won. Wireless has enormous cost advantages over cable, but suffered competitively initially as a result of its susceptibility to occasional interruptions caused by atmospheric conditions. The primary reason for the coexistence of the two systems, rather than the complete domination by wireless, stems from the sunk costs of the existing cable lines. However, after 1928, new capacity was satisfied by wireless. This is reflected in both the volume of international messages via cable and wireless (see Figure 5) and the fact that no new telegraph cable lines were added after 1928 (Coates and Finn, 1979).

The persistence of telegraphy, both wired and wireless, in contemporary times is at first sight rather surprising given the availability of both domestic and international phone services. However, this persistence reflects the critical role of distinct functionality provided by alternative technologies. One typically thinks of telegraphy in the context of Morse code transmissions. The modern application of telegraph technology, however, is the teletype, which is an application of telegraphy that encodes and transmits alphanumeric data. Indeed, starting from its inception in the early 1930s, teletype

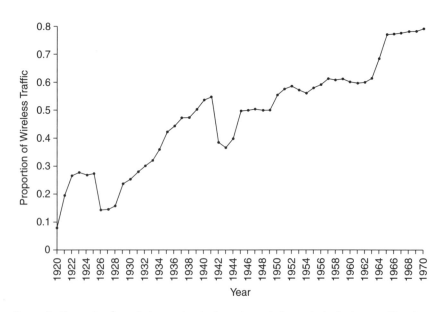

FIGURE 5. Competing forms in international telegraphy—wireless and wired telegrapy. (Data from Coates and Finn, 1979.)

messages have become the dominant use of telegraph services (Statistics of Communications Common Carriers, 1977).

The important functionality of the teletype that has led to its persistence in a wide array of business transactions is the fact that it provides a written record of any correspondence, making it preferred to voice communication for many purposes. Another advantage relative to telephone communication is the freedom to transmit without consideration for differences in time zones. It is the relatively recent development of the widespread application of fax technology and the even more recent development of widespread computer networks that is leading to a decline in teletype communication.

Wireless telephony has not been a substitute technology for wired telephone service, at least in competition with an existing wired network.[11] Rather, wireless telephony has opened up new possibilities for mobile communication. Initially, these applications were focused on public safety uses, such as police and emergency services. In more recent years, wireless technology has penetrated more mainstream, mass consumer markets. The speed with which mobile phone services developed was largely constrained by regulatory factors and the battle for access to the frequency spectrum. From a technological perspective, the 'cellular revolution' had been largely achieved by the 1940s, notwithstanding the dramatic commercial developments of the last decade.

At least initially, these commercial discontinuities took the form of providing communication services where none existed before rather than new technology for existing services. Such a pattern is likely to be prototypical, rather than peculiar to wireless communication. A new technology will be viable if it out-competes existing technologies on some performance criteria, whether an element of functionality or cost. It is unlikely that a new technology will be able to out-compete an established technology in its primary domain of application.

The technology finds an initial toehold for viability in the competitive ecology of alternative technologies in some specialized domain of application. In order to be viable, the technology must have some basis by which it is differentiated from the refined variants of existing technologies. Often that initial niche is applications, such as the military, where distinctive performance on some dimension of functionality is highly valued and provides a basis for competitive viability. However, in other cases, such as minimally invasive surgery or pen-based computing, the early domains of application are ones that not only value the distinctive functionality, but ones in which relatively crude forms of the new technology are sufficient to suit the needs of the

---

[11] There is the interesting possibility of wireless phone service being a viable competitor with a wired network in the context of emerging economies that lack a developed wired system.

application domain, such as gallbladder versus heart surgery in the case of minimally invasive surgery, or the use of pen-computing for structured forms rather than tasks that require handwriting recognition.

The above argument suggests the following possible patterns of technology development. Initially, the focus of activity is on the new, or peripheral niche that has provided the basis for the speciation event. A critical factor in the evolution of a technology is whether the technology, as it develops, is able to penetrate a broader set of niches. Figure 6 illustrates such a pattern. For instance, the video recorder was initially developed in the context of the distinct niche of broadcasters (application domain X). As the manufacturing process was refined and the product design simplified, it was possible to penetrate a new niche (application domain Y) of industrial and commercial users (Rosenbloom and Cusumano, 1987). Finally, this development continued to the point that the product was able to penetrate the mass consumer electronic market (application domain Z). It is important to note that, at each point in its development, video recording technology was commercially viable and profitable within the niche in which it was operating.

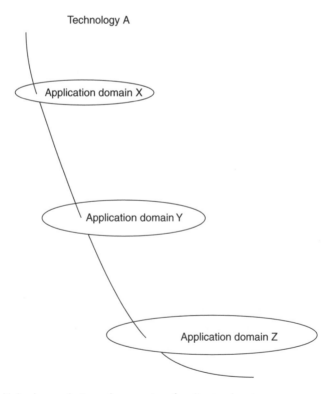

FIGURE 6. Technology evolution and penetration of application domains.

In the context of the history of the video recorder, we see a movement from a peripheral niche to penetration of the broad niche of the mass consumer market. In ecological terms, we might think of this as the artifact shifting from a specialist to a generalist. No longer must the video recorder look for resources for its survival and development to the narrow niche of television broadcasters, but the entire set of households becomes a basis for resources.

This need not be the only sort of pattern one might observe. It is quite possible that the technology is not able to go beyond the initial, peripheral market. For instance, gallium arsenide was heralded as a replacement for silicon in semiconductors in the early 1980s based on the superior speed that it provided. However, the technology has proved commercially viable only in the context of supercomputer applications and communications devices (Wiegner, 1988). Recently, the demand for Gallium arsenide has increased, but this demand is still in the context of communications devices, not mainstream computing applications (Ristelhueber, 1993).

4. Conclusion

An obvious limitation of the empirical analysis is the focus on the evolution of a particular technology—that of wireless communication. However, the choice of this technological domain was not based on its fit with the theoretical framework, but rather its fit with popular views of technological development consisting of radical or revolutionary changes.[12]

Yes, wireless communication technology has undergone extraordinary change in the hundred years since Hertz's experiments. However, the dramatic breakthroughs that set the technology on a new course were less technological in nature than discoveries of new domains of application. As noted by his Nobel Prize citation, Marconi's contribution to science was most importantly his demonstration of the possibilities for wireless telegraphy. The miracle of broadcast radio was initially demonstrated by ham radio operators, not the large corporate entities pursuing wireless telegraphy.

These 'speciation' events were, of course, made possible by wonderfully creative development efforts—development efforts that commanded tremendous amounts of time and financial resources. However, these efforts were supported within the existing application domains. Broadcast radio and wireless telephony could not have been possible in the absence of continuous-wave transmitters, but the impetus to develop that technology and the resources to do so came from efforts to enhance the distance and clarity of wireless

---

[12] A further criterion was the existence of a long and well-documented history of the technology's development.

telegraphy and AT&T's interest in developing an effective repeater for long-distance, wired phone service.

The framework developed here of speciation of existing technologies to new application domains with distinct resources and selection criteria provides a structure with which one can make sense of rapidly changing technological environments. In particular, it offers a bridge between the notion of the gradual cumulation of scientific knowledge and the phenomenon of dramatic transitions from one technological regime to another in the commercial sphere.

The dramatic commercial impact of technological change is not the result of singular, transformational events. Speciation, in an immediate sense, is technologically conservative; however, it may prefigure rapid technical and commercial changes. The commercial impact may reflect the growth of the technology in its new application domain, as was the case of broadcast radio. The ultimate commercial impact of the new technological form precipitated by the speciation event, however, may also reflect the penetration of other market niches and a Schumpeterian revolution of the competitive exclusion of prior technologies.

Acknowledgements

I thank Ron Adner for many enjoyable discussions on the subject of technological change. I have benefited from the comments of seminar participants at the University of Pennsylvania, Stanford University, Harvard University, Richard Rosenbloom, and two anonymous reviewers. This research was supported by the Sol Snider Center for Entrepreneurship, the Hunstman Center for Global Competition, the Reginald Jones Center at The Wharton School and the Division of Research, Harvard Business School.

References

Adner, R. and D. Levinthal (1997), 'Dynamics of Product and Process Innovations: A Market-based Perspective,' unpublished Working Paper, University of Pennsylvania.

Archer, G. (1938), *History of Radio to 1926*. American Historical Society: New York.

Aitken, H. (1976), *Syntony and Spark: The Origins of Radio*. Princeton University Press: Princeton, NJ.

Aitken, H. (1985), *The Continuous Wave: Technology and American Radio, 1900–1932*. Princeton University Press: Princeton, NJ.

Arthur, W. B. (1989), 'Competing Technologies, Increasing Returns, and Lock-in by Historical Events,' *Economic Journal*, 99, 116–131.

Basalla, G. (1988), *The Evolution of Technology*. Cambridge University Press: Cambridge.

Bush, G. (1975), 'Modes of Animal Speciation,' *Annual Review of Ecological Systems*, 6, 339–364.

Calhoun, G. (1988), *Digital Cellular Radio*. Artech House: Norwood, MA.

Cantelon, P. (1995), 'The Origins of Microwave Telephony—Waves of Change,' *Technology and Culture*, 36, 560–582.

Christensen, C. and R. Rosenbloom (1995), 'Explaining the Attacker's Advantage: Technological Paradigms, Organizational Dynamics, and the Value Network,' *Research Policy*, 24, 233–257.

Coates, V. and B. Finn (1979), *A Retrospective Technology Assessment: Submarine Telegraphy*. San Francisco Press: San Francisco, CA.

Colpitts, E. H. (1971), 'Radiotelephony,' in Martin Codel (ed.), *Radio and its Future*. Arno Press: New York.

D'Aveni, R. (1994), *Hypercompetition*. Free Press: New York.

David, P. (1985), 'Clio and the Economics of QWERTY,' *American Economic Review*, 75.

Dosi, G. (1983), 'Technological Paradigms and Technological Trajectories,' *Research Policy*, 11, 147–62.

Douglas, S. (1987), *Inventing American Broadcasting: 1899–1922*. Johns Hopkins: Baltimore, MD.

Dunlop, O. (1970), *Communications in Space*. Harper & Row: New York.

Eldredge, N. and J. Cracraft (1980), *Phylogenetic Patterns and the Evolutionary Process Method and Theory in Comparative Biology*. Columbia University Press: New York.

Erickson, D. (1973), *Armstrong's Fight for FM Broadcasting*. University of Alabama Press: Athens, GA.

Federal Communications Commission (1977), *Statistics of Communications Common Carriers*. Government Printing Office: Washington, DC.

Foster, R. (1986), *Innovation: The Attacker's Advantage*. Summit Books: New York.

Garratt, G. R. M. (1994), *The Early History of Radio*. Institute of Electrical Engineers: London.

Gersick, C. (1991), 'Revolutionary Change Theories: A Multilevel Exploration of the Punctuated Equilibrium Paradigm,' *Academy of Management Review*, 16, 10–36.

Goldschmidt, R. (1940), *The Material Basis of Evolution*. Yale University Press: New Haven, CT.

Gould, S. and N. Eldredge (1977), 'Punctuated Equilibria: The Tempo and Mode of Evolution Reconsidered,' *Paleobiology*, 3, 115–151.

Hawley, A. (1950), *Human Ecology*. Ronald Press: New York.

Inglis, A. (1990), *Behind the Tube: A History of Broadcasting Technology and Business*. Butterworth: Stoneham, MA.

Kargman, H. (1978), 'Land Mobile Communications: The Historical Roots,' in R. Bowers (ed.), *Communications for a Mobile Society*. Sage: Beverly Hills: CA.

Kodama, F. (1992), 'Technology Fusion and the New R&D,' *Harvard Business Review*, 70, 70–78.

Kotler, P. (1991), *Marketing Management: Analysis, Planning, Implementation and Control*. Prentice Hall: Englewood Cliffs, NJ.

Lancaster, K. (1966), 'A New Approach to Demand Theory,' *Journal of Political Economy*, 74, 132–157.

Lavin, D. (1996), 'Ionica Offers Second Line for Calls. Will Many Answer?,' *Wall Street Journal*, September 16, p. B4.

Lodge, O. (1902), *Signalling without Wires*. Van Nostrand: New York.

Mayr, E. (1963), *Animal Species and Evolution*. Harvard University Press: Cambridge, MA.

Maclaurin, W. R. (1949), *Invention and Innovation in the Radio Industry*. Macmillian Press: New York.

McGahan, A., L. Vadasz and D. Yoffie (1997), 'Creating Value and Setting Standards: The Lessons of Consumer Electronics for Personal Digital Assistants,' in D. Yoffie (ed.), *Competing in the Age of Digital Convergence*. Harvard Business School Press: Boston, MA.

Noble, D. (1962), 'The History of Land–Mobile Radio Communication,' *Proceedings of the IRE*, 50, 1405.

Ristelhueber, R. (1993), 'GaAS are Making a Comeback, but Profits Remain Elusive,' *Electronic Business Buyer*, 19, 27–28.

Rosenbloom, R. and M. Cusumano (1987), 'Technological Pioneering and Competitive Advantage: The Birth of the VCR Industry,' *California Management Review*, 51–76.

Rosenberg, N. (1976), 'Technological Change in the Machine Tool Industry, 1840–1910,' in N. Rosenberg (ed.), *Perspectives on Technology*. M. E. Sharpe: London.

Schumpeter, J. A. (1934), *The Theory of Economic Development*. Harvard University Press: Cambridge, MA.

Simpson, G. (1949), *The Meaning of Evolution*. Yale University Press: New Haven, CT.

Strickberger, M. (1996), *Evolution*. Jones & Bartlett: Boston, MA.

Susskind, D. (1964), 'Observations of Electromagnetic Wave Radiation before Hertz,' *Isis*, 55, 32–42.

Teece, D. (1987), 'Capturing Value from Technological Innovation,' in D. Teece (ed.), *The Competitive Challenge*. Harper & Row: New York.

Tushman, M. and P. Anderson (1986), 'Technological Discontinuities and Organizational Environments,' *Administrative Science Quarterly*, 31, 439–465.

Tushman, M. and E. Romanelli (1985), 'Organizational Evolution: A Metamorphosis Model of Convergence and Reorientation,' in L. Cummings and B. Staw (eds), *Research in Organizational Behavior*. JAI Press: Greenwich, CT.

Wiegner, K. (1988), 'Silicon Valley 1, Gallium Gulch 0,' *Forbes*, 141, 270–272.

Yoffie, D. (1996), 'Competing in the Age of Digitial Convergence,' *California Management Review*, 38, 31–53.

Technologies, Products and Organization in the Innovating Firm: What Adam Smith Tells Us and Joseph Schumpeter Doesn't

KEITH PAVITT

(Science Policy Research Unit, Mantell Building, University of Sussex, Brighton BN1 9RF, UK)

Adam Smith's insights into the increasingly specialized nature of knowledge production are crucially important in understanding the contemporary problems of managing innovating firms. Products and firms are based on an increasing range of fields of specialized technological understanding. Competition is not based on technological diversity, but on diversity and experimentation in products, etc. Firms rarely fail because of an inability to master a new field of technology, but because they do not succeed in matching the firm's systems of coordination and control to the nature of the available technological opportunities.

All the improvements in machinery, however, have by no means been the inventions of those who had occasion to use the machines. Many . . . have been made by the makers of the machines, when to make them became the business of a peculiar trade: and some by . . . those who are called philosophers, or men of speculation, whose trade is not to do anything but to observe everything: and who, upon that account are often capable of combining together the powers of the most distant and dissimilar objects. . . . *Like every other employment . . . it is subdivided into a number of different branches, each of which affords occupation to a peculiar tribe or class of philosophers; and this subdivision of employment in philosophy, as well as in every other business, improves dexterity and saves time.* (Smith, 1776, p. 8, my italics)

1. Setting the Scene

Evolutionary Theory and the Innovating Firm

Attempts over the past twenty years to build an evolutionary theory of the firm have grown in part out of a dissatisfaction with the inability of mainstream theory to deal satisfactorily with two important, interrelated and empirically observable characteristics of contemporary society: continuous technical change, and the central role of the business firm in generating learning, improvement and innovation, through deliberate and purposive action. At the beginning, concepts like 'technological trajectories' and 'routines' were introduced by Nelson and Winter (1977, 1982) to reflect the cumulative and path-dependent nature of technical change, the often tacit nature of the knowledge underlying it, and the trial-and-error behaviour of business practitioners trying to cope with a complex and ever-changing world.[1]

Since then, two influential streams of analysis have helped deepen our knowledge of the innovating firm. First, numerous attempts have been made to apply the tools and techniques of evolutionary theory (and particularly biological evolution) directly to modelling and understanding technical change (e.g. Dosi and Marengo, 1993; Metcalfe and de Liso, 1995). Second, numerous empirical studies have attempted to formulate generally applicable laws that explain when and why established firms succeed in innovation, and when and why they fail (e.g. Iansiti and Clark, 1994; Teece, 1996). This paper will argue that, whilst both schools have made notable contributions to understanding of both the nature of the innovating firm and the conditions for successful innovation, much remains to be done.

Multi-technology Products and Firms

In particular, greater care and attention needs to be devoted to the distinctions between the *artefacts* (products, etc.) that the firm develops and produces, the firm-specific technological *knowledge* that underlies its ability to do so, and the *organizational* forms and procedures that it uses to transform one into the other. We shall argue that, in the late twentieth century, lack of technological knowledge is rarely the cause of innovation failure in large firms based in OECD countries. The main problems arise in organization and, more specifically, in coordination and control.

This can best be understood if more attention is paid to what Adam Smith said about the division of labour, and less to what Schumpeter said about creative destruction. Smith's identification of the benefits of specialization in the production of knowledge has been amply confirmed by experience. Professional education, the establishment of laboratories, and improvements

---

[1] This paper concentrates on these aspects of firm behaviour, and not on the wider implications of evolutionary theory for the theory of the firm. For a concise evaluation of the latter, together with that of other recent theoretical developments, see Coriat and Weinstein (1995).

in techniques of measurement and experimentation have increased the efficiency of discovery, invention and innovation. Increasingly difficult problems can be tackled and solved.[2] Two complementary forms of specialization have happened in parallel.

First, new disciplines have emerged, with all the benefits of the division of labour highlighted by Smith himself at the beginning of this paper. These specialized bodies of knowledge have become useful over a growing range of applications, so that products incorporate a growing number of technologies: compare the eighteenth-century loom with today's equivalent, with its fluid flow, electrical, electronic and software elements improving the efficiency of its mechanical functions. In other words, products are becoming increasingly 'multi-technology', and so are the firms that produce them. Each specific body of technical knowledge cannot be associated uniquely with a single, specific class of product.[3] Products and related technologies co-evolve within firms, but their dynamics are different. For example, Gambardella and Torrisi (1998) found that the most successful electronics firms over the past ten years have been those that have simultaneously broadened their technological focus and narrowed their product focus. In other cases, firms have used their range of technological skills to create or enter new product markets (see Granstrand, 1982; Granstrand and Sjolander, 1990; Oskarsson, 1993; Granstrand and Oskarsson, 1994).

Second, in addition to the benefits of the cognitive division of labour into more specialized fields, the rate of technical change has been augmented by the functional division of labour within business firms, with the establishment of corporate R&D laboratories and similar groups devoted full-time to inventing the innovative activities. In addition to the Smithean benefits of specialization, professionalization and improved equipment, these laboratories enabled firms to monitor and benefit more systematically and effectively from the outside advances in specialized academic disciplines. And with growing experience in the development and testing of prototypes, they have allowed systematic experimentation with a wider range of products and processes than had previously been possible through incremental improvements constrained by established products and production lines. In fields of rich technological opportunity, firms have in consequence become multi-product as well as multi-technology.

---

[2] The classic texts on this are Rosenberg (1974), de Solla Price (1984) and Mowery and Rosenberg (1989). See, for example, the reasons why problems in mechanics were solved more easily than those in medicine.

[3] Amongst other things, this is a source of frustration for economists who would like to match statistics on inventions from technology-based patent classes with product-based trade and production statistics. See, for example, Scherer (1982).

Two Bodies of Knowledge

Hence the importance, in analysing the innovating firm, of distinguishing clearly artefacts (products) from the knowledge sources on which they are based.[4] Nelson (1998) identifies two, complementary elements in firm-specific knowledge. First, there is a 'body of understanding', based on competencies in specific technological fields, and reflected in the qualifications of corporate technical personnel, and in the fields in which they patent and publish.[5] The second element is what Nelson (1998) calls a 'body of practice', related to the design, development, production, sale and use of a specific product model or a specific production line. This firm-specific practical technical knowledge is often obtained through the combination of experimentation, experience, and information and other exchanges amongst different parts of the organization.[6] As such, it is an organizational task, so that 'a body of practice' consists largely of organizational knowledge that links 'a body of understanding' with commercially successful (or, more broadly, useful) artefacts.

Method

The starting point for our analysis is the large, multi-divisional manufacturing firm, with established R&D activities and a product range that has grown out of a common, but evolving, technological competence. In part, this reflects the focus of this author's recent research (Patel and Pavitt, 1997; Tidd *et al.*, 1997). More important for the purpose of this paper, large multi-divisional firms are the largest single source of the new technological knowledge on which innovation depends. They perform most of the R&D activities,

---

[4] For an earlier discussion of this distinction, see Archibugi (1988).

[5] For measurement of corporate technological competencies through the fields of qualifications of technical personnel, see Jacobsson and Oskarsson (1995); through patenting, see Patel and Pavitt (1997); and through scientific papers, see Narin and Olivastro (1992), Godin (1996) and Hicks and Katz (1997).

[6] The difference between the two forms of knowledge is nicely illustrated in the following passage from Iansiti and Clark (1994), in relation to the firm-specific capabilities for the design and development of dies used in the production of body panels for automobiles: 'The knowledge that underlies that capability includes an understanding of metallurgy, the flow of metal under pressure and the relationship between the characteristics of the material, the forces and pressures applied to the material and the surface properties that result. These kinds of knowledge pertain to the fundamental properties of the die and its production system. But the firm must also have knowledge about how the fundamental concepts can be operationalised into effective actions. These include knowledge of techniques of die design, die modelling, die testing and finishing, for example. Additionally, knowledge can take the form of the skill of die designers in anticipating processing problems, customised software that allows for rapid and effective testing, patterns of communication and informal interaction between die designers and manufacturing engineers that allow for early identification of potential problems, and an attitude of co-operation that facilitates coordinated action between the die designers and the tool makers that will build the dies. These elements (and many others) define an organisational capability for die design and development' (p. 560).

employ most of the qualified research scientists and engineers, perform and publish most of the corporate basic research, and maintain the closest links with academic research (Hicks, 1995). They also contribute to the development of knowledge and products for their suppliers of production equipment, components and software (Rosenberg, 1963; Patel and Pavitt, 1994). Finally, even when they fail in innovation themselves, they remain the major source of the technological and other competencies which enable new firms with different organizational approaches to succeed. Understanding the reasons for their success and failure therefore has the widest implications, not only for their managers, but also for the distribution of innovative activities amongst companies of different sizes and ages. It is not the main concern of this paper to argue in general for or against the large firm's ability to sustain radical innovation, but to understand better the reasons for its success and failure in trying to do so.[7]

We divide our analysis into four parts, reflecting four mechanisms identified by earlier analysts of the innovating firms: competition, cognition, coordination and control.[8] Table 1 sets out schematically how the division of labour, both in knowledge production and in corporate innovative activities, has influenced these four mechanisms. We argue in Section 2 that failure to distinguish between technologies and products has led to confusion in evolutionary writings about what kind of 'diversity' is desirable in competitive processes. In Section 3, we further argue that, although there are clear cognitive limits on the range of technologies that a specific firm is capable of mastering, failure in innovation in established firms is not the result of the destruction of their technological competencies, but of their inability to match the technological opportunities with organizational forms and procedures appropriate for their development and exploitation. In Sections 4 and 5, we analyse in greater depth how the appropriate forms of two organizational elements that are central to corporate innovative activities—mechanisms

---

[7] Many analysts in the evolutionary tradition are pessimistic about the ability of large firms to sustain radical innovation, pointing to recent spectacular failures and to the emergence of new organization forms: Teece (1996) recently identified four types of firm: conglomerate, multi-product integrated hierarchy, virtual corporation and 'high flex' Silicon Valley type. Others argue that the obituary of the large innovative firm may well be premature, since there remain many examples of their success in developing and exploiting major innovations: for example, according to Methe *et al.* (1996): 'established firms, including industry incumbents and diversifying entrants, play vital and underemphasized roles as sources of major innovations in many industries' (p. 1181). And now even the oldest and best established of capitalists—grocers (supermarkets) and moneylenders (financial services)—have become major players in the development and exploitation of information technology.

[8] These dimensions of the innovating firm emerge from the original work of Nelson and Winter (1982), and from later work by Cohendet *et al.* (1994). In the language of Teece and Pisano (1994), in their analysis of the 'dynamic capabilities' of the firm, out competitive mechanisms relate their notions of corporate *position*, cognitive mechanisms to corporate *paths*, and coordination and control mechanisms to corporate *processes*.

TABLE 1. Some Consequences of the Division of Labour in the Production of Technological Knowledge

	Technology ≠ products	Technological discontinuities ≠ product discontinuities	Technological diversity within firms, and within countries, but not within industries
Analytical implications			
Division of labour in knowledge production Laboratories Disciplines Trained scientists and engineers → Increasing output, range and usefulness of knowledge →	Multi-technology products →	Multi-technology firms →	Multi-product firms
Division of labour in business functions Specialized technical functions, inc. R&D labs → Increasing competence to understand and improve artefacts →			
Management implications	**Co-ordination** Organizational competence to experiment and learn across organizational boundaries	**Competencies** Technological competence enhancement > competence destruction	**Control** Organizational competence to reconfigure divisions and evaluate options in the light of technology characteristics

of coordination and control—depend in part on the nature of the technology itself.

2. *Competitive Mechanisms and Technological Diversity*

It is around the notion of diversity[9] that the distinction between technologies (bodies of understanding) and products (bodies of practice) is most confused—and potentially most misleading, given the central importance accorded to diversity in the evolutionary theory of technical change.[10] In recent research undertaken at SPRU on the technological competencies of the world's largest firms, we have used the level and distribution of corporate patenting by technical field as a measure of the corporate body of technological understanding (Patel and Pavitt, 1997; O. Marsili, in preparation). This showed that technological diversity is prominent in some dimensions, but virtually absent in others.

- Large firms are active in a range of technologies *broader* than the products that they make. This reflects the multi-technology nature of their products, and the knowledge required to coordinate in-house product innovation with innovation in related production systems and supply chains. What is more, the range of technological competencies mastered by large firms is increasing over time, as new technological opportunities emerge.
- There is *high* diversity amongst large firms in the level and mix of their technological competencies, depending on the products that they produce. These largely sector-specific mixes of technological competence change only slowly over time, again in response to changing technological opportunities.
- There is *low* diversity in the level and mix of technological competencies amongst large firms producing similar products. What is more, the degree of technological diversity is lowest in the product fields with the highest rate of technical change: computers and pharmaceuticals.

In other words, for the *individual firm*, technological diversity gives it the basis to make and improve its products. For the *economy as a whole*, more diversity amongst firms in their mixes of specialized technological knowledge enables them to explore and exploit a fuller range of product markets. But at the level of the *product market or industry*, there is similarity rather than

---

[9] A reading of the *Oxford Concise English Dictionary* suggests that the term 'diversity' is interchangeable with 'variety' and 'heterogeneity'.

[10] 'It is a basic proposition of evolutionary theory that a system's diversity affects its development' (Cohendet and Llerena, 1997, p. 227).

diversity in the level and mix of technological activities in competing firms, and especially in those with high rates of technical change. Technological diversity is certainly not a characteristic of competition amongst innovating firms.[11] The diversity exists downstream in the body of practice, namely the product and process configurations that can be generated from the same or very similar base of technological knowledge. We know that some of these configurations do not work out technically, and many more do not work out commercially (Freeman and Soete, 1997). What emerges is a world where firms with broad and stable bundles of technological competencies have the capacity to generate and experiment with a range of product (and process and service) configurations, some of which succeed, but many of which fail.

At any given time, advances in some fields of technology open major opportunities for major performance improvements in materials, components and subsystems (e.g. economies of scale in continuous processes, economies of miniaturization in information processing). The directions of these improvements are easily recognized, even if they require the commitment of substantial resources for their achievement, e.g. Moore's Law in semiconductors.[12] Thus, experimentation and diversity do not take place between different technologies. On the contrary, rich and well-known directions of improvement in underlying technologies[13] create opportunities for diversity and experimentation in product configurations. Technological opportunities create product diversity. There is no convincing evidence that technological diversity creates product opportunities.[14]

---

[11] A (frivolous) translation of these results into biological evolutionary terms might be (i) species need a range of genetic attributes for survival; (ii) since they live in different parts of the forest, the elephant and the mouse have different genetic mixes, which change only slowly; (iii) there is little room (or need) for genetic deviance when things are changing fast (and in predictable directions—see below).

[12] Recent comments by an IT expert make the point nicely: 'Precious little has happened in digital technology over the past five years. . . . Steady increases in processor speed and storage size have become as predictable as a child's growth. . . . Just as the computer industry is predicated on Moore's Law—that chips will double in speed every 18 months, which companies can literally plan on—the telecom industry can be predicated on the transparent network. . . . Change is routine and uneventful. . . . The fiber-optic backbone has joined the microprocessor on a steady predictable climb. Processing speeds will double every 18 months. Bandwidth will quadruple every two years. Corporate planners can rest easy' (Steinberg, 1998, pp. 80–84). In our framework, the conclusion of the last sentence does not follow from the preceding analysis. Such rapid if predictable change in underlying technology is bound to create a plethora of difficult-to-predict services.

[13] Nelson and Winter (1977) originally called these 'natural trajectories' and were roundly criticized by those arguing that technologies are socially constructed. But perhaps Nelson and Winter were right. The range of opportunities in different technological fields depends heavily on what nature allows us to do. Compare rates of increase of information storage capacity over the last 20 years with rates of increase in energy storage capacity. In the former, newsprint, punch cards and analogue recording have been overwhelmed by digital methods. In the latter, petroleum remains supreme, in spite of considerable technological efforts to develop better alternatives.

[14] In this context, a recent paper, Stankiewicz (1998) proposes the notion of interrelated 'design space' for artefacts, and 'operands' for the underlying knowledge base, techniques, etc.

3. *Cognitive Mechanisms and Creative Destruction*

Large firms may have competencies in a number of fields of technology but, in the contemporary world of highly specialized knowledge, the costs of mastering all of them clearly appear to outweigh the benefits. Firms develop their technological competencies incrementally, and constrain their search activities close to what that they already know. Thus, over the past 20 years, electronics firms have moved heavily into semiconductor technology (but not biotechnology), and drug firms into biotechnology (but not semiconductor technology). The firm's knowledge base both determines what it makes, and the directions in which it searches (Patel and Pavitt, 1997). In this sense, there are clear cognitive limits on what firms can and cannot do.

The central importance of firm-specific technological competencies has led some analysts to place technological discontinuities (i.e. major technological improvements) at the heart of the theory of the innovating firm. In particular, they argue that such discontinuities may either enhance established competencies and strengthen incumbent firms, or destroy established compet-encies and undermine them. Again, it must be stressed that technological discontinuities are not the same as product discontinuities, even if they are often treated as such. For example, perhaps the most influential paper on discontinuities by Tushman and Anderson (1986) talks of *technological* discontinuities in its title, whilst the basis for its empirical analysis are new products and processes (e.g. jet engines, oxygen steel-making).

Although they may have revolutionary effects, technological discontinu-ities rarely encompass all—or even most of—the fields of knowledge that feed into a product. Typically they may affect the performance of a key component (e.g. transistors vs. valves) or provide a major new technique (e.g. gene spli-cing). But they do not destroy the whole range of related and complementary technologies (e.g. sound reproduction in radios, memories in computers, molecular design in pharmaceuticals) that are necessary for a complete product.[15] Indeed, they create opportunities for product 'discontinuities' that often can be achieved only through improvements in complementary but long-established technologies (e.g. metal tolerances and reliability for robots).

Furthermore, as Gambardella and Torrisi (1998) have shown, corporate technological dynamics can have different dynamics from corporate product dynamics, with technological diversification going hand in hand with increasing product focus: for example (i) when a technological discontinuity is incorporated in a product family at the mature stage of its product cycle; or (ii) when a technological discontinuity provokes the emergence of radically new but technology-related product markets with different—but as yet

[15] On biotechnology, see McKelvey (1996).

ill-defined—characteristics; this is probably the case in the electronics industry studied by Gambardella and Torrisi (1998).

Finally, it should be noted that the predominance given to revolutionary technologies in the destruction of corporate competence has often been associated with the notion of paradigm shifts in technology (Dosi, 1982), similar to those in science (Kuhn, 1962). But this is a misinterpretation of the notion of paradigm. A new paradigm does not discredit and displace all the knowledge generated in the earlier paradigms, but instead adds to them. Newtonian physics still has major theoretical and practical uses, and at least a quarter of all the new technology created today is still in mechanical engineering. The development and commercial exploitation of technological discontinuities turns out to be a more cumulative process than is often supposed.

Certainly, there are many historical examples of firms that have failed because they did not master major emerging fields of technology (Cooper and Schendal, 1976). But competence-destroying technologies are the exception rather than the rule today, especially amongst large firms, who have demonstrated a strong capacity through their R&D departments to acquire and develop competencies in 'discontinuity-creating' technologies like computing and biotechnology (Patel and Pavitt, 1997). The key factors behind the success and failure of innovating firms must be sought elsewhere, in the organizational processes linking technologies, products, their production and their markets.

Cognitive mechanisms also underlie the taxonomy of innovation proposed by Abernathy and Clark (1985), which distinguishes four types: incremental, component, architectural and revolutionary. Based on an analysis of innovation in photolithographic aligners, Henderson and Clark (1990) argued that innovations in product architecture[16] destroy the usefulness of the architectural knowledge in established firms, and this is difficult to recognize and remedy. More recently, and based on analysis of innovations in computer disk drives, Christensen and Rosenbloom (1995) concluded that architectural innovations do not necessarily destroy established competencies. What does is a change in the 'value network' (i.e. user market) of the innovation.[17]

Whilst these studies throw interesting and important light on innovation processes within firms, they must be interpreted with care. An alternative reading of the Henderson and Clark story is that failure has less to do with cognitive failure by design engineers to recognize the value of alternative product architectures, than with organizational factors such as the inability of

---

[16] '. . . reconfiguration of an established system to link together existing components in a new way' (Henderson and Clark, 1990, p. 12).

[17] The authors liken a change in the 'value network' (i.e. disk configuration and user marker) to a paradigm shift, which implies a much broader definition of the notion of paradigm than that probably envisaged by Dosi (1982).

design engineers to recognize signals from users or the marketing department, or the unwillingness or inability of corporate management to establish a new design team or product division. Furthermore, it may be a mistake to generalize from the experience of US firms specialized in the IT sector to firms in other sectors and countries. In contrast, for example, to Christensen and Rosenbloom's emphasis on the difficulties of US firms making computer disk drives in switching end-user markets, most of the world's leading chemical firms have been very successful in the twentieth century in deploying their techniques and products deriving from organic synthesis in markets as diverse as textiles, building, health and agriculture (Hounshell and Smith, 1988; Plumpe, 1995).

4. Co-ordination Mechanisms and Learning Across Organisational Boundaries

One of the most robust conclusions emerging from empirical research on the factors affecting success in innovation is the importantce of coordinating learning and other change-related activities across functional boundaries (Burns and Stalker, 1961; Rothwell, 1977; Cooper, 1988; Wang, 1997).[18] Here we see the second major feature of the division of labour that is central to contemporary corporate innovative activities, namely coping with functional specialization, with the emergence of specialized departments for R&D, production, marketing, logistics, strategy, finance, etc. Such coordination cannot realistically be reduced to designing flows of codified information across functional boundaries. It also involves coordinated experimentation (e.g. new product launches), and the interpretation of ambiguous or incomplete data, where tacit knowledge is essential. As the observations of Iansiti and Clark in footnote 6 (p. 436) show, personal contacts, mobility and interfunctional teams are therefore of more central importance than pure information flows.

In our present state of knowledge, effective coordination belongs in the field of practice rather than the field of understanding. Unlike purely technological processes, organizational processes are difficult to measure and evaluate, and do not lend themselves readily to rigorous modelling and controlled experiments. In addition, the coordination processes in which we are interested are complex. Experimentation and learning across critical organizational interfaces are particularly difficult when combining knowledge from different functions, professions and disciplines, each with their distinct and different analytical

---

[18] Problems of such coordination have also figured largely in the works of Coase (1937), Penrose (1959), Aoki (1986) and Loasby (1998).

frameworks and decision rules—which is another reason why firms may try to compensate for greater technological complexity by greater market focus.[19]

In addition, the identification of the location of critical interfaces is not easy, for three reasons. First, there are potentially several such interfaces, involving a multitude of possible linkages between R&D, production, marketing and logistics within the firm, and a variety of sources of outside knowledge in universities, other firms (suppliers, customers, competitors, etc.) and other countries. Second, the interfaces that merit analysis and managerial attention vary considerably amongst technologies and products. Compare firms in pharmaceuticals and automobiles. In the former, strong interfaces between in-house R&D and the direct output of academic research (in medicine, biology and chemistry) are essential. In the latter, they are not, but strong interfaces between in-house R&D and production are of central importance. These differing characteristics have important implications for both the appropriate organizational forms, and geographical location of corporate innovative activities.

Finally, the key interfaces for organizational learning change over time, very often as a result of changes in technology-related factors themselves. Witness the growing importance for the pharmaceutical industry of the interface with research in academic biology, the consumer market interface for producers of telephones and computers, and of interfaces with software and materials technologies for firms in virtually all sectors. One major source of failure in innovation is likely to be inadequate recognition of the importance of these new interfaces, or the inability of management to take effective action to establish them. We should look for what Leonard-Barton (1995) calls 'core rigidities', when individuals and groups with the established competencies for today's products are either ignorant of, or feel threatened by, the growing importance of new competencies.

5. Control Mechanisms: Matching Strategic Styles with Technologies

The lack of a one-to-one link between each product and each technology has at least two major implications for organizational practice in business firms.[20] The first is that firms which master fields of rich technological opportunity

---

[19] Models of intra-corporate coordination have not got very far in grappling with these essential features of innovative activities. For example, in Aoki's models (1986), problems of coordination are in production and dealt with through information flows, rather than in learning and innovation mediated through tacit knowledge. Furthermore, sources of instability and change are in an exogenous environment, rather than created by the firms themselves.

[20] For more extended discussions, see Kay (1979), Prahalad and Hamel (1990), von Tunzelmann (1995) and Marengo (1995).

are often able to develop and produce several products based on the same body of knowledge. In other words, they compete and grow through technology-related diversification.[21] Second, the very existence of this broadly useful knowledge means that the classic M-form organization is unable to match tidily each field of its technology to one product or to one division.

As a consequence, systems of corporate control in the multi-product firm have a major influence on the rate and direction of its innovative activities. Chandler (1991) distinguishes two essential functions of corporate control: the *entrepreneurial* function of planning for the future health and growth of the enterprise, and the *administrative* function of controlling the operation of its many divisions.[22] The administrative function is normally exercised through systems of financial reporting and controls. The entrepreneurial function for technology is the capacity to recognize and exploit technology-based opportunities. This requires an ability to evaluate projects and programmes where the normal financial accounting techniques are often inoperable and inappropriate, since exploratory research programmes should be treated as options, rather than full-scale investments (Myers, 1984; Hamilton, 1986; Mitchell, 1986; Mitchell and Hamilton, 1988). It may also require the establishment of a central corporate research programme or laboratory, funded in part independently from the established product divisions (Graham, 1986). And it will certainly require the capacity to reconfigure the composition and objectives of established divisions in the light of changing opportunities (Prahaled and Hamel, 1990).

Different balances between the administrative and the entrepreneurial functions are likely to be appropriate to different levels of technological opportunity. In addition, the appropriate degree of decentralization of the entrepreneurial function within the corporation will depend in part on the nature of the firm's core technology.[23] The higher the costs of product development, the greater the need for central control of the entrepreneurial function. In other words, the appropriate system of corporate control will depend in part on the nature of the technology.

Thus, Table 2 suggests that firms with low technological opportunity are likely to be compatible with an emphasis on the administrative rather than the entrepreneurial function, and with more centralization with increasing capital intensity. Firms with high technological opportunities and high costs of product and process development—such as those in drugs and automobiles—are likely to be best suited to a strong entrepreneurial function at the corporate

---

[21] See Rumelt (1974). Numerous examples can be found in the electrical and chemical industries.

[22] See also the earlier pioneering work of Goold and Campbell (1987).

[23] Marengo (1995) models learning, and comes to some intuitively appealing conclusions about the balance between organizational centralization and decentralization. But his learning is also about changes in the environment, rather than about internally generated changes.

TABLE 2. Technology and Corporate Control

		Strategic style	
		Entrepreneurial	Administrative
Levels of decision-making	HQ	*High-tech opportunity + high costs of product development* • drugs • automobiles • bulk chemicals in 1960s → • mainframes in 1970s ↓	*Low-tech opportunity + high cost of investments* → GEC (UK) → ITT (USA) • aluminium • steel
	Division	*High-tech opportunity + low costs of product development* • consumer electronics • 3M	*Low-tech opportunity + low cost of investments* • conglomerates

level. Those with high technological opportunities, but low costs of product development—like those in consumer electronics and the 3M Corporation—will be best served by more decentralized entrepreneurial initiative.

Table 2 also shows that there can be mismatches between strategic style and the nature of technological opportunities. For example, tight financial control and emphasis on short-term profitability do not allow investments in exploring longer-term options emerging from new technological opportunities: this is one reason why GEC in the UK and ITT in the USA have progressively excluded themselves from many high-technology markets (*Economist*, 1995, 1996). Similarly, the characteristics of technology, and the corresponding organizational requirements, change over time. Thus, one reason for the recent deliberate demerger of ICI was the reduced technological opportunities in the previously fast-moving field of bulk chemicals (Owen and Harrison, 1995). Similarly, the high costs of mainframe computers in the 1960s and 1970s, and their specificity to the corporate office market, imposed centralized entrepreneurship. With the advent of the microprocessor and packaged software, the costs of experimentation tumbled and new markets emerged. Mainframe firms had great difficulty in adjusting in time to the requirements of greater decentralization.

6. Conclusions

The main argument of this paper is that—as foreseen by Adam Smith—specialization in knowledge production is a central feature of the innovating firm. It is therefore of great importance to distinguish products (and other artefacts) from the underlying bodies of technological understanding on which they are based. Although the two evolve together, they do not have the same dynamics. Inadequate care in distinguishing the two can result in mistaken policy prescriptions (e.g. Granstrand *et al.*, 1997). And it can lead to too much emphasis in evolutionary theorizing on the economic benefits of technological diversity, on the frequency and causes of creative destruction, and on the nature and implications of changes in technological paradigms.

The main challenge is to improve understanding of the organizational processes of coordination and control that make for a successful matching between the development and deployment of bodies of technological knowledge, on the one hand, and commercially successful (or useful) working artefacts, on the other. We have stressed that our practical and theoretical knowledge of these organizational processes are less well grounded than our knowledge of the processes of technological advance *per se*. This is why companies with outstanding technological competencies—Xerox and IBM in the early days of personal computers, for example—failed to develop organizational forms to exploit them. Nonetheless, large firms are capable of restructuring their activities to benefit from the new technological opportunities that they have mastered. 'Routines' can and do change. 'Creative destruction' is not inevitable.

The appropriate organizational processes will depend on the characteristics of the technologies, such as their sources, the rate and direction of their change, and the costs of developing and building artefacts based on them. And since technologies vary greatly in these characteristics, and they change over time, any improved knowledge that we acquire will be highly contingent. Nonetheless, the research of Woodward (1965) and Chandler (1977) on the organizational dimensions of changes in process technologies shows that such research can make a major difference to our understanding of innovation in firms. The following avenues of research appear to be particularly fruitful:

1. Bibliometric studies and surveys that map linkages between knowledge, products and organization in business firms over a range of sectors. This is essential given intersectoral variety. The great challenge is to develop measures of organization that are conceptually clear and empirically robust.

2. Detailed studies by historians and sociologists of the interactions between the development of the technological knowledge base, and the associated artefacts that emerge from them (e.g. Constant, 1998; Stankiewicz, 1998).

3. Case studies of the effects on firms, their organization and their products of the introduction of technological discontinuities, whether in the form of new sources of useful knowledge, or of order-of-magnitude improvements in the performance in one field. If then our analysis is correct, large

firms in advanced countries will have few difficulties in mastering the new technology, resultant product discontinuities will happen only after a extended period of learning,[24] and failure is likely to result from 'core rigidities', namely resistance from established groups within the organization.

Finally, our analysis suggests that truths about the real innovating firm will never be elegant, simple or easy to replicate. It is nonetheless to be hoped that formal theorizing will try to incorporate more real-world features of the innovating firm. In particular, evolutionary economics grew out of dissatisfaction with mainstream formalizations of technical change. It would be a pity if it ended up going down the same path.

Acknowledgements

The author has benefited greatly in the preparation of this paper from the comments of Stefano Brusoni, Mike Hobday, Patrick Llerena, Richard Nelson, Ed Steinmueller and two anonymous referees. The usual disclaimers apply.

References

Abernathy, W. and K. Clark (1985), 'Innovation: Mapping the Winds of Creative Destruction,' *Research Policy*, 14, 3–22.

Aoki, M. (1986), 'Horizontal vs. Vertical Information Structure of the Firm,' *American Economic Review*, 76, 971–983.

Archibugi, D. (1988), 'In Search of a Useful Measure of Technological Innovation,' *Technological Forecasting and Social Change*, 34, 253–277.

Burns, T. and G. Stalker (1961), *The Management of Innovation*. Tavistock: London.

Chandler, A. D. (1977), *The Visible Hand: The Managerial Revolution in American Business*. Belknap Press: Cambridge, MA.

Chandler, A. (1991), 'The Functions of the HQ Unit in the Multibusiness Firm,' *Strategic Management Journal*, 12, 31–50.

Christensen, C. and R. Rosenbloom (1995), 'Explaining the Attacker's Advantage: Technological Paradigms, Organisational Dynamics, and the Value Network,' *Research Policy*, 24, 233–257.

Coase, R. (1937), 'The Nature of the Firm,' *Economica*, 4, 386–405.

Cohender, P. and P. Llerena (1997), 'Learning, Technical Change and Public Policy: How to Create and Exploit Diversity,' in C. Edquist (ed.), *Systems of Innovation: Technologies, Institutions and Organisations*. Pinter: London.

---

[24] See Miyazaki (1995) for an account of the extended period that Japanese firms spent learning about opto-electronics. It might be argued that the personal computer began with a component innovation (the microprocessor) which, after a number of complementary component innovations (e.g. memories), and architectural innovations (internalizing the disk drive) and incremental improvements, created the conditions for the emergence of the revolutionary innovation that was the PC.

Cohender, P., P. Llerena and L. Marengo (1994),: 'Learning and Organizational Structure in Evolutionary Models of the Firm,' EUNETIC Conference 'Evolutionary Economics of Technological Change: Assessment of Results and New Frontiers,' Strasbourg.

Constant, E. (1998), 'Recursive Practice and the Evolution of Technological Knowledge,' in J. Ziman (ed.), *Technological Innovation as an Evolutionary Process*. Cambridge University Press: Cambridge (in press).

Cooper, A. and D. Schendel (1976), 'Strategic Responses to Technological Threats,' *Business Horizons*, February, 61–69.

Cooper, R. (1988), 'The New Product Process: A Decision Guide for Management,' *Journal of Marketing Management*, 3, 238–255.

Coriat, B. and O. Weinstein (1995), *Les Nouvelles Theories de l'Entreprise*. Livre de Poche, Librarie Generale Française: Paris.

de Solla Price, D. (1984), 'The Science/Technology Relationship, the Craft of Experimental Science, and Policy for the Improvement of High Technology Innovation,' *Research Policy*, 13, 3–20.

Dosi, G. (1982), 'Technological Paradigms and Technological Trajectories: A Suggested Interpretation of the Determinants and Directions of Technical Change,' *Research Policy*, 11, 147–162.

Dosi, G. and L. Marengo (1993), 'Some Elements of and Evolutionary Theory of Organisational Competencies,' in R.W. England (ed.), *Evolutionary Concepts in Contemporary Economics*. University of Michigan Press: Ann Arbor, MI.

Economist (1995), 'The Death of the Geneen Machine,' June 17, 86–92.

Economist (1996), 'Changing of the Guard,' September 7, 72.

Freeman, C. and L. Soete (1997), *The Economics of Industrial Innovation*. Cassel-Pinter: London.

Gambardella, A. and S. Torrisi (1998), 'Does Technological Convergence Imply Convergence in Markets? Evidence from the Electronics Industry,' *Research Policy* (in press).

Godin, B. (1996), 'Research and the Practice of Publication in Industry,' *Research Policy*, 25, 587–606.

Goold, M. and A. Campbell (1987), *Strategies and Styles: The Role of the Centre in Managing Diversified Corporations*. Blackwell: Oxford.

Graham, M. (1986), 'Corporate Research and Development: The Latest Transformation,' in M. Horwitch (ed.), *Technology in the Modern Corporation: a Strategic Perspective*. Pergamon Press: New York.

Granstrand, O. (1982), *Technology, Management and Markets*. Pinter: London.

Granstrand, O. and C. Oskarsson (1994), 'Technology Diversification in "Multi-tech" Corporations,' *IEEE Transactions on Engineering Management*, 41, 355–364.

Granstrand, O. and S. Sjolander (1990), 'Managing Innovation in Multi-technology Corporations,' *Research Policy*, 19, 35–60.

Granstrand, O., P. Patel and K. Pavitt (1997), 'Multi-technology Corporations: Why they Have "Distributed" rather than "Distinctive Core" Competencies,' *California Management Review*, 39, 8–25.

Hamilton, W. (1986), 'Corporate Strategies for Managing Emerging Technologies,' in M. Horwitch (ed.), *Technology in the Modern Corporation: A Strategic Perspective*. Pergamon Press: New York.

Henderson, R. and K. Clark (1990), 'Architectural Innovation: The Reconfiguration of Existing Product Technologies and the Failure of Established Firms,' *Administrative Sciences Quarterly*, 35, 9–30.

Hicks, D. (1995), 'Published Papers (1995) Tacit Competencies and Corporate Management of the Public/Private Character of Knowledge,' *Industrial and Corporate Change*, 4, 401–424.

Hicks, D. and S. Katz (1997), *The Changing Shape of British Industrial Research*, STEEP Special Report no. 6, Science Policy Research Unit, University of Sussex.

Horwitch, M. (ed.) (1986), *Technology in the Modern Corporation: A Strategic Perspective*. Pergamon Press: New York.

Hounshell, D. and J. Smith (1988), *Science and Corporate Strategy: Du Pont R&D, 1902–1980*. Cambridge University Press: New York.

Iansiti, M. and K. Clark (1994), 'Integration and Dynamic Capability: Evidence from Product Development in Automobiles and Mainframe Computers,' *Industrial and Corporate Change*, 4, 557–605.

Jacobsson, S. and C. Oskarsson (1995), 'Educational Statistics as an Indicator of Technological Activity,' *Research Policy*, 24, 127–136.

Kay, N. (1979), *The Innovating Firm*. Macmillan: London.

Kuhn, T. (1962), *The Structure of Scientific Revolutions*. Chicago: University of Chicago Press.

Leonard-Barton, D. (1995), *Wellsprings of Knowledge*. Harvard Business School Press: Boston, MA.

Loasby, B. (1998), 'The Organisation of Capabilities,' *Journal of Economic Behaviour and Organisation* (in press).

Marengo, L. (1995), 'Structure, Competence and Learning in Organisations,' *Wirtschaftspolische Blatter*, 42, 454–464.

McKelvey, M. (1996), *Evolutionary Innovations: The Business of Biotechnology*. Oxford: Oxford University Press.

Metcalfe, S. and N. de Liso (1995), 'Innovation, Capabilities and Knowledge: The Epistemic Connection,' in J. de la Mottre and G. Paquet (eds), *Evolutionary Economics and the New International Political Economy*. Pinter: London.

Methe, D., A. Swaminathan and W. Mitchell (1996), 'The Underemphasized Role of Established Firms as Sources of Major Innovations,' *Industrial and Corporate Change*, 5, 1181–1203.

Mitchell, G. (1986), 'New Approaches for the Strategic Management of Technology,' in M. Horwitch (ed.), *Technology in the Modern Corporation: a Strategic Perspective*. Pergamon Press: New York.

Mitchell, G. and W. Hamilton (1998), 'Managing R&D as a Strategic Option,' *Research-Technology Management*, 31, 15–22.

Miyazaki, K. (1995), *Building Competencies in the Firm: Lessons from Japanese and European Optoelectronics*. Macmillan/St Martin's Press: New York.

Mowery, D. and N. Rosenberg (1989), *Technology and the Pursuit of Economic Growth*. Cambridge: Cambridge University Press.

Myers, S. (1984), 'Finance Theory and Financial Strategy,' *Interfaces*, 14, 126–137.

Narin, F. and D. Olivastro (1992), 'Status Report: Linkage between Technology and Science,' *Research Policy*, 21, 237–249.

Nelson, R. (1998), 'Different Perspectives on Technological Evolution,' in J. Ziman (ed.), *Technological Innovation as an Evolutionary Process*. Cambridge: Cambridge University Press (in press).

Nelson, R. R. and S. G. Winter (1977), 'In Search of a Useful Theory of Innovation,' *Research Policy*, 6, 36–76.

Nelson, R. R. and S. G. Winter (1982), *An Evolutionary Theory of Economic Change*. Belknap Press: Cambridge, MA.

Oskarsson, C. (1993), *Technology Diversification—The Phenomenon, its Causes and Effects*. Department of Industrial Management and Economics, Chalmers University of Technology, Gothenburg.

Owen, G. and T. Harrison (1995), 'Why ICI Chose to Demerge,' *Harvard Business Review*, March–April, 133–142.

Patel, P. and K. Pavitt (1994), 'The Continuing, Widespread (and Neglected) Importance of Improvements in Mechanical Technologies,' *Research Policy*, 23, 533–546.

Patel, P. and K. Pavitt (1997), 'The Technological Competencies of the World's Largest Firms: Complex and Path-dependent, but not Much Variety,' *Research Policy*, 26, 141–156.

Penrose, E. (1959), *The Theory of the Growth of the Firm*. Blackwell: Oxford.

Plumpe, G. (1995), 'Innovation and the Structure of the IG Farben,' in F. Caron, P. Erker and W. Fischer (eds), *Innovations in the European Economy between the Wars*. De Gruyter, Berlin.

Prahalad, C. K. and G. Hamel (1990), 'The Core Competencies of the Corporation,' *Harvard Business Review*, May–June, 79–91.

Rosenberg, N. (1963), 'Technological Change in the Machine Tool Industry, 1840–1910,' *Journal of Economic History*, 23, 414–446.

Rosenberg, N. (1974), 'Science, Invention and Economic Growth,' *Economic Journal*, 84, 333.

Rothwell, R. (1977), 'The Characteristics of Successful Innovators and Technically Progressive Firms,' *R&D Management*, 7, 191–206.

Rumelt, R. (1974), *Strategy, Structure and Economic Performance*. Graduate School of Business Administration, Harvard University.

Scherer, F. (1982), 'Inter-industry Technology Flows in the US,' *Research Policy*, 11, 227–45.

Smith, A. (1776), *The Wealth of Nations*. Dent (1910): London.

Stankiewicz, R. (1998), 'Technological Change as an Evolution of Design Spaces,' in J. Ziman (ed.), *Technological Innovation as an Evolutionary Process*. Cambridge: Cambridge University Press (in press).

Steinberg, S. (1998), 'Schumpeter's Lesson: What Really Happened in Digital Technology in the Past Five Years,' *Wired*, January.

Teece, D. (1996), 'Firm Organisation, Industrial Structure and Technological Innovation,' *Journal of Economic Behaviour and Organisation*, 31, 193–224.

Teece, D. and G. Pisano (1994), 'The Dynamic Capabilities of Firms: An Introduction,' *Industrial and Corporate Change*, 3, 537–556.

Tidd, J., J. Bessant and K. Pavitt (1997), *Managing Innovation: Integrating Technological, Market and Organisational Change*. Wiley: Chichester.

von Tunzelmann, N. (1995), *Technology and Industrial Progress*. Elgar: Aldershot.

Tushman, M. and P. Anderson (1986), 'Technological Discontinuities and Organisational Environments,' *Administrative Science Quarterly*, 31, 439–465.

Wang, Q. (1997), 'R&D/Marketing Interface in a Firm's Capability-building Process: Evidence from Pharmaceutical Firms,' *International Journal of Innovation Management*, 1, 23–52.

Woodward, J. (1965), *Industrial Organisation: Theory and Practice*. Oxford: Oxford University Press.

Ziman, J. (1998), *Technological Innovation as an Evolutionary Process*. Cambridge: Cambridge University Press (in press).

Economic Experiments*

NATHAN ROSENBERG

(Department of Economics, Stanford University, Stanford,
CA 94305-6072, USA)

1. Introduction

This paper will offer a historical examination of a certain kind of freedom and
the economic consequences that have flowed from it. It will focus upon the
freedom to perform economic experiments, understanding the expression in
the broadest sense to include experimentation with new forms of economic
organization as well as the better-known historical experiments that have
been responsible for new products and new manufacturing technologies. It
will be argued that the freedom to undertake such experiments has been the
essential element accounting for the fact that industrialization has been,
uniquely, a historical product of capitalist societies.

The perspective suggested here is not, of course, entirely novel. Marx
understood very well that the new technology that was transforming Great
Britain in the century before the publication of *The Communist Manifesto*
(Marx and Engels, 1848) was inseparably linked to capitalist institutions.
Marx grasped a part of this story so firmly that his treatment must, necessarily,
be the starting point for this paper. However, as we will see, Marx missed
some fundamental parts of the story. Moreover, we now have the distinct
advantage over Marx of more than a century of further capitalist performance
and more than seventy years of history of a large socialist economy that
adopted a distinctly different posture toward the freedom to conduct organizational experiments. Thus, we start with Marx and the big issues connected
with the economic growth experience of the west.

The argument of the paper will be advanced through a consideration of
some of the salient features of western institutional history and more recent

* This paper is a substantial modification of a paper presented at a conference, 'What is Political
Economy?: Some Issues at the Foundation,' that was held at Claremont McKenna College, November 14–17,
1987. The paper draws heavily, in parts, upon N. Rosenberg and L. E. Birdzell, Jr., *How the West Grew Rich*,
Basic Books, New York, 1986. I would like to acknowledge my intellectual debt to L. E. Birdzell, Jr.,
from whom I have learned a great deal. The present paper has also benefited from the suggestions of several
anonymous referees of this journal.

developments in the east European socialist world. There is, of course, a considerable body of theoretical literature examining the weaknesses of market capitalism and the strengths of central planning. Market economies underinvest in research generally and private incentives may drive the pool of potential inventors into commitments of their resources that are socially suboptimal. Decentralized exploration of the technological frontier may lead to a 'lock-in' to an inferior path of technological development that is not subject to correction by market forces. On the other hand, one can postulate a central planning authority of a socialist society that appropriately addresses society's long-term interests, that can internalize positive economies external to the innovating unit, and can avoid the many pitfalls generated by profit-maximizing firms that consider only private and not social returns. Nevertheless, it now seems plausible, especially in view of the recent economic collapse of east European socialism, to render certain judgments on why the two systems have in fact performed so differently with respect to technological change.

The central argument of this paper is a simple one. The freedom to conduct experiments is essential to any society that has a serious commitment to technological innovation or to improved productive efficiency. The starting point is that there are many things that cannot be known in advance or deduced from some set of first principles. Only the opportunity to try out alternatives, with respect both to technology and to form and size of organization, can produce socially useful answers to a bewildering array of questions that are continually occurring in industrial (and in industrializing) societies.

2. *Marx on the History of Capitalism*

How does Marx (and Engels) account for the intimate historical association of capitalism and industrialism? How are these connected with the decline of feudalism? Is the independent variable technological or economic? Although Marx is sometimes portrayed as a technological determinist, he surely did not believe that it was technological changes that initiated social changes. Rather, as the economic determinist that he surely was, he visualized economic forces as shaping the forces of technology.

In the case of the rise of capitalism itself, its emergence was not directly associated with any major changes in the methods of production. Indeed, in Marx's view, capitalism arose in the 16th century, but the dramatic changes in technology that are associated with the industrial revolution only came more than two hundred years later, in the second half of the eighteenth century (Engels, 1910).

In the opening pages of *The Communist Manifesto*, Marx and Engels emphasize that it was the economic opportunities associated with the expansion of trade and overseas markets that provided the initiating impulses to the growth of capitalism and the unique technologies that capitalism brought with it.

> From the serf of the Middle Ages sprang the chartered burghers of the earliest towns. From these burgesses the first elements of the bourgeoisie were developed.
>
> The discovery of America, the rounding of the Cape, opened up fresh ground for the rising bourgeoisie. The East-Indian and Chinese market, the colonization of America, trade with the colonies, the increase in the means of exchange and in commodities generally, gave to commerce, to navigation, to industry, an impulse never before known, and thereby, to the revolutionary element in the tottering feudal society, a rapid development.
>
> The feudal system of industry, under which industrial production was monopolised by closed guilds, now no longer sufficed for the growing wants of the new markets. The manufacturing system took its place. The guildmasters were pushed on one side by the manufacturing middle class; division of labour between the different corporate guilds vanished in the face of division of labour in each single workshop.
>
> Meantime, the markets kept ever growing, the demand ever rising. Even manufacture no longer sufficed. Thereupon, steam and machinery revolutionized industrial production. The place of manufacture was taken by the giant, Modern Industry, the place of the industrial middle class, by industrial millionaires, the leaders of whole industrial armies, the modern bourgeois.
>
> Modern industry has established the world-market, for which the discovery of America paved the way. This market has given an immense development to commerce, to navigation, to communication by land. This development has, in turn, reacted on the extension of industry; and in proportion as industry, commerce, navigation, railways extended, in the same proportion the bourgeoisie developed, increased its capital, and pushed into the background every class handed down from the Middle ages (Marx and Engels, 1848).

Marx's account, therefore, emphasizes the growth in profit opportunities that were associated with the growth of overseas markets—it is, in fact, quite noteworthy that Marx and Engels pay no attention to the internal growth taking place in European markets. The feudal economy lacked the capability to respond to these market opportunities. The organization of its industry was fundamentally restrictive and conservative. The craft guilds that controlled handicraft industry severely restricted entry into specific trades, dictated the quality of the product, and controlled the relationship between buyer and seller, including the price at which a product could be sold. The feudal system is therefore overthrown by an emerging class of capitalists who sweep away feudal institutions and replace them with institutions of their own making.

Above all, these institutions accord a more prominent role to market forces than would have been possible in the middle ages.

Perhaps the most striking aspects of *The Communist Manifesto* are the passages calling attention to the unique role of capitalism in bringing about a historic growth in human productivity.

> The bourgeoisie has . . . been the first to show what man's activity can bring about. It has accomplished wonders far surpassing Egyptian pyramids, Roman aqueducts, and Gothic cathedrals . . .
>
> The bourgeoisie cannot exist without constantly revolutionising the instruments of production, and thereby the relations of production, and with them the whole relations of society. Conservation of the old modes of production in unaltered form, was, on the contrary, the first condition of existence for all earlier industrial classes . . .
>
> The bourgeoisie, by the rapid improvement of all instruments of production, by the immensely facilitated means of communication, draws all, even the most barbarian, nations into civilisation . . .
>
> The bourgeoisie, during its rule of scarce one hundred years, has created more massive and more colossal productive forces than have all preceding generations together. Subjection of Nature's forces to man, machinery, application of chemistry to industry and agriculture, steam-navigation, railways, electric telegraphs, clearing of whole continents for cultivation, canalisation of rivers, whole populations conjured out of the ground—what earlier century had even a presentiment that such productive forces slumbered in the lap of social labour? (Marx and Engels, 1848)

Why, according to Marx, is capitalism such an immensely productive system? (Note that, in the paean of praise in the last paragraph quoted, the great accomplishments cited are specifically creations of the bourgeoisie, not the Protestant Ethic or some other force exogenous to a particular form of economic organization.)

Marx's answer is that the bourgeoisie is a unique ruling class on the stage of world history. It is the first ruling class whose economic interests are inseparably tied to change and not the maintenance of the status quo. The bourgeoisie '. . . cannot exist without constantly revolutionising the instruments of production . . .' In essence, capitalism has created a very powerful set of incentives that drives the system in the direction of continuous technical change and capital accumulation. The market pressures of competitive capitalism force the capitalist to maximize the output from his labour force. These pressures compel the capitalist to plow back the profits that he has earned by adopting new, economically superior, labor-saving technologies as rapidly as possible.

It is not Marx's view that capitalism was, *ab initio*, a highly productive system, although some passages in his writings often sound that way. Such an interpretation overlooks the intermediate steps in Marx's historical analysis of capitalism because, in its earliest stages, it still made use of an essentially handicraft technology. This system—of manufacturing—was more productive than the handicraft system that it displaced, but not enormously so. While it involved a much more extensive division of labor, it did not yet utilize any drastically new technology. Capitalism did provide the necessary incentives to raise productivity. However, that great improvement in productivity was only realized when capitalism's more powerful incentive structure led to the emergence of Modern Industry. And that took a couple hundred years, in Marx's view.

Marx's argument here has an important component that was foreshadowed in the last quotation from *The Communist Manifesto*. The great increases in productivity are attained only when capitalism leads to a mode of production to which science can be directly applied. This is perhaps the most distinctive feature of what he refers to as Modern Industry. For Marx, then, the application of science to industry is the essential step to the rapid productivity growth of modern industrial societies, but it was uniquely capitalism that made that application possible. In fact, Marx's view is that modern science itself developed primarily in response to the problems that first expressed themselves historically in the sphere of production. Far from being some exogenous force, science arose out of the incentive structure and culture of capitalism.[1]

Thus, the Marxian view is that capitalism has served as a remarkable vehicle for the increase of human productivity because:

1. It provided powerful incentives to generate new technologies.
2. It generated high rates of investment that led to the rapid diffusion and exploitation of new technologies.
3. It generated incentives for the development of science as well as for the application of science to the problems of industry.

Of course it was also central to Marx's thinking that advanced capitalism would finally give way to socialism after it became caught up in its own internal contradictions, but also after it had brought about the vast increases in human productivity that it was, uniquely, qualified to bring about. It is perfectly obvious, from the present vantage point, that this was wrong. The fact of the matter is that socialism was never introduced into a country that had attained an advanced stage of capitalism—at least not without the assistance of the Soviet army. On the contrary, twentieth century socialist revolutions occurred only in societies that had not yet passed through the advanced stage of capitalism, with all of its attendant expansion of productive capacity.

---

[1] For an extended discussion of this point, see Rosenberg (1974). See also Schumpeter (1943).

One of the ironies of the twentieth century is that socialism was embraced not only as an anti-capitalist ideology; in addition, many socialists looked to Marx and his writings for guidance on how to organize a socialist society in order to generate rapid economic growth in poor countries. The irony, of course, is that Marx himself did not believe that this bypassing of the capitalist stage on the road to socialism was possible. Marx believed that a socialist revolution had to be preceded by a capitalist stage because only capitalism could bring about the improvements in productivity that would make it possible for socialist societies to be indifferent to *further* productivity growth. Socialist societies would not have to be concerned with raising productivity to high levels, because it was the historic mission of capitalism to accomplish precisely that. Marx was wrong in believing in the inevitability of that sequence. But at the same time, recent events in the socialist world suggest that Marx was at least right in believing that societies with socialist objectives could not so casually bypass the capitalist stage. As the recent joke in the Soviet Union goes: Question: 'What is communism?' Answer: 'The most painful of all possible roads from capitalism to capitalism.'

3. *Features of Technological Innovation*

Marx's account of the reasons why industrialization first occurred within a framework of capitalist institutions is incomplete, or at least incompletely specified. He is much more explicit about the importance of the special incentive mechanisms of capitalism—the large financial rewards—than he is about the specific forms that economic organizations have taken and why they have taken those particular forms. Capitalism's historic success in generating new technologies depended heavily upon its ability to fulfill certain other conditions. What were the additional features of capitalism that have rendered it such a powerful instrument for technological innovation? The general answer that has already been advanced is that capitalism has offered the freedom to engage in experiments of all sorts. But to see why that freedom has been so critical, it is first necessary to examine with greater care certain aspects of technological innovation.

The essential feature of technological innovation is that it is an activity that is fraught with many uncertainties. This uncertainty, by which we mean an inability to predict the outcome of the search process, or to predetermine the most efficient path to some particular goal, has a very important implication: the activity cannot be planned. No person, or group of persons, is clever enough to plan the outcome of the search process, in the sense of identifying a particular innovation target and moving in a predetermined way to its realization—as one might read a road map and plan the most efficient route to a historical monument.

If we wanted to push an analogy, we might say that achieving an attractive technological innovation is much more like a military engagement. Its execution cannot be completely planned in minute detail because the commanding officer does not know how the enemy will respond, or what the outcome to that initial response will be.

Without pushing the analogy too far (because, after all, a battle has a simple, unambiguous goal, whereas the search for a technological improvement typically has a number of possible tradeoffs) what innovation and military combat have in common is that decisions need to be made in a sequential way. That is to say, vital information will become available at some future point which cannot, in the nature of the case, be made available now. It would be folly to lock oneself into a predetermined pattern of behaviour, because this amounts to depriving oneself of the benefit of additional information, of a kind that may be decisive to success or failure, that can only become available in the future (Nelson, 1961).

It is inherent in the research process that information accumulates, even if it is only the information that certain alternatives are unproductive and should be discarded—i.e. dry wells. There is no way of knowing, in advance of the research (experiments), which alternatives are worth pursuing further and which are not. This is one reason why taking out a patent discloses valuable information to a firm's competitors, even though the award of the patent provides the owner with certain legal protections, and even though the contents of the patent document may not disclose sufficiently detailed information to permit imitation. The mere knowledge that something is possible (say, in pharmaceuticals), or that a particular procedure can achieve a particular end result, is likely to be extremely valuable. It is important evidence that research in certain specific directions, or employing certain specific methods, is likely to prove fruitful. The appropriate analogy here is to the information provided when someone has struck oil. A competitor may want to locate her drilling equipment as closely as possible to the successful well.

Thus it is in the nature of the research process that it is more likely to prove successful, and far more likely to proceed efficiently, if decision making is sequential in nature. However, it is also very important to realize that failed experiments often generate valuable information of a kind that is not exhausted by the analogy with the information produced by the drilling of a dry well. Those engaged in both search and research of an unsuccessful nature may accumulate a great deal of understanding along the way that may enhance their prospects for success in the future. The design of a new product does not proceed directly from scientific principles. Rather, product designers necessarily deal with multiple tradeoffs with respect to product characteristics, as well as tradeoffs between performance and cost. It is in the nature of the research process that it is more likely to be successful, and far more likely to proceed efficiently, if decision making is sequential in nature. It is also likely to be the case that experience with poorly designed products (or failed experiments) may contribute to the ability to produce superior designs in the future.

Moreover, quite independently of the improvement of skills, there is an additional tradeoff between time and cost. Proceeding more rapidly, and on a large scale, is costly. The reason is that, when one is allowed to proceed slowly and sequentially, one can keep numerous options alive. As new information becomes available from the ongoing research enterprise, and as uncertainties are reduced, options can be re-evaluated and more informed allocative decisions can be made. Unpromising avenues can be dropped. By committing larger amounts of money only at a later and better informed stage, research resources are utilized more efficiently.

The trouble with a War on Cancer, as with an SST, is that large amounts of money were committed to a particular project, or to a particular design, long before sufficient information was available to permit an intelligent evaluation of the research options. Where government funds are involved the problem is likely to be compounded by the failure to terminate a project, or a design, even after compelling evidence has accumulated that the thrust of R&D expenditures is in a direction that is unlikely to yield acceptable results. The post-war American experience is littered with such instances in nuclear energy, synthetic fuels, and the procurement of new military hardware of all sorts.[2] Although there may on occasion be a compelling case for rapid development, as in the Manhattan Project of World War II, the evidence is overwhelming that there is an inherent pathology of wastefulness in such an approach, as compared with a slower pace of development that permits frequent revision and redirection as new information becomes available.

There is an additional advantage to a system that encourages, or at least tolerates, multiple sources of decision making. Not only do human agents differ considerably in their attitudes toward risk; they differ also in their skills, capabilities, and orientations, however those differences may have been acquired. This heterogeneity of the human input, insufficiently stressed in microeconomics, constitutes a valuable resource that is much more readily enlisted into the realm of potentially useful experimentation by an organizationally

[2] Richard Nelson (1977) provides a valuable discussion of some of these issues.

decentralized environment. An economy that includes small firms and easy entry conditions is likely to benefit from this pool of human talent far more than one dominated by centralized decision making.

4. *Distinctive Features of Capitalism*

The relevance of this discussion for the historical efficiency of capitalist institutions in encouraging innovation is clear. Capitalism has provided multiple sources of decision making and initiative, strong incentives for proceeding one step at a time, and the possibility for drawing upon a wide range of human potential—all valuable features of activities that are carried out in an environment of high uncertainty. The notion that planning and centralization of decision making are likely to be more efficient appears to be the opposite of the truth when there is a high degree of uncertainty and when goals and objectives cannot be clearly defined *ex ante*.

One of the less-heralded but considerable virtues of competitive capitalism has been the speed with which firms have unsentimentally cut their losses as it became apparent that a particular direction of research was likely to prove unfruitful. Where funds come from the public sector, by contrast, monies are likely to be spent much longer on unpromising avenues. Inertia and the reluctance to admit failure publicly play important roles here, but so does the fact that the decision makers in government are not personally concerned over the financial losses involved.

The historical creativity of capitalism as an institutional mechanism for encouraging technological and organizational innovation has to be examined against this background of the centrality and pervasiveness of uncertainty. The uncertainties that are inherent in the search for new technologies have meant that the risks associated with this search could best be approached in certain specific ways. Capitalism historically has developed a cluster of novel organizational forms that have had the result of reducing certain intolerable risks to more tolerable levels. These were the risks that were unavoidably associated with the decision to commit financial resources to the search for technological improvements. These high levels of risk were inseparable from technological innovation because, as we have seen, the outcome of the search for new technologies was uncertain in the extreme. Moreover, even if one did succeed in developing a new technology that was a clear improvement over anything that already existed, the prospect of making any money out of it was still highly uncertain.

It is of particular interest to note that Marx himself recognized this uncertainty, although the recognition only made its public appearance in the third volume of *Das Capital*, published after his death and many years after the publication of the immensely influential first volume of that book. In the third volume Marx called attention to '. . . the far greater cost of operating an establishment based on a new invention as compared to later establishments arising *ex suis ossibus*. This is so very true that the trail-blazers generally go bankrupt, and only those who later buy the buildings, machinery, etc., at a cheaper price make money out of it.' (Marx, 1959). This is an extremely interesting passage, since it constitutes explicit recognition on Marx's part of the extreme vulnerability of the capitalist in his social role as a carrier of technological innovation. Had Marx given more attention to this vulnerability in Volume I of *Das Capital*, it would have been necessary to portray the capitalist in a distinctly different light. It would also have been necessary to face up more candidly to the painful tradeoffs that all societies must confront between greater equity and greater efficiency.[3] But such an examination would have highlighted the weakness of capitalists whereas Marx was intent on portraying their social power and their consequent capacity for exploiting others.

The history of capitalism involved the progressive introduction of a number of institutional devices that facilitated the commitment of resources to the innovation process by reducing or placing limitations upon risk while, at the same time, holding out the prospect of large financial rewards to the successful innovator. Among the most critical were new institutions, laws and legislation that (1) limited the liability of an investor in any particular enterprise, (2) provided for the easy marketability of ownership shares, (3) established stock markets which were essential to the achievement of ready marketability, (4) reduced risk by the fundamental technique of insurance, and (5) defined the obligations between principals and their agents.[4]

The emergence of business firms with limited liability for their owners, and ownership shares that were easily marketable, was central from the point of view of facilitating investment in risky undertakings. From the point of view of the individual investor, a limited liability corporation made it possible to convert a long-term risk involving large amounts of capital into a short-term risk that was limited to small amounts of capital Marketability of assets and the existence of efficient markets for the sale of these assets meant that owners were not undertaking commitments equal in duration to the life of long-lived capital assets. On the contrary, they could realize their financial gains or cut their financial losses whenever doing so appeared to be expedient. In this way a capitalist proprietor's long-term risk was converted into an investor's

---

[3] Insofar as Marx may be said to have dealt with the tradeoff between equity and efficiency, he did so by 'assigning' to capitalism the historical role of providing efficiency and to a later socialism the role of delivering equity.

[4] These matters are discussed in detail in Rosenberg and Birdzell, Jr (1986) especially Chapters 4–8.

short-term risk. At the same time, the ownership of the firm's assets was effectively divided into two levels: first, those of the corporation as an ongoing entity; and secondly, those of the shareholders who supplied the firm with its capital. The first-level risks remained as great as they always had been, but the second-level risks were of a different order and were much more readily acceptable. This division of risk obviously bears a close analogy to the redistribution of risk that takes place between a property owner and his insurance company.

Looking back on Marx, it is apparent that, although he had a profound appreciation for the technological dynamism of capitalism, he did not appreciate the extent to which this was due to such institutional measures that reduced risk and, by reducing risk, encouraged the experimentation that made innovation so commonplace under capitalism.[5] There has obviously been a close connection between reducing risk and encouraging experimentation. The willingness to undertake experiments in both the social and technological spheres depends upon some sort of limitation upon the negative consequences for the individual if the risky enterprise should fail, as it frequently did. The great technological dynamism of capitalism has been inseparable from the system's success in reducing risk to more tolerable levels while, at the same time, offering the prospect of huge financial rewards if the risky enterprise should succeed.

These technological achievements were thus based upon capitalist legal institutions, especially with respect to contracts and property rights, that legitimized the right to experiment with new organizational forms as well as with new technologies. The final arbiter of whether something new was socially desirable was not a government authority, or the religious clergy, or the guild members or the merchants whose personal interests might be adversely affected by some innovation. Rather, the final arbiter was the market place. Capitalism did legitimize innovation, but only if it could pass the market test. It was indeed, as Marx recognized, the first form of social organization in which economic life was dominated by groups whose economic interests caused them to threaten the status quo.

5. *Autonomony of the Economic Sphere*

The freedom to conduct experiments, in turn, required that yet other conditions be fulfilled. One of these conditions was that the economic sphere had to attain a higher degree of autonomy from external forces, especially freedom from arbitrary and unpredictable interventions by government authorities.

---

[5] Of course, it is also true that some of the risk-reducing innovations achieved their full development after Marx's main writings had been completed.

A critical aspect of this increasing autonomy was that new political institutions emerged that reduced the risk of arbitrary exactions and appropriations (or even expropriations) by a powerful ruler. The rise in western Europe of parliaments in control of government financial purse strings was an essential part of this story. So was the emergence of new legal concepts, precedents, and institutions for the enforcement of contracts and property rights generally. In this respect, the bourgeois political revolutions of the seventeenth and eighteenth centuries were central to the economic achievements of capitalism.

The swiftness and the extent to which business organizations were rendered free of government control in the early years of capitalism should not be exaggerated. Government approval, in the form of a charter or franchise, long remained the normal practice, at least for specific forms of organization—e.g. with limited liability—or for companies that wished to trade in certain regions—Hudson's Bay Company, East India Company, Muscovy Company, etc.—or for organizations providing certain particular kinds of services—such as canal building, road building, etc.[6] It was only in the course of the nineteenth century that business firms attained a reasonable degree of freedom in selecting new activities or new product lines. Nevertheless, the trend in western Europe and North America in the eighteenth and nineteenth centuries was in the direction of an expansion of the freedom of action of the enterprise.

The freedom to conduct experiments required not only a high degree of autonomy; it also required, as already discussed, a large number of decision makers, as opposed to a high degree of centralization and/or hierarchy. In effect this meant not only decentralization but also the inability of the experimenters to influence the outcome of the market evaluation of the new product. In fact, some of the most decisive failures of twentieth century socialism flow from the failure to allow experimentation, and from the consequent failure to benefit from the opportunity to observe the *outcome* of such experiments.

The need to expose investment decisions to the risk of being proven wrong implies the decentralization of decision making authority, since any central authority will have a strong motivation for withholding financial support from those who are bent on proving that the central authority made a mistake, or on imposing on the central authority the cost of scrapping splendid-looking facilities whose only fault is that some interloper has devised more productive facilities or discovered that the work done in the facilities can be accomplished more cheaply in some other country—or perhaps need not be done at all. The social costs and risks associated with such moves might be

---

[6] Of the regulated companies, which controlled so much of foreign trade even in the late eighteenth century, Adam Smith made the sardonic observation: 'To be merely useless, indeed, is perhaps the highest eulogy which can ever justly be bestowed upon a regulated company.' Smith (1937), p. 693.

well worth financing, but the costs and risks *to centralized decision makers* might well be prohibitive.

Historically, one of the most distinctive features of capitalist economies has been the practice of decentralizing authority over investments to substantial numbers of individuals who stand to make large personal gains if their decisions are right, who stand to lose heavily if their decisions are wrong, and *who lack the economic or political power to prevent at least some others from proving them wrong.* Indeed, this particular cluster of features constitutes an excellent candidate for *the* definition of capitalism. Its importance for western economic growth turns on the point that the choice of capital investments includes the selection of the proposals for innovation that are to be funded. The diffusion of authority to select programs for capital expenditure and the diffusion of authority to select projects for innovation thus cover much the same ground.[7]

6. *Organizational Diversity of Capitalism*

The historical outcome of this long-term freedom to conduct experiments which, as I have argued, has been the central feature of western capitalism, has been an economy characterized by a truly extraordinary pattern of organizational diversity. This diversity may usefully be thought of as the end result of a process of social evolution in which a wide range of organizational forms have been introduced, and in which firms have been allowed to grow to sizes that were influenced by underlying conditions of technology, location, market size, range of products, etc. The particular outcomes achieved with respect to firm size, pattern of ownership, product mix, etc., have been essentially determined by a market process in which the underlying conditions of different industries have generated patterns of survival reflecting their own special circumstances, not some *a priori* notion of a single best model to which they were expected to adhere.

It is very common to stress the importance, indeed the dominance, of large firms in western capitalist economies. This perspective has been particularly common among Marxists (although of course not confined to them) who have seen the trend toward bigness and greater industrial concentration as part of the 'inner logic' of capitalism. According to the Marxist version, the emergence of monopoly capitalism not only reflects the pervasive advantages of bigness; it also conveniently facilitates the transition to socialism through the mechanism of nationalization of giant firms. Unfortunately, the commitment to this view has absolved several generations of critics of the much more

---

[7] The last two paragraphs are drawn, with only slight modification, from Rosemberg and Birdzell, Jr (1986) pp. 234–35.

serious task of examining, and accounting for, the remarkable institutional complexity of contemporary capitalist societies. Had they done so, it would have been apparent that, for example, although large firms are the predominant employers of labor, organizational structures not only differ immensely among the agricultural, manufacturing, public utilities and services sectors, but immense differences also exist *within* each of these sectors. Giant corporations do indeed play a most important role, but so do millions of self-employed individuals. Any perspective that sees only giant corporations misses a most impressive feature of western economies: the great subtlety with which organizational modes have been adapted to, and modified by, the particularities of products and markets. Thus, even in those manufacturing industries that contain the largest firms, as measured by assets, size and sales—petroleum, automobiles, aircraft, chemicals, computers, photographic equipment—dozens, or even hundreds, of smaller firms also persist.

7. *Problems of 20th Century Socialism*

The discussion of organizational diversity as the outcome of a process of prolonged experimentation forms an appropriate bridge on which to cross over to a consideration of some of the economic problems of twentieth century socialism. The failure of these societies to permit experimentation was compounded by an undiscriminating ideological commitment to the economic advantages of bigness—a commitment that had its origins in the writings of Marx. The reluctance to allow organizational size and structure to be tailored to the specific needs of different economic activities was combined with an incentive system that is pervasively hostile to risk-taking. This combination goes a long way toward explaining one of the most fundamental, and perhaps surprising, difficulties of socialist societies: their failure to take full advantage of superior technologies.

It is, on first consideration, not so obvious why hostility toward experimentation and risk-taking should have created such serious obstacles toward the exploitation of better technologies. After all, in a world where technologically advanced capitalist economies already exist, a socialist economy has the invaluable option of acquiring such technologies from abroad. There are no compelling reasons why foreign capitalist economies cannot serve as sources for the more sophisticated technologies that socialist economies are unable to develop internally.

Of course, to a considerable extent, that is precisely what happened. The Soviet Union, beginning in the 1920s, has been, and continues to be, a large-scale importer of western technologies. Her inability to generate the incentives, or to provide the social space and opportunity for experimentation, was at least partially offset by the ability to import technologies developed by the technologically dynamic capitalist west. Thus, although Marx was wrong in arguing that socialism would arrive only in societies that had already passed through the state of mature capitalism, one might argue that this did not carry so severe a penalty as one might expect because advanced capitalism in the west has made its technologies universally available. This is, indeed, an important truth, and it should be further acknowledged, that *all* industrializing countries have managed to grow more rapidly by borrowing foreign technologies. This was, as is widely acknowledged, true of Japan in the twentieth century, but it was also a central element of America's rapid industrialization in the nineteenth century, an industrialization that built upon the already-existing technologies of metallurgy, power generation, railroads and textiles in Great Britain.

But even though twentieth century socialist societies did not have to develop their own technologies, the mode of organization of their economies imposed rather sharp limits to the economic benefits they could derive from the availability of foreign technologies. First of all, technology transfer is not simply a matter of shipping hardware from one location on the earth's surface to another. Rather, such borrowing presupposes a sizeable cadre of engineers, technicians and managers to modify, adapt, maintain and repair such technology. This implies a competent infrastructure of skills, organization and facilities. Unless these very considerable preconditions are reasonably fulfilled, the prospects for successful exploitation of foreign technologies are poor.

But there are other systemic considerations at issue here. Central planning, and the negligible freedom of action accorded to plant managers under the Soviet system, have been deeply hostile to the introduction of new technologies. New technologies are, by their nature, disruptive of established routines. Although they hold out the considerable promise of long-term improvements in productivity, they also exact a high short-term cost in terms of installation of new equipment, teaching of different skills, establishment of new work routines, working out of inevitable bugs with respect to product design and process technologies, developing new arrangements with suppliers of doubtful reliability, etc. However, the entire central planning apparatus has been geared to short-term goals. The success of a plant manager has been based relentlessly upon his ability to fulfill the annual output quota given to his firm by the central planners. Although there have been innumerable attempts to introduce greater flexibility into this system, those attempts have consistently failed. The system inflicted severe penalties upon the manager who failed to fulfill his annual output goal while, at the same time, the managerial reward for fulfillment or overfulfillment has been small—such as a modest, once-and-for-all bonus. Thus, risk aversion with respect to new technology has been endemic to the structure of incentives. The system not only lacked the capitalist incentive of large financial rewards, which Marx understood well; it also lacked the threat of competition, and the large risks of *failing* to innovate in an environment containing competitors who were likely to do so.

Indeed, the situation was typically even worse than this. Since the setting of annual targets was based upon the estimate made by the central planners of a plant's productive capabilities, it has been distinctly dangerous to the plant manager to reveal a capability considerably in excess of the most recent annual target. The plant manager has had a strong incentive to under-represent his capabilities in order to keep his future targets low and therefore easily attainable.

This managerial risk aversion and dissimulation was, of course, powerfully reinforced by a huge and well-entrenched Soviet bureaucracy. Drastic reforms in the direction of greater managerial discretion and autonomy would threaten both the power and the perquisites of that bureaucracy. Decentralization would carry with it a devolution of power to the regions and to the plant managers. For these reasons, a greater reliance upon the associated apparatus of markets and market-determined prices remained anathema to planners and bureaucrats.

In addition, the systematic neglect of the consumer or, at best, the attachment of a low priority to consumer needs, weakened even further the incentive at the plant level to introduce improved products.[8] It is notorious that, within the perpetual seller's market that the Soviet system created, selling the product was never a problem. As a result, the effort involved in improving a product, or the disruption involved in changing the productive apparatus in order to introduce an entirely new product that would be more attractive or useful to consumers, offered a zero payoff to the plant manager. His continual preoccupation has always been, not with the marketing of his product, but with the unreliability of his suppliers in providing him with the inputs essential to annual goal fulfillment.[9] Here again the system provided no incentive to innovation.

> The problem is the lack of institutions and organizations which despite all obstacles can effect the introduction of revolutionary new technical innovations, accepting all the risk concomitant with this work, including that of failure, the

---

[8] It has been a deliberate policy in the Soviet Union in the past to limit the number of models of a given product and the frequency of model changes. For a discussion of the impact of this policy, see Berliner (1976), pp. 195–98.

[9] One important by-product of supplier unreliability is an incentive to vertical integration in order to achieve greater control over the supply of inputs and thereby to reduce dependence upon others. This translates, of course, into another incentive to increase the size of the firm.

struggle against conservatism and deep-rooted habit. Why should an enterprise director accept this risk and take up a struggle when . . . he is able without such effort to sell the products of his firm easily? With the buyers lining up for the firm's old product, why take upon oneself all the trouble involved in the introduction of a new product? (Kornai, 1971)

The failure of socialist societies to learn from the conduct of experiments has been most conspicuous, of course, with respect to the uncritical acceptance of the desirability of large size, or what is sometimes referred to as 'giantism' in Soviet central planning. Giantism may be defined as an uncritical commitment to a belief in the existence of indefinitely continuing economies of large-scale production.[10] Its intellectual antecedents undoubtedly lie in Marx's admiration for the large-scale technologies of the British industrial revolution and his forceful articulation of the view that, in the competitive process, the larger-scale capitalist always beats out the smaller one. In Marx's words: 'The battle of competition is fought by cheapening of commodities. The cheapness of commodities depends, *caeteris paribus*, on the productiveness of labour, and this again on the scale of production. Therefore, the large capitals beat the smaller.'

Marx was certainly one of the first economists (together with John Stuart Mill) to call attention to the economic significance of large-scale production. He appreciated the importance of indivisibilities and pointed to numerous cases (especially in the capital goods sector) where economic advantages were derived from doing certain things on what he called a 'cyclopean scale'. Marx also pointed to the possibilities in certain industries, when the scale of production was sufficiently large, of utilizing wastes, or by-product materials.[11]

As a very careful and perceptive observer of the industrial scene, it is far from clear that Marx would have advocated indiscriminate giantism as that goal was to be pursued in the Soviet Union. There is evidence, moreover, that the thrust toward giantism was fed, during the Stalinist years, by a determination to emulate certain of the largest American establishments that were

---

[10] See Smolinski (1962). Smolinski asserts that giantism began with the first of the Five Year Plans in 1928. Giantism '. . . started in 1929 when the original draft of the First Five Year Plan was scrapped as being too conservative, and both the output goals and the size of the new projects, from which the bulk of the additional output was to come, underwent a series of drastic upward revisions. The sky was soon the limit. Coal mines of 10 million tons annual capacity were being designed (some 4 times larger than the world's largest mine and some 150 times larger than an average Soviet mine then in operation), the world's largest cement works of 930,000 tons, steam condensing power stations of 1 million kw., etc. At the same time, hundreds of smaller projects included in the original draft were being dropped, even when they were complementary to the "giants" themselves. Giantism reached its peak around 1932, was condemned in 1938, and revived, in a modified form, in 1950.' (pp. 139–40).

[11] 'The general requirements for the reemployment of these "excretions" are: large quantities of such waste, such as are available only in large-scale production, improved machinery whereby materials, formerly useless in their prevailing form, are put into a state fit for new production; scientific progress, particularly chemistry, which reveals the useful properties of such waste.' Karl Marx (1959), p. 100.

believed to be highly efficient—e.g. in the steel industry.[12] (It is tempting to say that, in their determined pursuit of the economies of large-scale production, the Soviet Union has provided the world with much additional evidence on the diseconomies of large-scale production.) Finally, as a matter of administrative convenience, central planners undoubtedly found it much simpler to deal with a small number of large plants rather than a large number of small ones. Bigness clearly served the interests of the central bureaucracy. This was most apparent in the disastrous experience in agriculture, the sector where bigness was least appropriate. However inefficient the large collective farm may have been in terms of the productivity of agricultural inputs, it served as a powerful organizational device for *collecting* an agricultural surplus that could then be made to serve the interest of rapid industrialization.[13]

An ironic historical outcome is that, whereas Marx predicted that bigness would emerge out of the competitive process under mature capitalism, the size distribution of industrial firms shows a far greater concentration of employment in large firms in the Soviet Union than in the US or Japan. Data for the 1960s indicate that 24% of Soviet enterprises had more than 500 employees. The corresponding figure for the US was only 1.4% and for Japan a mere 0.3%. At the other extreme, only 15% of Soviet enterprises had fewer than 50 employees, whereas 85% of American firms and 95% of Japanese firms had fewer than 50 workers.[14] Obviously, the larger size of Soviet firms has been imposed by deliberate government policy and was not the outcome of historical experience of an earlier, mature capitalism or socialist experimentation.

[12] Smolinski (1962), p. 141. For an account of some of the early Soviet difficulties in the establishment of large-scale industrial complexes, see Hughes (1989), chapter 6. Hughes documents the important role of American ideas, as well as the direct participation of American industrialists and engineers, in the early years of Soviet industrialization.

[13] China's dramatic improvement in food production after 1979 provides strong evidence of the earlier costs of collectivized agriculture.

[14] Berliner (1976), pp. 33–34. Some more recent World Bank data show a much greater concentration of industrial enterprises at the high end of the spectrum, with respect to number of employees, in Yugoslavia and Hungary as compared to south Korea and Japan. Mainland China occupies an intermediate position, reflecting the large number of small rural enterprises.

Size distribution of industrial enterprise (%)				
	China (1982)	S. Korea (1981)	Japan (1972)	Yugoslavia (1981)	Hungary (1981)
5–33 employees	59.2	70.6	80.2	6.6	2.2
33–75 employees	19.5	14.4	10.7	15.8	4.8
75–189 employees	12.2	9.2	6.1	32.1	18.7
189–243 employees	8.5	1.5	0.8	12.0	9.2
More than 243 employess	0.6	4.3	2.2	33.5	65.1

Source: World Bank, as reported in *The Economist*, August 1, 1987, China's Economy Survey, p. 10.

The purpose of experimentation, of course, is to provide useful information for answering certain kinds of questions. But Marxism, in at least some of its most influential twentieth century forms, has been unwilling to admit that the answers to some questions were subject to doubt. This has often taken the form of simply asserting the priority of ideological purity over technical expertise. In China, both the Great Leap Forward and the later, disastrous Cultural Revolution involved a denial of the role of technical expertise in the attainment of an efficient industrial society. Chairman Mao further claimed that a new socialist man would pursue economic efficiency and embrace an ideal of hard work merely out of a sense of commitment to socialism, and without any strong material rewards. His followers made important technical and economic decisions with no reference to technical specialists. The only litmus test for occupying important managerial and technical positions was an ideological one. It is fair to say that these episodes set back the industrialization of China by at least a generation.

(Curiously, the Great Leap Forward may be said to have involved experimentation of a very perverse sort: The attempt to set up backyard blast furnaces and chemical plants involved a 'test' of the non-existence of economies of large-scale production in precisely those sectors of the economy where they are of critical importance!)

The socialist preoccupation with bigness in industry has been hostile to technological innovation in another very fundamental way. Some of the disadvantages of bigness are minimal in an environment characterized by a high degree of stability and routine. But where the technology is changing rapidly or might be *made* to change more rapidly, bigness is much more likely to be a serious handicap. Many experiments are easier and less costly to conduct on a small scale. It is inherently difficult to experiment and to introduce numerous small changes, and to do so frequently, in a large hierarchical organizational structure where permissions and approvals are required from a remote central authority.

The history of industries that have recently been undergoing rapid technological change—such as electronics and biotechnology—suggests that the flexibility offered by small firms may be highly advantageous to experimentation and exploration, especially in the early stages of the development of a new technology. Large firms, operating through layers of management with rigid rules, are not well-suited for environments undergoing rapid changes and requiring frequent, on-the-spot decisions. Where technological uncertainties are high, it is often far more efficient to be able to conduct experiments in small firms on a small scale.[15]

[15] Of course, firms of different sizes are likely to differ with respect to the *kinds* of innovative activity in which they are most competent to engage. Given the varying requirements of different classes of

However, as Alfred Chandler has so extensively documented, as new technologies have gradually matured and entered commercialization on a national and eventually global scale, large firms have come to play a far more prominent role (Chandler, 1990). But what it is essential to realize is that the large western firms, which perform most of the R&D activity, bear little resemblance to large firms in socialist economies, although some parallels in the decision making process of large hierarchical organizations, with elaborate rules, are easy to find. In the Soviet economy the largest firms have commonly been single function plants or retailing organizations. Planning and coordination of the flow of goods have been the responsibility of government agencies such as Gosplan and Gosnab. By contrast, in western capitalist economies over the past century the large firm has been responsible for integrating production with distribution and has coordinated the flow of goods to the market. Equally important, the firm's current financial performance and future earnings expectations have powerfully influenced the commitment of resources to new product and new process development. Retained profits have played a major role in the financing of investment for expanding the firm's future capacity to produce new products and to deliver them to the appropriate markets. Large firms in socialist economies conspicuously lack these essential functions.

The Soviet thrust toward larger scale and centralization has even pervaded the organization of R&D activities within each of the ministries that has had planning responsibilities for major sectors of the economy. Among other consequences, this has resulted in the isolation of R&D from managerial decisions relating to production planning, and has thus intensified the difficulties, discussed earlier, of introducing new technologies.[16] It has also further isolated the findings of Soviet science from possible industrial applications. This is a consideration of great significance. Improving the links among the

---

innovation, it would be natural to expect patterns of specialization based upon size. Moreover, many innovations actually carried out by large firms, such as du Pont, have been based upon inventions originally made in small firms. For a suggestive analysis of the role of firm size in innovation, see Arrow (1983). Arrow's conclusion is '. . . that there is likely to be a tendency toward specialization—less costly and more original innovations will come from small firms, and those involving higher development costs but less radical departures in principle will come from larger firms.' (p. 16).

[16] Within each ministry, there is a separation between R&D and production. 'The decision was taken early in the development of Soviet economic institutions to pursue the presumed advantages of scale and specialization, and to concentrate R&D within branch institutions rather than to have individual R&D departments at each enterprise. This separation of R&D units from production units extends to the separate subordination of each to different channels of planning, finance, and supply. This has proved a considerable barrier to the transfer of new technology from the laboratory to production. Similar Western experience clearly demonstrates how important it is to maintain a close linkage between the management of production and that of R&D, to coordinate the two activities, and to ensure that the new technology is compatible with the technical production procedures and organizational characteristics and needs of the adopting enterprise.' Levine (1983).

separate components of the R&D process is crucial to success in innovation in all industrial economies (see Aoki and Rosenberg, 1989). In the case of the Soviet Union the costs of poor linkages have undoubtedly been very great, since much Soviet research at the basic end of the R&D spectrum is at the highest international standards.

This last point is in fact of more general significance than the specific context in which it has been raised. Institutional innovation can foster technical change, not just by the risk reduction that has received primary emphasis in this paper, but also by fostering improved communication among specialists with the needed knowledge. Such reductions in the cost of technological change in market economies have been achieved in various ways. The emergence of capital good sectors has, in some instances, brought about a concentration of technological communication that has proven to be highly efficient; and a great strength of many integrated firms has been their ability to integrate the R&D function with marketing as well as manufacturing and other functions. Thus, in technologically sophisticated economies, success in the innovation process is likely to depend strongly upon improved communication among a number of specialized agents, especially agents in different organizations. Carrying through an innovation may depend upon effective relations with a variety of organizations, such as universities and input suppliers, and especially upon feedbacks from marketing specialists. Put somewhat differently, the existence of incentives to facilitate the learning process underlying innovation can be found in only a highly attenuated form in socialist societies. The upstream diffusion of incentives that originate in perceived possibilities for larger profits in the market place has been a powerful source of incentives to improve communication and to reduce its costs in capitalist economies. This incentive has essentially been aborted in centralized socialist economies.

8. *Conclusion*

The purpose of this paper has been to assert the strategic role played by the freedom to experiment in the long-term process of economic growth and industrialization. It has been argued that a peculiar strength of capitalism, historically, has been the manner in which it has accommodated the special needs of the innovation process. It has also been argued that the failure to provide for such accommodation, in terms of organization and incentives, has been responsible for the persistent failure of socialism to generate new technologies or even to adopt technologies that already exist. It should be obvious that this discussion does not exhaust all the significant things that one might say about capitalism and socialism as alternative ways of organizing economic activity. However, it should also be obvious, as recent developments in eastern Europe and China have emphasized, that it is extremely difficult to make socialist societies more amenable to technological change without, at the same time, making them more capitalistic.

References

Aoki, M. and N. Rosenberg (1989), 'The Japanese Firm as an Innovating Institution'. In T. Shiraishi and S. Tsuru (eds), *Economic Institutions in a Dynamic Society*, Macmillan and the International Economic Association: London.

Arrow, K. (1983), 'Innovation in Large and Small Firms'. In J. Ronen (ed.), *Entrepreneurship*, D. C. Heath and Co.: Lexington, MA, chapter 1.

Berliner, J. (1976), *The Innovation Decision in Soviet Industry*. MIT Press: Cambridge, MA.

Chandler, A. D., Jr (1990), *Scale and Scope. The Dynamics of Industrial Capitalism*. The Belknap Press of Harvard University: Cambridge, MA.

Engels, F. (1910), *Socialism: Utopian and Scientific*, pp. 12–13.

Hughes, T. P. (1989), *American Genesis*. Viking Penguin: New York.

Kornai, J. (1971), *Anti-Equilibrium*, North Holland Press: Amsterdam, pp. 288–89.

Levine, H. (1983), 'On the Nature and Location of Entrepreneurial Activity in Centrally Planned Economies. The Soviet Case'. In J. Ronen (ed.), *Entrepreneurship*, D. C. Heath and Company: Lexington, MA, pp. 249–50.

Marx, K., *Das Capital*, The Modern Library Edition.

Marx, K. (1959), *Das Capital*, Volume III, Foreign Languages Publishing House: Moscow.

Marx, K. and F. Engels (1848), *The Communist Manifesto*. As reprinted in K. Marx and F. Engels, *Selected Works*, 2 vols. Foreign Languages Publishing House: Mascow (1951, vol. I).

Nelson, R. (1961), 'Uncertainty, Learning and the Economics of Parallel Research and Development Efforts'. *Review of Economics and Statistics*, 43, 351–64.

Nelson, R. (1977), *The Moon and the Ghetto*, W. W. Norton and Co.: New York.

Rosenberg, N. (1974), 'Karl Marx on the Economic Role of Science'. *Journal of Political Economy*, July–August. Reprinted in N. Rosenberg (1976) *Perspectives on Technology*, Cambridge University Press: New York.

Rosenberg, N. and L. E. Birdzell, Jr (1986), *How the West Grew Rich*, Basic Books: New York.

Smith, A. (1937), *Wealth of Nations*, Modern Library Edition.

Smolinski, L. (1962), 'The Scale of the Soviet Industrial Establishment', *American Economic Review Papers and Proceedings*, 52, 138–48.

Schumpeter, J. A. (1943), 'The Civilization of Capitalism'. *In Capitalism, Socialism and Democracy*, Allen and Unwin: London, chapter XI.

Heroes, Herds and Hysteresis in Technological History: Thomas Edison and 'The Battle of the Systems' Reconsidered

PAUL A. DAVID

(Department of Economics, Stanford University, Stanford, CA 94305, USA)

The history of this development is worth following—as an example of scientific and technological co-operation, of multiple invention, of progress by an infinitude of small improvements, of creative entrepreneurship, of derived demand and unanticipated consequences.
David S. Landes (1969, p. 284) on electric power.

A master's advice always is compelling. The story to be told here will be about the early period in the development of electric lighting and power supply networks. Since this tale is one whose broad outlines probably are familiar to many readers from previous and more skillful recountings,[1] I must have a special reason to return to it here. My motivation lies in the bearing which some less known details of the rivalry between direct current and alternating current systems of electricity supply will be seen to have upon a far broader, and more complex matter. That subject concerns the precise place to be accorded individual economic actions in the evolution of modern technological systems.

What causal role properly can be assigned to particular decision-makers in the build-up of those complex production systems that form the material

---

[1] Landes (1969), pp. 281–90, gives a concise and pithy account of the main electrical developments in Britain, France and Germany up to 1913, drawing largely on Jarvis (1967a, 1967b) for technical details. Among works appearing subsequently that deal primarily with the British and American parts of the story, in chronological order, see Hennessey (1971), Passer (1972), Byatt (1979), Hannah (1979), Bowers (1982), and Hughes (1983). The latter work by Thomas Hughes, also treats the experience of Germany.

infrastructure of modern societies? When do specific actions, taken purposively and implemented by identifiable agents (say, entrepreneurs) have the power significantly to alter the course of technological history? Ever? Or should we hold that the economic analyst of technical change, being occupied for the most part with the progress of armies which have few generals and need none, will find only misleading metaphors in the heroic deeds chronicled by traditional political and military historians?[2] Rather than being 'made' by anyone at any particular point in time, does not technology simply 'accumulate' from the incremental, almost imperceptible changes wrought by the jostling interactions among the herd of small decision-makers—the crowd of myriad dreamers and scientists, tinkerers and engineers, inventors and innovators, tycoons and managers, artisans and operatives, all of whose separate motions somehow have been coordinated and channelled by markets under the system of capitalism? Should we then not insist that the nature of technical progress is best conveyed by conceptualizing it as a continuous flow? Shall we therefore foreswear the reading and writing of narratives which would dwell on a succession of unique actions and discrete, historical 'events'? Inasmuch as recognition of such actions, and events, is required if we are to speak in a meaningful way about the occurrence of 'changes' in technological practice and economic organization, does it not appear that there is a high intellectual cost entailed in adopting a mode of discourse that suppresses them? These questions are daunting, indeed, and no definitive answers to them can be expected to come from this quarter. But, surely, they cannot be inappropriate ones to consider, especially now that 'innovation', 'entrepreneurship' and, indeed, 'intrapreneurship' are words on the lips of those in business and politics who concern themselves with preserving 'competitiveness' by fostering technological dynamism.

1. *Views of Technological Change—Herds or Heroes? Continuities or Events?*

From the way that my larger agenda of concerns has been phrased, one might surmise that I am preparing to plunge into the thick of the recurring debate over Schumpeter's representation of entrepreneurs as individuals who form a distinct sociological category—those heroic few to whom in each era is assigned the function of innovation, and without whom the capitalist

---

[2] On the argument's other side, Jonathan Hughes (1986, p. 3) writes: '. . . in too many accounts the economy lies silently in the background growing miraculously to support and nourish the actions of the gods and heroes the professional historians so love to study in war and politics. But just as men must be mobilized and led in war, voters organized and persuaded in politics, so economic resources must be mobilized and directed intelligently for economic growth to occur.'

economic system soon would settle down to a dismal stationary state.[3] But, I confess, I am too wary for that; I do not mean to focus squarely on the vexed question: what is it that entrepreneurs and 'bosses' do, really do, or may have done in the past?[4] Instead, I want to take up a different problem which, being more general, is logically antecedent to that subject of ongoing controversy among economic historians. When, if at all, in the development of society's technological knowledge and apparatus, could the actions of some individual participants in a market process be expected actually to exert a perceptible influence over the eventual outcome—in effect, determining the characteristics of the particular trajectory of diffusion and development along which some branch of technology becomes channeled?[5] For this, one must admit, there is no need that the vital actors be cast as visionary heroes, or essential contributors to enhancing economic efficiency. Scoundrels and fools, or merely men with weak stomachs for the perils of entrepreneurial voyages, might serve just as well in teaching us when it is that big consequences are most likely to flow from historical events petty enough to be the work of ordinary mortals.

Oddly enough, it would be quite uncongenial for many who now are studying technological and economic history to be asked to concentrate attention on the detailed actions of specific individuals, and so to emphasize the role those persons had in producing changes that were consequent upon 'events'.[6] At least two causes can be found for this state of affairs. For the first, there is the dominant historiographic tradition in regard to the progress of technology. As elsewhere in the writing of social science history, this tradition perpetuates

---

[3] See Clemence and Doody (1950), for a useful account of the Schumpeterian system, and the recent, sympathetic overview by Stolper (1981). Streissler (1981), pp. 65–7, makes the interesting observation that to have emphasized the creative role of the entrepreneur was no revolutionary intellectual departure on Schumpeter's part, nor even on the part of his main teacher, Friedrich von Wieser. Rather, what was novel and somewhat shocking to Schumpeter's contemporaries was the stress he placed on the destruction and disorder that entrepreneurs caused by their innovations. The potential for competing network technologies completely to displace one another in actual use, and the associated properties of randomness and unpredictability that adhere to such competitions, make the novel aspect of Schumpeter's untidy vision of economic development particularly congenial to the major themes of this essay.

[4] The long-standing controversy among economic historians over the nature and essentiality of the entrepreneur's role has most recently been renewed and refreshed by Landes's (1986) critique of Marglin (1974), and Temin's (1987) effort to distinguish questions about the genesis and advantages of large-scale, hierarchically structured production activities, from other historical questions concerning the control and management of hierarchical organizations, including those addressed by Clark (1984).

[5] David and Olsen (1986) provide a formal model of the generation of a 'diffusion-cum-development trajectory', along which the adoption and incremental improvement of a capital-embodied technology are intertwined. That analysis, however, leaves aside the mathematically more difficult stochastic aspects of the actual matter, which are the focus of interest here.

[6] I concede that I would have numbered myself among them, at least until 1975. Jonathan Hughes complained of this state of affairs among professional economists in his introduction to the 1965 edition of *The Vital Few*, and has reiterated it recently, while noticing the recent rejuvenation of interest in the subject of entrepreneurship among business and political circles. See Hughes (1986), pp. ix, 2.

Darwin's approach to the study of evolution. Its followers cling rather perversely to an essentially ahistorical concept of the modus operandi of change: natura non facit saltum. Changes, on this view, are produced by slow, continuous adaptations in an 'eventless' world.[7] It is, of course, a strong tradition that can draw upon Karl Marx, A. P. Usher, and C. S. Gilfillan for elaborations of the view of technical progress as a social process, consisting of the steady accretion of innumerable minor improvements and modifications.[8] It therefore supports the conceptualization of 'technology' as a powerful flux, a broad and mighty river reshaping the economic and social landscape and, in the process, sweeping puny individual actors—inventors, businessmen, workers, customers, politicians—along in its currents. Thus, although the dominant tradition in the historiography of modern technological change has firmly embraced the Schumpeterian vision of a distinctly capitalist process of development situated in historical time, its adherents paradoxically still resist Schumpeter's emphasis upon the discontinuous nature of technological progress—the driving force he saw at work within that process.

For a second cause we can turn closer to home. In the era of 'Cliometrics', especially, economic theory has not been without an influence upon the way that technological history has come to be studied.[9] Mainstream economics since 'the Marginalist Revolution', and certainly since Alfred Marshall, has subscribed to the characterization of change as being so incremental as to constitute an 'eventless' continuum. Moreover, although modern micro-economists show no hesitancy in producing formal theories of human action, they appear to be most comfortable with the assumption that actual individuals (in the past and present) somehow or other manage to cancel each other out, so that changes emerge from the ensemble of their behaviors—that is, from the action of the anonymous masses. As a consequence of the neoclassical economists' efforts to expose the workings of mechanisms that would cause invention and innovation

[7] This concept of change, as timeless and constant, of course, holds a strong grip on other areas of the natural sciences, and the social sciences that have made them their model—from whence, ironically, it has come to conflict with the narrative tradition in the writing of history. See the perceptive and too little noticed work of Teggart (1925), especially chapters 7–12, recent use of which has been made by Eldredge (1985), chapter 1 and pp. 141–46. In this respect it may be seen that the pioneering work of Nelson and Winter (1982) on 'evolutionary models' of economic change has been well-designed to influence economists at ease with the eventless Darwinian conception of continuous modification through (competitive) natural selection. The incorporation of the Markov property in Nelson and Winter's models has served the same purpose, as has been noted elsewhere, e.g. David (1975), p. 76.

[8] Gilfillan (1935b) explicitly stressed the Darwinian evolutionary analogy in placing 'the continuity of development' first among his 38 'social principles of invention,' and, in (1935a), documented it in extenso by references to the merchant ship. For Marx's views of technology, see Rosenberg (1976), who calls attention to their fruition in the emphasis Usher (1929) accorded to social processes in 'setting the stage' for invention, as well as in the cumulation of small improvements. This particular chain of influence extends at least one important link further: Landes (1986, p. 602), in a related context, declares himself to be among the descendents of the (intellectual) 'House of Usher'.

[9] See for example Rosenberg (1983), chapter 1, for a review.

to respond like other resource-using activities to signals and incentives emanating from markets, Adam Smith's metaphoric 'invisible hand' has now reached deep into the technological historians' bailiwick. The actions of many individual human minds and muscles are thus depicted naturally as being subject to coordination by non-hierarchical social organizations including markets, thereby permitting very substantial decentralization of control in the creation of technological achievements of great complexity.[10] On this view it would appear that no techno-economic entrepreneurs of extraordinary stature are required for the creation of such things as railroads, electrical supply systems, or telephone networks.

While prepared to demur from the latter opinion, I seek no quarrel with those who say that technological progress is a collective, social process, many important aspects of which are characterized by continuity. Nor would I dispute the case for treating invention and innovation as endogenous to the resource allocation process conducted by means of markets. But, I do want to counteract or at least to qualify the suggestion—one that is strongly conveyed by some recent contributions to the history of technology—that individuals essentially have no real points of leverage from which to control the outcomes of such a macrocosmic, societal process; that decision-making agents either are rationally moving with the tide of technical change, or, by failing to heed the proper signals, are running the risk of being swept aside by it.

There is another conceptualization of dynamical systems constituted of many elements or 'actors', in which the actions of individuals that appear to be autonomous and even extraneously motivated, nevertheless, can turn out to have exercised a profound and persistent influence upon the macrostate. These are dynamical systems in which local *positive feedback* mechanisms (e.g. in economics, dynamic increasing returns due to learning-by-doing) predominate over negative feedback mechanisms (e.g. increasing marginal costs), and which, therefore, are characterized as 'self-reinforcing' or 'auto-catalytic'. Stochastic systems of this kind in physics, chemical kinetics, and theoretical biology are perhaps not the most suitable paradigms for understanding economies composed of human agents, but they are nonetheless a source of insights into processes of change that are not 'eventless', and whose outcomes are *path-dependent*. As a result of the operation of local positive feedbacks which

[10] Williamson (1975, 1985), and related work on organizational structure, contracting, and hierarchical control, has, of course, been reactive against the more extreme formulations of this position—on the grounds that they left unexplained the boundaries between firms and the market, and the internal institutional features of modern business enterprises. Chandler (1977), while much occupied with the rise of large and complex business organizations within which were developed modes of resource allocation alternative to the market, casts the emerging technology of large-scale production in the role of the principal exogenous force inducing these organizational adaptations. Where the new technology was coming from, and whether its development was occurring primarily under the guidance of a visible hand (rather than its invisible, market counterpart), remains inexplicit in Chandler's scheme of things.

give rise to regions of instability, these systems typically possess a multiplicity of stable 'attractors', or possible asymptotic states (sometimes) referred to as 'emergent structures'. The initial state of the system, combined with random events, or 'channelled perturbations' arising from endogenous innovations or periodic fluctuations at the microcosmic level of the individual actors, serves to push the dynamics into the domain of one of these asymptotic states.[11] Consequently, even extraneous and transient disturbing events—far from 'averaging out', so that their influence may safely be abstracted from—act as historical selection mechanisms, 'selecting' the particular persisting structure or configuration that eventually emerges; the nature of the eventual outcome is thus not uniquely preordained, but, instead, is dependent upon the details of the sequence of small 'events' along the dynamic path.

In physics the term 'hysteresis' refers to the persistence of an altered state when the force that caused the alteration has abated. Positive feedback conditions of the kind just described are the very ones in which the actions of individual agents are most likely to give rise to hysteresis effects. Indeed, in social and economic systems where positive feedback dominates, the character and personality of individual actors takes on much greater importance than classical and neoclassical economic theory, long preoccupied as it has been with the analysis of negative feedback regimes, has been wont to acknowledge. Where interactions among agents tend to be reinforcing rather than counteracting, all the 'other-directed' agents end up having to adapt to the 'inner-directed' few who remain, for rational or irrational reasons, immune to the influence of their immediate socio-economic environment.[12] Under such conditions, the personal ambitions and subjective beliefs of inner-directed entrepreneurs, and the particular ideological convictions of public policy makers, become essential ingredients of the temporary historical contexts within which the long-run course of change may be pushed irreversibly in one direction rather than in another.

Rather than elaborating upon the foregoing general but highly abstract formulation of an alternative vision of the way the world (or at least some parts of the world) works—an approach that I have adopted elsewhere—I shall try here to advance my argument by means of a concrete historical illustration.[13]

[11] See for example Haken (1978), Prigogine (1980), Arthur *et al.* (1985, 1986), for formal mathematical analysis of dynamical systems with these properties; Prigogine and Stengers (1984) offer a less technical and more philosophical interpretation.

[12] This rather general proposition has been arrived at by analysts of quite a few, different economic contexts. For example, it has been demonstrated recently, using different arguments, by Akerloff and Yellen (1985), and by Haltiwanger and Waldman (1985).

[13] See for example David (1975, pp. 6–16, 50–91), and, more recently, (1987) and (1988), for formalizations of the underlying view of the nature of the stochastic process that generates path-dependent technological progress. The heuristic value of a vivid illustration, such as the tale of the QWERTY typewriter keyboard layout recounted in David (1986a), has been masterfully demonstrated by Gould (1987).

I will use the story of a technological rivalry—the 'Battle of the Systems', so-called, between the late nineteenth century commercial proponents of direct current and alternating current systems of electricity supply—to suggest that sometimes we should expect to find critical moments, or points of *bifurcation* in the dynamic process of technical change. Such points, really more like narrow windows in the time domain, are especially prone to appear at early stages of the incremental development of integrated production and distribution systems that are characterized by strong elements of localized positive feedback, or 'increasing returns' to the more extensive utilization of one or another among the available technical formulations. In this context, specific technical formulations represent variants of a particular technological system paradigm and tend to undergo further development and elaboration along rather narrowly defined trajectories which lead away from these historical bifurcation points.[14] It is at such junctures, I suggest, that individual economic agents do briefly hold substantial power to direct the flow of subsequent events along one path rather than another. Unfortunately, in the very nature of those circumstances it is difficult to gauge just how quickly seemingly similar paths may begin to diverge, or to foresee exactly the eventual alternative outcomes towards which they lead.

Looked at in retrospect, however, things often take on an appearance of having been rather more pre-ordained. In the case at hand, modern commentators have been inclined to downplay as historically insignificant the rivalry that arose in the late 1880s between Thomas Alva Edison and George Westinghouse, then the publically prominent champions, respectively, of direct current and alternating current electrical supply systems in the United States. The actors in these events hardly rank as pygmies on the stage of American technical innovation and entrepreneurship, and their supporting cast in this particular drama included the likes of Elihu Thomson, Nikola Tesla, Henry Villard, J. Pierpont Morgan, and Samuel Insull! Yet, such is the strength of the currently dominant historiographic tradition that some satisfaction has been taken in showing even an Edison to have been utterly without power to prevent the technical 'progress of civilization' from pushing

---

[14] This is a highly compressed and necessarily abstract statement of complicated matters that have been set out more fully elsewhere. See David (1975), chapter 1, on localized stochastic learning, the channelling of technical innovations along particular 'cones' in factor input space defining available production processes (techniques), and the influence of historical events in causing industries or economies to become committed to a particular path, or trajectory of development associated with such 'techniques.' The notion of a technological paradigm, which Dosi (1982, 1984) has introduced and elaborated upon, is quite usefully applied to the concept of a 'universal' electrical system, i.e., an integrated network for electricity supply and use. The latter concept, the paradigm, embraces variant technical formulations of such a system, notably, the alternative designs based upon d.c., single phase a.c., and polyphase a.c. Each of these, as will be seen, would carry some peculiar implications for the subsequent experience of the regions and economies that became committed to one or another specific 'trajectory' of technological and industrial development.

aside his own previous achievements in the field of direct current, and moving forward in the new form of polyphase alternating current. Edison has been portrayed as foolishly deluded, stubbornly egotistical, and worse, for launching a campaign against the Westinghouse electricity supply system on the grounds that it constituted a menace to public safety.[15] Most historians of the episode have supposed that the Wizard of Menlo Park and his colleagues meant to 'do in' their rivals by blocking the future commercial application of alternating current in the United States, and so they present Edison's failure to achieve that result (despite the employment of low strategems) as testimony to the proposition that there is not much scope for either individual heroism or knavery where technical change is concerned. This would tell us that the momentum of technological progress is overwhelming, that it raises up its 'heroes' and casts down those who try to thwart or redirect it for their own irrational ends. Although the thought may be comforting to some, I reject it as a myth that has encouraged flawed interpretations of the facts and the extraction of quite the wrong moral from the historical episode in question.

The reinterpretation of the 'Battle of the Systems' that I offer here argues for a different way of thinking about the process of technological change. We should become more consciously reconciled and, perhaps, even comfortable with its contingent nature, acknowledging that some and possibly many episodes in the progress of technology will be marked by a high degree of ex ante indeterminacy. Not all of them, of course, because the whole of the world of technology does not work that way. I would prefer to see careful qualifications placed around bald propositions such as: 'There is nothing in the character of a previous event or decision—the choice of one path or another—that implies reversibility. Even an accident changes the future irremediably.'[16] But, where localized positive feedback mechanisms *are* operative, there the element of 'chance' or 'historical accident'—in the form of idiosyncratic personal perceptions and predilections of the actors, as well as extraneous and transient circumstances surrounding their decision-making at such

---

[15] The following passage from Prout (1921), the American Society of Mechanical Engineers' official biographer of Westinghouse, exemplifies this tradition of interpretation: 'As soon as it became evident that Westinghouse proposed to exploit extensively the alternating-current system great opposition was developed. Looking back at history, one is surprised at the stupidity and puerility of some of this opposition. Men of great repute gave their names and their help to methods of which they must now be thoroughly ashamed. They know now that if they had succeeded, the progress of civilization would have been delayed—how much and how long we cannot even guess. . . . It is needless to enlarge upon this [battle of the systems] aspect of the development. Every well-informed human being knows Westinghouse was right, the alternating electric current being now used to generate and convey 95 percent of the electric use in power and lighting in the United States.' (p. 115). More recent versions, to be examined below, do not even contemplate the possibility that Edison could have succeeded—had it been his intention to block these developments.

[16] Landes (1986), p. 622, speaking of the historical evolution of the factory system.

junctures—is most likely to acquire sufficient power to shape the eventual outcomes. Such adventitious influences must render the task of prediction an unproductive one for all but the closest and most acute observers.

The point I wish to underscore by example is therefore a modest one, concerning the special scope which the development of *network technologies* creates for individual actors to influence the course of history, as innovating entrepreneurs, or in other roles. As a result, some important and obtrusive features of the rich technological environment that surrounds us may be the uncalculated consequences of actions taken long ago by petty heroes, and petty scoundrels. The accretion of technological innovations inherited from the past therefore cannot legitimately be presumed to constitute socially optimal solutions provided for us—either by heroic entrepreneurs, or by herds of rational managers operating in efficient markets. Before taking up the promised historical tale, it is important to explicitly consider why this should be particularly true in the case of a generic network technology.

2. *Network Technologies, Compatibility Standards, and 'Accidents' of History*

The recent wave of improvements in information, computing and communications technologies has heightened popular awareness of some of the special opportunities and difficulties created by competitions waged by commercial sponsors of alternative technical formulations for new, complex products and production methods. Brief reference to our contemporary experience therefore can assist in forming an intuitive appreciation for the highly contingent way in which the technology of the electrical manufacturing and supply industries came to be elaborated at the end of the nineteenth, and the significance of the rapid emergence in the United States of de facto technical standards for a universal electrical supply system based on alternating, rather than direct current. Recall that during the early 1980s, the burning issue in the market for video tape recorders (VCRs, more specifically) was whether to commit to the Betamax format developed and sponsored by Sony, or cast one's lot with the VHS format group that had formed around the Japan Victor Corporation.[17]

Who among us has not wrestled with the question of whether our desktop computer is to be an IBM PC-compatible system, or an Apple system like the Macintosh? Or, paused to consider the call of the International Dvorak Society

---

[17] A sequel now confronts the home video or 'cam-corder' enthusiast, and the manufacturers of video-camera and VCR equipment: is the current half-inch (12.7 mm) tape width for VCRs to be preserved as a standard, or is it better to switch to systems based on the 8 mm format pioneered by Sony? See Rosenbloom (1985) on the background: Cusumano (1985) on details of the VCR rivalry, from the producer's side.

to reconfigure our computer keyboards, learn to touchtype on the DSK keyboard patented in 1932 by August Dvorak and W. L. Dealey, and thereby escape a perpetual bondage to the inefficient QWERTY layout?[18] Such quandries seem all too commonplace nowadays.

Two features are significant about the prosaically modern choice-of-technique situations just instanced. First, they involve technologies characterized by increasing returns to scale of use or production, and second, they entail choices where considerations of technical interrelatedness among the components forming alternative systems cannot be ignored. These are attributes of 'network technologies', which, because they may give rise to pecuniary and technical externalities, create special problems as well as economic opportunities for private and public decision-makers. It is now quite widely recognized that users of a network technology are at the mercy of the social mechanisms available for maintaining efficient system performance by providing compatibility among all its constituent elements. Network technologies may, of course, be developed in a coordinated way through private commercial sponsorship of an integrated system: all the necessarily interrelated components of a product or production facility can, in many instances, be packaged together by a single provider who develops and maintains the required interface specifications. A difficulty can arise, however, when the entailed fixed capital costs are so large that they pose effective barriers to the entry of competitive formulations of the basic technology; the gains in operating efficiency assured by integrated supply then may be obtained at the expense of the inefficiencies that come with 'natural monopoly' and too little diversity to suit the varied needs of end-users. On the other hand, when coordination of a network or technological system is left to the decentralized resource allocation processes of competitive markets, the latter have generally led to an insufficiently high degree of standardization of 'compatibility' to avoid efficiency losses in systems operations.[19]

A different point, which has only lately come to be more fully appreciated among economic analysts, is that when private agents in pursuit of profits set about solving what seem to be reasonably straightforward problems of operating more efficiently with the technologies already at hand, the ensemble of suppliers and users can easily become committed to an unfavorable implicit 'trade-off' against dynamic gains from further basic innovations in

---

[18] See David (1985, 1986a) for the story of QWERTY.

[19] The normative literature on the economics of standardization recognizes that while the evident failure of markets would call out for remedies in the form of governmental efforts to promote the exploitation of economies of scale obtainable via network coordination and system integration, such interventions may result all too easily in choices of technology that prove to be 'mistakes.' See Brock (1975), Kindleberger (1983), Carlton and Klamer (1983), Katz and Shapiro (1985a, b), Farrell and Saloner (1985a, b, c). David (1986b) reviews this literature in fuller detail.

fundamental systems-design. When the relative attractiveness of adopting a technical solution tends to increase as that particular practice or device gains adherents, and durable commitments are being made sequentially by different agents under conditions of imperfect information, the ultimate outcome of the process can turn on the detailed timing of small events—even happenings of a nature so extraneous as to appear random in character.[20]

Such commitment, moreover, is most likely to occur within a narrow frame of time, positioned near the beginning of the technologic's trajectory of diffusion and development. What defines these critical phases, or windows in time, and causes them to close down quickly, essentially, is the growing weight that attaches to considerations of 'network externalities'—the shaping of individual technological choices by the contact formed through the prior decisions of other agents. For it is the distribution of the already 'installed base' that will come to count more and more heavily in determining choices about interrelated capital investments—which must be made in respect to both supplying and using the network technology.

Governmental intervention, therefore, is not the only potential source of 'standardization errors'; markers also can make early and costly technological mistakes which subsequently prove policy interventions, the existence of significant increasing returns to scale, or analogous positive feedback mechanisms such as 'learning by doing,' and by 'using,' can give the result that one particular formulation of a network technology—VHS-formatted VCRs, or QWERTY-formatted keyboards—will be able to drive out other variants and so emerge as the de facto standard for the industry. By no means need the commercial victor in this kind of systems rivalry be more efficient than the available alternatives. Nor need it be the one which adopters would have chosen if a different sequence of actions on the part of others had preceded their own.[21]

Yet, by the same token it is entirely conceivable that for reasons having little to do with the ability of economic agents to foresee the future, or with anything more than an accidental and possibly quite transitory alignment of their private interests with the economic welfare of future generation, technological development may take a particular path which does prove eventually to have been superior to any available alternative. This is a disquieting message for

---

[20] Under such conditions—where, as I observed more than a decade ago, 'marked divergences between ultimate outcomes may flow from seemingly negligible differences in remote beginnings' (David, 1975, p. 16)—market rivalries among variant technological systems do exhibit a strictly historical character. In the sense that they are non-ergodic, the dynamic process cannot shake itself loose from the grip of past events and its outcome therefore can properly be described as path-dependent.

[21] It should be emphasized that this form of (hindsight) recognition that rational decision-making had nonetheless resulted in an inferior path being mistaken for the 'right' one could not arise under conditions of constant or decreasing returns; in the latter cases the eventual outcomes would be path independent. See Arthur (1984, 1985), Arthur *et al.* (1985) for more formal (mathematical) treatment, and David (1986b) for further exposition.

those who normally find comfort in the Panglossian presumption that 'the invisible hand' of market competition—assisted sometimes by the visible hand of farsighted management—somehow has worked to shape ours into the most economically efficient of all possible worlds. Yet, recognition of the importance of network externalities naturally predisposes one to be extremely skeptical about the claims of that proposition to any general validity. We must acknowledge that where network technologies are involved one cannot justifiably suppose that the system which has evolved most fully is really superior to others whose development might have been carried further, but was not. Nor should we comfort ourselves with the presumption that the 'right economic reasons' were responsible for the emergence of a technological system that has in fact turned out to be superior to any of the alternatives available. These are lessons borne out by the curious events now to be recounted.

3. *Some History of 'Current' Affairs*

The years 1887–1892 witnessed an episode of intense rivalry involving the proponents of two technologies vying for the electricity supply market. The contestants were, on one side, the incumbent direct or 'continuous' current system sponsored by the complex of manufacturing and financial interests that had been built up around Edison's 1878 patent for a carbon filament incandescent lamp, and its sequelae;[22] and, on the other side, the challenging alternating current technology which at the time was represented on the American scene primarily by the Westinghouse and Thomson-Houston Companies. This was not a Competition of long standing, for the first commercial a.c. system was built during the fall of 1886 in Buffalo, NY, by the Westinghouse Electric Co., an enterprise that had received its corporate charter from the State of Pennsylvania only as recently as January of the same year.[23] George Westinghouse, whose fame and fortune already had been established by more than a score of patents which he had secured for railroad airbrake apparatus in the years 1869–1873, was thus a comparative latecomer to the young electrical lighting industry.[24] In 1886 the Edison Electric Light

---

[22] In 1882, according to Jones (1940), p. 41, this complex of enterprises included: (1) the Edison Electric Light Company, which had been formed to finance the invention, patenting, and development of Edison's electric-lighting system, and which licensed its use; (2) the Edison Electric Illuminating Company of New York, that being the first of the Edison municipal lighting utilities; (3) the Edison Machine works, organized to manufacture the dynamos covered by Edison's patents; (4) the (Edison) Electric tube Company, set up to manufacture the underground conductors for electric power distribution in the lighting system; and (5) the Edison Lamp Works.

[23] See Prout (1921), pp. 94–5, 113; Sharlin (1963), pp. 195–6.

[24] On the pre-electrical career of Westinghouse, see Leupp (1919), Product (1921).

Company already had been installing isolated plant electric supply systems for 5 years, and, having commercially implemented its system of incandescent lighting in 1882 by opening the Pearl Street Station, in New York City, and the Holborn Viaduct Station, in London, was well launched into the business of building 'central' generating plants.[25]

Although Thomas Edison's inspiration had propelled direct current into an early position of leadership as the basis for a commercially implemented technology for electricity supply and application, the fundamental principles of generating alternating current with dynamos were not new. Indeed, the invention of the first direct current dynamo, by H. Pixii, in 1832, had involved the addition of a commutator to the alternating current dynamo he had built immediately following Michael Faraday's discovery of the 'dynamo principle' in the preceding year. Furthermore, knowledge of the fundamental 'inductance', or self-induction property of electric conductors (which formed the basis for the technique of distributing alternating current at reduced voltage by means of 'step down' transformers) dated from the same era. It had been discovered by Faraday in 1834, and, even before him, by an American professor, Joseph Henry.[26] Commercial exploitation of a.c. had awaited the demonstration—by the Frenchman, Lucian Gaulard, and his English business partner, J. D. Gibbs—that by using highest voltage alternating current and step-down transformers it was possible to achieve substantial reductions in the costs of moving energy, while making electrical power available at the low voltages then suitable for application to incandescent lamps.[27] The beauty of the thing was that transformers could be used without entailing significant losses of power to substitute voltage for amperage. Doing so would reduce the need for the high conductivity, heavy gauge copper-wire transmission lines that were used to distribute current in the early d.c. lighting systems, thereby saving greatly on fixed capital costs. Step-down transformers could then be employed to reverse the process and make low voltage available for local distribution at points of consumption.[28] The critical portion of the detailed

[25] Fleming (1921), p. 225.

[26] See for example Sharlin (1963), pp. 136–47; Jarvis (1967a, b), for convenient reviews. More details of the history of alternating current technology prior to 1880 can be found in *Electrical World* (March, 1887); Sumpner (1890); *Encyclopaedia Britannica* (1910–11), vol. 9, pp. 179–203; Fleming (1921), p. 44.

[27] Sharlin (1963), pp. 192–3; T. Hughes (1983), pp. 86–91.

[28] A 'transformer,' in modern electrical parlance, refers to a device by which the electromotive force (e.m.f.) of a source of alternating current may be increased or decreased. [For the reader whose recollection of the introductory physics of electricity has grown as hazy as was mine: the difference in potential, which may be thought of as a kind of driving force behind the electrons forming the current, is sometimes called the e.m.f. and is measured by V, the voltage. Electric current is analogous to the flow of water through a pipe, the rate of flow being measured by I, the amperage. 'Power', P measured in watts in W/t, the time rate at which energy (W) is developed or expended.] Unlike a dynamo used in generation, a transformer needs no moving parts. It has a primary winding (whose terminals are attached to an a.c. source), and a secondary winding, both of which pass in coils around an iron 'core.' The first such device was the 'closed-core' transformer made by Faraday, the core of which had the form of an iron ring. 'Step-down'

chronology with which we shall be concerned (see Figure 1) is therefore the part that commences in 1882, when a patent was awarded to Gaulard and Gibbs in Britain.

There were, however, practical problems with the Gaulard-Gibbs transformer system, and it was not until 1885 that remedies were found for these. On the American side of the Atlantic, this was accomplished by William Stanley, an inventor in the private employ of George Westinghouse. In 1884, Westinghouse, having established himself during the preceding decade as the inventor and manufacturer of air-brake systems for railroad passenger trains, had become actively interested in the potentialities of alternating current, and had moved quickly in securing the American rights to the Gaulard-Gibbs transformer patent. Within the same year, 1885, S. Z. de Ferranti was installing an a.c. lighting system with transformers wired in parallel in London's Grosvenor Gallery.[29] The commercial use of alternating current for lighting in the United States followed close on the heels of these developments. An experimental lighting system had been set up by Stanley in Great Barrington, MA., and successfully demonstrated for Westinghouse in March, 1886; within six months Stanley's work was being put to use in Buffalo by the Westinghouse Electric Company.[30] Thus, on both sides of the Atlantic, Thomas Edison in 1886 was quite suddenly confronted by potential commercial rivals who had began to explore an alternative technological trajectory.

Initially, the two systems did not compete directly. Instead, they staked out distinct portions of the market which were determined primarily by the differences in their inherent technical constraints. Two distance-related problems hampered immediate widespread application of the d.c. technology. First, despite implementation (beginning in 1883) of Edison's three-wire distribution design which reduced the cost of wiring by two-thirds relative

---

transformers have a larger number of turns of wire in the primary winding than in the secondary winding, since the ratio of primary (or 'impressed') voltage to secondary voltage is equal to the ratio of the number of turns in the respective windings. Although it may seem, on first consideration, that the boost in voltage achieved by means of a step-up transformer somehow violates the conservation of energy law, such obviously cannot be the case; the power supplied at the primary is just equal to that delivered at the secondary. In general, when the voltage is stepped up (or, as English electrical engineers say, 'bumped up'), the current is 'bumped down' by the same proportion.

[29] See Stanley (1912), pp. 564–5; Passer (1972), pp. 136–8, on Gaulard and Gibbs, Stanley and Westinghouse, and the still more comprehensive account in T. Hughes (1983). pp. 95–105. The challenge of solving the practical problems arising from the connecting of the primary coils of the transformers in series by Gaulard and Gibbs drew an even earlier response from the Hungarian team of Zipernowsky, Deri, and Blathy of Budapest. Like Stanley, they found that transformers can be worked independently if the different primary circuits are arranged in parallel between two high voltage mains (1000 V in their patent), like the rungs on a ladder; the secondary circuits of the transformers were kept isolated, with incandescent lamps placed on them in parallel.

[30] T. Hughes (1983), pp. 101–5; Passer (1972), pp. 131–8.

Direct Current System Developments	Alternating Current System Developments
1878: December: Swan carbon lamp exhibited in Newcastle, England.	1878–1882: Different 'alternators' (a.c. generators) designed by Gramme, Ferranti, and others.
1879: Edison patents filament lamp in U.S. and Britain; builds bipolar dynamo.	
1880: Edison electric lighting 'system' at Menlo Park;	
: First commercial carbon filament lamps produced.	
1882: Edison central stations at Pearl St., N.Y., Holborn Viaduct, London.	1882: Gaulard and Gibbs file British patent for distribution by transformers.
1883: Edison–Hopkinson 3-wire distribution system, patented and installed.	1883: Parallel wiring of generators demonstrated, following Hopkinson.
1885: van de Poele streetcar system in New Orleans, South Bend, etc.	1885: Stanley patents improvement of GG transformer; Zipernowsky, Deri and Blathy also patent improvement.
	: Ferranti installs A.C. system with transformers in parallel in Grosvenor Gallery.
1886 November: Edison sanguine about Westinghouse competition, raises 'safety issue' in memo to Johnson.	1886 November: Westinghouse Co. completes first A.C. central station in Buffalo, N.Y.
: Villard returns with 'proposal'.	: March: Stanley demonstrates experimental A.C. system for Westinghouse at Gt. Barrington Mass.
1887: Sprague electric traction system successful in Richmond, Va.	1887: Induction motor research by Telsa, Ferraris.
: Edison and associates engaged in animal experiments at West Orange.	:Thompson-Houston enter production and sale of A.C. lighting system.
	: March: Bradley patents polyphase induction motor.
	: October: Telsa files first A.C. motor patent
1888: July: Brown demonstration at Columbia: campaign to presuade N.Y. legislature to set voltage limit.	1888: May: Bradley files for patent on rotary converter.
1889: January: Edison General Electric Co. organized.	: April–June: Shallenberger develops A.C. meter based on induction motor.
1890: Edison liquidates personal holdings in EGE Co.	: July: Westinghouse acquires Tesla patents.
	1890: Westinghouse Electric and Manufacturing Co. reorganized and refinanced by Belmont syndicate.
	1891: Westinghouse power system at Telluride.
	: Demonstration of transmission with 3-phase alternators driving synchronous motors, at Lauffen-Frankfurt.
1892: General electric formed by Thomson, Houston & Morgan-backing for acquisition of EGE Co.	: Niagra projects commits to electricity.
	1893: Westinghouse demonstrates 'universal' 3-phase system at Chicago World's Fair.
	: Westinghouse and GE submit A.C. generator designs for Niagra project.

FIGURE 1. Chronology of key events in the 'battle of the systems' episode in the US.

to the previous two-wire scheme,[31] the cost of copper wire in the transmission lines continued to define what constituted an economically viable distance in competition with illuminating gas. Moreover, even if lower cost conductors were to be found, or new wiring systems devised, the low voltage d.c. system was distance-constrained on technical grounds having to do with 'voltage drop'. In other words, the further the distance a current traveled, the larger the voltage loss on the lines between the point of generation and the point of consumption. The earliest Edison systems, which typically were confined to a fairly small service are (approximately one mile in diameter), made allowance for this problem by generating at 105–110 volts in order to insure the delivery of at least 100 volts at the point of consumption—the latter being the voltage for which household lamps and other appliances were then being designed.[32] Beyond a certain transmission distance, however, this type of adjustment would no longer prove adequate; the system would deliver too broad a spectrum of voltages along the transmission lines.

Like others, George Westinghouse had seen these limitations of the direct current system as leaving an opening through which the alternative, Gaulard-Gibbs formulation could be used to make a significant inroad into the promising electricity supply business dominated by Edison. Transmission of alternating current at higher voltages meant that with a given amount of generating capacity and a given weight of copper wire, the distance over which it remained economically feasible to deliver electric power would increase substantially. Indeed, for a given amount of power input, and a wire conductor of specified material and cross-sectional area, transmission distance increases as the square of voltage.[33] The economic implication of this was that expansion of supply from existing a.c. generating capacity—which allowed the further spreading of fixed capital charges—would be *comparatively* unconstrained by the costs of reaching customers over a wider area. Situating

---

[31] Josephson (1959), pp. 231–2; Jarvis (1967b), Ch. 10, p. 229; T. Hughes (1983), p. 83–4; Byatt (1979), p. 99.

[32] Jarvis (1976b), p. 229. The 110 volt standard for electricity consumption which came to be established in the United States was selected by Edison on the basis of electrical circuit theory and the maximum resistance lamp filament that he was able to obtain circa 1879. From 1883 onwards, however, the Edison 'three-wire' system was employing 220 volts for transmission of direct current. How the European following the Berliners' example, came to establish a 220 volt standard is another story. See Hughes (1983), p. 193.

[33] Using the standard notation introduced in note 26, above, the power equation for direct current is $p = VI$; but, for the case of alternating current, power has to be thought of in an 'average' sense and the equation takes the root mean square form: $P = V_{rms} I \text{ rms} \cos \phi$. Here $V_{rms} = V_{max}/(2)^{1/2}$ and $I_{rms} = I_{max}/(2)^{1/2}$. The power factor, $\cos \phi$, depends on the phase angle f, which measures the amount by which the electron current in the line leads or lags the impressed voltage. For current of any kind, however, Ohm's Law gives the resistance, R, measured in ohms, as $R = I/V$. Note that the resistance of a wire connecting two points is directly proportional to its length, L, and inversely proportional to its cross-sectional area, A, with the factor of proportionality being the 'resistivity', β:$R = \beta(L/A)$. This relation, combined with Ohm's Law, and the a.c. power equation, above, yields the voltage – distance relationship cited in the text: $L = (V^2/P)B$, where the constant is implicitly defined as $B = \{A(\cos \phi)\}/2\beta$.

generating facilities at locations where ground rents were not as high as those found in urban central business districts, where electric energy demand for lighting, generally was most concentrated, was another potential source of economic advantage. Transmitting alternating current at high voltage and then employing step-down transformers at sub-stations, or 'bumping down' at the point of consumption, also greatly ameliorated the voltage drop problem encounter in operating d.c. systems.

Nevertheless, at this stage, Edison's system remained the better positioned of the two to dominate the more densely populated urban markets. Part of the reason was that there peak load lighting demands could be matched with Edison's larger, more efficient generators, leaving the a.c. supply systems to work the surrounding territory. Reinforcing this territorial division were numerous absolute disadvantages which blunted the ability of the early, single-phase a.c. technology to penetrate the urban market in competition with d.c.

At least four generic difficulties with a.c. remained to be resolved at the end of 1886. First was the fact—alluded to already—that the early Westinghouse and Thomson-Houston 'alternators' (the a.c. equivalent to dynamo generators) were only 70 percent efficient, whereas 90 percent efficiency was being achieved with d.c. dynamos, especially the large, 'jumbo' design introduced by Edison. Second, the d.c. system was able to provide metered electric supply, whereas no a.c. meter had yet been developed—a deficiency that greatly reduced the system's attractiveness to central station operators. A third drawback for the a.c. technology at this stage of its development was that, although the principle of operating alternators in parallel had been demonstrated in 1883 (following the theoretical work of John Hopkinson), it remained to be translated into practical central station operations. The ability to connect dynamos in parallel rather than in series gave the d.c. system a distinct advantage: its generators could be disconnected and reconnected to the mains in response to varying load, thereby saving power inputs and wear and tear. Further, d.c. generators could be shut down for repair and maintenance— or might even be tolerated to break down—without disruption of the entire system.[34]

Fourth, at a time when central stations employing the Edison system were beginning to spread fixed generating costs by supplying electricity for power as well as lighting, the a.c. system's ability to compete in urban markets was restricted by the lack of any satisfactory secondary motor available to be used with alternating current.

In addition to depriving electricity supply companies who chose to install alternators of the ability to serve industrial and commercial power customers,

[34] Passer (1972), p. 137–44, 165–7; Byatt (1979), pp. 102–7; Evans (1892), p. 52.

the lack of a motor became an increasingly pronounced comparative disadvantage with the success of the experimental electric streetcar systems installed during 1885 by Charles J. Van Depoele in New Orleans, South Bend, and Minneapolis. Its ability to deliver high torque at low r.p.m. made the direct current motor particularly well suited in such applications as traction, where continuous speed control was important. The 'traction boom' based upon d.c. was well and truly launched in 1887, with the completion of the superior streetcar system developed for the City of Richmond, VA, by Frank J. Sprague—a talented but erratic inventor formerly employed by Edison—in partnership with another Edison associate, Edward Johnson. There would be 154 electric street railway systems in operation in the United States by the close of 1889.[35]

It should be emphasized that up until 1888 the underlying technological and economic considerations were not such as to allow great scope for the commercial realization of conventional scale economies and positive network externalities in the electricity supply business, as distinguished from the business of manufacturing electrical supply equipment and appliances, such as lamps. Within *local* territories served by utility companies, of course, there were significant fixed cost requirements for generation and transmission, and these were sufficient to produce some 'exclusion effects,' or 'first-move advantages,' which created incentive for racing between the sponsors of rival systems.[36] But, as has already been noted, rather than being symmetrically positioned with regard to every marker, d.c. and a.c. systems each could find some markets in which they would enjoy some advantages in preempting entry by the other. Furthermore, such economies of scale as each could exploit in the generation of current remained definitely bounded by rising marginal distribution costs, with the geographical bounds due to transmission costs being more tightly constricted around the central generating stations in the case of d.c. systems. On the other side of the ledger, the possibilities of enjoying economies of scale in generation by achieving greater 'load diversity', and consequently higher load factors for plants of given capacity, were far more limited for a.c. systems at this stage. The latter were still restricted to serving only the segment of the market (for incandescent lighting) that was characterized by very high peak-load in power usage. In the case of residential lighting demands, the load factor—defined as the ratio of the average load to the maximum load of a customer, group of customers,

[35] See Passer (1972), pp. 237–49 on Sprague and Johnson Particularly; pp. 216–55 on electric street railways: McDonald (1962), p. 36.

[36] And, also, between the main competitive suppliers of a.c. lighting plant—the Thomson-Houston, and Westinghouse Electric companies. On 'first-mover advantages', and incentives for pre-emption by suppliers of new technologies and goods and services based upon them, see the theoretical analysis developed by Fudenberg and Tirole (1985); and Bresnahan and David (1986), for an effort at empirical application.

or an entire system during a specified period—typically might be as low as 10–20 per cent.[37]

All things considered, in 1886 Edison was perhaps quite justified in his rather sanguine view of the challenge represented by a.c. and the recent entry by Westinghouse into the central station business. November of that year found him writing to Edward Johnson:

'Just as certain as death Westinghouse will kill a customer within 6 months after he puts in a system of any size. He has got a new thing and it will require a great deal of experimenting to get it working practically . . . None of his plans worry me in the least; only thing that disturbs me is that Westinghouse is a great man for flooding the country with agents and travelers. He is ubiquitous and will form numerous companies before we know anything about it.'[38]

One cannot be sure of the bases for Edison's sanguine assessment of the situation at this point. Had he been thinking primarily of the commercial advantages that his d.c.-based enterprises derived from their headstart in acquiring experience and expertise in engineering design, component manufacturing, and operation of central stations supplying incandescent lighting, he could have viewed the safety problem as indicative of some of the many practical improvements that remained to be made in the a.c. system. Quite possibly he had in mind also the disadvantage at which the a.c. lighting technology would be placed in competing against a more comprehensive ('universal') electrical system which could supply lighting, power, and traction customers—such as the one that was beginning to be implemented on the basis of d.c. under Edison's sponsorship.[39]

Data on the number of central station and lamps associated with each of the rival formulations suggests that by the years 1888 and 1889 the diffusion of a.c. technology was rapidly catching up with that of the d.c. technology in the United States. As of October, 1888, the Westinghouse Electric Co. already could count 116 central stations (some of which, however, actually were d.c. plants) with a total capacity to run 196 850 lamps, in comparison with the 185 Edison central stations operating 385 840 lamps. By 1891 a.c. had pulled ahead in the area of lighting, but the available estimates of generating capacity for that date indicate that when electricity supply for power

[37] See, for example T. Hughes (1983), pp 217–19. A 10–12 per cent load factor is given as the average for a simple lighting load in the article contributed by J. A. Fleming on 'Electricity Supply' in *Encyclopedia Britannica* (1910–1911), vol. 9, p. 194.

[38] Quoted in Josephson (1959), p. 346, italics added. Josephson's source was an Edison memorandum to E. H. Johnson, commenting on a report that had been obtained from the engineers of Siemens and Halske (Berlin), evaluating the version of the a.c. lighting system that had been developed by Zipernowski, Deri and Blathy (see note 27, above).

[39] According to Prout (1921), p. 95, Westinghouse had begun installing isolated d.c. lighting plants earlier in 1886, and had practically completed his company's first d.c. central station in Trenton, NJ in August. Direct current installations in other towns were underway. Quite probably, it was this bustle of activity—an incursion into markets that otherwise might 'naturally' fall to the Edison Electric Lighting Co.—which Edison felt was more disturbing than the first a.c. central station completed by Westinghouse Electric Co, in November.

and traction is included, d.c. remained preponderant.[40] The catch-up that occurred during the latter 1880s mainly reflected the a.c. companies' move into the electrification of smaller cities and towns not well served by d.c., rather than penetration into the Edison system's 'natural' territory in the spatially more dense urban lighting market.

There surely were some geographical markets in which the two variants were approximately balanced in their advantages, at least from the viewpoint of the cost of supplying electricity for lighting—larger territory for a.c. being offset by the impossibility of load balancing through connections to industrial power users, and traction companies. In such circumstances one might well expect that competition would feature the use of marketing tactics of all kinds, designed to tip the balance in one direction or another between competing system sponsors. And, in fact, it is precisely against this background of an apparent 'technological stand off' in the late 1880s that historians of technology and economic historians who have studied the electric supply industry have set the ensuing episode known as the 'battle of the Systems.' Nevertheless, the events which marked this period of intense and open rivalry between the proponents of direct and alternating current only become fully comprehensible, in my view, when they are seen to have been precipitated by a fundamental transformation of the underlying techno-economic situation. That disruption of the status quo ante occurred in 1887–1888.

4. The Electricity Supply 'Battlefield' Revisited

As it has been recounted by more than one historian of technology and business enterprise, the 'battle' that burst into public view during 1887–1892 was remarkable—even bizarre in some aspects—and regrettable in transgressing the normal boundaries for either market competition between different formulations of a new and highly promising technological paradigm, or professional disputation among scientists and engineers with regard to their comparative technical merits.[41]

Spilling over from the market-place and the academy into the legal and political arenas, the 'contest of the currents' between d.c. and a.c. took the form of courtroom struggles over patent rights, attempts to pass anti-competitive legislation, and public relations schemes aimed at discrediting the opposition and frightening their customers. The conjuncture of these events in time has contributed to the impression that they all were facets of a concerted and unbridled

[40] See Passer (1972), Table 19, p. 150 for lighting capacity data for the three leading companies in 1891.

[41] See, for a sample of the best modern accounts in each genre, Stillwell (1934); Passer (1972), Ch. 5; T. Hughes (1983), Ch. 6, esp., pp. 106–11; J. Hughes (1986), pp. 192–98. McDonald (1962), pp. 43–6 recounts the affair from the viewpoint of Samuel Insull.

counter-attack launched by the Edison camp, parts of an irrational effort to turn back the tide of technological progress that had brought an unwelcome influx of competition into the electrical supply business. But, some of the temporal coincidences in this instance are rather misleading. So it is necessary to begin by disentangling two of the major strands that appear intertwined in this fabric.

Throughout the late 1880s claims and counter-claims regarding infringement of electrical patent rights flew back and forth, both between members of the d.c. and the a.c. camps, and among parties belonging to the same camp.[42] Virtually from their inception the companies associated with Edison, and their financial backers, had approached the development and commercial exploitation of electricity for lighting and other uses within the paradigm of an integrated system—originally conceived of by the inventor through a conscious analogy drawn with existing systems of lighting, based upon the generation and distribution of illuminating gas.[43] The owners of these companies had an obvious collective motivation to block competition from a major variant system. In claiming patent rights to some components that were utilized by the a.c. alternative, the Edison interests might well have hoped to delay the marketing of a rival integrated electrical supply system, if only by inducing would-be competitors to take the time and trouble to 'invent around' Edison's patents. Indeed there were several occasions upon which Westinghouse's company was induced to go to great lengths in circumventing Edison patents, particularly those linked to the incandescent lamp.[44]

Legal contests of this form are not costless, however; time, energy and money were expended by all parties involved, and the costs often were deemed particularly steep by the more talented inventors, who were drawn away from their laboratories in order to defend proprietary rights to previous inventions—sometimes even though they had ceased to hold a major ownership stake in those putative rights.[45]

---

[42] For example, in addition to the patent suits mentioned below, Westinghouse filed claim for patent infringement against Thomson-Houston when the latter firm began production and sale of an a.c. incandescent lighting system. The two companies worked out an agreement under which control of the Consolidated and Sawyer-Man patents in possession of Thomson-Houston was relinquished to Westinghouse. See Passer (1972), p. 139.

[43] See T. Hughes (1983), pp. 22–3, and references therein, on Edison as a 'systems-inventor'—a point of some further significance below.

[44] Passer (1972), pp. 149–64.

[45] For example, Woodbury (1960), pp. 184–5, gives an account of the inordinate amount of time and worry that Elihu Thomson had to devote to problems connected with patent litigation. Josephson (1959, pp. 354–8) details Edison's vexations with the protracted 'war' with Westinghouse over the carbon filament patent of 1878, in which he was brought to testify during 1890. The suit cost the victorious Edison General Electric Co., holder of the patent, about $2 million by the time it was concluded in 1891—when the lamp patent had less than 3 years of life remaining. Sheer vanity aside, economically motivated reputational considerations can account for the willingness of inventors to spend time defending claims to proprietary rights which they have already sold; the value to purchasers of patent rights, which a self-employed inventor might wish to sell in the future, will be directly and indirectly affected by this form of commitment.

Edison's personal financial stake in patents he had received relating to lighting diminished greatly from the outset of his incandescent lamp project in 1878, when he had slightly over a 50 percent share; by 1886, after several rounds of raising more capital—first for the lighting enterprise, and then to expand his companies engaged in manufacturing components—he had sold nearly all his shares of the Edison Electric Lighting Co. The latter was the paper entity which legally held the patents and licensed use of the devices they covered to local light and power utilities.[46]

Throughout 1880–1885, neither Edison or the holding company's directors showed much interest in litigating over patent infringements, even though Edison maintained that his incandescent lamp invention preempted the claims of both Sawyer-Man and Maxim. Edison had been involved in enough patent litigation to know that such battles could stretch out over many years and entail very considerable expenses; it was also true that the Edison lamp at this time was far superior to the others being offered, and that during the pioneering phase of their development of the d.c. electric supply system the Edison people were more concerned with competing against gas than against the sponsors of rival electric lighting systems.

Moreover, the subsidary enterprises engaged in manufacturing dynamos, motors, conducting mains and components, lamps and other appliances required for lighting plants using the Edison system, were proving quite profitable even in these early years. The manufacturing part of the business constituted the primary source of income not only for the inventor, but also for his original colleagues at Menlo Park; Johnson, Batchelor, Upton, and Bergman had become responsible for the running of these subsidiary enterprises in which they had co-ownership interests with Edison.[47]

Beginning in 1885, however, the Edison Electric Light Co's passive stance vis-à-vis patent infringers was altered. At that time a reorganization of the board of the holding company occurred, which resulted in a weakening of the power of Edison and his original co-workers, particularly Batchelor and Upton. The new board were almost entirely representative of the financiers behind the company, and so were primarily interested in protecting the revenues derived from the proprietary rights of the Edison patents. A policy decision was therefore made to go after the infringers; law suits were initiated and customers were notified that the other sellers of lamps would be prosecuted.[48] The patent fights that reached the courts in the late 1880s and dragged on into the early

---

[46] See Josephson (1959), p. 351.

[47] See Josephson (1959), pp. 295–97; T. Hughes (1983), pp. 38–41.

[48] See Josephson (1959), p. 299; also *Electrical World* (January 1, 1887) for details on the eleven suits the Edison Electric Company began against the Westinghouse Electric Company on December 23, 1886 for injunctions and damages for the infringement of electric lighting patents; the patents in question covered the entire central station system.

1890s thus had been set in motion well beforehand and bore little direct connection with Edison's own responses to the intrusion of competition from the a.c. suppliers.

Of course, the patent litigation was only an aspect of the conflict and not the one that has caused the 'Battle of the Systems' to be characterized as bizarre. The most striking events of this episode revealed the lengths to which Edison and his immediate associates were prepared to go in order to convince the public that alternating current was an unsafe basis for an electricity supply system. Their campaign was waged through a barrage of 'scare' propaganda, supported by the grisly 'evidence' Edison and his immediate associates produced by experimenting with a.c. at their laboratory in West Orange, NJ. As Edison's biographer, Matthew Josephson, relates:

> There, on any day in 1887, one might have found Edison and his assistants occupied in certain cruel and lugubrious experiments: the electrocution of stray cats and dogs by means of high tension currents. In the presence of newspaper reporters and other invited guests, Edison and Batchelor would edge a little dog onto a sheet of tin to which were attached wires from an a-c generator supplying current at 1,000 volts.[49]

In July, 1888, Harold Brown, a former Edison laboratory assistant, electric pen salesman, and self-styled 'Professor', put on a demonstration of the harmful effects of a.c. at Columbia College's School of Mines: the electrocution of a large dog was featured.[50] Meanwhile, a scarlet-covered book had been issued under the title 'A Warning from the Edison Electric Light Company,' in which competitor-companies were accused of patent theft, fraud, and dishonest financing (including personal attacks on George Westinghouse); it gave descriptive details of the deaths, and in some instances the cremation by electrocution of unfortunates who came into contact with wires carrying alternating current.[51]

During 1888 the 'West Orange gang,' consisting of Edison, Johnson, and young Samuel Insull, aided by Brown and other assistants, succeeded in bringing off a related, stunning achievement in the art of negative promotion: they convinced the State of New York to substitute electrocution by administration of an alternating current for hanging as the means of executing convicted criminals. Edison himself had lobbied for this action before the New York legislature, and Brown—engaged as a consultant to the State on capital punishment by means of electrocution—surrptitiously purchased three Westinghouse alternators which he then announced had been selected as the

---

[49] See Josephson (1959), p. 347.
[50] See Josephson (1959), pp. 347–8; T. Hughes (1983), pp. 108–9; Woodbury (1960), p. 174.
[51] Woodbury (1960), p. 170–1.

type most suitable for such work.[52] The Edison group proceeded to milk the legislature's decision for all the publicity it was worth, circulating leaflets which, in warning the public about the dangers of high voltage a.c., used the term 'to Westinghouse' in referring to electrocution by alternating current.[53] Now, some warnings concerning the dangers involved with the new technology would not have been unwarranted when alternating current was first suggested as the basis of an incandescent lighting system. The source of the problem, however, lay not in the nature of the current, but rather in the fact that the proposed a.c. system would transmit energy on its mains at a higher voltage; direct current is always more deadly than alternating current at an equivalent voltage.[54]

Back in the fall of 1886, when the Westinghouse Electric Co. commercially introduced its alternating current lighting system, Edison therefore was only being overly optimistic in predicting that there soon would be some accidental electrocutions of Westinghouse's customers, which would bring about the new technology's natural demise. His view of the danger at the time was supported as reasonable by some experts within the a.c. camp.[55] In fact, Professor Elihu Thomson, co-founder of the Thomson-Houston Company, of Pittsburgh, PA, advised his company to refrain from marketing an a.c. lighting system for home use until better safeguards were developed; this, despite his having already employed alternating current in the company's commercial arc-lighting systems, and his development of an a.c. incandescent lighting system concurrently with the one that Westinghouse was proceeding to market. As one of Thomson's biographers has put it: 'There was enough truth in the contention [that h.v.a.c. is deadly] to hold the Pittsburgh firm back and use up much of its time and money in making counterclaims [to those of the Edison forces].'[56] Thus it was that while the Westinghouse Electric Co. and Edison-interests were engaged in head-to-head battle in the incandescent

---

[52] George Westinghouse, reportedly, was outraged. One of these alternators was in place at the Auburn State Prison in August 1890, where it produced the current lethal to the first victim of the 'electric chair,' William Kemmler, a convicted axe-murderer. See Leupp (1919), pp. 132–55, for details of the controversy over this execution, and the unfounded suspicions of the time that Westinghouse was financing the opponents of capital punishment who mobilized on the occasion.

[53] See Josephson (1959), pp. 348–9; Cheney (1981), p. 43; T. Hughes (1976), p. 108.

[54] See *Electrical World*, August 1887; September 1888; Woodbury (1960), p. 174. The lesser hazard of accidental electrocution from a.c. derives from the tendency of the current to repel a body from the mains, breaking the contact, whereas d.c. does not have this action. Although the text follows contemporary popular discussions by speaking of the harm done by high voltage, V, strictly, the damage done by a current is dependent upon the volume of the flow, i.e. the amperage, I. By Ohm's Law, however, the latter is proportional to the e.m.f., V—the proportionality constant being the resistance of the conducting body, R. See above, note 31.

[55] Josephson (1959), p. 345–5, 349. In addition to the early concern expressed by Elihu Thomson, Franklin Pope, in the US, and both Dr. Werner Von Siemens and Lord Kelvin—recognized 'scientific authorities' on electricity—warned against the dangers of the a.c. system of transmission at higher voltages.

[56] Woodbury (1960), pp. 169–72.

lighting field, the Thomson-Houston firm held off for a year and developed a simple method of preventing accidental electrocution in the unlikely event a transformer short-circuited.

Following this safety improvement, however, the Edison group did not relent in their propaganda campaign. Right through to 1889 Edison continued to participate in publicizing the undesirability of high voltage a.c. on grounds of safety, by criticizing the technical means given for rendering a.c. less hazardous. In an article on 'The Dangers of Electric Lighting,' published originally in the *North American Review*, Edison stated that the undergrounding of high voltage line (an often suggested means of increasing their safety) would serve only to make them more dangerous; further, he claimed that there was no means of effectively insulating overhead high-voltage wires, and concluded that 'the only way in which safety can be secured is to restrict electrical pressure (voltage).'[57]

With the benefit of hindsight, and a seeming pre-disposition towards the 'Whig' interpretation of technological history, previous chroniclers of this episode have been almost unanimous in portraying Edison as economically irrational in stubbornly championing the direct current system, and uncharacteristically, but nonetheless deplorably unscientific in his dogmatic public opposition to the rival alternating current technology sponsored by Thomson-Houston and the Westinghouse Electric Company.[58]

Harold Passer described Edison's transformation bluntly in the following terms: 'In 1879, Edison was a bold and courageous innovator. In 1889, he was a cautious and conservative defender of the status quo.'[59] More severe is the judgement offered by Jonathan Hughes' spirited account, according to which, by 1886–1887, Edison

had lost touch with the rapidly changing technology, or was fast losing touch. He had been a staunch, and then a rabid, opponent of alternating current transmission. . . . For some reason Edison could not comprehend the a.c. system. He was convinced that, transformers or not, the high-voltage of the a.c. system made it extraordinarily dangerous. . . . Arguments got nowhere with Edison on this issue. The fact that he considered the main proponents of the a.c. system to be

[57] *Electrical World*, November 2, 1889, pp. 292–3.

[58] See the influential account given by Josephson (1959), pp. 313–38, 349–50, 361–2, emphasizing Edison's resistance to the advice of others to follow Westinghouse and Thomson-Houston into the a.c. electricity supply field.

[59] Passer (1972), p. 74. This summation in Passer's 1954 study is quoted approvingly in the influential biography by Josephson (1959), p. 350. Alterations in the inventor's objective economic and institutional circumstances are cited by Passer in explanation of this transformation, whereas Josephson attributes Edison's unwillingness to pursue developments in a.c. technology to 'the fear that all the effort, equipment, and capital invested in the old system would quickly be made obsolete by the new'—seemingly without crediting Edison with an awareness that if his efforts could produce that result, it also could happen at the hands of others.

common thieves made him even more unwilling to see any virtue in their arguments. . . . There was no part of Edison's career that was so unworthy of the man and, in fact, sordid.[60]

Now, the reputation of Thomas Edison in American history-books is in all other respects so little in need of rehabilitation that there could scarcely be much call to repair it in this one regard, even if such a defense were plainly warranted by the facts. The concern here, accordingly, lies less with the way the conduct of the 'Battle of the Systems' has colored modern appraisals of Edison the man, and more with the proper appreciation of the strategic goals and constraints which shaped the decisions that he and his close associates made and implemented in this episode. Initial safety concerns about the hazards of a house-to-house incandescent lighting system based on (high voltage) a.c. were not irrational in view of the preceding history of faulty installations and consequent injuries with high voltage arc-lighting systems.[61]

Yet, practical experience in the industry soon revealed that grounding and improved insulation methods worked quite reliably.[62] It is therefore difficult to credit the view that Edison's original safety concerns were completely unwarranted, and that he continued to pronounce a.c. 'unsafe' because he remained ill-informed, or foolishly obstinate, or both. Indeed, so far was he from spurning high voltage as an unacceptably risky technology that the *Scientific American* for July 23, 1887 carried an article describing a new Edison

McDonald (1962), pp. 32–3, takes a different explanatory tack in suggesting that a profound psychological change had occurred with the death of Edison's wife, Mary Stilwell Edison, in 1884: 'Edison's creative period as an electric innovator [sic] ended with his wife's death, and in the future he not only contributed little to the success of his electric companies, but sometimes actually impeded their progress [by opposing alternating current applications]. From the greatest single asset a collection of electrical enterprises could possibly have, he suddenly became a burden.' An awkward fact, omitted from McDonald's account, is that within a year of Mary's death Edison had courted and successfully proposed marriage to Mina Miller, and appeared to his friends to have drawn a renewed vitality and pleasure in anticipating life with his second wife. (See Josephson 1959, pp. 301–8). As for the suggested waning of Edison's inventive powers, McDonald's assertion (p. 33, n. 16) that '[a]fter 1884, virtually all Edison's inventions were relatively trivial, and some of them were almost foolish' is refuted within 10 pages by his own, more accurate statement (p. 43): 'To be sure, some of his greatest achievements were yet to come—among them the perfected phonograph and the motion picture—but none of them was in the electric field.'

[60] J. Hughes (1986), pp. 193–4. This account bears indications of the influence of Josephson's (1959, p. 349) view that the 'whole dreadful controversy can be attributed only to an extreme bitterness of feeling towards his [Edison's] opponents that completely overbalanced his judgement.' Among the many previous histories of these events, the account provided by Thomas P. Hughes (1983) stands out in refraining from depicting Edison as ignorant and technologically reactionary on the subject of alternating current.

[61] Carlson and Millard (1987, pp. 267–77) call attention to Edison's earlier experience with the use of safety concerns as a competitive strategy—from the days when the illuminating gas companies had deployed such 'fear propaganda' against his own incandescent lighting enterprise. These authors offer an interpretation of Edison's motives in raising the 'safety question' which is quite different from the one put forward here. But nothing in the documentation they cite contradicts my contention that from 1887 onward Edison's actions were driven primarily by considerations of short-run expediency, rather than a long-run commitment to promoting the universal use of electricity by increasing the technology's safety.

[62] Woodbury (1960), pp. 172–3; Josephson (1959), p. 345.

high voltage d.c. distribution system. Presumably then he had a purpose in going on with the safety campaign against a.c. until 1889, but not continuing it beyond that year. Not surprisingly, the existence of some deeper, goal-directed strategy has been supposed even by some historians who have expressed their strong disapproval of the tactics used.[63]

An immediate purpose is not too hard to find. The objective of the animal execution demonstrations, the initiation of the electric chair, and the volumes of published material detailing the actual and potential hazards of a.c. was not, however, that of gaining sales in contested markets by influencing the choices made by purchasers of lighting systems, or their ultimate customers. Rather, the proximate goal was the creation of a climate of popular opinion in which further inroads by a.c. systems in the Edison companies' share of the incandescent lighting market might be prevented by legislative restraint, ostensibly justified on grounds that the public's safety needed protection. The gruesome promotional campaign was designed to persuade lawmakers to limit electric circuits to 800 volts, thereby stripping the rival system of the source of its transmission cost advantage. In at least two states, Ohio and Virginia, these efforts came closer to succeeding than in New York, where, having adopted the electric chair, the legislative balked at the intended sequel.[64]

If the events just recounted cannot be dismissed merely as the spiteful reactions of a short-sighted inventor who was being left behind in the onward march of technology, or simply as an unseemly tussle over marginal market territories between the respective suppliers of d.c. and a.c. lighting equipment, how should they be understood? What was Edison's underlying purpose, and, when was it formed? If Edison was quite sanguine in the face of the commercial initiation of Westinghouse's lighting system in Buffalo, NY, as his communication with Johnson in November of 1886 seems to indicate,[65] what had triggered the launching during the following year of the 'sordid' propaganda campaign aimed at crippling the a.c. technology with safety legislation? And, having once committed himself to this mode of competition, why did Edison discontinue it after 1889?

Although definitive answers to these questions about the motives of Edison and his associates are elusive, and may remain so even when the contents of the Edison Archives covering these years have become fully accessible, his actions can plausibly be construed as an economically rational, albeit cynical response on the part of an inventor-entrepreneur whose long-term plan to be the sole-sponsor of a 'universal' electrical supply system suddenly had gone away. On this view, Edison, far from being foolishly obtuse, was more likely

---

[63] See, for example McDonald (1962), p. 62; T. Hughes (1983), pp. 107–9.

[64] T. Hughes (1983), p. 108.

[65] See the extract from Josephson (1959), p. 346, quoted in the text above.

than any of the interested parties to have perceived during 1887 that the world in which he was operating had been abruptly altered; specifically, that a number of unexpected and serious blows had been dealt to his previous hopes of profiting greatly from control of the key technological components of a system that could supply energy for public arc-lamps, residential and commercial lighting, industrial power, and traction. This sudden reversal of his fortunes in the direct current electricity business came from the concatenation of two fundamentally unrelated sets of developments. One was a clustering of technological innovations that opened the way for alternating current to become the basis of an alternative, fully competitive universal electricity supply system; the other was the deterioration of Edison's personal financial position, along with that of the companies in which he was most directly involved. We have now to consider the nature of these critical technological and financial developments, taking them in turn. Coming together, they precipitated a course of action well-designed to salvage for Edison and his immediate associates as much as was possible before he would leave the industry to embark upon other ventures.

5. *The Advent of Polyphase A.C. and Its Significance*

The original 'stand-off' situation that had left d.c. and a.c. in 1885–86 with respective markets within which each held a clear, technically derived advantage was in reality a condition of transient equilibrium, a temporary balance soon disturbed by the realization of a differentially faster rate of technological advance along the a.c. system trajectory.[66] In the alternating current field, three new and interrelated innovations abruptly removed the disadvantages that had formerly restrained a.c. supply companies from penetrating the d.c. lighting and power markets: (1) the induction motor, (2) the a.c. meter, and (3) the rotary converter.

Between 1885 and 1888 Nikola Tesla, in the United States, Galileo Ferraris of Italy, and Michael Osipowitch von Dolivo Dobrowolsky, in Germany, each had discovered that two alternating currents differing in phase by 90 degrees, or a three alternating currents differing in phase by 120 degrees, could be used to rotate a magnetic field; that by placing in such

---

[66] See T. Hughes (1983), pp. 106–11 for a discussion suggesting that this differential rate of progress was somehow elicited because electrical engineers, having used a.c. to overcome the transmission cost constraints that encumbered the expansion of d.c. distribution networks, quickly encountered numerous obstacles in getting an a.c. electricity supply system to emulate the functions that existing d.c. systems were capable of performing—particularly, the provision of power to secondary motors. While such constraints may have served as 'focusing devices' (see Rosenberg, 1969), directing engineering efforts towards projects which were more likely to have high commercial payoff if the technical problems could be overcome, they could not have signalled the possibility of actually solving those problems.

a field a pivoted bar of iron, or a drum of laminated iron on which are wound self-closed coils of copper wire, one could construct a two- or three-phase induction motor.[67] Invention of the motor led directly to the development of a special polyphase generator and system of distribution.

Tesla's first two patents on the alternating-current motor were filed in October of 1887, and three more patents pertaining to the system were filed in November. The Westinghouse Electric Co. acquired these patents in July 1888, by which time Westinghouse already had persuaded Ferraris to permit it to file an American patent on the rotating magnetic field motor which he claimed he had built three years before.[68] Coincidentally, in April 1888, Oliver B. Shallenberger, an engineer working for Westinghouse, came upon the polyphase induction phenomenon and applied it to solve the problem of designing an effective meter for alternating current; by June he had shown that such meters could be built in quantity. Hence, by 1889, Westinghouse Electric Company was able to put into commercial production a meter which enhanced the scope for a.c. in central station lighting operations, and the technological basis for penetrating portions of the electric power market.[69]

While a.c. induction motor and meter posed an obvious threat, they did not immediately give rise to commercial challenges to Edison's manufacturing companies in urban markets where d.c. power supply was already established. Despite the greater than fifty percent market share that a.c. had achieved in the field of lighting by 1891, there was a considerable amount of momentum built into the growth of d.c. supply systems. Two forces were behind this momentum. First, where a local electric supply system did constitute a natural monopoly and there already existed an installed d.c. generating and distribution system, the unamortized investment in d.c. plant was so large that it discouraged replacement with polyphase a.c.; by adopting a mixed system the local utility would lose the scale advantages associated with a single system.[70] Second, as long as there was an important portion of the urban market held firmly by d.c.—namely, the market for traction power, and to a lesser degree industrial electrolysis, as distinguished from that for secondary-motor power for elevators, factories and other such applications—the local d.c. central stations meeting this (traction) demand would necessarily also supply the other

[67] See Fleming (1921), pp. 146–7 for details of motor development and their construction.

[68] T. Hughes (1983), pp. 115–17 gives full details on the filing, issuance and acquisition dates of the key Tesla patents, and others.

[69] See Prout (1921), pp. 128–9. Development of an a.c. meter was regarded as sufficiently important that Westinghouse himself filed patents on one such device, in June 1887, and on another, in October 1887, developed jointly with one of his engineers, Phillip Lange. Patents were issued for these meters in May 1888, but by then they had been superceded by Shallenberger's design.

[70] T. Hughes (1983), p. 120, notes also that the electrical equipment manufacturing companies also 'remained partially committed to direct current' by virtue of the specialized facilities, patent positions, as well as the experience and expertise they had built up in that field.

electricity needs in the area; rivals could not penetrate the market because the d.c. system with its load balancing advantage could under-price them. Hence, unless some 'gateway,' or interface technology emerged, a partial commitment to perpetuation of the d.c. technology would remain for some time to come.

Viewed from this perspective, it was another technical innovation, part of a new 'gateway' technology coincident to and dependent on the development of polyphase a.c., that was critical in delivering the coup de grace to a comprehensive electric supply system based entirely on a d.c. technology.[71] The rotary converter was a device which combined an a.c. induction motor with a d.c. dynamo to make possible the connection of high voltage a.c. transmission lines to d.c. distribution networks. A former Edison employee, Charles S. Bradley, who already had applied for a patent on a polyphase generator and a synchronous motor in March 1887 (actually before Tesla), successfully patented the rotary converter in the United States during the following year.[72]

The major significance of the rotary converter lay in the fact that it enabled the old d.c. central station and traction distribution networks to be coupled with new long distance high voltage a.c. transmission mains. These 'gateway devices' thereby made possible the formation of a more flexible 'hybrid' system, the advantages of which were recognized in the electrical engineering press as early as 1887.[73]

By the early 1890s Bradley had set up his own factory to produce the converter in Yonkers, NY, a plant that would soon be acquired along with the patent by the General Electric Company. The potential profitability of the business of supplying rotary converters likewise drew the Westinghouse Electric Company into further development work on such devices.[74] Converters were also developed to couple existing single-phase a.c. with the newer and more efficient polyphase technology. In fact, by the middle of the 1890s there would exist devices to convert in any direction. Conversion of d.c. to polyphase a.c. proved an immediately attractive application in some locales, such as Chicago, where Samuel Insull saw it would permit raising the load factors on existing d.c. plant by transmitting current over a much more extensive area in which the load was more diverse.[75]

---

[71] The role of 'gateway' innovations in network technology evolution is explicitly considered with reference to the rotary converter by David and Bunn (1988), and is discussed more generally in regard to standardization policy issues by David (1987).

[72] Passer (1972), pp. 300–1; T. Hughes (1983), p. 118. The courts eventually ruled against the patent application by Bradley for the generator and synchronous motor, on the ground that Tesla's patent was fuller and more complete.

[73] See Pfrannkuche (1887) for discussion of an 'all purpose' system involving d.c. dynamos and a.c. transmission.

[74] Lamme (1926), Chapter 6, recounts his early work for Westinghouse on rotary converters.

[75] See McDonald (1962), pp. 69–70, on the work of Chicago Edison's chief engineer, Louis Ferguson, circa 1894, who installed rotary converters at both the generating and local distribution ends—using

What had happened during 1887–88, in essence, was the dramatic appearance of a new technological variant—the polyphase a.c. system—induced by the opportunities inherent in the limitations of d.c. and singlephase a.c. as bases for a 'universal' electricity supply system. It was the polyphase a.c. technology that would diffuse rapidly, becoming the de facto network standard for electricity generation and transmission in the United States, penetrating the core urban markets for electric light and power, and thereby realizing the greater economies of scale which fostered the emergence of extensive 'natural monopolies' in the electric supply industry.

Although Edison may not have foreseen the whole evolution of the network technology that would be created to exploit the transmission cost advantages of alternating current, his course of action from 1887 onwards reflected, in my view, an astute grasp of the precarious, unstable nature of a competitive situation that was unfolding with unexpected speed from the successful experiments with polyphase a.c. motors. That perception would have reinforced whatever other considerations might have disposed him to leave the electricity industry, instead of girding himself to participate in an inventive race against the emerging a.c.-based universal system.[76]

As Thomas Parke Hughes has emphasized, Edison's talents inclined him toward the invention of devices that were interrelated within a system context, and he naturally preferred to work on components whose improvement would lead to enhanced performance and value throughout a system whose parameters he could control—and thereby draw the greater profit from.[77] Yet, in the circumstances of the electricity supply industry during 1887–1888, reasonable expectations of extracting significant rents on any incremental, strictly d.c.-compatible inventions had largely been vitiated by the developments leading to Bradley's rotary converter. Furthermore, the d.c. system elaborated under Edison's sponsorship was now at a disadvantage; additional research and development resources would have to be devoted to reducing distribution costs, just for it to be able to hold its own in competition with

polyphase a.c. for transmission only. On the technology of rotary (or, in some English usage, 'rotatory') converters, as well as rotary transformers (used in changing the voltage of direct current), and the Ferranti rectifier (used in transforming an alternating single-phase current into a direct pulsating current for arc lighting), see the article on 'Transformers' contributed by J. A. Fleming in _Encyclopedia Britannica_ (1910–1911), vol. 27, pp. 178–9. More generally, on the significance of converters, see T. Hughes (1983), pp. 121–2.

[76] Edison, in a 1908 encounter with George Stanley, the son of William Stanley, whose improvement on the Gaulard Gibbs patent had been the basis for Westinghouse's a.c. system, is said to have remarked: 'Oh, by the way, tell your father I was wrong.' Josephson (1959, p. 349) in reporting this interprets Edison to have thereby acknowledged that he had made 'his greatest blunder' by not following Westinghouse into the a.c. technology. Putting aside the issue of whether Edison had made a blunder or a justifiable decision, it remains quite unclear exactly what Edison felt he had been 'wrong' about. Possibly it was his mistaken expectation, in 1886, that a great deal of experimenting and a long period of further practical development would be needed before a system based on a.c. could be brought to the point of challenging his own.

[77] See T. Hughes (1983), pp. 22–3.

polyphase a.c. systems. What profit to an inventor undertaking that uncertain mission, when the limiting value of the improvement would be that set by the cost of the rotary converters installed to transform d.c. to a.c. and/or a.c. back to d.c. for local distribution and traction uses? Edison had more tempting projects in which to engage his laboratory staff and his own inventive genius.[78]

The unorthodox and rather desperate tactics adopted by the 'West Orange Gang' in their 'safety campaign' against Westinghouse takes on a different appearance when set in this context, especially their focus upon invoking some regulatory intervention to deprive alternating current-based systems of the transmission advantages deriving from use of high voltages. The campaign looks more like a temporary 'holding operation,' meant to delay the competition so as to permit Edison to stage a more orderly and profitable exit from the industry, and less like a serious counter-offensive. Had it been Edison's hope and intention to permanently cripple the competitive system of electricity supply, it would hardly have made sense for him to accelerate his withdrawal from the business of manufacturing and selling the key components of the d.c. system that would be left in command of the field. Yet, that is precisely what he was proceeding to do.[79] It was a decision, however, that owed something also to the financial straits in which Edison unexpectedly found himself just when he was moving into research and development projects in other areas, pursuing costly undertakings that were still quite far from the commercialization stage.

6. *The End of the Sponsored-Systems Rivalry*

Edison's decision to get out of the electricity business was significant, because it would lead shortly to the disappearance from the United States' electrical

---

[78] Thus, it is not surprising that after the spring of 1887 Edison should have allowed himself to become increasingly pre-occupied with renewed experimental work on his phonograph—entering an inventive race against workers in the laboratory of Alexander Bell who had undertaken to improve upon the original Edison device of 1877. Josephson (1959), pp. 317–31 relates the story of this project, which was brought to a successful culmination by Edison's famous 72-hour frenzy of non-stop work in June, 1888; and of the disappointing sequel, in which J. Lippincott and Edison's unscrupulous associates swindled the inventor out of a major part of the value of the rights to the new phonograph patent and an exclusive manufacturing license.

[79] In response to this interpretation, Jonathan Hughes in private correspondence with the author (March 5, 1987) writes: 'I hope you're right about how clever Edison was in getting out of the way of the ac "juggernaut". So far as actual verbal evidence goes, Edison could have done what he did for no more reasons than ignorance and cunning. . . . I am willing to grant that he had a certain peasant cunning (Bauernschlauheit) that would make him see that a campaign of dust-in-your eyes about ac would allow him to sell out and get out. It is reasonable. The evidence that he was running from what he did not and could not understand is pretty strong too.' Bauernschlauheit, no less, and from a fellow of mixed Scottish and Dutch descent!

manufacturing industry of a commercial sponsor having proprietary interests exclusively in the d.c. technology.[80] It had its roots not only in the burst of polyphase a.c. developments just reviewed, but in the evolution of Edison's relationship with the holding company (Edison Electric Light) in charge of his lighting patents and the various entities such as Edison Lamp, and (Edison) Machine Works, that actually manufactured the components of the system and serviced them. Recall that by the mid-1880s Edison and his immediate associates had little stake in, and less control of the holding company that drew royalties on the use of the lighting patents by central station companies and other companies set up to license the construction of isolated lighting plants; whereas, Edison remained the principal owner of the factories, from which he and his immediate associates had been drawing their main income. During 1886–1888, however, the precarious financial situation of the latter group of enterprises came to be perceived as tremendously burdensome to their owners. Much of the equipment supplied previously by the manufacturers to central stations had been paid for with hard-to-negotiate shares in those fledgling enterprises, resulting in severe cash flow problems for the Edison concerns. With the recovery from the business recession of 1885, electrical equipment orders were coming in faster than the factories had resources to produce and deliver. But, it was proving difficult to finance the expansion on short-term credit, and to solve this problem by permitting the Morgan banking group (who already dominated Edison Electric Light) to extend their control over the manufacturing enterprises in exchange for long-term loans was hardly an appealing prospect. Thus, at the same time that Edison was fretting over the possibility that his over-expanded manufacturing businesses might be forced into bankruptcy, he was also sending his financially skillful young associate, Samuel Insull, off to borrow the extra sums needed for the West Orange, NJ laboratory's expanding program of non-electrical researches.[81]

Consequently, the return of Henry Villard from Germany in 1886, bearing a commission from the Deutsche Bank to negotiate with Drexel, Morgan and Company about the acquisition of holdings in American businesses, came at a most fortuitous moment. Edison was much relieved to be presented soon thereafter with Villard's proposed plan for the consolidation of all the Edison-related enterprises (including the patent-holding company, and Sprague Electric Railway and Motor Company) into one new corporation with backing from the Deutsche Bank, the Allgemeine Elektrizitats Gesellschaft, and the firm of Siemens and Halske, of Berlin. The inventor saw in this a welcome

---

[80] See Josephson (1959), pp. 350–66, and McDonald (1962), pp. 30–39 for a fuller account of the formation of the Edison General Electric Co., and then, the General Electric Co.

[81] See Josephson (1959), p. 340; McDonald (1962), p. 38.

opportunity to both extricate himself from the worries and distractions of managerial and financial responsibility for the manufacturing business, and raise sufficient capital to place his laboratory on firmer financial foundations.[82] Ultimately, the terms to which J. P. Morgan was willing to agree turned out to be somewhat less favorable to Edison and the manufacturing company owners than those initially proposed, and, not surprisingly, more generous to the holders of the lighting patent with whom Morgan was directly involved. Nevertheless, they gave the inventor $1750 000 in cash, 10 per cent of the shares, and a place on the board of the new company.[83]

In this way the Edison General Electric Co. came to be organized in January 1889. Within a few months the consolidations were formally effected, and Edison himself no longer had direct influence in the running of the manufacturing side of the business. By 1890 he had largely completed the liquidation of his remaining 10 per cent shareholding in the new company, was taking no active role on its board of directors, and was writing to ask Villard not to oppose his 'retirement from the lighting business, which will enable me to enter into fresh and congenial fields of work.'[84] The propaganda war against the Westinghouse a.c. system, which had been brought to its peak in the midst of the consolidation negotiations, was rapidly wound down in 1889. It would seem to have served the real purpose of supporting the perceived value of the Edison enterprises which were at the time wholly committed to manufacturing the components of a d.c.-based electric light and power system, and thereby improving the terms on which Edison and his close associates were able to 'cash out.'

Elements within the American financial community, among which the Morgan interests were most prominent, were moving at this time to consolidate and hence 'rationalize' another network industry—the railroads.[85] The control and consolidation of the electrical manufacturing and supply business represented a parallel undertaking. A major step was effectively accomplished by joining Thomson-Houston Company and the Edison General Electric Company; in 1892 the first of these, under the leadership of Charles A. Coffin, received Morgan's support in buying out the second, thereby forming the General Electric Company.[86] This turn of events meant that by 1892

---

[82] Josephson (1959), pp. 351–3. On Villard's role, see also, McDonald (1962), pp. 39–40, and T. Hughes (1983), pp. 76–7.

[83] See McDonald (1962), pp. 40–1.

[84] Josephson (1959), p. 361, quoting a letter dated February 8, 1890.

[85] See for example Daggett (1908), Campbell (1938), Kolko (1965), Chapter IV, esp. pp. 64–7.

[86] See McDonald (1962), pp. 48–51. Villard, at the head of E.G.E. previously had sought a consolidation with the Westinghouse Electric Company, but when priority was awarded to Edison's carbon filament patent in 1891, he felt his hand sufficiently strengthened to seek to acquire a supposedly weakened competitor, and opened negotiations with Thomson-Houston. In the end, Morgan agreed with Coffin that Thomson-Houston was in a stronger financial position, and so should purchase E.G.E. There is a nice, but

Edison—who had earlier been adamantly opposed to the idea of forming a combine with Thomson-Houston and doubtless would have remained so—had withdrawn entirely from the business, so that no solely d.c.-oriented manufacturing entity existed in the American market.

Westinghouse's enterprise, however, was able to elude the Morgan group's aspirations for an all-encompassing 'rationalization' of the industry, paradoxically because its shaky condition had forced it to put its affairs in order and line up banking support from other quarters at the very beginning of the decade. Finding his business under-capitalized to weather the aftermath of the Baring 'crisis' in 1890, and unable to obtain a half-million dollars on satisfactory terms from the Pittsburgh business banking community, George Westinghouse was obliged to turn for backing to a New York-based financial syndicate headed by August Belmont and to reorganize his company.[87] Work on the development of Tesla's induction motor and 3-phase system was brought to a halt during these difficulties in 1890–1891, but, it soon was resumed—once Tesla had been induced not to hold Westinghouse to the terms of the royalty agreements concluded between them in 1888–1889.[88]

The electrical manufacturing business in the United States thus came to be dominated by two large firms from 1892 onward, but the industry also had become essentially homogeneous with regard to the basic formulation of its technology. By 1893, the General Electric and the Westinghouse Electric and Manufacturing Companies both were marketing some version of a polyphase alternating current system, and both had entered the profitable business of manufacturing rotary converters.[89] The era of rivalry between commercial

---

unresolved, and probably unresolvable question: whether E.G.E.'s comparatively weaker financial condition owed something to the effect of Edison's propaganda campaign against a.c., which supported an inflation of the price E.G.E. paid for its constituent d.c.-system companies.

[87] See Leupp (1919), pp. 157–61. Under Belmont's direction, two electric lighting companies that had been controlled by the Westinghouse interests (the United States and the Consolidated) were absorbed into the reorganized firm, and their stockholders were given the new preferred and common stock issued by the Westinghouse Electric and Manufacturing Co. The stockholders of the main company surrendered 40 per cent of their old stock, and were asked to take second preference shares in the reorganized firm in lieu of the rest. By these measures the original outstanding liability of more than $10 million (on which the annual interest charges exceeded $180 000) was reduced to less than $9 million—all in equity.

[88] See Cheney (1981), pp. 48–9. According to the memos exchanged between Westinghouse and Tesla in 1888 and 1889, the former was to pay the Tesla Electric Co. $2.50 per h.p. of electric power sold. It was said that by 1893 the accrued royalties that would have been owed Tesla under these agreements would have amounted to $12 million—considerably more than the assets of the Westinghouse Electric and Manufacturing Co. at that date. Tesla, by then, had already been talked out of his royalties by George Westinghouse, who, reportedly had told him: 'Your decision determines the fate of the Westinghouse Company.' Were Tesla not to give up his contract, Westinghouse suggested, there was nothing to assure that his inventions would be implemented commercially: 'In that event you would have to deal with the bankers, for I would no longer have any power in the situation.'

[89] Passer (1972), pp. 298–303; Sharlin (1963), pp. 187–8. Bradley's patents and facilities were bought up by General Electric and the Westinghouse Electric Company developed their own rotary converters over the same period.

sponsors of technologically distinct systems in the United States' electrical supply industry was brought to a close within six years of its commencement.

7. *Diffusion of the New Technology—and the Path Not Taken*

Yet, the question of the superiority of one form of current over the other remained unresolved within the engineering community. Whether direct or alternating current was to be generated by the hydroelectric power project being undertaken at the Niagara Falls was still very much an open question during 1892.[90] The proponents of d.c. at Niagara had argued that for conditions of varying load, as was the case in a lighting system, d.c. was much the more efficient of the two.[91] While this may have held true in 1890, following the 1891 demonstration by Oscar Muller and the Swiss firm of Brown Boveri & Co. that polyphase current could be transmitted the 110 miles from Lauffen on the upper Neckar River to Frankfurt-am-Main, Germany,[92] and the equally impressive Westinghouse Electric Company polyphase system exposition (including the rotary converter) at the Chicago World's Fair in 1893, it was evident that lighting was no longer the only factor to consider when discussing the load and efficiency characteristics of the a.c. and d.c. system variants.[93]

With the extension of a.c. to power users, and to traction users as a result of the invention of the rotary converter, the decision between a.c. and d.c. came down to the one which could distribute power over a distance most efficiently and cheaply. And, as the distance from Niagara to the nearest concentration of customers in Buffalo, NY, was 20 miles, a.c. could reduce the loss of power on transmission lines to a far greater extent than was possible with d.c. In 1893, both the Westinghouse Electric Company and the newly formed General Electric Company submitted plans to the Cataract Construction Company (which was pioneering the Niagara development), specifying an a.c. system consisting of generators, transformers, and transmission lines.[94]

Beginning in 1896, central stations began being converted into substations hooked up to a.c. transmission lines, and by 1898 a constant current transformer had been developed to make possible the linking up of arc lighting

---

[90] Fleming (1921), pp. 238–9.

[91] 'One engineer estimated that under such conditions, the d.c. system would be twice as efficient as an a.c. system.' Sharlin (1963), p. 200, quoting from a statement in 1900 by the British electrical engineering authority, J. A. Fleming.

[92] See Landes (1969), p. 286, and Fleming (1921), pp. 238 ff. for technical details.

[93] On the Westinghouse exhibit at The Columbian Exposition in 1893, see for example Prout (1921), pp. 134–40; Sharlin (1963), pp. 206–11.

[94] See Sharlin (1963), pp. 195–210 for discussion of the choice of technology at Niagara.

distribution networks with a.c. transmission lines.[95] Hence, the flexibility and capabilities of this new coupling technology led to a rapid diffusion of the a.c. polyphase technology and the integration of smaller urban electricity supply systems into larger networks which eventually formed regional grids.[96] Once the systems competition had tipped in this direction, lighting plant also came to be replaced with a.c. technology as the previous d.c. distribution networks wore out; other things being equal, transformers stepping-down high voltage a.c. were a much simpler and cheaper technology for lighting purposes than the use of rotary converters to feed local d.c. distribution networks from high voltage a.c. transmission lines.[97] Converters continued to be employed well into the 20th century, however, most notably in the traction field where d.c. remained the current preferred at the point of consumption.[98]

A *de facto* standard in the form of alternating current as the basis of a 'universal' electrical supply system had emerged by the 1920s, both in the United States and abroad. While diffusion data for the 1890s is not available, the figures assembled in Table 1 show that in America the fraction of central station generating capacity accounted for by a.c. rose from 69 percent in 1902 to 95 percent in 1917. Moreover, one can discern in this the large role played by the rotary converter. This appears from the absolute rise in rotary converter capacity installed and also from the fact that the d.c. share of end-use capacity fell far less sharply than its share in generating capacity. Indeed, the former remained essentially unchanged after 1907. At the engineering level, therefore, the 'battle of the systems' did not end with the capitulation and withdrawal of one of the contenders, as the Edison-Westinghouse business rivalry had done. The technological denouement has been described by Thomas Parke Hughes[99] as a peaceful resolution to the conflict: no outright defeat for d.c.; rather, a graceful and apparently efficient absorption within a transitional 'mixed' system, prior to its gradual disappearance from the American electrical scene.

The perspective of hindsight may impart to this story an impression of inevitability, and even a supposition of optimality, both of which should be resisted. Meaningful global evaluations of efficiency are difficult if not impossible

---

[95] National Electrical Manufacturers Association (1946), p. 74.

[96] See Byatt (1979), pp. 114; Bowers (1982), pp. 162; Lardner (1903) for discussion of regional grid development.

[97] See Byatt (1979), p. 76.

[98] See Byatt (1979), chapter 4; Sharlin (1963), pp. 185, 188.

[99] T. Hughes' (1983), pp. 120–21, succinct formulation bears quotation: 'Because "the battle of the systems" had become far more complicated than a technical problem awaiting a simple technical solution, it ended without the dramatic vanquishing of one system by the other, or a revolutionary transition from one paradigm to another. The conflict was resolved by synthesis, by a combination of coupling and merging. The coupling took place on the technical level; the merging, on the institutional level.'

TABLE 1. Distribution of Generating and End-Use Electric Capacity between Direct Current and Alternating Current, Excluding Power Generation by Electric Railways, in the United States, 1902–1917.

	Kilowatt Capacity (thousands)			
	1902	1907	1912	1917
Dynamos:				
d.c., constant voltage	330.1	406.5	432.4	418.6
a.c. and polyphase	736.3	2221.8	4689.2	8557.7
Rotary converters	232.2	363.4	1009.1	1898.6
Transformers	560.4	1693.5	4103.9	9499.0
d.c. share in total generating capacity[a]	0.31	0.16	0.08	0.05
d.c. share in end-use[b] capacity	0.53	0.29	0.28	0.26
Ratio of transformer capacity to a.c. capacity	0.76	0.76	0.88	1.11

[a] d.c. share in generating capacity is calculated by dividing d.c. dynamo capacity into the sum of d.c. and a.c. dynamo capacity.

[b] d.c. share in end-use capacity is calculated by subtracting rotary converter capacity from the a.c./polyphase dynamo capacity, adding rotary converter capacity to d.c. dynamo capacity, and then recalculating d.c.'s share of total capacity.

Sources: Dynamo data: Bureau of Census (1920), Table 40, p. 63 for 1907, 1912, and 1917; transformer data: Bureau of Census (1920) Table 110, pp. 170–1, for 1917; Bureau of Census (1915) Table 65, p. 104 for 1912; Bureau of Census (1906) Tables 118 and 119, pp. 134–7 for 1902. Note that the horsepower data from Tables 74 and 75 has been converted to kilowatts according to 1 h.p. = 0.746 k.w.

to make between alternative technological systems whose influences ramify so widely and are so profound that they are capable of utterly transforming the economic and social environments into which they have been introduced.[100] As a guard against the strong temptation to suppose in matters of technological advance that 'what is, ought to have been', it is always useful to at least notice the existence of other paths that were not taken.

From the technical journals and magazines of the period it is apparent that no immediate consensus emerged on the engineering merits of the two currents; there were well-respected inventors and scientists, many of whom were founders of the industry, who would not testify to the technical superiority of alternating current.[101] For, the d.c. technology also showed itself quite capable of being

[100] This is a difficulty with which efforts to quantify the effects of major transport innovations, such as the canal and railroad systems, have had to contend [see for example David (1975), Chapter 6]; I am grateful to Edward Constant, who has reminded me of its relevance in the present connection.

[101] Throughout the 'Battle of the Systems' electrical engineers debated the advantages and disadvantages of the variant systems in the pages of the *Electrical World* [see for example Duncan (1988) and February 26, 1887; January 21, 1888; March 31, 1888]. In addition to Lord Kelvin, and Dr Werner von Siemens, two of the more distinguished industry personalities who argued on behalf of direct current until late in the 19th century, there were many other engineers continuing to debate the merits of the two systems at the turn of the century; see for example Barstow (1901) and Scott (1901).

further elaborated, in directions that both heightened its special advantages and broadened the range of conditions under which it was economically competitive. As was the case with a.c., the possibility of lowering the cost of the d.c. systems by raising the voltage was being actively explored. As early as 1883 Charles F. Brush had attempted a high voltage d.c. system that could more fully utilize fixed generating capacity and increase the radius of profitable transmission, by using 'accumulators' (storage batteries) to handle some of the peak lighting load and to accomplish the reduction of voltage for local distribution. Due to a combination of problems associated with the battery technology available at the time, the dangers of operating a high potential system having dynamos wired in series, and the usual run of financial difficulties, this particular project never took off and the concept was not pursued further in the United States.[102]

Abroad, however, the English from the mid-1880s onwards attempted to implement a variety of h.v.d.c. electricity supply schemes.[103] The earliest of these met much the same fate as that of Brush—too many troubles with expensive primitive batteries and a myriad of financial woes arising from inadequate demand and insufficient capital. But several innovations introduced late in the 1880s did prove successful. Notable among these was the 'Oxford system,' an approach first employed in 1889, which transmitted high voltage d.c. to substations where it was 'bumped down' to usable voltage levels via either a battery arrangement or a direct current transformer.[104] On balance, the major advantages of the h.v.d.c.-battery technology lay in ensuring continuity of supply when generating plants failed or were shut down for maintenance, and in reducing the amount of fixed capacity required to meet peak loads on the system.[105] In Britain, then, the story unfolded along lines very different from those in the United States; there, the 'competition of the

---

[102] Stanley (1912), p. 565.

[103] The voltages these involved were much lower than those in modern high voltage direct current systems, which recently have re-emerged as a technological area of active research and development interest to the electricity industry in the United States. See, for example, Alvarado and Lansetter (1984), Weeks (1981), Zorpette (1985).

[104] See Parsons (1940), chapter IV, pp. 52–70, for discussion of early h.v.d.c. systems in England. According to the *Encyclopedia Britannica* (1910–1911), vol. 9, p. 196, the 'Oxford system' was distinguished by the use of 'continuous' (direct) current transformers to accomplish the drop in voltage from the 1000–2000 v. range at which the current was transmitted from the generating stations to the 100–150 v. supplied by distributing mains to users. Although 3000 v. came to be regarded as the practical limiting voltage for individual d.c. dynamos (due to the problems of sparking at the commutator brushes when running at faster speeds) two or more such machines could be wired in series in order to secure much greater voltages for purposes of transmission. In France, for example, on the Thury direct current system energy was transmitted a distance of 115 miles (between Moutiers and Lyons) at voltages upwards of 45 000 v., using four groups of dynamos in series, each group consisting of four machines in series. See *Encyclopedia Britannica* (1910–1911), vol. 8, p. 778.

[105] Byatt (1979), p. 100. One additional advantage of the 'Oxford system' was that existing d.c. arc-lamps for street lighting could be worked off the high voltage mains in sets of 20 to 40. See *Encyclopedia Britannica* (1910–1911), vol. 9, p. 196. See also Lineff (1888).

currents' was tipped during the 1890s towards d.c. by the possibility of using accumulators in combination with high voltage.[106]

Concurrently, on the European Continent, M. Thury was developing a system of transmitting direct current at very high voltages from constant current generators worked in series, and commonly coupled mechanically in pairs or larger groups driven by a single prime mover. This offered advantages in easier line insulation than was required at half the voltage with alternating current, and removal of difficulties of line inductance and capacity encountered in high voltage a.c. transmission. High voltage constant current plant lent itself to greater ease of operation in emergencies (over a grounded circuit, for example) and permitted the design of comparatively simple and inexpensive switchboard arrangements. Notwithstanding the fact that the direct current generators used in this system were relatively expensive and their individual output was inconveniently small for large transmission work, around 1910 even a contemporary American authority gave it as his view that 'the possibilities of improvement in the system have by no means been worked out, and although it has been overshadowed by the enormous growth of polyphase transmission it must still be considered seriously.'[107]

Unlike the battery-using h.v.d.c., the a.c. version of the 'universal' electricity system concept inexorably pushed Samuel Insull and others who pioneered it in the US towards 'load balancing' as the way to mitigate the wastage imposed by having to build enough generating capacity to meet peak loads. The search for a diversified load over a wider region, with high fixed costs in place, created problems of natural monopolies which would not have existed to the same degree under the h.v.d.c. battery technology. Of course, it must be acknowledged that without strong increasing returns effects via load balancing, a d.c. battery-d.c. technology might simply have allowed more leeway to the forces making for too great a degree of diversity in voltages, current and a.c. frequencies. Such could be said to have been the experience

---

[106] Landes (1969), p. 285–6 summarizes this with the statement that 'The two systems competed fiercely in Britain for many years. In the long run, however, victory lay with centralized generators and long-distance transmission.' Although the latter is indisputable, there is a point in noticing that the 'victory' was not an indigenous evolutionary outcome. It came in the 1920s, with the transplantation to Britain of the electric utility system technology which had become the dominant engineering style in the United States. The interruption of WWI had contributed to leaving Britain's electricity supply industry in a rather dilapidated state, considerably behind American practice in terms of generator size and efficiency, and load factors. Compared with British 'average practice' c. 1920, American methods looked far superior. But the long-run outcome of the British 'contest' cannot be offered in support of the optimality of the course of technological evolution which the industry had followed in the United States. It was not an independent experiment; indeed, had the a.c.–d.c. rivalry not been resolved in the American market so far before, allowing time for much improvement in the design and actual operation of electricity networks, borrowing technology from the United States might hardly have been so attractive to the British in the 1920s.

[107] Louis Bell, 'Power Transmission', in *Encyclopedia Britannica* (1910–1911), vol. 22, p. 234. Bell was Chief Engineer of the Electric Power Transmission Department of General Electric Co., and former editor of *Electrical World*. See also Weeks (1981), pp. 267–71.

of the industry in Britain. Yet, if regulatory intervention is accepted as a proper solution to the natural monopoly problem which soon arose in the United States in the case of electric utilities, presumably public intervention could have imposed some standardization of d.c. voltages to permit realization of scale economies in the production of motors, lamps, and other end uses. Moreover, further down the road, when social efficiency was deemed to be achieved through the development of a larger network or 'grid', the US state and local regulatory structure which by then had actually been imposed in response to the condition of local monopoly would prove to have discouraged local utilities from integrating and supplying still wider geographical markets.

Such skepticism about the long-run economic optimality and consequent inevitability of the de facto standard that emerged in the United States is, of course, reinforced by the foregoing detailed recounting of its historical roots in 'battle of the systems'. Given the urgency of the utility companies' drive to achieve scale economies in electric supply, their move to the polyphase a.c.-based 'universal' system was certainly little affected by weighing the potentialities for long-run technical improvement offered by alternative systems. Just as short-run liquidity considerations had figured prominently in Edison's decisions during the formation of Edison General Electric, so short-run maximization of rents on the existing stock of proprietary technology seems to be the best algorithm descriptive of the course of action pursued by the dominant successor-firms engaged in manufacturing and marketing electric supply equipment in the US during the years before the First World War.

8. *Reflections on Network Technologies and Schumpeterian Entrepreneurs*

The 'battle of the systems' has been presented by previous narrators as a colorful and cautionary tale. Many of them, it seems, would have us find in it the moral that even an individual possessing extraordinarily inventive and entrepreneurial talents may sink to foolish knavery by exchanging the role of technological progress's steadfast champion to become, instead, a defender of the status quo; and a vain fool in the bargain. As we have had to be taught that the progress of invention and technical change is a complex social and economic process which transcends the intentions and efforts of individual men and women, and that technology is best regarded as 'socially constructed'— a cumulative result of the work of many minds and hands under the guidance of unseen forces, we naturally suppose ourselves to have a clearer view than that held by the individual participants in the process. In a sense this leaves one pre-disposed to fault even Thomas Alva Edison for his supposed hubris in hoping single-handedly to stay this advance.

Although there are contexts in which such a moral is well worth remembering, it does not strike me as the best one to recall in conjunction with this particular episode in technological and industrial history. Indeed, the perspective which recent contributions to economic theory offer on the early phases of the evolution of a paradigmatic network industry like electricity supply should prepare us to recognize the degree to which discrete 'events' of a largely adventitious nature, among them the specific courses of action chosen by individual agents occupying key decision-making positions, really do have the potential to set important technological parameters defining the industry's future trajectory. This is not to say that great consequences can be expected to follow from every move made by the drama's principal human actors; only that if we are concerned to understand a thing such as how and why one particular technical variant rather than some other eventually came to be widely adopted and further elaborated, recognition of the presence of 'localized positive feedback effects' should make us especially skeptical of modes of explanation that presuppose the inevitability of one outcome and the impotence of individual agents to alter it. The latter, in such circumstances may well have the power to take early actions which, in effect, will turn out to have strongly directed the ensuing course of developments.

In the story as retold here, the actions of Edison and the group of his immediate associates during the years 1887–1892 do not stand out as having run counter to an imminent flow of events leading the electrical supply industry in America away from direct current and rapidly toward a 'universal' integrated system designed around polyphase alternating current. Rather than vainly seeking to block the further development of the competitive a.c. electrical supply technology and so preserve a monopoly of the field for his d.c. system, Edison, in our account, sees the juggernaut of a competitive technical system bearing down upon his own immediate economic interests with a swiftness that he had not anticipated. And so, he undertakes expedient actions aimed to slow the pace of its advance enough to allow him quickly to get his inventive resources and financial assets safely out of the way. The propaganda campaign thus launched against high voltage a.c. in general and Westinghouse in particular, with its threat of crippling restraints by safety legislation, made considerable economic sense in the context, however unscrupulous it may have been.

Did it also make more sense than the other, more direct, and probably more reliable modes of commercial competition that were available to the Edison enterprises, but apparently went untried? That remains less clear, for it seems that Edison had reasons for seeking to exit from the industry promptly. A supplier of direct current dynamos, lighting and other appliances and traction motors who had sought to hold onto a dominant market share might have moved immediately to explore ways in which the new rotary converter technology could be supplied cheaply for application in lowering the costs of transmission (via high voltage a.c. mains) between d.c.-based generating plant and end-users. As has been shown, this kind of mixed, or 'patched' system, which was already being discussed in the engineering periodicals in 1887, was entirely feasible and came to be implemented by electric utility companies in the following decade.

Additionally, or alternatively, 'promotional' pricing of d.c. generators and compatible equipment by the Edison manufacturing companies might well have sufficed in the late 1880s to further entrench that system in urban markets. The principal immediate beneficiaries from this short-run revenue sacrifice, it is true, would have been the financiers around Morgan, because it was they who held the rights to the patent royalties on sales of d.c. central stations and isolated electrical plants. But, had Edison wanted to remain in the business, the occasion of the negotiations opened by Villard during 1887–1888 might have been used to arrange to share in some of the royalties that would thereby be secured during the remaining 7–8 years of life on his basic lighting patents. Perhaps it would have proved impossible ultimately to negotiate such an arrangement. What is significant is that there are no indications from the published sources based on the relevant archives that Edison and those around him ever considered it, or were actively exploring other ways of using their substantial initial market position to compete against the commercial sponsors of alternating current equipment. Westinghouse, if not Thomson-Houston also, might well have proved vulnerable to attack at just that point. The former enterprise evidently was under-capitalized to meet the head-on challenge of a price war, so much so that George Westinghouse found himself obliged during 1890–1891 to turn for financial help from August Belmont, and to persuade Nikola Tesla to relinquish his legal claim to a fortune in patent royalties.

Yet, far from fighting to drive out the competition or, at least, to curtail their ability to finance research and development directed towards improving the polyphase a.c. technology, Edison responded to the cluster of innovations related to the a.c. induction motor by refusing to engage the opposition in an economically costly market rivalry; instead, he conducted a rapid but orderly financial withdrawal—under the diversionary cover of a 'talking war.' I have suggested that it was not unreasonable in the circumstances, much less irrational, for Edison to have seized upon the Villard proposal to consolidate all Edison-related electrical enterprises, as a fortuitous opportunity to exit profitably from the electrical manufacturing business. The evidence presented here, however, does not speak to the question of whether or not, in withdrawing and turning his attention to the improvement of his phonograph, the movies, and mining technology, the inventor was following an expected-private wealth-maximizing strategy. Evidently Edison's decision was influenced by the short-run asset constraints, indeed, by the distracting liquidity constraints, under which both the manufacturing operations and the laboratory at West Orange, NJ were perceived to be working. In any event, had he chosen otherwise, or been prevailed upon by others to remain in the industry and sacrifice short-run earnings in an attempt to block the commercial development of universal electricity supply systems based entirely upon polyphase a.c., the outcome could well have been very different from that which transpired.

The bunching of related induction-motor inventions by Tesla, Shallenberger, and Bradley, which appears as the most probable cause of Edison's precipitate retirement from the electricity business, had a direct bearing on the outcome, which is also worth keeping in mind.[108] The induction motor made polyphase a.c. a rival standard around which to develop a 'universal' system of electricity generation, transmission, distribution and application, such as was originally conceived by Edison. This was so in large measure because it permitted comparatively inexpensive conversion from a.c. to d.c. for application to high torque–low r.p.m. motors most suitable for traction work. Yet, by the same principle, the rotary converter could have been used more extensively to expand the market territory served by existing d.c. central stations, thereby depriving commercial a.c.-generation technologies of part of the widening basis for incremental improvements that they came to enjoy. Just as d.c. traction motors became a specialty application of electrical energy through the mediation of rotary converters, so converters could have been employed to transform d.c. into a.c. for specialized application in textile mills, mines and other industrial contexts where 'sparkless' a.c. motors were advantageous. The resulting system by 1914 would quite probably not have been more efficient in an engineering sense than the one that was in existence in the United States at that date; it would, perhaps, have resembled the situation that obtained in Britain. But, that is beside the main point—which is that the advent of polyphase a.c. generators and motors brought into existence a multiplicity of feasible equilibria in the design and configuration of electricity supply systems.

Might-have-beens are difficult for the historian to articulate, in that they call for very precise specifications of the contingent unfolding structure of counterfactual worlds. There was nothing foreordained, much less evidently optimal, about the selection that Edison's reactions contributed to making from among these possibilities. Holding more closely to what did happen in

---

[108] The significance of the rotary converter as an example of a neutral 'gateway innovation,' which may have important effects in tipping the balance between a sponsored rivalry, is further explored by David and Bunn (1988).

this particular episode, I should simply say that those who seem to view with approval the outcome of the 'Battle of the Systems' in the United States have unjustifiably withheld from Edison due recognition for his inglorious part in the avoidance of what could have been a protracted market competition of uncertain result between the contending currents.

Little is taken from this conclusion, even by granting that a.c. really was the economically and technically superior basis for a universal electricity supply system rather than being simply the more cost effective form of current for long-distance transmission work. 'Good guys' are not automatically winners when network technologies compete. One may note that if a new network technology would be economically superior to an incumbent system when everyone had switched to it, complete information in the possession of all agents would be sufficient to induce everyone to decide independently to make the necessary switchover. But, given the state of uncertainty and conflicting opinion among the scientists and engineers of the day, complete information simply was not in the cards.[109] One may also note that technological 'sponsorship' sometimes will be adequate to prevent the installation or retention of an inferior network technology as the unintended consequence of mere 'accidents of history'. Where patent-holdings give commercial sponsors property rights in particular technical standards, as in the case at hand, they may be able to capture the benefits that otherwise could accrue to producers and users from subsequent network expansion. A firm convinced that the system whose benefits it can internalize will be superior in the future to the presently incumbent system therefore may find it well worthwhile to subsidize the initial adoption of its technological variant by pricing the equipment or service below costs.[110] On the other hand, an incumbent confronted by challengers sponsoring a potentially superior technology (the benefits of which it cannot expect to fully share) may successfully defend its position if it has enough financial resources to engage and outlast those rivals in a war of attrition.

In view of the latter possibility, I have thought it important in the foregoing account to indicate some reasons why Edison apparently turned away from such

[109] See Farrell and Saloner (1985a). The indicated route of escape from being 'locked in' to a suboptimal technological system depends upon a rigorous backward induction process, which leads the last decision-making unit to switch, given that all others have switched; and the next-to-last to correctly anticipate the decision of the last, and so to switch, given that all before him have already switched; and so on, back to the first decision-maker, who will rationally switch in the expectation that all following him will do likewise. It is a pretty piece of logic, but incomplete information readily breaks this chain, and therefore would prevent it from even beginning to form.

[110] This point has been developed by Katz and Shapiro (1985b). Westinghouse is said to have acted from just such considerations: submitting a successful but money-losing low bid for the contract to light the Columbian Exposition in Chicago in 1893, conscious that the demonstration value would ultimately pay off, possibly by affecting the outcome of the competition for the contract to build a.c. generators for the Niagara Project. See Leupp (1919), pp. 162–70.

a course of action. Although these have been sufficiently idiosyncratic to underscore my emphasis upon the working of chance, one should observe that the strategy of counter-attack in such circumstances generally would require access to financial backers with 'deep pockets' and widely diversified portfolios.[111] Lacking that, short-run asset constraints may prevent superior technologies from acquiring sponsors with sufficient capital to unseat inefficient incumbents, just as they may precipitate the premature capitulation of an established technology-sponsor faced with the entry of an alternative technology.

Thus, while exercises in applied microeconomics can tell us that rather special circumstances are required for an inefficient formulation of a technological system to become accidently 'locked in', we may also see that these were the very conditions which historically obtained when the electricity supply business—and possibly some other paradigmatic network industries in the fields of transportation and communications—were beginning to take shape. Most of the complex, multi-component and multi-agent systems of production with which we are familiar did not emerge full-blown in the forms that they have, respectively, come to assume. Large scale technological systems such as railroads, electrical utilities, and telephone networks, have been built up sequentially, through an evolutionary process in which the design and operation of constituent components undergoes both continuous and discrete adaptations to the specific technical, economic and politico-legal circumstances in which new opportunities and problems are perceived. And those perceptions, in turn, are often formed on the basis of experience acquired through the operation of pre-existing systems having some of the same functions, or ones directly analogous to the technology in question. So it was that Edison in the 1870s had before him the model of then-existing illuminating gas supply systems—with their generators, distribution mains, meters, and lamps—when he conceived of an integrated lighting and power system based upon electricity. To recognize this calls for acknowledgement of the importance of chance factors in the precise timing of events, including, naturally enough, the sequential development of technical and organizational innovations that shape the competitive strategies followed by commercial sponsors of different network formulations. But, as traditional historians intuitively have understood, the timing and character of 'small events' is more likely to be capable of exerting real leverage when these occur close to the beginnings of a sequential development process.

Of course, the temporal location and brevity of those critical phases, in which there is greatest scope for individual decision-makers to alter the

---

[111] Moreover, just those bankers with the financial resources adequate to the task may be the ones most concerned, as was J. P. Morgan, to avert 'destructive' price competition, and to seek the pooling of patent rights as a basis for the cartelization, or outright monopolization of the industry in question.

direction of a decentralized process of technology diffusion and development, must be a relative matter. The comparison indicated here is with the full course of the market competition which may ensue as one system or another progresses towards establishment as the de facto universal standard for the industry. Actual temporal durations depend upon the rate at which system suppliers and users become sequentially committed to one technical formulation, with its attendant compatibility requirements, or another; cyclical booms, during which high rates of investment are undertaken to embody specific technologies in long-lived physical facilities, thus can contribute to narrowing the time-window within which truly formative decisions can occur. Viewed from this angle, it is the fleeting context created by an emergent network technology that creates the opportunity for one or another innovating agents to take specific initiatives which can be held to have directed the subsequent course of events.

Although I began with the question of what role individual entrepreneurial actions could have on the social construction of technological progress, I should therefore close with the observation that the relationship of interest now appears to be a reflexive one. A special kind of competitive struggle, involving the formation of technological or organizational systems characterized by localized positive feedback, holds a special role in the creation of Schumpeterian innovators. This is so if only because these 'battles' evolve as dynamic processes in which chance actions on a human scale can prove determinative. Moreover, as such actions are more likely to be those which have occurred before battle lines became clearly drawn and large forces were engaged, if archetypal entrepreneurs are to be found anywhere by retrospective observers, surely they can be singled out more readily from among the ranks of the early participants in emergent network industries. 'Innovation,' then, in the sense of an unanticipated impulse imparting a cumulative motion to the economic system, is perhaps less a product of uniquely creative individual attitudes and special social incentives, and more a matter of being pivotally situated during those comparatively brief passages of industrial history when the balance of collective choice can be tipped one way or another. Thomas Edison demonstrated this, as much by abandoning the electric manufacture and supply business as by his launching of it.

Acknowledgements

The research assistance of Julie Bunn was indispensible to me in preparing this essay. Much of the historical material presented here has been drawn (without further attribution) from sections of our collaborative paper, David with Bunn (1987). Numerous debts incurred in that connection have been acknowledged in the proper place. An earlier version of the present paper was presented at the Conference on Economic Growth, Past and Present, held in honor of David S. Landes, at the Villa Serbelloni, Bellagio, Italy, 30 August–4 September, 1987. It remains a pleasant necessity to record here my thanks to Patrice Higgonet and Henry Rosovsky, the organizers of that conference, and to Peter Temin, among other conference participants, for their excellent advice about the structure of my exposition; to Jonathan Hughes for sharing insights into Edison's nature, and generously welcoming disagreement over points of emphasis; to Thomas Parke Hughes for a fine mixture of encouraging comments, technical corrections, and references to sources that I otherwise would have missed; to W. Edward Steinmueller and Gavin Wright for characteristically perceptive and helpful suggestions of ways to sharpen the formulation of my arguments. Financial support for this research was provided under the High Technology Impact Program of the Center for Economic Policy Research at Stanford University. I wish also to thank Kenneth S. Ryan for a personal gift of pertinent reference materials, which proved to be a considerable convenience to me in this research.

References

Akerloff, G. A. and J. L. Yellen (1985), 'Can Small Deviations from Rationality Make Significant Differences to Economic Equilibria?', *American Economic Review*, 75, 708–720.

Alvarado, F. L. and F. H. Lansetter (1984), 'Methodology for Analysis of Multi-Terminal HVDC Systems', in C. W. Buyllard and P. J. Womelodoff, eds, *Trends in Electric Utility Research*, Pergamon Press, New York pp. 210–30.

Arthur, W. B. (1984), 'Why a Silicon Valley?: The Pure Theory of Locational Choice,' Technological Innovation Project Workshop paper, Department of Economics, Stanford University, November.

Arthur, W. B. (1985), 'Competing Technologies and Lock-in by Historical Small Events: The Dynamics of Allocation Under Increasing Returns,' Technological Innovation Project Working Paper No. 4, Center for Economic Policy Research (Publication No. 43), Stanford University.

Arthur, W. B., Y. M. Ermoliev and Y. M. Kaniovski (1985), 'Strong Laws for a class of Path-dependent Urn Processes,' in *Proceedings of the International Conference on Stochastic Optimization, Kiev, 1984*, Springer-Verlag, Munich.

Arthur, W. B., Y. M. Ermoliev and Y. M. Kaniovski (1986), 'Path-dependent Processes and the Emergence of Marco-structure', *European Journal of Operations Research*, 30, 294–303.

Barstow, W. S. (1901), 'Notes on the Alternating Current System of Distribution,' *AIEE Transactions*, Volume XVIII, pp. 849–53.

Bowers, B. (1982), *A History of Electric Light and Power*, Peter Peregrinus Ltd, New York.

Bresnahan, T. R. and P. A. David (1986), 'Strategic Effects in the Diffusion of Innovations: Testable Implication and Preliminary Findings for the Case of Automatic Teller Machines in U.S. Banking Markets,' a paper presented to the Conference on Innovation Diffusion, held at the University of Venice, Italy, March 17–22, 1986. (Technical Papers Series of the High Technology Impact Program, Center for Economic Policy Research at Stanford University, Stanford, CA.)

Brittain, J. E. (1977), *Turning Points in American Electrical History*, IEEE Press, New York.

Brock, G. (1975), 'Competition, Standards and Self-Regulation in the Computer Industry,' in R. Caves and M. Roberts (eds), *Regulating the Product: Quality and Variety*, Ballinger Publishing Company, Cambridge, MA.

Bureau of the Census, US Department of Commerce and Labor (1906), *Special Reports of the Bureau of Census: Electrical Industries 1902*, Government Printing Office, Washington, DC.

Bureau of the Census, US Department of Commerce and Labor (1910), *Special Reports of the Bureau of Census: Electric Light and Power Station 1907*, Government Printing Office, Washington, DC.

Bureau of the Census, US Department of Commerce (1915), *Census of Electrical Industries 1912*, Government Printing Office, Washington DC.

Bureau of the Census, US Department of Commerce (1920), *Census of Electrical Industries 1917*, Government Printing Office, Washington, DC.

Byatt, I. C. R. (1979), *The British Electrical Industry, 1875–1914: The Economic Returns in a New Technology*, Clarendon Press, Oxford.

Campbell, S. G. (1938), *The Reorganization of the American Railroad System, 1893–1900*, New York.

Carlson, W. B. and A. J. Millard (1987), 'Defining Risk in a Business Context: Thomas A. Edison and Elihu Thomson, and the A.C.-D.C. Controversy, 1885–1900', in B. B. Johnson and V. T. Covello, (eds), *This Social Cultural Construction of Risk*, D. Reidel, Dordrecht.

Carlton, D. W. and J. M. Klamer (1983), 'The Need for Coordination Among Firms, with Special Reference to Network Industries,' *The University of Chicago Law Review*, 50, 446–465.

Chandler, A. E., Jr (1977), *The Visible Hand: The Managerial Revolution in American Business*, Harvard University-Belknap, Cambridge, MA.

Cheney, M. (1981), *Tesla: Man Out of Time*, Prentice-Hall, Inc., Englewood Cliffs, NJ.

Clark, G. (1984), 'Authority and Efficiency: The Labor Market and the Managerial Revolution of the Late Nineteenth Century', *Journal of Economic History*, 44, 1069–83.

Clemence, R. V. and F. S. Doody (1950), *The Schumpeterian System*, Addison-Wesley Press, Cambridge, MA.

Cusumono, M. (1985), 'Note on VTR Industry and Market Development: Japan, the U.S., and Europe, ca. 1975–1985,' Harvard Business School.

Daggett, S. (1908), *Railroad Reorganization*, Boston.

David, P. A. (1975), *Technical Choice, Innovation and Economic Growth: Essays on American and British Experience in the Nineteenth Century*. Cambridge University Press, New York.

David, P. A. (1985), 'Clio and the Economics of QWERTY,' *American Economic Review*, 75, 332–337.

David, P. A. (1986a), 'Understanding the Economics of QWERTY: The Necessity of History,' in W. N. Parker (ed.), *Economics History and the Modern Economist*, Basil Blackwell, Oxford.

David, P. A. (1986b), 'Some New Standards for the Economics of Standardization in the Information Age', in P. Dasgupta with P. L. Stoneman (eds), *Economic Policy and Technological Performance*, Cambridge University Press, Cambridge.

David, P. A. Bunn (1988), 'Path-Dependence: Putting the Past into the Future of Economics', *Institute for Mathmatical Studies in the Social Sciences Technical Report 533*, Stanford University.

David, P. A. with J. A. Bunn (1987), ' "The Battle of the systems" and the Evolutionary Dynamics of Network Technology Rivalries,' High Technology Impact Program Working Paper No. 15, Center for Economic Policy Research, Stanford University.

David, P. A. and J. A. Bunn (1988), 'The Economics of Gateway Technologies and Network Evolution: Lessons from Electricity Supply History,' *Information Economics and Policy*, 3, 165–202.

David, P. A. and T. E. Olsen (1986), 'The Equilibrium Dynamics of Diffusion when Incremental Technological Innovations are Foreseen,' *Ricerche Economiche* (Special Supplement on Innovation and Diffusion), n. 4, October–December.

Dosi, G. (1982), 'Technological Paradigms and Technological Trajectories. A Suggested Interpretation of the Determinants and Directions of Technical Change,' *Research Policy*, 13, 3–20.

Dosi, G. (1984), *Technical Change and Industrial Transformation*, Macmillan, London.

Eldredge, N. (1985), *Time Frames: The Rethinking of Darwinian Evolution and the Theory of Punctuated Equilibria*, Simon and Schuster, New York.

Electrical World (articles without identified authors):

(1887), 'Edison vs. Westinghouse,' January 1, pp. 7–8.

(1887), 'Incandescent Lights on High Tension Circuits,' February 26, p. 110.

(1887), 'The Distribution of Electricity by Secondary Generators,' March 26, pp. 156–8.

(1887), 'Report on the Committee on Electrical Distribution by Alternating Currents,' August 20, pp. 92–3.

(1888), 'Alternating Current or Storage Battery,' January 21, p. 25.

(1888), 'Alternating vs Continuous Current,' March 31, p. 159.

(1888), 'The Comparative Danger of Alternating vs. Direct Current, 'September 8, p. 126.

(1889), 'Mr. Edison on the Dangers of Electric Lighting,' November 2, pp. 292–3.

The Encyclopedia Britannica. A Dictionary of Arts. Literature and General Information (1910–1911), Eleventh Edition. 29 vols. The Encyclopedia Britannica Co., New York.

Evans, G. T. (1982), 'Some Phases of the Alternating Current,' *Electrical World*, January.

Farrell, J. and G. Saloner (1985a), 'Standardization, Compatibility and Innovation,' *Rand Journal*, 16, 70–83.

Farrell, J. and G. Saloner (1985b), 'Economic Issues in Standardization,' Working Paper No. 393, Department of Economics, Massachusetts Institute of Technology, October.

Farrell, J. and G. Saloner (1985c), 'Installed Base and Compatibility, with Implications for Product Preannouncements,' Working Paper No. 385, Department of Economics, MIT, August.

Fleming, J. A. (1921), *Fifty Years of Electricity: The Memories of an Electrical Engineer*. Published from the offices of Wireless World, London.

Fudenberg, T. and J. Tirole (1985), *Dynamic Models of Oligopoly* (Fundamentals of Pure and Applied Economics, Volume 3: Theory of the Firm and Industrial Organization Section), Harwood Academic Publishers, London.

Gilfillan, S. C. (1935a), *Inventing the Ship*, Foller, Chicago.

Gilfillan, S. C. (1935b), *The Sociology of Invention*, Foller, Chicago.

Gould, S. J. (1987), 'The Panda's Thumb of Technology,' *Natural History*, 1987, no. 1, 14–23.

Haken, H. (1978), *Synergetics*, 2nd Ed., Springer-Verlag, Berlin.

Haltiwanger, J. and M. Waldman (1985), 'Rational Expectations and the Limits of Rationality: An Analysis of Heterogeneity', *American Economics Review*, 75, 326–340.

Hannah, L. (1979), *Electricity Before Nationalism: A Study of the Development of the Electricity Supply Industry in Britain to 1948*. Johns Hopkins University Press, Baltimore.

Hennessey, R. A. S. (1971), *The Electricity Revolution*, Oriel Press Ltd, Newcastle Upon Tyne, UK.

Hughes, J. (1986), *The Vital Few*, Oxford University Press, New York.

Hughes, T. P. (1983), *Networks of Power: Electrification in Western Society. 1880–1930*, The Johns Hopkins University Press, Baltimore.

Jarvis, C. M. (1967a), 'The Generation of Electricity,' in C. Singer, E. J. Holmyard, A. R. Hall and T. I Williams, (eds), *A History of Technology, Volume V: Late 19th Century. 1850–1900*, The Clarendon Press, Oxford, p. 177–207.

Jarvis, C. M. (1967b), 'The Distribution and Utilization of Electricity,' in C. Singer, E. J. Holmyard, A. R. Hall and T. I. Williams, (eds), *A History of Technology, Volume V: Late 19th Century. 1850–1900*. The Clarendon Press, Oxford, pp. 208–234.

Josephson, M. (1959), *Edison: A Biography*, McGraw-Hill, New York.

Jones, P. (1940), *A Power History of the Consolidated Edison System*, New York Consolidated Edison, New York.

Katz, M. L. and C. Shapiro (1985a), 'Network Externalities, Competition and Compatibility,' *American Economic Review*, 75, 424–440.

Katz, M. L. and C. Shapiro (1985b), 'Technology Adoption in the Presence of Network Externalities,' Discussion Paper in Economics No. 96, Woodrow Wilson School, Princeton University.

Kindleberger, C. P. (1983), 'Standards as Public, Collective and Private Goods,' *Kyklos*, 36, 377–396.

Kolko, G. (1965), *Railroad and Regulation 1877–1916*, W. W. Norton and Company, New York.

Lamme, B. G. (1929), *Benjamin Garver Lamme, Electrical Engineer: An Autobiography*, Putnam's Sons, New York.

Landes, D. S. (1986), 'What Do Bosses Really Do?' *Journal of Economic History*, 46, 585–624.

Landes, D. S. (1969), *The Unbound Prometheus: Technological Change and Industrial Development in Western Europe from 1750 to the Present*, Cambridge University Press, New York.

Lardner, H. A. (1903), 'Economical and Safety Limits in the Size of Capital Stations,' *A.I.E.E. Transactions*, 21, pp. 407–416.

Lineff, W. (1888), 'Accumulators versus Direct Currents for Electric Traction,' *Electrical World*, April 14.

Leupp, F. E. (1919), *George Westinghouse: His Life and Achievements*, John Murray, London.

MacDonald, E. (1962), *Insull*, University of Chicago Press, Chicago.

Marglin, S. (1974). 'What Do Bosses Do? Part I,' *The Review of Radical Political Economy*, 6, 60–112.

National Electrical Manufacturers Association (1946), *A Chronological History of Electrical Development*, NEMA, New York.

Nelson, R. R. and S. G. Winter (1982), *An Evolutionary Theory of Economic Change*. The Belknap Press of Harvard University, Cambridge, MA.

Parsons, R. H. (1940), *The Early Days of the Power Station Industry*, Cambridge University Press, Cambridge.

Passer, H. C. (1972), *The Electrical Manufacturers: 1875–1900: A Study in Competition, Entrepreneurship, Technical Change, and Economic Growth*, Arno Press, New York.

Pfrannkuche, A. (1887), 'Long Distance Distribution of Electric Energy,' *Electrical World*, April 2.

Prigogine, I. (1980), *From Being to Becoming: Time and Complexity in the Physical Sciences*, W. H. Freeman, New York.

Prigogine, I. and I. Stengers (1984), *Order Out of Chaos*, New Science Library, Boulder.

Prout, H. G. (1921), *A Life of George Westinghouse*, The American Society of Mechanical Engineers, New York.

Rosenberg, N. (1969), 'The Direction of Technological Change: Inducement Mechanisms and Focusing Devices,' *Economic Development and Cultural Change*, 18, No. 1 (October).

Rosenberg, N. (1976). 'Marx as a Student of Technology,' *Monthly Review*, 28, 56–77.

Rosenberg, N. (1983), *Inside the Black Box: Technology and Economics*, Cambridge University Press, New York.

Rosenbloom, R. (1985), 'Managing Technology for the Longer Term,' in K. Clark *et al.* (eds), *The Uneasy Alliance*, Praeger, New York.

Scott, C. F. (1901), 'Alternating Current as A Factor in General Distribution for Light and Power,' *AIEE Transaction*, XVIII, 843–48.

Sharlin, H. I. (1963), *The Making of the Electrical Age*, Abelard-Schuman, New York.

Stanley, W. (1912) 'Alternating Current Development in America,' *Franklin Institute Journal*, 68, 568–73.

Stillwell, L. B. (1934), 'Alternating Current Versus Direct Current,' *Electrical Engineering*, 53, 708–10.

Stolper, W. F. (1981), 'Aspects of Schumpeter's Theory of Evolution,' in H. Frisch, (ed.), *Schumpeterian Economics*, Praeger Publishers, New York.

Streissler, E. (1981), 'Schumpeter's Vienna and the Role of Credit in Innovation,' in H. Frisch, (ed.), *Schumpeterian Economics*, Praeger Publishers, New York.

Sumpner, W. E. (1890), 'Some Peculiarities of Alternate Currents,' *Electrical World*, January.

Teggart, F. J. (1925), *Theory of History*, Yale University Press, New Haven.

Temin, P. (1987). 'Bosses and Technical Change.' Paper presented at the Conference in Honor of David S. Landes, In Bellagio, Italy, August 30–September 4, 1987.

Usher, A. P. (1929. 1954), *A History of Mechanical Inventions*, 2nd edition. Harvard University Press: Cambridge, MA.

Weeks, W. (1981), *Transmission and Distribution of Electrical Energy*, Harper and Row, Publishers, New York.

Williamson, O. E. (1975), *Markets and Hierarchies: Analysis and Anti-Trust Implications*, Free Press, New York.

Williamson, O. E. (1985), *The Economic Institutions of Capitalism*, Free Press, New York.

Woodbury, D. O. (1960), *Elihu Thomson: Beloved Scientist, 1853–1937*. The Museum of Science (1944, 1960), Boston.

Zorpette, G. (1985), 'HVDC: Wheeling Lots of Power,' *IEEE Spectrum*, June, 30–36.

Patents and Welfare in an Evolutionary Model

(US General Accounting Office, Washington, DC 20548, USA)

1. Introduction

This paper addresses two related problems, one at the level of general theory, the other a specific policy issue. The first is that of conceptualizing and modeling innovative opportunity. Any theoretical model of invention or innovation must include a model of inventive/innovative opportunity—though the model may be as simple as the assumption 'there is a single invention that could be made'.[1] The policy issue is the desirability of patents and the appropriate duration of patent protection. The question is whether very short-lived patents, or even no patents at all, might in some contexts yield higher economic welfare than the patent rights conferred under existing institutional arrangements.

The two problems are intimately related. A conceptual framework specific enough to provide a structured approach to answering the patent policy question is necessarily one that involves strong commitments regarding the nature of inventive opportunity. Yet the problem of modeling inventive opportunity in a realistic way—appropriate to the very real policy problem—is extremely challenging. Granted, in specific fields of activity, invention often follows identifiable 'trajectories' or 'paradigms' associated with the use of particular classes of heuristic methods for bringing about improvements (David, 1974; Dosi, 1984; Nelson and Winter, 1982; Pavitt, 1986; Rosenberg, 1969). Understanding of the trajectories being followed at a particular time may yield qualitative predictions about the nature of the improvements that are likely to be forthcoming in the near future. But when it comes to the question of the pace of advance, and particularly to the question of when a trajectory will top out, it becomes problematic to even identify the knowledge base that is relevant.

* This paper is based on a presentation delivered at the Conference on Innovation Diffusion held in Venice, Italy in March 1986. The present written version is a revision of one produced in the summer of 1988. The views expressed herein do not necessarily represent those of the US General Accounting Office, where the author serves as Chief Economist.

[1] This is the model in Arrow's classic paper (1962).

However difficult such assessments may be, they are logically indispensable to the economic case for any definition of property rights in productive knowledge. The case for recognizing and protecting such rights rests on the assumption that resources for advancing knowledge are scarce. The appropriate level of rents for such property rights depends on the scarcity of the resources and the benefits they can yield; we would like to know how much difference it makes, at the margin, if the quantity of resources devoted to advancing knowledge is a little higher or a little lower. This sort of question simply cannot be answered without reference to a model of inventive opportunity.

In section 3 of this paper, I describe a model of inventive opportunity employed in previous simulation work of Nelson and Winter; specifically, the model we referred to as the 'science based case'. Section 4 then describes briefly how the model simulated in the earlier work has been expanded into a model of industry evolution. Section 5 adds the patent policy instrument to the model, and sets forth the results of a simulation experiment comparing industry evolution with and without patent protection. Section 6 offers concluding comments appraising the significance of the results. Before proceeding to the main business of the paper, however, it will be helpful to review some of the theoretical background.

2. *Approaches to Modeling Innovation and Diffusion*

At the risk of reworking familiar ground, let me briefly characterize the models of innovation and diffusion that orthodox economists have explored over the past few decades. In the orthodox view, the production possibilities available to a firm, an industry or an economy at a particular time may be characterized by a production set—S_0, say. All techniques within S_0 are perfectly known. Initially, there are no other techniques. Alternatively, economic actors know that there are techniques not in S_0, and perhaps some of the characteristics of those techniques. They know nothing at all, however, about how to accomplish such results in practice.[2] At some subsequent time, one or more 'innovations' occur; this means that the production set becomes S_1, of which S_0 is a proper subset. The problem of the economics of *innovation* is to describe the role of economic factors in determining why S_1 is what it is, and why the change occurs when it does. The problem of the economics of *diffusion of innovation* is to explain (on economic grounds) why economic actors choose to adopt techniques in S_1–S_0 when they do. In particular, if it is assumed that the new techniques are economically superior at prevailing prices, the diffusion

<hr>

[2] Rather than elaborate the evolutionary critique of this orthodox construct, I refer the reader to Nelson and Winter (1982, esp. Chapter 3), Nelson (1980), Winter (1982).

problem is to explain why every actor who faces this situation does not adopt such techniques immediately.

There is something inherently awkward about the notion of constructing an economics of innovation within the orthodox framework. If economic factors are relevant to the change of production sets; if resources can be applied with the intention of bringing about such change, what has happened to the notion that the production set itself is a 'given' and comprehensive description of technical possibilities? This difficulty has been dealt with in different ways over the years. In the age of golden ages (that is, when the old growth theory was in vogue), the puzzle was in most cases avoided by eschewing the subject entirely. Technical change of various sorts was usually assumed to fall from the heavens, or from the progress of science. It affected the economic system but was not in turn affected by the system. In other cases, higher level choice possibilities were conceived to provide the basis for an economic rationalization of innovative change: such devices as meta-production functions, innovation possibility frontiers, and the like come to mind. While some models addressed the problem of socially optimal investment in costly research, there was little attention to the question of how self-interested economic actors operating in competitive environments could cover the costs of innovation. This problem has recently received more attention in the 'new growth theory' (e.g. Romer, 1986, 1990).

Reflecting its origins in macroeconomic concerns, the modeling of technical change in the old growth theory at least had the virtue of addressing large-scale questions of considerable social and historical importance, and doing so in a way that established at least a few significant connections between theory and empiricism (Solow, 1970).

Subsequently, a substantial literature grew up that dealt with the theoretical economics of innovation. This literature consisted primarily of various elaborations and extensions of Arrow's seminal paper of 1962. In these models, the set S_1 typically differs from the set S_0 by one possible innovation, and the questions are whether this innovation will be made or not, when it will be made, who will make it, what the welfare consequences will be, and what market structure has to do with all of this. A parallel stream of activity starting from the same simple formulation of technological opportunity explored the problem of optimal patent life (Nordhaus, 1969; Scherer, 1972).

Barzel (1968), with an assist from Hirshleifer (1971), contributed tremendously to the interest of these questions by introducing countervailing considerations to the formerly presumptive inadequacy of incentives for innovation. This set the stage for a variety of theoretical analyses exploring the balance between the forces producing inadequate incentives and the forces providing excessive incentives. In these studies, the absence of first-best optimality was a foregone conclusion and the occurrence of an optimal second-best standoff between the different forces seemingly a low probability event (see Reinganum, 1988, for a survey covering much of this work).

Whatever the complexities they address in other respects, these models typically have an extremely stark and simple characterization of technological opportunity at the center of the story. They are 'one bit models' in the sense that only two possible production sets are envisaged. With efficient coding, it only takes one bit of information to describe which technological state of affairs obtains. This feature, by itself, is a considerable impediment to translation of the lessons of the models into realistic contexts.

The problem of modeling diffusion is, superficially, not as problematic in orthodox economic theory as the problem of modeling innovation itself. Theoretical manipulations can go forward on the assumption that 'the innovation' and 'adoption of the innovation' are well-defined concepts—and one can point to examples in the world where these assumptions seem reasonably justified. The basic puzzle of 'why doesn't everybody adopt immediately' can be solved in various ways that are within the restrictive bounds of the orthodox paradigm of optimization in equilibrium. For example, the answer 'because the potential adopters are in relevant respects not a homogenous population' has a lot of appeal on its face, and models of rational non-simultaneous adoption have been constructed on this foundation.

In the older literature that had its origins in rural sociology, the answer was 'because not everybody hears about the innovation right away from sources they consider reliable'. There is certainly nothing fundamentally irrational about the behavior portrayed in this sociological explanation. Concerns about the credibility of information sources are entirely appropriate in the real world, and economic actors adopt a variety of strategies to economize on the effort devoted to processing unreliable information. Because there are two types of error to be balanced, some valid information is undoubtedly rejected by these strategies. There is little doubt, I think, that both the heterogeneous actors models and the information diffusion models are highly relevant in explaining some real situations, and the fruitful questions to ask relate not to methodological issues but to the identification of the situations in which one or the other or both of the mechanisms are operative.

What is more to the point for my present purposes is the critique of the basic conceptual structure of 'diffusion of innovation' that arose, in large part, from the attempt to subject various models and hypotheses to empirical test. An important part of the critique is that 'adoption' of a pre-existing 'innovation' often seems very much like innovation itself (Downs and Mohr, 1976). The same set of facts can often be plausibly viewed in either way, depending on the extent of the difficulties that must be creatively overcome by an adopter. The greater those difficulties—or the greater the emphasis one chooses to place on them—the more the adopter looks innovative and the more the adoption looks like an innovation. The version of this ambiguity that bedevils the patent office and the courts is the question of whether result of an adopter's efforts to make a patented invention more useful to himself and others is (a) an infringement of the original patent if done without a license, (b) a patentable invention in its own right, (c) both a and b, (d) neither a nor b.

There is, in short, ample reason to think that the subjects of innovation and diffusion are not as separate as they are often made out to be, and that a unified theory is called for. The proper subject matter of this unified theory is the growth and diffusion of productive knowledge. Innovation itself is in part a process of diffusion, since it inevitably draws on pre-existing productive knowledge and diffuses that knowledge in a new form. What is needed is a much richer theory of productive knowledge and its changes.[3] What follows is a small contribution in this direction.

3. *Technological Opportunity and the Latent Productivity Model*

Embedded in the simulations of Schumpeterian competition that Nelson and I reported in our book (1982, Part V) is a simple stochastic, dynamic model of the way in which R&D effort produces innovations by drawing upon exogenously given technological opportunities. In terms of the survey above, this model contains as special cases the 'manna from heaven' models of standard neoclassical growth theory and the 'one bit' models of the later literature on incentives. (I refer here to the way in which technical change *per se* is modeled, not about the other features of these various models.) Particular versions emphasizing the stochastic process features were studied by Horner (1977); Iwai (1984a, b) did interesting work on a deterministic 'large numbers' limiting case of the model, unifying it to some degree with the deterministic model in Chapter 10 of my book with Nelson. Here, I am going to re-expound the model and its rationale, isolated from the complexities introduced by other features of the simulation model.

So far as the rationale is concerned, the first point worthy of emphasis is that innovative effort generally takes place in a social context that both sets goals for the effort and provides solution fragments upon which the innovator may draw in pursuit of those goals. In common with the great bulk of the

[3] My essay on production theory (Winter, 1982) puts forward a more substantial argument to this same effect.

theoretical literature, this model treats the motivational context as that of a for-profit firm facing constant input prices. Following further in the familiar tradition, the model abstracts from the details of elements upon which the innovator draws and of the processes by which a 'new combination' of these elements leads to innovation.

The results of successful innovative effort are represented by their direct economic consequences for the firm; further, these consequences are represented by a single number. In this mode, the single number is output per unit capacity (in a particular time period), and it is assumed that variable input coefficients are affected in the same proportion (Hicks neutrality).

Technological opportunity at a point of time is characterized by a probability distribution of possible alternative values of the productivity variable. Expenditures on innovative R&D efforts yield results in terms of draws from this distribution. More precisely, the probability of a draw occurring in a particular period is proportional to the expenditure level in that period.[4] R&D effort in the model, as in reality, is subject to a double uncertainty: (i) a given level of expenditure maintained for a period of time may or may not yield a technically successful development (a draw); (ii) even if a technically successful development is achieved, it may not be an economic success (the productivity level yielded by the draw may not surpass the firm's prevailing productivity level). Note also that this modeling approach implies in one sense constant returns to R&D effort: the expected number of technical successes achieved (draws) is proportional to R&D expenditure. Yet, in another sense, returns to R&D are diminishing: if the probability distribution of draw outcomes in constant, higher rates of expenditure yield results higher and higher in the probability distribution over time, and it thus becomes more and more improbable that a technical success achieved by future R&D will surpass what has already been achieved.

Within this general approach to modeling innovative R&D, Nelson and I worked primarily with a model that involves a specific commitment regarding the probability distribution: it is log normal in the productivity level, with a constant standard deviation over time. The central tendency of the distribution may change over time; it is characterized by the mean of the logs, denoted $L(t)$, or by $\exp[L(t)]$, called 'latent productivity'. In general, latent productivity may be presumed to be improving over time, as the fields of knowledge relevant to the industry are advanced by processes other than the

---

[4] The constraint that the probability of a draw not exceed one is avoided by an appropriate choice of parameter values. In this respect and others, the simulation model actually implemented is best thought of as a discrete time approximation to an underlying continuous time model, with the simulation model's time period chosen short enough so that single period binomial processes can adequately represent the Poisson processes of the underlying model.

industry's own research. A much more specific commitment is typically made for modeling purposes: $L(t)$ is increasing as a linear function of time; productivity growth is exponential.

$$L(t) = L_0 + \gamma(t - t_0) \tag{1}$$

The kinship of this formulation to neoclassical growth theory may be noted. If the standard deviation of the distribution were zero, and if 'draws' were costless, the assumptions made would bring us to the familiar Hicks-neutral, disembodied, exogenously determined, exponentially-rising productivity case of neoclassical growth theory. In this case, there is no economics of R&D to discuss and no interesting role for individual firms.[5] The interesting issues arise precisely because costly and uncertain activities undertaken by individual firms intermediate between exogenously given opportunities and actual realization of the economic benefits latent in those opportunities. The 'science based case' is distinctive in that the opportunities are strictly exogenous for the industry as a whole; the _only_ role for private innovative R&D is to realize those opportunities. The case of 'cumulative' R&D explored in the earlier work is, by contrast, one in which there is no exogenous component to technological opportunity at the industry level, and from the individual firm's point of view the only options are direct imitation of other firms and the gradual, cumulative advance of its own competence. There are, obviously, many intermediate cases in which the innovative/imitative success of an individual firm depends in varying degrees on its own efforts, on the accomplishments of rivals, and on the expansion of technological opportunity from sources external to the industry.[6]

4. _Birth and Evolution of an Industry_

This paper extends the model presented in my 1984 paper, which was itself an extension of earlier work done with Nelson. The earlier Nelson–Winter work on Schumpeterian competition was concerned with evolutionary 'contests' among firms with different strategies, and also with the development of concentration in initially unconcentrated industries. For both purposes, it was appropriate to start the model from highly stylized and symmetric initial conditions. The phenomena of industry evolution, on the other hand, are largely a reflection of the fact that the situation of an industry as its founding firm

---

[5] As the literature amply illustrates, there is an economics of innovation to discuss in the 'one bit' models. These have their counterpart in our model of opportunity when the standard deviation is zero, latent productivity is _constant_ at a level above prevailing productivity, and innovative R&D is costly.

[6] See Jaffe (1986) and Levin and Reiss (1988) for empirical explorations of the effects of technological opportunity and spillovers on R&D intensity and patenting.

appears is a very specific sort of situation and one that is typically remote from long run equilibrium. The same fundamental adjustment laws that would be operative in the vicinity of a long run equilibrium presumably drive the process from the start; it is the peculiarity of the initial conditions that fundamentally defines the subject matter.

In general, then, a theory of industry evolution must be based on a set of commitments regarding those special features of the data of the system that distinguish early periods from later periods. More specifically, a theory of industry evolution must include a theory of industry birth.

A plausible structure for such a theory of birth can be sketched by a series of linked observations. First, if industry birth is to be identified empirically with the appearance of the first firm(s) producing the product or products in question, the theory must include an account of this initial entry. If initial entry is not to be treated as a *sui generis* event—a methodological path that would impose severe limitations on the explanatory power of the resulting theory—it must be an instance reflecting a more general set of theoretical commitments regarding entry. Such is the case with the model here; the first building block to be described is the general model of entry.

Suppose a potential entrant has in hand a technique with productivity level A_E. He or she will choose to create a firm and go into production if it is anticipated that the product can be sold at a price P that covers production cost with something left over. This criterion is modeled as

$$P A_E u > c + r_E, \text{ or} \tag{2}$$
$$\log A_E + \log u > \log (c + r_E) - \log P \tag{2a}$$

Here, u is a random variable reflecting the fact that it is not possible to assess the productivity of the technique completely accurately without creating the firm and trying it. This variable is assumed to have mean log zero (and specifically, in the simulations, to be log normal). The role of r_E in the model is to provide for entry decisions being influenced by some crude anticipation of the industry's future, as well as by the prevailing price—so that such decisions need not be thought of as totally myopic. This limited foresight might be derived, for example, from observation of the historical development of other new industries. What crucially distinguishes an evolutionary from an orthodox approach here is that r_E is not conceived as the result of an informed rational expectations calculation *specific to this industry*. Hence, nothing in the model will guarantee that the early development of the industry does not turn out to be a fiasco regretted by all entrants or, alternatively, a brilliant success that makes others say 'why didn't *we* do that?'

An important feature of this model of entry is that the entrant is assumed to confront the situation with a *technique* in hand. An alternative assumption would be that all the entrant has in hand is a way of acquiring a technique—an R&D strategy. Such a strategy might consist of an approach to acquiring a single technique that would make profitable entry possible, or it might involve an approach to generating a continuing sequence of innovations—constituting, in effect, a long-term plan for competing in the industry. While the 'technique in hand' approach seems more generally descriptive of entry processes, the area of biotechnology provides many contemporary examples of firms created primarily on the basis of the promise of their R&D resources rather than on the demonstrable profitability of innovations in hand.

Where does the potential entrant's technique in hand come from? Like the technical advances achieved by existing firms, it may be the fruit of innovative R&D or it may be the result of direct imitation of an existing firm. Unlike existing firms, however, potential entrants do not apply resources in the hope of discovering techniques (the alternative assumption would lead to the 'R&D strategy' entry model). Rather, the techniques are conceived to arise from a pool of continuing activity, some innovative and some imitative, that is financed and carried on without regard to the prospects for commercial success in the industry in question. This activity is called 'background R&D', and its mechanisms in the model are directly analogous to the R&D of firms in being, except that the activity level is constant over time, determined by model parameters conceived as equivalent expenditure levels. Innovative background R&D may be thought of as the fruits of the activity in, for example, university research settings, the workshops of individual inventors, or perhaps the laboratories of firms in other industries. Imitative background R&D may be thought of as the sort of diffuse search for revealed profit opportunities that implicitly underlies the usual idea of free entry, although in the present model such activity is conceived as costly and hence limited in amount in each time period. Only when background R&D generates a technique is the possibility of creating a firm considered, and only when a firm is created and entry occurs does the bookkeeping begin and the long run breakeven constraint come into play.

The founding firm must be an innovative entrant, there being no existing firm to imitate. Aside from that, the only feature that distinguishes the founder is the fact that it cannot look to a functioning market for the value of output price to use in the entry test. In many cases, uncertainty about the initial price might contribute significantly to errors in decision making, occasionally giving rise to 'premature birth' of an industry and perhaps to the early failure of the founder. Here it is assumed, however, that the novelty of the industry derives entirely from the technological basis of its production techniques, and not at all on the function performed by the industry's product. Specifically, it is assumed that there exists a perfect substitute for the

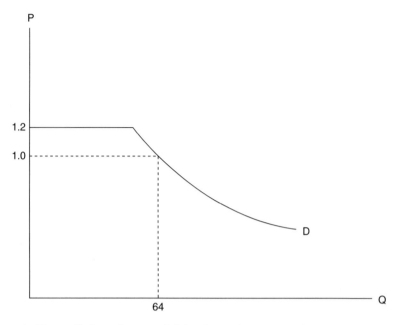

FIGURE 1. The specific demand curve underlying the simulations reported.

industry's product, and that the given price of this substitute translates into a critical price of P_0 per unit for the new product. Above P_0 there is zero demand for the new product, at P_0 precisely the market may be shared between the new product and the old; below P_0 the new product takes the entire market. The result is a demand curve of the general character shown in Figure 1.

In fact, Figure 1 portrays the actual demand curve employed in the simulation reported below. Units choices aside, its significant feature is that it is of unitary elasticity below P_0. Thus, industry sales will be constant once the price has fallen below P_0 ($=1.2$ in Figure 1). Continuing technological progress, although it reduces the prices of the product, neither increases nor decreases the aggregate size of the market. Informational economics of scale, which play a fundamental role in Schumpeterian competition and industry evolution, do not rise or decline in importance over time, once the industry has 'grown up' and price is below P_0. For this and other reasons, the special demand condition assumed is one in which the potential exists for the industry to move toward a stochastic growth equilibrium path with output, price and productivity changing at the rate of latent productivity growth. This property is interesting theoretically and a convenient simplification of the experimental context explored below, but its importance in the theory of industry evolution is that it is a special case marking the boundary between quite different evolutionary paths.[7]

The model of industry birth that emerges from the foregoing may be summarized as follows. Taking entry condition (2a), substituting $L(t) + \log v$ for log A_E, taking $L(t)$ from (1), and using P_0 for P, we have the following condition:

$$L_0 + \gamma(t - t_0) + \log v > \log (c + r_E) - \log P_0 - \log u, \text{ or} \qquad (3)$$

$$\log u + \log v > \log (c + r_E) - \log P_0 - L_0 - \gamma(t - t_0) \qquad (3a)$$

The industry is founded at the first time when background R&D yields a technique 'ahead of the state of the art' (log v large) and this technique is sufficiently optimistically appraised (log u large) so that the combination leads to a decision to enter. Both log u and log v are assumed to be normally distributed, mean zero, and they are independent. There is a time t^* defined by

$$t^* = t_0 + (1/\gamma) [\log (c + r_E) - \log P_0 - L_0] \qquad (4)$$

Time t^* may be interpreted as the time when it is an even money bet that a single draw will lead to a decision to enter, or, alternatively, as the time when the mean log revenue expected from the technique yielded by an entry draw just covers log costs per unit capital (log $(c + r_E)$).

Figure 2 illustrates the determinations of the time of industry birth. The normal densities relevant to three times log t^1, t^* and t^2 are shown [to be interpreted as rising above the $(t, \log A)$ plane]. The shaded areas show the probability that a single draw at the time in question will lead to the founding of the industry, if it has not been founded earlier. At t^1 the probability is small, at t^* it is 0.5, and at t^2 it is large. Of course, the expected date at which the industry is founded depends not only on the single draw probability but also on the frequency of draws—that is, on the level of background R&D. If, for example, background R&D is high, then the industry may come into being well before t^*, at a time when the probability that a single draw would lead to entry might be quite low.

After the industry is founded, additional innovative or imitative entry occurs to populate the industry with firms. The relative rates of the two forms of entry depend on, among other things, the levels of the two forms of background R&D and the existence or non-existence of patent protection.

An actual entrant must have not just a technique in hand, but also a capital stock and an R&D policy. In the model, new firms' capital stocks are drawn from a truncated normal distribution specified by model parameters. The assumptions with respect to R&D policies are more complex. The policies of the founder are

---

[7] The general condition characterizing this boundary situation is that the rate of latent productivity advance (γ), the elasticity of demand (η) and the growth rate of demand (α) combine in such a way that there is no trend in the amount of capital employed in the industry: $\alpha + \gamma(\eta - 1) = 0$. (Nelson and Winter, 1978, note 3, with a change of notation.)

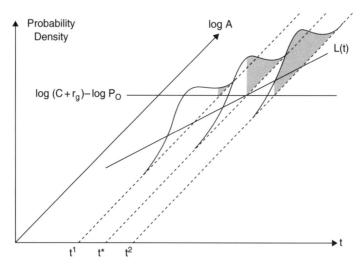

FIGURE 2. The determinants of the time of industry birth.

specified as model parameters. Subsequent entrants determine their policies by adding a random deviation to the capital-weighted average of the policies of existing firms. Firms in being that are persistently below average in profitability also change R&D policies; they add a random deviation to a convex combination of their previous policy and the industry average. Thus, through a combination of search and selection effects, industry average R&D policies respond to the industry environment and to the range of behaviors actually tried.

The position and size of that range, however, is part of the exogenous 'sociology' of the model rather than the economics. For example, the R&D policy specified for the founder will have a strong effect on the early development of the industry. If that policy is radically out of line with the realities of the environment, the industry's evolutionary path may be interpretable as a gradual repudiation of that policy. Such a case provides a good illustration of the contrast between an evolutionary and an orthodox approach. A decision made under uncertainty may be a mistake, by perfect information standards. Mistakes can have important lasting consequences. It is at least as interesting to explore how mistakes are slowly corrected by realistic selection and adaptation mechanisms as it is to circumvent the whole issue by some strong foresight assumption.

5. Simulation of the Effects of Patents

In the particular simulation runs described here, the effect of patents on welfare in a 'science based' technological regime is investigated. As patent protection is represented in the model, a patented production technique cannot be imitated by other firms during the life of the parent, here chosen as 3 years.[8] Nothing, however, prevents a firm from generating through its own innovative R&D a technique that yields a productivity level equal, approximately or exactly, to that of a patented technique. The patent system characterized in the model is thus a very strong one in the sense that it totally prevents other firms from benefiting from an innovator's R&D during the life of the patent, and it does so at no cost. On the other hand, the standards of 'Novelty' and 'utility' implicitly applied do not reach the question of whether an invention actually represents an economic advance over the prior art. Given the fact that techniques are described in the model only by the productivity levels to which they give rise, this approach seems appropriate and virtually inevitable.

More realistically, a patented invention might be thought of as occupying a region in a space of technological attributes; a firm seeking to invent around the patent must avoid encroaching upon that region regardless of whether the knowledge it draws upon is acquired by imitation or not, and regardless of whether its alternative is economically inferior or superior to the patented one. In general, the need to avoid the technological region occupied by the patent might be expected to raise the cost of making an economically comparable invention; on the other hand, the availability of some of the information disclosed in the patent might lower that cost (even given the need to avoid infringement). The net effect might, in reality, be approximately zero. The model treats it as precisely zero.[9]

After a patent has expired, the technique involved does not become instantly available to all other firms, but rather is subject to being acquired by them through costly imitative effort. As noted below, the need to incur these costs should be considered reflective of the innovator's continuing antipathy to being imitated and, relatedly, of the fact that the application for the now-expired patent involved less than perfect disclosure of the technique actually employed.

The welfare consequences of 3-year patents (versus no patents) are described here in terms of the percentage of 'reference surplus' achieved. Reference surplus is the total discounted present value of consumer's and producers' surplus, as measured from the ordinary supply and demand curves, that would be achieved under first-best socially optimal conditions. The calculation of this social optimum assumes that the only barriers to diffusion of technology are ones that are deliberately created to defend against the imitative efforts of

---

[8] The reason for the short patent life will be discussed subsequently.

[9] As noted in Levin *et al.* (1987, pp. 810–11), there is evidence that in some cases, at least, patenting reduces costs of duplication of a competitor's advance.

other firms; thus imitation costs are not a factor in the calculation of the social optimum. It assumes also that it is unfeasible to vary R&D intensity from time period to period according to the prevailing relationship between actual and latent productivity; industry R&D intensity is constrained to be constant over time. Reference surplus may thus be thought of as the surplus generated when there is a single firm, constrained to meet the demand at marginal production cost in every period, and operating at a constant R&D intensity calculated to maximize the present value of the total surplus.[10] The maximized total surplus involves a negative producer's surplus because pricing at marginal production cost implies that the firm does not recover its R&D costs. Finally, in both reference surplus and actual surplus calculations, costs associated with the advance of latent productivity and the existence of background R&D are ignored, and the calculation of reference R&D expenditure takes into account the fact that some R&D—background R&D—is available at no cost to the industry. This treatment is consistent with the interpretation that the technological opportunity that gives rise to the industry is a byproduct or 'spinoff' of other social activities pursued for other reasons, and similarly that background R&D is not financed for reasons involving specific anticipations of profitability in this industry.

The numerous parameter values that characterize these simulation runs are similar to those explored in Winter (1984); readers interested in the details of the runs should consult that paper and its appendix for further explanation of the model and interpretation of the parameters.

Among the particularly significant features of the numerical setting are the following. First, there is a relatively high rate of the latent productivity growth, 6% per year, and the standard deviation of the draws distribution corresponds to 3 years of latent productivity growth. Thus, a single draw has only about a 5% probability of yielding a technique that is more than 6 years ahead of the 'state of the art' as represented by the log latent productivity. (Note, however, that the industry may actually be following a track well above or below the latent productivity track). Second, the interest rate used in discounting surplus is 6%, which is also the private rate of return on capital. Discounting is done to the same absolute date regardless of when the industry is actually born; random differences in industry birth date are thus among the many sources of random variation in outcomes among runs.

---

[10] Actually, the R&D intensity used in the calculation of reference surplus in the runs reported is an approximation to the true optimum, and the approximation method used is biased toward understating the productivity of innovative R&D expenditure. It probably underestimates, therefore, both the level of optimized surplus and the optimal level of R&D. Since the runs compared in the present paper are all conducted under identical technological opportunity conditions (and hence have the same reference surplus value), the fact that the reference surplus value is itself approximate merely attaches a minor caveat to assessments of how big the run-to-run differences are.

Results

Table 1 summarizes the results of five runs under each parameter setting. The 3-year patents have a strong negative effect on total surplus, amounting to about 10% of reference surplus. This change is the net result of a decline of 25% of reference surplus obtained by consumers and an increase of 15% of reference surplus obtained by producers.

Additional comparisons between the two sets of runs are shown in Table 2; these provide some insight into the mechanisms producing the welfare effect. The large swing in producers' surplus shown in Table 1 indicates that, in a straightforward sense, patents are effective in protecting gains from innovation. Table 2 provides some weak indication that firms respond to this 'incentive' by increasing their R&D intensity. In the evolutionary model, of course, such a behavioral change is a reflection of selection and search effects operating on behavioral alternatives actually tried, rather than of *ex ante* calculations. That is, the change is partly a matter of superior growth by firms that choose high R&D intensity as they enter, and partly a matter of imitative, adaptive policy change by firms whose profitability performance is below average. Although the five run average changes in the right direction, the extent of run-to-run variation within experimental conditions indicates that neither adaptive learning nor

TABLE 1. Surplus With and Without Patents[a]

	Total	Consumers'	Producers'
No Patents	88.0	93.2	−5.2
	(7.2)[b]	(6.3)	(1.7)
3-Year patents	78.1	68.4	9.7
	(6.4)	(6.9)	(3.0)

[a] Five run averages, expressed as per cent of reference surplus.
[b] Figures in parentheses are standard deviations.

TABLE 2. R&D and Industry Structure[a]

	R&D Policy[b]	N_H[c]	R&D expenditure[d]
No patents	3.68	16.87	369.7
3-Year patents	4.48	9.21	302.9

[a] Five run averages.
[b] Capital-weighted average of firm policies (designed as expenditure/capital ratios), end of run
[c] Herfindahl numbers equivalent, end of run.
[d] Total (undiscounted) R&D expenditure over run.

selection is a particularly powerful mechanism shaping R&D policy—the feed-back is very noisy, and the cost levels are in any case small in relation to sales.

More importantly, however, there is actually over 20% more total R&D performed, on average, without patents than there is *with* patents. Relatedly, best practice productivity levels tend to be higher without patents.

The greater volume of total R&D performed in the no-patents condition is a minor, and comparatively inconsequential, reflection of the major mechanism by which patents affect welfare in these simulations. The mechanism is to restrict imitative entry and lead to a generally less competitive industry—an industry that may be somewhat more R&D intensive per unit of capital employed, but involves fewer firms, employs less capital, produces less output, and earns substantial excess returns. Also, the restriction of imitation among existing firms leads to a substantially lower ratio of average to best practice productivity than is true in the no-patents condition; the welfare impact of this effect drawfs that of the different R&D intensity.

The data on average draws in Table 3 extend this story. Three-year patents, given the context of relatively rapidly advancing latent productivity, are sufficient to almost eliminate imitation as a method of technology transfer among firms. In the absence of patents, imitation accounted for 74% of the technique adoptions by existing firms, and 87% of the techniques adopted by entrants. In the presence of 3-year patents, these numbers change to 9% and 24%. The effect mostly takes the form of reducing successful imitation draws to very low levels; hardly anything on which the patent has expired is worth imitating. It is clear that much longer patent lives would make very little difference; even moderately longer patent lives would eliminate imitation entirely. The 3-year life was, in fact, chosen to preserve some small role for imitation.

Notice that there are substantially more innovations adopted under the patents condition—68% more in fact. However, this greater 'innovativeness'

TABLE 3. Innovation and Imitation Draws[a]

	Innovation		Imitation	
	Total	Accepted[b]	Total	Accepted[b]
Existing firms				
No patents	192	27	184	77
3-year patents	142	39	156	4
Potential entrants[c]				
No patents	52	4	105	26
3-year patents	55	13	100	4

[a] Five run averages.
[b] Implies change of technique if by an existing firm, entry if by a potential entrant.
[c] Excluding founder.

basically represents the necessary recourse to independent invention as a means of acquiring technology, given that patents block imitation. It is, in fact, a reflection of the inferior industry performance the patents cause: best practice is worse, not better; average practice is much worse still; more innovations are brought into use because more of them surpass these lower standards.

6. Concluding Comments

The simulation results illustrate vividly the possibility that the patent system can be counterproductive from a social welfare point of view. It is easy to imagine, nevertheless, that the system might have its defenders in the simulated world. That world presents strong incentives for self-interested advocacy of the patent system, and at least some of the arguments such advocates might advance—e.g. that patents lead to more innovations—are correct. From the social welfare point of view, however, their case as a whole is incorrect. First, it overlooks the possibility [originally emphasized by Barzel (1968)], that patents can cause inefficiencies by providing private incentives to seize exogenously improving opportunities at dates that are too early from a social point of view. A related inefficiency illustrated in the present model is that the process of diffusion of the knowledge represented by the exogenous opportunities may involve an increased proportion of expensive innovative R&D relative to cheap imitative R&D. Finally, and most importantly, the assessment of patents in the context of industry evolution (and using discounted surplus as the welfare criterion) underscores their possible adverse effects on industry structure and output.

Both the quantitative and qualitative patterns in the simulation outcomes reflect, of course, the assumptions of the model and the particular parameter values chosen. In considering what significance to attach to these numerical examples, it is important to distinguish two quite different questions: (i) are these results likely to be representative or typical of the actual welfare effects of the patent system as a whole? (ii) are these results illustrative of real mechanisms that may imply significant negative consequences for the patent system in some industrial contexts? My own responses are a tentative *no* for question (i) and a more vigorous *yes* for (ii). Both responses are consistent with the general view that there are large and important differences among industries with respect to the characteristics of productive knowledge, the sources of technological opportunity and the mechanisms of appropriability.[11] There is abundant reason to think that there are real situations that have little in

---

[11] For illustrative evidence in support of this point, see Levin *et al.*, 1987. The Yale survey partially reported in that report contains a good deal of additional evidence along the same line.

common with the simulated environment, little reason to think that the simulation outcomes correspond to the central tendency of real outcomes (whatever that might mean), but nevertheless good reason to think that the key features of at least some real environments may correspond sufficiently closely to the simulated world to make the simulation results relevant.

Four features of the simulated world principally account for the poor showing of the patent system. The first, of course, is the exogeneity of technological opportunity. Returns to innovative R&D are diminishing at any point of time as exogenously given opportunities are exhausted; this obviously limits the benefit from the patent system's stimulus to innovative R&D. Secondly, the assumed existence of background R&D means that some innovative R&D takes place, producing results sufficiently practical to motivate the founding of firms, regardless of whether the private returns are sufficient to cover the R&D costs. This reduces the marginal significance of the additional R&D that is funded in anticipation of net private gains. Relatedly, since it is background R&D that gives rise to the birth of the industry, the surplus transfers brought about by the patent system do not create effective incentives to found the industry earlier—this might conceivably be a significant source of benefit from the patent system in reality.

The two features just noted might be subsumed under the heading 'major influences from the broader social context of technological change'. The industry analyzed is not an island complete unto itself from a technological point of view. Perhaps some industries can reasonably be thought of as such islands, but certainly the theoretical literature has drastically (albeit implicitly) overemphasized the importance of these cases relative to industries whose technological development is significantly intertwined with that of the wider society.

A third feature underlying the results is the fact that the patents characterized in the model serve only to bar imitation, and do not serve as a basis for licensing agreements. (If they did, presumably such agreements would eliminate the inefficient substitution of innovative for imitative R&D.) This feature of the model may be rationalized by reference to a point made previously: the patents in the model do not fully disclose the technology; a prospective licensee needs the undisclosed technology as well as the licensed technology, and the prospective licensor is reluctant to strike such a deal because secrecy is considered more reliable than the legal protections of the patent system. Whatever the specific rationale, there are good theoretical and empirical grounds for thinking that in *some* sectors of the economy, patents function about as they do in the model.[12]

---

[12] Based on survey of high-level R&D executives, Levin *et al.* (1987) emphasize the diversity across industries in the working of the patent system and other mechanisms for protecting the gains from innovation. Overall, the executives scored patents as more effective in 'preventing duplication' than in 'securing royalty

Finally, the negative impact of patents on discounted total surplus is partly attributable to the slowing of the industry's early growth caused by the suppression of imitative entry. Much of this effect would not occur if the innovator-founder were assumed to enter at profit-maximizing scale, 'saturating' the market at P_0. This would require that the innovator-founder's decision rules reflect knowledge of the market demand at P_0; under the assumptions of the model this is not the case. Given this restriction, a tentative approach to initial entry scale seems plausible. With uncertainty about the demand at P_0, an orthodox model deriving entry scale from optimization calculations would probably yield a similar result: the more contenders for the market, the larger initial industry capital would tend to be.[13]

Changing these various assumptions would change and perhaps overturn entirely the simulation results. As noted above, while different assumptions might be more realistic for some industrial contexts, they would be less realistic for others.

Those who call for stronger protection of intellectual property—a common theme particularly among US policymakers in recent years—often seem to regard the desirability of such change as virtually axiomatic, perhaps on a par with the desirability of less crime. As economists are well aware, even the desirability of less crime is not axiomatic if the only available means to the end is the devotion of additional resources to law enforcement. The present paper emphasizes that the desirability of stronger intellectual property protection is far from axiomatic, even abstracting from the significant issue of enforcement. It illustrates the fact that specific features of the knowledge environment of an industry may be critical in determining how that particular industry is impacted by a policy change. A more flexible and discriminating approach to the modeling of technological opportunity is called for if economists are usefully to come to grips with these important issues.

References

Arrow, K. J. (1962), 'Economic Welfare and the Allocation of Resources for Invention,' in R. R. Nelson (ed.), *The Rate and Direction of Inventive Activity*, Princeton University Press: Princeton.

Barzel, Y. (1968), 'Optimal Timing of Innovations,' *Review of Economics and Statistics*, 50, 348–355.

David, P. A. (1974), *Technical Choice, Innovation and Economic Growth*. Cambridge University Press: London.

Dosi, G. (1984), *Technical Change and Industrial Transformation*. St. Martin's Press: New York.

---

income'. The belief that licensing could generally circumvent the adverse effects of patents on diffusion is one that fails to come to grips with the transactional difficulties in the market for intellectual property.

[13] Alternatively, the effect would at least be diminished if the imitative entry blocked by the innovator's patent were somehow transformed into innovative entry capable of 'inventing around' the patent. This would, of course, be a departure from the model's 'background R&D' story of how innovative entry occurs.

Downs, G. W. and L. B. Mohr (1976), 'Conceptual Issues in the Study of Innovation,' *Administrative Science Quarterly*, 21, 700–712.

Hirshleifer, J. (1971), 'The Private and Social Value of Information and the Reward to Inventive Activity,' *American Economic Review*, 61, 561–574.

Horner, S. (1977), *Stochastic Models of Technology Diffusion*. Unpublished dissertation, University of Michigan.

Iwai, K. (1984a), 'Schumpeterian Dynamics: Part I, An Evolutionary Model of Innovation and Imitation,' *Journal of Economic Behavior and Organization*, 5, 159–190.

Iwai, K. (1984b) 'Schumpeterian Dynamics: Part II, Technological Progress, Firm Growth and "Economic Selection"', *Journal of Economic Behavior and Organization*, 5, 321–351.

Jaffe, A. B. (1986). 'Technological Opportunity and Spillovers of R&D: Evidence from Firms' Patents, Profits and Market Values,' *American Economic Review*, 76, 984–1001.

Levin, R. C. and P. Reiss (1988), 'Cost-reducing and Demand-creating R&D with Spillovers,' *Rand Journal of Economics*, 19, 538–556.

Levin, R. C., A. K. Klevorick, R. R. Nelson and S. G. Winter (1987), 'Appropriating the Returns from Industrial Research and Development,' *Brookings Papers on Economic Activity: Special Issue on Microeconomics*, 783–820.

Nelson, R. R. (1980), 'Production Sets, Technological Knowledge and R&D: Fragile and Overworked Constructs for Analysis of Productivity Gowth?' *American Economic Review*, 79, 62–67.

Nelson, R. R. and S. G. Winter (1978), 'Forces Generating and Limiting Concentration under Schumpeterian Competiton,' *Bell Journal of Economics*, 9, 524–548.

Nelson, R. R. and S. G. Winter (1982), *An Evolutionary Theory of Economic Change*. Harvard University Press: Cambridge, MA.

Nordhaus, W. D. (1969), *Invention, Growth and Welfare: A Theoretical Treatment of Technological Change*. MIT Press: Cambridge, MA.

Pavitt, K. (1986), ' "Chips" and "Trajectories": How Does the Semiconductor Influence the Sources and Directions of Technical Change?', in R.M. MacLeod (ed.), *Technology and the Human Prospect: Essays in Honour of Christopher Freeman*. Frances Pinter: London.

Reinganum, J. (1988), 'The Timing of Innovation: Research, Development, Diffusion,' in R. Schmalensee and R. Willig (eds), *Handbook of Industrial Organization*. North-Holland.

Romer, P. M. (1986), 'Increasing Returns and Long-run Growth,' *Journal of Political Economy*, 94, 1002–1037.

Romer, P. M. (1990), 'Endogenous Technological Change,' *Journal of Political Economy*, 98, S71–S102.

Rosenberg, N. (1969), 'The Direction of Technological Change: Inducement Mechanisms and Focusing Devices,' *Economic Development and Cultural change*, 18, 1–24.

Scherer, F. M. (1972). 'Nordhaus Theory of Optimal Patent Life: A Geometric Interpretation,' *American Economic Review*, 68, 422–427.

Solow, R. M. (1970), *Growth Theory: an Exposition*. Oxford University Press: New York.

Winter, S. G. (1982), 'An Essay on the Theory of Production,' in S. H. Hymans (ed.), *Economics and the World Around It*. University of Michigan Press: Ann Arbor.

Winter, S. G. (1984), 'Schumpeterian Competition in Alternative Technological Regimes,' *Journal of Economic Behavior and Organization*, 5, 287–320.

Corporate Strategy, Structure and Control Methods in the United States During the 20th Century*

ALFRED D. CHANDLER, JR

(Graduate School of Business Administration, Harvard University, Soliders Field,
Boston, MA 02163, USA)

The title of this session is 'National Patterns—an historical analysis in terms of organizational forms, strategies, and control methods, etc'. My assignment is to review the United States' experience. Such organizational forms, strategies and control methods were responses to specific business challenges. As the papers that follow emphasize, responses to these challenges differed from nation to nation reflecting different national business, economic, political and cultural environments.

Nevertheless, all these national patterns are historically modern ones. They begin with the coming of the modern business enterprises—those that employed a number of full-time salaried managers—that first appeared in the mid-19th century. Before the building of modern transportation and communication systems the movement of goods, information and people was so slow and uncertain that there was no need to create enterprises directed by teams of salaried managers.

For centuries business organizational forms, structure and control methods in the Western World remained little changed. The partnership that came and went with the lives and changing activities of a small number of individual partners was still the standard organizational form. Double-entry bookkeeping and handwritten correspondence were the methods of control. As a study of Baltimore merchants, the Olivers, at the beginning of the 19th century noted, their 'form of organization, and their method of managing men, records and investment would have been almost immediately understood by the 15th century merchant of Venice.'[1] Even the great trading companies of the

---

* Presented at the conference on Organization and Strategy in the Evolution of the Enterprise, Milan, October 3–5, 1991.

[1] Quoted in Alfred D. Chandler, Jr, *The Visible Hand: The Managerial Revolution in American Business* (Cambridge, MA: Belknap Press/Harvard University Press, 1977), p. 16.

17th and 18th centuries rarely employed more salaried managers than a small local business enterprise of today.

1. *The Coming of the Modern Business Enterprise*

In the United States the railroad and its handmaiden, the telegraph, pioneered in the modern forms of organization, control and strategy. Their managers did so because they had to. Railroad construction and operations raised completely new sets of challenges. The capital required to build a major railroad was greater than that of any earlier business enterprise (and from the 1840s on not one but many such enterprises were demanding such unprecedented amounts of capital at the same time) and their operation was far more complex than any previous business enterprise. Not only were the sunk costs unprecedented, so too were the fixed costs—those that did not vary with the flow of traffic and, therefore, income. Moreover, unless the movement of trains and the flow of goods were carefully monitored and coordinated, accidents occurred, lives were lost and goods moved slowly and with uncertainty. Hierarchies of salaried managers had to be recruited and trained if railroad and telegraph enterprises were to achieve their promise of providing a high volume, fast, scheduled flow of goods, services and information.

In meeting these challenges American railroad managers brought into being many of the institutions and practices of the modern corporate world. In the United States their financing created its modern capital markets— Wall Street and the financial instruments traded on that national exchange. Their size and high fixed costs led to the coming of modern oligopolistic competition and with it the American brand of government regulation of individual business enterprises. Their size also led to the coming of modern labor relations with collective bargaining between national trade unions and the managers of the new enterprises. Most important of all, for the subject in hand, these executives pioneered in creating the first large multi-level managerial hierarchies and developing brand new techniques of controlling operations and of determining costs and profits. Finally, during the period of construction and consolidation, when managers were building the giant inter-regional systems, they concentrated on outmaneuvering their rivals through carefully considered strategic moves to protect their large investment and to maintain and increase their revenues.[2]

---

[2] Alfred D. Chandler, Jr, *The Railroads: The Nation's First Big Business* (New York: Harcourt, Brace & World, Inc., 1965), especially Parts II, III, and V. Thomas C. Cochran, *Railroad Leaders: The Business Mind in Action* (Cambridge, MA: Harvard University Press, 1953), especially Ch. 6 'The Foundations of Management,' and Ch. 9 'The Strategy of Railroad Expansion.'

The railroad, and to a lesser extent the telegraph, not only pioneered in the new ways of corporate organization, control methods, strategy, finance and labor and government relations. They also provided the essential base or infrastructure on which modern large-scale production and distribution rested.

In distribution the unprecedented speed, volume and regularity of flows brought into being the modern wholesaler who took title to goods and made profit on mark-up rather than by selling on commission. Quickly too came the mass retailer—the department stores, mail-order houses and chain stores—whose profits were based on low price and high 'stock-turn'. That is, the number of times stock 'inventory' was sold and replaced within a specified time period. The higher the stock-turn with the same working force and equipment, the lower the unit costs, the higher the output per worker and the greater the profit.[3]

In production the new speed, volume and certainty of flows of materials and information stimulated a wave of technological innovations that swept through western Europe and the United States. Old industries such as food processing and metal making were transformed. New ones were created, including oil, rubber, heavy machinery, light machinery (such as sewing, agriculture, construction and business equipment), chemicals (such as man-made dyes, medicines, fertilizers and materials), and electrical equipment for light, industrial power and urban transportation. In these industries 'throughput' (that is the amount of materials processed within a production facility during a specified period of time) determined profit much as stock-turn did for the new mass retailing. Up to its rated capacity a production establishment's unit costs fell as the speed of throughput increased and rose as it decreased. Thus, the cost advantages of the economies of scale reflected both capacity of a facility and the intensity in which it was used. Another source of unit cost reduction came from the economies of scope. That is, by producing more products in a single establishment that used similar raw and semi-finished materials and much the same processing equipment, the cost of each individual product was lowered.[4]

In nearly all these cases, these new or transformed industries with capital-intensive, technologically complex processes of production were quickly dominated by a small number of 'first movers'. These were those pioneering enterprises which invested in production facilities large enough to exploit fully the potential cost advantages of scale and scope of the new technologies, which built product-specific national and then international marketing and distribution networks and which recruited and trained teams of managers

[3] Chandler, *The Visible Hand*, p. 223.

[4] Alfred D. Chandler, Jr, *Scale and Scope: The Dynamics of Industrial Capitalism* (Cambridge, MA: Belknap Press/Harvard University Press, 1990), p. 24.

essential to monitor and coordinate the flow of goods through the enterprise. Such first movers began to compete oligopolistically—that is, they competed for market share and profit less on price and more by functional effectiveness (improved manufacturing, research and development, marketing and distribution, and labor relations) and by strategically moving more quickly into new markets and out of old ones.[5] These large managerial integrated enterprises continued to dominate the industries of the 1880s and 1890s that transformed the economies of their day. They played a similar role in the later transforming industries such as motor vehicles in the 1920s and 30s and computers after World War II.

These long-lived dominant firms in these industries led the way during the twentieth century in shaping strategies of growth and competition, in developing the most complex of organizational forms and control of systems. Therefore, I concentrate this historical analysis on these industrial enterprises. But let me stress, where the technologies of production did not foster cost advantages of scale and scope—in industries such as textiles, apparel, lumber, furniture, printing and publishing, shipbuilding and mining—companies had less needs for such relatively complex organizational forms and methods.

2. Strategy, Structure and Control Methods in the Years of Enterprise Growth

The development of corporate strategies, structures and control systems in the US firms in modern capital-intensive industries rested on three sources—those developed in the management of railroads, those that came from the management of units of production (the factory or works) and finally those created by the corporate managers themselves. Because the railroad so dominated the US industrial scene in the late 19th century and because American industrialists had fewer business or governmental models upon which to draw, the railroad had a greater impact on organizational and control forms and possibly on strategic planning in the large industrial enterprise than was the case in Britain or on the continent.

From the railroad came a three-level organizational structure. On the railroads the lower level managers included division superintendents (responsible for roughly 100 miles of track) who reported to middle managers, the general superintendents (responsible for roughly 500–1000 miles of track). Each had the same set of staff executives for traffic (freight and passengers), maintenance of locomotives and rolling stock, maintenance of way and telegraph

[5] Alfred D. Chandler, Jr, *Scale and Scope: The Dynamics of Industrial Capitalism* (Cambridge, MA: Belknap Press/Harvard University Press, 1990), pp. 34–36.

and those for purchasing and accounting. At the top were 'the Vice President and General Manager' responsible for transportation and the vice presidents in charge of traffic and finance. In the new industrial structures the lower level managers become responsible for an operating unit (a factory, sales office, purchasing unit or laboratory) and reported to middle managers who were responsible for coordinating and monitoring multi-unit functional departments (those for production, sales, purchasing, and research and development and also for financial control). At both the railroads and the new industrials the vice presidents for functional activities with the president were responsible, not only for overall monitoring and coordinating current departmental activities but also planning and allocating resources for future operations.[6]

From the railroads, too, came the line and staff definition of the duties of the managers on each level. On the railroads the line of authority ran from the Vice President and General Manager to the general superintendents and then to the division superintendents. The staff executives were responsible for maintenance and repair, for establishing systems for the movement of goods and passengers, analyzing methods, checking quality and maintaining accounts. At the new industrials the line of authority ran from the functional vice presidents to the managers of factories or sales offices or laboratories. The staff executives provided supporting activities. Thus Harrington Emerson, an early factory management consultant with long railroad experience, urged the appointment of factory staff executives for personnel, plant and machinery, materials (purchasing), accounting and operational methods.[7]

The new industrials also took over from the railroads the structure of the top policy-making office—the corporation's Board of Directors. On both full-time executives—the president and heads of the major functional departments—made up the Executive Committee of the Board. They were soon known as the 'inside directors'. Part-time representatives of large shareholders—outside directors—made up the Finance Committee.[8] Because the inside directors set the agenda for the Board's monthly meetings, provided the information discussed and were responsible for implementing decisions taken and because the part-time outside directors were almost always involved in their own full-time business or professional activities, the inside directors—the Executive Committee—dominated top level decision making.

---

[6] Chandler, *The Visible Hand*, pp. 94–109 describes the development of railroad organizational forms; Chandler, *Scale and Scope*, pp. 31–34 the development of the U-Form in industry.

[7] Chandler, *The Visible Hand*, p. 277.

[8] By the 1870s the New York Central and the Pennsylvania Railroad had their Executive and Finance Committees; by the 1880s these committees of the boards of directors had become standard on major US railroads. Industrial first-movers quickly adopted the form—including such firms as Standard Oil, General Electric, Du Pont and US Rubber.

In their control methods the new industrial corporation modified only slightly railroad accounting practices to meet their own somewhat different needs. As did the railroad managers, the industrial managers made a careful distinction between capital and operating costs and between fixed and variable costs. In accounting for depreciation, they relied, as did their counterparts on the railroads, on 'renewal accounting'. That is, they considered depreciation as an operating cost and charged all maintenance and repairs to operating accounts. In addition the industrial managers set up monthly rates for depreciation so as to account for technical obsolescence and unexpected fire or accidents. In determining profit and loss they used comparable balance sheets and looked on the 'operating ratio,' which the railroads had used since the 1850s, as the criterion for financial performance. For the railroads quickly learned that the dollar value of earnings was not enough. Earnings had to be related to the volume of business. So the ratio between earnings and operating costs or, as the railroads defined it, earnings from operations required to meet operating expenses became the critical measure of financial performance. The executives of the new industrials first used earnings (revenues from sales minus costs) as a percentage of costs and then, more often as a percentage of sales.[9]

The factory—particularly those establishments in processing metals or metal making machinery—was a source for modern control methods, but not for strategy or organizational forms. First came a more precise definition of a factory's direct costs based on determining standard costs and standard volume through 'scientific' methods. Here Frederick W. Taylor was a pioneer. Then came the determination of indirect costs or 'factory burden,' particularly those that fluctuated with the volume of output. Here such consultants as Alexander Hamilton Church and Henry Gantt were the innovators. They realized that the critical item in determining indirect costs was throughput. When throughput was lower than standard volume, say, 80% of rated capacity, the increased unit costs were termed 'unabsorbed burden' and when it was over, decreased unit costs were termed 'over-absorbed burden'.[10] Over and unabsorbed burdens soon became major items on factory cost sheets. By 1910 the internal cost control methods for a single factory or works in the United States had been effectively defined.

But Taylor and other management experts of the first years of the 19th century rarely went beyond factory accounting. They paid little attention to the overall costs of running a multi-function enterprise that integrated

[9] Chandler, *The Visible Hand*, pp. 110–112, 445; William Z. Ripley, *Railroads: Finance and Organization* (New York, NY: Longmans, Green, 1915), pp. 612–615; Thomas Johnson and Robert S. Kaplan, *Relevance Lost: The Rise and Fall of Management Accounting* (Boston, MA: Harvard Business School Press, 1987), pp. 8, 37, 90.
[10] Chandler, *The Visible Hand*, pp. 278–279.

production and distribution. Nor did they consider the financial accounting needed for capital budgeting for the enterprise as a whole. Here innovations came from the corporate executives themselves.

Especially innovative were the managers of the E.I. du Pont de Nemours Powder Company formed by three du Pont cousins in 1903 to consolidate the American explosives industry. Du Pont managers realized that in defining overall corporate financial performance the modified railroad operating ratio was not enough. As one Du Pont executive argued: 'The true test of whether the profit is too great or too small is the rate of return on the money invested in the business and not the percent of profit on the cost. A commodity requiring an inexpensive plant might, when sold only 10% above its cost, show a higher rate of return on the investment than a commodity sold at double its cost, but manufactured in an expensive plant.'[11] To obtain an accurate figure of investment Pierre du Pont, the youngest of the three cousins and the new company's treasurer, made the distinction between 'permanent investment' and working capital used in operations. To determine the former he reviewed the valuations of the properties that were brought into the 1903 merger. Then he set up a 'permanent investment' account to which all new construction (and dismantle assets) were charged.

By 1910 one of Pierre du Pont's subordinates, Donaldson Brown, had refined this approach. Brown stressed that if prices remained the same, the rate of return on invested capital increased as volume rose and decreased as it fell. The higher the throughput and stock-turn, the greater the rate of return. Brown termed this rate of flow 'turnover'. He then multiplied turnover by the accepted older definition of profit—earnings as a percent of sales. Figure 1 provides an oversimplified, but still valid, description of how the Du Pont Company determined their ROI. (In this formula over and under absorbed burden were listed as part of working capital.) As two present day accounting experts point out, 'the formula . . . shows how return on investment is affected by a change in any element of either the income statement (via the operating ratio) or the balance sheet (via the turnover ratio).'[12]

Besides its use in evaluating, coordinating and planning divisional operations, the ROI formula became central to the capital budgeting process. Even before World War I, capital appropriation procedures in the industrial enterprises were being systematized. At Du Pont, for example, as early as 1908 proposals for capital expenditures had to include detailed blueprints, cost data, market studies and, most important of all, a breakdown of expected rate of return. In addition, plant sites had to be approved by the sales, purchasing and traffic departments to assure that the costs involved had been factored in.

[11] *Ibid*, pp. 446–447.
[12] Johnson and Kaplan, *Relevance Lost*, p. 84.

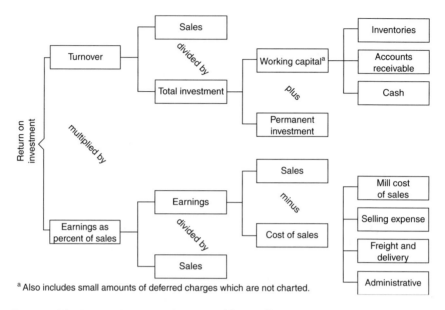

^a Also includes small amounts of deferred charges which are not charted.

FIGURE 1. The Du Pont Company: relationship of factors affecting return on investment.

Source: T. C. Davies (1950), 'How the du Pont Organization Appraises Its Performance,' in American Management Association, *Financial Management Series*, No. 94:7.

Once a project was underway, a member of the Executive Committee was responsible for reviewing and acting on the regularly scheduled flow of reports as to its progress.[13] These control methods in which Du Pont pioneered were adopted by other industrial enterprises in the 1920s. They were valuable in assisting American firms to carry out strategies of growth after World War I.

In the United States modern industrial enterprises grew in four ways. They merged with competitors in the same market (horizontal combination) or they obtained suppliers or distributors (vertical integration). But these moves were usually in response to specific, more immediate business situations. The continuing long-term strategy of the still relatively new large enterprises in the capital-intensive industries was to grow by moving into distant markets (geographical expansion) or into related markets (product diversification). They did so by moving into markets—markets in which their organizational learning based on the initial product- and process-specific investments in production and distribution gave them a competitive advantage. Those companies whose organizational capabilities were honed by exploiting the economies of scale tended to move into new more distant geographical markets and became increasingly multi-national. Those whose capabilities were

---

[13] Chandler, *The Visible Hand*, pp. 460–461.

based on the economies of scope tended to enter related product markets and became multi-industrial.

This strategic growth brought into being a new basic organizational form or structure. In the interwar years, US firms rationalized the management of their multi-market businesses by adopting some version of the multidivisional structure (the M-Form) which had a corporate headquarters and a number of product or geographical operating divisions.

The M-Form was a response by senior managers operating through existing centralized, functionally departmentalized U-Form structures to the demands of implementing their strategy of growth. They quickly realized that they had neither the time nor the necessary information to coordinate and monitor day-to-day operations, or to devise and implement long-term plans for the several product or geographical divisions. The administrative overload had become simply too great. Du Pont in 1921 (here again Du Pont was an innovator), and then other new multibusiness enterprises, turned over the responsibility for monitoring and coordinating production and distribution (and often product development) to the division managers. The major role of the new corporate headquarters became, and remained, that of maintaining the long-term health (usually defined as continued profitability) and growth of their firms.[14]

To implement this role the executives at the new headquarters carried out two closely related functions. One was entrepreneurial or value-creating, that is to determine strategies to maintain and then to utilize for the long-term the firm's organizational skills, facilities and capital and to allocate resources—capital and product-specific technical and managerial skills—to pursue these strategies. The second was more administrative or loss-preventive. It was to monitor the performance of the operating divisions; to check on the use of the resources allocated; and, when necessary, redefine the product or geographical lines of the divisions so as to continue to use more effectively the firm's organizational capabilities.

The administrative tasks of monitoring were, of course, intimately related to the entrepreneurial task of strategic planning and resource allocation. For monitoring provided the essential information about changing technology and markets, and the nature and pace of competition in the different businesses. And it permitted a continuing evaluation of the performance of divisional operating managers.

The control systems developed before World War I were even more essential to the management of the new M-Form than they had been to the U-Form. At Du Pont until well after World War II the Executive Committee

---

[14] Alfred D. Chandler, Jr, *Strategy and Structure: Chapters in the History of the Industrial Enterprise* (Cambridge, MA: M.I.T. Press, 1962), Ch. 2.

met every Monday in the 'Chart Room' with a division manager and his staff to review divisional operations. From the Chart Room's ceiling 'hung large, metal-framed charts displaying the overall return on investment and each of the constituent parts of the ROI formula for each of the divisions. A system of tracks and switches allowed any one of the 350 charts to be moved to the center position. There the committee, seated in a semi-circle, could view and discuss trends for a given division or for two or more divisions.'[15] At these meetings the Committee reviewed seriatim the operating performance of the company's several divisions (in the interwar years Du Pont operated through 8–10 divisions), checked on the implementation of approved capital projects and considered future capital expenditures.

The cost management and budgetary procedures adopted at Du Pont and at other large industrial enterprises were not seen as pictures of reality but rather as guidelines to understanding reality. The continuing close interaction between the top and operating managers was a learning process for both. It enhanced product- and process-specific management and technical skills of the company as a whole and created organizational capabilities that were not only specific to the enterprise but to the industries in which it operated.

Facilitated by the adoption of the M-Form and refinement of earlier control methods, the size and number of US multimarket firms—both multinational and multiproduct—grew before World War II and expanded more rapidly after that war. So too did the number of the markets they entered, and therefore the number of the divisions in which they operated. Moreover many dominant firms in the capital-intensive industries in Europe followed much the same strategy of growth, although they rarely adopted the M-Form structure until after World War II. I document the extent of this expansion into new geographical and product markets in the United States, Great Britain and Germany between the 1880s and 1940s in *Scale and Scope*. Bruce Scott, in 1973, summarized the several studies of continuing diversification into new markets between 1950 and 1970 in France and Italy as well as United States, Britain and Germany.[16] By the 1960s the multibusiness enterprise had become the norm in most modern capital-intensive, technologically complex industries.

Such strategies of growth into new markets obviously intensified interfirm competition. Until the 1960s, however, world events—the two global wars and the massive global depression of the 1930s—held back the full impact of international and inter-industry competition. The two wars weakened the competitive strength of the US firms' most powerful foreign rivals, particularly the

---

[15] JoAnne Yates, *Control Through Communication: The Rise of System in American Management* (Baltimore: Johns Hopkins University Press, 1989), pp. 266–267.

[16] Bruce R. Scott, 'The Industrial State: Old Myths and New Realities,' *Harvard Business Review*, March–April 1973, 133–145.

Germans. And the Great Depression reduced markets and brought economic autocracy. It was not, therefore, until the 1960s after the economic health of the European nations had been fully restored, and after Japan, following a massive transfer of technology, began to industrialize rapidly, that the international competition which had been developing before 1914 became a full-fledged reality. In these same years US enterprises, which had begun to enter closely related product markets during the interwar years, began to expand in this manner more aggressively. For example, by the 1960s, agricultural, mining, industrial, and construction machinery as well as truck and automobile companies had moved into each other's industrial markets and glass, rubber, and food firms had expanded their activities in chemicals. Rapidly growing R&D expenditures intensified such interindustry competition.

3. *The Impact of Continuing Growth and Intensified Competition*

In the 1960s continued growth and intensified competition began to affect the organizational structure, the strategy of growth, and the control methods of large US industrial firms. Continued growth by the adding of new product lines and to a lesser extent moving into distant geographical markets forced structural change in much the same manner as had the initial product diversification and overseas expansion. The decision-making overload soared at both the corporate and divisional headquarters. So senior executives at Du Pont reviewing the company's problems in the 1920s and those of the late 1960s.[17] The solution at Du Pont and many other companies was to form functionally integrated business units (often termed profit centers) within their enlarged divisions to coordinate and control a single product or very closely related product lines. In others it was to place a number of divisions under the control of a larger 'group' office.

But whatever the name used, by the 1970s most large multibusiness enterprises had at least three (not just two) levels of autonomous planning and administrative offices—the business unit, the division and the corporate headquarters. The first normally operated through functional U-Form structures, while the divisions, like the corporate office, operated through a version of the M-Form structure with its senior line executives supported by an extensive staff responsible for profit, market share, and other measurements of performance.

---

[17] David A. Hounshell and John K. Smith, *Science and Corporate Strategy: Du Pont R&D, 1902–1980* (New York: Cambridge University Press, 1988), p. 586.

The corporate office continued to define growth paths and goals for the corporation as a whole and to monitor the performance of the subordinate operating units. In these same years the headquarters' role as mediator with government agencies and other public bodies increased sharply with new regulatory legislation.

In the same years that brought structural modifications many US industrial enterprises began to alter their strategies. Intensified competition resulting from new players from abroad and from related industries gave US companies the greatest competitive challenge they had had to face since their founding, often decades earlier. The long-established strategies of growth were difficult to maintain. New markets where an enterprise's organizational capabilities gave it a competitive advantage were harder to find. Even new ventures such as those carried out at Du Pont, Hercules, General Electric and Westinghouse, based explicitly on perceived organizational capabilities, too often proved unprofitable.[18]

The strong revival of powerful firms abroad made direct overseas investment more risky for US firms; while expansion from firms in related industries began to crowd their markets at home. Excess capacity increased. Prices fell, costs rose, ROI dropped. Many managers responded, as their predecessors had done particularly in the depression years, to investing revenue into improving product and the performance of their functional activities. But others looked for investment opportunities in industries that appeared to show greater profit potential even though their operations called for a very different set of organizational capabilities—of different facilities and skills.

For the first time in American industrial history firms now began to grow by entering businesses in which their enterprises had little distinctive competitive advantage. Because of their lack of knowledge of the operations of the target industries, they rarely moved, as they had earlier into related industries, through direct investment, that is, by building their own factories and hiring or transferring their own workers and managers. Instead they obtained facilities and personnel by acquisitions or, less often, by merger.

There were, of course, other reasons besides intensifying competition for the new strategy of growth through mergers and acquisitions into distantly related or unrelated markets and industries. With the passage of the Cellar-Kefauver Act in 1950 the federal government's antitrust forces began to tighten restrictions

---

[18] H. D. Fast, *The Rise and Fall of New Corporate Venture Divisions* (Ann Arbor, MI: MI Research Press, 1977). Hounshell and Smith, *Science and Corporate Strategy*, Ch. 22. Davis Dyer and David R. Sicilia, *Labors of a Modern Hercules: Evolution of a Chemical Company* (Boston, MA: Harvard Business School Press, 1990), pp. 363–372. At G.E. the CEO, Reginald Jones, referred in 1975 to the 'venture mess', and 'the venture problems', quoted in Alfred D. Chandler, Jr, and Richard S. Tedlow, *The Coming of Managerial Capitalism: A Casebook on the History of American Economic Institutions* (Homewood, IL: Richard Irwin, 1985), p. 785.

on enterprise growth through horizontal and vertical mergers.[19] Even moves into closely related industries became suspect. Furthermore, accounting practices under existing tax laws often made mergers and acquisitions profitable. Railroads, pipe lines, and utility companies could not enlarge their existing markets and had few resources that might be transferred to other businesses. To grow they had to acquire firms in distantly or unrelated businesses. This was also the case for manufacturing firms in such industries as textiles, shipbuilding and railroad equipment whose capabilities were also difficult to transfer to other product markets.

Nevertheless, the primary motive for the acquisition and mergers in the 1960s was the desire of managers to assure continuing growth of their enterprises by entering industries that promised higher ROIs and lesser competition than did their own. Because of the wartime expansion and early post-war success, many of that generation of managers overrated the potential of the product-specific organizational capabilities of their enterprises. The growing flood of business school graduates had been trained to believe that what they had learned for one set of industries could be easily transferred to another. The computer created new flows of information and new techniques to analyze these data as to both current and future operations. The information revolution reinforced the beliefs of the new 'scientific' approach to corporate management. As one careful observer noted in 1969, 'the new science of management is the primary force behind conglomeration.'[20]

In that year, 1969, the drive to growth through merger and acquisition in related industries had become almost a mania. In 1965 the number of mergers and acquisitions was just over 2000. Managerial hubris and to a much lesser extent, antitrust laws, tax advantages and in some industries obvious limits to enterprise growth raised the number to 4500 in 1968 and then to over 6000 in 1969. Then the mania waned. By 1974 the number of mergers had dropped to 2861. During the period 1963–1972 close to three-fourths of the assets acquired were for product diversification. One-half of these were in unrelated product lines. In the years 1973–1977 one-half of all assets acquired through merger and acquisition came from those in unrelated industries.[21]

This new strategy of acquisitions of or mergers with firms in distantly or unrelated businesses often weakened the effectiveness of the enlarged M-Form

[19] Neil Fligstein, *The Transformation of Corporate Control* (Cambridge, MA: Harvard University Press, 1990), ch. 6 provides an excellent review of the impact of antitrust policies on corporate strategy after World War II.

[20] Neil H. Jacoby, 'The Corporate Conglomerate Corporation,' *The Center Magazine*, Spring 1969, reprinted in Chandler and Tedlow, *The Coming of Managerial Capitalism*, p. 739. The next few paragraphs follow closely pages in my 'Competitive Performance of U.S. Industrial Enterprise: A Historical Perspective,' in Michael E. Porter, ed., *Time Horizons in American Industry* (a tentative title) to be published in 1992.

[21] David J. Ravenscroft and F. M. Scherer, *Mergers, Sell-offs, and Economic Efficiency* (Washington, DC: Brookings Institution, 1989), ch. 6.

organization and of the existing control systems. Increasingly top managers at the corporate office—the executives responsible for coordinating, monitoring, and planning and allocating resources for the enterprise as a whole—lost touch with the middle managers responsible for maintaining the competitive capabilities of the operating divisions in the battle for market share and profits. This disconnection of corporate from operating management affected the competitive strength of American companies and industries far more than the separation of ownership control and management ever had. For it undermined top managers' ability to carry two of their basic functions—the monitoring and coordinating of current operations and the allocation of resources for future ones.

Diversification by acquisition led to such separation for two reasons. First, the top managers often had little specific knowledge of, and experience with, technological processes and markets in many of the businesses they had acquired. The second was simply that the large number of different businesses acquired created a still greater overload in decision-making at the corporate office. Whereas before World War II the corporate office of large diversified international enterprises rarely managed more than ten divisions and only the largest had as many as 25, by 1969 numerous companies were operating from 40 to 70 divisions and a few even more.

Because few senior executives had either the training or experience necessary to evaluate the proposals and monitor the performance of so many divisions in so many different activities, they had to rely more and more on impersonal statistics to maintain their link with operating management. But, as Thomas Johnson and Robert Kaplan point out in their *Relevance Lost: The Rise and Fall of Managerial Accounting*, 1987, such data were becoming increasingly less pertinent to realistically controlling costs and understanding the complexities of competitive battles. Too often management cost accounting as taught in colleges and graduate schools and as practiced by accountants became divorced from the complex operating needs of the decentralized, multidivisional organization. 'Cost accounting textbooks and academic research continued to concentrate on highly simplified, frequently abstract representations of cost systems.' Such representations were 'in stark contrast' to actual practice in firms. Historical cost procedures in 'generally accepted accounting principles (G.A.A.P.)' permitted plenty of leeway for managers to adjust accounts to meet budget and cost targets. 'As a result,' the authors conclude, 'cost accounting and management systems found in most U.S. companies in the 1980s are of little use for determining product cost, for enhancing cost control, or for encouraging the creation of long-term economic wealth.'[22]

---

[22] Johnson and Kaplan, *Relevance Lost*, pp. 169, 197, 221. They comment on the impact of the growth of the enterprise and other institutional changes in recent years on the use of ROI in evaluating divisional performance, pp. 203–204.

Even so problems lay less in the quality of the data and more in their use. Many divisions had themselves become multiproduct and multiregional and the number of business units (profit centers) increased impressively. In the 1960s, for example, GE had 190 and ITT over 200 such units. At GE the 190 business units were managed by 46 divisions which in turn came under the supervision of 10 groups whose heads looked to the corporate office for supervision.[23] This meant that the statistical ROI data were no longer the basis for discussion between corporate and operating management as to performance, profit and long-term plans. Instead ROI became a reality in itself—a target sent down from the corporate office for division managers to meet. Divisional offices, in turn, sent comparable targets to the business units or profit centers. Since managers' compensation and promotion prospects depended on their ability to meet targets, these middle managers had a strong incentive to adjust their data accordingly.[24] As dangerous to competitive success, they rarely had the chance to review with top management the implications of the numbers.

In the post-war years capital budgeting, like the monitoring of performance, became more statistically based. In the late 1950s a capital budgeting model began to be used in determining long-term ROI of proposed capital projects. The new concept was a more precise determination of the earning rate required to make a project profitable. The model was used to determine cost of time, and then took into account the risk involved; the longer the time, the greater the risk, the larger the rate.[25] Such seemingly precise estimates of anticipated project costs, if taken literally, could shorten managers' investment time horizons. Although experienced executives understood that this calculation of the required earning rate was only the place to begin discussions, its use may account for the fact that US managers appear to require a higher threshold or 'hurdle' rate of return for financially justifiable projects than do Japanese or Continental European managers.[26]

Finally, increase in the size and the number of operating divisions forced the systematizing and indeed the bureaucratizing of strategic planning procedures. The senior corporate officers now had to allocate resources on the basis of strategic plans and capital budgets developed by scores of business

[23] Francis J. Aguilar and Richard Hamermesh, 'General Electric, Strategic Position-1981,' in Chandler and Tedlow, *The Coming of Managerial Capitalism*, p. 777.

[24] I analyze these changes and systematizing and bureaucratizing of the strategic planning process in my 'The Functions of the HQ Unit in the Multibusiness Firm', *Strategic Management Journal* (forthcoming), 1992.

[25] Johnson and Kaplan, *Relevance Lost*, pp. 163–165. Robert N. Anthony, 'Reminiscences About Management Accounting,' *Journal of Management Accounting Research*, 1:7–9 (Fall, 1989).

[26] James M. Poterba and Lawrence H. Summers, 'Time Horizons of American Firms: New Evidence from a Survey of CEOs,' Porter, *Time Horizons*. They found the average hurdle rate for U.S. firms to be 11.6% for manufacturing firms and 12.2% for all firms in their sample. Japanese reported hurdle rates of below 10%.

units. Those strategic planning reports were initially reviewed and culled by the division headquarters in which the units operated. Those offices, in turn, sent divisional plans to corporate headquarters, sometimes via group head-quarters. Thus the top executives at the corporate office not only lost personal contact with the operating managers of divisions and business units; but also they set budgets and targets and allocated resources on the basis of written often statistical data distilled by at least two levels (and sometimes three) of planning staffs.

Moreover, these capital budgeting and strategic review processes, like the statistical evaluations of ROI, too often failed to incorporate complex non-quantifiable data as to the nature of specific product markets, changing pro-duction technology, competitor's activities and internal organizational problems—data that corporate and operating managers had in the past discussed in their long person-to-person evaluation of past and current performance and allocation of resources.[27] Top management decisions were becoming based on numbers, not knowledge. In too many cases the existing control methods no longer guided discussions between corporate and operating managers. Instead they became devices for setting targets—ROI and budget targets decided by the corporate managers who had little or no direct contact with operating realities.

The strategy of unrelated or distantly related mergers and acquisitions and the resulting weakening of organizational structure and control systems can account in part for the unprecedented numbers of divestitures that occurred in the years that followed the mergers of the late 1960s. Before that merger move-ment, divestitures were rare. By the early 1970s they had become common-place. In 1965 there was only one divestiture for every 11 mergers; in 1969, at the height of the merger wave, the ratio was 1 to 8; by 1970, 1 to 2.4; and then for four years 1974 to 1977 the ratio was close to or even under 1 to 2.[28]

The unprecedented number of mergers and acquisitions followed so shortly by an unprecedented number of divestitures helped to bring into being another new phenomenon—the buying and selling of corporations as an established business, and a most lucrative one at that. Although industrial-ists pioneered in this business, the financial community prospered from it.

The new business of buying and selling companies and, with it, the result-ing change in the basic role of US investment banks from underwriting long-term corporate investments to profiting from the greatly increased merger and acquisition activity was further stimulated by the rise of a new set of financial intermediaries—the mutual and pension funds administered by professional

---

[27] Carliss Baldwin and Kim Clark, 'Strategic Capital Budgeting: The Case of New Product Introductions,' in Porter, *Time Horizons*.

[28] W. T. Grimm & Company, *Mergerstat Review*, 1988 (Chicago, IL: Grimm & Company, 1988), pp. 103–104.

managers. With their rise came an unprecedented change in the nature of the 'ownership' of American industrial companies. After World War II, increasingly larger amounts of the voting shares of American industrial enterprises came to be held in the portfolios of pension and mutual funds. These funds, which had their beginnings in the 1920s and suffered severely during the depression years of the 1930s, began to come into their own in the 1960s. The success of the managers of these funds was measured by their ability to have the value (dividends and appreciation) of their portfolios outperform the Standard & Poor's index of the value of 500 companies. To meet their portfolio objectives, they had constantly to buy and sell securities—transactions made far more on the basis of short-term performance than on long-term potential. As time passed, these portfolio managers—the new owners of American industry—increasingly traded securities in large blocks of 10 000 shares or more. Block trading accounted for only 3.1% of total sales on the New York Stock Exchange in 1965. By 1985 it accounted for 51% of sales. In those years, too, the volume of total transactions rose on the Exchange from close to one-half a billion shares annually in the early 1950s to three billion at the end of the decade and to 27.5 billion by 1985.[29]

The great increase in the total volume of transactions, the rise in the turnover rate, and the growth of block sales made possible still another new phenomenon—the coming of an institutionalized market for corporate control. For the first time individuals, groups, and companies could obtain control of well-established enterprises in industries in which the buyers had no previous connection simply by purchasing their shares on the stock exchange. Large blocks of stock were being traded regularly; and such buyers had difficulty in raising funds for these purchases from financial institutions and financiers.

Thus, the diversification of the 1960s, the divestitures of the 1970s, the business of buying and selling corporations stimulated by the shift in ownership, and finally the coming of the market for corporate control greatly facilitated the ease with which the modern managerial enterprise could be restructured. Such firms could now be bought, sold, split up, and recombined in ways that would have been exceedingly difficult before the acquisition wave of the 1960s.

During the 1970s a new financial environment and the continuing intensifying battle for markets brought a basic change in the strategies of many large multimarket US industrial firms. Their managers appreciated that an era of competition demanded different responses than did one of growth. They were learning that competitive advantages in highly contested markets

---

[29] *New York Stock Exchange Fact Book, 1987* (New York, NY: New York Stock Exchange 1988), p. 71.

required close attention to the competitive potential of their companies' distinctive capabilities—of their specialized organizational facilities and skills. So the senior executives of these multimarket enterprises began to restructure and size down the portfolio of the businesses in which they competed. This restructuring was facilitated by the new institutionalized market for corporate control. In these same years these managers were learning that competitive success also depended on the ability of their corporate offices to carry out the basic functions of monitoring the performance of the operating units and planning and allocating resources for future production and distribution. As they redefine their strategies, they also reshape their organizational structures and attempted to revitalize their control methods.

In carrying out their restructuring strategies corporate and operating executives continued to learn more about the specific nature of the enterprises' organizational capabilities and how their product, process, and managerial labor and technical skills might best be used. This process of restructuring was usually one of trial and error. As a result the spinning off of existing operating units was often accompanied by the acquisition of other product or service lines.

During the mid- and late 1970s such corporate restructuring was carried out almost wholly by senior executives at corporate headquarters. Investment bankers and other financial intermediaries happily profited from their new role of financially facilitating the transactions involved in the spinning off of existing operations and acquiring the new ones. In these transactions the corporate managers preferred friendly takeovers; but if they determined the acquisition was valuable in their long-term strategic plans, they were willing enough to acquire it without the target company's support. Hostile takeovers, until then rare in American business, became commonplace as the decade came to a close.

During the 1980s financial intermediaries and entrepreneurs became more aggressively involved in corporate restructuring. They began to instigate mergers and acquisitions in order to profit from the transactions themselves, rather than from long-term strategic gains. These were the years of the highly profitable transaction-oriented mergers and acquisitions carried out by raiders, greenmailers, and the instigators of 'bust-up' transactions (i.e. the purchasing of companies for the purpose of selling off their parts).[30] Even so, as one study points out, companies, divisions or subsidiaries involved in these transaction-oriented mergers and acquisitions usually ended up in the hand of firms with similar or closely related products and processes. In these

---

[30] I review the negative impact of such transactions-oriented mergers and acquisitions in my 'Competitive Performance of U.S. Industrial Enterprises' in Porter, *Time Horizons*.

transaction-oriented deals the financiers acted as brokers, making profits (and often extravagant ones at that) in carrying out the brokerage function.[31]

But even in the mid-1980s when such transaction-oriented mergers and acquisitions peaked, they were still outnumbered by those carried out by managers of industrial enterprises involved in the long-term strategic reshaping of the portfolios of the businesses they managed. In the 1980s these corporate restructurings involved more than just acquisitions and divestitures. In that decade corporate managers carried out more joint ventures and other alliances with foreign companies in global markets and domestic firms in related ones than had ever occurred in earlier years.

In some industries such corporate restructuring was successful. In others it was less so. These variations reflect the nature and the intensity of competition.[32] In industries where new product development has been critical for continuing success, restructuring has been the most effective. In such industries as chemicals, pharmaceuticals, aerospace, computers and some electrical equipment—industries in which R&D expenditures have been the largest—companies have succeeded in maintaining and expanding their positions in some markets as they have moved out of others, using the funds they received from selling off to enter new product lines. Thus, chemical firms have moved away from petrochemicals and other commodities (turning these over to oil companies) into a wide variety of specialty chemicals. Makers of over-the-counter drugs and toiletries have transformed themselves into modern capital-intensive, research-intensive, pharmaceutical companies. Aerospace companies have been moving from defense to commercial products.

In the low-tech industries where research and development expenditures are low and where competition has been based much more on marketing and distribution than on production and R&D, leading companies have successfully completed their cycle of expansion and contraction. One reason why the companies in food and drink, tobacco, lumber, furniture, publishing and printing were successful in making these strategic moves was that foreign and interindustry competition was much less intensive than it was in the stable and high tech industries. By the end of the 1980s these firms had pulled back to producing and distributing products on which their core capabilities had long rested.

It was in the stable tech industries—stable because their final products remain much the same—that restructuring has been the most difficult.

---

[31] Sanjai Bhagat, Andrei Schleifer, Robert W. Vishney, 'Hostile Takeovers in the 1980s: The Return to Corporate Specialization,' *Brookings Papers on Economic Activity: Microeconomics* (Washington, DC: The Brookings Institution 1990), p. 55.

[32] The differences in the basic nature of competition in these three categories (high, low and stable tech industries) and the relative success and failure in restructuring in each of these categories is spelled out in my 'Competitive Performance of U.S. Industrial Enterprises,' in Porter, *Time Horizons*.

In these industries R&D and capital expenditures, concentrated mostly in cost-cutting procedures, were still essential to competitive success and here both international and interindustry competition was the most intensive. In such industries as motor vehicles (especially trucks, parts and accessories); light machinery (agricultural, industrial, mining and construction equipment) tires, glass, steel and nonferrous metals a number of leading US firms failed to meet the challenges and disappeared. These include International Harvester, Allis-Chalmers, Singer Sewing Machine, United Shoe Machinery, US Rubber, Libbey-Owens Glass, American Can and Continental Can. On the other hand, others like John Deere, Caterpillar, Dresser Industries, Ingersoll-Rand, Cooper Industries, FMC, Pittsburgh Plate Glass, 3M, Alcoa, Gillette, and the leading oil companies have readjusted their product lines and remain effective competitors in global markets.

During these years of strategic restructuring organizational forms and control methods were modified. Nearly all of the leading firms have gone through a major reorientation of their organizational forms. For multimarket firms the M-Form is still standard, but the number of levels has been reduced. The divisions and business units remain, while group offices have been dropped as have been many of the smaller business units within the divisions. As these operating offices were being reshaped, the relationships between them (particularly between those on different levels of management) were being redefined so as to permit the enterprise to respond more swiftly and effectively to worldwide competition and rapid technological change. As the information revolution continues to transform the speed, accuracy and the flow of data, the size of the staffs in the operating units and corporate offices has been reduced.[33]

Control methods are also being redefined to take advantage of new, computer-based technologies and to meet the cost-cutting demands created by continuing powerful international and interindustry competition. The development of flexible, computer-aided manufacturing systems have sharply reduced labor, variable and other direct costs and proportionally increased indirect, fixed and sunk costs require a thorough rethinking of cost accounting. Similar challenges are reorienting the data that make up ROI and other measures of operating and financial performance. Budgeting and other control measures are being rethought.

---

[33] The recent reorganizations at Du Pont and GE are described in my 'The Functions of the HQ Unit in the Multibusiness Firm.' For adjusting control methods to meet new needs and structures see Johnson and Kaplan, *Relevance Lost*, chs. 9–11; Robert S. Kaplan, 'One Cost System Isn't Enough,' *Harvard Business Review* (January–February 1988); and Robin Cooper and Robert S. Kaplan, 'Activity Based Usage Models,' Harvard Business School working paper, July 25, 1991. The new information-based manufacturing technologies include Computer-Aid-Design and Engineering (CAD/CAE), Computer Integrated Manufacturing (CIM), and Flexible Manufacturing Systems (FMS). For changes in capital budgeting, see Baldwin and Clark, 'Strategic Capital Budgeting,' Porter, *Time Horizons*.

I can say little more about the reshaping of structures and the revising of control methods that are the response to the strategic restructuring of US corporate businesses in recent years. The reshaping process is still going on. Information about these changes is not yet fully compiled and has only begun to be analyzed. The task of examining and understanding current development is, as the format of this conference indicates, one for economists and students of management rather than for historians. I would hope, however, that students of recent developments would place their finding in the different national historical frameworks outlined in this, the third, session of the conference.

The development of organizational forms, strategies and control methods has differed from nation to nation. This was because the national environments differed in many ways when over a century ago modern business enterprise first appeared and also because each nation was differently affected by continuing economic growth and transformation and by the great and smaller wars and the depressions and recessions of the past century. We still have much to learn about the historical evolution of corporate organizational forms, strategies and control methods. We know something about these changes during the period of rapid enterprise growth that began in the late 19th century and came to a close in the 1960s. We know much less about the ways in which firms adjusted their structures, strategies and accounting techniques in the new era of intensified international and interindustry competition. By learning more about present practices we can better appreciate their roots in the past and better understand continuing different national patterns of corporate change.

INDEX

Note: Information in notes is signified by n, followed by note number